Keynes and his Battles

To Marielle
To the memory of Tom Asimakopulos

Keynes and his Battles

Gilles Dostaler

Université du Québec à Montréal, Canada

An augmented and revised edition of *Keynes et ses Combats*
Paris, Albin Michel, 2005, translated by Niall B. Mann

Edward Elgar
Cheltenham, UK • Northampton, MA, USA

Published by
Edward Elgar Publishing Limited
Glensanda House
Montpellier Parade
Cheltenham
Glos GL50 1UA
UK

Edward Elgar Publishing, Inc.
William Pratt House
9 Dewey Court
Northampton
Massachusetts 01060
USA

A catalogue record for this book
is available from the British Library

Library of Congress Cataloguing in Publication Data

Dostaler, Gilles.
    [Keynes et ses combats. English]
    Keynes and his battles / Gilles Dostaler.
       p. cm.
    "An augmented and revised edition of Keynes et ses combats, Paris, Albin Michel, 2005, translated by Niall B. Mann."
    Includes bibliographical references and index.
    1. Keynes, John Maynard, 1883–1946. 2. Economists—Great Britain—Biography. I. Title.
    HB103.K47D6713 2005
    330.15′6092—dc22   2006026425
    [B]

ISBN 978 1 85898 266 3 (cased)

Typeset by Cambrian Typesetters, Camberley, Surrey
Printed and bound in Great Britain by MPG Books Ltd, Bodmin, Cornwall

Contents

1. Introduction

The master-economist must possess a rare *combination* of gifts. He must reach a high standard in several different directions and must combine talents not often found together. He must be mathematician, historian, statesman, philosopher – in some degree. He must understand symbols and speak in words. He must contemplate the particular in terms of the general, and touch abstract and concrete in the same flight of thought. He must study the present in the light of the past for the purposes of the future. No part of man's nature or his institutions must lie entirely outside his regard. He must be purposeful and disinterested in a simultaneous mood; as aloof and incorruptible as an artist, yet sometimes as near the earth as a politician.
Keynes, 'Alfred Marshall (1842–1924)', (1924-25, pp. 173–4)

Maynard is a great man, I rather think. They had caught three mice in one trap; this excited him to the verge of hysteria. Now thats true of greatness; combined as it is with buying a whole flock of sheep; ditto of cows; he had been also dictating a letter to the *Times*; is overcoming the innumerable actors and actresses [at his Cambridge Arts Theatre] who won't act Phedre; they will act Phedre; had also a complete knowledge of Tuberculosis in cows; meanwhile gave permission for Auntie to drive with Edgar [chauffeur] to Lewes to buy stockings; all details are referred to him; yet he remains dominant, calm; intent as a terrier to every word of L's [Lydia Lopokova-Keynes] play; spotted at sight things Id never seen from sheer vacancy; and left me crushed but soaring with hope for a race that breeds men like Maynard. And I kissed him and praised to the skys his Memoir Club paper ['My early beliefs']; by which, most oddly, to my thinking, he was really pleased.
Virginia Woolf, letter to Vanessa Bell, 8 October 1938 (Woolf, 2003, p. 415)

John Maynard Keynes was one of the most influential figures of the twentieth century. His *General Theory of Employment, Interest and Money*, published in 1936, stands alongside Adam Smith's *Wealth of Nations* or Karl Marx's *Capital* as one of the most important works in the field of economic and social thought. And yet Keynes's work is much more than this single book. He was a man of action, fully engaged in the problems of his time. Economics, inseparable from the social and the political, was only one of his preoccupations. The economic reforms he advocated were but one (however major) element in a process of political and social transformation necessary to save a world threatened by war, revolution and all forms of extremism. Keynes proposed a global vision of society, its evils and the means to overcome them.

After World War Two, his ideas became an essential part of economic, political and social thought. Keynes appeared to many at the time to be responsible for preserving capitalism. But this view changed in the 1970s, when the Welfare State was being called into question and neoliberalism started gaining ground.[1] Keynesian policies then came to be seen as responsible for the evils of contemporary economies, and some economics students were discouraged from seeking awareness of his theories and recommendations.

I believe that reading Keynes's work while studying his engagements with the issues of his times is of the highest interest, from a historical point of view, but also for an understanding of our own times. Keynes's thought has often been reduced to a series of mechanical prescriptions which, in some cases, contradict his understanding of society. More pragmatic than dogmatic, Keynes claimed to provide a diagnosis of the state of modern economies, but did not claim to provide remedies for their ills applicable to all times and places. And, as we shall see, the economy did not occupy centre stage in his conception of society. The first quotation above, an obituary note Keynes wrote for his professor Alfred Marshall, can be read as a self-portrait, illustrating the fact that an economist must be more than an economist to understand his time. As the second quotation above shows, his friend Virginia Woolf described with humour the multiple facets of this surprising figure.

Keynes's name has been used to refer to a revolution, a current of thought, states and policies. However, what is called 'Keynesianism' arises from a rather complex relationship with Keynes's ideas. As is generally the case with schools of thought, their founders' works have often been simplified, vulgarized and dogmatized by disciples. The Keynesianism associated with the postwar economic boom and called into question in the 1970s has in many regards little in common with most of Keynes's arguments. Moreover, intellectual inheritances frequently give birth to virulent quarrels. As such, several variants, from radical to moderate, exist within Keynesianism.

This book is devoted to Keynes and not to Keynesianism, and to a Keynes who is far from reducing himself to a mere theoretician of the economy. It is hoped that the reader will be convinced of the accuracy of the positions advanced above, particularly the distance separating Keynes and Keynesianism and Keynes's contemporary relevance, which will be discussed in the Conclusion.

WAR OF WORDS

Keynes left behind an enormous body of work. It is of substantial literary quality and extends across many fields, from philosophy and economics to history and politics. He excelled in all genres: abstract treatises or pamphlets, academic or newspaper articles, official reports or personal correspondences, statistical analyses, biographical essays. A master of the spoken as well as the written word, his effectiveness as lecturer, conference speaker, member and president of boards of directors, political activist, member of various commissions and committees, negotiator of private and public, particularly international, affairs, was unmatched. Accounts attesting to his skill at verbal jousting abound. He made use of brutality and seduction alternatively, exploiting a voice that fascinated his listeners in spite of a light stutter he transformed into an asset. For his friend Leonard Woolf, husband of Virginia, 'he could outwit a banker, business man, or Prime Minister as quickly and gracefully as he could demolish a philosopher or crush an economist . . .; he might, at any moment and sometimes quite unjustifiably, annihilate some unfortunate with ruthless rudeness' (L. Woolf, 1960, pp. 144–5).[2]

This paradoxical figure, though physically fragile, was a man of action as much as thought, economics and politics comprising only part of his meticulously organized schedule. With an eye constantly on the clock, he never seemed pressed for time to those around him. He always found a moment to share confidences and gossip, which constituted one of the preferred activities of the circle of friends to which he belonged and which has come to be known as the 'Bloomsbury Group'. With the exception of Keynes and Leonard Woolf, this group counted no economists or politicians among its members, who were artists, writers, art critics, journalists, biographers and psychoanalysts.

Keynes maintained a sharp division between his public and private lives. The latter was devoted, in addition to romantic and friendly relationships, to an important involvement in the art world, to activities as a collector of paintings and rare books, to gardening and the work of being a gentleman farmer. His public life involved politics, in which he intervened both as party militant and government adviser, and of course economics, in which he acted as theoretician, but also as financier, speculator and administrator. He claimed to accord priority to his private universe, even though in the end he devoted most of his energy to the public sphere. The exhausting negotiations he led with the United States in the name of Great Britain during the Second World War probably hastened his end. In the spring of 1934, Virginia Woolf composed what she called 'a biographical fantasy' of Keynes which began by enumerating words characteristic of his centres of interest: 'Politics. Art. Dancing. Letters. Economics. Youth. The Future. Glands. Genealogies. Atlantis. Morality. Religion. Cambridge. Eton. The Drama. Society. Truth. Pigs. Sussex. The History of England. America. Optimism. Stammer. Old Books. Hume' (V. Woolf, 1934, p. 274).

His life was characterized by combats and battlefields. If there exists one common thread throughout Keynes's kaleidoscopic activities, it is that of a permanent struggle to convince his contemporaries, particularly political and economic leaders, of the urgent necessity of radical transformation in preventing the collapse of a fragile and threatened civilization. Poverty, intolerable inequalities of income and fortune, unemployment, crises and international conflicts were all conditions favourable to the rise of extremism, of which Fascism and Bolshevism represented two of the most dangerous forms. These economic calamities were not consequences of inescapable natural laws, but the result of human error and irrational impulses buried in the unconscious, much like the love of money. It was not only possible but essential that major reforms be undertaken to confront such perils, to master such demons. Keynes defined himself, not as a professor, economist or politician, but as a spreader of ideas, a publicist[3] and a prophet of misfortune. He gave the title *Essays in Persuasion* to a 1931 collection of articles and book extracts, describing their contents as follows:

> Here are collected the croakings of twelve years – the croakings of a Cassandra who could never influence the course of events in time. The volume might have been entitled 'Essays in the Prophecy and Persuasion', for the *Prophecy*, unfortunately, has been more successful than the *Persuasion*. But it was in a spirit of persuasion that most of these essays were written, in an attempt to influence opinion. (1931-1, p. xvii)[4]

Keynes displayed here his customary false modesty; in fact, he entertained few doubts on his capacity to influence public opinion. It was necessary for him to struggle against the threats looming over society. And economic difficulties were but one of these. In an ideal society, 'the economic problem will take the back seat where it belongs, and . . . the arena of the heart and head will be occupied, or reoccupied, by our real problems – the problems of life and of human relations, of creation and behaviour and religion' (ibid., p. xviii). But this struggle, however pitiless, must remain peaceful. The rejection of violence was a fundamental principle for Keynes. It prevented him from joining Labour, a party some of whose values he shared but which included in its ranks advocates of the violent overthrow of the social order. It also brought him, like most of his Bloomsbury friends, to claim objector of conscience status during the First World War.

At the age of 20, Keynes, then a student at Cambridge, presented a paper written during the winter of 1902–1903 before a King's College literary society. Its subject was Abelard, lover of Eloise.[5] He emphasized the former's struggles against the established political and religious powers of his time. He praised the 'dialectical skill' (1903-1, p. 27) of this philosopher who investigated the logic of language and religious discourse and composed numerous hymns. But mostly he admired him for having been inclined 'rather to the war of words than to the war of arms' (ibid., p. 14). Keynes clearly felt kinship with the medieval philosopher. Like Abelard, he rejected violence in spite of the glaring injustices he denounced throughout his life and led a relentless war of words against the dominant views of his time, as much in morality as in politics and economics.

OUTLINE OF THE BOOK

The following pages are devoted to an exploration of several of Keynes's struggles, bringing out both their specificities and their interactions. The struggle against Victorian morality that he waged with his Bloomsbury friends was not unrelated to his struggle against the gold standard or against classical economics.

The present work does not propose a new biography of Keynes. In addition to Skidelsky's monumental biography (1983, 1992 and 2000),[6] those of Moggridge (1992), Harrod (1951), Hession (1984) and Felix (1999), essays published by his nephew Milo Keynes (1975) and several other biographical articles are available to the reader.[7] It does, however, contain several biographical elements. As it will refer frequently to Keynes's life, a detailed chronology is provided in Appendix 1 which sets out the stages of his life and the major contemporary events in British and, where relevant, world history. Keynes's ideas are thus placed in their biographical and historical context. Awareness of this context is indispensable. A section on the Bloomsbury Group and the Cambridge Apostles and another on British political history are also included. The first outlines the context of Keynes's private life; the second that of his public life. These 'Interludes' are placed, respectively, after Chapters 2 and 4, with whose contents they are closely linked.

The following eight chapters cover four main axes in Keynes's thinking and action. The first axis is philosophy. Keynes's important contributions to this field are little known to the non-specialist. Chapter 2 discusses the question of ethics and the struggle of Keynes and his Bloomsbury friends against Victorian morality. Chapter 3 tackles a more difficult problem, but one essential to understanding Keynes's thought, namely that of knowledge. This chapter traces the influence of his father's ideas, his work on the logical foundations of probabilities, his conception of the 'moral sciences' and economics, and his critique of their mathematization. While in Chapter 2, the philosophers Sidgwick and Moore occupy an important place, in Chapter 3 Bertrand Russell, Frank Ramsey and Ludwig Wittgenstein take centre stage – all close friends of Keynes.

The second axis concerns politics. Chapter 4 presents Keynes's political vision, starting with its genesis in little known early works, such as an important paper on Burke. This chapter examines Keynes's attitude toward conservatism, labourism and liberalism, his complex relations with Marx and Soviet communism, and his unflinching condemnation of Fascism. Chapter 5 is devoted to Keynes's actions and attitudes on war and discusses both the Boer conflict and World War One. It evokes the question of conscientious objection, with Keynes's position having raised a lively controversy. It describes the struggle he led, and lost, during the Paris Peace Conference. The latter gave birth to the Treaty of Versailles; Keynes believed it iniquitous and denounced it in *The Economic Consequences of the Peace*, a work that made him a world celebrity. His important activities during World War Two are evoked in the chapter relating to international monetary relations.

Three chapters are devoted to the field in which Keynes is best known, economics. Chapter 6 deals with his personal relations with and his conception of money. This chapter also evokes the relationship between Keynes and Freud. Chapter 7 analyses the heart of Keynesian economic theory, the question of employment. It presents the 'classical' arguments Keynes criticized, before presenting the evolution of his own conceptions up to the system presented in *The General Theory of Employment, Interest and Money*. His proposed policies to combat unemployment are also evoked. Chapter 8 discusses international monetary relations, first by recounting Keynes's unsuccessful struggle against Britain's return to the gold standard in the 1920s, and second by relating the events leading up to the Bretton Woods Agreement.

Chapter 9 saves for last an important field neglected by Keynes's interpreters and specialists, namely that of art. Starting with ethics, the book finishes with aesthetics. This chapter evokes Keynes's efforts as patron and organizer of the arts, notably in his role in the creation of the Arts Council of Great Britain. It also describes his activities as an art lover, particularly as a collector of paintings. The chapter begins with an unknown though still important part of Keynes's thought, namely the conception of aesthetics he developed in a series of unpublished papers written during his time as an active member of the Apostles' Society – a conception that has lost none of its relevance.

Each chapter contains analytical, biographical and contextual elements. There are numerous connections among these elements from one chapter to another. This interconnection makes some repetition inevitable as the same subjects are studied from different angles. An effort has been made to render the present work accessible to the non-specialist, interested in the problems with which contemporary societies are confronted. This is why detailed entry into some of the extremely specialized controversies that Keynes's theories have aroused has been avoided.

Most Keynes scholars are economists. Several among them believe that studying his political or philosophical thought, or exploring his life and the context in which it unfolded, is of interest only in light of the theoretical revolution he achieved in economics. It is also believed that his economic thought can be understood independently from other aspects of his world vision. On this view, *The General Theory*, conceived as the culmination of this thought, results exclusively from Keynes's reflection in the domain of economic analysis, as if theories reproduce themselves independently of the conditions in which they were conceived. It is hoped that this book will help invalidate such positions. In effect, Keynes's influence is connected, not only to his economic theories, but also to a political vision and a philosophic conception which he skilfully integrated into his activities as publicist, adviser and theoretician. Moreover, Keynes's influence does not date from the publication of *The General Theory*. Thus, even if economics occupies an important place in this book, it is neither a work of economic theory nor a history of economic thought.

QUOTATIONS AND BIBLIOGRAPHY

Keynes's writings, both published and unpublished, are quoted frequently here. Secondary literature, which is extraordinarily abundant, has been consulted and referred to on various occasions.[8] The concluding bibliography is a guide for the reader interested in exploring Keynes's work in greater depth. It includes two parts, Keynes's work and a secondary bibliography. The reader is advised to refer to the bibliography's introduction before reading from the start. Regarding the secondary bibliography, the author-date system has been used to indicate references. The referral date is, in most cases, the work's original date of publication. When another edition is used, it will be indicated in the bibliography. In case of possible confusion, for example if two other editions are mentioned, both dates – that of the original edition and that of the one used – will be given in the text. When two or more people have the same name, such as Leonard and Virginia Woolf, a first name initial will be given in the reference indication.

The sources of Keynes's writings quoted are indicated by date of publication (or writing, for an unpublished text), followed by a figure allowing the reader to relocate this entry in the bibliography. The following page numbers refer either to one of the 30 volumes of the *Collected Writings of John Maynard Keynes*, published between 1971 and 1989, or to archival documents. In a certain number of cases, these rules could not be followed. Regarding correspondence or other documents, such as lecture notes or private diaries kept over long periods of time, the following method has been adopted. When a letter is quoted without mentioning the source in the text, this signifies that it has been consulted by the author in the Keynes archives. If a letter, or any other unpublished document of Keynes or another author, has been quoted in another publication, this secondary source is given in the text by using, as in Keynes's bibliography, the code JMK to indicate Keynes's *Collected Writings*. If these documents have been taken from other archives, this has been indicated in the text. The reader will find at the beginning of the bibliography an explanation of the codes used.

ACKNOWLEDGEMENTS

During much of my research I benefited from the financial support of the Social Sciences and Humanities Research Council of Canada. With my colleagues Robert Nadeau, Robert J. Leonard and Maurice Lagueux, I participated in a study group on the history and philosophy of economics in the twentieth century financed by the Fonds québécois de recherche sur la société et la culture.

I thank the Provost of King's College, Cambridge, for permission to quote from the Keynes, Charleston and J.T. Sheppard archives as well as the British Library and the Society of Authors as agents of the Strachey Trust, which authorized me to quote passages from Lytton Strachey's archives and from the correspondence between Keynes and Duncan Grant; Palgrave Macmillan for permission to quote *The Collected Writings of John Maynard Keynes*. Jacqueline Cox and Rosalind Moad, archivists at King's College Library, always welcomed me with kindness and efficiency in the reading room. I much appreciated being able to visit Keynes's apartment at King's College thanks to Mrs Cox. My sister Isabelle facilitated my stays in Cambridge by generously offering me her flat. Robert Skidelsky kindly received me at Tilton, Keynes's country house which he now owns.

I am grateful to the following persons who read, commented and suggested corrections, at different stages in the writing of my book: Steve Ambler, Robert Armstrong, Roger Backhouse, Michel Beaud, Joanna Bauvert, Gilles Bourque, Ghislain Deleplace, Alfred

Dubuc, Bernard Élie, Angelica Garnett, Craufurd Goodwin, Frédéric Hanin, Sid Ingerman, Luce Jean-Haffner, Monique Larue, Maria Cristina Marcuzzo, Bernard Maris, Catherine Martin, Robert Nadeau, Jean-Marc Piotte, Louis-Bernard Robitaille, Pierre Rochon, Robin Rowley, Christian Schmidt, Christian Tutin, Jeffrey Weatherhead. I am obviously responsible for any faults in the final product.

I was invited to present preliminary chapters of this book to the following research centres and universities: PHARE (Universities of Paris 1 and Paris 10), GRESE (University of Paris 1), CEPN (University of Paris 13), LEREPS (University of Toulouse), CEPERC (University of Aix-en-Provence), CEPSE (University Pierre Mendès-France, Grenoble), CREUSET (University Jean-Monnet, Saint-Étienne), CRIISEA (University of Picardie Jules-Verne, Amiens), HEC-DEEP (University of Lausanne), LED (University of Paris 8), CEPN (University of Paris 13), Institut d'Études Politiques de Toulouse, Institut d'Études Politiques de Bordeaux, Faculty of Economic Sciences at the University of Barcelona, Economics Department of the Wirtschaftsuniversität (Vienna), Institute of Economic Research of Hitotsubashi University (Tokyo). It is impossible here to name all the colleagues whose commentaries and questions allowed me to improve my work.

Hélène Jobin, Bernard Maris and Ianik Marcil authorized me to use works we carried out together. For this I thank them. I was welcomed on several occasions throughout this work by the Laboratoire d'Études et de Recherches sur l'Économie, les Politiques et les Systèmes Sociaux (LEREPS). The final stage of writing was accomplished during a stay in Paris at the invitation of the Pôle d'Histoire de l'Analyse et des Représentations Économiques (PHARE). I thank the members of these institutions, particularly Daniel Diatkine, Claude Dupuy, François Morin, Jean-Pierre Gilly and Anne Isla for their warm welcome. The Université du Québec à Montréal, with which I have been associated since 1975, assisted me in various ways in pursuing my research. The École des Sciences de la Gestion and the Département des Sciences Économiques of this establishment provided me with financial assistance for the English translation of this book, a translation carried out with care and professionalism by Niall B. Mann.

I would especially like to express my gratitude to Marielle Cauchy. Not only did she provide support and encouragement during the difficult moments of this work, but she also contributed greatly to its realization by carefully correcting the manuscript in its entirety.

NOTES

1. On this subject see Beaud and Dostaler (1995).
2. See Dostaler (2002a).
3. Keynes used the term 'publicist' to characterize himself. This term, which today signifies a publicity agent or public relations officer, formerly referred to a political writer or a journalist.
4. See the end of the Introduction for an explanation of this reference.
5. Peter Abelard (1079–1142) was castrated on the orders of Canon Fulbert, uncle of Eloise (1101–1164), whom he had secretly married. From her convent, Eloise maintained with Abelard a long correspondence in which philosophical discussions mixed with romantic outpourings.
6. Skidelsky (2003) is a condensed version of the three initial volumes.
7. Among these biographies, the most serious are those of Skidelsky, Moggridge and Harrod, although the last, as the biography 'authorized' by Keynes's family, chooses to overlook several aspects of Keynes's private life. See Dostaler (2002b).
8. Numerous articles on Keynes are collected in Blaug (1991), McCann (1998) and Wood (1983, 1994). Among books on Keynes published in the last twenty years, see Carabelli (1988), Clarke (1988), Dimand (1988),

Fitzgibbons (1988), Meltzer (1988), O'Donnell (1989), Barrère (1990a), Blaug (1990), Littleboy (1990), Asimakopulos (1991), Herland (1991), Abraham-Frois (1991), Orio and Quilès (1993), Davis (1994a), Mini (1994), Cartelier (1995), Felix (1995), Bateman (1996), Verdon (1996), Henry (1997), Parsons (1997), Ventelou (1997), Combemale (1999), Maris (1999), Bousseyrol (2000), Poulon (2000), Castex (2003, vol. 3) and Davidson (2007). Also see the following collections: Thirlwall (1982), Eatwell and Milgate (1983), Harcourt (1985a), Lawson and Pesaran (1985), Poulon (1985a), Vicarelli (1985), Deleplace and Maurisson (1985), Boismenu and Dostaler (1987), Thirlwall (1987), Zerbato (1987), Barrère (1988, 1989 and 1990), Eltis and Sinclair (1988), Hamouda and Smithin (1988), Hillard (1988), Maurisson (1988), Hill (1989), Bateman and Davis (1991), O'Donnell (1991), Gerrard and Hillard (1992), Cottrell and Lawlor (1995), Crabtree and Thirlwall (1993), Marzola and Silva (1994), Davis (1994b), Dow and Hillard (1995), Harcourt and Riach (1997), Benetti, Dostaler and Tutin (1998), Sharma (1998), Pasinetti and Schefold (1999), Dostaler and Nadeau (2003), Runde and Mizuhara (2003), Backhouse and Bateman (2006).

2. Ethics: the sources of Keynes's vision

> We repudiated entirely customary morals, conventions and traditional wisdom. We were, that is to say, in the strict sense of the term, immoralists. The consequences of being found out had, of course, to be considered for what they were worth. But we recognised no moral obligation on us, no inner sanction, to conform or to obey. Before heaven we claimed to be our own judge in our own case . . . Yet so far as I am concerned, it is too late to change. I remain, and always will remain, an immoralist.
> 'My Early Beliefs' (1938-12, pp. 446–7)

> Birth control and the use of contraceptives, marriage laws, the treatment of sexual offences and abnormalities, the economic position of women, the economic position of the family – in all these matters the existing state of the law and of orthodoxy is still medieval – altogether out of touch with civilised opinion and civilised practice and with what individuals, educated and uneducated alike, say to one another in private.
> 'Am I a Liberal?' (1925-17, p. 302)

Victoria acceded to the throne of Great Britain and Ireland in 1837, at the age of 18, and became Empress of India in 1871. She would reign until 1901.[1] Her diamond jubilee, in 1897, symbolized the triumph of Victorian England. Her reign accompanied the victory of laissez-faire within British borders. The 1846 abolition of laws hampering wheat importation marked the victory of free trade, which was completed by the repealing, in 1849 and 1854, of the protectionist navigation laws, the first of which was proclaimed by Cromwell in 1651.[2] Demanded since the end the eighteenth century by industrialists, supported by most economists, in particular by David Ricardo, and fought against by landowners, the repeal of the Corn Laws announced the rise in power of the industrial bourgeoisie. A free trade treaty between France and England, hereditary enemies, was signed in 1860. Industrialization, which began at the end of the preceding century, accelerated, stimulated by the arrival of the railway in 1825. In 1834, an amendment to the Poor Laws, which linked assistance to the destitute with internment in workhouses in which conditions were intentionally difficult, accelerated the formation of the modern labour market.[3] The working class started to organize. The Combination Acts of 1824 and 1825, though with several restrictions, including the prohibition of the right to strike, facilitated the creation of trade unions. The People's Charter, published in 1838, demanded universal male suffrage and gave birth to the Chartist Movement which would be active for about ten years.

The Vienna Congress, which met at the end of the Napoleonic Wars between September 1814 and June 1815, marked the beginning of an enormous movement of colonial expansion for England, an expansion which saw the surface of its empire double in a century. England ruled over, on the eve of the First World War, a quarter of the planet's population. Beyond the borders of this colonial empire, the City of London financially dominated the world. The international monetary system rested on the gold standard and a pound sterling whose gold value, fixed in 1717 by Isaac Newton, then Master of the Royal Mint, would not change, excluding a few crisis periods, until 1931. After the Franco-Prussian War of 1871, the gold standard system, adopted by the United States in 1873, would gradually be imposed around the world. Victoria left on her deathbed in 1901 a country which had become the world's foremost economic, political and military power.

In a paper from his youth, dating probably from the summer of 1899, Keynes, then an Eton student, praised the 'the stable and constitutional rule of Victoria' (1899-1, p. 4), which allowed England to enjoy peace and prosperity, brought about the triumph of free trade and assured the progress of morality and education, under the beneficial influence of the Church. Later, however, Keynes and his Bloomsbury friends would become merciless critics of the Victorian order. In the book that made him famous, *The Economic Consequences of the Peace*, published in 1919, Keynes masterfully portrayed this golden age of laissez-faire and of the gold standard, all the while showing that this system was an idol with feet of clay. He also dissected the ideology which held it together.[4]

VICTORIAN MORALITY

In accordance with the rules of constitutional monarchy established at the end of the seventeenth century, Queen Victoria reigned while her ministers governed, with power alternating between liberals and conservatives, then called 'Whigs' and 'Tories'. This arrangement did not prevent Victoria from closely following the nation's affairs and exercising, during her long reign, a certain political power.[5] But most importantly, she enjoyed her role of guardian of institutions, as symbol and conscience of the nation, and it is in this sense that she gave her name to an ensemble of social, cultural and ideological phenomena which accompanied the golden age of English capitalism.

The word 'Victorian' refers to all that relates to Victoria's reign and in particular to its cultural and social characteristics. We thus speak of Victorian literature, poetry, painting or decorative art. But it is above all to morality that this expression refers. Victorianism is in part a reaction against the perceived immorality of the Regency period preceding it. It refers to the the domination of puritan values, prudery, moral strictness, particularly in the domain of sexual affairs. Sexuality, considered dangerous, was to be linked exclusively to procreation. Homosexual relations were of course condemned. In 1885, while Parliament debated a law aimed at raising the age of legal consent for heterosexual relations, MP Henry Labouchere proposed an amendment by virtue of which all acts of 'gross indecency' between men, in private or in public, would be considered criminal and punishable by two years of forced labour.[6] It was as a result of this amendment that Oscar Wilde was condemned in 1895 to two years of forced labour, after which he went into exile in France where he died one year before Victoria. Keynes and his friends were preoccupied by this situation.[7] He was panic-stricken when rumours of his homosexual activities started to circulate while he was working at the India Office. He wrote to Lytton Strachey on 12 April 1907: 'I have always been a model of discretion – neither word nor hint . . . So I have no doubt now, that, although they are too polite to mention it, everybody in England is perfectly well aware of everything . . . But – in the present state of public opinion – damn and damn and damn'.

This conception of sexuality was associated with a perception of the family as a closed universe ruled by strict laws, and a hierarchy in which man occupies first place and children are considered parents' possessions. At the same time, Victorianism was characterized by a hypocrisy which inspired a number of literary works and of which Lytton Strachey, in

Eminent Victorians (1918) and *Queen Victoria* (1921), offered a vitriolic portrait. This hypocrisy allowed one to keep up appearances, all the while liberating urges which, otherwise, would lead to dangerous and sometimes mortal neuroses.[8] Within certain circles, sexual indiscretions were public knowledge. Everyone knew about Victoria's son, the future Edward VII's playboy reputation, but his mistresses were never spoken about in public.

Beyond sex and family, Victorian ideology also sought to organize social relations, in particular the codes that governed relations between social classes, between families and their servants. Despite being the first country to have achieved its bourgeois revolution, England, like several other European countries, remained a stratified society. The education system was one of the instruments that perpetuated social divisions; sons of factory workers were unlikely to attend public schools.[9] Even leisure was differentiated.

Victorian morality, particularly in the sexual domain, did not apply equally through all classes. The upper middle classes were the main target. The lower classes, considered deprived of virtue and will, could compensate their miserable lot in life with alcohol and sex. The situation of the very rich was also different from that of the middle classes. Victorian morality was also addressed first and foremost to women. It was admitted implicitly that men, even honourable men, could satisfy certain urges with women of ill-repute. Prostitution, both female and male, flourished in Victorian London.

While Keynes and the Bloomsbury iconoclasts rejected some sexual and some familial traditions, they remained attached to the social divisions of the Victorian universe.[10] As regards workers, they manifested a paternalist condescension mixed with scorn. Most, however varying their income levels, had at their service two or three servants, often more, as was the case with Keynes. At his birth, his parents employed three people – one of whom had the full-time job of looking after the newborn. Neville Keynes's diary describes numerous complications regarding staff management. That of Virginia Woolf is full of remarks on the difficulties she encountered with her servants from the 'lower classes'.[11] This attitude extended to relations between nations, between England and the world. Victorian imperialism was impregnated with the consciousness of the natural superiority of the English nation. For Keynes and his friends, the centre of civilization was situated somewhere between Cambridge, London and Sussex.[12] The further one travels away from this centre, the more the enlightened spirit loses its lustre.

Morality also applied to the economy. For Keynes, as for Freud, questions of sex and of money are closely linked and subject to the same hypocrisy.[13] Adam Smith wrote that a nation, like an individual, enriched itself by working and saving. He opposed frugality to prodigality and bad conduct: 'every prodigal appears to be a public enemy, and every frugal man a public benefactor' (Smith, 1776, vol. 1, p. 263). Capital grows 'silently and gradually . . . by the private frugality and good conduct of individuals, by the universal, continual, and uninterrupted effort to better their own condition' (ibid., p. 267). This vision is part of the Victorian economic morality. The frugal entrepreneur is one of the mythical figures of this universe, alongside the alcoholic and vulgar factory worker, who lacks those very virtues giving him access to a better world.

Keynes never stopped denouncing this 'psychology of society' to which he devoted some of his most eloquent pages:

Thus this remarkable system depended for its growth on a double bluff or deception . . . The duty of 'saving' became nine-tenths of virtue and the growth of the cake the object of true religion. There grew round the non-consumption of the cake all those instincts of puritanism which in other ages has withdrawn itself from the world and has neglected the arts of production as well as those of enjoyment. (Keynes, 1919-1, pp. 11–12)

MORALITY WITHOUT RELIGION

Thinkers of the Victorian Age were far from unanimous as regards the ideology whose main traits we have just outlined. The foundation of this ideology was religious. But, for several of these thinkers, God was dead or in the process of dying. Anglicanism, the established Church of England, which had taken its definitive form with the promulgation in 1563 by Elizabeth I of the 39 Articles to which members of English universities, as all those holding civil office, were obliged to declare allegiance, was in crisis. The Oxford movement sought to break the link between Church and State by moving closer to Catholicism, to which the future Cardinals Newman and Manning had converted in 1845 and 1851 respectively.[14]

Since its inception, Anglicanism has not been the only denomination in the British religious arena. During the reign of Elizabeth I, Puritans, of whom Presbyterians and Congregationalists constituted the main branches, criticized the Anglican episcopacy and pushed for a simplification of rites and a return to the sources of faith and morality which had earned them their name. Cromwell was one of the most illustrious representatives of this community which gained power during the English civil war.[15] But during the following Restoration, harsh legislation against the Puritans, in particular the Clarendon Code of 1661–1665, led to the departure of many of them from the Church of England. They were then called 'nonconformists', and, following the Toleration Act of 1689, 'Protestant dissenters'. From there on, these expressions have been used to characterize all Protestants who did not conform to the doctrine and discipline of the Anglican Church, such as Baptists, Quakers and Unitarians. Methodism, started by John Wesley and associated with industrial cities, separated from the Church of England in the late eighteenth century. It is an important step in the rise, in the next century, of evangelicalism, which stresses public morality.

As the Tories were in favour of the acts excluding non-conformists from public and military office, as well as from university degrees, while the Liberal Party advocated civil and religious liberty, dissenters were closer to the latter party. Dissidence gave birth, at the end of the eighteenth century, to a political–philosophical movement known as radicalism, which would play an important role in nineteenth century England.[16] Influenced by the French and American revolutions, radicals, who were called English Jacobins or rationalist dissidents, advocated liberalism and the pursuit of happiness, proclaimed their faith in reason, progress and the natural rights of man and demanded universal suffrage. They were in favour of a radical reform of the educational system to prevent it from being dominated by religious orthodoxy and political conservatism and to enable it to form individuals capable of freely realizing their desires and of attaining happiness.

In 1828 nonconformists were accorded the same political rights as Anglicans; a year later, equality was accorded to Catholics, while Jews would have to wait until 1858. One finds several persons close to Keynes who belonged to the nonconformist community, starting with his parents. Keynes's maternal grandfather, John Brown, was considered the nonconformist bishop of his region.[17]

Bentham and John Stuart Mill

While many believed that Great Britain's success came from divine will and the faith of her Majesty's subjects, it was outside religion that several of the nineteenth century's most important thinkers sought to give new foundations to morality, by reconciling the individual's pursuit of self-interest and private happiness with collective well-being. In the preceding century, Adam Smith, more moral philosopher than economist, led the way with his parable of the invisible hand.[18] Shortly thereafter, Jeremy Bentham, philosopher, jurist and economist, laid the grounds for utilitarianism, whose objective was to establish the conditions for achieving the greatest happiness for the greatest number of individuals. Bentham founded this doctrine on the conviction that individuals rationally calculate pleasure and pain, on the principle of psychological hedonism according to which individuals seek to maximize their satisfaction. Bentham believed that quantities of pleasure and pain were measurable. In the economic sphere, he enumerated the domains in which public powers could act and those in which the market should take over. Friend of Ricardo, James Mill and Malthus, Bentham was an important influence on both classical and neoclassical economics. Partisan of extending the right to vote, he was one of the principal forces behind radicalism.[19]

Son of James Mill, John Stuart Mill was one of the admirable figures of the Victorian period. Like Smith, he was a philosopher and moralist before he was an economist. Conciliatory, he sought to synthesize, in ethics, utilitarianism with moral intuitionism, in epistemology, inductivism with deductivism, and in politics, liberal capitalism with socialism, which he increasingly espoused toward the end of his life. Founder at the age of 16 of the Utilitarian Society, he published in 1861 *Utilitarianism*, in which, while developing Bentham's arguments, he gave the latter a completely different scope than that found in Bentham or in most of the classical economists who were inspired by them. For Mill, happiness is the ultimate goal of all human activities, but that in no way justifies the egoism whose affirmation figures at the base of classical political economy. Utilitarianism is thus not contradictory to a certain idealism.[20] Even on the admission of God's absence, human beings need faith in goals that transcend individual existence. Society's progress must not be limited to material wealth or, still worse, to the accumulation of massive amounts of money. Progress must be as much moral and spiritual. Classical economists, in particular Ricardo, anticipated that the accumulation of capital would inescapably entail, in the long term, a reduction of profit rates leading to a stationary state, which was to be feared. Mill accepted this analysis but considered stationary states in a radically different way. On the contrary, he welcomed this state of society in which people stopped chasing after money to concentrate on matters of the soul and mind. Some of Mill's most eloquent passages seem written for the present times:

> I confess I am not charmed with the ideal of life held out by those who think that the normal state of human beings is that of struggling to get on; that the trampling, crushing, elbowing, and treading on each other's heels, which form the existing type of social life, are the most desirable lot of human kind, or anything but the disagreeable symptoms of one of the phases of industrial progress. (Mill, 1848, vol. 2, pp. 261–62)

His book, *On Liberty* (1859) is not an apology for laissez-faire and economic liberalism, but above all a radical critique of an ideology which imposed on individuals a code of good conduct on the moral level. It is a denunciation of Victorian respectability. Mill forcefully proclaims freedom for all, not only to think, talk and write as one sees fit, without constraint, but also to live according to one's inclinations, even if the latter risks causing scandal. In fact, Mill is a precursor to and inspirer of Bloomsbury's revolt against Victorian morality. On another question, that of women's status in society, Mill also adopted an attitude diametrically opposed to the dominant vision of his time, including that of opponents of Victorian morality and even of capitalism. Author of *The Subjection of Women* (1869), Mill radically condemned the domination of men over their wives and children.[21] Feminist before his time, Mill was also an ecologist, drawing attention to the destruction that economic growth was provoking in the environment.

Sidgwick and Marshall

After Mill, an important moral philosopher of the Victorian era was Henry Sidgwick, a pastor's son.[22] He was a colleague and close friend of John Neville Keynes. Maynard had the opportunity of meeting him and played golf with him. John Neville corrected the proofs of the first edition of Sidgwick's *Principles of Political Economy*, published in 1883, the year of John Maynard's birth.

Elected member of the Cambridge Apostles in 1856,[23] named fellow of Trinity College after his studies, in 1859, Sidgwick belonged to that generation of Cambridge intellectuals to have lost faith during the 1860s. The 1859 publication of Darwin's *On the Origin of Species*, stimulating the debate on the relation between science and religion, played a crucial role in this process. Sidgwick renounced in 1861 the religious career for which his father had prepared him. In 1869 he quit his position at Trinity College, no longer able to maintain allegiance to the 39 Articles of Anglican dogma that he had to proclaim when he was hired. Two years later, in 1871, the Test Act abolished this obligation. It is said that Liberal Prime Minister Gladstone had been influenced in his decision by Sidgwick's stepping down.[24] The latter continued teaching at Cambridge, where he was named professor of moral philosophy in 1882. Partisan of the radical reform to an antiquated university system, Sidgwick was the principal architect behind opening the university to women, contributing to the foundation of Cambridge's Newnham College for women. Thanks to his efforts women were admitted to sit university exams.[25] Sidgwick was closely associated with Keynes's father in these struggles.[26]

Sidgwick's intellectual efforts consisted in finding a substitute for God and Christianity to guide and reconcile individual and social, private and public life. He pursued in this goal Mill's project, which tended to combine moral and social philosophies and give them a scientific foundation. Published in 1874, *The Methods of Ethics* is his main attempt in this direction. Sidgwick sought to reconcile the two forms of hedonism he distinguishes. Universalist hedonism, advocated by Bentham and his disciples, is in fact utilitarianism. Sidgwick amends it by including in the search for the greatest happiness for the greatest number, the equal repartition of happiness. Egoistic hedonism considers actions as means to attain individual pleasure or happiness. In the final analysis, Sidgwick does not succeed in reconciling these various dimensions of human life: 'It seems, then, that we must conclude [. . .] that the inseparable connexion between Utilitarian Duty and the greatest happiness of the individual who conforms to it cannot be satisfactorily demonstrated on empirical grounds' (Sidgwick, 1874, p. 503). It is impossible for an individual to act altruistically, for him to obey rules of conduct, unless he is rewarded by a god. This failure led Sidgwick to turn toward more esoteric speculations and to conclude that immortality is the necessary condition for the resolution of these contradictions. He was one of the founders and president, from 1882 to 1885 and from 1888 to 1893, of the Society for Psychical Research, which investigated parapsychological phenomena. Confronted with a great depression and the aggravation of social problems in the 1880s, Sidgwick was convinced moreover that some form of moderate socialism was inevitable.

At the time of the publication of Sidgwick's autobiography, Keynes wrote to Lytton Strachey on 8 March 1906: 'What were they all doing fussing themselves to death about God, when it's perfectly obvious that they knew quite well all the time that there was no such person?'. To Bernard Swithinbank, one of his friends from college, he wrote on 27 March, of this book: 'Very interesting and depressing and, the first part particularly, very important as an historical document dealing with the mind of the period. . . . He never did anything when young but wonder whether Christianity was true and prove it wasn't and hope that it was'. Keynes's judgement is severe and cursory, all the more so since he was influenced, albeit indirectly through Moore, by Sidgwick. He mocked Sidgwick's parapsychological investigations, while he himself participated in the Society for Psychical Research's activities.

Contemporary, colleague and friend of Sidgwick, as of John Neville Keynes, Alfred Marshall also played a role in this story. Author of *Principles of Economics* (1890), influential teacher, and founder of the Cambridge school of economics, Marshall was primarily interested in ethics. He saw in the economy a means of assuring the moral elevation of the working class. He had regarding society's evolution a vision heavily influenced by Darwin. He asked himself the same questions as Mill and Sidgwick. His responses were different, which would lead to important tensions between Sidgwick and Marshall. Marshall thought ethics could not give scientific foundations to social life, but that economics could do so. It is in this perspective that he pushed for the creation of an economics programme independent of the moral philosophy programme at his university, which was realized in 1903. In the end economics took the place of the lost religion for Marshall. At the same time, he was morally more Victorian than Mill or Sidgwick. He was opposed to attributing complete university status to women, as he was opposed to much of the other university reforms proposed by Sidgwick.[27] Denouncing excessive income inequality, favourable to the cooperative movement, Marshall was at the same time critical of trade unionism. He played a major role in Keynes's formation as an economist, sponsoring him, but it was in large part against him that Keynes affirmed his positions, as much in ethics as in economics.[28]

G.E. MOORE, BLOOMSBURY'S PROPHET[29]

George Edward Moore was born in 1873, ten years before Keynes. He was admitted to Trinity College at Cambridge in 1892. There he met Bertrand Russell. Together they studied Kant and Hegel, taught to them by John McTaggart. McTaggart at Cambridge and Francis H. Bradley at Oxford were, with Bernard Bosanquet and Thomas H. Green, the chief artisans of the Hegelian reaction to the arguments of Mill and Sidgwick. Moore recalls in his autobiography that, around 1893, 'Russell had invited me to tea in his rooms to meet McTaggart; and McTaggart, in the course of conversation had been led to express his well-known view that Time is unreal. This must have seemed to me then (as it still does) a perfectly monstrous proposition, and I did my best to argue against it' (Moore, 1942, pp. 13–14). Russell and

Moore would thus, at the turn of the century, criticize and reject McTaggart's Hegelianism and lay the ground for what would become known as analytic philosophy.[30] Moore published in 1903 his famous 'Refutation of Idealism', concluding that the suppositions of the idealist, for whom '*esse est percipi*', are 'as baseless as the grossest superstitions' (Moore, 1903b, p. 44).

Moore also attended Sidgwick's lectures and was interested in the ethical problems that the latter left unsolved. Although Sidgwick's personality was unappealing to him and the lectures were boring, he admitted learning much from *Methods of Ethics* (Moore, 1942, p. 16). It is from Sidgwick that Moore began the line of thinking that would lead him to publish in October 1903, the same year as his article against idealism, *Principia Ethica*, undoubtedly one of the works that greatly influenced Keynes. In 1894, Moore was admitted into the Apostles,[31] of which he became one of the most influential members. He had the reputation of not tolerating ambiguity or vague and meaningless statements. This stance became a trademark of the Apostles, but Moore pushed it to its highest degree. His most frequently asked question, which terrorized his listeners, was: 'what do you mean exactly?'.

As much as his exceptional intelligence, it was Moore's personal qualities of integrity, honesty, politeness and a certain naïveté that explain the influence he exercised over his entourage, who likened him to Socrates, Jesus or the prince Mychkine. Leonard Woolf wrote in his autobiography: 'George Moore was a great man, the only great man whom I have ever met or known in the world of ordinary, real life' (L. Woolf, 1960, p. 131). Moore, who was according to Leonard the only philosopher to have been read by Virginia Woolf, appeared in the latter's first novel as a man called Bennett, 'very lonely, very simple, caring only for the truth of things, always ready to talk, and extraordinarily modest, though his mind was of the greatest' (V. Woolf, 1915, p. 189). Harrod described him in the following way:

> His devotion to truth was indeed palpable. In argument his whole frame was gripped by a passion to confute error and expose confusion. To watch him at work was an enthralling experience. Yet, when the heat of argument died down, he was the mildest and simplest of men, almost naïve in unphilosophical matters. He was friendly to the young, approaching them on natural or equal terms. Despite his *naïveté*, he seemed to have understanding. In human question he had none of that intolerance or crabbedness which so often marks the academic man of thought. (Harrod, 1951, p. 76)

In 1898 Moore was named fellow of Trinity College after having prepared a dissertation on Kant's ethics. That same year, he started organizing annual reading parties in the country. An invitation to these meetings of pastoral meditation depended entirely on Moore's will, and was considered a great honour. Keynes was invited to participate for the first time in 1907. Arriving in Cambridge, he attended lectures of both McTaggart and Moore. The detailed notes he kept from this attendance show that several of *Principia Ethica*'s essential arguments had already been circulating for some time. In his lectures, Moore defines the science of ethics as having to respond to two questions: 'what things are good in themselves?' and 'what is it that everybody ought to do?' (1903-4, p. 3). Goodness is described as 'entirely simple – therefore unanalysable' (ibid.). Regarding the links between ethics and politics, we read in these notes that the 'whole of politics [is] in a sense subordinate to e[thics]' (ibid., p. 10) and that 'politics and law [are] more closely connected with e[thics] with regard to what is good as a *means*' (ibid., p. 9). We also find in these notes criticisms of those arguments which Moore would develop fully in his book: hedonism, intuitionalism, evolutionary and metaphysical ethics.

'Principia Ethica', Bloomsbury's Bible

Paraphrasing one of Kant's titles, Moore presents *Principia Ethica* as 'Prolegomena to any future Ethics that can possibly pretend to be scientific' (Moore, 1903a, p. 35). Ethics is for Moore a philosophical discipline unto itself, rigorous and systematic. It is not derived from theology or any other science, such as psychology. In ethics, one must first discover 'precisely *what* question it is which you desire to answer' (ibid., p. 33) before one can respond. This is in contrast to what has been done in the past, which has most often confused two questions: firstly, what goodness is, what good things are in themselves; secondly, what actions to be accomplished, their just character, the nature of duty. Goodness can thus be considered an end or a means. Once these questions are clarified, we may know 'what is the nature of the evidence, by which alone any ethical proposition can be proved or disproved, confirmed or rendered doubtful' (ibid., p. 34).

The nature of good

The first and most fundamental inquiry is thus: what is good? Moore's answer 'is that good is good, and that is the end of the matter. Or if I am asked "How is good to be defined?" my answer is that it cannot be defined, and that is all I have to say about it' (ibid., p. 58). This disappointing answer, he says, is at the same time of extreme importance. Only Sidgwick formulated it before him, by saying that goodness was a non-analysable notion. In philosophical terms, this statement signifies that propositions dealing with goodness are of a synthetic nature and non-analytic. As for goodness in itself, it is a simple notion, of the same nature as for example the colour yellow. For Moore, we may no more explain what is yellow than we may explain what is good: '"Good" then, if we mean by it that quality which we assert to belong to a thing, when we say that the thing is good, is incapable of any definition, in the most important sense of that word' (ibid., p. 61).

Good cannot thus be defined by something external to it. It is a common error in moral philosophy to want to give reasons for why something is good. Moore qualifies this error as a 'naturalistic fallacy'.[32] This error is shared by several lines of thought which contradict each other. Thus hedonists, among whom Moore cites Bentham, Mill and Sidgwick, confuse goodness with pleasure, in that everything else, virtue, knowledge or beauty, is but a means to attain pleasure, the only thing that is good in itself. Hedonism confuses the end with the means, whether it is egoistic hedonism, for which the greatest pleasure of the individual is the only good, or utilitarian hedonism, for which the greatest pleasure of all is the only good. Following the Stoics, naturalist ethics, of which Rousseau was a famous representative, considers that goodness is what is true to nature, and therefore that one must live in accordance with nature. Yet nothing indicates, for example, that the process of evolution described by Darwin leads to results that can be qualified as good. To confuse 'more evolved' and 'better' is a naturalist error. The metaphysical ethics put forth by Plato, Spinoza, Kant or Hegel suffers from analogous contradictions, even if the metaphysicians had the merit to recognize that our knowledge is not limited to what we can grasp by our senses. Good is identified by them with a suprasensible reality, which also results in naturalistic fallacy. On this basis, Kant commits the error of conceiving the moral law as an imperative.

Only intuition allows one to grasp what is good. Moore admits that Sidgwick, among others, had recognized this reality. He is careful, however, to underline that emphasizing intuition does not make him an adept at intuitionism as a philosophic doctrine.[33] It is only in the last chapter, 'The Ideal', conceived and added on at the last minute, that Moore gives an answer to the first ethical question, 'What is good?', after having criticized the false answers to this question. Intuition teaches us that the greatest imaginable goods are states of consciousness associated with aesthetic pleasure, with the appreciation of beautiful objects, on the one hand, and with personal affections on the other:

> By far the most valuable things, which we know or can imagine, are certain states of consciousness, which may be roughly described as the pleasures of human intercourse and the enjoyment of beautiful objects. No one, probably, who has asked himself the question, has ever doubted that personal affection and the appreciation of what is beautiful in Art or Nature, are good in themselves; nor, if we consider strictly what things are worth having *purely for their own sakes*, does it appear probable that any one will think that anything else has *nearly* so great a value as the things which are included under these two heads. (Moore, 1903a, p. 237)

These objects have as their characteristic the fact that they constitute complex 'organic unities' and provoke emotions. By 'organic', Moore understands that a whole has an intrinsic value different from the sum of its parts. A totality can also include parts, some of which are good and some of which are bad. Moore calls 'mixed goods' these entities in which ugliness or nastiness can themselves contribute to bringing about a good state of mind. Poverty is like this for the reformer. Keynes would apply this argument to the study of tragedy, in which the vision of evil stimulates good states of mind, in a paper given before the Apostles (1910-8).[34]

Rules of action
What of ethics' second question: what are good actions? This issue is a matter of seeing if something is good as a means, of judging its effects. Causal relations are at stake here, complex relations since we are in the domain of human relations. Even in the domain of natural phenomena, few definitive laws have been established. A correct action is an action that produces good results. One must act in such a way that one's action produces the greatest possible good and the least possible evil in the Universe. Here one comes up against a major problem, which will be a central theme of the reflections leading Keynes to his *Treatise on Probability*.[35] It is a matter of knowledge: 'we never have any reason to suppose that an action is our duty: we can never be sure that any action will produce the greatest possible value possible' (Moore, 1903a, p. 199). It is impossible to have knowledge of the totality of long-term results of all possible actions:

> But it is quite certain that our causal knowledge is utterly insufficient to tell us what different effects will probably result from two different actions, except within a comparatively short space of time; we can certainly only pretend to calculate the effects of actions within what may be called an 'immediate' future . . . in general, we consider that we have acted rationally, if we think we have secured a balance of good within a few years or months or days. Yet, if a choice guided by such considerations is to be rational, we must certainly have some reason to believe that no consequences of our action in a further future will generally be such as to reverse the balance of good that is probable in the future which we can foresee. This large postulate must be made, if we are ever to assert that the results of one action will be even probably better than those of another. Our utter ignorance of the far future gives us no justification for saying that it is even probably right to choose the greater good within the region over which a probable forecast may extend. (Moore, 1903a, p. 202)

According to Moore, one cannot affirm with certitude that an action will have a given, predictable result. An ethical law can only have a probable character.[36] Even regarding the ban on murder, one cannot be certain that in the long term it is better than the law of the jungle. That said, following humanity's long evolution, one finds that common sense punishes murder, rape or stealing. In a situation of uncertainty, it is wise to go back to observing a certain number of rules of conduct, of the morality of common sense: 'If, then, we ask what rules are or would be useful to be observed in the society in which we live, it seems possible to prove a definite utility in most of those which are in general both recognized and practiced' (ibid., p. 209). Moore goes as far as affirming that it is probably useful to adhere to an existing custom, even if it is bad (ibid., p. 213). In the same vein, he adds that egoism can be preferable to altruism. He also affirms that it is better to seek to attain a good in the near than distant future.

A RELIGION WITHOUT MORALITY

The publication of Moore's *Principia Ethica* in October 1903 unleashed an almost delirious enthusiasm among the Apostles. A group of Cambridgians, among them Russell and Hawtrey, came up with the idea of publishing a book which would make accessible its arguments to the common man. Lytton Strachey wrote to his friend on 11 October 1903:

> I have read your book, and want to say how much I am excited and impressed. I think your book has not only wrecked and shattered all writers on Ethics from Aristotle and Christ to Herbert Spencer and Mr Bradley, it has not only laid the true foundations of Ethics, it has not only left all modern philosophy bafouée – these seem to me small achievements compared to the establishment of that Method which shines like a sword between the lines. . . . I date from Oct. 1903 the beginning of the Age of Reason. (quoted by Levy, 1979, p. 234)

Writing to Bernard Swithinbank on 7 October, Keynes wrote: 'I have just been reading Moore's *Principia Ethica* which has been out a few days – a stupendous and entrancing work, *the greatest* on the subject'. To Lytton Strachey, he wrote on 21 February 1906:

> It is *impossible* to exaggerate the wonder and *originality* of Moore; people are already beginning to talk as if he were only a kind of logic chopping eclectic. Oh why can't they see! How amazing to think that we and only we know the rudiments of a true theory of Ethics; for nothing can be more certain than that the broad outline is true. What is the world doing?

Thirty years later, in a paper read before his friends at the Bloomsbury Memoir Club, 'My Early Beliefs',[37] he wrote:

> I went up to Cambridge at Michaelmas 1902, and Moore's *Principia Ethica* came out at the end of my first year . . . its effect on *us*, and the talk which preceded and followed it, dominated, and perhaps still dominate, everything else . . . The influence was not only overwhelming; but it was the extreme opposite of what Strachey used to call *funeste*; it was exciting, exhilarating, the beginning of a renaissance, the opening of a new heaven on a new earth, we were the forerunners of a new dispensation, we were not afraid of anything. (1938-12, p. 435)

Identifying good in affective relations and in aesthetic contemplation constituted a total reversal of Victorian morality. This shift legitimized the lifestyle chosen by those who would soon form the Bloomsbury Group. Nothing counted for them but states of mind:

These states of mind were not associated with action or achievement or with consequences. They consisted in timeless, passionate states of contemplation and communion, ... The appropriate subjects of passionate contemplation and communion were a beloved person, beauty and truth, and one's prime objects in life were love, the creation and enjoyment of aesthetic experience and the pursuit of knowledge. Of these love came a long way first (ibid., pp. 436–7).

Keynes added that, under the influence of Moore's rigorous puritanism, the love then in question was not physical love, even if certain among them had already shared such love.

On the nature of good, Keynes and his friends had certain knowledge: 'How did we know what states of mind were good? This was a matter of direct inspection, of direct unanalysable intuition about which it was useless and impossible to argue' (ibid., p. 437). This knowledge of good and evil placed them above their contemporaries. In this ethereal world, they were not interested in riches, power or success, which was even scorned at. One of the paradoxes of Keynes's life was that he always maintained this moral position, in particular regarding money, while at the same time acquiring considerable wealth, power and success.[38] What Moore's disciples would at that time do was to evaluate their states of mind by applying the doctrine of organic unities, by wondering whether, for example, an intense and fleeting love was preferable to a quieter, more longlasting love, or still to consider more complicated cases, which would often characterize Bloomsbury's love affairs:

If A was in love with B and believed that B reciprocated his feelings, whereas in fact B did not, but was in love with C, the state of affairs was certainly not so good as it would have been if A had been right, but was it worse or better than it would become if A discovered his mistake? If A was in love with B under a misapprehension as to B's qualities, was this better or worse than A's not being in love at all? If A was in love with B, because A's spectacles were not strong enough to see B's complexion, did this altogether, or partly, destroy the value of A's state of mind? (1938-12, p. 439)[39]

Keynes presented Moore's vision of good, taken from the chapter 'The Ideal', as a religion, which replaced the one on which Victorian morality was founded. Thirty years later, it still appeared to him as the right religion, remaining closer to the truth than the others with which he was familiar: 'It was a purer, sweeter air by far than Freud cum Marx. It is still my religion under the surface' (ibid., p. 442). Next to this religion, 'the New Testament is a handbook for politicians . . . I know no equal to it in literature since Plato' (ibid., p. 444). He saw no reason to diverge from the fundamental intuitions of *Principia Ethica*, intuitions which allowed his generation to free itself of Benthamite tradition, which he now considered 'as the worm which has been gnawing at the insides of modern civilization and is responsible for its present moral decay' (ibid., p. 445). Bentham's perspective contributed moreover, according to Keynes, in overvaluing economic calculations in human affairs, to the detriment of Moore's ideals. It constituted the philosophic foundation for classical economics. It was, in his view, at the same time the basis of Marxism, which he considered as the *reductio ad absurdum* of Benthamism.[40] Marx, as much as Ricardo, overestimated the importance of the economic factor.

There was more than the ideal in *Principia Ethica*, and it was a biased and partial reading that the Apostles and Keynes made of this work, as the latter admitted:

Now what we got from Moore was by no means entirely what he offered us. He had one foot on the threshold of the new heaven, but the other foot in Sidgwick and the Benthamite calculus and the general rule of correct behaviour. There was one chapter in the *Principia* of which we took not the slightest notice. We accepted Moore's religion, so to speak, and discarded his morals. Indeed, in our opinion, one of the greatest advantages of his religion, was that it made morals unnecessary – meaning by 'religion' one's attitude towards oneself and the ultimate and by 'morals' one's attitude towards the outside world and the intermediate. (1938-12, p. 436)

As we have seen, Moore believed that, considering our ignorance of the future, one must submit to tradition, to rules of proper conduct, to common sense, and thus to dominant moral- ity, in order to guide our action. It is in this sense that he had one foot in the world of Bentham, Sidgwick and even in Victorian morality. Keynes did not see this element on his first reading, but it is what constituted the beginnings of his epistemological reflection which would lead to A *Treatise on Probability*, which we will present in the following chapter. Keynes could not accept that Moore's edifice was crowned by a call for submission to tradi- tional morality. He believed that Moore's religion could do without morality. Keynes declared in the quote cited at the beginning of this chapter that he and his friends were at that time immoralists and that, as far as he was concerned, it was too late for him to change. This immoralism has two characteristics. It consists firstly of a refusal of the external imposition of all norms of behaviour: the individual is the sole judge of what he must do. It consists secondly of a rejection of the conventional norms of Victorian morality, in particular regard- ing sexuality. Thus was the ethos of Bloomsbury.

But Keynes and his friends' views on human being changed over time. They discovered Freud,[41] which led to the belief that rationality and the moral qualities of human beings had been overestimated. It was wrong to believe, which was in fact at the basis of the ethics of self-interest, that human nature was reasonable. One barely understood oneself, let alone others, once an absent rationality had been attributed to emotions and behaviour. It had not been understood that human actions could just as well originate in spontaneous and irrational explosions,[42] and even wickedness could be the source of worthy situations. Thus, Keynes considered in 1938 that 'the attribution of rationality to human nature, instead of enriching it, now seems to me to have impoverished it. It ignored certain powerful and valuable springs of feeling' (ibid., p. 448). It followed, by a curious reversal, that rules and conventions did finally have a role to play in the preservation of society: 'We were not aware that civilisation was a thin and precarious crust erected by the personality and the will of a very few, and only maintained by rules and conventions skillfully put across and guilefully preserved. We had no respect for traditional wisdom or the restraints of custom' (ibid., p. 447).

PRIVATE HAPPINESS AND PUBLIC DUTY

Keynes's reflections were subject to various criticisms, coming in particular from his contem- poraries. For Quentin Bell (1995), present at the meeting in which Keynes read his paper, the auto-proclamation of immoralism was explained by the fact that Keynes, then an imposing figure of the British establishment, was considered by some of his younger listeners (Quentin included) as a conservative. For Leonard Woolf, Apostle at the same time as Keynes, 'his recollection and interpretation are quite wrong about Moore's influence' (L. Woolf, 1960, p. 146). In fact, Woolf believed that the Apostles were not immoralists, that they were very preoccupied by codes of conduct and consequences of their actions. For Richard Braithwaite, a more recent Apostle, 'whatever Keynes implies to the contrary in his memoir, he always kept to that part of the 'morals' of *Principia Ethica* which requires that actions should be judged by their consequences' (Braithwaite, 1975, p. 245).[43]

It is clear that Keynes's actions, throughout a life whose many episodes will be evoked in the following chapters, contradicted certain principles affirmed in 'My early beliefs'. From Victorianism he retained a keen sense of duty which had been inculcated by his parents, among the 'presuppositions of Harvey Road'. He asked himself on 24 February 1906 before the Apostles in a paper entitled 'Egoism', if one should sacrifice oneself for the good of humanity, and answered negatively: 'I see, in fact, no reason for supposing that the good of the Universe is inextricably bound up with mine; and why should not the Universe go to the devil if one saves one's own soul alive?' (1906-3, p.11). The course of his life contradicted this remark, since it was made up of a continual struggle to save his society rather that his soul, to work toward the construction of a new world which would allow humanity to free itself from the economic problem and to devote itself to the art of living, to the contempla-tion of beauty, to the culture of friendship and love. It was still a matter of pursuing the ethi-cal ends described by Moore, though this entailed engaging in collective action, on political, economic and social levels. In regards to ultimate goods, which can only be enjoyed individ-ually, one must in fact add collective goods of the second order, such as full employment and justice in the distribution of incomes and fortunes.

Keynes's ethical reflection was situated within the context of the philosophical, religious and ethical debates of nineteenth century England, evoked at the beginning of this chapter. He sought to resolve the same problems confronted by Bentham, James and John Stuart Mill, Sidgwick, Leslie Stephen and Moore. Like Mill, he gave absolute priority to the individual's freedom to think and live as he sees fit. Bentham's solution, the calculation of pleasure and pain by a rational individual, was for him unacceptable. It was at the basis of an economic vision that he would be moved to criticize with increasing severity. Sidgwick, for his part, did not really succeed in liberating himself from religious thought that brought him to conclude that the soul's immortality was the solution to the ethical problem. In *Principia Ethica*, Moore put forth a conception of good which satisfied Keynes. However, Moore advocated follow-ing norms of conventional morality, taking into account the consequences of our actions. Not accepting this solution, Keynes would develop a theory of the logical foundations of proba-bilities to show how one may act in an uncertain context.[44]

Neither Keynes nor his Bloomsbury friends were exempt from contradiction in their atti-tudes regarding Victorian morality. Rejecting it in principle, they kept from it in practice several elements. Keynes, for his part, would come to accord to traditions and conventions an important role in the preservation of civilization. Here is what he wrote for a discussion of functioning of the British Treasury: 'In some ways I think Treasury control might be compared to conventional morality. There is a great deal of it rather tiresome and absurd once you begin to look into it, yet nevertheless it is an essential bulwark against overwhelming wickedness' (1921-17, p. 299).

One must not underestimate, in the enthusiastic adhesion to Moore's ideas, the sexual dimen-sion. Keynes and several of his friends belonged to what was considered a criminal minority in turn of the century England.[45] Homosexual relations were punishable on conviction by two years of forced labour. Bloomsbury was a major ground for revolt against this situation. *Principia Ethica* was considered as a work that was opening the way to tolerance and accep-tance of behaviours that did not correspond to the norms of the majority. But this was also to be found before in, among other books, Mill's *On Liberty* and Sidgwick's *Method of Ethics*.

Keynes married in 1925, and after this date nothing is known about further homosexual affairs. But he fought until the end of his life to change those customs and laws he considered medieval. As we will see in Chapter 4, he made such a fight a major axis in the programme of New Liberalism. Keynes was a very organized man, who carefully filed all his papers. He chose to conserve an immense correspondence, with Lytton Strachey and others, which leaves no doubt as to his sexual orientation and activities. This archiving was most certainly pursued with the intention that it be read in the future.[46]

When, with the publication of the first volume of Keynes's biography by Skidelsky, the veil was further lifted on this aspect of his life, several economists tried to associate Keynes's sexual life with what they considered his economic errors, in particular his rejection of savings as a motor of growth.[47] Schumpeter had already made the link between Keynes's philosophy of life, his advocacy of monetary management and the fact that he had no children (Schumpeter, 1946, p. 506). For his part, Hayek wrote that Keynes's declaration of immoralism, which he denounced on several occasions and linked to his economic errors, lost much of its significance once one realized that 'the majority of the members of the group about which Keynes spoke, including himself, were homosexual, which is probably a sufficient explanation of their revolt against ruling morals' (Hayek, 1970, p. 16).

At this moment, Keynes's struggle for women's equality, for the right to contraception and abortion, for the recognition of homosexuality, is far from being won in most parts of the world, including in certain of the most powerful and in principle most 'evolved' countries. Contrary to the convictions of the first great liberal thinkers, the radical liberalism which is being imposed today is very much at home with puritanism and moral conservatism, with religious fundamentalism, as well as with political authoritarianism and disregard for human rights. The struggles of Locke, Voltaire, John Stuart Mill, Keynes and the Bloomsbury group are not yet over.

NOTES

1. In 1840, she married her cousin Prince Albert of Saxe-Coburg and Gotha, and the couple would have nine children. Albert, named Prince Consort in 1857, played an important role of his own and as adviser to his wife. His premature death in 1860 plunged Victoria into 40 years of mourning, which surely has something to do with the 'Victorian morality' we will talk about.
2. By virtue of the Navigation Act of 1651, all merchandise imported into England had to be on board an English vessel.
3. The first Poor Law dates from Elizabeth's reign, in 1597. The workhouse system was established in 1722, halfway between an asylum and a prison. In 1795, in light of the rise of wheat prices provoked by the French Revolutionary Wars, the so-called Speenhamland amendment – named after the locality where this decision was made – linked the amount of aid accorded to both the price of basic foodstuffs and family size. Harshly criticized by Malthus and other classical economists, this system was repealed in 1834. On this subject, see Polanyi (1944), a masterful fresco of the transformations briefly evoked here. On Victorian England, see Kitson Clark (1966), Thomson (1950) and Young (1977).
4. We will return to the circumstances of this book's creation and to its contents in Chapter 5.
5. See Craig (2003).
6. This amendment was not repealed until 1967.
7. The philosopher Lowes Dickinson, fellow of King's College and friend of Keynes, wrote in a 1905 account of Oscar Wilde's *De Profundis* in the *Independent Review*: 'Every society has a duty . . . to control sexual relations in the interest of the children to be born of them. But everything beyond that is a question of private morals and taste . . . And our law on that matter in question is a mere survival of barbarism, supported not by reason but by sheer prejudice' (quoted by Wilkinson, 1980, p. 51).
8. See Chesnay (1970) and Gay (1993).

9. Otherwise known as 'senior independent schools', the term 'public' comes from their charitable origins, preceding the establishment of a state-run education system. Keynes did his pre-university studies at Eton College, a public school.
10. See the following Interlude.
11. Lydia Lopokova, who became Keynes's wife in 1925, was considered too familiar with servants.
12. On the relation of Keynes with Cambridge, see Marcuzzo (2006).
13. We will return to these questions in Chapter 6.
14. Manning was one of Lytton Strachey's targets in *Eminent Victorians*.
15. Keynes devoted one of his early writings, to which we will return in Chapter 4, to Cromwell (1901-1). On this period of England's history, see Hill (1972).
16. See Halévy (1901–04).
17. See Brown (1988).
18. But it is a mistake to attribute to Adam Smith the concept of *homo oeconomicus* motivated solely by self-interest. It is in fact a matter of self love, inspired by the Stoics, and, next to this sentiment, Smith accorded as much importance to altruism, to the analysis of which he devoted a book, *The Theory of Moral Sentiments*. Smith is thus more a precursor of Mill and Keynes than of Ricardo, Hayek or Friedman. See Fitzgibbons (1995) and Dostaler (2000).
19. On Bentham, see Halévy (1901–1904), Harrison (1983), Cot (1992) and Sigot (2001).
20. It is evidently not a question of idealism as philosophical doctrine, which we will discuss in the next chapter, but of the moral character of individuals aspiring to elevated ideals.
21. One of the most merciless critics of the Victorian conception of sexuality, Freud, who, when a student, translated one volume of Mill's works (edited by Gomperz) including 'Enfranchisement of Women', warned his fiancée against the latter's ideas of male–female relations. In a letter to Martha Bernays from 15 November 1883, Freud wrote that Mill, 'the man of the century most capable of freeing himself from the domination of the usual prejudices . . . lacked the sense of the absurd, on several points, for instance in the emancipation of women and the question of women altogether . . . It seems a completely unrealistic notion to send women into the struggle for existence in the same way as men. Am I to think of my delicate sweet girl as a competitor? . . . I will make every effort to get her out of the competitive role into the quiet undisturbed activity of my home' (Freud, 1961, pp. 90–91).
22. See the intellectual biography of Schultz, who stresses the influence of Sidgwick on Moore and Bloomsbury: 'Moore, Russell, Strachey, Keynes, and Virginia Woolf . . . simply realized some – by no means all – of Sidgwick's hopes for future generations' (Schultz, 2004, p. 7).
23. On the Cambridge Conversazione Society, better known as The Apostles, which played a very important role in Sidgwick's life, as in Moore and Keynes, see the following Interlude. The three of them were leading Apostles in their days.
24. On Gladstone, see the Second Interlude.
25. Called 'tripos' in Cambridge University jargon.
26. Only in 1947 were women able to attain full Cambridge University status.
27. Marshall's father was author of a pamphlet entitled *Man's Rights and Woman's Duties*. Marshall's wife, Mary Paley, was the first woman to teach economics at Cambridge. She renounced her career for her husband. She co-signed with him a book of which she was the principal author and she closely contributed to other works by her husband without the latter's acknowledgement. Keynes noted in a biographical article on Mary Paley's death in 1944, in which one reads: 'In spite of his early sympathies and what he was gaining all the time from his wife's discernment of mind, Marshall came increasingly to the conclusion that there was nothing useful to be made of women's intellects' (1944-4, p. 241). See also Mary Paley's memoirs (M.P. Marshall, 1947).
28. On Marshall, see Keynes (1924-25), Groenewegen (1995a) and (1995b), Maloney (1985) and Gerbier (1995).
29. This expression, 'Bloomsbury's prophet' is from Regan (1986). See also Levy (1979) on relations between Moore and the Apostles.
30. One wonders if this assault had anything to do with the actions of McTaggart, who became an ardent militarist, in taking the leading part in the expulsion of Russell, an ardent pacifist, from Trinity College in 1916 (Dickinson, 1931, p. 116).
31. McTaggart was an Apostle from 1886 and Russell from 1892.
32. Nadeau (1999, p. 655) characterizes the naturalistic fallacy as 'a presumably incorrect form of reasoning based on the supposition that it is basically possible to define all ethical terms using only natural terms.'
33. On intuition, intuitionism and Moore's ethical intuitionism, see the corresponding entries in Nadeau (1999).
34. See on this subject Carabelli (1998) and O'Donnell (1998).
35. See the following chapter.
36. On the meaning of probability, see the next chapter.
37. This paper is, along with an account of his relations with the German financier and negotiator Carl Melchior, the only one Keynes wanted published posthumously. See David Garnett's 'Introduction to two memoirs', in JMK 10, pp. 387–8.

38. See on this subject the first part of Chapter 6.
39. These kinds of considerations led Bertrand Russell to write that Keynes and Strachey, 'degraded his [Moore's] ethics into advocacy of a stuffy girls-school sentimentalizing' (Russell, 1967, p. 71).
40. A passage in a letter Keynes addressed to George Bernard Shaw on 1 January 1935 announced that his coming book, *The General Theory*, would destroy the Ricardian foundations of Marxism. We will come back to this, quoting the letter, in Chapter 7.
41. See on this subject Dostaler and Maris (2000).
42. In *The General Theory*, Keynes speaks of 'animal spirits' to describe the grounds for making decisions by, among others, entrepreneurs.
43. See also Levy (1979), O'Donnell (1989) and Regan (1986). On relations between Moore and Keynes, see Bateman (1988), Coates (1996), Davis (1991) and Shionoya (1991).
44. See Chapter 3.
45. As much as Keynes's belonging to a sexual minority cannot be neglected when trying to understand certain aspects of his behaviour, still we cannot follow authors such as Mini (1994), Felix (1999) and especially Hession (1984) when they make of his homosexuality a key to his work. Hession stresses 'the importance of Keynes's mothering and of his homosexuality and androgyny as factors in his creative personality' (pp. 106–7).
46. This correspondence was made accessible in 1986. Inheritor of a portion of these letters, Keynes's brother Geoffrey wanted to destroy them, while James Strachey, executor of his brother Lytton's will, judged it necessary to make them accessible to the public. On this, see Holroyd (1994, pp. 695–8), who had access to this correspondence in writing his biography of Lytton Strachey. The first edition of 1967 revealed for the first time Keynes's sexual activities. Harrod hides the latter carefully in his biography, making subtle cuts in the letters he quotes.
47. See the papers mentioned in the preface to the American edition of Skidelsky (1983), pp. xv–xix.

First Interlude: Bloomsbury and the Apostles

Bloomsbury is the name of an area in London with the British Museum located at its southern border. It contains a number of attractive, tree-filled squares. The oldest of these, Bloomsbury Square, was established in 1661. The others (Fitzroy, Bedford, Brunswick, Tavistock, Russell and Gordon Squares) date from the nineteenth century. From the end of the eighteenth century, this residential area was frequented by many of the greater figures in English literature and art. Bloomsbury gave its name to a set of artists, writers and intellectuals who lived mainly in this quarter during the first half of the twentieth century.[1] This ensemble was not a structured organization or school of thought, but a group of friends (and lovers) who shared certain values and who profoundly marked British cultural life. Keynes was closely associated with it until the end of his life, as were many of his closest friends. It was his private world.[2]

The group's centre consisted, apart from Keynes, of Vanessa and Clive Bell, Virginia and Leonard Woolf, Molly and Desmond MacCarthy, Adrian Stephen, Lytton Strachey, Duncan Grant, Roger Fry, E.M. Forster and Saxon Sydney-Turner.[3] Several others would, at varying distances, gradually attach themselves to this core group. Of course, as it was not a structured group, the delimitation of its borders varies according to commentators. Certain of the group's founding members, such as Clive Bell, would deny its very existence. This attitude undoubtedly had something to do with the fact that, as early as the 1920s, Bloomsbury was the object of increasingly vigorous attacks on the part of critics who described it as a sect, a clan, a mafia or a mutual admiration society.

The common values of the Bloomsbury Group were also objects of discussion and controversy. The cult of friendship occupied centre stage. The members of this group expressed themselves, most often with great talent, sometimes even genius, in paintbrush and pencil, though words were its favoured means of communication. Bloomsbury was above all a set of individuals who seldom stopped talking, discussing and gossiping. They generally had a great sense of humour and could laugh at themselves. They were also merciless critics of each other, without letting such criticism get in the way of friendship. Indeed no holding back was tolerated. Anything could be said, although it took some time before certain subjects were approached. Virginia Woolf recalled, in a paper prepared around 1922 for the Bloomsbury Memoir Club, how the group started talking about sex. She found herself with her sister and other friends in a drawing room:

> Suddenly the door opened and the long and sinister figure of Mr. Lytton Strachey stood on the threshold. He pointed his finger at a stain on Vanessa's white dress.
> 'Semen?' he said.
> Can one really say it? I thought and we burst out laughing. With that one word all barriers of reticence and reserve went down. A flood of the sacred fluid seemed to overwhelm us. Sex permeated our conversation. The word bugger was never far from our lips. We discussed copulation with the same excitement and openness that we had discussed the nature of good. (V. Woolf, 1922, p. 54)

Nothing was to be taken for granted. At the same time, frankness and the most absolute sincerity were required of all. Each was asked to speak truthfully. Keynes found himself in difficulty during the war when he was suspected by his friends of betraying his private beliefs.[4] They cultivated scepticism, while maintaining belief in the power of reason, in the progress of civilization, in the perfectibility of human nature. Aesthetes, the Bloomsburians placed art at the top of human accomplishments. Hedonists, they loved parties, travels, food and wine. Francophiles, they imported into England artistic and culinary recipes from across the Channel, and discovered then little-known corners of the Mediterranean coast, such as Saint-Tropez and Cassis.

Leaders in the revolt against Victorian morality, they derided those institutions it honoured (the army, the Church and the State) and rejected the social conventions, and in particular the sexual morality that it implied. Bloomsbury unions were far from conformist. Homosexuality was not only tolerated but practised within the group.[5] The most singular couples and trios formed and dissolved in a milieu that scandalized contemporaries.[6] Bloomsbury was a sort of family, a commune before its time, which its adversaries sometimes compared to a brothel. Friendship survived the ending of intimate relationships, even if it was not without consequences. Bloomsbury was characterized above all by the fact that its members stayed closely united and committed to each other until the end of their lives, in spite of the inevitable conflicts, disagreements and crises that sprang up periodically. In this lofty milieu, politics, especially in the beginning, was at times a very remote concern. Only Keynes and Leonard Woolf immersed themselves in this arena. Most, as Keynes, thought themselves as liberals; some, as Woolf, were labourites. All, however, situated themselves on the left, at least in terms of the political spectrum in Britain.

They were above all industrious, moulded by a very Victorian sense of duty inherited from their families. Endowed for the most part with sharp wit and exceptionally cultured, they were leaders in all domains in which they intervened: literature, painting, biography, literary criticism and art criticism, journalism, publishing, political writing, economics, psychoanalysis. In these fields, they criticized, destroyed and reconstructed according to the new norms of what is sometimes called 'modernism', and of which, elsewhere, Proust, Joyce, Musil, Cézanne, Matisse or Picasso – artists and writers admired by Bloomsbury – were shaping other contours.

The best way to present Bloomsbury is to tell its story, a story that accompanies that of Keynes, particularly his romantic life. Following a tradition initiated by members of the Group, we will distinguish between 'Old Bloomsbury', which developed before the war, and 'New Bloomsbury', which came about after the war. We will start with a presentation of the Apostles Society, which played a major role in the intellectual life of Keynes. Through this story the Group's world vision and aesthetic conceptions will be revealed. Finally, we will evoke the important links between Bloomsbury and psychoanalysis.[7]

THE CAMBRIDGE APOSTLES

Bloomsbury was born of two sources: on the one hand, Cambridge University, in particular the Cambridge Conversazione Society, better known as 'The Apostles' or simply 'The Society';[8] on the other hand, the Stephen family, whose father Leslie, writer and biographer, author of *Essays on Free Thinking and Plain Speaking* (1873), editor of the *Dictionary of*

National Biography (1885–1891), was a great Victorian intellectual and Anglican pastor turned agnostic.[9] He had, from his second marriage to Julia Duckworth, four children, Vanessa (who would become Vanessa Bell), Thoby, Virginia (the future Virginia Woolf), and Adrian.[10] One might say that Bloomsbury was the result of the meeting of a few Cambridgians, most of them Apostles, and of two exceptional women, Vanessa and Virginia Stephen.[11] Bloomsbury has been compared to a matriarchy with Vanessa as its head.

Among the numerous student societies, some secret, others less so, which proliferated at Cambridge and other English universities, the Apostles was one of the oldest and most important.[12] It was founded in 1820 by George Tomlinson, then student of St John's College, who would become bishop of Gibraltar. He formed this discussion group with 11 friends of his college, hence the name Apostles. It was in principle a secret society. Belonging to the Society could only be revealed after an Apostle's death, or to a wife. Of course, the nature of the discussions were to be kept secret.[13]

From the start, the Society adopted a peculiar set of working rules and an esoteric jargon. Following Kantian terminology, the Apostles, who called themselves 'brothers', distinguished between the external, phenomenal world from their noumenal world. One needed in order to be admitted into the latter, exceptional moral and intellectual qualities. The Apostles observed newly arrived students and recruited 'embryos' judged suitable for election.[14] The election of an embryo to the status of Apostle had to be unanimous. It was done on the proposition of a father and was called a birth. Like the birth of Christ, which, as many believed, occurred without a father, so that of an Apostle occurred without a mother, at least until 1985, when the first woman was elected into the Society, which still exists. Each newly elected member was associated with a number.

An Apostle was elected for life, Ludwig Wittgenstein being one of the few who resigned from the Society.[15] The Apostle was required, during university semesters, to participate in Society meetings, which took place every Saturday evening in the apartment of the 'moderator', who would read a paper. After this reading, a drawing of lots determined the order of brothers' commentaries. Discussion was followed by a vote on a question, normally but not necessarily relating to the theme of the moderator's paper, each vote being registered in the Society's records. Other than tea and coffee, 'whales' (sardines on toast), were consumed. Before adjourning, they drew lots to choose the next moderator, who then proposed four subjects for the brothers to choose. When a moderator came unprepared, by recycling an old text for example, he was condemned to paying for his brothers' dinners.

The themes debated varied, but they were mainly questions of an existential nature, on the meaning of life, morality, religion, art, literature and philosophy. And it was one's attitude towards the debate, the sincerity and disinterested search for truth, that counted, rather than content. Freedom of expression was a fundamental principle and no subject was to be considered taboo. In an autobiographical text dictated on his deathbed, Sidgwick described his adhesion to the Society in 1856 as 'an event [. . .] which had more effect on my intellectual life than any one thing that happened to me afterward', and thus described the state of mind of its members:

> I can only describe it as the spirit of the pursuit of truth with absolute devotion and unreserve by a group of intimate friends, who were perfectly frank with each other, and indulged in any amount of humorous sarcasm and playful banter, and yet each respects the other, and when he discourses tries to learn from him and see what he sees. Absolute candour was the only duty that the tradition of the society enforced. No consistency was demanded with opinions previously held – truth as we saw it

then and there was what we had to embrace and maintain, and there were no propositions so well established that an Apostle had not the right to deny or question, if he did so sincerely and not from mere love of paradox. The gravest subjects were continually debated, but gravity of treatment, as I have said, was not imposed, though sincerity was. (Sidgwick, 1906, pp. 34–5)

When he was no longer able to participate regularly in the weekly meetings, generally because he had finished his studies and was about to enter the phenomenal world to earn his living, the Apostle 'took wings' and became an 'angel'. The angel was to be replaced by a new Apostle, in such a way that their number remained constant. Other than Sidgwick, the Apostles Society counted among its ranks several figures of England's intellectual elite. One finds, among the elected of the nineteenth century, James Clerk Maxwell, Arthur Hallam, Frederick Maurice, Oscar Browning, F.W. Maitland, Alfred Tennyson, Alfred Whitehead, Bertrand Russell, J.E. McTaggart, Roger Fry, Ralph Hawtrey and George E. Moore,[16] who occupied at the turn of the century the post of secretary of the Society, which he then led. The thirty or so papers Moore presented constituted the outline of the philosophical vision that would be affirmed in *Principia Ethica* and in 'A refutation of idealism'. His thought played a capital role in the emergence of the Bloomsbury Group. Among the future associates of Bloomsbury, Roger Fry, who graduated from Cambridge in 1888, was elected in 1887. Elected in 1896, Desmond MacCarthy became the closest of Moore's friends.

OLD BLOOMSBURY

The story of Bloomsbury begins with the arrival at Trinity College, in October 1899, of five students (called 'freshmen'), Lytton Strachey, Leonard Woolf, Saxon Sydney-Turner, Thoby Stephen and Clive Bell. Rapidly becoming close friends, they founded in February 1900 a reading and discussion society, as was then common, which met Saturdays at midnight in Clive Bell's room, hence the name 'Midnight Society'. They met at this time since a few members of the group belonged to another society, the 'X', which met earlier on Saturday evenings. The Stephen sisters, duly chaperoned, visited their brother in Cambridge on the occasion of 'May weeks'[17] and met his friends and their future husbands. Leonard Woolf was dazzled by their beauty. The core of Bloomsbury started to form.

In February 1902, Lytton Strachey, 'discovered' by Bertrand Russell and Desmond MacCarthy, was elected Apostle at the same time as John Sheppard,[18] who would become close to Bloomsbury and a great friend of Keynes. His first paper, 'Ought the father to grow a beard', read on 10 May, dealt with the limits of art. Here he declared that everything, including the most taboo and delicate subjects, could be treated by art.[19] Strachey imposed himself rapidly as the new leader of the society, of which he would soon become secretary. Homosexual, he introduced to the Apostles the free discussion of sexuality in all its forms.[20] The expression 'higher sodomy' would designate a platonic homosexuality considered as the superior form of love. In Keynes's correspondence with Strachey, 'apostolic' was sometimes used as a codeword for homosexual.

In October, Saxon Sydney-Turner and Leonard Woolf made their entry into this coveted circle into which, to their vexation, Clive Bell and Thoby Stephen were not admitted. A short time later, Lytton Strachey and Leonard Woolf visited a new arrival at King's College, who appeared to them as an exceptional embryo, Maynard Keynes. John Sheppard brought him for tea in Moore's apartment, without whose agreement no embryo could be born. Moore agreed, and Keynes became on 28 February 1903 Apostle number 243, under the paternal protection of Sheppard.[21] Until November 1910, when he took wings,[22] Keynes read 20 or so papers to the Society. Most were devoted to matters of philosophical nature, in particular ethical, aesthetic and epistemological questions. It was in this context that he began the reflection that would lead him to write *A Treatise on Probability*. This reflection was stimulated by the 1903 publication of Bertrand Russell's *Principles of Mathematics* and especially, in October, of Moore's *Principia Ethica*.[23]

Leslie Stephen died on 22 February 1904, after a long illness. Depressive since the loss of his wife, he was very demanding towards his daughters, particularly Vanessa, who was required to maintain the house. The children decided to visit Italy in May. On the way back, they stopped in Paris, where Clive Bell was based, and he invited them to visit Rodin's studio. They heard for the first time of Cézanne, Gauguin, Bonnard and Matisse. Virginia fell into a severe depression, as was the case after the death of her mother, in 1895. She attempted suicide by throwing herself from a window.

Vanessa set about looking for new lodgings to escape the memories and sombre, suffocating atmosphere of the family residence in the fashionable quarter of Kensington. She found a big and bright house overlooking Gordon Square, in the heart of the Bloomsbury district. This address would become the headquarters of the Group and, from 1916 until his death in 1946, Keynes's London residence.[24] Gradually, the friends would settle in other parts of Bloomsbury, and find houses elsewhere in the English countryside and on France's Mediterranean coast.

Shortly after moving to Bloomsbury, Thoby Stephen, to keep in touch with his friends from Cambridge and others who began to become dispersed, organized weekly 'at home' meetings, which started on Thursdays at nine o'clock.[25] According to Virginia Woolf's recollections, the first meeting was held on 16 March 1905, which may be considered the official date of Bloomsbury's birth. The most regular participants were Saxon Sydney-Turner, Clive Bell and Lytton Strachey, who occasionally brought his sisters Marjorie, Pippa and Pernel.[26] Of the Cambridgians, only Leonard Woolf was absent; he had been a civil servant in Ceylon since 1904. Other participants included Desmond MacCarthy, Theodore Llewelyn Davies, Robin Mayor, Hilton Young, Charles Tennyson, Jack Pollock, Neville Lytton, Edward Marsh, then private secretary to Winston Churchill, and Gerald Duckworth.

During the summer of 1905, Vanessa started her own club, which brought together on Friday evenings mainly artists to discuss painting and eventually to organize exhibitions. She met the painter Duncan Grant, cousin of Lytton Strachey. Grant, who had met Clive Bell and Thoby Stephen in 1903, was returning from a year's stay in France. Although they were not painters, Virginia, Thoby and Sydney-Turner were admitted to the 'Friday Club', which attracted many. This club served until the start of the Great War as a meeting place for progressive painters and continued to organize exhibitions until the beginning of the 1920s.

Following a trip to Greece and Turkey by the Stephen family in September and October 1906, Thoby contracted typhoid fever, which was not correctly diagnosed, and he died on 20 November. It was a hard blow for his family and friends. The chief organizer of Bloomsbury had abruptly disappeared. Two days after her brother's death, Vanessa agreed to be married to Thoby's closest friend, Clive Bell, whom she had twice refused. The marriage took place on 7 February 1907. Two children would come of it, Julian in 1908 and Quentin in 1910.[27] Adrian and Virginia moved to 29 Fitzroy Square, in order to give the newlyweds privacy.

After a few months, they resumed the initiative of the Thursday evening salons, attended by new participants such as Duncan Grant, Henry Lamb and Charles Sanger. Keynes was integrated at this time into Bloomsbury, being invited to the group's meetings by Duncan Grant.

Keynes and Grant began an affair in May 1908, much to the dismay of Lytton Strachey, who was in love with his cousin.[28] The following year, Lytton proposed to Virginia Stephen, who immediately accepted. Just as quickly, both protagonists realized they were headed for disaster and decided to cancel their engagement. In the Bloomsbury circle, Virginia and Lytton remained close friends until the end, despite Virginia's jealousy of Lytton's literary success. After the failed marriage episode, Lytton suggested to Leonard Woolf, still in his post in Ceylon, to consider marrying Virginia. In 1910, it was Keynes's turn to be heartbroken in his relationship with Grant when the latter revealed to him that he had fallen in love with Adrian Stephen.

Grant, Adrian and Virginia Stephen were among the organizers of one of Bloomsbury's first public manifestations on 10 February 1910. The Dreadnought, pride of the British Navy, then moored at Weymouth, was the most imposing warship in the world. Adrian Stephen and his companion from college, Horace Cole, organized a false visit by the emperor of Abyssinia to the ship. Virginia Woolf and Duncan Grant disguised themselves as members of the emperor's retinue, personified by one of Cole's friends, Anthony Buxton, while Adrian played the role of translator. They learned some Swahili. The ship's commander Admiral William Fisher and his acolytes were fooled, and welcomed the band on board with much pomp. Invited to eat, the pseudo-Abyssinians refused citing religious considerations, but really fearing the effects the meal would have on their make-up and fake beards. Once the hoax became known, the affair caused a stir in the press and debates in Parliament. Cole and Grant received a few symbolic lashings to save the Navy's honour. Learning later that the incident led to a reinforcement of security measures concerning the official visitors, Virginia Woolf proclaimed that she was happy to have thus served her country. It was at this time that the expression Bloomsbury came about to designate the group of friends. Lytton Strachey, in a journal entry dating from 8 March 1910, called his friends the 'Bloombies'. In 1910 or 1911, in a letter, Molly MacCarthy called them 'Bloomsberries'.

'On or about December 1910 human character changed'

It was first in the realm of visual arts that Bloomsbury came to the attention of English society, before becoming known in literature, biography, economics and psychology. One man, older than the others, elected Apostle in 1887, and who came late to the group, played a key role. In January 1910, Roger Fry met Clive and Vanessa Bell by chance, on the platform at Cambridge train station.[29] Their conversation on the London-bound train is a key moment in Bloomsbury history. They discovered a common vision of art and civilization. Fry was already an esteemed painter and recognized art critic. He shared with them his intention of organizing an exhibition devoted to latest tendencies of French painting. One of the first Bloomsberries, Desmond MacCarthy, assisted him in this task. Held in London's Grafton Gallery, between 8 November 1910 and 15 January 1911, the exhibition was christened, after several discussions, 'Manet and the Post-Impressionists'.[30] Other than paintings by Manet, one could also admire 21 Cézannes, 37 Gauguins, 20 Van Goghs, as well as works by Matisse, Picasso, Derain, Rouault, Vlaminck and Maurice Denis. The exhibition outraged polite society and most critics. Spectators cried out in horror, others laughed. At best, the works were found incomprehensible; at worst, they were considered more pornography than art. There were a few positive critiques, one of whom predicted that such works would cost a fortune in 20 years. In the end, the scandal assured the exhibition's success. Desmond MacCarthy described the event as the 'Art-Quake' of 1910, and Virginia Woolf undoubtedly had it in mind when she declared on 8 May 1924, before the Cambridge Heretics Society: 'On or about December 1910 human character changed'.[31]

A troubled period of important social, political and economic transformations,[32] marked by important workers' agitation, the rise of the Labour Party, Liberal reforms, the struggle to extend the vote to women, in which the Bloomsberries were very involved, the end of the Edwardian period, which was also characterized by the easing of Victorian constraints, was marked by major cultural transformations, which are associated with the term 'modernism'. These transformations were not limited to painting, but characterized the whole art world and that of literature. The arrival of post-impressionism in England was accompanied by that of the *Ballets Russes*, who would revolutionize the world of dance.[33] Keynes, who would marry 15 years later a star dancer from Diaghilev's troop, was an avid consumer of these new productions.[34] The theatre world was also touched.[35] This process was far from being a purely English phenomenon. Paris and Vienna were, more than London, at the cutting-edge. Bloomsbury would be one of the points of entry for Parisian and Viennese influences in London.

From the end of the nineteenth century, Fry, lecturing at Cambridge, taught that in art, treatment is more important than subject. In 1909 he published 'An essay in aesthetics'. If Moore's *Principia Ethica* inspired Bloomsbury's ethical vision, this essay articulated its aesthetic principles. Among the Bloomsberries, Fry was the one who was the least impressed and influenced by Moore.[36] These two lines of thinking were thus independent, even if they came together in many regards. Contrary to the ideas of John Ruskin, for whom art and morality came together, Fry sought to liberate aesthetics from ethics: 'As to the value of aesthetic emotion – it is clearly infinitely removed from those ethical values to which Tolstoy would have confined it. It seems to be as remote from actual life and its practical utilities as the most useless mathematical theory' (Fry, 1920, p. 211).[37] Morality, he wrote, appreciates emotion by virtue of the action resulting from it. Art appreciates emotion in and of itself. As a consequence, art should not seek to imitate nature. It acts on what Fry called our 'imaginative life', which must be distinguished from 'actual life', which refers in large part to 'instinctive reactions to sensible objects' (Fry, 1909, p. 13). The experience of beauty in nature and beauty in art must not be confused. In order to unleash emotions in the spectator, the artist combines forms and colours.

Taking up and developing these ideas, which he discussed with Fry on the train from Cambridge to London in 1910, Clive Bell published *Art* in 1914. The central idea is that of 'significant form':

> What quality is common to Sta. Sophia and the windows at Chartres, Mexican sculpture, a Persian bowl, Chinese carpets, Giotto's frescoes at Padua, and the masterpieces of Poussin, Piero della Francesca, and Cézanne? Only one answer seems possible – significant form. In each, lines and colours combined in a particular way, certain forms and relations of forms, stir our aesthetic emotion. (C. Bell, 1914, p. 23)

There can be no objective validation of an aesthetic system. Founded on personal experience, it is by nature subjective. Bell does not use the term 'beauty' because it might refer to an objective conception. In his memoirs, published more than 40 years later, Bell indicates that 'significant form' can be replaced by any other expression, 'provided that what you mean by your name is a combination of lines and colours, or of notes, or of words, in itself moving, i.e. moving without reference to the outside world' (C. Bell, 1956, p. 72).

'Notes' refer to music and 'words' to literature. This conception of visual arts can thus apply to other arts. It is moreover more immediately applicable to music than to any other form of artistic expression. Except for Sydney-Turner, who was a good pianist, there were no musicians in the group, but most were music lovers. James Strachey, who became a psycho-analyst, remained until the end of his life a keen musicologist, writing opera programmes for the Glyndebourne Festival. This aesthetic vision also applies to the novelistic art of Virginia Woolf, as it does to Proust, Musil or Joyce. Responding to a question, Virginia Woolf claimed that her writing came more from texture than from structure, and that she handled her pen as others do their paint brush. She ridiculed, in *Mr. Bennett and Mrs. Brown* (1924), the typical Victorian novel which sought to tell a story for the moral elevation of its readers. It was no longer a matter of painting reality as faithfully as possible, but of creating in the reader an aesthetic emotion by describing 'streams of consciousness'.[38] In this process, time stops flowing regularly toward the future. It dissolves. One goes backward and takes shortcuts. Such is also the technique Lytton Strachey would use to describe the neuroses of great Victorians in *Eminent Victorians*. Keynes was also a master in the art of psychological biographies, which are found for example in the *Economic Consequences of the Peace* and in his *Essays in Biography*, one of his more remarkable books. And, even if we are far from aesthetics, one finds in his approach to economic processes, where 'animal spirits', irrational urges, uncertainty and fear of the future play a role, an analogous vision to that which is revealed in the pages of Virginia Woolf or Lytton Strachey.

After the first post-impressionist exhibition, Fry was severely criticized, treated as a charlatan and sorcerer's apprentice. This reception, far from discouraging him, stimulated him and, with the help of Clive Bell and Leonard Woolf, the exhibition's secretary, he repeated this performance in 1912 with a second exhibition, whose stars were Picasso and Matisse. The latter, who one conservative critic described as one of Cézanne's degenerate offspring, was represented by 34 works, including *Danse*. Several paintings from Russia were displayed. Russian ballets, music and literature were in vogue. Paintings by Duncan Grant, Vanessa Bell and Roger Fry were also hung on the walls of the Grafton Gallery. The exhibition made fewer waves than the preceding one. There were more visitors and more sales. Within the exhibition, Leonard Woolf organized sessions during which French and English writers read their works. This arrangement served to illustrate the convergences between transformations in the visual arts world and those which marked literature.

Indefatigable, Fry organized trips to France, Italy and Turkey to study painting and architecture. During a trip to Turkey in April 1911 with H.T.J. Norton[39] and her husband, Vanessa Bell fell seriously ill. Fry, whose wife had recently been confined for mental illness, showed himself to be more attentive and effective toward Vanessa than Clive Bell. Shortly after their return, Roger Fry and Vanessa became lovers, until about two years later, when the latter fell in love with Duncan Grant, which caused Roger considerable upset. But, as was Bloomsbury's rule, friendship would prevail over romantic spite, and the three of them would often be seen in various places, travelling and painting together.

The year 1911 also brought with it another structural change in Bloomsbury's geography. Although they were brother and sister, or perhaps because of it, Virginia and Adrian Stephen were in perpetual conflict over domestic issues. They decided to solve the problem by moving into bigger lodgings at 38 Brunswick Square and by sharing them with Gerald Shove,[40] Grant and Keynes. The latter took responsibility for the lease. A complex domestic system was put in place for, among other things, the organization of meals. On his return from Ceylon in June 1911,[41] Leonard Woolf moved in with them. In August 1912, he married Virginia. She was then finishing, after several rewrites, her first novel, *The Voyage Out*, which would be published in 1915. The end of this work, in 1913, was followed by a new and serious mental crisis which would last until 1915. On 9 September 1913, she swallowed a strong dose of sleeping pills that Leonard had neglected to keep locked away, and only escaped death due to the presence of Maynard's brother Geoffrey Keynes, who was a doctor.

In 1913 Roger Fry founded a venture whose goal was, on the one hand, to assure subsistence to young artists having difficulty to sell their work and, on the other, to fusion art with everyday life in decorative art.[42] Fry, who published 'Art and Socialism' in 1912, believed that the distinction between fine art and applied art was erroneous and that the greatest art was communal. The Omega Workshops, as it was named, sought, given the depressing uniformity of industrial products, to transform domestic objects – dishes, pottery, rugs and furniture – into works of art, and to decorate houses with frescos inspired by Byzantine art, which greatly impressed Fry and his friends. Grant, Vanessa Bell and Fry were the three directors of the Omega Workshops, which set up shop at 33 Fitzroy Square on 8 July 1913, and were announced as a limited company 'for applying Post-Impressionism to domestic decorations and furniture' (quoted in Collins, 1983, p. 47). Keynes, E.M. Forster and G.B. Shaw were among the shareholders. Like the post-impressionist exhibitions, Omega's creations were subject to sharp criticism denouncing their immoral character. But at the same time, the workshops would enjoy the financial support of a few rich patrons, mostly women such as Ottoline Morrell,[43] Lady Cunard, Lady Hamilton, Madame Vandevelde or Princess Lichnowsky. The first two hosted receptions frequented by Bloomsbury. Like other projects of this type, Omega's creations were influenced by the vogue of Russian ballet. In October 1913, Omega's contribution to the Ideal Home Exhibition aroused strong reactions. At the same time, the painter Wyndham Lewis left abruptly with four other members of the group,[44] accusing Fry of favouring his Bloomsbury friends. It appears that Lewis did not accept the rule of anonymity in force for Omega's productions. He became, for the next 30 years, one of the most virulent adversaries of Bloomsbury, which he never stopped attacking in his writings and conferences.[45] He accused Bloomsbury of running a veritable dictatorship in the art world, and of being responsible for the ostracism of which he was victim. In 1916, Vanessa Bell and Duncan Grant left London for Wisset Lodge, in Suffolk, and then in Charleston, in Sussex,[46] so that their involvement in the Omega Workshops was much diminished. The enterprise was closed during the summer of 1919. Omega started to decline when, at the beginning of the war, Vanessa Bell and Duncan Grant stopped working there.[47]

WAR AND COUNTRYSIDE

The war was a brutal shock to a group of friends who already saw themselves as architects of a new civilized, rational society, one liberated from moral constraints and devoted to the quest for beauty and truth. Their first works started to appear. Bloomsbury's painters and art critics became regulars in Paris, where in 1913, at Gertrude Stein's home, Duncan Grant met

Picasso, who would become close to the group. At the same time, they amused themselves intensely. Bloomsbury was the centre of a night life marked by parties and often extravagant receptions, in which dressing up in fancy dress or drag was common. Without being very rich, they lived comfortably. They started to colonize Sussex, moving there with their servants. Virginia Stephen was the first, renting in 1911 a house in the village of Firle, near Brighton. She named it 'Little Talland House' after Talland House at St Ives in Cornwall, which her parents had rented from 1882 to 1894.[48] In 1912 she discovered close by a house which would play an important role in Bloomsbury's story over the next few years, Asheham House.[49] The house warming party took place on 11 February in the presence of those who would become frequent occupants: Vanessa and Clive Bell, Adrian Stephen, Grant, Fry and Leonard Woolf. It was at Asheham, visited by as many French as English painters, where the second post-impressionist exhibition was prepared. Virginia first shared this house with her sister Vanessa, who would often paint there with Grant. After her marriage to Leonard Woolf in August 1912, it was the Bells who would become, for three years, the principal occupants, followed by the Woolfs[50] until 1919. They then took possession of Monks House, which was surrounded by a very large garden, in the village of Rodmell, in the same region. It was there that Virginia Woolf wrote a large part of her work, in a little pavilion that she had made in the garden. A renowned gardener, Leonard Woolf would win prizes for the quality of his fruits and vegetables.[51]

Confronted with the unleashing of hostilities, the friends' positions fluctuated, so much so that Maynard, always optimistic, predicted that the conflict would be of short duration. At Bloomsbury's limits, two extreme attitudes were represented by the poet Rupert Brooke, who took arms and died on the Aegean Sea on 23 April 1915,[52] and Bertrand Russell, whose pacifism and radical anti-militarism would put him in prison. Clive Bell thought at first of joining the army, before publishing in 1916 *Peace at Once*, which would be burned on the orders of London's mayor. Adrian Stephen thought of volunteering before becoming secretary of a group founded in autumn 1914 to combat conscription, the No Conscription Fellowship. Duncan Grant considered joining Artists Rifles, before becoming a conscientious objector. It was the introduction, for the first time in British history, of conscription in January 1916 that created Bloomsbury's consensus regarding the war. This matter was discussed during a New Year's party at Asheham. Without necessarily being pacifists, all refused to accept that the State could require them to bear arms. Several would be very active within the No Conscription Fellowship and National Council against Conscription. Keynes, who was exempted from military service because of his work at the Treasury, testified in favour of his friends when they were called to stand trial as conscientious objectors. There was nevertheless considerable tension between him and the rest of Bloomsbury. His departure from the British Delegation at the Paris Conference, followed by his writing of *The Economic Consequences of the Peace* would see him reconciled with them.[53]

During the war, the Garsington manor, near Oxford, acquired by Philip and Ottoline Morrell in 1915, became the meeting place for 'conchies', or conscientious objectors. In an uninterrupted succession of brilliant receptions, the Bloomsberries came into contact with other artists, writers and students, but also with politicians, including Prime Minister Asquith, who was himself opposed to conscription.[54] But it was the Charleston farmhouse that would become, from 1916, Bloomsbury's second centre.[55] In spring 1916, Grant and David Garnett[56] established themselves with Vanessa Bell at Wisset Lodge farm near Halesworth, in Suffolk, to participate in agricultural work in hopes of softening the tribunal before their appearance as conscientious objectors. After the failure of their first appearance, in spite of the presence of Philip Morrell and Keynes, Grant and Garnett obtained in an appeal, on 28 June, exemption from active service on the condition that they carry out work of national importance.[57] As this work could not be carried out at Wisset Lodge, where the farmers were hostile to conscientious objectors, they found an employer in Sussex, near Asheham. It was Virginia who, during one of her walks near the village of Firle, discovered Charleston, which is at the foot of Firle Beacon, one of the summits of the South Downs. With Keynes's financial contribution – he kept a room there from 1916 to 1926 – the trio rented the farmhouse belonging to Lord Gage and moved in October 1916. It was a singular *ménage à trois*, typical of Bloomsbury, in which Vanessa Bell was in love with Duncan Grant who was in love with David Garnett who sought to seduce Vanessa. And, to crown it all, in 1942, David Garnett married Angelica, the daughter of Vanessa Bell and Duncan Grant, the identity of whose father would remain hidden for 17 years.[58] Angelica and David Garnett had four children.

The living conditions at Charleston were rudimentary, without running water, gas or electricity, but these deficiencies did not prevent Vanessa Bell from finding the place a paradise. Her overflowing energy completely transformed Charleston into what became a veritable museum, with her mural decorations and those of Duncan Grant, to which the children Julian, Quentin and Angelica also contributed, as well as furniture and accessories from Omega. Charleston's renovation was the putting into practice of their aesthetic principles and those of Omega. Vanessa would live there for 44 years and Duncan for 62, until their death.[59]

Besides Charleston and other parts of Sussex, Tidmarsh in Berkshire would become another of Bloomsbury's meeting places. Lytton Strachey, who also claimed himself conscientious objector, had been judged unfit for combat.[60] After finishing *Eminent Victorians*,[61] he moved to Tidmarsh in December 1917 with Dora Carrington,[62] living in Mill House, whose rent Keynes would again help to pay. It was another strange couple. In 1918 Carrington met Ralph Partridge,[63] who fell in love with her. Shortly after, Mill House became the site of another *ménage à trois*, in which Lytton Strachey was attracted to Ralph who, finally, would marry Dora Carrington in 1921. Shortly after the marriage, Dora would become close to one of Ralph's friends, Gerald Brenan.[64] As for Ralph, he began living in 1926 with Frances Marshall,[65] whom he would marry after Dora's death in 1933. Throughout these events, which have Mill House, and then Ham Spray, near Hungerford, in Wiltshire, as backdrop, Dora Carrington remained deeply attached to Lytton Strachey. She committed suicide with a hunting rifle a few months after Lytton's death on 11 March 1932.

The year 1917 also saw the birth of another important Bloomsbury institution, the Hogarth Press, which took its name from the house where Leonard and Virginia Woolf lived in Richmond, outside London. It was conceived from the start by Leonard as a therapeutic support for his wife, something to distract her from her writing and counter her depressive moods. It was often after completing a novel that Virginia would find herself battling against her demons. In fact, the Hogarth Press became a major publishing house, printing, not only the works of Bloomsbury,[66] including several pamphlets by Keynes, but also several major works, foreign as well as English.[67] We will return below to the publication of Freud's works.

On the painting scene, Bloomsbury remained very active during the war. An exhibition entitled 'The New Movement in Art' was held in July in Birmingham and moved to London in September 1917. Works by Fry, Grant, Vanessa Bell and several contemporary French works were shown. Omega continued to function until 1919 despite the departure of Bell and Grant. Fry remained an indefatigable organizer and driving force on the London arts scene.

NEW BLOOMSBURY

A movement thus far relatively confidential and little known by the public, Bloomsbury became an imposing presence in British and Western cultural life between the wars. This new Bloomsbury was composed of the founding core plus new generations of artists, writers and other intellectuals who attached themselves at varying distances. In 1920, on Molly MacCarthy's instigation, the 13 members of the initial group formed the Bloomsbury Memoir Club. Initially, it intended to pressure Desmond MacCarthy into creating the literary work that everyone expected of him. They abandoned this attempt on realizing that the pages he seemed to be reading were blank! The meetings of the Memoir Club were held after dinner, two or three times a year, at the home of one of its members, and were occasions on which one or two of its members read something autobiographical. The Memoir Club was a structured group which co-opted members.[68] In 1921 Keynes read his paper on Melchior and, in 1938, 'My early beliefs'. Generally, the papers were of high literary quality. In 1943, Vanessa Bell painted a canvas representing a Memoir Club meeting depicting Duncan Grant, Leonard Woolf, Vanessa and Clive Bell, David Garnett, Maynard and Lydia Keynes, Desmond and Molly MacCarthy, Quentin Bell and E.M. Forster. This canvas also depicted a wall on which three deceased members, Virginia Woolf, Lytton Strachey and Roger Fry, were represented as portraits. The Club's last meeting took place in 1956, attended by four of its original members, Vanessa Bell, Duncan Grant, Leonard Woolf and E.M. Forster.

Bloomsbury's first literary works appeared during the First World War, if one excludes E.M. Forster, whose first novel, *Where Angels Fear to Tread*, was published in 1905. *The Voyage Out*, whose completion was followed by a suicide attempt by Virginia Woolf, appeared in 1915. A series of innovative novels would follow which would establish her as one of the major writers of the twentieth century, particularly *Mrs Dalloway*, *To the Lighthouse* and *The Waves*. The regular diary she kept from 1915 is among other things a chronicle of Bloomsbury. Leonard Woolf also tried his hand at writing a play, *The Hotel*, and novels, *The Village in the Jungle* in 1913 and *The Wise Virgins*, in 1914, a portrait of Old Bloomsbury, but he soon realized it was best to leave such matters to his wife. He turned instead to literary criticism, a genre which Virginia practised as well, and especially to political writing, putting forward from 1916 the creation of an international political organization. *Eminent Victorians*, a psychological dissection of four heroes of the Victorian age, appeared in 1918 and assured the fortune and fame of Lytton Strachey. This book, which renewed the art of biography, was a very great selling success. It would be followed by portraits of Queen Victoria and Queen Elizabeth. The following year, Keynes himself attained international recognition with another best seller, *The Economic Consequences of the Peace*, which contained a tableau of the protagonists of the Paris peace conference using techniques similar to those of Strachey. In the inter-war period, it was the Keynes–Strachey–Virginia Woolf trio which was most familiar to the public.

Bloomsbury continued to impose itself on the world of art and most particularly on painting, as much in criticism and exhibition organization as in creation. Duncan Grant had his first individual exhibition in 1920 and Vanessa Bell in 1922. Several others would follow. The two artists also became the most influential force during the inter-war years in the area of decorative art. They were commissioned to decorate the Sands home in Dieppe, two churches[69] and even a passenger liner, the Queen Mary. However, in this last case, Duncan Grant's production would be rejected by Cunard, the ship's owner. The company felt it was not appropriate for the type of passengers travelling on such a vessel. One of their most important creations was the music room situated over the Lefebvre Gallery, on King's Street, in Saint James, which opened in December 1932. Its inauguration was marked by a famous Bloomsbury reception, organized by Vanessa and Virginia, celebrated by the press as the shining stars in the literary and artistic world and uncrowned queens. Roger Fry also continued his artistic production in addition to pursuing his activities as critic, writer, teacher and organizer. A friend of Bloomsbury, Kenneth Clark, was named director of the National Gallery in 1933.

While, at the end of the war, modern painters from France and other European countries started to be exhibited, appreciated and bought in London,[70] in large part thanks to Bloomsbury's efforts, the group's painters started to be exhibited in Paris, particularly at Charles Vidrac's gallery. The links between Bloomsbury and France, important since the turn of the century, intensified after the war.[71] This translated into frequent stays by the Bloomsberries in France.[72] Vanessa Bell and Duncan Grant discovered Saint-Tropez in 1921 and spent a few months there painting. In April 1927, the Woolfs stayed for the first time in Cassis, which Roger Fry had discovered in 1915, and which Vanessa Bell called later 'Bloomsbury-sur-Méditerranée'. Vanessa and Duncan obtained in 1927 the lease of a small villa, 'La Bergère', situated in the wine producing lands of the Château de Fontcreuse. They stayed at this 'reconstructed Charleston' on several occasions until 1938. This house helped them escape the downside of their growing notoriety in England. 'La Bergère' was naturally a place where other Bloomsbury members stayed.

While Bloomsbury became increasingly important for the odd gathering of painters who formed the London Group,[73] Keynes founded in 1925 (with Samuel Courtauld, Hindley Smith and L.H. Myers) the London Artists' Association, with the goal of providing artists with a regular income.[74] Grant and Vanessa Bell were involved, before withdrawing at the beginning of the 1930s. Very active as a Bloomsbury propagandist, in 1923 Keynes, along with progressive liberal friends, took control of the periodical *Nation and Athenaeum*. He became chairman of the board of directors and named Leonard Woolf the literary director. This monthly review included a section on politics and economics, in which he himself published a number of articles, and an arts and literature section largely dominated by Bloomsbury writers.

Theatre, music, opera and especially ballet were other domains with which Bloomsbury was involved. Returning in 1918, accompanied by Igor Stravinsky, Ernest Ansermet, André Derain and Picasso, the *Ballets Russes* continued to fascinate, achieve great success and influence the Bloomsberries. In return, the latter also influenced the ballet's decorators and costume makers.[75] Links were established between the inhabitants of the two worlds, with Ottoline Morrell often acting as go-between. Roger Fry would become friendly with Larionov and Goncharova. Two new stars appeared. The great dancer and choreographer Massine visited Duncan Grant in his studio. Several Bloomsberries were found in Lydia Lopokova's dressing room, which André Gide[76] also visited. Picasso sketched the Russian dancers several times, including Lydia Lopokova.[77] Diaghilev called upon his services to design decors and costumes. During the reception following the production of *Sheherazade*, in October 1918, Keynes met for the first time the woman who would become his wife in 1925. The evening of the Armistice, in November 1918, in the collector Montague Shearman's house at Adelphi, brought together most of the Bloomsbury friends, Diaghilev, Massine, Lopokova, D.H. Lawrence, Augustus John and several others. One of Bloomsbury's most memorable postwar soirées was organized by Clive Bell and Keynes at 46 Gordon Square on 29 July to mark the end of the season and to bring together their friends, as well as other artists and writers and the members of Diaghilev's troop, including Olga Kokhlova and her husband, Picasso, Derain, Massine, Ernest Ansermet, Aldous Huxley and Drieu La Rochelle, who would be later politically compromised by his association with Nazis. The invitation card indicated that the hosts were Madame Picasso, Mr Keynes and Mr Clive Bell. Thirty-three people were present.

Absent was Lydia Lopokova, who disappeared suddenly on 10 July 1919, only to return in April 1921. No one knows exactly what she did during this time; some believed her to be in the US, others in Russia. The most likely hypothesis is that she was fleeing Randolfo Barocchi, administrator of the *Ballets Russes*, whom she married in 1916. Keynes started seeing her in December 1921. This relationship caused complex problems with Bloomsbury, which illustrate well the familial nature of the Group. The correspondence between Keynes, Vanessa Bell, Virginia Woolf and Duncan Grant on this subject is fascinating. At first, Keynes went to Vanessa for advice in his attempt at seducing Lydia. Vanessa then explained to Keynes, who wanted to bring Lydia to Charleston, that, in a group as close-knit as Bloomsbury, a newcomer is not so easily admitted. Between them, Keynes's friends lamented the possibility of a wife and children which could only serve to gentrify him even more and, Virginia added, fatten a man who had already started to distance himself from his Apostolic and Bloomsburian ideals during the war. Having obtained her divorce in 1925, Lydia married Keynes on 4 August of the same year, the latter forcing a very reluctant Duncan Grant to act as witness. Bloomsbury's geography changed again with this marriage, with Clive Bell leaving 46 Gordon Square, where he had a room, and the Keyneses taking total possession of the flat. Keynes obtained, at the same time, the lease of the Tilton farmhouse, situated 500 metres from Charleston. It was there that he wrote his major works, and it is there that he passed away. There were now three Bloomsbury axes in Sussex: Charleston, Monks and Tilton. Even though Lydia was poorly received into the group, Keynes's receptions were considered Bloomsbury's best, along with those of Duncan Grant. Lydia Keynes would finally be admitted, in 1930, into the Bloomsbury Memoir Club.

BLOOMSBURY AND PSYCHOANALYSIS

It is not surprising that Freud and Bloomsbury came together.[78] Psychoanalysis and the culture of Bloomsbury sprang from the same context, in reaction to the same type of society and to the same culture, against religious obscurantism and the sexual morality that was associated with it. Moreover, Bloomsbury's complex, tortured, and generally self-obsessed personalities were fertile ground for this new discipline. For Moore and his friends, as for Freud and his disciples, speech played a central role. It was the way by which one reaches consciousness, and especially the unconscious. In 'My early beliefs', Keynes, recounting his youth with the Apostles, describes himself and his friends as 'pre-Freudian', and as having 'completely misunderstood human nature, including our own' (1938-12, p. 448). But his words are in part contradicted by those of Leonard Woolf, relating the events of a period anterior to Keynes's arrival. Like the latter, he admitted that he knew nothing of Freud at that time. But he recounted how he developed, with Lytton Strachey, a 'method' to explore psychology and thus to improve interpersonal relations, making them more authentic:

The 'method' referred to in the conversation had been invented by Lytton and me; it was a kind of third-degree psychological investigation applied to the souls of one's friends. Though it was a long time before we had any knowledge of Freud, it was a kind of compulsory psychoanalysis. It was intended to reveal to us, and incidentally to the victim, what he was really like; the theory was that by imparting to all concerned the deeper psychological truths, personal relationships would be much improved. Its technique was derived partly from Socrates, partly from Henry James, partly from G.E. Moore, and partly from ourselves. (L. Woolf, 1960, pp. 113–14)

Psychoanalysis made its official entry in England with the 1913 foundation by Freud's disciple Ernest Jones of the London Psychoanalytic Society, a branch of the International Psychoanalytical Association created in 1910.[79] Freud's thought had already made an incursion, notably through the Society for Psychical Research, which elected the founder of psychoanalysis as an honorary member in 1912.[80] In 1914 the English translation of *The Psychopathology of Everyday Life* was published, which was read and discussed at Bloomsbury. Lytton Strachey composed a short dialogue, 'According to Freud' (Strachey, 1972, pp. 112–20) the same year and Leonard Woolf published an account of the book in the *New Weekly*. In May, in preparation for his review, Woolf read *The Interpretation of Dreams*. Appearing in June 1914, this review was the first writing on Freud in England in a non-medical journal. This date may be considered the beginning of an association between Bloomsbury and Freud which would intensify in the following years.

Adrian Stephen, a member of Bloomsbury's initial circle, was the first to delve into the new discipline. He married Karin Costelloe in 1914, and the couple decided to study medicine with the goal of practising psychoanalysis. They started their new profession in 1926. Here is how Virginia described to Vanessa, on 22 May 1927, the activity of their younger brother: 'I creep up and peer into the Stephen's dining room where any afternoon, in full daylight, is to be seen a woman in the last agony of despair, lying on a sofa, burying her face in the pillow, while Adrian broods over her like a vulture, analyzing her soul' (V. Woolf, 2003, p. 228).

Lytton Strachey's younger brother James made the same decision at the end of the war, deciding to reveal his unconscious directly to the observation of the master. He travelled to Vienna in June 1920 with his wife Alix Florence-Sargant. Freud, deviating from freudian orthodoxy, agreed to see them both.[81] He judged them fit to practise in 1922, although Alix would continue her cure for many years. But it was on another level that the couple's practice of analysis would leave its mark. Freud, unsatisfied with his American translator, A.A. Brill, asked them to translate his writings. This request would be the start of a gigantic undertaking.[82]

Keynes was to preside over the annual Apostles dinner in June 1921 and he invited, as was the custom, every former Apostle still alive. James Strachey wrote to him on 6 June: 'I'm sorry to say that I shan't be back in England in time for the Dinner. It's sickening to miss it – but the Professor's scalpel is still probing the recesses of my *verdrängten Unbewussten* [repressed unconscious]'. Keynes preceded the reading of this letter, in his presidential speech, with the following commentary: 'James Strachey, who is being disintegrated at the hands of Professor Freud, rendered immortal by Professor [unintelligible word], and fitted out with a more than ordinarily complete sex apparatus at the expense of the poorer classes of Vienna, writes as follows' (1921-2, p. 3).[83]

James and Alix Strachey's stay in Vienna was the occasion for an indirect exchange between Freud and Keynes. On 22 February 1921, Lytton Strachey wrote to his friend:

The enclosed, from James, may amuse you. Apparently your fame in Vienna is tremendous, & Dr Freud says that he has got far more notoriety from a mention of his name by you somewhere than from anything else. He received several letters of congratulations on the occasion. Otherwise he is unknown in Austria.

The mention of Freud is found in Chapter 3 of *The Economic Consequences of the Peace*, in which Keynes traces the portrait of the protagonists at the Paris Conference and writes, regarding President Wilson: 'In the language of medical psychology, to suggest to the President that the treaty was an abandonment of his professions was to touch on the raw of a Freudian complex' (1919-1, p. 34). Freud himself attempted, at the end of the 1920s, to write a psychological portrait of President Wilson, with the American journalist and diplomat William Bullitt, who suggested the idea to him. The book, which was finished in 1932, was only published in 1966, after the death of President Wilson's second wife. In his preface, Bullitt indicated that both read Keynes's book while preparing their own (Freud and Bullitt, 1966, p. vii).

A reader of Keynes and undoubtedly of Virginia Woolf, Freud was also a reader of Lytton Strachey. He wrote to him after the publication of *Elizabeth and Essex*, on 25 December 1928:

I am acquainted with all your earlier publications, and I have read them with great enjoyment. But the enjoyment was essentially an aesthetic one. This time you have moved me more deeply, for you yourself have reached greater depths. You are aware of what other historians so easily overlook – that it is impossible to understand the past with certainty, because we cannot divine men's motives and the essence of their minds and so cannot interpret their actions . . . As a historian, then, you show that you are steeped in the spirit of psychoanalysis. (quoted in Meisel and Kendrick, 1985, p. 332)

In reality, when he was writing *Eminent Victorians* and *Queen Victoria*, Lytton Strachey was reticent regarding Freud, about whom he knew little. The influence came from sources other than psychoanalysis, such as Dostoievsky, whom he regarded, like Virginia Woolf, as one of the world's greatest novelists. Freud recognized that great writers had preceded him in the direction he explored. This awareness shows how the cross-influences between Freud, Strachey, Keynes and Woolf were not simple or linear. In Vienna as in London, in Paris and elsewhere in the world, the beginning of the twentieth century saw the emergence of a new vision of the world, of relations between individuals and society, of the motivations of human action, of the perception of time and the streams of consciousness, in art, literature and science. Borders became blurred. New forms of relationships were being explored. People realized they were living in a changing and unstable universe characterized by uncertainty and in which they must make decisions in the dark.

The coming together of Bloomsbury and the Viennese master which began in 1914 led to a more formal alliance in 1924,[84] one in which Leonard Woolf would once again play a determinant role. He was approached by James, early in 1924, to be editor of Freud's *Collected Papers*, a collection of four volumes to be published in a translation by a team composed of Alix, James and Joan Rivière as principal architects. Leonard immediately accepted this risky gamble, which Unwin publishers had already refused. Published in 1924 and 1925, the four volumes became an immense success, in the USA as much as in England, and remained in circulation for 40 years.[85] Keynes read this edition, as did most of his Bloomsbury friends. A controversy over Freud developed in the columns of the *Nation and Athenaeum*, to which Keynes contributed on 29 August 1925 under the pseudonym Siela:

Professor Freud seems to me to be endowed, to the degree of genius, with the scientific imagination which can body forth an abundance of innovating ideas, shattering possibilities, working hypotheses, which have sufficient foundation in intuition and common experience to deserve the most patient and unprejudiced examination, and which contain, in all probability, both theories which will have to be discarded or altered out of recognition and also theories of great and permanent significance. (1925-19, p. 392)

From 1924 until Freud's death, the Hogarth Press published all the English translations of his books, as well as all works by the Psycho-Analytical Library, associated with the London Institute of Psychoanalysis, in all about 70 titles. Three months after the *anschluss*, Freud succeeded in leaving Vienna and arrived in London in June 1938. On 28 January 1939, he received the Woolfs for tea at his new home in Hampstead. For Leonard, 'He was not only a genius, but also, unlike many geniuses, an extraordinarily nice man' (L. Woolf, 1967, p. 166).[86] On their arrival, the elderly man, 'extraordinarily courteous in a formal, old-fashioned way' ceremoniously offered a daffodil to Virginia: 'There was something about him as of a half-extinct volcano, something sombre, suppressed, reserved. He gave me the feeling which only a very few people whom I have met gave me, a feeling of great gentleness, but behind the gentleness, great strength' (ibid., p. 169). From her side, Virginia described Freud as 'a screwed up shrunk very old man: with a monkeys light eyes, paralysed spasmodic movements, inarticulate but alert . . . an old fire now flickering' (V. Woolf, 1977–84, vol. 5, p. 202).

Freud died a few months after this meeting, shortly after the beginning of the war, on 23 September 1939. It was at this moment that the publication of his complete works was conceived. The work of translating and editing would be undertaken by James Strachey, whose physical resemblance to Freud, at the end of his life, was striking. The 24 volumes of the Standard Edition were published from 1953 by the Hogarth Press. James died in 1967, after the publication of the 23rd volume, just before being awarded a prize for this monument of erudition which became the basic reference on Freud, surpassing even the German edition.

It was after her meeting with Freud that Virginia Woolf began seriously reading his works 'to enlarge the circumference, to give my brain a wider scope; to make it objective; to get outside' (V. Woolf, 1977–84, vol. 5, p. 248). She claimed this reading enabled her to see more clearly into her ambivalent relationship toward her parents, into that mixture of love and hate that Freud showed to be natural. But in fact, she discovered this ambivalence earlier, and one finds traces of it in her first writings.

Virginia Woolf would soon follow Freud to the grave. Upon completion of *Between the Acts* and fearing a new attack of madness, she crossed, on 28 March 1941, the few hundred metres separating Monks House from the Ouse River and walked in carrying heavy stones in her fur coat pockets. A group of adolescents found her body on 18 April. Already distraught by the brutal death of Julian in 1937, Vanessa Bell would never completely recover from the shock of her sister's suicide. But Bloomsbury went on. In 1969, Leonard Woolf, the last witness of the group's beginnings, disappeared. He died shortly after finishing the last volume of his autobiography.

BLOOMSBURY PORTRAITS

BELL, Clive (1881–1964): descended from a rich family of mine owners, Clive Bell was a hedonist, hunter and unrepentant womanizer. After studies at Cambridge, he spent a year in

Paris in 1904 where he discovered French painting and learned art criticism. He would make several more trips to France, a country he loved and which would make him a member of the Légion d'honneur in 1936. He became the friend of several artists, including Picasso. He married Vanessa Stephen in February 1907, but their married life would become one of friendship after a few years and they would share Charleston with Duncan Grant. He had several affairs, with, among others, Mary Hutchinson, Molly MacCarthy, Barbara Bagenal and Benita Jaeger. He is author of *Art* (1914), *Peace at Once* (1915), *Since Cézanne* (1922), *Proust* (1928), *Civilization* (1928), *Warmongers* (1939) and *Old Friends* (1956), recollections of Bloomsbury. Socialist and pacifist during the First World War, he evolved toward increasingly conservative positions. On Clive Bell, see Bywater (1975).

BELL, Vanessa, née Stephen (1879–1961): eldest daughter of Leslie Stephen and Julia Duckworth, Vanessa Bell may be considered the soul of Bloomsbury, the fixed point around which everything revolved and the maternal organizer toward whom everyone turned to share their problems. Keynes called her 'Ludendorff Bell'. She married Clive Bell in February 1907, a few months after the death of her brother Thoby. Julian in 1908 and Quentin in 1910 would be born of this union. After an affair with Roger Fry, Vanessa, who had acquired the lease of the Charleston farmhouse, in Sussex, would live there with Duncan Grant from 1916 until her death, dividing her time between Sussex, London and the South of France. She had a daughter with Duncan Grant, Angelica, born in 1918, the identity of whose father would not be revealed until her eighteenth birthday, a role until then assumed by Clive Bell. Vanessa Bell left behind a considerable work as a painter and decorator. She had her first solo exhibition in 1922. She was profoundly affected by the brutal death of her son Julian in 1937 and by the suicide of her sister Virginia Woolf, in March 1941. She died at Charleston on 7 April 1961. A commemorative exhibition of her works was organized by the Adams Gallery in London in October 1961. A part of her correspondence was published in 1998. On Bell, see Spalding (1983).

FORSTER, Edward Morgan (1879–1970): as a student at Cambridge, Edward Morgan Forster was elected Apostle in February 1901. He considered himself more at the group's periphery than at its core. As close friend of the Woolfs, Lytton Strachey and Roger Fry, often spending time at Charleston and Monks House, and as member of the Memoir Club, he must be considered a member of Bloomsbury. He was the first of the Group's writers to be published, starting with *Where Angels Fear to Tread* in 1905, which was followed by *A Room with a View* (1908), *Howard's End* (1910), and *A Passage to India* (1924), his most famous novel. Published posthumously, *Maurice* (1971) is the story of a homosexual love affair widely read by Bloomsbury. He was prolific as an author of literary criticism. He lived with his mother, a very conformist Victorian, at Abinger Hammer, until the latter's death in 1945. In 1946 he was made honorary fellow of King's College, Cambridge, where he remained until his death. His eightieth birthday in January 1956 was the occasion of a moving reunion of Bloomsbury's survivors. On Forster, see Furbank (1979).

FRY, Roger (1863–1934): painter, teacher, critic and historian of art, friend of Picasso and Matisse, Roger Fry was Bloomsbury's oldest member, which he became in 1910. After studying natural sciences, he turned to painting and studied in Paris in 1892. Elected Apostle in 1887, he worked at the Metropolitan Museum of Art of New York in 1906–1907. In 1910 and 1912 he organized two London exhibitions of mostly French post-impressionist works, the first of which caused a scandal. In 1913 he founded the Omega Workshops with the aim of uniting artistic activity and home decoration. After his wife's confinement to a mental hospital, he had an affair with Vanessa Bell between 1911 and 1914. He remained very attached to her, and they often painted and travelled together with Duncan Grant. He lived with Helen Anrep, née Maitland, wife of the Russian Mosaicist Boris Anrep, from 1926 until his death. He was named Slade Professor of Fine Art at Cambridge in 1933. He is author, among others of *Giovanni Bellini* (1899), *Vision and Design* (1920), *The Artist and Psycho-analysis* (1924), *Art and Commerce* (1926), *Transformations* (1926), *Cézanne* (1927), *Henri Matisse* (1930), *Reflections on British Painting* (1934). His letters were published in 1972. Several of his writings have been collected by Reed (1996) and Goodwin (1998). On Fry, see V. Woolf (1940), Spalding (1980).

GRANT, Duncan (1885–1978): of Bloomsbury painters, Duncan Grant was the best known, affirming himself from the pre-war period as a leader in the progressive and post-impressionist movement. Descended from a family of Scottish aristocrats, he was a cousin of the Stracheys. His father was an army officer stationed in India, where Duncan spent a part of his childhood. After three years at the Westminster School of Art, from 1902 to 1905, he continued his artistic formation in Paris. His affair with Keynes, from 1908, would transform itself after a few years into a lasting friendship. Keynes would help him financially until the end of his life, guaranteeing him an income in his will. From 1916 he lived with Vanessa Bell, staying with her in Charleston, London and the South of France, while pursuing numerous homosexual affairs. He continued to live in Charleston after Vanessa's death in 1961 until the end of his life. He had his first individual exhibition in 1920. The Tate Gallery organized a retrospective exhibition of his work in 1959. On Grant, see Spalding (1997).

MACCARTHY, Desmond (1877–1952): a student at Cambridge, Desmond MacCarthy was elected Apostle in 1895 and became from this date a close friend of the philosopher George Moore. His marriage to Mary Cornish in 1906 was the first Bloomsbury marriage. A literary and theatre critic and brilliant conversationalist, he never succeeded at realizing his novelistic ambitions. He signed his articles the 'affable hawk'. He was secretary of the first post-impressionist exhibition organized by Roger Fry and composed the introduction to its catalogue. He published among others *Remnants* (1918), *Portraits* I (1931), *Leslie Stephen* (1937) and *Memories* (1953). On Desmond MacCarthy, see Cecil (1990).

MACCARTHY, Mary, née Warre-Cornish (1882–1953): painter, Mary Warre-Cornish was called Molly by her friends. She married Desmond MacCarthy in August 1906. She would later have an affair with Clive Bell. Molly MacCarthy was the first to use the term 'Bloomsberries' to describe the members of what would be called the Bloomsbury Group. She was founder of the Bloomsbury Memoir Club in 1920. Her initial objective was to force her husband to write a novel equal to that of Proust or Tolstoy. She was author of the novel *A Pier and A Band* (1918), an autobiography, *A Nineteenth-Century Childhood* (1924) and biographical sketches. She was very close to Vanessa Bell and Virginia Woolf. On Mary MacCarthy, see Cecil (1990).

STEPHEN, Adrian (1882–1948): the youngest of the Stephen family. In 1907 he moved in with his sister Virginia at 29 Fitzroy Square, where he received the Bloomsbury friends on

Thursday evenings. He was one of the organizers of the Dreadnought hoax in 1910, during which he and his friends passed themselves off as the Emperor of Abyssinia and his entourage, and under this title visited the greatest warship of the British Navy. In 1911 he replaced Keynes in the affections of Duncan Grant before marrying Karen Costelloe in 1914. He and his wife studied to become doctors and then psychoanalysts, and started practising this activity in London in 1926.

STRACHEY, Lytton (1880–1932): Giles Lytton Strachey descended from a well-known Victorian family, in a milieu very similar to that of the Stephens. His brothers and sisters occupied an important place in British cultural life. His brother James was a translator of Freud and his sister Dorothy a translator of Gide. An eccentric and flamboyant personality, studying at Cambridge, he was elected Apostle in 1902. He met Keynes the same year; the two became very close and maintained a lengthy correspondence. After having failed to obtain a Cambridge fellowship, he became journalist and literary critic. Connoisseur of French literature, he published in 1912 *Landmarks in French Literature*. Published in 1918, *Eminent Victorians* was an immense success. Two other biographies would follow: *Queen Victoria* (1921) and *Elizabeth and Essex* (1928). Affirming his homosexuality, Strachey nevertheless lived from 1916 until his death with the painter Dora Carrington, even after the marriage of the latter with Ralph Partridge in 1921. He died in his country home of Ham Spray in Wiltshire of an undiagnosed intestinal cancer on 22 January 1932. On 11 March of that year, Dora Carrington committed suicide with a hunting rifle. On Strachey, see Holroyd (1994), on which Christopher Hampton's film *Carrington* (1995) is based. Part of his correspondence has been published (Strachey, 2005).

SYDNEY-TURNER, Saxon (1880–1962): while studying at Cambridge, Saxon Sydney-Turner was elected Apostle in October 1902. A founding member of Bloomsbury and undoubtedly the most faithful participant in the Group's meetings and activities, Sydney-Turner was at the same time one of its most atypical elements. In this milieu of talkers, he rarely spoke, if at all. A poet, opera lover and pianist, he was the most musically endowed of the Group's members. He left no musical or literary work behind him, and led a quiet career as a civil servant at the British Treasury, the institution against which his friend Keynes fought with such vigour throughout much of his professional life.

WOOLF, Leonard (1880–1963): descended from a Jewish family, Leonard Woolf studied at Cambridge, where he was elected Apostle in October 1902. He resided as a civil servant in Ceylon from 1904 to 1911. He married Virginia Stephen in August 1912. Without his attentive watch and constant care, it is doubtful whether his wife could have completed her work. An active member of the Labour Party, for which he unsuccessfully tried to become MP, he worked for 28 years as secretary of its advisory committee on international and colonial questions. As such, he was a tireless advocate for the establishment of an international political organization to preserve peace. Editor and literary critic, he founded in 1917 the publishing house of Hogarth Press. An author of few novels, Leonard Woolf was especially known for his numerous political writings, including: *International Government* (1916), *Co-operation and the Future of Industry* (1918), *Economic Imperialism* (1920), *Socialism and Co-operation* (1921), *Imperialism and Civilization* (1928), *Quack, Quack!* (1935), *Barbarians at the Gate* (1939), *The War for Peace* (1940), and *Principia Politica* (1953). His autobiography, published in five volumes between 1960 and 1969, is the best account of Bloomsbury by one of its core members. A part of his correspondence was published in 1990, as well as his letters to Trikkie Ritchie Parsons, who was his companion after Virginia's death, published in 2001. On Leonard Woolf, see Meyerowitz (1982).

WOOLF, Virginia, née Stephen (1882–1941): second daughter of Julia and Leslie Stephen, Virginia received, like Vanessa, her education at home. Her mother's death in 1895 sparked the first in a series of serious psychological crises, punctuated by suicide attempts, the last of which would be fatal, when she drowned in March 1941. Renowned literary critic, she published her first novel, *The Voyage Out*, in 1915, at the age of 33. *Night and Day* (1919), *Jacob's Room* (1922), *Mrs Dalloway* (1925), *To the Lighthouse* (1928), *Orlando* (1927), *The Waves* (1931), *The Years* (1937), *Between the Acts* (1941), as well as numerous short stories would follow. These works made her one of the twentieth century's major novelists. Her diary, published in five volumes between 1977 and 1984, and her correspondence in six volumes from 1975 to 1980, are also literary *chefs-d'oeuvre* and precious accounts of Bloomsbury and English cultural life. She also published in 1940 a biography of her friend Roger Fry, and two famous essays on the situation of women, *A Room of One's Own* (1929) and *Three Guineas* (1938). She took the name Woolf on marrying Leonard Woolf in August 1912. It was in large part thanks to him that she was able to overcome her internal demons through several years and produce her work. Virginia left him this letter, before taking leave of her life: 'I want to tell you that you have given me complete happiness. No one could have done more than you have done. Please believe that. But I know that I shall never get over this: and I am wasting your life. It is this madness. Nothing anyone says can persuade me. You can work and you will work much better without me. You see I can't write this even, which shows I am right. All I want to say is that until this disease came on we were perfectly happy. It was all due to you. No one could have been so good as you have been, from the very first day till now. Everyone knows that' (V. Woolf, 2003, p. 443). On Virginia Woolf, whose life and work have given rise to an imposing body of literature, see the biography of her nephew Quentin Bell (1972) and Lee (1996).

NOTES

1. The 1989 edition of the *Oxford English Dictionary* defines 'Bloomsbury' as 'a set of writers, artists, and intellectuals living in or associated with Bloomsbury in London in the early 20th century; a member of this set' (second ed., vol. 2, p. 311). Since the 1970s, literature devoted to Bloomsbury has expanded tremendously. The reader interested in knowing more about it might start with Rosenbaum (1995), a collection of writings on Bloomsbury including contributions by members of the group. Rosenbaum is the author of wide-ranging and scholarly studies of Bloomsbury seen as a literary movement (1987, 1993, 1994, 1998, 2003). Q. Bell (1997) and A. Garnett (1998) are accounts by Vanessa Bell's children. After Johnstone (1954), Gadd (1974) and Edel (1980) are among the first authors outside the group to study it. Later interesting descriptions include Palmer and Palmer (1987), Naylor (1990), Blot (1992), Reed (2004), Shone (1993, 1999), Marsh (1995), Richardson (1989), Stansky (1996) and Bradshaw (2001), some of which are embellished with iconographies taken from the works of Bloomsbury's painters. Green (1999), Robins (1997) and Shone (1999) are catalogues of exhibition of Bloomsbury's works. Marler (1997) offers a critical survey of the literature on Bloomsbury. Danièle Roth's novel (2001) depicts Bloomsbury as seen by Nelly Boxall, one of the Woolfs' servants from 1916 to 1934. The Bloomsbury Workshop, founded in London in 1986 by Tony Bradshaw, is an art gallery specializing in the works of Bloomsbury. Since 1990, the Charleston Trust has published biannually the *Charleston Magazine: Charleston, Bloomsbury and the Art*. Other than biographies on Keynes, Crabtree and Thirlwall (1980), Skidelsky (1982), Mini (1991), Annan (2002) and Goodwin (2006) study his relations with

Bloomsbury. The autobiographies, personal journals and correspondences of the Bloomsbury founders constitute the main source of information. Although part of this material has been published or is about to be published, there still remain many documents found only in remote archives around the world.

2. His public persona will be presented in the Second Interlude.
3. One will find at the end of this Interlude brief biographical sketches of these friends of Keynes. Other biographical information will be given in the endnotes.
4. See Chapter 5.
5. This was obviously the case outside Bloomsbury too. Homosexual activities were tolerated, in Victorian as much as Edwardian England, but generally they were hidden and seldom spoken of. See Cook (2003).
6. Here is a characteristic passage from a letter Keynes wrote to Lytton Strachey, on 10 December 1905: 'Lamb was full of rather dull (to me) gossip about Henry and the Stephens – how Henry Lamb is in love with Vanessa and Vanessa with Nine? and Adrian with Nine? And, I suppose, all the other possible and impossible Sapphic, sodomitic and incestuous relationships'. Correspondences between Bloomsbury members teem with often crude passages. For example, Keynes wrote to Lytton Strachey while visiting Ireland with a delegation of Liberal MPs on 12 October 1911: 'The Irish show some perspicacity. The following notice met my eyes in Cork: "All Englishmen, men, youths and boys, wish to be fucked up their assholes, and the bigger the prick the better they like it". But whether or not it was intended to be an argument for Home Rule, I don't know'. On 19 April 1914, Vanessa Bell wrote to Keynes, who hosted her and Clive during Easter in Sussex: 'Did you have a pleasant afternoon buggering one or more of the young men we left for you? . . . I imagine you, however, with your bare limbs intertwined with him and all the ecstatic preliminaries of Sucking Sodomy – it sounds like the name of a station' (V. Bell, 1998, p. 163).
7. We will return, in particular in Chapter 6, to the links between Freud and Keynes. Chapter 9 will deal with Keynes's aesthetic conceptions and activities in the arts.
8. This is how Keynes refers to it in his correspondence.
9. On Stephen, who many consider one of Bloomsbury's spiritual fathers, and who Keynes read closely, see Annan (1986).
10. When she married Leslie Stephen in 1879, Julia Duckworth, née Jackson, had three children from a previous marriage, Stella, Gerald and George. The presumed sexual aggressions by her half-brothers could have played a role in the psychological instability of Virginia Woolf. See on this subject De Salvo (1989). Caramagno (1992) believes that Virginia Woolf suffered from a manic-depressive disorder.
11. On the complex relations between the sisters, see Dunn (1996).
12. On the Cambridge Apostles, see Levy (1979), Deacon (1985) and Lubenow (1998). Accounts of the Society are also to be found in the biographies of several of its members.
13. In the Bloomsbury Group, Keynes usually respected this rule, while Roger Fry and Desmond MacCarthy were less discreet. As for Moore, he never told his parents that he belonged to the Society.
14. This activity of recruiting embryos occupied Keynes considerably for several years. The physical appearance of candidates sometimes counted as much as their moral and intellectual qualities.
15. See on this subject the following chapter.
16. Not all were distinguished. Thus, according to one of the numerous conflicting hypotheses in this dark story, James Kenneth Stephen, cousin of Virginia Woolf, elected Apostle in 1879, who died in an asylum in 1892, was Jack the Ripper (Harrison, 1972). According to Abrahamsen (1992), Stephen committed his crimes with the complicity of Prince Albert Victor, grandson of Queen Victoria. According to other 'ripperologues', the latest of which is Patricia Cornwell (2002), the serial killer was the painter Walter Sickert, who was close to Bloomsbury, friend of Roger Fry and Clive Bell, protégé of Keynes (see Chapter 9). Bell described him warmly in his memoirs (Bell, 1956, pp. 13–24), and Virginia Woolf published in 1934 *Walter Sickert: A Conversation*. The identification of Jack the Ripper with Sickert is strongly contested in the latter's biography (Sturgis, 2005, pp. 625–45).
17. This Cambridge custom is composed of a series of wine soaked festivities held during the first two weeks of June.
18. John Tressider Sheppard (1881–1968) studied classics. Elected fellow of King's College in 1908, he was provost from 1933 to 1954, after having taught classics. He was frequently Keynes's guest at Tilton.
19. He likewise discussed defecation, 'that mysterious and intimate operation . . . that mystic unburdening of our bodies' (quoted by Holroyd, 1994, p. 81), in one of his papers read before the Apostles.
20. Lytton's younger brother, James Strachey, elected Apostle in 1906, wrote to Martin Kallich on 2 October 1956: 'As is generally known, my brother was to a very large extent homosexual . . . His attitude was strongly in favour of open discussion . . . There is a large amount of unpublished material – including a very great deal of delightful correspondence – which I hope will become accessible with the gradual advance of civilized opinion. For this advance we owe a good deal, I believe, to Lytton's own influence . . . on his contemporaries, and, of course, more than anything to that of Freud' (quoted by Holroyd, 1971, p. 10).
21. Keynes was chosen over Thoby Stephen, who was called 'the Goth'. This choice was later regretted by Leonard Woolf. He wrote to Strachey from Ceylon on 23 October 1908: 'I detest Keynes don't you? Looking back on

him from 4 years, I see he is fundamentally evil if ever anyone was. God! fancy electing him & not the Goth' (L. Woolf, 1990, p. 140). Woolf's hatred was circumstantial and temporary. He had a grudge against Keynes following letters in which Strachey complained that Maynard was stealing his friends. They were reconciled in the end.

22. He nevertheless continued, until the end of the 1930s, to participate, schedule permitting, in the Saturday evening meetings. He presided, in 1921, over the Society's annual dinner.

23. An inspiration behind Bloomsbury, Moore was very close to its members, particularly after his return from Scotland, where he taught from 1904 to 1911. However, he was not considered a member of the group, or at least part of its inner core. His puritanism fit poorly with Bloomsbury's ways. Russell too was associated with the group, but not considered one of its members. He was probably kept out by his homophobia. Strachey wrote to Keynes on 24 November 1905: 'It's just occurred to me how shocked Russell would be if he read our correspondence'.

24. Neither Keynes nor the other members of the group generally owned the lodgings they occupied.

25. Chapter 4 of Virginia Woolf's *Night and Day* was inspired by one of these meetings, 'this fortnightly meeting of a society for the free discussion of everything' (V. Woolf, 1919, p. 39), most of whose participants 'proposed to spend their lives in the practice either of writing or painting' (ibid., p. 46).

26. Brilliant and energetic women, they could not compete however with the Stephen sisters for their appearance. On the Strachey family, see Lubenow (2003).

27. Teacher, writer and poet, Julian joined the International Brigades and died in Spain in July 1937. Quentin, artist and writer, was professor of history and art theory at Leeds University, and then at Sussex University. Author of several writings on Bloomsbury (1995, 1997) and of a two-volume biography of his aunt Virginia Woolf (1972), he died in 1996.

28. Three years earlier, Keynes angered Lytton Strachey by 'stealing' an embryo on which he had his heart set, Arthur Hobhouse, elected Apostle in 1905. Discovering the following year that Grant and Hobhouse were lovers, Keynes wrote to Strachey on 13 April 1906: 'It's more wild and more mad than anything that ever happened in the world before. Oh and we have created it. It has sprung and sprouted from the tips of our penes – from yours and mine'.

29. According to contradictory accounts of the three protagonists, there may have been other, less important meetings before this date. There were sometimes, in Bloomsbury, different accounts of the same event.

30. The expression 'post-impressionist' was coined on this occasion. Exasperated by a three-way discussion, with MacCarthy and a journalist, which sought to come up with a name, Fry is recorded as saying: 'Oh, let's just call them post-impressionists; at any rate, they came after the impressionists.' (MacCarthy, 1995, p. 76). See Watney (1980).

31. See Stansky (1996).

32. See the Second Interlude.

33. The *Ballets Russes* were created in 1909 by Serge Diaghilev, who directed them until the end, in 1929. After passing through Paris in 1909 and 1910, they gave their first London season in 1911.

34. It is thus a mistake to link his interest in ballet to his marriage. This interest in ballet had many dimensions. He wrote to Strachey on 17 July 1911: 'When Cambridge becomes too dull I slip up to London for a night and view M. Nijinsky's legs. Really, he's almost my ideal of . . . beauty – isn't he yours?'. Nijinsky, the great star of the *Ballets Russes* and one of the greatest dancers of the twentieth century, met Grant the same year. His *Cahiers* (1995), a fascinating chronicle of the development of his madness, describes his meetings with the Bloomsberries.

35. Founder of the *Nouvelle Revue Française* and of the Vieux-Colombier Theatre, Jacques Copeau, who attended the exhibition, was received at Gordon Square by the Bells. Later he would call on Duncan Grant to design the decors and costumes of his productions.

36. Goodwin (2006) considers that Fry's influence on the worldview of Bloomsbury and Keynes was more important than that of Moore, who did not play a role in shaping its social values or norms of conduct.

37. In spite of this criticism, Fry admitted owing much to the conception of aesthetics developed in Tolstoy's *What is Art?* (1898), particularly to his criticism of traditional conceptions linking art to an abstract criterion of beauty, when it was more a matter of communicating emotions between human beings.

38. This expression is found in work by her contemporary, James Joyce.

39. Henry Tertius James Norton (1886–1937), close friend of Keynes, had like him studied at Cambridge and Eton. Elected Apostle in 1906, brilliant mathematician, he was elected fellow of Trinity College in 1910.

40. Elected Apostle in 1909, Gerald Shove (1887–1947) taught economics at Cambridge from 1923 until the end of his life. He became a fellow of King's in 1926. His 1913 dissertation was titled 'Notes on the Application of G.E. Moore's System of Ethics to Some Problems of Political Economy'. Close friend of Keynes, he often assumed the task of the latter's teaching, which meant that he published little.

41. What was meant to be a temporary return to Britain became permanent, as Woolf left his post in Ceylon the following year.

42. On the Omega Workshops, see Collins (1983) and Shone (1993), pp. 90–117.

43. Ottoline Morrell, née Cavendish-Bentinck (1873–1938), was a flamboyant personality, a famous hostess and patron of artists and writers. Her husband, Philip Morrell, Liberal MP, was a pacifist. Their marriage was unconventional, and Ottoline Morrell engaged in several affairs, one of which, long and tumultuous, was with Bertrand Russell. From 1906 to 1915, the Morrell house, on Bedford Square, became a meeting place for artists, writers and politicians. Several Bloomsbury members attended regularly. From 1915, the receptions took place in their Garsington manor, near Oxford, which the Morrells bought in 1913 and where pacifists and conscientious objectors could find refuge. Taking generous advantage of Ottoline's table and wines, the friends of Bloomsbury never totally considered her one of their own and often made fun of her in private, Virginia Woolf excelling in this art. Only Keynes, whom Ottoline cared for during a convalescence, did not play this game. On Morrell, see Seymour (1992).
44. They will form the Vorticists group.
45. See in particular *The Apes of God* (1931).
46. See next section.
47. Keynes showed the Omega Workshops to a star dancer of the *Ballets Russes*, Tamara Karsavina, and offered her a bracelet of coloured pearls.
48. It forms the backdrop to the autobiographical novel *To the Lighthouse*.
49. In spite of important protests, Asheham House was destroyed in 1994 by Blue Circle Industries cement factory so that the latter could expand its burying grounds. Asheham is the background to *A Haunted House* by Virginia Woolf. The house was reputed to be haunted.
50. Their friends called them the Woolves.
51. The ashes of Leonard and Virginia Woolf were buried in the garden of Monks House, while the corpses of Vanessa Bell, Duncan Grant and Quentin Bell are buried in the cemetery at Firle. Keynes's ashes were dispersed close by on the slope of Firle Beacon.
52. Born in 1887, elected Apostle in 1908, Rupert Brooke was a famous poet. He found himself at the centre of a group in many regards similar to Bloomsbury, which Virginia Woolf, who was close to the poet, nicknamed the 'Neo-pagans'. More politically active, Brooke's friends were close to the Fabian Society (see Second Interlude). Sportsmen, they enjoyed the outdoor life and organized summer camps which the Bloomsberries, including Keynes, would sometimes join. Keynes's brother Geoffrey was a close friend of Brooke. His death caused strong emotions and made the author of the poem 'The Soldier' a hero.
53. We will return in much more detail to these events in Chapter 5, which deals with Keynes's action during the war.
54. See on this subject the Second Interlude.
55. See Q. Bell et al. (1987).
56. At first close to Rubert Brooke and the 'neo-pagans', David 'Bunny' Garnett became a part of the Bloomsbury Group in 1915. He was among the 17 invited by Keynes to celebrate his engagement at the Treasury on 6 January: 'Maynard put me between Vanessa and Duncan. I was a little shy of Vanessa, whose beauty and strong character had always attracted me. However, Maynard had ordered plenty of champagne and confidence soon returned' (Garnett, 1955, p. 21). After the war he founded with Francis Birrell a bookshop frequented by all the Bloomsberries. Novelist, he published in three volumes (*The Golden Echo*, 1953; *The Flowers of the Forest*, 1955; and *The Familiar Faces*, 1962) memoirs which are an important source of information on Bloomsbury. Dedicated to Duncan Grant, his first novel, *Lady into Fox* (1924) is a strange and troubling tale.
57. See Garnett's account in Chapter 5.
58. See her somewhat bitter account, A. Garnett (1984).
59. Of course, here as elsewhere, servants played an essential role. In particular, Grace Higgins was employed as a cook from 1921 to 1971. Since 1986, after a careful restoration, one may visit the site.
60. When Her Majesty's prosecutor asked him the standard question: 'What would you do if you saw a German soldier trying to rape your sister?', he responded: 'I should attempt to come – [significant pause] – between them' (Strachey, 1972, p. xiii). This response unleashed a wave of laughter among his friends present.
61. He read two of its chapters 'Cardinal Manning' and 'Florence Nightingale' at Charleston, where Keynes would read, shortly after, his portrait of the protagonists of the Paris Conference.
62. One of this world's most colourful personalities, the painter Dora Carrington (1893–1932) studied at London's Slade School of Arts of London. She belonged to a group of young women called the 'cropheads' because they wore their hair short. She fell in love with Lytton Strachey whom she met at Asheham at the end of 1915. This event provoked a physical aggression against Lytton Strachey from painter Mark Gertler, her colleague at Slade, who was in love with her. Keynes helped separate the two men. Friend of Ottoline Morrell and the Woolfs, Gertler killed himself in 1939. On Carrington, see Gerzina (1989) and Christopher Hampton's 1995 film *Carrington*.
63. Ralph Partridge (1894–1960), an athlete and energetic soldier, practised several vocations, including that of an actor, and worked for the Woolfs' publishing house, the Hogarth Press.
64. A writer, Gerald Brenan (1894–1987) lived in a remote Spanish village, where he received the Carrington–Strachey–Partridge trio and the Woolfs. His memoirs, *South from Granada* (1957) and *Personal Records: 1920–1972* (1974) retrace his links with Bloomsbury.

65. Born in 1900, Frances Marshall came in contact with Bloomsbury while working at Birrell and Garnett's book-shop. Chronicler of Bloomsbury romances (Partridge, 1981), she was the author of a number of other works and an important diary. Her death in 2004 marked the disappearance of one of the last witnesses of Bloomsbury's golden age.
66. Vanessa Bell designed the covers of all the novels published by her sister Virginia.
67. It started, however, on a regrettable decision. In 1918 the Hogarth Press was offered the manuscript of James Joyce's *Ulysses*, which was refused because of its length.
68. Bunny Garnett as well as Julian and Quentin Bell were admitted, as was Lydia Keynes.
69. The side chapel of the Lincoln Cathedral and a small Berwick church, near Charleston. We will return in Chapter 9 to Keynes's interventions in this last and complicated affair.
70. Matisse was very surprised to see his paintings quickly sold at the Leicester Gallery in 1919. He had to call Charles Vidrac to assist him in bringing other works.
71. See on this subject Fawcett (1977) and Caws and Wright (2000).
72. They often stopped at the Château d'Auppegard, near Dieppe, owned by the American painters Ethel Sands and Nan Hudson who, without being Bloomsbury members themselves, were close friends with several of them.
73. This gathering of progressive painters hostile to academism was founded in 1913.
74. We will come back to this subject in detail in Chapter 9.
75. Bloomsbury also influenced the ballet in the United States through Bunny Garnett and Lincoln Kirstein.
76. André Gide had close ties of friendship with several Bloomsbury members, particularly Clive Bell. *La Nouvelle Revue Française*, of which he was a founder in 1909, had points in common with Bloomsbury. Lytton Strachey and Gide participated together in one of the meetings at the Cistercian abbey of Pontigny, which, from 1910 to the 1930s, brought together French intellectuals. Lytton's sister Dorothy, who married the French painter Simon Bussy, became Gide's translator, and her love for him was unrequited. Fry painted Gide's portrait in 1918. Duncan Grant designed the decors and costumes for his piece, *Saül*, brought to the stage by Copeau in 1922.
77. Grant and Vanessa Bell were received by Picasso in his Paris studio on returning from a trip to Italy with Keynes in May 1920. They saw each other often after this, until 1937. On this occasion, Picasso showed them what he was then working on, *Guernica*. Julian Bell was killed the same year while driving an ambulance in Spain. Picasso continued to meet Clive Bell until the 1950s. In 1971, he sent Duncan Grant a sketch on a post-card to wish him well on his ninetieth birthday.
78. On the links between Bloomsbury and psychoanalysis, see Winslow (1990), Mini (1991), Caine (1998) and Dostaler and Maris (2000), from which this section borrows certain elements. Apart from Freud, Bloomsberries were interested in the works of many other psychologists, including Trotter, Jung and Ross.
79. Following conflicts with Jung's disciples, Jones dissolved the Society in 1917 and established, in 1919, the British Psychoanalytical Society. In 1914 the British Society for the Study of Sex Psychology was also founded. Lytton Strachey assisted in the latter's activities. Virginia Woolf also considered joining the society (V. Woolf, 1977–1984, vol. 1, p. 110).
80. Founded, as we mentioned in the preceding chapter, by Sidgwick, and to which Keynes belonged. The Society, which still exists, had over the years, among its presidents, C.D. Broad, Henri Bergson, Arthur Balfour, William James and Charles Richet.
81. In a letter to his brother Lytton, on 6 November 1920, James described Freud as 'most affable and as an artis-tic performer dazzling' (quoted in Meisel and Kendrick, 1985, p. 29), and the session as 'an organic aesthetic whole' (ibid., p. 30).
82. But see Caine (1998), according to whom the Stracheys decided and even began to translate Freud before meet-ing him.
83. James Strachey belonged to the list of partners whose name Keynes noted for the years 1906, 1907 and 1908 (KP, PP/20A; see Moggridge, 1992, pp. 838–9). It is likely that Freud had privileged access to the Keynes's sex life.
84. That year, Fry published, at the Hogarth Press, a short essay entitled *The Artist and Psycho-analysis*.
85. A fifth volume would be published in 1950.
86. Only the philosopher Moore merited such marked praise from Leonard Woolf, normally almost as reserved as his wife in his appreciation of others.

3. Knowledge: uncertainty, probabilities and the moral sciences

> The hope, which sustained many investigators in the course of the nineteenth century, of gradually bringing the moral sciences under the sway of mathematical reasoning, steadily recedes – if we mean, as they meant, by mathematics the introduction of precise numerical methods. The old assumptions, that all quantity is numerical and that all quantitative characteristics are additive, can no longer be sustained. Mathematical reasoning now appears as an aid in its symbolic rather than in its numerical character. I, at any rate, have not the same lively hope as Condorcet, or even as Edgeworth, *'éclairer les Sciences morales et politiques par le flambeau de l'Algèbre'*.
> *A Treatise on Probability* (1921-1, p. 349)

> We are merely reminding ourselves that human decisions affecting the future, whether personal or political or economic, cannot depend on strict mathematical expectation, since the basis for making such calculations does not exist; and that it is our innate urge to activity which makes the wheels go round, our rational selves choosing between the alternatives as best we are able, calculating where we can, but often falling back for our motive on whim or sentiment or chance.
> *The General Theory of Employment, Interest and Money* (1936-1, pp. 162–3)

> The pseudo-analogy with the physical sciences leads directly counter to the habit of mind which is most important for an economist proper to acquire.
>   I also want to emphasise strongly the point about economics being a moral science. I mentioned before that it deals with introspection and with values. I might have added that it deals with motives, expectations, psychological uncertainties.
> Letter to Harrod (16 July, 1938, JMK 14, p. 300)

The passage from *A Treatise on Probability* quoted above appeared in slightly modified form in the first version of the dissertation on probabilities that Keynes presented in December 1907 as part of his attempt to obtain a fellowship at King's College. Contrary to Keynes's prediction, the efforts to bring 'the moral sciences under the sway of mathematical reasoning' were not receding at that time, particularly in economics. This drove him, three decades later, to criticize sharply the tendency towards the mathematization of economics and particularly the emerging field of econometrics.[1] And if Keynes were resurrected today, it would be to discover that the subordination of the moral sciences to mathematics has been further consolidated, not only in economics, which increasingly resembles a branch of applied mathematics, but in several other social sciences as well.[2]

We are here in the realm of the theory of knowledge, a battleground on which Keynes waged war against orthodox economics which he called classical theory.[3] He accused the classical theory of errors in its analysis of the functioning of economies and in the solutions it put forth to solve their problems, such as proposing to lower wages in order to increase employment. He accused this theory of not taking into account to a sufficient degree history and institutions. He considered these errors to be the result of a mistaken conception of science and an incorrect method of analysis. To support this view, Keynes relied on a reflection that went beyond the boundaries of economics and that concerned the nature of knowledge and the connections between knowledge and action. John Neville Keynes also made important contributions to logic and the epistemology of economics. These contributions certainly influenced his son's thought, which is why we will begin here with the father. We will then examine Keynes's theory of probabilities, his subsequent critique of statistical inference in the field of social science and his conception of economic thought.

THE PATERNAL INHERITANCE

John Neville Keynes (1852–1949), a nonconformist Victorian intellectual, was a tireless worker and a tortured individual who suffered periods of intense depression, the details of which are found in a private diary covering much of his life.[4] He kept in the latter a detailed account of hours spent working, subdivided according to type of activity,[5] his financial situation, his results at golf, bridge and chess, his stamp and butterfly collections, letters he received, the weight and height of his children. His career at Cambridge was essentially administrative. He occupied, with an efficiency appreciated by his peers, the highest positions in the hierarchy of the university: secretary of the Council of the Senate, its governing body, from 1893, and Registrar, the most important administrative post, from 1910. He led fierce battles to reform the university, particularly to increase its powers and resources in relation to those of the colleges.[6]

In opposition to his friend Alfred Marshall, he fought for the complete integration of women into the university. It was in 1874 that Neville Keynes met for the first time Marshall, who would be his professor before becoming a colleague with whom relations would nevertheless become increasingly tense. He was called to arbitrate in numerous conflicts between Marshall and his colleagues, particularly Sidgwick and Herbert Foxwell.[7]

Even though he continued giving lectures in the moral sciences programme until 1911, John Neville Keynes more or less renounced from the start of the 1890s the scientific career that began with the publication of two well received works: *Studies and Exercises in Formal Logic* (1884) and *The Scope and Method of Political Economy* (1890). He composed a few entries for the *Dictionary of Political Economy* edited by R.H. Innis Palgrave between 1894 and 1899. While accepting membership in the council of the British Economic Association,[8] founded in 1890, he refused to yield to Marshall's pressures to edit the Association's journal, *The Economic Journal*, which Maynard would subsequently direct from 1911. He never published anything in this journal despite pressure from the first editor, Francis Edgeworth.[9]

Neville Keynes always devoted much time to his family, and particularly to Maynard's education, following his career step by step and helping him prepare for examinations, over which he agonized more than his son. In a certain way it was Maynard who would fulfil Neville's own disappointed intellectual ambitions. According to Victorian tradition, fathers had the task of administering corporal punishment to children guilty of reprehensible behaviour. Maynard was sometimes victim of this. For one of his biographers, David Felix (1999), one may interpret Keynes's life and work in light of these events, the *Treatise on Probability* being thus written in reaction against his father's theoretical works. There is, however, no testimony that this was the case in Keynes's writings, which demonstrate on the contrary great affection for a man thus described, on the occasion of his ninetieth birthday, in August 1942:

elegant, mid-Victorian high-brow, reading Swinburne, Meredith, Ibsen . . . loved entertaining, wine, games, novels, theatre, travel; but the shadow of work gradually growing, as migraine headaches set a readiness to look on the more gloomy or depressing side of any prospect. And then his withdrawal, gradual, very gradual, to his dear wife and the bosom of his family . . . a perfect lovable, dependable parent, generous, reserved and shy, leaving you always to your own will and judgment but not concealing his own counsel. (1942–44)

A student at Cambridge from 1872, Neville Keynes chose the moral sciences over mathematics, despite strong pressure to choose the latter, considered superior at forming the intellect and more promising as a career plan. Even Sidgwick, the patron of moral sciences teaching, considered their study less demanding than that of mathematics. In 1876, Neville Keynes was named fellow of Pembroke College, a situation that he kept for six years, and began teaching logic and political economy.[10] He contemplated submitting his candidacy to the chair of political economy at University College London, which had been left vacant by Jevons in 1880, but, always hesitant and timorous, he failed to do so and the chair went to Foxwell. In 1884 he obtained a teaching post in moral sciences at Cambridge. This same year saw the publication of *Studies and Exercises in Formal Logic*, the result of seven years' teaching. The book reflects the character of its author, moderate, fearful of conflicts and extremes, in short, the opposite of his son, who wrote to his father on 2 July 1906, after the publication of the fourth edition, to whose preparation he contributed: 'The worst of your book is that when one is reading it everything seems so hopelessly obvious and uncontroversial'.

Neville Keynes's book was well received by the critics. Still, he was reproached for his use of traditional logic, initiated by Aristotle, and for not taking into account more recent developments. This possible deficiency did not prevent the work from being widely used as a manual, in print until 1945, and his definition of logic from appearing in the respected *Vocabulaire Technique et Critique de la Philosophie*:

> Logic may be defined as the science which investigates the general principles of valid thought. Its object is to discuss the characteristics of judgments, regarded not as psychological phenomena but as expressing our knowledge and beliefs; and, in particular, it seeks to determine the conditions under which we are justified in passing from given judgments to other judgments that follow from them . . . It may accordingly be described as a normative or regulative science. This character it possesses in common with ethics and aesthetics. (J.N. Keynes, 1884 [1906], p. 1)[11]

These first sentences of John Neville's book, published one year after the birth of his son, are similar to those which open the latter's *Treatise on Probability* nearly 40 years later. It suffices to replace 'judgment' by 'proposition'. There is nothing surprising here. There is a filiation from the father's book to that of the son, transmitted by, among others, the work of W.E. Johnson, neighbour and friend of Neville, who started his own studies on probabilities with a critical reading of *Studies and Exercises*.[12] For their part, Russell and Moore pursued their reflections starting with Johnson while Keynes was writing under the influence of the latter two. Among the logicians who most influenced him, Neville Keynes mentions Jevons, Augustus de Morgan[13] and John Venn,[14] authors who figure widely in the *Treatise on Probability*.

The Method of Economics

After pure logic, John Neville turned to the methodological foundations of economic theory. The best known previous works in this domain were Nassau Senior's *An Introductory Lecture on Political Economy* (1827), John Stuart Mill's 'On the Definition of Political Economy; and on the Method of Philosophical Investigation in that Science' (1836) and John Elliott Cairnes's *The Character and Logical Method of Political Economy* (1857). The lively controversies which opposed historicists, and soon Marxists, to classical and neoclassical economists flowed from oppositions on the level of methodology as much as from economic and political disagreements. Moreover, when Neville Keynes was starting his research in political economy, the latter was starting to undergo transformations known under the expression 'the marginalist revolution', which would gradually give birth to the neoclassical economics that would dominate the discipline in the following century. In England, 'new political economy' was being used to describe this novel vision, which Marshall promoted over after Jevons, Menger and Walras.[15] While some scholars, such as Jevons, saw a fundamental rupture between classical political economy and the new scientific economics, others, such as Marshall, saw a continuity linking the disparate elements.

Such continuity is also the position of Neville Keynes. He was trying to find grounds of agreement, to show that despite differences, the main rival schools in economics resembled each other, having been built on the same foundations and following the same objectives. Here still, the contrast is striking between John Neville and Maynard, who refused the injunctions of Harrod and others urging him to moderate the tone of his attacks against classical economics in *The General Theory*.[16] For Maynard, this classical vision has been codified, among other places, in Marshall's *Principles of Economics*, whose genesis was parallel to that of his father's book, the two works being published six months apart, each author being the attentive reader and critic of the other's work in progress. After seven years of exile in Bristol and Oxford, Marshall returned to Cambridge in 1885 to hold the chair of political economy left vacant after the sudden death of Henry Fawcett[17] the previous year. Marshall took hold of economics instruction and left a small share of elementary courses to Neville Keynes.[18]

While Marshall's *Principles* develops the theoretical aspects of the new political economy, Neville Keynes's book establishes its methodological foundations. It sought to put an end to the debates, whose acrimonious character Neville Keynes deplored, that marked the discipline in the last decades of the nineteenth century, particularly the debate known as *Methodenstreit*, opposing Schmoller, his colleagues within the German historical school and its foreign counterparts,[19] to Menger and his disciples of the Austrian school. Following the publication of his first book, Neville Keynes pointed out that research into method in economics is dependent on applied logic: 'The discussion that follows belongs, then, to what may be called the philosophy or logic of political economy, and does not directly advance our knowledge of economic phenomena themselves' (J.N. Keynes, 1891, p. 3). The word 'economy' signifies 'the employment of our resources with prudence and discretion, so that we may derive from them the maximum net return of utility' (ibid., p. 1). Although he probably did not agree with this definition, Maynard would follow his father, however, when the latter, following John Stuart Mill, emphasized that economic science dealt with more complex and less uniform phenomena than the natural sciences, such that one does not find laws as certain and universal as one does in the world of nature, and that erroneous reasoning is more frequent than elsewhere. It is a science that deals with tendencies rather than with precise facts, and in which one is forced to disregard a number of accidental, singular and superficial factors.

Neville Keynes considered that there are two ways to approach economics. The first approach is positive, abstract and deductive and the second one is ethical, realist and inductive.

The first characterizes the great classical economists, such as Ricardo and Mill. The second is the defining feature of, among others, Malthus, members of the historical school in Germany and elsewhere, among whom were friends of Neville Keynes and Marshall. While expressing his preference for the first approach, Neville Keynes did not reject the second. He even believed that some of the greatest economists, Adam Smith being first among them, were inspired by both. Smith was a man who rejected dogmas and extremes, who occupied the middle ground between partisans of a priori reasoning and those of a posteriori reasoning in such a way that 'the support of his authority has been claimed on behalf of both the schools above referred to. It has been said of him that he first raised political economy to the dignity of a deductive science. But he has also been regarded as the founder of the historical method in political economy' (J.N. Keynes, 1891, p. 10). Maynard Keynes, who sharply criticized Ricardo, Marshall, Pigou and several others, always manifested the greatest deference towards Adam Smith, right up until his last article, published posthumously (1946-4, p. 445).[20]

Neville Keynes felt it is an error, in economics as in all other social sciences,[21] to hold on dogmatically to one method to the exclusion of others. This brought him, in a famous passage from his book, to distinguish three manners of approaching economics. This distinction is supported by an idea put forth by David Hume and applied to political economy by Nassau Senior, who differentiated, in his 1827 book, between positive science and the normative art of political economy:

> As the terms are here used, a *positive science* may be defined as a body of systematized knowledge concerning what is; a *normative* or *regulative science* as a body of systematized knowledge relating to criteria of what ought to be, and concerned therefore with the ideal as distinguished from the actual; an *art* as a system of rules for the attainment of a given end. The object of a positive science is the establishment of *uniformities*, of a normative science the determination of *ideals*, of an art the formulation of *precepts*.
>
> . . . It is, nevertheless, important to distinguish economic enquiries according as they belong to the three departments respectively; and it is also important to make clear their mutual relations. (J.N. Keynes, 1891, pp. 34–5)

This classification allows for the protection of the core of neoclassical theory, focused on uniformities, while rejecting the attacks of historicists, institutionalists, Marxists and other heterodox thinkers influenced by ideals and precepts. Like his first book, Neville Keynes's work was very well received, in England and abroad, and became a standard textbook for methodological questions, replacing Cairnes's *Character and Logical Method of Political Economy*.[22] More than 60 years after its publication, one of Keynes and Keynesianism's main critics, Milton Friedman, began his famous methodological essay by praising the 'admirable book' (Friedman, 1953, p. 3) of the elder Keynes, from whom he borrowed his definitions of positive economics and normative economics: 'Positive economics is in principle independent of any particular ethical position or normative judgments. As Keynes says, it deals with "what is", not with "what ought to be" . . . In short, positive economics is, or can be, an "objective" science, in precisely the same sense as any of the physical sciences' (ibid., p. 4). This position, as we will see, would not have been congenial to Maynard. He held, on the distinction between positive and normative economics, the opposite view of his father's positions in a perspective quite similar to those defended by Myrdal in *The Political Element in the Development of Economic Theory* (1930) and the economists associated with institutionalism, according to which it is impossible to isolate so-called positive economics from the values defended by its theoreticians: 'economics . . . employs introspection and judgments of value' (letter of Keynes to Harrod, 4 July 1938, in JMK 14, p. 297).

There was, however, an important feature in Marshall's inaugural lecture of 1885 at Cambridge, 'The Present Position of Political Economy', adopted by Neville, to which Maynard would remain faithful. This feature was the conception of economics, not as a set of ready-made truths, but as an instrument, a toolbox with which to discover concrete truths. Thus Keynes wrote, in his editorial introduction to the Cambridge Economic Handbooks collection: 'The theory of economics does not furnish a body of settled conclusions immediately applicable to policy. It is a method rather than a doctrine, an apparatus of the mind, a technique of thinking, which helps its possessor to draw correct conclusions' (1922-35, p. 856).

UNCERTAINTY AND PROBABILITY

First Works: from Ethics to Epistemology

In the field of ethics, it is necessary, according to Moore, to distinguish reflection on the nature of good from that which concerns the action required to achieve such good. In 'My early beliefs' (1938-12), Keynes qualifies as a religion, as we saw, the conception of good that Moore gives in the final chapter of *Principia Ethica* entitled 'The ideal'. He calls the answer to the second question moral. It is formulated in the chapter entitled 'Ethics in relation to conduct', the chapter in which Moore introduces the notion of probability. We cannot in effect foresee with certitude the result of our actions. It is impossible to know if a given action will bring about in the long term more good than evil. We have no means of concluding that, when we must choose between two actions, one will bring about more good than the other: 'we can certainly have no rational ground for asserting that one of two alternatives is even probably right and another wrong' (Moore, 1903a, p. 203). Moore concludes from this that one must resolve to follow conventions and traditional morality. For Keynes, Moore's conclusion is unacceptable. One must be able to judge the rightness of an action, and thus act, but without knowing with certitude its consequences. On the basis of ethical problems, which confront societies as much as individuals, Keynes moves towards reflection of an epistemological nature.

The theme of uncertainty is present in Keynes's thought from beginning to end of his adult life.[23] Before his encounter with Moore, in the first essays he composed while studying at Eton, the young Keynes already insisted on the importance of time, on the precariousness and transitory character of human affairs and on the uncertainty in the context of which man acts.[24] One must act, in one's private as well as one's public life, in spite of the fog clouding our path. It is here that the idea of probability comes in. In 1904, he presented to the Apostles an important paper dealing with Chapter 5 of *Principia Ethica*, 'Ethics in relation to conduct'.[25] This paper contains some of the main ideas of the *Treatise on Probability* as well as the argumentation that Keynes would use in his debates with Pearson and Tinbergen, which we study below.

To counter Moore's argumentation and demonstrate that an individual can act in a situation of uncertainty, Keynes turned to the concept of probability. For Keynes, the numerical comparison between a number x of occurrences of a given event and the number y of elements of a set of reference, which is the conception used by Moore, is far from exhausting the meaning given to the term probability. Moreover, probability does not admit a rigorous and satisfying definition and can only be grasped by intuition: 'Any adequate definition of probability I have never seen, and I am unable to give one' (1904-3, p. 3).[26] However, he adds, 'it is possible to try to refute definitions and to find out the real question at issue' (ibid.). A good part of the task he would accomplish from this date consisted of criticizing and sharply attacking several of his predecessors, as he would do with economists in *The General Theory*.

Keynes had alternative names for the conception of probabilities he criticizes: frequentist, quantitative, mathematical and statistical.[27] It is based on the principle of non-sufficient reason that he would call in *A Treatise on Probability* the principle of indifference. Equiprobability and the law of great numbers[28] reflects the same idea: 'According to this view "x will probably happen" means "I do not know whether x will happen in any particular case, but, if a large number of cases be taken, I do know for certain that x will happen more often than not"' (ibid., p. 3). Keynes relates that Karl Pearson[29] spent one of his holidays tossing a coin 25 000 times and noted that it fell roughly half the time heads, which allowed him to affirm the probability of such an occurrence as 50 per cent. Repeating this experiment with the roulette wheel at Monte Carlo, Pearson observed the results did not seem to obey the same rules, which brought Keynes to conclude: 'it is about time that men of science reconstructed their theory of probability' (ibid., p. 9). The problem comes from the fact that probabilities are most often considered in relation to games of chance. Now, these situations are not the most typical when it is a matter of applying probabilities. According to Keynes, very few cases can be dealt with mathematically in light of the law of great numbers.

Probability is linked to the fact that man must make decisions without knowing what the future will entail. Ignorance, which is at the heart of the human condition, must not prevent us from judging the rectitude of an action and of acting:

> Probability implies ignorance; it is because we do not know for certain that we use the word at all; and the fact that it is possible (in the sense that it is not self contradictory) that every action producing a balance of good in the immediate future, may produce a vast balance of evil on the whole, is no bar to our assertion, until we have further evidence, that such an action is probably right. (1904-3, p. 14)

We want to say 'x is probably right', Keynes insisted, even if there is no way of knowing what the total consequences of our action will be in 100 years from now. The situation is complicated by the fact that there exists what Keynes, following Moore, calls organic unities. Even when it concerns nature, the atomic hypothesis which organic unities oppose is most often denied. The presence of organic unities is still more evident when it is a question of social, human, psychic events, which are most of the time complex in nature and composed of more simple elements. A characteristic of a given set is not necessarily the sum of the characteristics of its elements. For example, most often, if b stands for goodness, $b(x + y)$ is certainly different from $b(x) + b(y)$. Keynes discusses the doctrine of organic unities in several writings, and particularly in a set of notes composed between July and September 1905 entitled 'Miscellenea ethica' in which he alludes to economic theory, whose great authors he started to read systematically at that time:

As I understand this doctrine, it prevents our drawing any conclusion as to the value of a whole by a consideration of the value of the parts. The goodness of a whole is not the sum of the goodness of its parts, nor is the value of a group of individuals necessarily the same as the sum of their values taken severally . . . The fact that utility belongs to this class leads to difficulties in the pure theory of economics. (1905-1, pp. 20–21)

From Dissertation to Book

In December 1907, Keynes submitted the first version of his dissertation, entitled *Principles of Probability*, to King's College in the hope of obtaining a fellowship. This writing contains much of what would be found in the 1921 book. He affirms from the start that this work is a matter of logic and not mathematics. He launches a general attack on the manner of seeing probabilities inspired by Laplace and emphasizes 'the extraordinarily immature condition in which the student still finds the logic of Probability' (1907-1, p. 3). Following Laplace's logic, one is able to demonstrate God's existence as easily as the law of gravitation. It is not difficult, for example, 'to confound Professor Pearson's theories and mock at his laws' (ibid., p. 228). The confusions surrounding the definition and interpretation of induction have never been dissipated (ibid., p. 260). One can demonstrate that, on these questions, the main conclusions of Condorcet, Laplace, Poisson, Cournot, De Morgan and Boole are demonstrably false (ibid., p. 336). Of the 445 works figuring in his bibliography, Keynes writes with 'a feeling of melancholy' that less than 100 are still worth reading: 'The time is rapidly approaching when the labours of research should be lightened, wherever it is possible, by the existence of an accredited *Index Expurgatorius*' (ibid., bibliographical annexe, p. 5).

It is not surprising that this dissertation from a young man of 24 could have irritated a few elders. In his report to those voting on the post of fellow, A.N. Whitehead[30] underlined that the controversial nature of the subject led the candidate to commit several errors. Whitehead considered Keynes's criticism of the Venn and Crystal school superficial; but he was careful to add that his judgement was perhaps biased because he himself adhered to the frequentist school rejected by Keynes. Anticipating a criticism that would often be made against Keynes, he wrote: 'He invariably considers the arguments in its favour at their stupidest, and never attempts to make the theory work by any added subtlety of his own. In short he dismisses the theory in the most dogmatic unconvincing manner' (KP, TP/4/2). Curiously, Whitehead considered the philosophical part the weakest and the purely mathematical contributions the most significant, while concluding that Keynes's work was remarkable. The other examiner, W.E. Johnson, was more favourable than Whitehead. The voters decided nevertheless to choose a candidate other than Keynes for the position, which did not mean that Keynes's dissertation was refused. He was free to present himself again the following year with a revised version of his work. This resubmission is what Keynes did. The polemical tone was attenuated; the candidate underlined, however, that it was difficult to avoid controversy. In a new report, Whitehead wrote that there had been a tangible improvement in Keynes's writing and added that he understood it better. In fact, his own future works, like those of his co-author Russell, would be somewhat influenced by Keynes: 'Accordingly I now accept his contention that probability cannot be solely derived from ideas of "frequency", more or less obscurely present in the mind' (KP, TP/4/8).[31] Moreover, Whitehead, while praising the Keynes 'charming literary style', reproached him for confusing literary style and one appropriate to logic and philosophy.

On the basis of the second version of his work, Keynes was named fellow of King's College. He had left his job at the India Office a few months earlier and started teaching at Cambridge without being certain of obtaining the position. In 1910, he signed a contract with Cambridge University Press for the publication of the reworked version of his dissertation. The contract was cancelled in 1912 on Keynes's request, who would from then on publish all his books with Macmillan. The considerable effort he devoted to reworking his thesis may be followed step by step in his correspondence. Like his works to come, this effort was not done in solitude. Keynes submitted his chapters and discussed them with friends and colleagues. Among others, Russell contributed. While Keynes indicated that he was largely inspired by his friend's *Principles of Mathematics* in the preparation of his dissertation, Russell was one of the first to make public Keynes's theses in *The Problems of Philosophy*, published in 1912: 'I have derived valuable assistance from unpublished writings of G.E. Moore and J.M. Keynes: from the former, as regards the relations of sense-data to physical objects, and from the latter as regards probability and induction' (Russell, 1912, p. 6). Keynes wrote to his father on 19 July 1914:

> I had 5½ hours with Johnson on Friday and got some most useful criticisms and suggestions. From conversations with Russell and Broad I have got less. I have been very much encouraged by Johnson's and Russell's reception of my Theory of Induction. They are both exceedingly complimentary. I finished this two or three years ago, but no one has read it until now.

In his autobiography, Russell wrote that although he did not have contact with Keynes in what concerned his political and economic works, 'I was considerably concerned in this *Treatise on Probability*, many parts of which I discussed with him in detail' (Russell, 1967, p. 71). Moore also helped in the correction of the book's proofs during a summer excursion (letter to his father, 26 July 1914). Clive Bell, who lived in the same house as Keynes at the time the latter was putting the final touches on his manuscript, recalled: 'And after that war, when he took up the manuscript of his old dissertation with a view to making a book, he would . . . occasionally hand me a much corrected sheet saying . . . "can you remember what I meant by that?" ' (C. Bell, 1956, p. 59).

A Treatise on Probability

Keynes's *Treatise on Probability* is not a textbook of probability theory. It is, affirms the author in the first, 1907, version of his writing, a work of logic, whose main object is a reflection on knowledge and the '*laws of thought*' (1921-1, p. 144; Keynes's italics) in relation to action. Keynes was first inspired by Leibniz who conceived, in a dissertation composed at the age of 23, of probability as a branch of logic. In this sense, Keynes pursued the reflection began by his father in 1884 and similarly went on to apply it to economics. More precisely, probabilities constituted 'that part of logic which deals with arguments which are rational but not conclusive' (ibid., p. 241). Most of these arguments arise from induction and analogy. Almost all empirical sciences, but also decisions which must be taken in everyday life, both private and public, rest on this type of argumentation. The field of application is thus vast.

A probability is not an objective, natural fact, as the frequentist interpretation implies. It expresses the degree of belief that it is reasonable to hold toward a set of propositions *a*, in light of a set of propositions *h*: 'it is concerned with the degree of belief which it is *rational* to entertain in given conditions' (ibid., p. 4). The probable is that in which it is reasonable to believe, in light of our knowledge: 'To this extent, therefore, probability may be called subjective. But in the sense important to logic, probability is not subjective. It is not, that is to say, subject to human caprice' (ibid.). It is a logical relation between two propositions or two sets of propositions manifested in the mind of individuals. It is not a relationship between a statement and a reality: 'Probability begins and ends with probability' (ibid., p. 356). A relationship of probability can be expressed by the symbol 'a/h'. The knowledge of a situation in which '$a/h = 1$' is certain. A situation in which '$a/h = 0$' constitutes an impossibility. This figure is situated between 0 and 1. And, in the majority of cases, numbers have only an ordinal meaning. By this, Keynes means that it is often impossible to quantitatively compare two probabilities and to affirm, for example, that the chances of one event taking place are x times higher than the chances of another event taking place. Moreover, it is possible that two probabilities be incomparable: 'it is not always possible to say that the degree of our rational belief in one conclusion is either equal to, greater than, or less than the degree of our belief in another' (ibid., p. 37). And one is inclined to think that, in social and human reality and perhaps even in the natural world, probabilities are in most cases non-quantifiable and incommensurable, all the more so since they are bound by the limited power of human reason.[32] Even when individual probabilities are numerically measurable, we cannot go very far in mathematical reasoning. It is moreover difficult to eliminate intuition and direct judgement from the consideration of probabilities (ibid., p. 56). This difficulty restricts the scope of frequentist probabilities founded on the law of great numbers. Even in the domain of natural sciences, intuition and analogy play a more important role than the manipulation of statistical frequencies.

The quotation at the beginning of this chapter, and of which one finds a version as early as 1907, gives evidence of this. Keynes believed that several great thinkers – Condorcet, Bernoulli, Bentham, Laplace, Edgeworth and others – were mistaken in thinking that one could apply principles coming from equiprobability to the moral sciences and thus mathematically quantify, measure and formalize social reality. In the domain of ethics, one was brought to believe 'that degrees of goodness are numerically measurable and arithmetically additive' (ibid., p. 343), while the question of right action arises from intuitive judgement. Keynes denounced this 'mathematical charlatanry' which had undermined for a century theoretical statistics (ibid., p. 401) and was supported by a total confidence in statistical inference. In economics, we will see that this error is supported by the quantification illusion according to which things such as utility can be quantified, measured, added and subtracted. This error leads to an abusive use of statistics which, as a means of quantitatively describing reality, transformed itself into an instrument of prediction.[33]

Among the many additions to the published version of his manuscript, one would resurface in his economic analysis, namely the question of the 'weight of arguments', which Keynes defined as the quantity of evidences on which a set of propositions is based. It must be distinguished from the more or less favourable character of evidences, their probability in the strict sense. Thus, the probability of an error does not necessarily go down as the weight of an argument goes up. Like probability, weight cannot generally be measured. This element in *A Treatise on Probability* is the only one to which *The General Theory* (1936-1, p. 148) would explicitly allude.[34] But the influence of the *Treatise* on Keynes's work in economics goes beyond this question. It includes several other elements such as the principle of risk, in accordance to which it may be more rational to aim at a lesser good that can be obtained with more probability, than a greater good associated with less probability.[35] But, more globally, it is the vision of knowledge that is at stake.[36]

Criticisms and Revisions: Ramsey and Wittgenstein

The *Treatise on Probability* would acquire a singular destiny. Published well before the unleashing of the Keynesian revolution, it was remarked on by a few economists at the time of its publication[37] but went unnoticed by most. This situation would last until the 1970s. The editors of the *Collected Writings* decided to publish this book not in chronological order as they did for Keynes's other seven monographs, but as an eighth title. They included in it an editorial foreword signed by philosopher and friend of Keynes, R.B. Braithwaite, so as to facilitate its access to economists. The situation changed at the start of the 1980s, with works by Skidelsky (1983), Bateman (1987), Carabelli (1988), Fitzgibbons (1988), and O'Donnell (1989),[38] who inaugurated a body of work investigating the relations between philosophy and economics in Keynes as well as the continuity of his philosophical vision.[39]

Amongst mathematicians and philosophers, on the contrary, there was much interest. In the months following its publication, critical reviews were numerous. Keynes's book, 'the first systematic work in English on the logical foundations of probability for 55 years' (Braithwaite, 'Editorial foreword' in 1921-1, p. xv) became a reference to this day. For Braithwaite, 'the originality of Keynes's approach lay in his insistence that probability, in its fundamental sense, is a logical relation holding between propositions which is similar to, although weaker than, that of logical consequence' (ibid., pp. xvi). In the 'Probability' article of the important 1967 *Encyclopedia of Philosophy*, we can read: 'Keynes, whose eloquent defense of the logical approach against its rivals is largely responsible for its present vogue, wished to treat the ultimate relation between"proposal" and "supposal" as indefinable' (Black 1967, p. 475). Black lists Keynes's books among the half-dozen that anybody coming to the subject must read: 'A *Treatise on Probability* must be read by all serious students of the subject. Like von Wright's book, it is also valuable for its historical remarks' (ibid., p. 478). Walley writes, in a more recent book entitled *Statistical Reasoning with Imprecise Probabilities*: 'The first major effort to construct a theory of imprecise probability was made by Keynes (1921). Keynes aimed to develop an inductive logic, based on a logical interpretation of probability as a "degree of rational belief" . . . Since Keynes, a large literature has grown up concerning the mathematics and interpretation of imprecise, epistemic probabilities' (Walley, 1991, pp. 44–5).

The non-frequentist conception of probabilities conceived as relations between propositions was also the focus of critics. Bertrand Russell affirmed that this book, 'undoubtedly the most important work on probability that has appeared for a very long time' (Russell, 1922, p. 119), could not be praised enough, even though he did not accept probabilities as indefinable and, in the majority of cases, non-numerical. Probabilities constituted according to him a branch of mathematics and not, as Keynes believed, a branch of logic. He reproached the latter for presenting him as the sole author of *Principia Mathematica*, all of whose passages result from a joint effort between himself and Alfred Whitehead. In one of the most detailed reviews, C.D. Broad wrote that Keynes's long-awaited book 'will at once take place as the best treatise on the logical foundations of the subject', and declared himself 'substantially in agreement with him' (Broad, 1922, p. 72).

One of the most serious criticisms came from a young mathematician of genius, Frank

Ramsey,[40] for whom Keynes had great admiration. Ramsey accused Keynes of confusing the existence of relations of probabilities with their perception. There is no necessary correspondence between the two:

> But we are concerned with the relation which actually holds between two propositions; the faculty of perceiving this relation, accurately or otherwise, we call insight, perfect or imperfect. Mr Keynes argues that owing to the possibility that our insight may be all wrong we should talk not of the relation which actually holds, but of the relations which, we have reason to suppose, holds. (Ramsey, 1922, p. 4)

Ramsey returned to this attack during a conference, 'Truth and probability', given before the Cambridge Moral Science Club in 1926 and published posthumously in 1931. For him, probabilities do not concern objective relations between propositions, but rather degrees of belief. Calculating probabilities consists in establishing a set of rules permitting degrees of belief to form a coherent system. Relations of probability as described by Keynes do not exist:

> I do not perceive them, and if I am to be persuaded that they exist it must be by argument; moreover I shrewdly suspect that others do not perceive them either, because they are able to come to so very little agreement as to which of them relates any two given propositions. (Ramsey, 1926, p. 161)

Regarding his Cambridge critics, Keynes wrote to Broad on 31 January 1922:

> But what I really attach importance to is, of course, the general philosophical theory. I am much comforted that with that you are in general agreement. But I find that Ramsey and other young men at Cambridge are quite obdurate, and still believe that *either* Probability is a definitely measurable entity, probably connected with Frequency, *or* is of merely psychological importance and is definitely non-logical. I recognise that they can raise some very damaging criticisms against me on these lines. But all the same I feel great confidence that they are wrong. However, we shall never have the matter properly cleared up until a big advance has been made in the treatment of Probability in relation to the theory of Epistemology as a whole. (KP, TP/1/1)

It was this very general philosophical vision that was then being transformed at Cambridge. The Cambridgians mentioned by Keynes were at the time influenced by a young Austrian philosopher who had resided at Cambridge from 1911 to 1913 and who had made a strong impression on, among others, Russell, Moore and Keynes: Ludwig Wittgenstein.[41] Elected Apostle in November 1912,[42] he was unable to tolerate the group's atmosphere and decided to leave before the year's end, which did not prevent him from rising to the status of 'angel' on his return to Cambridge in 1929.[43] Voluntarily enlisted in the Austrian army during the War, he wrote on the front and during military leave what he presented to Russell as 'a book called "Logisch-Philosophische Abhandlung" containing all my work of the last six years. I believe I've solved our problems finally' (letter from 13 March 1919, in Wittgenstein, 1974, p. 68).[44] He finished in August 1918, two months before being taken prisoner in Italy, the only book that would be published in his lifetime, in 1922, under the title *Tractatus Logico-Philosophicus*, a title suggested by Moore in reference to Spinoza's *Tractatus Theologico-Politicus*.[45] He claimed to have solved in this work both the main questions of logic and philosophy. In June 1919 he sent a copy to Russell and thus summarized its central message in a letter from 19 August:

The main point is the theory of what can be expressed (gesagt) by propo [sition]s – i.e. by language – (and, which comes to the same, what can be *thought*) and what can not be expressed by prop[osition]s, but only shown (gezeigt); which, I believe, is the cardinal problem of philosophy. (ibid., p. 71)

Ramsey was one of the two English translators of this work, which would leave its mark on modern philosophy and contribute, by its description of metaphysical statements as meaningless, to the birth in Vienna of logical positivism, from which Wittgenstein would soon distance himself. By putting into question the existence of obvious truths, by affirming that philosophy could not claim to attain reality, by writing that necessary truths are meaningless tautologies, Wittgenstein called radically into question some of Moore's central ideas, as well as ideas of those whom he inspired, such as Keynes. For Wittgenstein, logic is unable to describe the truth, or ethics the good. By questioning the relationship between language and reality, he contributed to the philosophy of language and to the constructivist view which would be developed during the last decades of the twentieth century. For Wittgenstein, philosophy becomes a critique of language; thought is language.

Wittgenstein, for whom delicacy in interpersonal relations was not the first quality, wrote to Keynes from Cassino, where he was taken prisoner, on 12 June 1919:

Please kindly forward the enclosed letter to Russell's address. I wish I could see him somehow or other, for I am sure he won't be able to understand my book without a very thorough explanation, which can't be written. Have you done any more work on probability? My M-S. contains a few lines about it which, I believe – solve the essential question. (Wittgenstein, 1974, p. 112)

This remark did not seem to upset Keynes any more than Ramsey's criticism. To the extent that he could remorselessly crush and humiliate an individual he considered mediocre, he also respected those whom he judged to be of superior intelligence. Such was manifestly the case with Wittgenstein, regarding whom he wrote to Lydia Lopokova on 4 May 1924: 'I have a letter from Frank Ramsey about the mad philosopher genius Wittgenstein. It seems that three of his brothers have committed suicide; so perhaps it is better not to be so wise and to be unphilosophical'. When Wittgenstein announced his imminent arrival in Cambridge, Keynes wrote on 18 November 1928 to his future wife: 'He . . . wants to come to stay with me here in about a fortnight. Am I strong enough? Perhaps if I do no work between now and then, I shall be'. After his guest's arrival, he wrote on 18 January 1929: 'Well, God has arrived. I met him on the 5.15 train. He has a plan to stay in Cambridge *permanently*. . . . I see that the fatigue is going to be crushing. But I must not let him talk to me for more than two or three hours a day'. On 20 January he added: 'I would willingly exchange my guest for yours! – though we are really getting on very well and I must not complain. Sometimes it is almost unbearable – the fatigue'.

In fact, Keynes had been Wittgenstein's protector for some time, the latter having renounced his father's enormous inheritance. He intervened so that he could correspond, receive and send manuscripts while he was prisoner in Italy in 1919. He paid for the trips that allowed Ramsey to meet him in the Austrian villages where he taught primary school in the 1920s.[46] He sent money to help him get to Cambridge in 1925, where he stayed at a country house in Iford, near Lewes, that the newly wedded Keynes had rented for the summer.[47] He organized his return to Cambridge in 1929[48] and, himself an elector, was the main advocate of Wittgenstein's election as successor to Moore to the chair of moral philosophy in 1939. He also helped him in the process of obtaining British citizenship.

Keynes and Wittgenstein met on numerous occasions after the latter's return to Cambridge.[49] The content of these discussions is unknown, but it is possible that Keynes was among the first to assist in the transformations of Wittgenstein's philosophical vision, in the reevaluation of logical positivism and in the development of the theory of language games. Language was henceforth understood as a social practice, language games a new philosophical technique designed to clarify the grammar of our statements. Some believe that Wittgenstein's 'second philosophy', particularly in regards to the role played by rules and conventions in relation to individual intuition, had a significant influence on the Keynes of *The General Theory.*[50]

Keynes's Response

It was only after Ramsey's death that Keynes publicly responded to his critics and recognized in part their legitimacy in regards to the subjective nature of probabilities:

> Thus the calculus of probabilities belong to formal logic. But the basis of our degrees of belief – or the *a priori* probabilities, as they used to be called – is part of our human outfit, perhaps given us merely by natural selection, analogous to our perceptions and our memories rather than to formal logic. So far I yield to Ramsey – I think he is right. But in attempting to distinguish 'rational' degrees of belief from belief in general he was not yet, I think, quite successful. (1931-26, p. 339)

Nevertheless, recognizing the important progress made by Ramsey and Wittgenstein in the field of formal logic in regards to Russell's first works, Keynes believed that 'the gradual perfection of the formal treatment . . . had been, however, gradually to empty it of content and to reduce it more and more to mere dry bones, until finally it seemed to exclude not only all experience, but most of the principles, usually reckoned logical, of reasonable thought' (ibid., p. 338). While Wittgenstein came to see philosophy as a sort of non-sense, Ramsey arrived at a pragmatism that was repugnant to the former. Keynes was not ready to admit that all his first philosophical intuitions were to be rejected. Even though religious and political certitudes disappeared with the war, this was no reason to abandon all common goals, all objective principles, he wrote in the last of a series of articles he edited for the *Manchester Guardian Commercial*: 'Progress is a soiled creed, black with coaldust and gunpowder; but we have not discarded it. We believe and disbelieve, and mingle faith with doubt . . . Our newest Spinoza gives us frozen comfort' (1923-3, pp. 448–49). He quoted a passage of the *Tractatus*, whose arguments he tried unsuccessfully to explain to the Apostles in November 1925: 'Last night, I tried to explain the philosophy of Ludwig to my Society, but it escapes the mind – I could only half remember it' (letter to Lydia, 15 November 1925).

He wrote to Wittgenstein on 29 March 1924 that he waited a year before responding to the latter's letter because he wanted to succeed in understanding his book 'yet my mind is now so far from fundamental questions that it is impossible for me to get clear about such matters. I still do not know what to say about your book, except that I feel certain that it is a work of extraordinary importance and genius' (Wittgenstein 1974, p. 116). On *A Treatise on Probability* which he sent him at the same time, he wrote: 'I fear you will not like it' (ibid.), a fear that was not unjustified. Wittgenstein had a better appreciation for Keynes's political economic works, particularly *The Economic Consequences of the Peace* and *A Short View of Russia.*[51]

In his obituary note on Ramsey, Keynes wrote that, having lived longer, he might 'have exchanged the tormenting exercises of the foundations of thought and of psychology, where the mind tries to catch its own tail, for the delightful paths of our own most agreeable branch of the moral sciences, in which theory and fact, intuitive imagination and practical judgment, are blended in a manner comfortable to the human intellect' (1930-6, p. 335). Let us now turn to these moral sciences.

ALCOHOLISM AND ALCHEMY: THE CRITIQUE OF STATISTICAL INFERENCE

The fifth and last part of *A Treatise on Probability*, composed of five chapters, is devoted to statistical inference. Its contents were almost entirely elaborated after the 1907 and 1908 dissertations, which end with a chapter devoted to the relations between ethics and probabilities. In the book, this chapter, the 26th, 'The application of probability to conduct', from which this chapter's first quotation was taken, precedes Part Five. For Keynes, statistics fulfil two functions. The first role is descriptive, consisting of numerical and graphic techniques used to describe in a condensed manner certain determinant characteristics of large sets of phenomena. The second function is inductive: 'It seeks to extend its description of certain characteristics of observed events to the corresponding characteristics of other events which have not been observed' (1921-1, p. 359). It is this second function that he calls statistical inference. It is founded on Bernoulli's theorem on a priori probabilities, which allows us to deduce 'general laws amongst masses of phenomena, in spite of the uncertainty of each particular case' (ibid., p. 369). Keynes did not believe there was 'any direct and simple method by which we can make the transition from an observed numerical frequency to a numerical measure of probability' (ibid., p. 400). He had already expressed his scepticism in this regard in the second version of his dissertation by underlining the danger of applying this method to political questions: 'Statistical-correlation affords a valuable method of summarising a certain kind of evidence. But we must not incautiously accept conclusions which depend on nothing but the observation of high statistical-correlation, when they are offered in solution of practical problems of politics or science' (1908-4, p. 252).

In every set of events, including in the natural world, possible contingencies are too numerous to allow for exact and certain conclusions: 'Although nature has her habits, due to the recurrence of causes, they are general, not invariable' (1921-1, p. 402). Keynes quotes approvingly a passage from Leibniz, demanding 'not so much mathematical subtlety as a precise statement of all the circumstances' (ibid.). Statistics arise from observation: 'The ultimate basis of the theory of statistics is thus not mathematical but observational' (ibid., p. 413). It is thus invalid to apply 'mathematical methods, . . . to the general problem of statistical inference' (ibid., p. 419). Keynes considers that among the great statisticians, Wilhelm Lexis, Ladislaus von Bortkiewicz and Alexander Tschuprow were conscious of the problems that he raised. Others are 'the children of loose thinking, and the parents of charlatanry' (ibid.). The claim to be able to exactly measure the probability of an induction and to proclaim the certainty of our predictions would have been universally rejected long ago, in the majority of cases, 'if those who made it had not so successfully concealed themselves from the eyes of common sense in a maze of mathematics' (ibid., p. 424). Such are the ideas Keynes would use in a series of methodological debates which would place him in opposition to a number of his contemporaries from the writing of his dissertation until his death.

After having been named a fellow of King's College on 16 March 1909, Keynes started on a paper on price indexes, a subject with which he had already dealt in the first essay he wrote for Marshall as an economics student in 1905. He finished this long paper while on holiday in Versailles in April 1909 and submitted it to a competition for the Adam Smith prize, which he won. Unpublished until the release of the *Collected Writings*, 'The method of index numbers with special reference to the measurement of general exchange value' (1909-4), would in part be used in *A Treatise on Probability* and *A Treatise on Money*.[52] Inspired by his reflections from 1904 on knowledge and probabilities, this paper deals with the methodological problems linked to the nature of quantities in economics and to their measurement, but it applies to all social sciences, where elements are measurable with great difficulty. Keynes soon had occasion to use his reflections in a controversy with Pearson, whom he had already criticized in his dissertation.[53]

Keynes against Pearson

Economics was only one of many of statistical inference's fields of application. This method spread from the middle of the nineteenth century, at the same time as a determinist vision gave way to a probabilistic world vision, in both the natural and social domains. Francis Galton, Francis Y. Edgeworth, George U. Yule and Karl Pearson[54] figured among those who made the most important contributions to the use of statistics in the social sciences.

In May 1910, the Francis Galton Laboratory for National Eugenics published a report prepared by Ethel M. Elderton with the assistance of Karl Pearson, dealing with the influence of parental alcoholism on the physical and intellectual characteristics of children, and based on population samples from Manchester and Edinburgh. Counter to the general intuition, the report concluded that there was no significant relation between the two sets of data. In short, children of alcoholics were not more disadvantaged than the others from the start. This study, summarized in *The Times* for 21 May, unleashed a lively controversy in the newspapers, Pearson, Keynes and Marshall being its main protagonists. Marshall, who believed in the evils of alcohol and the importance of parental influence, wrote a letter to *The Times* on 'Alcoholism and efficiency', published on 7 July, to which Pearson answered on 12 July. In his letter, Marshall hoped that someone more competent than himself would criticize the methodology of the study. This is what Keynes engaged in. He sent two letters to *The Times*, which were not published (1910-3, 1911-1). He published a review of the study in the July edition of the *Journal of the Royal Statistical Society* (1910-4). Marshall published a second letter in *The Times* of 2 August, drawing on Keynes's writings, to which Pearson answered on 10 August. Marshall intervened for the last time on 19 August, affirming that Pearson did not show conclusively that parental alcoholism has no effect on children's degeneration. Pearson answered Keynes, as well as Marshall, in September in a 26-page supplement to the report, subtitled: 'A reply to the Cambridge economists'. Keynes replied in a letter to the *Journal of the Royal Statistical Society* in December (1910-7), and he responded in February 1911 (1911-3) to a last intervention by Pearson in January, in which he wrote about Marshall's preconception in this debate.

Keynes's attack was directed at the use made of statistics by the report's authors and is based on the main conclusions of his dissertation on probabilities. The appreciation of probabilities, of the weight of arguments, of risk, must be based on judgement, which brings us to choose, define, and classify data according to our intuitions. It is not a question of facts, but of the nature and validity of the arguments employed. Now, Elderton and Pearson's conclusions go totally against judgement and common sense. It is known for example, according to Keynes, that alcoholism seriously diminishes potential income. The arguments on which the study is founded concluding definitively that the environment has little influence on an individual's character are both insufficient and poorly constructed, despite all their useless efforts at statistical compilation. The study 'is a salient example of the application of a needlessly complex mathematical apparatus to initial data, of which the true character is insufficiently explained, and which are in fact unsuited to the problem in hand' (1910-4, p. 195): 'The methods of "the trained anthropometrical statistician" need applying with much more care and caution than is here exhibited before they are suited to the complex phenomena with which economists have to deal' (ibid, p. 205).

The vigour of Keynes's attack is doubtless the result, not only of methodological considerations, but also of his prejudices, anchored in the Victorian universe and the 'presuppositions of Harvey Road', according to which alcoholism in the lower classes was a hereditary defect. He had much admiration for the economist Irving Fisher, who campaigned against alcohol consumption,[55] and himself even juggled with the idea of forbidding alcohol consumption: 'I expect that the prohibition of alcoholic spirits and of bookmakers would do good' (1925-17, p. 303).

Keynes against Tinbergen[56]

Some elements of the debate with Pearson reappear nearly 30 years later in a controversy which opposes the now famous economist to one of the founders of econometrics, Jan Tinbergen. In a long study of business cycle theory appearing in 1935 in the journal of the new Econometric Society, Tinbergen qualifies the systems of Keynes and Hayek as 'open systems' which do not lend themselves well to mathematical translation, even if one can formulate certain hypotheses and relations with mathematical precision. The number of variables discussed is superior to the number of relations which are exposed precisely and explicitly (Tinbergen, 1935, p. 264).[57] Tinbergen opposed this type of system with 'some business cycle theories that form macrodynamic closed systems and are formulated mathematically' (ibid., p. 268). His own work, like that of Frisch and Kalecki, is a part of this second group, which represented for Tinbergen the way of the future.

At the League of Nations' request, at the end of the 1930s, Tinbergen undertook an empirical testing of business cycle theories. The results were published in 1939 in two volumes, the first of which presented his method of empirical testing and the second the first macroeconomic model of the American economy (Tinbergen, 1939). Keynes was asked to comment on Tinbergen's first book. His reaction was virulent and gave birth to a severely critical account in *The Economic Journal* (1939-9), to which Tinbergen would reply (1940) before a final blow from Keynes (1940-3). Tinbergen's econometrician colleagues, particularly Koopmans (1941) and Haavelmo (1943), would take up their pens to denounce Keynes's incomprehension of the new discipline. Keynes was effectively engaging himself in a virulent attack against the practice of econometrics such as it would be developed, as well as the misuse of statistics in economics and the social sciences in general.

For Keynes, the problem was fundamentally methodological in origin. He rejected 'the logic of applying the method of multiple correlation to unanalysed economic material, which we know to be non-homogeneous through time' (letter to R. Tyler, 23 August 1938, JMK 14,

p. 285–6). He reproached Tinbergen for postulating that the future state of an economy can be calculated as the result of past statistics. As a result, the uncertainty which constitutes an essential element of economic and social reality disappears from sight and non-quantifiable factors 'such as inventions, politics, labour troubles, wars, earthquakes, financial crises' (ibid., p. 287), what he calls in his article 'political, social and psychological factors' (ibid., p. 309), cannot be taken into account. He described Tinbergen's book to Kahn as 'such a mess of unintelligible figurings' (letter from 23 August 1939, JMK 14, p. 289). He wrote to Harrod on 21 September that 'the whole thing is charlatanism in spite of T.'s admirable candour' (ibid., p. 305).

Of all economic problems, that of the business cycle was for Keynes the least suited to statistical and mathematical treatment. This dismissal holds particularly in the case of investment determination, whose central role in *The General Theory* will be examined below. But more generally, Tinbergen's error, in Keynes's view, was to apply to economics methods of analysis conceived for other objects. Economic data lack the required permanence and stability for successful implementation. One cannot draw up an exhaustive list of causal factors of a given situation. Several fundamental elements simply cannot be measured. Even if this were the case, units of measurement are not necessarily homogeneous. When an effect can in turn react on the cause, one comes up against fallacious correlations and insoluble complications. In his model, Tinbergen is forced to postulate among his variables a linear dependency which does not correspond to reality: 'indeed, it is ridiculous' (1939-9, p. 312). Keynes's conclusion that 'the successful application of this method to so enormously complex a problem as the business cycle does strike me as a singularly unpromising project in the present state of our knowledge' (ibid., p. 317) is hardly surprising.

It is significant that one finds here one of Keynes's rare public allusions to his first research into probabilities. Reproaching Tinbergen for preferring the labyrinths of arithmetic to those of logic, he described himself as someone whose tastes in statistical theory followed the opposite path (ibid., p. 307). And more explicitly, he added: 'Thirty years ago I used to be occupied in examining the slippery problem of passing from statistical description to inductive generalization in the case of simple correlation; and today in the era of multiple correlation I do not find that in this respect practice is much improved' (ibid., p. 315). In his response to Tinbergen's polite reply, Keynes wrote that he doubted 'that this brand of statistical alchemy is ripe to become a branch of science . . . But Newton, Boyle and Locke all played with alchemy. So let him continue.' (1940-3, p. 320).[58]

In Praise of Statistics

Keynes's criticism of Tinbergen's econometrics did not prevent him from associating with the institution of econometrics from its beginnings, six or seven years earlier. In 1933 he accepted participation in the group of the 30 founders of the Econometric Society, before being appointed a member of its board the following year. He also sat on the board of editors of *Econometrica*, the Society's journal. And finally he became the Society's president in 1944–45. This mixture of rejection and participation illustrates the complexity of the man.

The Society was defined in its founding document as 'an international society for the advancement of economic theory in its relation to statistics and mathematics . . . Its main object shall be to promote studies that aim at a unification of the theoretical-quantitative and the empirical-quantitative approach to economic problems and that are penetrated by constructive and rigorous thinking similar to that which has come to dominate in the natural sciences' (quoted in *Econometrica*, vol. 1, 1933, p. 1). Now, Keynes agreed at least in part with this objective. He considered that statistics had an important role to play in the description of phenomena, in economics as elsewhere. And during his whole career, he never stopped fighting for improvements in methods of statistics collecting. Statistical data abound in his writings. On 18 December 1908 he confided to Duncan Grant while he was composing his first academic article on the Indian economy, that the production of statistics 'makes me into a tremendous state of excitement – like the excitement of the scientist who watches the result of his experiments . . . Nothing except copulation is so enthralling' (BL, 57930A). There is in Keynes's involvement with statistics a psychological dimension. He inherited from his father the habit of keeping accounts of everything: finances, work hours, hours of reading, game results. He even attempted a complex tabulation of his sexual activities.[59]

He never stopped, alone and with other colleagues in the 1920s and 1930s, complaining about the dearth of statistical data on the British economy, in comparison with the situation in the United States, where the National Bureau of Economic Research (NBER), founded by Wesley Clair Mitchell in 1920, and other institutions, were carrying out this task. In 1919 he signed a Royal Statistical Society petition destined for the Prime Minister calling for an inquiry into methods of statistics collection and presentation.

Informing the public with the most complete and reliable information possible constituted one of the important elements of the Liberal programme with which he opposed, in the 1920s, that of the Conservatives. Statistics appeared to him as an essential instrument for the rational mastering of the economy. It was in response to this need that he established in 1923 with his colleagues Hubert Henderson, William Beveridge and Arthur Bowley, the London and Cambridge Economic Service, which attempted, at a time when nothing resembling statistical series existed, to make available to businessmen information helping them to make their decisions. This project was similar to the objective pursued by Wesley Clair Mitchell and his colleagues at the National Bureau of Economic Research on the other side of the Atlantic. The group established by Keynes and his associates elaborated new economic indicators and presented them in tables and graphs in monthly bulletins and special reports. Actively implicated in the work of the Service until 1938, Keynes composed seven detailed memorandums on stocks of staple commodities (JMK 12, pp. 267–647).

Keynes led his crusade in favour of collecting statistics in the 'liberal yellow book', *Britain's Industrial Future*, published in January 1928 in view of the following year's elections.[60] In the Macmillan Committee report of 1931 and to which he was one of the main contributors, he called for the establishment of a system of public statistics. He pursued his campaign in the Economic Advisory Council alongside Colin Clark, a pioneer with Simon Kuznets in the establishment of national accounts statistics. In 1931 the Prime Minister Macdonald formed a Committee on Economic Information, linked to the Economic Advisory Council. In 1938 Keynes was appointed member of the council and governor of the new National Institute of Economic and Social Research. The following year he wrote to the Institute's director Noel Hall that it was urgent to pressure the government into collecting statistics not yet gathered in an adequate manner (Stone, 1978, p. 84). This institute established the Cambridge Research Scheme, presided over by Keynes, who undertook detailed statistical research with the intention of studying the process of England's economic transformation.

The General Theory contains a few statistical data, taken from the works of Clark and Kuznets, with which Keynes sought to illustrate some of his intuitions, particularly those relative to the size of the multiplier. The concepts elaborated by Keynes – the consumption function, the investment function, the multiplier, money demand – call for statistical testing and constitute a framework for national accounts. Economists rapidly began working on this. Keynes contributed himself in his book *How to Pay for the War*, published in 1940. To support his proposals to finance the war, he estimated the income potential of Great Britain with his statistical assistant Erwin Rothbarth and published the results in the December 1939 issue of *The Economic Journal* (1939-14).

From 1940, Keynes was closely associated with the British war effort and in particular with all its economic aspects, including the conditions of postwar reconstruction.[61] The same year in June, James Meade, a close friend of Keynes, entered into the service of the war cabinet's Economic Information Service and began working on drawing up tables of national accounts in the analytic framework provided by Keynes. He was joined by Richard Stone in August, and the two men sent their work to Keynes in December. Keynes was enthusiastic and it was in 1941 that the famous White Book on the budget containing an analysis of the financial sources for the war, written by Keynes, and tables of national income and expenditures prepared by Meade and Stone, was published. For many this date marks the true beginning of the Keynesian revolution in Great Britain.[62]

When the White Book on Employment Policy was published in 1944, Keynes wrote that 'the new era of "Joy through statistics" (I do not write ironically) can begin. Theoretical economic analysis has now reached a point where it is fit to be applied' (1944-1, p. 371). At the same time the Department of Applied Economics at Cambridge was founded. This department, whose creation Keynes proposed in 1939, focused on quantitative economics. Here is how the first director of the new department, Richard Stone, describes Keynes's attitude to econometrics:

> His ambivalence on the role of theory and his hostility to the use of mathematics in economics were the outcome, I think, of his background and early experiences and reflect the critical bystander in him. With his rhetorical style there is no difficulty in finding overloaded, not to say outrageous, quotations. But they are representative of the young self; the actions of the old self belie them. Despite many hard words, there is no doubt in my mind that he should be counted among the benefactors of econometrics. (Stone, 1978, p. 88)

ECONOMICS: MORAL SCIENCE, ART AND DISCOURSE

Keynes wrote little on the nature and method of economic sciences. His main reflections are found in letters, in brief passages in his books, particularly in his criticisms of classical economics. His implicit positions can be deduced from some of the writings we have discussed in the present chapter. A first conviction, affirmed very early and constantly repeated, is that economics must not be confused with physical sciences. It is a social science or, to use an older designation, a moral science:

> I also want to emphasize strongly the point about economics being a moral science. I mentioned before that it deals with introspection and with values. I might have added that it deals with motives, expectations, psychological uncertainties ... It is as though the fall of the apple to the ground

depended on the apple's motives, on whether it is worth while falling to the ground, and whether the ground wanted the apple to fall, and on mistaken calculations on the part of the apple as to how far it was from the centre of the earth. (Letter to Harrod, 16 July 1938, JMK 14, p. 300)

Keynes was convinced of the fact that methods used in the physical sciences cannot be applied to the moral sciences: 'It seems to me that economics is a branch of logic, a way of thinking; and that you do not repel sufficiently firmly attempts à la Schultz to turn it into a pseudo-natural science . . . economics is essentially a moral science and not a natural science. That is, it employs introspection and judgments of value' (Letter to Harrod, 4 July 1938, JMK 14, pp. 296–7).[63] Keynes discusses here the presidential discourse that Harrod was to present in August 1938 to the F section of the British Association for the Advancement of Science[64] entitled 'Scope and method of economics', and published in the September edition of *The Economic Journal*. Harrod responded to him on 6 July: 'I am not sure that I agree altogether with your hostility to the idea of economics as a natural science' (quoted in JMK 14, p. 297). Unanimity was far from being the rule on this point in the Keynesian camp.

In the moral sciences, the unit of analysis is the human being, acting within the fog of history. The economist works with material that is 'in too many respects, not homogeneous through time' (letter to Harrod, 4 July 1938, JMK 14, p. 296), with judgements of value, such that the distinction, formulated by his father John Neville, between positive and normative economics must be rejected. Time occupies a central place. The future is uncertain and undetermined. Anticipation, anguish and fear play a crucial role, as we will see in Chapter 6, in the analysis of money and the preference for liquidity. One observes as early as Keynes's first writings the rejection of determinism, the conviction that movement constitutes the essence of social and human reality, the belief in the transitory nature of life and states of mind, in the precariousness of human and social realities.[65] These ideas were by no means unique to Keynes. They were shared by, among others, his Bloomsbury friends.

The consequences, even immediate, of our actions cannot be predicted with certitude. Now one finds in economics that results occur in a very distant future, which makes this discipline particularly unsuited to treatment by methods from the natural sciences:

Actually, however, we have, as a rule, only the vaguest idea of any but the most direct consequences of our acts . . . Now of all human activities which are affected by this remoter preoccupation, it happens that one of the most important is economic in character, namely wealth. The whole object of the accumulation of wealth is to produce results, or potential results, at a comparatively distant, and sometimes at an *indefinitely* distant, date. Thus the fact that our knowledge of the future is fluctuating, vague and uncertain, renders wealth a peculiarly unsuitable subject for the methods of the classical economic theory. (1937-4, p. 113)

Uncertain knowledge, Keynes states in this methodological postscript to his *General Theory*, must not be confused with what allows for the distinction between the certain and the probable.

The game of roulette is not subject, in this sense, to uncertainty; nor is the prospect of a Victory bond being drawn. Or, again, the expectation of life is only slightly uncertain. Even the weather is moderately uncertain. The sense in which I am using the term is that in which the prospect of a European war is uncertain, or the price of copper and the rate of interest twenty years hence, or the obsolescence of a new invention, or the position of private wealth owners in the social system in 1970. About these matters there is no scientific basis on which to form any calculable probability whatever. We simply do not know. (1937-4, pp. 113–14)

In *The General Theory*, he wrote regarding the uncertainty which characterizes the taking of economic decisions and particularly the decision to invest, which cannot be founded on a rational calculation of costs and benefits: 'By "very uncertain" I do not mean the same thing as "very improbable"' (1936-1, p. 148).

We must nevertheless act, in economics as in life's other domains 'in a manner which saves our faces as rational, economic men' (1937-4, p. 114). This we do by assuming that the present is a good guide for the future, that the present state of opinion is based on correct future prospects and by conforming to the behaviour of the majority: 'The psychology of a society of individuals each of whom is endeavouring to copy the others leads to what we may strictly term a *conventional* judgment' (ibid.). Now this is a 'flimsy foundation, . . . subject to sudden and violent changes' (ibid.). What goes on in the real world is not the outcome of processes envisaged by orthodox economic theory:

> New fears and hopes will, without warning, take charge of human conduct. The forces of disillusion may suddenly impose a new conventional basis of valuation. All these pretty, polite techniques, made for a well-paneled board room and a nicely regulated market, are liable to collapse. At all times the vague panic fears and equally vague and unreasoned hopes are not really lulled, and lie but a little way below the surface. . . . I accuse the classical economic theory of being itself one of these pretty, polite techniques which tries to deal with the present by abstracting from the fact that we know very little about the future. (1937-4, pp. 114–15)

Moreover, this theory postulates an illusory being that exists only in the mind of those who conceive it. This character is the *homo œconomicus* of Bentham's imagination and has become, according to Keynes, the cornerstone of the utilitarianism which constitutes the implicit philosophy of economists. For Bentham, man's behaviour is influenced by calculating pleasure and pain, advantages and disadvantages 'supposed to be capable of reducing uncertainty to the same calculable status as that of certainty itself' (ibid., pp. 112–13). Classical economists do not see 'how far the initial assumptions of the marginal theory stand or fall with the utilitarian ethics and the utilitarian psychology' (1926-10, p. 260). Keynes opposes this vision with one in which beings are motivated by their instincts, impulses, their 'animal spirits': 'a large proportion of our positive activities depend on spontaneous optimism rather than on a mathematical expectation, whether moral or hedonistic or economic.' (1936-1, p. 161)

Causality and Modellization

Yet one should not content oneself with stigmatizing the impotence of orthodox economic theory, but try to explain what happens in reality. Keynes attempted to do this in a number of writings destined for both the lay person and the theoretician or specialist. Here again, he did not explain his method at length, but rather put it into practice. It is based primarily on what he called, borrowing approvingly a formulation of Harrod, 'a vigilant observation of the actual working of our system' (letter from 4 July 1938, JMK 14, p. 296).[66] One must start with contemporary reality.[67]

Keynes opposed the conception of the economy in terms of a general atemporal equilibrium, which gradually became dominant in the twentieth century, with an approach in terms of causality inscribed in historical time. Historical time is opposed to the logical time of physics. History is irreversible. The past is bygone. Economic analysis must be based on a given concrete situation in which agents are constrained by the results of decisions made in the past. This is the case, for example, for investment spending. The past cannot be erased at each new phase in the development of an economy.

One of the main instruments of analysis is the model: 'Economics is a science of thinking in terms of models joined to the art of choosing models which are relevant to the contemporary world' (letter to Harrod, 4 July 1938, JMK 14, p. 296). Constructing models involves 'segregat[ing] the semi-permanent or relatively constant factors from those which are transitory or fluctuating so as to develop a logical way of thinking about the latter, and of understanding the time sequences to which they give rise in particular cases' (ibid., pp. 296–7). Progress in economics involves gradual improvements in the choice of models. Keynes considers the art of choosing good models a talent with which few are endowed. It is safe to say that he considered himself among such a happy few that were favorably endowed.

A model does not involve the juxtaposition of separate and independent atoms. It is an organic unity. The characteristics, particularly those quantifiable, of the unity are not the sum of the characteristics of its elements: 'The atomic hypothesis which has worked so splendidly in physics breaks down in psychics' (1926-10, p. 262). This organic vision is manifest, in the *General Theory*'s model for example, in the paradox of savings, according to which the attempt by people to increase the savings taken from their individual income translates into a decrease in effective demand leading to a decrease in national income and thus a decrease in global savings.[68] Keynes had already underlined, in 'Miscellanea Ethica' from 1905, the difficulties created by organic unities in economics. Utility is thus a part of this class of qualities for which the value of the whole differs from the value of its parts. In the second version of his dissertation on probabilities, Keynes shows how this notion allows one to justify a more egalitarian distribution of incomes, about which he would return later with his theory on the propensity to consume: 'It is at the root of all principles of equality. It is behind the numerous arguments that an equal distribution of goods is better than a very unequal distribution. If this is the case it follows that, the sum of the goods of each part of a community being fixed, the organic good of the whole is greater the more equally the goods are divided amongst the part' (1908-4, pp. 352–3).

Numbers and Intuition

For a model to be useful and generalizable, Keynes felt it is not enough to replace variables with real values. The utility of statistics 'is not so much to fill in missing variables with a view to prediction, as to test the relevance and validity of the model' (letter to Harrod, 4 July 1938, JMK 14, p. 296). Statistics are for Keynes undeniably important, useful and, as we have seen, even amusing. But they do not play in his economic vision the same role as in econometrics and more generally in mathematical economics. For Keynes, statistical data are essential for helping businessmen, union leaders and governments to make enlightened decisions. But they can in no way allow them to predict with certitude the results of alternative decisions. In what concerns economic theory, statistics can illustrate models, but they cannot, according to Keynes, allow for their transformation into instruments of prediction. Transforming an economic model into a quantitative formula destroys its utility (ibid., p. 299). In addition to the misuse of statistics, Keynes condemns the 'symbolic pseudo-mathematical methods of formalising a system of economic analysis' (1936-1, p. 297): 'Too large a proportion of recent "mathematical" economics are merely concoctions, as imprecise as the initial assumptions they rest on, which allow the author to lose sight of the complexities and interdependencies of the real world in a maze of pretentious and unhelpful symbols' (ibid., p. 298).[69]

In choosing sensible models, intuition, imagination and the researcher's common sense should play the main role. On Keynes's intuitive approach, Austin Robinson gave the following surprising explanation: 'For I have long felt that Keynes' economic thinking was, in reality, intuitive, impressionistic, and in a sense feminine rather than precise, ordered, and meticulous' (A. Robinson, 1964, p. 90). Many economists have reproached Keynes in the same way for his lack of theoretical rigour. Keynes believed that his approach was that of all great scientists, including those in the natural sciences. The following three examples show that his position on this subject did not change from his early philosophical writings to the end of his life.

In *A Treatise on Probability*, Keynes wrote that it was neither through logical process nor statistical inference but rather through intuition that Darwin arrived at his hypothesis that all living species evolved from a few primitive forms into which life was first breathed: 'Not only in the main argument, but in many of the subsidiary discussions, an elaborate combination of induction and analogy is superimposed upon a narrow and limited knowledge of statistical frequency. And this is equally the case in almost all everyday arguments of any degree of complexity' (1921-1, pp. 118–19). The long-term natural evolution studied by Darwin cannot be submitted to laboratory tests or described by means of demonstrative logic.

We quoted above in the First Interlude the article, signed 'Siela', in which Keynes praises the genial scientific imagination that allowed Freud to put forth a series of innovative ideas, ideas founded on intuition and experience. We did not reproduce the passage in which he writes that the validity of Freud's hypotheses depends very little on inductive verifications:

> I venture to say that at the present stage the argument in favour of Freudian theories would be very little weakened if it were to be admitted that every case published hitherto had been wholly invented by Professor Freud in order to illustrate his ideas and to make them more vivid to the mind of the reader (1925-19, p. 393).

One of Keynes's late writings deals with Newton, several of whose manuscripts he acquired in 1936.[70] In it he continued to develop his argument on the primordial role of intuition in scientific work, including the field of 'hard science'. Newton's experiments 'were always, I suspect, a means, not of discovering, but always of verifying what he knew already' (1947, p. 366). And he concludes that the gap so many others see between Newton's alchemical investigations and his serious scientific work does not exist. For Newton as for Freud, for Darwin so for Keynes, intuition rather than induction is the first step in the process of knowledge.

In short, even if, according to some scholars, Keynes's epistemological position can be qualified as realist,[71] it certainly cannot be associated with empiricism, any more than with pragmatism, according to which the value of a theory is linked to the value of its results, of the predictions that are deduced from it.[72]

Art and Language

Explaining to his mother the disappointment he felt at the publication of his *Treatise on Money*, Keynes warned her that 'Artistically it is a failure' (JMK 13, p. 176). In a paper written for the Apostles Society (1909-2), he wrote that if talent had been given to him, he would have preferred to have been an artist than a man of science.[73] But, according to him, there are more similarities than differences between the artistic and the scientific ways of apprehending reality, and he sometimes defined economics as an art.[74] In particular, imagination and intuition belong to both worlds. The world described in works of art and literature, like those dealt with by biographers and psychologists, is a changing, unstable world, one in which the most important decisions are made in uncertainty. It is a world in which individual, subjective experiences are confused and fragmented, in which individuals are not led by rationality. This vision of things applies to both everyday life and artistic creation, to social interactions and economic phenomena. For this reason, traditional scientific language cannot be applied to material with which he who seeks to describe society and the economy is confronted.

Moreover, language and reality, like form and content, do not constitute two separate entities, as Russell, Wittgenstein and several others have shown. Language is in reality, and reality lets itself be seen through language. Beyond this there is a conception of the world, of society, of human beings, developed at the turn of the century in England and elsewhere, which is sometimes qualified as 'modernism' and whose defining characteristics we examined in the Interlude devoted to Bloomsbury. Art and literature transform the world they describe. Post-impressionism appeared as the form adapted to the new universe, like the narrative style developed by Proust, Joyce, Musil or Woolf. It was in this context that Keynes elaborated his own language. It constituted, by its form as much as its content, an instrument in his struggle to transform social and economic reality.[75] Virginia Woolf praised his literary talents by writing to him on 23 December 1937 regarding his paper on her nephew Julian Bell, who died during the Spanish Civil War:

> I liked the notice on Julian very much . . . I wish you'd go on and do a whole portrait gallery, reluctant as I am to recognise your gift in that line when it seems obvious that nature gave me none for mathematics. Please consider it. Is portrait writing hard work compared with economics? (V. Woolf, 1975–80, vol. 6, pp. 192–3).

NOTES

1. But, as we will see later in this chapter, Keynes's attitude to econometrics was ambiguous.
2. At the beginning of the century at Cambridge, what was called the moral sciences included four subjects: moral and political philosophy, logic, philosophy of mind (which was in fact psychology) and political economy. In what follows, 'moral sciences' and 'social sciences' will be used synonymously.
3. The word 'orthodoxy' must of course be used with caution. It varies with time and place.
4. See Deane's biography (2001). See also Machlup (1957), Moore (2003) and Tilman and Porter-Tilman (1995).
5. In his diary entry of 1 January 1911, one reads: 'Last year's work 2068. Omitting Sundays and allowing 5 weeks holiday this is a full 8 hour day for the rest of the year' (Deane, 2001, p. 279).
6. The 31 Cambridge colleges, most of which are several centuries old (there were 23 colleges at the end of the nineteenth century, and eight have been founded since 1954), bring together fellows who live and eat at each college's 'high table'. Students pursue courses and sit examinations in departments of the university, the only body authorized to award diplomas, but their studies are supervised by tutors, who are fellows of the college to which they belong. To study at Cambridge, a student must necessarily be admitted to a college. University professors are generally attached to a college, but not necessarily. Inversely, a fellow is not necessarily a professor, which was Keynes's case.
7. On Sidgwick see Chapter 2. Herbert Foxwell (1849–1936) was a neighbour of Keynes's parents at Cambridge. On Foxwell, a fanatical bibliophile (he accumulated 70 000 books, which served as basis for Harvard University's famous Kress library), Keynes wrote that he was one of the first English economists to appreciate the importance of Marx (1936-9, p. 271). He undertook research on the first English socialist economists and always manifested sympathy for heterodoxy, particularly for institutionalism. Convinced of the instability of

capitalism, which produced both wealth and poverty, but fearing social revolution, he advocated State intervention. Foxwell opposed the idea of considering economics as a branch of logic or mathematics. Such reasons might explain why Marshall preferred Pigou to Foxwell as his successor to the chair of political economy at Cambridge in 1908, something which Foxwell never forgave. Foxwell succeeded Jevons in 1881 as chair of political economy at University College London.

8. An association which would become the Royal Economic Society.

9. Professor at Oxford, Edgeworth (1845–1926) may be considered one of Marshall's main rivals. Their personal rivalry symbolizes that between Oxford and Cambridge. Author of *Mathematical Psychics: An Essay on the Application of Mathematics to the Moral Science* (1881), he criticized in *New and Old Methods of Ethics* (1877) the arguments of Sidgwick. Keynes succeeded Edgeworth as director of the *The Economic Journal* in 1911, but from 1915, because of his wartime activities, Edgeworth assisted him as editor: 'As his fellow-editor I received a final letter from him about its business after the news of his death' (1926-10, p. 255). Keynes recognized Edgeworth as a principal promoter of the mathematization of the moral sciences: 'I do not think it can be disputed that for forty years Edgeworth was the most distinguished and the most prolific exponent in the world of what he himself dubbed *Mathematical Psychics* – the niceties and the broadnesses of the application of quasi-mathematical method to the Social Sciences' (ibid., p. 256).

10. In his autobiography, Bertrand Russell wrote: 'When I was young, Keynes's father taught old-fashioned formal logic in Cambridge. I do not know how far the new developments in that subject altered his teaching. He was an earnest Nonconformist who put morality first and logic second' (Russell, 1967, p. 71).

11. This passage does not appear in the first edition and it is present under a slightly different form in the second edition, in 1887. See Lalande (2002), p. 573.

12. Johnson was thanked, in the Preface, among those whose critiques helped improve Neville Keynes's book. In an obituary notice on Johnson, Maynard Keynes wrote: 'He had been recognised for many years as one of the acutest philosophers in Cambridge, and had an immense influence through his love of discussion and conversation on almost all Cambridge moral scientists of the last 40 years . . . it may be said that he was the first to exercise the epistemic side of logic, the links between logic and the psychology of thought' (1931-7, p. 349).

13. A pioneer in the integration of mathematics and logic, Augustus De Morgan defined the latter, in *Formal Logic*, as 'the examination of that part of reasoning which depends upon the manner in which inferences are formed, and the investigation of general maxims and rules for constructing arguments, so that the conclusion may contain no inaccuracy which was not previously asserted in the premises' (De Morgan, 1847, p. 1).

14. Author of *The Logic of Chance* (1866), Venn penned in *Mind* the first review of *Studies*, which he believed marked a decisive advance on Jevon's *Studies in Deductive Logic* (1880) (Deane, 2001, p. 117). Neville Keynes considered Jevons's book the closest rival to his own.

15. The divergences between the three founders of the marginalist revolution are as important as their convergences (see Jaffé, 1976). And among the disciples of Menger and Walras today, the divide is undoubtedly as great as those between Walrasians and the successors of either Marx or Veblen.

16. See for example Keynes's letter to Harrod on 27 August 1935: 'my assault on the classical school ought to be intensified rather than abated' (JMK 13, p. 548).

17. Henry Fawcett (1833–84) held the chair of political economy at Cambridge from 1863. Liberal parliamentarian from 1864, he was a disciple of John Stuart Mill. His *Manual of Political Economy* (1863) taught Smith's economics through the eyes of Mill. Fawcett was not interested in the new marginalist economics. His wife Millicent, who survived him until 1929, founded in 1897 the National Union of Women's Suffrage Societies (see Second Interlude).

18. Maynard would be better treated when he returned to Cambridge, since he would teach advanced courses from 1909.

19. There was a strong historicist group in Britain.

20. It was in 1910 that Keynes read Smith for the first time, on the occasion of a trip to Greece and Turkey: 'I have read nearly half of Adam Smith. It is a wonderful book' (letter to his father, 22 March 1910).

21. Neville Keynes considered economics as a 'department of sociological speculation' (1891, p. 14).

22. It is of course difficult to ascertain if the book was really read or only present on reading lists.

23. But not every one agrees on this. See in particular Bateman (1996) who argues that Keynes rejected the use of the idea of uncertainty in the period when he was writing *A Treatise on Money*, coming back to it later.

24. We will return to these first reflections in the following chapter.

25. When the paper, which does not carry a title, was written is uncertain. Skidelsky (1983, p. 152) and O'Donnell (1989, p. 10) claim it to be on 23 January 1904, while Moggridge (1992, pp. 131–6) believes it could have been written two years later.

26. On the multiple meanings of probability, see Nadeau (1999); on probabilities in economics, Hamouda and Rowley (1996).

27. There were important changes in the frequentist perspective after 1905, as French, Soviet and US mathematicians tried to remove the inadequacies of limited frequences on a basis for probability. It does not seem that Keynes kept abreast of these developments. On the other side, there is a large literature on intuitive and other

non-frequentist perspectives. See for example Walley (1991).

28. The law of great numbers, formulated by Jacob Bernoulli at the beginning of the seventeenth century, states that in any chance event, when the event happens repeatedly, the actual results will tend to the calculated, or planned result. In other words, repeated actions over time will produce the results we seek. In Keynes's words, Bernoulli showed that 'if the *a priori* probability is known throughout, then . . . *in the long run* a certain determinate frequency of occurrence is to be expected' (1921-1, p. 365).

29. Regarding Karl Pearson, refer to the section below that presents his debate with Keynes.

30. Alfred North Whitehead (1861–1947), mathematician and philosopher, taught successively at Cambridge, London and Harvard. He was a member of the Apostles. A long collaboration with Bertrand Russell gave birth to their famous *Principia Mathematica* (1910–13) which founded mathematics on logic. In *The Concept of Nature* (1920), he sought to reconcile the perception of nature and its analysis by science, the reddish glow of sunset and the movement of molecules and waves which explains it.

31. This does not mean that Whitehead accepted Keynes's notion of logical probability. Frequentism was rejected at that time by the newly developed axiomatization of probability and ergodic theory.

32. On this idea, as on several other elements of Keynes's thought, Hume's influence is important. He sought in his book to solve questions left in suspense by the great Scottish philosopher. He was unable to accept the conclusions to which Hume's scepticism led.

33. On these questions, see Porter (1986) and (1995).

34. See also the correspondence on this subject with Hugh Townsend in JMK 29, pp. 289–94.

35. We will see the important role this idea will play in Keynes's political vision. On the relation between uncertainty and risk, see Lavoie (1985a).

36. Frank Knight's *Risk, Uncertainty and Profit* was published the same year as Keynes's book. There are some analogies between the two authors in what concerned the difference between measurable probabilities, that Knight calls 'risk', and non-measurable probabilities, that he calls 'uncertainty'. They derived, however, very different consequences on the level of economic analysis. A founder of the Chicago School, Knight was an advocate of laissez-faire and believed that in the long term, economic competition would bring an end to the harmful consequences of uncertainty. See Greer (2000), Netter (1996) and Schmidt (1996b).

37. See for example Pigou (1921), who thus concludes his review: 'For the problems which Mr. Keynes has touched he has not only illuminated with a marvelous lucidity of style, but has also substantially advanced. Economists will recognise with pride what one of their number has accomplished in another field, and will look forward with added zest to his next essay in their own' (Pigou, 1921, p. 512). Pigou's critique of *The General Theory* would be much less praiseworthy.

38. O'Donnell's book is a revised and expanded version of a Ph.D. thesis completed in Cambridge in 1982. This thesis is thus the first extensive examination of the links between Keynes's philosophy and his economics and politics, on the basis of archival researches.

39. See for example Backhouse and Bateman (2006), Bateman (1996), Bateman and Davis (1991), Benetti, Dostaler and Tutin (1998), Cottrell and Lawlor (1995), Davis (1994a) and (1994b), Dow and Hillard (1995), Gerrard and Hillard (1992), Lawson and Pesaran (1985), Marzola and Silva (1994), Muchlinski (1996), O'Donnell (1991), Parsons (1997), Runde and Mizuhara (2003) and Verdon (1996). Several important articles have been reproduced in Wood (1994). On Keynes and probabilities, one may consult, among others, Carvalho (1988), Cottrell (1993), Dow (2003), Favereau (1988a), Gillies (2000), Lawson (1985), McCann (1994), Meeks (1991), Muchlinski (2003), O'Donnell (1990a), Rotheim (1988) and Schmidt (2003).

40. Author of two influential articles on savings and taxation, Ramsey, a Cambridge student, Apostle, fellow of King's College from 1924, died in 1930 at the age of 26. For Keynes, he was 'certainly far and away the most brilliant undergraduate who has appeared for many years in the border-country between Philosophy and Mathematics' (Letter to Broad, 31 January 1922, KP, TP/1/1). On Ramsey, see Gaspard (2003) and Newman (1987).

41. Born in 1889 to a wealthy family of the Viennese bourgeoisie, Wittgenstein studied engineering and started building a plane motor before becoming interested in the logical foundations of mathematics and meeting Frege who suggested that he study with Russell at Cambridge. After an unfavourable first impression, Keynes wrote to Duncan Grant, 15 November 1912: 'Wittgenstein is a most wonderful character – what I said about him when I saw you last is quite untrue – and extraordinarily nice. I like enormously to be with him' (BL, Add. MS 57931). Wittgenstein's work gave rise to an immense secondary literature and his complex personality has been described in numerous works – biographies, memoirs, novels – and even in a film. Monk (1990) may be the best introduction to his life and thought.

42. It was Keynes who led the campaign for his election, while Russell stressed that Wittgenstein would not be at ease in the group, which became apparent immediately. But Keynes and his friends believed that Russell wanted 'to keep Wittgenstein for himself' and prevent him from falling under the influence of Moore, whose relationship with Russell had become increasingly tense.

43. It was again Keynes who would organize Wittgenstein's reintegration into the Society's ranks.

44. He began this work in 1911 at Cambridge and continued it in the Norwegian village in which he found solitary

refuge in October 1913. He would go back to Norway in August 1936, living in an isolated house which he had built for himself near a lake.

45. The first German version had been published in 1921 under the title *Logisch-Philosophische Abhandlung*, but Wittgenstein was horrified by this edition, which he qualified as 'pirated'. From then on he considered the 1922 English version as the first true edition of his book.

46. Ramsey wrote to Keynes in 1924 that Wittgenstein, then living in Vienna and on bad terms with Moore and Russell, would only come to Cambridge to see Keynes, Hardy and perhaps Johnson (Wittgenstein, 1974, p. 117).

47. To Sheppard, one of their numerous guests in this house, Keynes wrote on 22 August: 'Wittgenstein is here! He came two days later than I expected with the result that he will still be here until Wednesday. I think he would drive you mad. So it would be much better if you didn't come until Wednesday. But if it suits you better to come on Tuesday, I daresay that would be all right and that you could survive the one day' (J.T. Sheppard Papers, JTS/2/112).

48. Wittgenstein submitted the *Tractatus* in June 1929 to obtain a doctorate of philosophy. Moore, who was one of its examiners, wrote: 'It is my personal opinion that Mr Wittgenstein's thesis is a work of genius; but, be that as it may, it is certainly well up to the standard required for the Cambridge degree of Doctor of Philosophy' (quoted by Monk, 1990, p. 272).

49. On relations between Keynes and Wittgenstein, see, in addition to the correspondence reproduced in Wittgenstein (1974), Coates (1996) and Monk (1990). For the latter, the two men did not have as close a friendship as, for example, there existed between Wittgenstein and Sraffa, which suited Keynes for 'being Wittgenstein's *friend* demanded more time and energy than he was able, or prepared, to give' (Monk, 1990, p. 262). A memorable lunch brought together Ramsey, Wittgenstein, Sraffa and Keynes to discuss the *Treatise on Probability* (Newman, 1987, p. 42).

50. See Favereau (1985), Davis (1994a) and Lavialle (2001). Wittgenstein indicated, in the Preface of his posthumous *Philosophical Investigations*, that criticisms from the economist Piero Sraffa, a close friend of Keynes, constituted the most important stimulation to his work. Sraffa and Wittgenstein met for discussion at least once per week, from the beginning of the 1930s until 1946. Sraffa then decided, to Wittgenstein's great dismay, to put an end to these meetings. On these two authors' relations, see Marion (2005).

51. Wittgenstein envisioned in the 1930s moving to the USSR as a manual worker and even started the procedures to this effect, asking for help from Keynes, whose book *A Short View of Russia* played a role in his decision. This project was never carried through. During a stay in the USSR, it was made known to him that he would be welcome as a professor of philosophy but not as a worker.

52. Keynes would publish from this the second appendix under the title 'The principal averages and the laws of error which lead to them' in *The Journal of the Royal Statistical Society* (1911-2).

53. We will return in Chapter 6 to the relations between this paper and the criticism, by Keynes, of the quantity theory of money.

54. Karl Pearson (1857–1936) studied at King's College, Cambridge. He was appointed in 1884 professor of applied mathematics and mechanics at University College London. He started his work in the field of biometrics in the 1890s. He also undertook research in psychology. He is the author of the widely read *The Grammar of Science* (1892) and one of the founders of the review *Biometrika*. In 1911, with the death of Francis Galton, he became the first holder of the chair of eugenics for whose establishment the latter made a donation to the University of London. Founder of the Department of Applied Statistics at the University College, London, in 1911, the first university statistics department in the world, he was one of the foremost statisticians of the century. He was an active controversionalist. David Garnett knew the Pearsons well, being friends of his parents. His description of them is interesting: 'Both were Rationalists and for some reason felt it necessary on that account to live up to stricter moral standards than the older type of puritans who faced the divine sanctions of brimstone and hell fire' (Garnett, 1953, p. 113).

55. Prohibition was in force in the United States from 1920 to 1933. Fisher campaigned with vigour against its repeal.

56. See Dostaler and Jobin (2000), from which the two following sections borrow certain elements.

57. The *Treatise on Money* is being referred to here and not *The General Theory*, which had not yet been published. But this comment applies equally to the latter work.

58. In literature pertaining to the Keynes–Tinbergen controversy, and more generally on Keynes's relations with econometrics, consult Bateman (1990), Bodkin et al. (1988), Hendry (1980), Patinkin (1976b), Rima (1988), Rowley (1988), Stone (1978) and the papers brought together in Lawson and Pesaran (1985).

59. See KP, PP/20A, partially reproduced in plates 9 and 10 of Moggridge (1992).

60. On the political context of the events related in this paragraph, see Second Interlude. We will return to the Macmillan Committee in Chapter 6.

61. On this, see Chapter 8.

62. On Keynes and national accounting, see Stone (1978), Klotz (2003) and Suzuki (2003).

63. Henry Schultz (1893–1938), author of *The Theory and Measurement of Demand* (1938), born in Russia, was

appointed at the University of Chicago in 1926. He was a pioneer in the development of quantitative method and econometrics. He studied under Karl Pearson at London University College in 1919.

64. The British Association for the Advancement of Science was founded in 1831 by scientists disenchanted with the elitism and conservatism of the venerable Royal Society, founded in 1660. The F section brings together economists.

65. See the following chapter.

66. Marshall, whose vision on the methods of economics is very different, for example, from the Walrasian vision, would probably agree with this. Here as elsewhere, Keynes does not pay due credit to his predecessors.

67. Keynes would thus be radically opposed to Friedman's vision, according to which the realism of a scientific theory's hypotheses is of no importance so long as empirically testable predictions can be deduced from them (Friedman, 1953).

68. See Chapter 6.

69. On the interpretation and use of mathematics by Keynes, see O'Donnell (1990b).

70. Newton's descendents auctioned off in London several of Newton's documents, among others those dealing with alchemy. Keynes bought 'almost everything which ought to remain in Cambridge ... Amongst other things I bought Sir Isaac Newton's death mask, which is extraordinarily interesting' (letter from Keynes to his father, 15 July 1936, JMK 21, p. 382).

71. See for example Lawson (2003).

72. Moore published in 1908 a critique of William James's pragmatism, a critique with which Keynes agreed. Frank Ramsey was on the contrary favourable to pragmatist arguments and, on this, Keynes did not follow him. For a different point of view on the relation between Keynes and pragmatism, see Berthoud (1998).

73. We will come back to this paper in the last chapter, devoted to art, and in which we will analyse Keynes's artistic conceptions.

74. His friend Roger Fry, painter and art critic, had also a scientific formation, and thought also that art and science are closely linked.

75. See on this subject Dostaler (2002a), Johnson (1978a), Marzola and Silva (1994) and O'Donnell (2004). On the relation between Keynes's and Woolf's writing, see Wicke (1994).We will return in Chapter 7 to the language of *The General Theory*, and to Keynes's response to those who accused him of imprecision in his use of words.

4. Politics: beyond liberalism and socialism

The true socialism of the future will emerge, I think, from an endless variety of experiments directed towards discovering the respective appropriate spheres of the individual and of the social, and the terms of fruitful alliance between these sister instincts.
'Does unemployment need a drastic remedy?' (1924-14, p. 222)

I am sure that I am less conservative in my inclinations than the average Labour voter; I fancy that I have played in my mind with the possibilities of greater social changes than come within the present philosophies of, let us say, Mr Sidney Webb, Mr Thomas, or Mr Wheatley. The republic of my imagination lies on the extreme left of celestial space.
'Liberalism and labour' (1926-8, pp. 308–9)

The question is whether we are prepared to move out of the nineteenth-century *laissez-faire* state into an era of liberal socialism, by which I mean a system where we can act as an organised community for common purposes and to promote social and economic justice, whilst respecting and protecting the individual – his freedom of choice, his faith, his mind and its expression, his enterprise and this property.
'Democracy and efficiency' (1939-1, p. 500)

Ethics is primarily concerned with individual behaviour and considers the nature of good and appropriate rules of conduct. For G.E. Moore and the Bloomsbury Group, ethics is a question of attaining good states of consciousness through friendship, intimate relationships, the contemplation of beauty, and the quest for truth. Of course, life does not stop there. Man is a political animal. Besides individual happiness, there is also the matter of realizing the conditions necessary for bringing about collective well-being. The two are connected. Attaining good states of consciousness and perfecting the art of living are impossible in a world of poverty marked by violence, injustice, lack of freedom, the domination of a few over the majority and the resolution of international conflict through war. For Keynes, the world will become a happy place only when class and international wars have been brought to an end. Issues of class will be discussed in the present chapter, and international relations in the following chapter.

We have thus passed from ethics to politics, one of Keynes's main battlefields. The economic theory he developed, known more appropriately as 'political economy', was subordinate to politics and aimed at resolving practical problems. It was a question of reforming society in order to avoid the traps of reaction and revolution threatening to engulf an already precarious civilization. Keynes's open letter to United States President Franklin D. Roosevelt on 31 December 1933 is particularly eloquent in this regard:

You have made yourself the trustee for those in every country who seek to mend the evils of our condition by reasoned experiment within the framework of the existing social system. If you fail, rational change will be gravely prejudiced throughout the world, leaving orthodoxy and revolution to fight it out. But if you succeed, new and bolder methods will be tried everywhere, and we may date the first chapter of a new economic era from your accession to office. (1933-31, p. 289)

Keynes's life was marked by the constant effort to convince his fellow citizens of the urgent need to effect essential changes in order to assure progress and well-being. Paradoxically, few of his writings were explicitly and entirely devoted to politics in general, that is, the art, technique, science and practice of government. Of course, the writings are filled with remarks of a political nature. But these passages are most often brief comments or incidental remarks. One exception is a paper devoted to Edmund Burke which Keynes wrote in 1904 at the age of twenty-one.

In fact, Keynes's involvements in politics, from his early days at Eton to his last days on the benches of the House of Lords, never ceased. His political involvement was not limited to advising decision makers or intervening in the print media, activities that took up much of his time and energy. This also included political activities and work at a practical level.

His positions have been subjected to very diverse and contradictory interpretations. For some, Keynes was on the far left of the political spectrum. Many conservatives viewed him as a crypto-communist. On the other hand, communists and Marxists considered him a conservative all the more dangerous because he presented himself as a friend of the working class and criticized Conservative policies. Between these two characterizations, one finds the complete range of positions imaginable. New Liberal, progressive and radical, for some, Keynes is a centrist liberal of rightist persuasion for others. He himself seemed to take pleasure in stirring things up by describing himself at times as moderately conservative and at other times as left of the Labour Party. He finished one article by saying that he hoped to have succeeded in pleasing conservatives, liberals, moderate socialists and revolutionaries (1930-3, p. 16)!

Keynes's political thought was nourished by many sources. It was issued from a family context characterized by what his biographer Harrod called the 'presuppositions of Harvey Road', a mixture of elitism and radical liberalism, of nonconformism and attachment to tradition, of rationalism and artistic sensibility. Keynes, like his Bloomsbury friends, came from a well-to-do middle class background whose values he retained until the end of his life. The events of his time – the economic and social upheavals marking the end of Victoria's reign and that of Edward VII – would reinforce a vision to the left of the liberalism to which Keynes adhered and would make him, to some extent, a friend of Labour and resolutely opposed to the Conservatives. Next to John Stuart Mill and the New Liberal theoreticians,[1] Burke played an important role in forming Keynes's vision. Our presentation of Keynes's political philosophy will therefore accord an important place to its genesis, to the ideas he developed as a young man in his twenties. On Burke, he wrote that most great social thinkers elaborated their political philosophy before the age of thirty. This remark applies to Keynes himself as well. The Interlude that follows the present chapter will provide a concise overview of Britain's political history from 1883 to 1946, and Keynes's place therein.

GENESIS OF A POLITICAL PHILOSOPHY[2]

History and its Progenitors

The curriculum at Eton, where Keynes studied from 1897 to 1902, revolved around classics and mathematics. Keynes excelled in mathematics. Though it comprised only a small part of the curriculum, Keynes was also keenly interested in history, an early interest that he pursued throughout his life. He was interested in ancient and modern history, the Middle Ages, the Reformation and the Renaissance, in factual history and the theory of history, the history of great men and nations, and the evolution of institutions and structures. On 18 November 1894, at the age of eleven, he wrote in his diary that Stanley Weiman 'is a splendid historical novel writer' (KP, PP/34, p. 5).[3] The young Keynes read a great many historical novels as well as more substantial works such as Plutarch's *Life of Caesar*, Trevelyan's *American Revolution* and Lecky's *History of the Eighteenth Century*. In his diary entry for 7 August 1900, his father wrote: 'altogether history seems to have a great attraction for him' (KP, PP/43, p. 161). In 1900, Maynard began genealogical research on the Keynes family, something he would pursue for many years, and would lead him as far back as William the Conqueror.[4] His first published writing (unsigned), dating from 1903, is a review of Volume 7 of *The Cambridge Modern History* (1903-6). In preparation for his Civil Service examinations in 1906, he immersed himself in historical documents. From 1920 to 1926, he conducted extensive research on the history of money and ancient currencies, research that delayed work on his *Treatise on Money*.[5] He mastered the art of writing short biographies, especially of economists but also of politicians and scientists.[6]

Many of Keynes's early essays deal with historical subjects, such as the Stuarts, Cromwell, and Queen Victoria. Ideas that would become important in later works, such as his rejection of determinism, are already present. History is not circular or repetitive, nor does it evolve toward a given end. There are no natural laws of evolution in history, just as there are no natural laws in society and the economy. This theme immediately sets Keynes in opposition to many economists, who, since Quesnay and the other founders of the discipline, believe that natural laws play a role in human affairs.[7]

The rejection of determinism was closely linked to his insistence on the presence and role of uncertainty in history and elsewhere, which became a major theme in his economic thought. In 1900, in a paper dealing with the Stuarts, he wrote about 'that uncertainty in events which baffles alike the historian, who studies the past, the politician who watches the present, and the statesman whose eye is on the future' (1900-1, p. 1).[8] If historians, politicians and statesmen are confused by uncertainty, it is not surprising that ordinary men contemplate the future as a continuation of the past: 'So strangely incapable is the human intellect of conceiving a changed condition of affairs before such a change has taken place, that to most men so great a transformation as that from peace to war seems scarcely possible until it is actually upon them' (1901-2, p. 2). In the preceding text, Keynes described Europe's political and economic climate at the beginning of the century, concluding that war was much closer at hand than believed by most people. There was also the threat of revolutionary uprisings, particularly in Germany and France: 'About France it is always dangerous to prophesy . . . But take for granted that popular feeling is excited by some revolutionary movement, it is not unlikely that the government will move to war in a wild attempt to regain popularity similar to that of 1870' (ibid., p. 7). Since the future is shrouded in uncertainty, it follows that the past is the only basis for prediction: 'history is to be taken as the basis of prophecy, and we are to judge the future by the past' (1900-2, pp. 4–5).

If there are no natural laws in history, which has no determinate future, individual actors must play an important role. These actors are the decision makers: statesmen, concerned with the distant future, and politicians, concerned with immediate problems. Both groups are influenced and guided by the ideas of philosophers and social thinkers. The psychological traits of individuals in a position to change the course of events is of considerable importance in history. The history of the Stuarts, the Scottish dynasty that ruled England from 1603 to 1714, illustrates this fact: 'The first three representatives of the House of Stuart on the English throne were not ungifted intellectually, nor were they obsessed by dangerous ambition; yet the first lost his dignity, the second his head, the third his character, and the fourth his crown' (1900-1, p. 1).[9] Keynes recalled this tragic outcome in a paper combining historical, political and psychological considerations in a way that foreshadowed his famous portraits of the participants in the Paris Peace Conference in *The Economic Consequences of the Peace*.[10] Even if destiny is not written in stone, heredity plays its role: 'Fortune is not such a capricious goddess as most represent her to be; the unfortunate man has, in most cases, some trait that logically leads to ill-fortune . . . So the unhappy house of Stuart seems to have had some characteristics which inevitably led to misfortune' (ibid., p. 9).

Among other things, the statesman's task is to transcend class struggles and prevent revolutions. Charles I and Louis XVI, though they were not bad people, were mediocre statesmen, according to Keynes. It is important to distinguish between individuals' 'moral character' and their 'historical character'. Keynes described the tragic consequences of Stuart weakness in the same way he later attributed the failures of the Versailles Treaty to US President Wilson's psychological fragility, and, more generally, the catastrophes, crises and wars, which are neither natural calamities nor divine retributions, to the mediocrity of statesmen and politicians. As a great statesman, President Roosevelt averted the dual trap of reaction and revolution and thereby atoned for the disastrous consequences of Wilson's weakness. As rulers during an important transitional period in British history, the Stuarts were unable to govern as responsible statesmen:

> Secondly they came at the transition stage of English history, and they suffered the usual fate of a man who refuses to move from his position on the beach when the tide comes up. It is true that the greatest statesmanship could not have prevented an upheaval, but it must be remembered that there was a Restoration; a dynasty with even the smallest insight or strength could have prevented the Revolution. (1900-1, p. 12)

Such was not the case for Cromwell, 'one of the ablest despots of all history', the 'originator of modern strategy', who exhibited toleration 'towards all sects except the Papists', and 'never lost sight of the fact that no government which did not give England liberty could obtain any real stability' (1900-3, pp. 3, 5, 6). The only stain on his accomplishments was Charles I's execution, 'but it is impossible to believe that he perpetrated this act except under uncontrollable pressure from his own followers . . . it is incredible from the point of view of expediency that the most consummate politician of the time should have of his own free will taken so impolitic a step' (ibid., p. 6). Noteworthy here is the word 'expediency', whose central place in Burke's political philosophy will be examined below.

History comprises long periods of relatively stable progress, crisis and transition, the latter often lasting for decades or even centuries. In 'Modern civilisation' (1905-3), Keynes wrote that the beginning of Christianity, the transition from the Roman Empire to the Middle Ages, and the end of the Middle Ages, were periods of transition. During such periods, one must adapt to rapid change; if not, one risks, to use Keynes's expression, finding oneself in the perilous situation of being immobile before a rising tide. Great men perceive in what direction the wind is blowing, and usually oppose the established order:

There seem to be certain periods in human history, when a spirit of discontent and of reaction and revolt against the established is everywhere abroad, when men, howsoever they may differ in natural temperament and surroundings, take up a new fearlessness of utterance whether against the current religion and morality, or against the settlement of the civil power.

Such a renaissance as this was the most striking characteristic of the twelfth century. (1902-1, p. 33)

Bernard de Cluny and Abelard were such men, and the young Keynes devoted considerable study to them.[11] Both were revolted by the political and religious orthodoxies of their time, and for this they paid dearly. Both served as examples of the important 'undercurrent of history' (ibid., p. 31) that plays a key role in periods of transition, such as that of the twelfth century. Bernard de Cluny was aware of living in a dark age. He also appreciated the great civilizations of antiquity, their art, literature and philosophy, which nourished the Reformation and Renaissance. The Renaissance returned to ancient traditions whose spirit was kept alive in mediaeval monasteries: 'The spirit of the Renaissance and the Reformation was not the parentless creature it appears at first. This spirit had never died; it lived on in these mediaeval monasteries and it was surely this that found voice in this satire of Bernard's' (ibid., p. 31).

Keynes considered the total condemnation of the Middle Ages excessive and believed that despite its horrors and iniquities, 'it is nevertheless impossible to deny a great, calm beauty to the mediaeval world' (ibid., p. 33). Such interest and respect for ancient traditions is usually associated with the mature Keynes; we see here that it appeared much earlier. The twelfth century was a great epoch for France, associated with Hildebert, Abelard, Peter the Venerable, Adam St Victor, Bernard de Cluny and Bernard de Clairvaux.[12] Keynes, however, reproved these great minds for 'their complete acceptance of the fact of misery, of pessimism with regard to this life, without any corresponding Joblike outburst against the deity for permitting it, or any theological doctrine explaining and excusing him' (ibid., pp. 65–6). He also reproached them for their 'absolute and complete disbelief in progress and in this world's future' from which followed the 'feeling of the utter insignificance of anything this world has to give, of the futility and of the hopelessness of all human activity' (ibid., pp. 65–6). The contemporary world has revised its approach on such matters: 'An age which can know and appreciate the past, which looks forward to an unlimited futurity, has been naturally compelled to modify its dogma, or at least to slur over a question which their predecessors faced without a qualm' (ibid., p. 66).

Phases of transition are followed by periods, however long, of stability. The Victorian Age was one such period. In 1815 the Congress of Vienna ended the Napoleonic Wars and ushered in a century-long period of European peace, though this did not prevent the spread of local wars and suffering, the regular occurrence of economic crises and the intensification of social struggles, some of which gave rise to violent uprisings and revolution. Though not totally exempted from all of this, Britain was less affected than the continent. In a paper referred to in Chapter 2 (1899-1), Keynes attributed this to the stability of Queen Victoria's reign. But he also explained it by evoking some of the innate characteristics of his native country. In 'The English national character', a paper written around 1900, he wrote that 'the English take more intelligent interest in political questions than their continental neighbours. The average Englishman probably knew more about the Dreyfus case than the average Frenchman' (1900-3, p. 3).[13] England is more disposed to progress and stability because of its 'great continuity of history and institutions' and 'owes her safe political position to this moderation; her typical citizen is neither reactionary nor radical' (ibid., p. 2). Even the revolution that enthroned William III was moderate, as were constitutional changes:

> An Englishman's whole political outlook is affected by his feeling that his institutions have at any rate the sanction of time and that, although they should not be lightly abolished, they nevertheless require adaptation as time goes on. He is in consequence liberal but not radical, adverse to sudden change, but reconciled to it when he is once satisfied of the necessity for it. (1900-3, p. 2)

Like most Western intellectuals of 1900, Keynes believed in the West's superiority over the Orient. On many occasions during his career, such as at the Bretton Woods negotiations, he was observed making comments that verged on racism regarding certain delegations' abilities to comprehend the heart of the discussions. In 'The difference between East and West: will they ever disappear?', he contrasted the West, birthplace of democracy, where the individual is all-important, and the East, where the masses predominate, where autocracy and despotism are prevalent: 'from this trampling down of the personality of the individual, we may trace that lack of humanity and that abominable cruelty, which flashes out at intervals from the normal Oriental stagnation' (1900-2, p. 2). There is also a passage on a people who were buffeted back and forth between Asia and Europe:

> The Jews have been scattered over Europe for many hundred years; they have, at any rate in modern times, done their utmost to make themselves indistinguishable from Europeans, and they have signally failed. It is not that the Jews are traditionally the accused race that makes anti-Semites; it is because they have in them deep-rooted instincts that are antagonistic and therefore repulsive to the Europeans and their presence amongst us is a living example of the insurmountable difficulties, that exist in merging race characteristics, in making cats love dogs. (1900-2, p. 3)

Comments of this kind were common at the time, even in a milieu such as that provided at Bloomsbury, which included Jews, such as Leonard Woolf, among its members. Some of Keynes's closest friends – Melchior, Sraffa, Kahn, Montagu and Wittgenstein – were Jewish. Keynes was also very actively involved in the reception of Jewish refugees once Hitler's persecutions began. But this did not prevent him from uttering occasional anti-Semitic remarks up the end of this life.[14]

Philosophical interlude: the nature of time

The question of history is linked to that of time. Time occupied a central place in Keynes's worldview, particularly its economic dimension. As we shall see,[15] he defined money as a bridge between the present and the future. Expectations and uncertainty are closely linked to time.

As an individual, Keynes was acutely aware of the psychological dimension of time's passing and of the precariousness of all things. He shared this awareness with his Bloomsbury friends. For Virginia Woolf, time was the writer's primary material. In 'Modern fiction', she wrote that the writer must forget 'the life of Monday or Tuesday' and describe 'the atoms as they fall upon the mind in the order in which they fall . . . however disconnected and incoherent in appearance' (V. Woolf, 1925, pp. 160–61). As if to combat the anguish this perception might arouse, Keynes organized his time meticulously, leaving nothing to chance and recording many of his activities. His life, divided between Cambridge, London and Tilton, was organized with clockwork precision. He always had one eye on his watch. Incapable of remaining inactive, and perhaps even of relaxing, he was convinced that one must act quickly, very quickly, in order to get things done, since one could die tomorrow.

Keynes's relation to time was rooted in his personal experience. But it was also, from a very early age, the object of philosophical reflection with traces found in many of his writings. He has left one paper dealing explicitly with the question of time, probably his first philosophical essay, which consists of a 20-page manuscript, written for a presentation on 8 May 1903 before the Parrhesiasts Society. The Parrhesiasts Society, one of the many clubs to which Keynes belonged, consisted of students at King's College, where he was in his first year when he wrote the essay. In preparing this essay, Keynes read H. Sidgwick (*A Dialogue on Time and Common Sense*), Hyslop (*Kant's Doctrine of Time and Space*), Calkins (*Time as Related to Causality and to Space*), McIntyre (*Time and the Succession of Events*) and Schiller (*The Metaphysics of the Time Process*). At that time, he attended lectures by McTaggart, who proclaimed that time is unreal: 'When I have attended Dr McTaggart's lectures, I have felt the plunge from ordinary life into metaphysics a very violent one; it usually takes me an appreciable time to gather my wits for a sustained dialectical outlook upon the Universe' (1903-2, p. 3). In his lecture notes one reads: 'Can the solution be founded in a *timeless* state compared with which things *in time* would be unreal? In which all experience might be experienced at once as being perfect' (1903-5, p. 47); 'Perhaps time is a reality not so independent of the content as is generally supposed' (ibid., p. 62).

Keynes begins his presentation in the following manner: 'In the three papers that have preceded me we have discussed the opposite banks of Life and Death, and the bridge of Sex that joins the two; tonight we are to consider the noise of Time that flows between' (1903-2, p. 1). He described time as 'one of the greatest stumbling blocks in every metaphysical system' (ibid., p. 2). His main point addressed 'the essential relativity of all time measurement, and especially . . . the essential interconnection of the ideas of time and change' (ibid., p. 7). The measurement of time is based on the unverifiable hypothesis according to which the intervals between two recurrent events of a certain type are equal. There is nothing absolute in time, whose concept is closely linked to change: 'If you admit the existence of a background of empty time, beyond and apart from change, you have no right to deny the possibility of the elapse of a million, million years between the utterance of my last two words' (ibid., p 8). Rejecting Kant's vision of time, Keynes added that the common sense conception of time is illusionary. In reality, Keynes's conception of time is closer to Kant than to Hegel. The reconciliation of inner subjective time with the progression of uncertain history is Kantian in the sense that it approaches the problem of psychology's passage into history. It is a question of synthesizing historical time, external to the subject, and psychological time. In trying to bridge the gap between the immutable ideal and changing materiality, Kant conceived time as a formal a priori condition of phenomena, as a category of understanding.

Kant tried to reconcile the principle of causality and human liberty in order to show that if man is a link in a causal historical chain, he is also the cause of his own actions. Consequently, actors play a primordial role in history, which leads to Keynes's political vision, to the themes discussed in the previous section, and to that which follows. Man emerges as a political being, as a civic animal, once he is able to take charge of his destiny, once his place in the universe is not determined by some sort of spiritual transcendence or forever fixed within nature's static order of things.[16]

Praise and Criticism of Burke

Of Irish origin, Edmund Burke (1727–1797) was one of eighteenth century England's most important writers and politicians. A liberal in economic matters, he was one of the first to present his friend Adam Smith's ideas to the British Parliament. Opposed to Britain's colonial policies under the reign of George III (1760–1820), he was at the same time a stout adversary of the French Revolution, which he criticized in *Reflections on the Revolution in France* (1790).[17] A member of the Whig Party, he was in many ways politically a conservative. He deplored the decline of the traditional social structure, in which man submits to the order of things, and the rise of a modern order founded on the Enlightenment and abstract human rights. Like all conservative thinkers, he was suspicious of reason's claims for governing society. He nevertheless adhered to certain fundamental principles of liberalism, to English political liberties and to the separation of powers. The liberal conservative Benjamin Disraeli, Queen Victoria's favourite Prime Minister (1868, 1874–80), may be considered one of Burke's spiritual disciples.

In 1901, Maynard bought a twelve-volume edition of Burke's works. In February 1902, he read Burke's speech on the East India Bill in period costume at a speech contest. In 1904, during his second year at Cambridge, he prepared an 86-page typed paper, 'The political doctrine of Edmund Burke', for which he obtained the University Members Prize for English Essays. As with his papers on Abelard and Bernard de Cluny, he devoted an enormous amount of research to the development of his text. It was the longest and most important paper that Keynes ever wrote on political philosophy.[18] His intention was to describe the 'consistent and coherent body of political theory' (1904-2, p. 1) inherent in Burke, a very contradictory man: simultaneously conservative and liberal, free-trader and imperialist, advocate of the English revolution and adversary of the French revolution. Keynes's positions often appeared contradictory.

According to Keynes, Burke's major contribution to political philosophy is his doctrine of 'expediency': 'In the maxims and precepts of the art of government expediency must reign supreme' (ibid., p. 36); 'In politics, it is true, he holds that there is no specific act which ought always to be performed; and herein lies no small part of his claim to fame' (p. 9). There are no ultimate ends in politics:

> He did not look to establish his ultimate goods by political considerations; those he sought for elsewhere; the science of politics is with him a doctrine of means, the theoretical part of a device intended to facilitate the attainment of various private goods by the individual members of a community. It is his antagonism to those who maintain that there are certain ends of a political nature, universally and intrinsically desirable, that occasions his constant attacks on 'metaphysical speculations', 'abstract considerations', 'the universals of philosophers', and the like. But there is another type of general principles to which he does not offer the same hostility; there is no universal end in politics except that of general happiness, but there are many general principles and maxims of wide validity which it is the business of political science to establish. (1904-2, p. 6)

For Burke, politics is concerned with the means for achieving various ends, one of these being the well-being of the greater number. Keynes qualified him as a political utilitarian. Well-being involves material comfort, security and liberty:

> Physical calm, material comfort, intellectual freedom are amongst the great and essential means to these good things; but they are the means to happiness also, and the government that sets the

happiness of the governed before it will serve a good purpose, whatever the ethical theory from which it draws its inspiration. (ibid., p. 81)

Such ends are not attained through violent and painful transformations: 'He does not think of the race as marching through blood and fire to some great and glorious goal in the distant future; there is, for him, no great political millennium to be helped and forwarded by present effort and present sacrifice' (ibid., p. 86). Here is a characteristic passage from *Reflections on the Revolution in France*:

> It is this inability to wrestle with difficulty which has obliged the arbitrary assembly of France to commence their schemes of reform with abolition and total destruction. But is it in destroying and pulling down that skill is displayed? Your mob can do this as well at least as your assemblies. The shallowest understanding, the rudest hand, is more than equal to that task. Rage and phrenzy will pull down more in half an hour, than prudence, deliberation, and foresight can build up in a hundred years. The errors and defects of old establishments are visible and palpable. It calls for little ability to point them out; and where absolute power is given, it requires but a word wholly to abolish the vice and the establishment together. (Burke, 1790, pp. 279–80)

In this quotation, one finds a central idea in Keynes's political thought, an idea at the source of his hostility toward Marxism and communism: revolution, like any form of violent social transformation, must be rejected not only because violence is bad and risks bringing people to power who do not have the requisite skill to govern, but also because, given the nature of uncertainty, it is dangerous to sacrifice a present well-being for a future good. Keynes attributed this idea to Edmund Burke, but it also drew on his reading of Moore and his work on probabilities:

> Our power of prediction is so slight, our knowledge of remote consequences so uncertain, that it is seldom wise to sacrifice a present benefit for a doubtful advantage in the future. Burke ever held and held rightly, that it can seldom be right to sacrifice the well-being of a nation for a generation, to plunge whole communities in distress, or to destroy a beneficent institution for the sake of a supposed millennium in the comparatively remote future. We can never know enough to make the chance worth taking, and the fact that cataclysms in the past have sometimes inaugurated lasting benefits is no argument for cataclysms in general. (1904-2, pp. 14–15)

Even though there are no final ends in politics, there are nevertheless principles that governments must respect. These principles are linked to ethical considerations that are, in Burke's case, 'his preference of peace over truth, his extreme timidity in introducing present evil for the sake of future benefits, and his disbelief in men's acting rightly, except in the rarest occasions, because they have *judged* that it is right so to act' (ibid., p. 10). The principles of government are grouped into four major categories (ibid., pp. 82–4):

1. 'It is not wise to look too far ahead; our powers of prediction are slight, our command over remote results infinitesimal . . . The part that reason plays in motive is slight'.
2. Individual freedom must be respected, especially in economic matters: 'in this field the individual must be left completely unfettered'.
3. Property must be respected: 'There is no rule in the whole of science to be preserved so rigorously as that of the sanctity of property and of prescription'.
4. A variety of rules must be respected dealing with 'the special modes and contrivances of government': the establishment and respect of the constitution, the taking into account of public opinion, the fight against despotism and corruption.

Keynes was most critical of Burke's second point, which is typical of economic thinking 'dominated by laisser-faire': 'But he certainly holds that there is a point beyond which no individual ought to be interfered with on any pretext whatever, and that there are certain spheres, in particular those of property and commerce, which ought, absolutely and without exception, to be left to individual action' (ibid., p. 20). Keynes criticized Burke's justification of inequalities and his argument in favour of laissez-faire:

> Most defenders of the rights of property are ready to admit the evils of a very unequal distribution; but this difficulty caused Burke no qualms. He declared that no alternative distribution would produce any appreciable increase of good, and urged that it is of the essential nature of property to be unequal. This is a line of argument of which Burke is overfond and which leads him into more than one fallacious position. (1904-2, pp. 22–3)

As far as Keynes was concerned, the State must not allow people to die of hunger. One of the glories of the French Revolution, to which Burke was hostile, was to have ended the serfs' subordination to nobles and reduced the extent of misery in the French countryside. Misery generates violence.

Reform must occur without violence. The enlightened exercise of power relies on public opinion. But public opinion is not spontaneously enlightened, which led Burke to criticize self-government and democracy. Without completely endorsing Burkes's views, Keynes shared his scepticism of the people's ability to understand great political issues. For Burke, 'the people *must* surrender the executive and legislative functions' (ibid., p. 51), because 'it is most dangerous that the people should, under normal conditions, be in a position to put into effect their transient will and their uncertain judgment on every question of policy that occurs' (ibid., p. 53). The government should not tyrannize people, but instead respect public opinion, all the while trying to influence it. It should be clement towards its citizens, but 'the selection of particular means and policies must be wholly beyond their competence' (ibid.).

Keynes criticized the excessive nature of Burke's ideas, while insisting on the educational power of democracy. But he agreed with part of Burke's analysis. He was and would always remain convinced that only an intellectual elite, of which he undoubtedly considered himself a gifted member, could understand the complex mechanics of economics and politics and would thus be able to implement the reforms necessary to achieve happiness or, at least, eliminate the reasons for revolt.[19] Twenty years after his essay on Burke, Keynes wrote:

> I believe that in the future, more than ever, questions about the economic framework of society will be far and away the most important of political issues. I believe that the right solution will involve intellectual and scientific elements which must be above the heads of the vast mass of more or less illiterate voters . . . With strong leadership the technique, as distinguished from the main principles, of policy could still be dictated above. (1925-17, pp. 295–6)

KEYNES'S POLITICAL VISION

Keynes's political vision is clearer in what it rejects than what it espouses. On the one hand, Keynes led the struggle against classical liberalism transformed into conservatism. Its extreme form was Fascism and Nazism. On the other hand, he rejected radical forms of socialism, Bolshevism amd communism. One must navigate between reaction and revolution.

Such was the mission of the 'third way', qualified alternatively as new liberalism, social liberalism or liberal socialism, of which he casts himself as the propagandist.[20]

Laissez-faire and Conservatism

Keynes probably read Veblen and other economists in the institutionalist tradition, thinkers who inspired him but whose influence he did not acknowledge. John R. Commons was an exception to this rule.[21] On several occasions, in particular during a 1925 conference given in the USSR (1925-22), Keynes presented and approved of Commons's schema illustrating the long-term evolution of Western societies. Commons distinguished three phases in this evolution. The first is an age of scarcity bringing together 'the minimum of individual liberty and the maximum of communistic, feudalistic or governmental control through physical coercion' (Commons quoted in 1925-17, p. 304). This period is marked by violence, inefficiency, incessant wars, the reign of superstition and the weight of tradition. It lasted from humanity's origins until the fifteenth or sixteenth century. The second phase is one of abundance, which starts with the beginnings of the accumulation of capital in the sixteenth century, and which Keynes says 'was initially due to the rise of prices, and the profits to which that led, which resulted from the treasure of gold and silver which Spain brought from the New World into the Old' (1930-17, p. 323). This period, bringing together 'the maximum of individual liberty, the minimum of coercive control through government, and individual bargaining takes the place of rationing' (Commons quoted in 1925-17, p. 304) reached its height in nineteenth century Britain with the triumph of laissez-faire and classical liberalism. Great Britain was henceforth engaged in the first phase of an economic transition that generated great suffering. The third phase is one of stabilization, in which 'there is a diminution of individual liberty, enforced in part by governmental sanctions, but mainly by economic sanctions through concerted action, whether secret, semi-open, open, or arbitrational, of associations, corporations, unions, and other collective movements of manufacturers, merchants, labourers, farmers, and bankers' (Commons quoted in 1925-17, p. 304). This period is marked, at the level of political organization, by two extremes: Fascism on the one hand and Bolshevism on the other.

A series of exceptional circumstances assured, he believed, for a half century, a prosperous and economically stable Europe under British domination: 'Very few of us realise with conviction the intensely unusual, unstable, complicated, unreliable, temporary nature of the economic organisation by which Western Europe has lived for the last half century' (1919-1, p. 1). Laissez-faire was the ideology of the day. Early on, Keynes distanced himself from this ideology, as his text on Burke demonstrated. In a 1908 review of a study on social and industrial problems in West Ham compiled by E.G. Howarth and M. Wilson, he wrote:

> Anyone who is interested in the effect which unbridled individualism and *laissez-faire* in such matters may have on the development of a community should turn to the account given in this volume of the doings of swarms of small builders, working with little or no capital for immediate profits, and unhindered by bye-laws or by an ordered scheme of development' (1908-1, 174).

According to Harrod, John Sheppard, a student at King's College and member of the Apostles, observed that Keynes, who was 'violently opposed to *laissez-faire*', proposed the following definitions of Conservatives and Liberals in a speech given at a Liberal gathering: 'let there be a village whose inhabitants were living in conditions of penury and distress; the typical Conservative, when shown this village, said, "It is very distressing, but, unfortunately, it cannot be helped;" the Liberal said, "Something must be done about this." That was why he was a liberal' (Harrod, 1951, p. 192).

In a pamphlet derived from conferences at Oxford in 1924 and Berlin in 1926 and published by Hogarth Press as *The End of Laissez-faire*, one finds one of Keynes's most famous attacks against laissez-faire and classical liberalism, the latter being identified with conservatism. A foundation of classical political economy of which Ricardo is the principal representative, laissez-faire was born out of the combination of two currents of thought: conservative individualism and democratic socialism, or egalitarianism. This apparent oxymoron permitted economists to associate private gain with public good. Individualism and laissez-faire thus became, and remain in Keynes's time, the Church of Great Britain. The power of this myth, besides conforming to business interests, results from weaknesses in the arguments opposing it: Marxist socialism and protectionism. For it is a myth. The 'principle of diffusion', as Keynes called it (1925-22, p. 440), of the automatic adjustment of prices and employment upheld by many economists, never existed except in the minds of these economists:

> Let us clear from the ground the metaphysical or general principles upon which, from time to time, *laissez-faire* has been founded. It is *not* true that individuals possess a prescriptive 'natural liberty' in their economic activities. There is *no* 'compact' conferring perpetual rights on those who Have or on those who Acquire. The world is *not* so governed from above that private and social interest always coincide. It is *not* so managed here below that in practice they coincide. It is *not* a correct deduction from the principles of economics that enlightened self-interest always operates in the public interest. (1926-1, pp. 287–8)

In short, Adam Smith's invisible hand, as it was then and is now generally understood,[22] does not exist: 'The old view, that the self-interest of individuals, operating without interference, will always produce the best results, is not true' (1923-29, p. 149). Based on a naturalistic illusion, the belief in laissez-faire was shared, prior to the twentieth century, by Liberals and Conservatives, the latter, however, being in favour of protectionism in the realm of international trade. It then became a Conservative dogma, justifying policies that deliberately increase unemployment in order to lower wages.

Keynes is sometimes presented, often by his friends, as radical in his youth and more moderate, if not conservative, as he aged.[23] This is questionable, as we will see in the Interlude that follows. Keynes resolutely condemned laissez-faire at the end of his career as he had at the beginning. He wrote on the subject in 1941: 'To suppose that there exists some smoothly functioning automatic mechanism of adjustment which preserves equilibrium if only we trust to methods of *laissez-faire* is a doctrinaire delusion which disregards the lessons of historical experience without having behind it the support of sound theory' (1941-1, pp. 21–2).

However, Keynes believed until the 1920s that free trade was an essential element of British prosperity during the previous century, and that it was important to maintain: 'I regarded departures from it as being at the same time an imbecility and an outrage. I thought England's unshakable free-trade convictions, maintained for nearly a hundred years, to be both the explanation before man and the justification before heaven of her economic supremacy' (1933-22, pp. 233–4). His change of mind on the free trade issue in 1931 is one of the elements that contribute to accusations of inconsistency. He responded by saying that when circumstances change, or someone convinces him that he is wrong, his ideas change. In this case, he discovered that free trade should not be considered an end in itself, but rather a means that, under certain circumstances, could have negative consequences: 'Neither free trade nor protection can present a theoretical case which entitles it to claim supremacy in practice' (1932-17, p. 210). His position radicalized following the 1933 World Economic Conference, during which he painted a picture of what he called individualist capitalism: 'The decadent international but individualistic capitalism, in the hands of which we found ourselves after the War, is not a success. It is not intelligent, it is not beautiful, it is not just, it is not virtuous – and it doesn't deliver the goods' (1933-22, p. 239).

This capitalism that creates unemployment also 'destroys the beauty of the countryside because the unappropriated splendours of nature have no economic value' (ibid., p. 242). It is now important to liberate oneself 'of world forces working out, or trying to work out, some uniform equilibrium according to the ideal principles, if they can be called such, of *laissez-faire* capitalism' (ibid., p. 240). It is particularly important that the control over financial markets remains national. In the presence of technical progress, Ricardo's theory of comparative advantages is less and less applicable, so that, far from being retrograde and conservative, the demand for a margin of national self-sufficiency is progressive and contributes more to world peace than Montesquieu's '*doux commerce*'. A country unable to provide its own art and agriculture, inventions and traditions is a country in which it is not worth living.

From conservatism to fascism

The major conflict in the 1920s appeared to be the opposition between Bolshevism and bourgeois capitalism. For Keynes, this was not true. Certainly, this opposition was important, but it was secondary in relation to the conflict opposing, from the middle of the nineteenth century,

> that view of the world, termed liberalism or radicalism, for which the primary object of government
> and of foreign policy is peace, freedom of trade and intercourse, and economic wealth, and that other
> view, militarist, or, rather, diplomatic, which thinks in terms of power, prestige, national or personal
> glory, the imposition of a culture, and hereditary or racial prejudice (1922-3, p. 373).

It was only after the victory of liberal forces that the world's main political combat would become the opposition between capitalism and communism. The real threat to civilization, at least during the 1920s and 1930s, apparently came from militarism and nationalism.

Like liberalism and socialism, conservatism is a complex nebula with currents and undercurrents. It tended, during the postwar period's economic difficulties, towards radicalization. Keynes often called this radicalization 'reaction'. Such was the case for Italian Fascism, followed by German Nazism, and similar movements around the world. In Britain, the Union of British Fascists was founded in 1932 by Oswald Mosley, former Labour Party member and one of Keynes's disciples.[24] For Keynes, this political movement was the very incarnation of evil. And this evil, resulting from unemployment and economic difficulties, was a real danger, since a growing percentage of the population was rallying to both left and right-wing extremism. Of course, British Fascism remained a marginal phenomenon, compared to, for example, its French equivalent. But the struggle against Fascism became an absolute priority for Keynes. In a letter written on 10 November 1937, he reproached Kingsley Martin for an angelic pacifism that played into the hands of Hitler and his allies. Himself a pacifist and conscientious objector during the First World War, Keynes became a defender of armed resistance against Fascism and Nazism and denounced the Munich Pact. This was another illustration of the principle of 'expediency' he borrowed from Burke as a young man.

Marxism and Bolshevism

Keynes and Marx

Keynes was born in London a little less than three months after Marx's death. It was in London that Marx produced most of his work. Keynes had little appreciation for Marx, even if he read and was sometimes inspired by him, ranking him in *The General Theory* as one of the rare heretics recognizing the importance of effective demand.[25] He considered that Marxism, like laissez-faire economics, originated in Benthamite utilitarianism.[26] Marx was inspired by Ricardo, whose economic determinism he adopted: 'Indeed, Marxism is a highly plausible inference from the Ricardian economics, that capitalistic individualism cannot possibly work in practice' (1934-10, p. 488). In this latter paper, derived from a radio broadcast in which he declared himself a heretic, Keynes claimed that Marxism was a form of orthodoxy. Like conservatism, communism 'enormously overestimates the significance of the economic problem. The economic problem is not too difficult to solve. If you leave it to me, I will look after it' (1934-9, p. 34).

Moreover, both communists and conservatives believed that capitalism continued in the 1930s to function as it had before 1870, with communists believing that only a violent revolution could solve the economic problems by overthrowing the bourgeoisie. Other than the fact that he was opposed to any form of violent social transformation, for reasons already mentioned, Keynes believed that power had changed hands since the nineteenth century. It passed from captains of industry to a class of wage-earners, which was not the proletariat: 'Revolution, as Wells says, is out of date. For a revolution is against personal power. In England to-day no one has personal power' (1934-9, p. 34). Erroneous at a political level, the communist project was also based on false theoretical foundations:

> How can I accept a doctrine which sets up as its bible, above and beyond criticism, an obsolete economic textbook which I know to be not only scientifically erroneous but without interest or application for the modern world? How can I adopt a creed which, preferring the mud to the fish, exalts the boorish proletariat above the bourgeois and the intelligentsia who, with whatever faults, are the quality in life and surely carry the seeds of all human advancement? (1925-2, p. 258)

Ten years later, in a 2 December 1934 letter to George Bernard Shaw, Keynes compared *Das Kapital* to the *Koran*:

> My feelings about *Das Kapital* are the same as my feelings about the *Koran*. I know that it is historically important and I know that many people, not all of whom are idiots, find it a sort of Rock of Ages and containing inspiration. Yet when I look into it, it is to me inexplicable that it can have this effect . . . How could either of these books carry fire and sword round half the world? (JMK 28, p. 38)

When Joan Robinson published *An Essay on Marxian Economics* in 1942, one of the first works sympathetic to Marx written by a member of the academic establishment, Keynes wrote to her on 20 August:

I found it [your book on Marx] most fascinating . . . This is in spite of the fact that there is something intrinsically boring in an attempt to make sense of what is in fact not sense . . . I am left with the feeling, which I had before on less evidence, that he had a penetrating and original flair but was a very poor thinker indeed, – and his failure to publish the later volumes probably meant that he was not unaware of this himself. (KP, L/42)

These remarks did not prevent Keynes, on several occasions, from highlighting some of Marx's important insights.[27]

Keynes and the USSR

Similarly, Keynes's relation to Soviet communism, which claimed to put Marx's project into practice,[28] fluctuated. At first he applauded the Bolshevik Revolution, about which he wrote to his mother on 30 March 1917: 'I was immensely cheered up and excited by the Russian news. It's the sole result of the war so far worth having'. On 24 December, after the government announced food rationing measures, he wrote to her:

My Christmas thoughts are that a further prolongation of the war, with the turn things have now taken, probably means the disappearance of the social order we have known hitherto. With some regrets I think I am on the whole not sorry. The abolition of the rich will be rather a comfort and serve them right anyhow. What frightens me more is the prospect of *general* impoverishment. In another year's time we shall have forfeited the claim we had staked out in the New World and in exchange this country will be mortgaged to America.
    Well, the only course open to me is to be buoyantly bolshevik; and as I lie in bed in the morning I reflect with a good deal of satisfaction that, because our rulers are as incompetent as they are mad and wicked, one particular era of a particular kind of civilisation is very nearly over. (JMK 16, pp. 265–6)

On 23 February 1919, he wrote, again to his mother, that the Russian government had offered him a decoration: 'Being a Bolshevik, however, I thought it more proper to refuse' (JMK 16, p. 267). At the same time, he angered his Bloomsbury friends by rejoicing at the establishment of a liberal Russian government at Archangel, following advances by Alexander Koltchak's White Russian troops and armed intervention from the Allies. After Koltchak's defeat and execution, he recognized this policy as a mistake.[29] In 1921 he proclaimed the failure of the Bolshevik experiment, in which the European working classes had placed so much hope (1921-12, pp. 269–70). The following year, after having studied in detail the USSR's economic situation as well as having met and admired the country's Minister of Foreign Affairs, Chicherine, he wrote:

An extraordinary experiment in socialism is in course of development. I think that there may be solid foundations on which to build a bridge. Revolutions are not kid-glove affairs, particularly in Russia. But a mere disgust and moral indignation, which has not even the curiosity to discover the facts, is never by itself the right reaction to a great historical event. (1922-15, p. 408)

He wrote to Gorky that having the correct emotional and intellectual reaction to Bolshevism was difficult, as the following phrase from an article published on 10 April in the same newspaper shows: 'Bolshevism is such a delirium, bred by besotted idealism and intellectual error out of the sufferings and peculiar temperaments of Slavs and Jews' (1922-3, p. 373). In 1925, Keynes and Lydia Lopokova travelled to the USSR for their honeymoon, Lydia's family residing in Petrograd. He was also invited to represent Cambridge University at the bicentenary of the Russian Academy of Sciences. There he delivered a speech in which he described the limits of his new liberalism and recognized as a positive aspect of Bolshevism the fact of having eliminated the love of money as a motor for human action: 'We in the West will watch what you do with sympathy and lively attention, in the hope that we may find something which we can learn from you' (1925-22, pp. 441–42).

On his return, he wrote three articles, published as a pamphlet in December by the Hogarth Press under the title *A Short View of Russia*. In it he was less diplomatic than he was before the Academy of Sciences. He described Leninism as a mixture of religion, mysticism and idealism. The USSR was led by a fanatical minority whose policies were applied with religious fervour. Keynes predicted serious problems for the peasantry. He nevertheless considered that the Soviet economy could survive by transforming itself. For example, the Soviets realized that money could not be abolished since it was indispensable for economic calculations and the distribution of goods and services. Problems with prices indicated that 'a lesson of bourgeois economics [is] being equally applicable in a Communist state' (1925-2, p. 265). The regime would undoubtedly survive and attain some form of political and economic stability, for, in addition to relying on a messianic and persecutory religion, it was an economic experiment. And Lenin was a pragmatic experimenter in economic matters, unafraid of tampering with the fundamental principles of his faith, as demonstrated by the New Economic Policy (NEP) (1922-21, 437).[30]

As he explained to his Russian listeners, there was one level on which Bolshevism could help capitalism resolve one of the most significant moral problems of our time, namely, the love of money, the fact that money is the measure of success: 'But in the Russia of the future it is intended that the career of money-making, as such, will simply not occur to a respectable young man as a possible opening, any more than the career of a gentleman burglar or acquiring skill in forgery and embezzlement' (1925-2, p. 260). This change of attitude towards money constitutes 'a tremendous innovation' (ibid., p. 261) whereas 'modern capitalism is absolutely irreligious, without internal union, without much public spirit, often, though not always, a mere congeries of possessors and pursuers' (ibid., p. 267).

Clearly, the cost of this experience, violent revolution followed by political oppression and lack of freedom, was unacceptable, and one must hope that the West will solve its moral problem by other means. As the years went by and Bolshevism was transformed into Stalinism, Keynes became more and more allergic to the USSR and increasingly placed Stalinism in the same camp as Fascism. Chair of the Board of Directors of the liberal progressive periodical *New Statesman and Nation*, he criticized his editor Kingsley Martin on various occasions, as well as other friends, such as George Bernard Shaw, for their complacency towards Stalin and Bolshevism. On 11 August 1934, he wrote in *New Statesman and Nation*: 'Marxists are ready to sacrifice the political liberties of individuals in order to change the existing economic order. So are Fascists and Nazis . . . My own aim is economic reform by the methods of political liberalism' (1934-7, pp. 28–9).

In a letter to Martin on 25 July 1937, he reminded the latter that Stalin was destroying the old Communist Party, 24 per cent of whose members had been executed, arrested, exiled or fired. He added: 'Stalin's position will soon be indistinguishable from that of the other dictators, and it would seem to be entirely in character that his foreign policy will be opportunist, and an eventual agreement between him and Germany by no means out of the question, if it should happen to suit him' (JMK 28, p. 72). Keynes was often wrong in his political predictions, but here he displayed remarkable foresight, two years before the German–Soviet Pact. He concluded this letter by stressing the increasing similarity of totalitarian states.

Keynes's hostility to Soviet communism did not prevent him from sympathizing with the young communists he frequented at the Apostles and in the Left Book Club,[31] as well as supporting the freedom of speech of the communists' sympathizers. When Harold Laski, a London School of Economics professor and member of the Labour Party, of which he became President in 1945, was threatened with a demotion and a reduction in salary as a result of comments made in the Soviet Union that were favourable to communism, Keynes was indignant at such a monstrous idea and vigorously defended a man to whom he was opposed:

> Too many of the younger members of the Left have toyed with Marxist ideas to have a clear conscience in repelling reactionary assaults on freedom. Thus the importance of impressing the minds of the Right and of the Left alike that not the smallest breach should be allowed in the fortifications of liberty. (1934-6, p. 27)

New Liberalism and Socialism

For Keynes, conservatism and communism constituted two dead ends greatly endangering the future of civilization. There remained but one path, that of liberalism, but of a deeply renewed liberalism. The word 'liberalism' refers to at least three dimensions of human activity: individual freedom, which lies within the domain of morality, political freedom and economic freedom. The first dimension is the most important, while the third is the most problematic. In *On Liberty*, John Stuart Mill explained that the doctrine of trade does not rest on the same ground as the principle of individual liberty.[32] He advocated public intervention to assist the disinherited, accepted that property rights be circumscribed and limited, favoured inheritance taxation and regulation of hours of work, and supported the nascent cooperative movement. If it turned out that, even with these amendments, economic freedom ceased to be the most efficient means for assuring prosperity and justice, then Mill considered that socialism would be justified.

Mill's thought falls within the radical trend in English liberalism, and is linked to nonconformism in religion. Within the Liberal Party, this radical trend was opposed by a more conservative and laissez-faire tradition of Whiggism, the Liberals' original name. A moderate or centrist current existed between these two. Toward the end of the nineteenth century, radical liberalism became known as 'new liberalism' and was advocated by thinkers such as Leonard Hobhouse (1864–1929), author of *Liberalism* (1911), John A. Hobson (1858–1940), author of *The Evolution of Modern Capitalism* (1894) and *Imperialism* (1902), Seebohm Rowntree, author of *Poverty, A Study of Town Life* (1901), C.P. Scott, editor of the *Manchester Guardian*, in which Keynes regularly collaborated in the 1920s, and Graham Wallas.[33]

For this new liberalism, individual freedom was no longer the ultimate value. Individual freedom was transformed into social freedom and finally into social justice, which became its primary objective. For Hobhouse, old liberalism's task was the realization of political democracy and that of new liberalism the realization of social democracy. For the latter, property rights, laissez-faire and even free trade were no longer absolute and indisputable dogmas. New Liberal thinkers did not believe in absolute efficiency of the market. Faced with rising social problems, economic crises, unemployment, deep inequalities of income and fortune, poverty and misery, they proclaimed the end of laissez-faire and advocated interventionist measures not unlike those that would later be associated with the Welfare State. The period from 1873 to 1895, sometimes described as the 'Great Depression', was a propitious time for the emergence of these arguments, as it was for a rise in the power of unions and workers' parties. It was a question of profoundly transforming the economic liberalism that had engendered high social costs in the Victorian era and risked provoking working class uprisings. New liberalism presented itself as an alternative to socialism, collectivism and Marxism. New liberals rejected the class struggle as the motor of social transformation. They adhered to a form of liberal socialism, that might be called social-democratic, at least in the sense that this expression took on after the schisms within working class parties at the beginning of the Second World War.

Of course, this new liberalism was the exact opposite of what is known today as neoliberalism, which is above all an ultraliberal reaction against Keynesian interventionism. Keynes's political convictions were closely linked to new liberalism, which he often mentioned, though nowhere did he cite Hobhouse:[34] 'The transition from economic anarchy to a régime which deliberately aims at controlling and directing economic forces in the interests of social justice and social stability, will present enormous difficulties, both technical and political. I suggest, nevertheless, that the true destiny of New Liberalism is to seek their solution' (1925-17, p. 305).

Keynes believed that liberalism's traditional objectives had been attained, namely 'the destruction of private monopoly, the fight against landlordism and protection, the development of personal and religious liberty, the evolution of democratic government at home and throughout the Empire' (1927-1, p. 638). The time had come for money to be managed rationally and to exercise control over an economy that could not be left to its own devices. Keynes's programme, which will be discussed in Chapter 7, consists of diverse policies of State intervention in the economy, but it also calls for the socialization of investment and the euthanasia of the rentier. But this economic aspect was not, in Keynes's mind, his programme's most important element: 'I believe that there are many other matters, left hitherto to individuals or to chance, which must become in future the subject of deliberate state policy and centralized state control' (1925-22, p. 441). The main problem in organizing the polity is distinguishing between what should be the responsibility of the State and what should be left to individual initiative, what Bentham called the agendas and non-agendas of public power. In *The End of Laissez-faire*, Burke is quoted in support of this idea: 'one of the finest problems in legislation, namely, to determine what the State ought to take upon itself to direct by the public wisdom, and what it ought to leave, with as little interference as possible, to individual exertion' (1926-1, p. 288).

In 'Am I a Liberal?', Keynes ranked economic questions fifth and last in order of importance to new liberalism's programme. The first question was that of peace, to which we will return in the following chapter: 'let us be pacifists to the utmost' (1925-17, p. 301). The second concerned government organization, which Keynes wished to see decentralized. In *The End of Laissez-faire*, he evoked the 'semi-autonomous bodies' of which the universities, the railway companies and the Bank of England were models. In short, we are far from the centralized bureaucracy to which Keynesian management is often compared. The third group he described as 'sex questions', which 'are of the utmost social importance':

Birth control and the use of contraceptives, marriage laws, the treatment of sexual offences and abnormalities, the economic position of women, the economic position of the family – in all these matters the existing state of the law and of orthodoxy is still medieval – altogether out of touch with civilised opinion and civilised practice and with what individuals, educated and uneducated alike, say to one another in private. (1925-17, p. 302)

There was then the question of drugs, which included the problem, always a preoccupation for Keynes, of alcoholism and gambling. He asked himself: 'How far is bored and suffering humanity to be allowed, from time to time, an escape, an excitement, a stimulus, a possibility of change? – that is the important problem. Is it not possible to allow reasonable license, permitted saturnalia, sanctified carnival . . .?' (ibid., p. 303)

This programme was not a socialist programme. It was possible to be in favour of planning without being a communist or a socialist (1932-7, p. 84). However, this did not prevent Keynes from writing, in *The End of Laissez-Faire*: 'The battle of Socialism against unlimited private profit is being won in detail hour by hour' (1926-1, p. 290). He did, on several occasions, speak of a 'semi-socialism' or even the true socialism of the future, in which the public and private spheres would be clearly delimited: 'But we must keep our minds flexible regarding the forms of this semi-socialism' (ibid.). In opposition to state socialism, he proposed liberal socialism. In an interview with Kingsley Martin published in *The New Statesman* on 28 January 1939, he said that the only practicable solution for the present circumstances was an 'amalgam of private capitalism and state socialism' (1939-1, p. 492). In 'The dilemma of modern socialism', taken from a 13 December 1931 conference before the Society for Socialist Inquiry, he wrote:

> For my part I should like to define the socialist programme as aiming at political power, with a view to doing in the first instance what is economically sound, in order that, later on, the community may become rich enough to *afford* what is economically unsound.
>   My goal is the ideal; my object is to put economic considerations into a back seat; but my method at this moment of economic and social evolution would be to advance towards the goal by concentrating on doing what is economically sound. (1932-10, p. 34)

The long-term future

New liberalism can be viewed as a programme of transition towards a distant, and, it is hoped, more radiant future. Keynes expressed himself on this subject in a lyrical text entitled 'Economic possibilities for our grandchildren', published during the Great Depression's worst moments. The Depression provoked 'a bad attack of economic pessimism' (1930-17, p. 321). It was not, however, a matter of old-age rheumatism, but rather of growth pains. The lack of insight into the fundamental causes of the crisis explained the pessimism of reactionaries and revolutionaries. What was experienced in 1930 was a momentary interruption in a process of extremely rapid technical advancement: 'All this means in the long run *that mankind is solving its economic problem*' (ibid., p. 325). In Keynes's mind, the long run here corresponded to a century. We could envisage a world in which basic needs would be met and in which one's energies would be devoted to non-economic ends. We would then be faced with a problem that risks engendering a universal nervous depression: how to make best use of one's liberty? One would be able to produce in three hours per day what is required to meet life's basic needs:

> Thus for the first time since his creation man will be faced with his real, his permanent problem – how to use his freedom from pressing economic cares, how to occupy the leisure, which science and compound interest will have won for him, to live wisely and agreeably and well . . . But it will be those peoples, who can keep alive, and cultivate into a fuller perfection, the art of life itself and do not sell themselves for the means of life, who will be able to enjoy the abundance when it comes. (1930-17, p. 328)

Bloomsbury was undoubtedly for Keynes a laboratory for this future Eden, inhabited by 'the delightful people who are capable of taking direct enjoyment in things, the lilies of the field who toil not, neither do they spin' (ibid., p. 331). The economy would become secondary, economists 'humble, competent people, on a level with dentists' (ibid., p. 332). Around the same time, he wrote in the preface to his *Essays of Persuasion*:

> And here emerges more clearly what is in truth his central thesis throughout – the profound convic-
> tion that the economic problem, as one may call it for short, the problem of want and poverty and
> the economic struggle between classes and nations, is nothing but a frightful muddle, a transitory
> and an *unnecessary* muddle. For the western world already has the resources and the technique, if
> we could create the organisation to use them, capable of reducing the economic problem, which now
> absorbs our moral and material energies, to a position of secondary importance. (1931-1, p. xviii)

One can therefore speak of a Keynesian utopia, which would not be unlike the Marxist utopia that Keynes opposed. Marx described a future world in which one would produce what is necessary to the satisfaction of one's primary needs in a few hours a day. A communist society 'thus makes it possible for me to do one thing today and another tomorrow, to hunt in the morning, fish in the afternoon, rear cattle in the evening, criticize after dinner' (Marx and Engels, 1845–1846, p. 169). Of course, Marx's pastimes did not resemble those of Keynes. Nevertheless, the two authors foresaw the emergence of a world from which the chrematistics denounced by Aristotle would be eliminated, in which the economy would be embedded in society and culture. The resolution of the economic problem would make possible the extension of freedom, the disappearance of social constraints and hierarchies, of exploitation and oppression, of 'this consolidation of what we ourselves produce into an objective power above us, growing out of our control, thwarting our expectations, bringing to naught our calculations' (ibid.).

The development of science and technology would make possible the realization of this utopia, the end result of a process of transformation that should be undertaken immediately. Obstacles linked to the existing social structures are what prevent the resolution of the problems of poverty and underdevelopment, of alternating phases of expansion, crisis and depression. It is with respect to the means of transformation that Keynes and Marx part ways. For Marx, the class struggle is not 'confusion without necessity', but the motor of history. In capitalism, this struggle places the bourgeoisie against the proletariat, the agent of transformation. Only a violent upheaval, which would give power to the proletariat, will pave the way for a classless society. Keynes and Marx therefore espouse two strategies of transformation that conflict with one another, while there are some analogies in their long-term objectives.

The Road to Transformation: Political Parties

Keynes inherited an elitist attitude from his parents and his education that persisted until the end of his life. Things will improve once an intellectual aristocracy takes charge of the nation's affairs. In reality, power is exerted by professional politicians and rarely by intellectuals. So one must push for cohabitation at the top, uniting authority and powerful leadership with the acuity of intelligence. As we will see in the Interlude, this is the role that Keynes tried to play all his life by frequenting and advising powerful political personalities such as Lloyd George or Winston Churchill. Convinced of his intellectual powers, domineering and self-assured, Keynes was at the same time fascinated with political power, by its aura and symbols, and clearly enjoyed mixing with the decision makers, abroad and at home.

Political life, however, is not limited to the prince and his adviser. There is also the voting population on whom the identity of those who exercise power depends. One must convince, not only the decision makers, but also public opinion of the necessity for transformation: 'Even if economists and technicians knew the secret remedy, they could not apply it until they had persuaded the politicians; and the politicians, who have ears but not eyes, will not attend to the persuasion until it reverberates back to them as an echo from the great public' (1922-19, p. 427).

Since the abolition of absolute monarchies, the political game is played out through the competition of parties based on ideologies, principles and worldviews: 'I believe in the depth and reality of the great traditional divisions between parties, – that they depend on principles which are forever reappearing in changing circumstances' (1922-30, p. 1). Men preoccupied with collective well-being, and even advisers to Princes, can hardly avoid belonging to a party:

> If one is born a political animal, it is most uncomfortable not to belong to a party; cold and lonely and futile it is. If your party is strong, and its programme and its philosophy sympathetic, satisfying the gregarious, practical, and intellectual instincts all at the same time, how very agreeable that must be! – worth a large subscription and all one's spare time – that is, if you are a political animal. (1925-17, p. 296)

If no political party engages one's passion, one must proceed by a process of elimination. Such was Keynes's situation. From the beginning he eliminated the Conservatives who 'offer me neither food nor drink – neither intellectual nor spiritual consolation' (ibid.). Of course, the Conservative party contained factions some of which were more enlightened than others.[35] The Labour Party was clearly more attractive.[36] Some of Keynes's closest friends were members or sympathizers. But it also contained factions. Next to the moderate socialists with whom he got on rather well, there were syndicalists, and especially extremists attracted by Bolshevism. This latter 'party of catastrophe' called for violent revolution and exercised considerable influence on Labour. Keynes criticized Labour for not concerning itself with monetary questions, a criticism that would lead it, once in power, to implement orthodox policies similar to those of the Conservatives. Labour remained a class-based party:

> To begin with, it is a class party, and the class is not my class. If I am going to pursue sectional interests at all, I shall pursue my own. When it comes to the class struggle as such, my local and personal patriotisms, like those of every one else, except certain unpleasant zealous ones, are attached to my own surroundings. I can be influenced by what seems to me to be justice and good sense; but the *class* war will find me on the side of the educated *bourgeoisie*. (1925-17, p. 297)

There was, by default, only one party left: 'On the negative test, I incline to believe that the Liberal Party is still the best instrument of future progress – if only it had a strong leadership and the right programme' (ibid., p. 297). This party had also, as we have seen, navigated among Whig, moderate and radical factions. Keynes identified himself with the latter, and believed the ideal political line to be situated somewhere between radical liberalism and moderate Labour: 'A Whig is a perfectly sensible Conservative. A radical is a perfectly sensible Labourite. A Liberal is anyone who is perfectly sensible' (1926-20, p. 542).

Keynes often dreamed of 'a party which shall be disinterested as between classes, and which shall be free in building the future both from the influences of diehardism and from those of catastrophism, which will spoil the constructions of each of the others' (1925-17, p. 300). He found it deplorable 'that the progressive forces of the country are hopelessly divided between the Liberal Party and the Labour Party' (1926-8, p. 307):

> The political problem of mankind is to combine three things: economic efficiency, social justice, and individual liberty. The first needs criticism, precaution and technical knowledge; the second, an unselfish and enthusiastic spirit, which loves the ordinary man; the third, tolerance, breadth, appreciation of the excellencies of variety and independence, which prefers, above everything, to give unhindered opportunity to the exceptional and to the aspiring. The second ingredient is the best possession of the great party of the proletariat. But the first and third requires the qualities of the party which, by its traditions and ancient sympathies, has been the home of economic individualism and social liberty. (1926-8, p. 311)

On 5 May 1923, in the first issue of *Nation and Athenaeum*, as chairman of the Board, Keynes wrote:

> We shall be very much Liberal and not Labour. We are absolutely convinced that, whatever conclusions calculations of early office may lead to, there must in the long run be a place for Liberalism which has no commerce whatever with Conservative opinion, however moderate. Although we believe that the doctrinaire part of the Labour party is completely inadequate for the solution of our present troubles, we do sympathise with Labour in their desire to improve and modify the existing economic organisation so as to minimise what ought to be avoidable distress due to recurring trade depression and unemployment. (1923-9, pp. 122–3)

After the 1924 elections put an end to the first brief Labour government, he wrote in this periodical on 8 November 1924:

> We are not likely to see, for many years to come, a progressive Government of the Left capable of efficient legislation, unless Radicals and Labour men stop cutting one another's throats and come to an agreement for joint action from time to time to carry through practical measures about which they agree. (1924-29, p. 327)

On 17 November 1923, he wrote: 'Labour cannot accomplish anything at present which is not on Liberal rather than on Labour lines' (1923-27, p. 145).

In 1918, the party in which Keynes placed his hopes entered into a decline, that placed the two great class-based parties head to head:

> if Liberalism was to decay, we should be left with one party representing Wealth and Conservatism up against another party representing Labour and Discontent. No Government lives forever, and I conceive nothing worse for all of us than a see-saw struggle on class lines between the Haves and the Have-Nots. (letter to F.R. Salter, 18 October 1924; JMK 19, p. 324)

What Keynes dreaded happened, as we will see in the Interlude. The decline of the Liberal Party in the 1920s placed Labour and Conservatives face to face, a situation that continues to the present day. This position did not, however, exacerbate the class struggle. In 1924 and again from 1929 to 1931, Labour governments subsequently implemented some orthodox economic policies denounced by Keynes. The latter thus found himself on several occasions on the left, not only of the Liberal Party, but also of the Labour Party.

This said, it is not easy to identify Keynes's political position. As with Burke, Keynes's vision is complex and at times contradictory. The rejection of violence as a means of social transformation is one of its main tenets and forms the basis of his condemnation of Nazism and Fascism as well as of Bolshevism. He was also wary of radical trade union activism, even though he sometimes supported strikes. At the same time, he rejected laissez-faire, which he considered obsolete, and believed that governments should not hesitate to use radical measures to ensure full employment and a more equitable distribution of income and fortune. In *The General Theory*, he would go so far as to promote the euthanasia of the rentier and the socialization of investment. Throughout his life, he criticized conservatism on all levels, moral, social and economic, with a vehemence as great as that directed at the communists, some of whose company he rather enjoyed. But this position did not prevent him from advising both Conservative and Labour governments. Keynes considered that one should adapt to circumstances and avoid adopting the worst possible line in order to attain one's own ends. His elitism led him to believe that social and economic problems will be resolved by talented intellectuals who, to some extent, are positioned outside party lines. He inherited this elitism from his family. It permeated the Bloomsbury group and was combined with both a certain paternalism and a mild contempt for the working people, whom he considered incapable of managing their own affairs.

NOTES

1. On New Liberalism, see later in this chapter and next Interlude.
2. A first version of this analysis was presented in Dostaler (1996).
3. On 16 February 1896, he wrote in his diary: 'I begin to make to-day a list of all the chief books I have read with authors' (KP, PP/34, p. 8). On 5 April of the same year, he wrote that 'the list of books which I have read has now reached 133' (p. 10).
4. Keynes's mother also conducted research of this type and made use of her son's discoveries: 'The account of the early Keynes family is based mainly upon research carried out by my elder son, Lord Keynes, in the Library of Eton, while he was at school, and as an undergraduate' (F.A. Keynes 1950, p. vii).
5. Fragments of these works have been published in JMK 28, pp. 223–94.
6. Most of these texts have been collected in JMK 10.
7. Of course, the historical school, that was very influential during much of Keynes's life, rejected this idea of natural law.
8. Another passage of this text constitutes a premonitory response to the accusations of contradictory positions often brought against him: 'A man who can only see one side of a question enters into the struggle of life with one eye blind' (1900-1, p. 12).
9. One should of course understand 'the first four representatives'.
10. See the next chapter.
11. Bernard de Cluny (also known as Bernard de Morlaix) was a Benedictine monk who lived during the first half of the twelfth century. A composer of hymns, a satirist and a poet, he authored the famous *De contemptu mundi* [On the contempt of the world], a bitter satire against the moral disorders of his time and which fearlessly attacked the Church. Little is known of his life.
12. A theologian and Cistercian monk, Bernard de Clairvaux (1090–1153) was in charge of responding to the dangerous teachings of Abelard.
13. Keynes himself closely followed the Dreyfus affair that divided France between 1894 and 1906.
14. On Keynes's alleged anti-Semitism, see Chandavarkar (2000) and Reder (2000).
15. Chapter 6.
16. Ideas on relations between Kant and Keynes have been developed in a paper presented by Dostaler and Marcil at a congress on 'Time in economic thought' (York University, Toronto, June 1996). See also Muchlinski (1996).
17. The response of his friend and adversary Thomas Paine is found in *The Rights of Man* (1791), an impassioned plea in favour of Republicanism and universal suffrage.
18. Skidelsky (1983) brought attention to this paper, also analysed by Fitzgibbons (1988), Helburn (1991), Moggridge (1992) and O'Donnell (1989).

19. In his essay on Victoria's reign, he wrote: 'It is very well to encourage a labourer to think for himself and to take an interest in things outside himself but when his "little knowledge" leads to strikes, it must be admitted that it is a dangerous thing' (1899-1, p. 2).
20. For an earlier presentation of these ideas, see Dostaler (1987). On Keynes, liberalism and laissez-faire, see Berthoud (1989), De Brunhoff (1990), Herland (1998), Lagueux (1998) and the papers collected in Thirlwall (1978). On his relations with socialism, see O'Donnell (1999a) and Potier (2002).
21. On the relations between Keynes and Commons, see Atkinson and Oleson (1998).
22. It is far from evident, in fact, that for Smith, author of *The Theory of Moral Sentiments*, the invisible hand has the meaning generally attributed to it, that of a justification of laissez-faire. On this, see Viner (1927).
23. Quentin Bell judged that, following a marriage decried by his Bloomsbury friends, Keynes became 'more socially ambitious and more reactionary in his politics' (1995, p. 97). For his biographer Skidelsky, the Keynes of the 1930s became radicalized intellectually, but more conservative socially and politically (Skidelsky, 1992, p. 437). This was also the opinion of Joan Robinson (1975, p. 128).
24. For details on this story, see the Interlude that follows.
25. See Chapter 7.
26. See, for example, the passages quoted in Chapter 1 from 'My early beliefs' (1938-12, p. 446) and the letter Keynes addressed to George Bernard Shaw on 1 January 1935 (JMK 28, p. 42).
27. We will return to these in Chapters 6 and 8.
28. Of course, Marx, Marxism, parties claiming Marxist ideology and 'real socialism' are each very different realities. Keynes referred to them all as one, as was common at the time.
29. On this subject, see Garnett (1979), p. 138 and Bell (1995), p. 78, who described the row between Garnett and Keynes 'in one of those fits of political euphoria to which he was subject'. On a monetary mechanism designed by Keynes to finance the anti-Bolshevik war, see Ponsot (2002).
30. Keynes wrote to Lenin in 1922 asking him to write an introduction to a series of articles on USSR that he was editing for *The Manchester Guardian Commercial*. Lenin's poor health prevented him from doing so.
31. See the following Interlude.
32. Mill would therefore have been opposed to the idea held by many contemporary thinkers, such as Milton Friedman, that there is no political freedom without economic freedom.
33. On New Liberalism, see, for example, the studies of Clarke (1978) and Freeden (1978 and 1986). Each author's interpretations, and his manner of linking Keynes to this tradition, are different.
34. He did praise Hobson's theory of under-consumption in *The General Theory*.
35. See, for example, Keynes's gracious words for former Prime Minister Balfour, after his death (1930-14, p. 43), or for Bonar Law, forced to leave office because of illness (1923-14, p. 33). Quotations are provided in the Interlude.
36. On Keynes's relations of with Labour, see Durbin (1988) and Toye (1999).

Second Interlude: The political history of Great Britain during the time of Keynes

As we shall presently see, there is no one-to-one correspondence between political parties, which bring together groups of people seeking power, and the ideologies with which they are associated. Parties generally defend the interests of certain social categories, even if most claim to represent the population as a whole. Between a government's discourse and practice, the gap is often very wide. Individuals coming together for political action have varying and contradictory interests and opinions. All liberals are not members of liberal parties and liberal parties do not bring together only liberals. The same incomplete matching holds true for socialists. The words 'liberalism' and 'socialism' carry multiple meanings. They refer to a vision of the world, particularly to relations between individuals and society, and to ideological positions, programmes, policies and economic theories. Political ideologies are complex ensembles intersected by various currents of thought. The borders between these currents are far from being clear cut and impassable.[1]

THE TRIUMPH OF IMPERIALISM

Since the nineteenth century, the political history of Great Britain has been characterized by the changeover of political power between two great parties. Heir to the Tories, the Conservative Party took this name in the 1830s, while the Whigs took the name of Liberal Party in the1860s. The origins of these two political formations go back to the seventeenth century, with the English Civil War and Glorious Revolution. The Whigs (from whiggamor, or cattle driver), a name first given to those hostile to the restoration of the Stuarts, were disciples of Locke, favourable to the Declaration of Rights, opposed to royal absolutism and partisans of parliament. They were found in large part among the moneyed classes and religious dissenters. The Tories (from the Irish word for outlaw), associated with the landed gentry, were partisans of the Crown and of the Church of England. These terms continue in colloquial use today to refer to Liberals and Conservatives.

When Keynes was born, the Liberal Party was in power, led by William Ewart Gladstone (1809–1898), who had been at its head since 1865, after having started his career as a Tory in 1832. He had already been Prime Minister from 1868 to 1874, before losing to his great adversary, the Conservative leader Benjamin Disraeli, defender of protectionism and imperialism and promoter of an alliance between the landed aristocracy and the working class against the middle class. Gladstone returned to power in 1880 at a time when Britain was suffering, for more than five years, from an economic slowdown which would last until the middle of the 1890s and which some historians would describe as the Great Depression. It was at the apex of the British Empire that the British economy began its relative decline, an economy whose share in world industrial production fell from 32 to 20 per cent between 1870 and 1900, primarily because of developments in the United States and Germany.

Deeply religious and led by moral ideals, Gladstone followed a policy of social and parliamentary reform and free trade. He also sought to resolve the Irish question by negotiating with the nationalist leader Charles Parnell.[2] These negotiations failed and his government was defeated in June 1885 following an alliance between the Irish Nationalists and Conservatives over a problem involving the budget. Queen Victoria then appointed as Prime Minister Robert Cecil, Lord Salisbury, head of the Conservative Party. Elections held in November 1885 gave a majority to the Liberals, but with an equal number of seats as the Conservatives and Irish Nationalists. The latter joined the Liberals to defeat the Conservatives, who announced they would maintain Ireland's union to Great Britain.

Named Prime Minister once again, Gladstone led a vigorous campaign in favour of giving Ireland the autonomous parliamentary system known as Home Rule. This project provoked a split in the Liberal Party, 93 of whose MPs, regrouped around Joseph Chamberlain, President of the Board of Trade, joined the Conservatives to bring it down on 7 July 1886. Gladstone stepped down and the elections of July 1886 gave a large majority to those Conservatives associated with the new Liberal Unionist movement.[3] Lord Salisbury became Prime Minister once again.

In the following July elections of 1892, Conservatives and Liberals were practically tied. Gladstone became Prime Minister for the fourth time with the help of the Irish Nationalists. He made a second attempt to introduce the Home Rule law in 1893. Voted by parliament, the project was rejected by the Lords. This failure led to Gladstone's withdrawal from political life in 1894. Archibald Philip Primrose, Lord Rosebery, succeeded him as Prime Minister. Rosebery belonged to a movement within the Liberal Party known as 'imperialist liberal', which favoured maintaining a strong British empire. Conservatives won the elections of July 1895 by a large margin. Prime Minister again, Lord Salisbury appointed Joseph Chamberlain his Colonial Secretary. Under this title, Chamberlain promoted an aggressive imperialism and led the Boer War, declared in 1899 and ended in 1902.[4]

In the October 1900 elections, known as the Khaki Election,[5] the Conservative Party obtained, with the Liberal Unionists, a crushing majority. Weakened by age and illness, Lord Salisbury ceded power to his nephew Arthur Balfour*[6] in July 1902. At the same time preparations were being made for Edward VII's coronation, following the death the previous year of his mother Victoria. Strengthened by his success as Colonial Secretary, Joseph Chamberlain unleashed a vigorous campaign in favour of imperial preference based on tariffs. After having divided the Liberal Party in 1886, Chamberlain thus provoked division of the Conservative Party over the question of protectionism or free trade. In May 1904, Conservative minister Winston Churchill, a free trade advocate, crossed the floor and joined the Liberals. Chamberlain stepped down from government in September 1903 to free himself for his tariff reform campaign. A heart attack ended his political life in 1907.[7] On 4 December 1905, faced with party divisions and union and education crises, Balfour resigned as Prime Minister. He remained head of his party until 1911, and was then replaced by Andrew Bonar Law*. Henry Campbell-Bannerman*, Liberal leader since 1899, was called to form a new government. He called elections for 12 January 1906 over the question of free trade. A wide victory went to the newly united Liberals. The Conservative Party's protectionist campaign and government-tolerated anti-trade union attacks from employers and the judiciary[8] were fatal blows. At the same time, a new party was coming into being.

THE EMERGENCE OF LABOUR

The 1880s were marked in Britain as in most of Europe by strong worker agitation. The ideas of adopted Londoner Karl Marx and those of anarchist and other socialist movements became increasingly influential. London had long since been the central meeting point for socialist leaders from around Europe. The International Federation of Working Men, known as the First International, was founded there in 1864.[9] Bringing together British trade unions in 1868, the Trades Union Congress (TUC), which led the struggle to extend union rights, had in 1890 1.5 million members. It housed within it a more radical tendency called Syndicalism. Syndicalists created the Labour Representative League, which succeeded in electing two socialist MPs in 1874. They became a part of the Liberal parliamentary group and thus became known as the 'Lib-Labs'. In 1881 Henry Hyndman, a professed Marxist, founded the Democratic Federation,[10] which would become in 1884 the Social Democratic Federation (SDF). Close to anarchism, William Morris created the Socialist League in 1889, after having been a member of the SDF. That same year the Fabian Society was born. The Society sought to establish a non-Marxist socialism to be arrived at through gradual transformation rather than violent revolution.[11] It counted among its influential members famous artists and intellectuals such as George Bernard Shaw,[12] who composed its manifesto and who would later become a friend of Keynes. Beatrice and Sidney Webb, the leading influences within the Society, would also cross Keynes's path on several occasions.[13]

Keir Hardie, a Scottish miner and active member of the TUC, established the Scottish Labour Party. Elected to the House of Commons in 1892, he founded in January 1893 the Independent Labour Party, with the help of the Fabian Society, the Socialist League and the Social Democratic Federation, who came together at a conference in Bradford. In 1900, these movements united with the Trades Union Congress to form the Labour Representative Committee. The Committee, whose secretary was future Prime Minister Ramsay Macdonald*, succeeded in electing two candidates in the 1900 elections. In 1903 Macdonald and the Liberal chief whip Herbert Gladstone negotiated an electoral agreement between the two parties, which was called the Progressive Alliance. Under this agreement, the Liberals would not present candidates against those of the Representative Committee in 50 constituencies. In the 1906 elections, which saw the Liberals take power back from the Conservatives, the Committee succeeded in electing 30 of its 50 candidates, including Macdonald, almost all of whom benefited from the electoral alliance. Of the 30 elected, seven belonged to the radical branch of the Independent Labour Party, while the rest were moderates. The Committee took the name of Labour Party. An unstoppable ascension began, in which Labour's Liberal allies would soon be their first victims.

THE KEYNES FAMILY AND POLITICS

John Neville Keynes and Florence Ada were both liberals, but they did not share the same orientation. While the father tended toward Whig-like conservatism, the mother, attracted by Labour philosophy, was resolutely in the radical camp. Here as elsewhere, the son was closer to his mother than to his father. From his father, he nevertheless inherited the taste for decorum, respect for traditions, and attraction to frequenting figures of high standing. John Neville was proud of having once lunched with Gladstone, as Maynard would boast of playing cards with Prime Ministers. On the Irish question, the father was unionist, which brought him to break with Gladstone and vote Conservative in 1886. He then rallied to the Liberal Unionists and defended Chamberlain's position, which his son opposed, during the Boer war. He was radically opposed to all forms of socialism. When his son seemed to be approaching the Fabians by speaking out in favour of Sidney Webb's motion on socialism, his horrified father wrote in his diary in September 1911: 'Maynard avows himself a Socialist and is in favour of confiscation of wealth' (quoted in Moggridge, 1992, p. 190).

There was, however, one question on which father, mother and son came together, namely that of women's right to vote, which divided England as vigorously as the Boer war or protectionism. While the 1885 electoral reform had extended the right to vote, with several restrictions, to all men of voting age, women were totally excluded from the process. During Victoria's Diamond Jubilee in 1897, Millicent Fawcett founded the National Union of Women's Suffrage Societies, the 'suffragists'. In 1903, Emmeline Pankhurst and her daughters Christabel and Sylvia, considering the movement too moderate, founded the Women's Social and Political Union, which demanded, in addition to the right to vote, total equality between men and women. The movement was known as the 'suffragettes'. Women's struggle to obtain the right to vote, with which Keynes and his Bloomsbury friends were closely associated, would take on spectacular forms and bring about police confrontations. Women finally obtained this right in 1918, but only from the age of 30. Another ten years would have to pass before they could vote from the age of 21.

It was at Eton that Maynard became initiated into debating public affairs and that his political thought was formed. The Boer war and protectionism were his two fields of battle. He was from the beginning unhesitatingly pro-Boer and anti-protectionist.[14] He was not content to watch the political agitation on the outside. He was elected in December 1901 a member of the Eton Society, called 'College Pop', in which he pronounced speeches on various political questions. Arriving in Cambridge in the autumn of 1902, he joined the Cambridge Union Society and University Liberal Club. He became president of both associations. He was thus aware of the transformations taking place in a Liberal Party weakened by the 1895 split. He was witness to the rise of a new liberalism opposed to classical Gladstonian economic liberalism, attached to laissez-faire, balanced budgets and the gold standard. He actively participated in the electoral campaign of 1906.

THE LIBERAL REFORMS

At the beginning of the century, Leonard Hobhouse and John Hobson, the main thinkers behind New Liberalism, were members of the Liberal Party. Included in this branch were those known as the 'Young Liberals', among them William Beveridge, who would play an important role in the Keynesian revolution during the Second World War.[15] Though opposed to Marxist socialism, they advocated active State intervention to solve economic problems and create social justice. It was this radical branch that dominated the Liberal Party when it won a dazzling victory in the elections of January 1906, taking 400 of the 670 seats. It was a period of close alliance, as ideological as it was political, between the Liberal and Labour Parties, more particularly between the radical branch of the former and the moderate branch of the latter.[16]

Appointed Prime Minister, Campbell-Bannerman formed a government in which the three branches of liberalism – Whig, moderate and radical – were represented. It counted in its ranks three major personalities and future prime ministers to whom Keynes would be close: Herbert Asquith*, David Lloyd George*, whose principal adviser he would become in the 1920s, and Winston Churchill*, whom he would advise during the Second World War after having sharply criticized him in the 1920s.

Illness forced Campbell-Bannerman to resign on 5 April 1908. He was replaced by Herbert Asquith, who named Lloyd George as Chancellor of the Exchequer. Beveridge was one of his chief advisers. The implementation of a series of economic and social reforms, initiated in 1906 and largely inspired by new liberalism, was accelerated. In 1906, the Trade Disputes Act suppressed the legal responsibility of unions for damages caused during strikes, and the Workmen's Compensation Act provided for indemnities in case of work-related accidents. That same year, the Provision of School Meals Act authorized local authorities to provide meals at no cost to school children, which was until then illegal. In 1908 the Children Act regulated child labour, while the Miners' Eight Hours Act, as its name suggests, limited daily work in mines to eight hours. The Old Age Pensions Act guaranteed an income to all persons over the age of 70. This income, varying between one and five shillings per week, was only paid to those whose incomes were less than 12 shillings. Labourites criticized the non-universal character and meagre level of the sums paid. In 1909 the House and Town Planning Act provided for the destruction of slums and the improvement of workers' housing. The Trade Boards Act accorded a minimum wage to the most vulnerable of workers. Other measures increased trade union powers.

The Old Age Pensions Act fell, in the spirit of its promoter Lloyd George, within the scope of the fight against the Poor Laws which forced the most destitute into workhouses. To finance it, Lloyd George proposed on 29 April 1909 his 'People's Budget', calling for an increase in tax revenues of 8 per cent – 16 million pounds sterling per year – by means of an increase in taxation of the highest incomes. While those with incomes of more than £3000 per year were required to pay one shilling two pence per pound, the lowest incomes were taxed at the rate of nine pence per pound. Lloyd George even proposed a surcharge of six pence per pound on incomes superior to £5000 per year, increased taxation of wealthy landowners' inheritances and high taxes on profits generated from possession and sale of properties.

This budget was rejected by the Conservative-dominated House of Lords on 30 November. The Conservatives were opposed to these measures of wealth redistribution. Lloyd George defended them vigorously by touring working class regions, accusing aristocrats and the 'haves' of refusing to pay the poor pensions that were 'rightfully' theirs. Asquith then decided to put it to the electors. In the elections of 14 January 1910, Conservatives and Liberals were practically tied, the latter only able to govern with the help of Labour and the Irish Nationalists.

The country was at a constitutional impasse that could only be resolved by institutional reform limiting the House of Lords' power. In order to accept its sanctioning, Edward VII, followed by his successor George V, who came to the throne on 6 May, demanded a new election, which took place on 2 December. Liberals and Conservatives obtained exactly the same number of seats. Keynes participated actively in both electoral campaigns, making several speeches, one before 1200 people.

Thanks to the support of Labour and the Irish Nationalists, Asquith was able to govern and put through the Parliament Act, sanctioned by the King in August 1911, which reduced the powers of the House of Lords. The path was open for the adoption of the National Insurance

Act, which established a system of insurance against unemployment and illness. All wage earners aged from 16 to 70 were required to join the health system. Each wage-earner paid four pence per week, employers paying three pence and the State two pence. Medical costs, including drugs, were free. Workers contributing to this fund received seven shillings per week, for 15 weeks during one year, on becoming unemployed. Home Rule, which accorded some autonomy to Ireland, was adopted by Parliament on 28 September 1912. Rejected by the Lords on 30 January 1913, it was nevertheless sanctioned by the King on 18 September 1914, thanks to the Parliament Act, which reduced the Lords' vetoing rights. Its application would be suspended until the end of the war.

THE WAR AND THE BREAK-UP OF THE LIBERAL PARTY

At the outbreak of war in 1914, Keynes began his career as 'adviser to the Prince' in addition to that of civil servant, which position he had already occupied at the India Office between 1906 and 1908.[17] At this point in his career, Edwin Montagu*, Liberal minister, played a determinant role. He was Financial Secretary to the Treasury from February 1914. When he died, Keynes wrote to Lydia Lopokova on 16 November 1924:

> I am a little sad at the death of Edwin Montagu. I owed – rather surprisingly – nearly all my steps up in life to him . . . It was he who got me called to the Treasury in 1915 during the War. It was he who got me taken to Paris in February of that year for the first inter-Ally Financial Conference and so established me in my war work. It was he who introduced me to the great ones (I first met Lloyd George in a famous dinner party of 4 at his house; I first met McKenna through him; I first met Margot sitting next to her at dinner in his house.) It was he who got me invited to the dinners of the inner-secretaries during the early part of the war (private gatherings of the secretaries of the Cabinet and of the chief ministers who exchanged the secret news and discussed after dinner the big problems of the war). He was the Minister to whom I was responsible during the first part of the Peace Conference. (1989-1, p. 256)

Keynes thus entered another world, different if not opposed to that of Bloomsbury, namely that of high politics. To a certain extent he led a double life. He soon became familiar to several ministers and to the first among them, Herbert Asquith, whom he met at one of Ottoline Morrell's dinner parties.[18] Asquith wrote to his friend Venetia Stanley on 11 February, regarding a committee on food prices over which he presided: 'We have a clever young Cambridge don called Keynes as Secretary, upon whom I rely for my brief tomorrow' (Asquith, 1982, p. 425). From the autumn of 1915, Keynes was regularly invited by the Prime Minister and his wife Margot, who was very fond of him, to 10 Downing Street or to their country residence, The Wharf. He also frequented Reginald McKenna* and his wife. He enjoyed frequenting elite circles. In letters to his parents he described them in detail. On 15 October 1915, he complained to his father of being 'exceedingly done up . . . It was a combination of work and excitement . . . I've been moving in very high life most of the week . . . and I am spending the weekend with the Prime Minister'. His *amour propre* was flattered by the attention that these personalities gave him.

With the outbreak of war, Asquith's government was supported by most Liberals, a majority of Conservatives and Labourites, then led by the syndicalist Arthur Henderson who replaced Ramsay Macdonald. The latter, with some Labourites and Liberals, defended a pacifist position and founded the Union of Democratic Control, promoting peace through international cooperation. On 25 May 1915, Asquith implemented a coalition government made up of Liberals, Conservatives and the Labour leader Henderson, who was named President of the Board of Education. He entrusted Munitions to Lloyd George, and McKenna became Chancellor of the Exchequer. Following the death on 5 July 1916 of the Secretary of State for War, Lord Kitchener, whose cruiser hit a mine while on his way to Russia,[19] Lloyd George succeeded him. He was determined to obtain total victory. He started a campaign in favour of conscription, to which Asquith, McKenna and the moderate Liberals were opposed. The majority of the cabinet decided on 28 December in favour of conscription, which came into effect on 27 January 1916.[20]

Tension grew between Lloyd George and Asquith, accused of lacking firmness in the conduct of the war. On 8 November, a vote in the House of Commons saw the majority of Conservatives oppose the government, while Lloyd George, the Conservative leader Bonar Law and the leader of the Irish Unionists engaged in secret talks in view of forming a small war committee excluding Asquith. His position having become untenable, the latter resigned and Lloyd George was appointed Prime Minister on 6 December, uniting the majority of Labourites and 120 Liberal MPs, 150 other members remaining faithful to Asquith, who stayed on as leader of the party. The main Liberal leaders, including McKenna, were excluded from the new coalition government. The split between Asquith Liberals and those who supported the coalition would be fatal to the Liberal Party. Bonar Law obtained the Treasury and became, after McKenna, Keynes's boss.

Keynes was not at all impressed by the new government appointed on 6 December, even if his own powers would increase. While his relationship to Asquith was good, his relationship to Lloyd George was bad. He qualified Lloyd George as a 'crook' in a letter to his mother (14 April 1918) and in a letter to Beatrice Webb, as an ' autocratic Prime Minister' (11 March 1918, in JMK 16, p. 295). Nevertheless, he would get on well with Bonar Law, who himself would increasingly confide in his young civil servant. They took up playing bridge together. When Bonar Law succeeded Lloyd George as Prime Minister in 1922, he would call on Keynes for advice, even though the latter had campaigned against him.

On 16 December Lloyd George formed a War Cabinet of five members, composed of himself, Arthur Henderson (Minister without Portfolio), Bonar Law (Chancellor of the Exchequer), Lord Curzon (leader of the House of Lords) and Lord Milner (Minister without Portfolio). Meeting daily, this cabinet became power's true centre of gravity. It ceased to exist in October 1919. On these events, Keynes wrote 12 years later, about Asquith: 'In the controversy as to the conduct of the war, which culminated in the downfall of the first Coalition Government at the end of 1916, I believed then, and I believe now, that he was largely in the right' (1928-3, p. 39).

In July 1917, Keynes participated in the creation of the Tuesday Club, which brought together for several decades on the third Tuesday of each month at London's *Café Royal*, financiers from the City, politicians, civil servants, journalists and academics to discuss economic and political questions following a presentation given by one of its members. He would be member until 1942. He opened discussion on 14 occasions, using this as a tribune to test his ideas on different subjects as well as to keep himself informed of his peers' opinions. In 1927, in spite of his crusade against Churchill's policies, Keynes would be admitted into the Other Club, founded by Churchill,[21] then a Liberal MP, and the Conservative MP Frederick Smith, to discuss political problems beyond partisan borders. Keynes considered these meetings an important way to frequent and influence those in power.

In September, following Asquith's refusal to sit with the government, a refusal which made official the split in the Liberal Party, Lloyd George and Bonar Law signed an electoral accord between Liberal dissidents, coalition supporters and Conservatives, a minority of whom rejected this accord. Three days after the armistice on 14 November 1918, the Prime Minister announced parliament's dissolution for 25 November and general elections for 14 December, elections in which the problem of Germany constituted the central element. Keynes severely judged this useless electoral campaign, which was called in his view to satisfy Lloyd George's personal ambition and political opportunism as 'a sad, dramatic history of the essential weakness of one who draws his chief inspiration not from his own true impulses, but from the grosser effluxions of the atmosphere which momentarily surrounds him' (1919-1, p. 87).

He dismissed both Asquith's independent Liberals and Lloyd George's Unionists for agreeing on imposing on Germany exaggerated reparation payments (ibid., p. 91). These elections gave 478 out of 707 seats to Lloyd George's coalition, which included 335 Conservatives, 133 Liberals and 10 Labourites. Labourites opposed to the coalition obtained 63 seats and the 'official' Asquith Liberals 28 seats. For the first time, a woman was elected under the banner of Sinn Fein, but she refused to sit in Westminster. These results depressed Keynes, who wrote to his mother on 16 December: 'every voice should be lifted, however vainly, against this dishonouring Coalition'. On 10 January 1919, Lloyd George formed a new government which included 12 Conservatives, seven Liberals and one Labourite. Austen Chamberlain* became Chancellor of the Exchequer and Bonar Law was appointed Lord Privy Seal. The Labourite George Barnes, Pensions Minister, stepped down for health reasons in January 1920.

Keynes was approached by Sidney Webb to be a Labour candidate for Cambridge University in a partial election:[22]

> I venture to hope you will not dismiss the idea. If you do not peremptorily do so, some Cambridge people will put in hand a requisition to you, which we are sure would be very numerously signed by the younger men. Of course, we are not expecting you to be returned! But you would certainly poll a very respectable minority; and it would do a great deal of good to the atmosphere (letter from 14 January 1918, JMK 16, p. 266).

He had already been asked on 27 April 1916, 'to represent the younger and less Tory section of the academic world' (letter from 27 April 1916, JMK 16, p. 267). New pressures intervened in 1920: 'Here, my book's publication [*Economic Consequences of the Peace*] is followed by congratulations from half the Cabinet, and invitations from three parties to stand for Parliament!' (letter to Norman Davis, 18 April 1920; JMK 17, p. 40). The East Walthamstow Central Liberal and Radical Association asked him to be a replacement candidate for Sir John Simon in a partial election on 2 March 1920. The following is Keynes's portrait of what was then being drawn in *Time and Tide*, on 8 July 1921:

> At present he has returned to Cambridge and withdrawn from any sort of political activity. Those who at one time hoped that he would join the Labour Party, did not know their man . . . From the Labour Party Mr Keynes is removed by a vast gulf – the gulf of his moral attitude . . . He does not accept the economic theory of the Socialists: more important is his rejection of their human claim, their belief in an altered standard of values, their optimism . . . With Liberalism he has social affinities and much more intellectual sympathy; but the entanglements of the Liberal Party are not of a kind [in] which he is inclined to involve himself. (quoted in JMK 17, p. 240)

CONSERVATIVE RULE AND THE RISE OF LABOUR

After having dominated the Paris Conference, which concluded in June 1919 with the Treaty of Versailles' imposition of heavy sanctions on Germany, Lloyd George was at the summit of his popularity. His fall would be all the more brutal. It was provoked by the creation of the Free State of Ireland, Eire. A large section of Conservative MPs were hostile to this decision. They met on 19 October 1922 at the Carlton Club and decided to withdraw their support from Lloyd George, who had no choice but to step down. The Conservative leader Bonar Law succeeded him on 23 October, formed a government composed exclusively of his party members and called for elections which gave him an absolute majority. This date marked the start of Conservative Party rule that would, alone or in coalition with others, determine Britain's fortune almost continually until the end of the Second World War. Another major event resulting from this election was the Labour Party's new status as Official Opposition, with 142 MPs, while the Lloyd George and Asquith's Liberals obtained 54 and 62 seats respectively.

Keynes, who did not intervene in these elections, met with the new Prime Minister, his old boss, on 19 October and proposed to him a plan on 23 October to solve the reparations problem. Suffering from throat cancer, Bonar Law resigned in May 1923. Lord Curzon[23] was expected to succeed him, but, as he was not an MP, the King preferred Stanley Baldwin*,[24] Chancellor of the Exchequer. On 24 May, Keynes wrote to his friend Melchior that the new Prime Minister is 'a very nice and sensible man who will always behave well and fairly (I know him intimately)' while 'Lord Curzon is a bad influence' (quoted in Johnson, 1978b, p. 55) regarding the resolution of the reparations problem. On 26 May, Reginald McKenna, another personality well known to Keynes, was appointed Chancellor of the Exchequer. On 30 May, Keynes met Baldwin and McKenna separately before travelling to Germany to join Chancellor Cuno, Foreign Affairs Minister von Rosenberg and Melchior to help prepare their response to Britain's proposition to settle the reparations question.[25]

With Lloyd George's fall, divisions within the Liberal Party started to subside after seven years of infighting. The Party's reunification was concluded in November 1923, under Asquith's direction, Lloyd George accepting to make available to the Party the funds he had amassed after the split. Pre-war New Liberalism was reborn and transformed. One of its main vectors was the Liberal Summer School, established in 1921 to provide the Party with a modern and progressive platform. Keynes, as well as Hobson and Beveridge, was involved in its first meeting at Grasmere. The Summer School would meet until 1939, alternating between Cambridge and Oxford. In the 1920s, Keynes's speeches would be a high point of these events. In January 1923, Keynes, with a group of Liberals associated with the Summer School, took control of the progressive liberal weekly *The Nation*, founded in 1907, which absorbed *The Athenaeum*, whose history goes back to 1828. He became president of its board of directors; Hubert Henderson was its editor-in-chief and Leonard Woolf its literary editor. The first edition of the *Nation and the Athenaeum* appeared on 5 May 1923 with articles by Lytton Strachey and Leonard Woolf. It would bring together politics, economics and Bloomsbury. In addition to his board leadership and financial support,[26] Keynes would contribute a number of articles, several of which were anonymous and some signed under the pseudonym of Siela. On 17 November 1923, in an article entitled 'The Liberal Party' (1923-27), he expressed hope that the Liberals, at last united, would attract moderates from both parties and win the elections. This hope would be disappointed. In 1931, the review would merge with the *New Statesman*, founded in 1913 by Fabians such as Shaw and the Webbs, to become the *New Statesman and Nation*. Keynes held on to his post as president of the board of directors, and Kingsley Martin became the chief editor.

The Labour Party's rise had for several years paralleled the Liberal Party's decline. Some former 'New Liberals', including Hobson, would join its ranks. Close allies before the war, the two parties became adversaries all the more bitter since they competed for support from the same electorate. Composed by the Webbs, the 1918 Labour manifesto, *Labour and the New Social Order*, opposed socialism to liberalism. For his part, Lloyd George insisted on the gap separating Labour and Liberals, close to the Conservatives. For Asquith, on the contrary, there was no logical antithesis between liberalism and Labour.

On 25 October 1923, Baldwin announced fiscal reforms that forced a return to the electorate, given the commitments of Bonar Law in 1922. The elections of 6 December would consecrate the reunited Liberal Party's defeat. With 159 seats, it came in third behind the Labour Party, which obtained 191 seats. It was a major shift in the political history of Great Britain, with power henceforth alternating between Conservatives and Labour. With 258 seats, the Conservatives lost their absolute majority. Since the Liberals refused to support Baldwin's protectionist cause, Baldwin's government was defeated in the House of Commons on 21 January 1924. King George V called on Labour leader Ramsay MacDonald to form the government, which eventually included five syndicalists, several members of the left wing of his party, but also some former Liberals. Philip Snowden, Chancellor of the Exchequer, showed himself in favour of a very Gladstonian liberalism, of budgetary rigour and a return to the gold standard, which Keynes criticized vigorously.

The Labour government fell in October 1924 following a censorship vote that was provoked by the Government's refusal to sue J.R. Campbell, editor of a communist newspaper calling for the army not to use force against strikers. At the same time, the fake Zinoviev letter, in which the leader of the Communist International called on British communists to rise up, contributed to the Conservatives' victory. They returned to power on 4 November, after the elections of 29 October 1924, with 415 seats against 151 for Labour and 40 for the Liberals.[27] Once again Prime Minister, Baldwin named Winston Churchill, who had just returned to Conservative ranks, his Chancellor of the Exchequer. The return to the gold standard at pre-war parity which the latter announced in May 1925 led to, as Keynes predicted, particularly in *The Economic Consequences of Mr Churchill*, a fall in exports and an increase in unemployment.[28] On 1 May 1926, coal mine owners decreed a lock-out after their workers refused to accept a decrease of wages and an increase in work hours. A general strike, launched on 3 May in support of the miners and mobilizing nine million workers, came to an end on 12 May without desired results. The miners remained in lock-out for several months before accepting, in November, wage cuts and increased daily hours. The following year, the Conservative government decided on an important restriction of union prerogatives.

The general strike provoked a new and very lively conflict between Asquith, who supported tough action against the illegal strike, and Lloyd George, who maintained a conciliatory attitude toward the unions. Lloyd George refused to attend a shadow cabinet meeting because of his opposition to the incendiary statements made against strikers by Asquith supporters. He was threatened with exclusion. In a letter published on 19 June in the *Nation and the Athenaeum*, Keynes, while admitting Lloyd George had made several errors during his political career, recognized his obvious qualities: 'He is naturally and temperamentally a radical, happiest when his lot lies to the left. . . . He is a great politician – an engine of power for the big public' (1926-18, p. 538). Opposed to Lloyd George's exclusion, Keynes came out, for the first time in a long while, in agreement with the former's political stance, implying a radicalization of the Party and a *rapprochement* with Labour. The Liberals were at their strongest when the Whig branch, represented by Asquith, and the radical branch, represented by Lloyd George, were able to cohabit within the same party. The letter provoked the rupture between its author and Asquith, who never saw each other again. Already, an invitation for a visit to the Asquiths' country house on 28 May was withdrawn. After having suffered a mild stroke on 12 June, Asquith decided to resign as Liberal leader. He announced this decision in a letter published on 15 October 1926. He died 16 months later. The obituary note that Keynes wrote in *the Nation* reconciled him with Margot Asquith.

Lloyd George became leader of the Liberal Party, which sought to regain power with a radical project, including public works, largely inspired by Keynes and his Summer School friends. In July, Lloyd George gave money for the creation of a Liberal Industrial Inquiry, presided over by Walter Layton, with the aim of preparing the Party's new programme. Keynes was member of the Inquiry's Executive Committee, and chaired the committee on industrial and financial organization. There were meetings until the end of 1927, some of which were held in Lloyd George's country house. The committee's report, *Britain's Industrial Future*, called the Yellow Book of the Liberal Party, was published on 2 February 1928. It carries a strong imprint of the ideas of Keynes, who composed several pages and inspired several others. From him came the proposition of establishing both an Economic General Staff, which would be put into practice in modified form by the Labour government in 1930, and a Board of National Investment with wide powers of control on public investments and the support of private investors. He also proposed a reform of the government's budget accounts which would not come about until 1945. The report suggested control of insider trading.[29] New modalities of managing public or semi-public enterprises and the setting up of public corporations to manage electricity, railways and public transport in the London region were also proposed. In short, Keynesian policies were formulated before elaboration of the theory that would support them.

This report would constitute the basis of the party's electoral programme. Keynes convinced Lloyd George to solemnly engage himself in favour of full employment before an assembly of ministers and Liberal candidates on 1 May. A special committee to which Keynes belonged concretized this engagement by publishing a document entitled *We Can Conquer Unemployment*, which became known as the Orange Book. On 10 May 1929, Hubert Henderson and Keynes published, in support of the Liberal campaign, *Can Lloyd George Do It?* (1929-1). Keynes appeared henceforth as the main inspiration behind the Liberal programme. Summoned by Baldwin to reveal the names of his experts, Lloyd George mentioned Keynes, Layton and Samuel.

During the winter of 1928, Keynes was once again approached to be Cambridge's Liberal candidate. He first refused but later accepted, under pressure of his parents and friends, to reconsider the matter. Finally, in a letter to F.A. Potts, on 14 October 1928, he refused: 'From many points of view I am tempted, and I don't know when I have vacillated more about making a decision' (JMK 19, p. 773). He explained his decision by referring to the work required to finish *A Treatise on Money*. He would nevertheless make several speeches during the campaign. In one speech, he affirmed having worked for four years on preparing the Liberal programme, spending long hours with Lloyd George. In the end, Hubert Henderson would be a candidate for one of the two seats of the Cambridge University constituency.

FROM LABOUR TO NATIONAL GOVERNMENT

Labourites were perplexed and divided regarding Keynes's propositions, and it was without a clear and explicit economic programme that they confronted the 1929 election. They won it, but again without an absolute majority. Although they saw their percentage of the vote pass from 17.8 at the 1924 elections to 23.6 per cent, the Liberal Party only obtained 59 seats. Labour wanted this time to escape from its Liberal tutelage. Keynes, who had once again gambled on the Liberal Party, lost much money, though he won £10 at Winston Churchill's expense. This detail shows that personal relations between both men were not bad in spite of their disagreements. Keynes was obviously disappointed by the results of a campaign into which he had invested so much effort and hope: 'I have relapsed into rather a depressed state about the Election. I can't see that anything satisfactory can possibly result from it. Anyhow I am glad that I shan't be mixed up in it in the House' (letter to Lydia, 3 June 1929).

The Macdonald–Snowden duo regained power in June 1929, a few months before the outbreak of an unprecedented economic crisis.[30] On 5 November, the government set up a Committee on Finance and Industry, the Macmillan Committee, of which Keynes was a part. He was invited to lunch with the Prime Minister on 2 December and met him several times thereafter. On 24 January 1930, the Economic Advisory Council was created.[31] Presided over by the Prime Minister, it counted Keynes among its members. Keynes thus occupied a central position in the first commission to inquire fully into the British economy and the first organization charged with advising the government on economic questions. He also convinced Macdonald to set up, in June 1930, a small committee of economists within the Economic Advisory Council. It was particularly through the Macmillan Committee, in which he spent many hours and made long interventions as witness, that he then sought to influence both the decision-makers and public opinion. There he exposed the arguments of his *Treatise on Money*, published in October 1930.[32] The committee was dominated by a triumvirate formed by Keynes, McKenna and the union leader Ernest Bevin.[33]

The aggravation of the crisis, on both the international and national scale, did not allow these organizations to be useful and would be fatal for the Labour government. The government would be incapable of surmounting the crisis and would follow orthodox policies, counter to Keynes's suggestions. On 7 March, he proposed, in a resounding article in the *New Statesman and Nation* (1931-9) proofs of which were sent to both Prime Minister and Chancellor of the Exchequer, raising tariff barriers. Sharply criticizing Snowden's budget in the *Evening Standard* of 28 April, he wrote: 'The first Socialist Chancellor is also the last adherent of true blue *laissez-faire*' (1931-16, p. 523).

On 8 May 1931, the bankruptcy of Credit Anstalt, the biggest bank in Austria, unleashed an international financial crisis which would be catastrophic for Great Britain. During the summer, the pound sterling came under very strong pressure. In February, the government set up an inquiry commission into the situation of public finances, presided over by George May, of the Prudential Insurance Company. Published on 31 May, the May Committee Report proposed strong cuts in public spending and social programmes, particularly a 20 per cent reduction in unemployment benefits. Asked by the Prime Minister his opinion of this report, Keynes responded from Tilton on 5 August that the proposals to lower wages and salaries constituted 'a gross perversion of social justice' (JMK 20, p. 590).

Unable to convince his party and the unions of the necessity of imposing these cuts in order to obtain foreign credit, Macdonald resigned on 24 August. George V asked him the same day to form a National Government. This act provoked a splintering of the Labour Party with only three ministers remaining in office. Arthur Henderson succeeded Macdonald as Labour's leader, the latter being excluded from the party with all those who supported or were a part of the National Government, which decided on 27 August to implement a programme of tax increases and expenditure cuts, with unemployment benefits reduced by 10 per cent. In notes for a speech pronounced before parliamentarians on 6 September, Keynes declared: 'In my opinion the Govt's programme is one of the most wrong and foolish things which Parliament has deliberately perpetrated in my lifetime' (1931-21, p. 608). He evaluated with defeatism his influence on public affairs: 'During the last 12 years I have had very little influence, if any, on policy. But in the role of Cassandra, I have had considerable success as a prophet' (ibid., p. 611). During this time, the drain of gold continued and, on 21 September, the convertibility of the pound was suspended, before the adoption of protectionist measures in November.

Elections were called for 27 October 1931, Keynes having sought to convince Macdonald to defer this consultation (JMK 20, pp. 617–19). To Lloyd George, he wrote on 1 October: 'I hope that if this ridiculous Government does force things to an election in any shape or form, you will lead the Liberal party – or what is left of it – into the fight in an honourable alliance with Labour' (JMK 20, pp. 619–20). The results were disastrous for the Labour Party, which obtained 52 seats: 'It will be good for them to go out into the wilderness for a time to find their soul again' (letter to Walter Case, 2 November 1931, JMK 21, p. 10). Henderson ceded leadership to George Lansbury. The Liberals divided into three groups obtaining a total of 72 seats: the National Liberals, led by John Simon, close to the Conservatives (35 seats); the Liberal Party proper, led by Herbert Samuel (33 seats), who broke with the National Government in 1932; and the Independent Liberals of Lloyd George (4 seats), who joined the first group in 1935 in opposition to the National Government. Macdonald formed a National Government consisting of a few ex-Labourites defining themselves as 'National Labour', Liberals, and a majority of Conservatives. Strongly attacked by his former Labourite colleagues and his health declining, he ceded power to the Conservative leader Stanley Baldwin, who became Prime Minister in June 1935. The latter dissolved parliament on 25 October and called elections for 14 November. The Conservatives won a decisive victory. The National Government was in practice a Conservative government.

Fearing Soviet communist expansion in Europe, Baldwin showed sympathy for the Franco rebellion and successfully pressured Léon Blum, French Prime Minister, to renounce intervention in favour of the Spanish Republicans. He succeeded in getting 27 countries, including the USSR, Germany and Italy, to sign a non-intervention agreement. The latter three countries would not respect the agreement. The Spanish Civil War, one of whose victims would be Julian Bell, son of Vanessa and to whom Keynes was very attached, aroused lively debate in the columns of the *New Statesman*. At first opposed to intervention, towards which several of his friends were favourable, Keynes finished by rallying with them. He suspected certain members of government of seeking closer ties with Hitler and Mussolini at the expense of Spanish democracy (1937-9, p. 74). Moreover, he pronounced himself in favour of imposing economic sanctions against Japan following the latter's aggression against China. In an article in the *New Statesman* entitled 'A positive peace programme' (1938-5), he admitted having believed with others that a negative pacifism would win out against a positive militarism.

After having managed the crisis leading to Edward VIII's abdication,[34] Baldwin stepped down as Prime Minister in May 1937, shortly before George VI's coronation. Neville Chamberlain* succeeded him. He pursued a policy of non-intervention in Spain, all the while sending an emissary to the pro-Franco leadership in Burgos. When, in May 1938,[35] Blum again manifested his intention of ending the French policy of non-intervention, Chamberlain and the Foreign Secretary became attentive and interested observers of the French campaign in which the forces of the Right tried to unseat the Prime Minister, who was finally replaced by Edouard Daladier, opposed to Spanish intervention and in support of appeasement with Germany. Disagreeing with Chamberlain's policies, the Foreign Affairs minister Anthony Eden stepped down in February 1938, and was replaced by Lord Halifax. The *Anschluss*, proclaimed on 13 March 1938 in violation of the Treaty of Versailles, brought Eden and Churchill to demand that Chamberlain take stronger measures against Hitler. In September 1938, Chamberlain, Daladier, Hitler and Mussolini signed the Munich Pact, in accordance with which Czechoslovakia was forced to evacuate the Sudetenland, abandoned to the Nazis, and to dismantle border fortifications. A majority of Britons believed the Pact had allowed Britain to avoid war with Germany, which was not the opinion of either Eden or Churchill, who declared 'They accepted dishonour to have peace. They'll have both war and dishonour'. Keynes condemned the Pact, in which the intrigues of England's Nazi supporters had played a role (letter to Kingsley Martin, 1 October 1928, JMK 28, p. 122).

Hitler invaded Czechoslovakia on 15 March 1939. After announcing in August the Non-Aggression Pact between the USSR and Germany, the latter's army entered Poland on 1 September. On 3 September, Chamberlain, who had pledged to protect Poland's independence, was forced to sign a declaration of war against Germany, and the Second World War began. Chamberlain's fate was similar to that of Asquith during the First World War. He was accused of being too soft in his handling of the conflict. In May 1940, members of the Liberal and Labour Parties refused to take part in his proposal for a National Union government. He stepped down and was replaced by Winston Churchill, who appointed him Lord President of the Council, but illness forced him to resign from this position and he died on 9 November. The coalition government that Churchill then formed, and which was more left-leaning than the previous government, included, among others, the future Labour Prime Minister Clement Attlee, who succeeded Lansbury as Labour Leader in 1935 and would be appointed Deputy Prime Minister in 1942.

Keynes between Liberals and Labourites

The 1930s were for the Labour Party a time of major mutation and, for the Liberal Party, one of continuous decline. The British electoral system favoured bipartisanism. The Liberal Party, which refused to change the electoral modality when it dominated British political life, now became a victim. Labour's transformation was marked by the growing influence of Keynes's ideas. The economists Evan Durbin and Hugh Gaitskell contributed to the introduction of Keynesianism into Labour philosophy, even if they were both critical of Keynes's political positions.[36] Members of the New Fabian Research Bureau, set up in 1931 by G.D.H. Cole and Hugh Dalton, included, as well as Gaitskell and Durbin, such friends of Keynes as Colin Clark, Roy Harrod, Richard Kahn, James Meade, Joan Robinson and Leonard Woolf. This committee sought to renovate the Labour programme.

In 1934 the Party adopted a new platform, 'For socialism and peace'. Its most radical aspects would be suppressed after the 1935 electoral defeat and the new programme adopted in 1937 would be known as 'Labour's immediate programme'. The latter borrowed several elements from the Keynesian approach. But it was not until 1944 with the adoption of a document prepared by Dalton, Durbin and Gaitskell, called 'Full employment and fiscal policy', that the objective of full employment and the methods proposed by Keynes to bring it about would be definitively adopted by the Labour Party, the day before its first majority victory.

For the Liberal Party, the 1930s were marked by splits and decline. Liberal ministers were briefly part of the National Government in 1932, with right of dissent on the question of tariffs, but they resigned in 1933. Twenty Liberal candidates were elected in 1935. Keynes made bitter comments regarding the Party's split, which pushed him away in the 1930s and caused him to move closer to Labour, whose positions he often supported in the *New Statesman and Nation*. The 1929 electoral campaign was the last in which Keynes actively participated. He also stopped attending the Liberal Summer School. He withdrew in 1931 his financial support to the National League of Young Liberals, of which he was until then vice president. When the Liberal MP Herbert Samuel requested financial support for the 1935 elections, he refused by responding on 23 October: 'But alas, I scarcely know where I stand. Somewhere, I suppose, between Liberal and Labour, though in some respects to the left of the latter . . . I should be glad to see a stronger representation of either of the above two parties in the next Parliament' (Letter to Herbert Samuel, 23 October 1935, JMK 21, pp. 372–3). He made a donation to the Labour candidate and economist Colin Clark,[37] and, for the first time in his life, he voted Labour.

The Liberal Party started to reorganize in 1936. Keynes wrote to its leader Archibald Sinclair on 4 April 1938 that, given the new circumstances, the Liberal Party needed to become the centre of gravity for progressive forces, even though Labourites constituted the dominant group. The latter were in reality 'progressively more liberal in their general outlook' (JMK 28, p. 107).

Communists and Fascists

The British political scene was not limited to the Conservative–Liberal–Labour trio. Founded in July 1920, the Communist Party was a member of the Third International created by Lenin. It succeeded in electing one MP in the 1922, 1924 and 1935 elections. The number of its members and militants would never be important, but its influence exceeded its limited electoral presence. From 1930 it published the *Daily Worker*, which found some echo among workers as the Depression worsened. It held a place in the trade union world as well as in the intellectual and university world. We find its influence extending to the Apostles, who counted in their ranks in the 1930s several communists. Even the young generation of Bloomsbury was affected. Far from being scandalized by this evolution within the Society in which he had long been active, Keynes welcomed it:

> There is no one in politics today worth sixpence outside the ranks of liberals except the post-war generation of intellectual Communists under thirty five. Them, too, I like and respect. Perhaps in their feelings and instincts they are the nearest we now have to the typical nervous nonconformist English gentleman who went to the Crusades, made the Reformation, fought the Great Rebellion, won us our civil and religious liberties and humanized the working classes last century. (1939-1, pp. 494–5)

It was discovered later that eight Cambridge students were recruited as Soviet spies, four of whom – Anthony Blunt,[38] Guy Burgess, Leo Long and Michael Straight – were Apostles.

Keynes was close to the first two, and he also mixed with the communists of the Left Book Club, which he described as 'one of the finest and most living movements of our time' (ibid., p. 496). Regarding this club, Keynes wrote to Stafford Cripps on 9 February 1939: 'I fancy that a spontaneous coming together of Liberals and of Left Book Clubbers to make an attempt on persuading the Labour Party is psychologically the best way the thing could have happened' (JMK 21, p. 502).[39]

On the other extreme of the political scene, Oswald Mosley founded in 1932 the Union of British Fascists.[40] This event was the arrival point of a very peculiar path. Conservative MP from 1918 to 1922, Mosley was elected an independent in 1922, then a Labourite in 1926. In 1927 he became member of the National Executive Committee of the Labour Party. When Labour took power in 1929, he was appointed Chancellor of the Duchy of Lancaster.[41] Like Keynes, whose arguments he tried to impose in the Labour Party, he was opposed to the government's economic policy, which he considered too moderate. He proposed a radical memorandum on socio-economic reforms close to Keynesian positions. The rejection of his propositions by the Labour leadership brought him to leave the Party in May 1930 and found the New Party, which obtained the support of 17 MPs and several intellectuals. John Strachey, Lytton Strachey's cousin, another Labourite defector who would later turn to the Communist Party, was among them.

Mosley was dazzled by his meeting with il Duce in 1932 and transformed his new party into the British Union of Fascists. At first financially supported by Mussolini's Italy, the Union then became closer to Nazi Germany. Mosley, who defended increasingly open racist, anti-Semitic and antiparliamentarian positions, became friendly with Goebbels and Hitler.[42] The Union set up bands of 'black shirts' who organized violent attacks on Jewish immigrants living in London's poorer East End. Following the Cable Street Riot, the government proclaimed in 1936 the Public Order Act to repress these groups' violent action.

Mosley harangued in his meetings audiences of several thousand people. He was able to enjoy some support within the British upper classes, notably of the man who reigned briefly as Edward VIII before becoming the Duke of Windsor. Mosley was also able to count on the protection of Lord Halifax, successively Viceroy of India, several times minister and wartime British ambassador to the United States. The party dissolved on 30 May 1940 and Mosley was detained with his wife until November 1943. After the war the couple withdrew to France, not far from their friends the Duke and Duchess of Windsor. Great Britain, as elsewhere, swarmed with various fringe groups, but none had any considerable audience. Even the Fascist Union never represented a serious threat.

LABOUR'S VICTORY

In preparation for by-elections for the seat of Cambridge University in 1940, Keynes was again asked to present his candidacy, which was backed by the three parties. He hesitated, consulted his physician and finally refused, giving a response that highlighted his conception of the relationship between directly political action and the type of work he pursued with intensity during the war: 'The active political life is not my right and true activity. I am indeed an extremely active publicist. And that is just the difficulty. I am on lines along which I can operate usefully and have my full influence if I am aloof from the day to day influence of Westminster' (letter to A.B. Ramsay, 24 November 1939, JMK 22, p. 38). Made a peer in

1942, Keynes became Baron of Tilton and choose to sit with the Liberals in the House of Lords. There he gave a few important speeches in support of negotiations that he had led in the United States, in particular those held at Bretton Woods.[43]

On 31 October 1944, Churchill announced that general elections, the first since 1935, would be held once Germany was defeated. Upon Labour's withdrawal from the government coalition on 23 May 1945, he called for elections on 5 July. The Conservative programme defended individualism and private enterprise against nationalization and interventionism. The Labour programme, 'Let us face the future', was on the contrary radical, proposing economic planification, important areas of nationalization and a vast social programme so as to realize the 'Socialist commonwealth of Great Britain'. The Liberal programme was situated between the two, insisting on continuity rather than rupture. In a letter to the Liberal candidate Violet Bonham-Carter, Keynes wrote on 16 May: 'I should view with great alarm a substantial victory by either of the major Parties' (JMK 28, p. 210).

Churchill led a blundering campaign by violently attacking his former allies, accusing Labourites of being doctrinaire socialists and their leader, Clement Attlee, of being a union puppet. Labourites, for their part, decided out of respect for wartime Britain's leader not to present any candidate against Churchill. The Conservatives were favoured to win, and the announcement of the results on 26 July took many by surprise. Labour secured a clear victory with 48 per cent of the vote and 393 seats. The Liberals collapsed with 9 per cent of the vote and 12 seats, while the Conservatives obtained 35 per cent of the vote and 197 seats. Clement Attlee was named Prime Minister and the economist Hugh Dalton, professor at the London School of Economics and defender of Keynes's theses within the Labour Party, became Chancellor of the Exchequer.

Mandated by a new political power, Keynes continued to lead, tenaciously and with desperate energy, negotiations with US representatives to reduce Britain's debt and obtain financial aid. In a letter to Kingsley Martin on 3 January, he explained that one of his motivations for this effort was to give the Labour government, which would not have resisted breaking with the United States, a chance. He questioned whether the intransigence of some was not due to ulterior motives:

> If the negotiations had broken down and we had not got the loan, I do not believe the Labour Government could have lasted a year . . . I personally felt this as an additional reason for insisting on an agreement. It seems to me it would have been a real disaster if, for the second time, a Labour Government should be destroyed by an external financial situation, for which they could scarcely be regarded as primarily responsible. (JMK 28, p. 220)

Keynes would not live long enough to see the Labour government put into practice the revolution that bears his name. By a ruse of history, half a century later and in the aftermath of Thatcherism, it would be New Labour which would go about partially liquidating the Keynesian heritage. The 'third way' of Prime Minister Tony Blair and his advisers is in effect very far from Keynes's new liberalism.

PORTRAITS

ASQUITH, Henry Herbert (1852–1928): a barrister, Herbert Asquith was elected Liberal MP in 1886. He was Home Secretary in Gladstone's government between 1892 and 1895.

Between 1899 and 1901 he belonged to the group of 'Liberal imperialists' who supported Britain's war against the Boers. Chancellor of the Exchequer from 1905 to 1908, he became Prime Minister in 1908, after Henry Campbell-Bannerman's resignation. Architect of the Parliament Act and Irish Home Rule, he was opposed to women's suffrage. He formed a coalition government in May 1915 and was forced to cede power to Lloyd George in December 1916, but remained leader of a divided Liberal Party. Defeated in the 1918 elections, he regained his seat in 1923. In 1926 he gave up Liberal Party leadership to Lloyd George. Having become Lord Oxford, he died in 1928, publishing that same year *Memories and Reflections*. For Keynes, who was close to him and his second wife Margaret Tennant ('Margot', 1864–1945), Asquith was a naturally conservative man who showed himself, during the eight years of his government, as 'the perfect Whig for carrying into execution those Radical projects of his generation which were well judged' (1928-3, p. 39).

ATTLEE, Clement Richard (1883–1967): born into a bourgeois family, a student of Oxford, made barrister in 1906, Clement Attlee began teaching at the London School of Economics in 1913. He was seriously wounded during the war. A Labourite, he was elected mayor of Stepney in 1919, then MP in 1922. He was Under Secretary of State for War in the Labour government of 1922, then Postmaster General in 1929. Refusing to follow Ramsay Macdonald in the 1931 National Union government, he became Labour Party leader in 1935. Advocating intervention against Franco in the Spanish Civil War, he visited the International Brigades on the front. Lord Privy Seal from 1940 to 1942, Secretary of State for the Dominions from 1942 to 1943, he was named deputy Prime Minister in 1942 and Lord President of the Council from 1943 to 1945. In 1945, he became leader of the first majority Labour government, which put into practice a programme of nationalization, social security and the emancipation of part of the British Empire. Leader of the opposition after the short electoral defeat of 1951, he stepped down in 1955, but remained active in the House of Lords until his death.

BALDWIN, Stanley (1867–1947): a cousin of Rudyard Kipling, the industrialist and gentleman-farmer Stanley Baldwin entered parliament as a Conservative in 1906. Financial Secretary to the Treasury (1917–21), President of the Board of Trade (1921–22), he became Chancellor of the Exchequer in 1922 and Prime Minister in 1923. He returned to this post, after the Labour episode of 1924, from 1925 to 1929, leading a policy of confrontation with the trade unions. Lord President of the Council from 1931 to 1935, he replaced Ramsay Macdonald as Prime Minister in 1935 and stepped down in 1937, after having led a policy of appeasement towards Hitler and non-intervention in the Spanish Civil War. He imposed the abdication of King Edward VIII, who insisted on marrying a divorced commoner. He led the Conservative Party from 1923 to 1937.

BALFOUR, Arthur James (1848–1930): elected Conservative MP in 1874, Balfour was appointed Chief Secretary for Ireland in 1887, First Lord of the Treasury in 1892 and that same year, leader of the House of Commons. Resolutely opposed to Home Rule, he became known as 'Bloody Balfour' by Irish Nationalists. In 1902, he replaced his uncle Lord Salisbury as Prime Minister. He resigned in 1905 following divisions within the Conservative Party over the question of protectionism, while staying on as Party leader until 1911. He was named First Lord of the Admiralty in the coalition government led by Asquith in 1915. Lloyd

George entrusted him the following year with the Ministry of Foreign Affairs, which he left in 1919. He was author of the 'Balfour Declaration' of 2 November 1917, calling for the creation of a national Jewish homeland in Palestine. From 1925 to 1929 he was Lord President of the Council. A student of Sidgwick, who became his brother-in-law, Balfour was also a philosopher and economist and was the first vice-president of the Royal Economic Society. In his obituary note, Keynes described his hesitations between laissez-faire and protectionism and presented him as 'supremely well-informed, brilliantly dialectical, open-minded conservative, perfectly poised between the past and the future' (1930-14, p. 43).

BONAR LAW, Andrew (1858–1923): born in Canada, Bonar Law was a Presbyterian of Scottish and Ulster origin who resolutely defended protectionism and the union of Great Britain and Ireland. He was elected MP in 1900 and named Secretary to the Board of Trade in 1902. Defeated in the 1906 elections, he became leader of the Conservative opposition in 1911, before being named Colonial Secretary in the National Union government formed in 1915, then Chancellor of the Exchequer (1916–18) and Lord Privy Seal (1918–21). He succeeded Lloyd George as Prime Minister in 1922, but throat cancer forced him to resign in May 1923, a few months before his death. On the death of Bonar Law, Keynes wrote: 'We shall not easily find another leader of the Conservative Party who is so *unprejudiced* . . . Yet, in truth, he was almost devoid of Conservative principles' (1923-14, p. 33).

CAMPBELL-BANNERMAN, Henry (1836–1908): an industrialist, Henry Campbell-Bannerman was elected Liberal MP in 1868. Named by Gladstone as Chief Secretary for Ireland in 1884, he attained a cabinet position as Secretary of State for War in 1886. In 1898, he became leader of the House of Commons and leader of the Liberal Party in 1899. Opposed to the Boer War, he vigorously criticized the treatment of prisoners in concentration camps, which caused tensions within his party. Edward VII called on him to form a government following Balfour's resignation in 1905. After the Liberal victory in 1906, he started implementing an ambitious programme of social reform, but illness forced him to resign on 4 April 1908.

CHAMBERLAIN, Joseph Austen (1863–1937): son of Joseph Chamberlain and half-brother of Neville Chamberlain, elected as a Liberal Unionist MP in 1892, he joined his father in the Conservative ranks and became Chancellor of the Exchequer between 1903 and 1906, before returning to this post from 1919 to 1921. Leader of the Conservative Party from March 1921 to October 1922, he was Foreign Secretary from 1924 to 1929. Appointed First Lord of the Admiralty in Macdonald's National Union government in 1931, he decided to withdraw from the elections. He obtained the Nobel Peace Prize of 1925 in recognition of his diplomatic efforts in the Locarno treaties guaranteeing the respect by all nations involved of the borders fixed by the Treaty of Versailles.

CHAMBERLAIN, Arthur Neville (1869–1940): son of Joseph Chamberlain and half-brother of Austen Chamberlain, Arthur Neville Chamberlain managed for seven years one of his father's plantations in the Bahamas and then went into the copper industry in England. Mayor of Birmingham (1915–16), elected Conservative MP in 1918, he was Postmaster-General (1922), Chancellor of the Exchequer (1923–24), Minister of Health (1924–29) and again Chancellor of the Exchequer from 1931 to 1937. In May 1937, he succeeded Stanley Baldwin as Prime Minister. A signatory of the Munich Pact along with Deladier, Hitler and

Mussolini, he presided over Britain's entry into the war, but was obliged to resign in May 1940, after the Liberals and Labour parties refused to recognize him as leader of a National Union government.

CHURCHILL, Winston Leonard Spencer (1874–1965): born into the aristocratic Marlborough family, Winston Churchill was one of the most famous and colourful statesmen of the twentieth century. After a military education, he fought in India and the Sudan. He left the army in 1899 and became correspondent for the *Morning Post* in South Africa, where he was imprisoned by the Boers and from whom he orchestrated a daring escape. Elected Conservative MP in 1900, he joined the ranks of the Liberal Party in 1904 in disagreement over his party's protectionist stance. Elected in 1906, he was successively Under-Secretary of State for the Colonies (1906), President of the Board of Trade (1908), Home Secretary (1910–11), and First Lord of the Admiralty (1911). As First Lord, he was responsible for the catastrophic Dardanelles campaign in 1915 and was forced to resign in May. In 1916, Lloyd George named him successively Minister of Munitions, Secretary of State for War, and Secretary of State for Air for the coalition government. Defeated in the 1922 elections and disappointed by the divisions within his party, Churchill returned to the Conservative Party and was elected in 1924. He was named Chancellor of the Exchequer and decided on Britain's return to the gold standard in 1925. After his electoral defeat in 1929, he retired from politics and devoted himself to writing, before leading public opposition to the British government's policy of appeasement towards Germany. At the outbreak of war, he was again named First Lord of the Admiralty. On 10 May 1940, after Neville Chamberlain's resignation, Churchill was called on by George VI to form a coalition government in which Labour leaders occupied key positions. On 13 May he declared to parliament: 'I have nothing to offer but blood, toil, tears and sweat'. Having won the war, Churchill lost the 1945 elections and became leader of the opposition in the first majority Labour government. He regained power in the 1951 elections. He was forced to retire from political life for health reasons in 1955. A Nobel laureate for literature in 1953, a talented painter, this extraordinary personality, who was a lover of alcohol and cigars, was endowed with exceptional energy. Keynes was often opposed to him on political issues, but respected him and met with him often, especially in the Other Club, which Churchill founded in 1911.

LLOYD GEORGE, David (1863–1945): a Welsh nationalist, David Lloyd George started his career as a barrister. Advocating land reform and influenced by the Fabian Society, he became in 1890 the youngest MP in the House. Liberal Party leadership distrusted his populist radicalism as much as his exceptional talents as an orator, having been educated as a nonconformist preacher. He opposed the Boer War. In 1906, Henry Campbell-Bannerman named him President of the Board of Trade. In 1908 he became Chancellor of the Exchequer, succeeding Asquith, who became Prime Minister. In 1909 he proposed a 'People's Budget' to finance an important programme of social measures. At first opposed to the war, he changed his position and became Minister of Munitions in 1915 and then Secretary of State for War in 1916. He allied himself with the Conservatives, forced Asquith to resign, provoking a split in the Liberal Party and became, in December 1916, Prime Minister of a coalition government. He was, with US President Wilson and French Prime Minister Georges Clemenceau, one of the three great players of the Paris Conference which led in July 1919 to the Treaty of Versailles. In October 1922, he was forced to resign by Conservatives who were unhappy with the 1921 creation of the Free State of Ireland. In 1926 he replaced Asquith as leader of the Liberal Party and led the 1929 electoral campaign on a programme inspired by John Maynard Keynes. The campaign was a failure. Lloyd George retired in 1931, wrote his memoirs and refused Churchill's proposition to enter his cabinet in 1940. He was given the nickname 'Goat' in reference both to his political stamina and to his many romantic adventures. Keynes, who became Lloyd George's ally in the 1920s, detested him for his bellicose attitude during World War One:

> He detested his demagogy. I remember his cutting from a French paper . . . a photograph of 'the goat' as he always called him, in full evening dress and smothered in ribbons, speaking at a banquet in Paris; and I remember his writing under it 'Lying in state'. He pinned it up in the dining-room at forty-six (C. Bell, 1956, p. 47).

MACDONALD, James Ramsay (1866–1937): an illegitimate child of modest origin, the Scottish journalist James Ramsay Macdonald started his political life in the Fabian Society and joined in 1894 the ranks of the Independent Labour Party. He was appointed in 1900 secretary of the Labour Representation Committee, which became the Labour Party in 1906. He was elected that same year and became leader of the Labour group in 1911. He was forced to resign in 1914, marginalized by his pacifist positions. Defeated in the 1918 elections, he was re-elected in 1922 and became in January 1924 Prime Minister of a minority Labour government overturned in October of the same year. Prime Minister once again in 1929, he was confronted with a crisis within his party in 1931 and subsequently led from August a National Union government dominated by Conservatives. This led to his exclusion from the Labour Party. He resigned as PM in June 1935 and lost his seat in the November elections. Re-elected in a partial election in 1937, he died on a sea passage to South America. An active member of the Second International, Macdonald frequented Bebel, Jaurès, Adler and Lenin. He was the author of several books, including *Socialism and Society*.

MCKENNA, Reginald (1863–1943): A mathematics-educated banker, Reginald McKenna was elected Liberal MP in 1895. He was appointed Secretary of the Treasury in Campbell-Bannerman's government in 1905, and then President of the Board of Education in 1907, First Lord of the Admiralty (1908–11), Home Secretary (1911–15), and Chancellor of the Exchequer (1915–16). Opposed to conscription, he resigned from government in 1916. Loyal to Asquith, he lost his seat in 1918, left politics and became president of Midland Bank from 1919 until his death. In *The Times* of 15 September 1943, Keynes emphasized 'his immense kindness and the true intimacy he gave to some of those who found themselves working for him' (1943-9, p. 58).

MONTAGU, Edwin Samuel (1879–1924): a Liberal MP from 1906 to 1922, Edwin Samuel Montagu was Under-Secretary of State for India (1910–14), Financial Secretary to the Treasury (1914–16), Minister of Munitions (1916) and Secretary of State for India (1917–22). He favoured Irish independence and was responsible for the Government of India Act which, in 1919, accorded some governmental autonomy to the great British colony. Opposed to Zionism, he was successful in having the Balfour Declaration modified. In his obituary published on 29 November 1924 in *Nation and Athenaeum* (1924–30), Keynes wrote a fascinating description of what appeared to be his manic-depression. Montagu was, in the British political universe, Keynes's main defender.

NOTES

1. Different aspects of the story being traced here are dealt with in the following works: Bogdanor (1983), Clarke (1978) and (1996), Durbin (1985), Freeden (1978) and (1986), Wilson (1966) and Winch (1969). Some events are described in more detail in other chapters, particularly Chapter 5.
2. Coming from an English protestant family, Charles Stewart Parnell (1846–91), elected to parliament in 1874, was head of the Home Rule Party and president of the Irish National Land League. He was called the 'uncrowned king of Ireland'.
3. The Liberal Unionist movement would fuse with the Conservative Party in 1912.
4. See the following chapter.
5. An allusion to the colour of military uniforms, a reference to the fact that these elections were dominated by the question of the Boer War.
6. An asterisk follows, on their first appearance, the names of personalities whose portraits will be presented at the end of this chapter. While the Bloomsbury portraits were those of personal friends of Keynes, the latter are portraits of men that Keynes frequented in his public life. Some of them were also his friends.
7. He died in 1914. His son Austen was appointed Chancellor of the Exchequer in 1903. Another of his sons, Neville, would occupy the same position in 1923–24 and from 1931 to 1937, before becoming Prime Minister.
8. For example, in 1901, following the suit of the Taff-Vale Railway Company against the Amalgamated Society of Railway Servants, the courts held that a union could be held responsible for damages caused by the actions of its officials in industrial disputes.
9. It was dissolved in 1876 following conflicts between anarchists and Marxists, which provoked its moving to the United States. The Second International, which still exists, was founded in Paris in 1889.
10. Eleanor Marx, daughter of Karl Marx, was a member. However, Marx and Engels refused to become involved in this undertaking.
11. The Society took its name from the Roman politician Fabius, known as Cunctator or 'the Delayer' (275–203 BC), who owes his name to the war of attrition against Hannibal.
12. The Irishman Shaw (1856–1960), recipient of the Nobel Prize for literature in 1925, was also interested in economic theory.
13. The economist Sidney Webb (1859–1947) founded in 1895 the London School of Economics to counterbalance the teaching of Alfred Marshall at Cambridge. He became a member of the Labour Party's National Executive in 1915. His wife Beatrice, née Potter (1858–1943), was also an economist. In one of history's ironies, the London School would become for some time, with Robbins and Hayek, the centre of laissez-faire's struggle against Keynesian interventionism.
14. We will return in detail, in the following chapter, to the episode that was the Boer war.
15. See Cutler, Williams and Williams (1987).
16. In particular, new liberalism was close to Fabianism. It differed from the latter over the question of imperialism and free trade. Several important Fabians, such as Shaw, were advocates of British imperialism and a protectionism which, to their eyes, would have allowed for the acceleration of social reforms in England.
17. On details of Keynes's wartime activities, see the following chapter.
18. Through this dinner, Ottoline Morrell hoped to bring Bloomsbury to the attention of the Prime Minister, who had shown an interest in meeting Bertrand Russell, also present for the occasion (Seymour, 1992, p. 264).
19. Keynes was supposed to have taken part in this delegation but was called to other tasks at the last minute. In his journal, John Neville Keynes wrote on 6 June: 'News of the death of Lord Kitchener and his party off the Orkneys on their way from London. It is only a chance that Maynard was not with him and we have felt it very much' (quoted in Deane, 2001, p. 290). See also the story as remembered by his mother, F.A. Keynes, 1950, p. 88.
20. See on this subject the following chapter.
21. Churchill was also a member of the Tuesday Club.
22. MPs representing some of the most important universities were a feature, abandoned since 1950, of the United Kingdom electoral system.
23. A Conservative MP since 1886, George Curzon (1859–1925) had been Viceroy of India (1899–1905), Lord Privy Seal (1915–16), Lord President of the Council (1916–19 and 1924–5) and Foreign Secretary (1919–24).
24. Following Queen Victoria's example, George V played a more political role than most British sovereigns, not hesitating to take a stand, both on the national and international scene, notably to calm tensions.
25. See on this subject Chapter 5.
26. From 1923 until 1931, this review would cost him personally £7000.
27. The number of votes obtained by Labour went up while its number of seats declined.
28. See Chapter 8, where these events are described in detail. In spite of his opposition to Churchill, Keynes had much admiration for him, as indicated by his praiseworthy comments in the books *The World Crisis, 1916–1918* (1927-5) and *The World Crisis: The Aftermath* (1929-7): 'Mr. Churchill's was, perhaps, the most

acute and concentrated intelligence which saw the war at close quarters from beginning to end with knowledge of the inside facts and of the inner thoughts of the prime movers of events' (1927-5, p. 46).

29. Passages of the report, most certainly written by Keynes, in which the manipulation of information by business leaders is denounced, are quite striking in the present context.
30. On these events, see Skidelsky (1967).
31. On this, see Howson and Winch (1977). Also see, on the history of monetary policy in England between the wars, Howson (1975) and on Keynes on monetary policy from 1910 to his death, Moggridge and Howson (1974).
32. We will return in Chapter 7 to these events and in particular to the contents of Keynes's involvements.
33. Ernest Bevin (1881–1951), then general secretary of the Transport and General Workers Union, became Minister of Labour and National Service under Churchill's wartime government, representing Great Britain in the Postdam conference, and subsequently Foreign Secretary of the postwar Labour Government.
34. Edward VIII succeeded his father George V, who died in January 1936. He announced to the Prime Minister his intention to wed Wallis Simpson, a two times divorced American. Baldwin had, as Prime Minister, the power to refuse the King permission to marry a divorced commoner, a power that he used in virtue of his Christian and monarchist convictions. Edward VIII chose to abdicate and would become the Duke of Windsor. His brother succeeded him as George VI.
35. Coming to power on 5 June 1936, Blum stepped down on 21 June 1937 and then returned to his functions in March 1938.
36. Durbin was a member of the teaching staff of the LSE during the 1930s.
37. Colin Clark was a pioneer in national accounting. Keynes used his works in *The General Theory*.
38. On Blunt, and his relationship with Keynes, see Carter (2001).
39. Stafford Cripps, a member of Labour's left wing and future Chancellor of the Exchequer (1947), was excluded from the party in 1939 and attempted to start a movement with the international situation as its focus. He wrote to Keynes asking him to sign a petition and give financial support. Keynes accepted, though revealing scepticism in regards to the creation of new movements not affiliated with political parties.
40. On Mosley (1896–1980), see Skidelsky (1975).
41. The Chancellor of the Duchy of Lancaster, member of government without departmental work, represented the King.
42. In 1936, in the home of his close friend Josef Goebbels, Mosley married Diana Mitford, who frequented the Bloomsbury Group before joining the circle that formed around Hitler, present at the wedding, of whom she said: 'I particularly appreciated his sense of humour. He was extremely fascinating and intelligent' (Obituary, *Le Monde*, 15 August 2003). Diana had five well-known sisters, one of which, Unity, was also a regular visitor of the Nazi leaders, while Jessica was socialist (see Lovell, 2001).
43. See Chapter 8.

5.   War and peace: from the Boer War to Versailles

I claim complete exemption because I have a conscientious objection to surrendering my liberty of judgment on so vital a question as undertaking military service. I do not say that there are not conceivable circumstances in which I should voluntarily offer myself for military service. But after having regard to all the actually existing circumstances, I am certain that it is not my duty so to offer myself; and I solemnly assert to the Tribunal that my objection to submit to authority in this matter is truly conscientious. I am not prepared on such an issue as this to surrender my right of decision, as to what is or is not my duty, to any other person, and I should think it morally wrong to do so.
Application to the Holburn Tribunal, 28 February 1916 (1916-2)[1]

But as it is, men have devised ways to impoverish themselves and one another; and prefer collective animosities to individual happiness.
The Economic Consequences of the Peace (1919-1, p. 62)

The first duty of foreign policy is to avoid war. Its second duty it to ensure that, if it occurs, the circumstances shall be the most favourable possible for our cause.
'British foreign policy' (1937-8, p. 63)

There are no issues on which the rights of the majority are so paramount as in the case of war and peace.
Letter to Kinsgley Martin, 10 November 1937 (JMK 28, p. 94)

In his preface to *Essays on Persuasion*, Keynes wrote that the biggest part of his book deals with 'the three great controversies of the past decade, into which I plunged myself without reserve – the Treaty of Peace and the war debts, the policy of deflation, and the return to the gold standard, of which the last two, and indeed in some respects all three, were closely interconnected' (1931-1, pp. xvii–xviii). In reality, war, gold and employment preoccupied Keynes's mind and drained his energy throughout his career. Peace is the necessary condition to assure the coming of a better world. War is the main symptom of disorder in human affairs. It is thus normal that this social pathology be the first target in his crusade. It was during the Boer War that the young Keynes awoke to politics and affirmed his opposition to the patriotic and militaristic orthodoxy to which his father was susceptible. The First World War brought him into close contact with political power and made someone who considered himself unknown outside Cambridge in 1913 an internationally recognized personality. The present chapter will highlight such events and place special emphasis on biographical considerations.

THE BOER WAR

The young Keynes arrived at Eton College, one of England's most prestigious public schools, in September 1897. Founded in the fifteenth century by Henry VI, the College has remained one of the main training grounds for the English ruling class. The Second Boer War broke out during his third year at Eton. The Boers, or Afrikaners, descended from Dutch farmers, who in 1652 founded the Cape Colony, annexed by the British following the Treaty of Paris in 1814.[2] After largely abandoning the Cape, they founded three new States – Natal, Transvaal and the Orange Free State – the first of which was annexed by Britain in 1844. The discovery of an important gold deposit in the Transvaal prompted Cape Prime Minister Cecil Rhodes, a eulogist for Anglo-American world domination, to seek unification of Britain's African colonies and annexation of those Boer territories still independent. The Boers, united under the leadership of Transvaal President Paul Kruger, resisted the British imperialist undertaking. The Transvaal, in alliance with the Orange Free State, declared war on Great Britain in October 1899. British troops clashed with very mobile combatants who practised guerilla warfare in a land they knew much better than their British counterparts. Pretoria, Transvaal's capital, was taken in June 1900, but it was only in May 1902 that the Boers capitulated to General Kitchener and the Treaty of Vereeniging was signed, anticipating the creation, in 1910, of the Union of South Africa uniting the Cape, the Orange Free State, Natal and Transvaal. The British army lost 22 000 lives in this war and the Boers 7000. The Boers estimated at 30 000 the number of mortalities out of a total of 200 000 men, women and children, interned in concentration camps, a term first used in this occasion. The erection of these camps was facilitated by the recent invention of barbed wire. This internment raised lively protest in Britain and abroad.

This war had the effect of igniting British nationalism, patriotism and the popularity of imperialist arguments. A minority of Britons and a section of world public opinion supported the Afrikaners' struggle, seeing the Boer War as an act of aggression by a great imperialist power against a small people. For their part, anti-Boers underlined the reactionary and retrograde character of this racist community. British patriotism was particularly intense in places such as Eton. Keynes found himself in an awkward position, with some of the contradictions which would often characterize his life already coming to the fore. He thus accepted British imperialism, rejoicing, in a paper on Queen Victoria, that 'It is only during the present reign that we have begun to realise the responsibilities of Empire and to see our duties to subject races. We have begun to see that Great Britain may have a high destiny and a great future before her' (1899-1, p. 4). Victoria was continuing Elizabeth's legacy: 'By his feeble foreign policy he [James I] brought England from the glorious position she had held in Elizabeth's reign to an entirely mediocre place amongst the nations' (1900-1, p. 3).

Keynes perceived the British Empire as an inescapable reality. He held on to this position until the end of his life. But, if he was not anti-imperialist, he declared himself very early an anti-militarist. Obviously, it remains to be seen how an empire can be built and maintained without military force and without war. The Eton student followed events in austral Africa closely, as his diary, which he kept from 1894 (KP, PP/35) bears witness. Its 23 August 1899 entry reads: 'The newspapers are interesting just now owing to the Dreyfus case and the difficulties in the Transvaal'. On 5 October he wrote: 'War in the Transvaal seems quite inevitable now ... I can't get clear about the rights of the case' (ibid.); on 16 October: 'the war is marvellously uneventful so far'; on 20 October: 'The war seems to have really begun at last now that we have news of the battle of Glencoe. Chamberlain's speech in reply to various members of the opposition was very good indeed' (ibid.). On 1 November, he learned of Mayor Myers's death, the Eton volunteers' warrant officer: 'This is the first war that I can remember in which the British have suffered serious losses ... we see lists of dead and wounded every morning in the papers'. On 16 December he wrote: 'The news from South

Africa is bad now that Buller's reverse has come so quickly after the other two. We console ourselves by thinking what much greater reverses and losses we sustained in the Peninsula War, a hundred years ago, and yet came out successful' (ibid.).[3]

Maynard wrote to his father on 8 October: 'I do not know what to think about this Transvaal business, but I think I am getting more and more anti-war'. His father, who had subscribed an important sum to a war loan, wrote to him on 1 October: 'We cannot quite convince ourselves that Great Britain is going to wage a righteous war'. In a 17 December letter, Maynard explained to his father that it was necessary to relativize British losses in a world in which information circulates faster, so much so that light losses seem much more catastrophic than the enormous losses suffered in past wars: 'I agree with you that the news from S. Africa is bad, especially this last reverse of Buller. But we console ourselves with History which makes our losses and reverses seem puny . . . Seventy men killed in a battle is terrible for their families but it is tiny loss for a nation of thirty million'.

At the beginning of the year 1900, college leadership informed students that it was their duty to join the ranks of volunteers, the Corps, fighting in South Africa. Maynard wrote to his father on 29 January 1900: 'Am I to join? I am not keen and the drills will be a nuisance, but I am perfectly willing to do so if I ought. It would be unpleasant to be almost the only non-shooter'. Keynes's parents were torn between their convictions and their fear of losing a son. To their relief, Maynard decided to resist the sirens of 'this marvellous martial ardour that has seized the school': 'About the volunteers – I have not joined . . . Some say that patriotism requires one to join the useless Eton shooters but it seems to me to be the sort of patriotism that requires one to wave the Union Jack' (letter to his father, 4 February 1900). He observed with ironic detachment the explosion of enthusiasm and chauvinistic manifestations which followed the British victories of Kimberley and especially of Mafeking, liberated after 218 days of siege:

> It is evident that the whole nation has gone in for what we call at Eton an organised rag . . . I do not think that we are quite such hypocrites here. Most of us know that Mafeking is a glorious pretext for a whole holiday and for throwing off all discipline. We do not break windows because we are mad with joy, but because we think that under the circumstances we can do so with impunity. (Letter of Keynes to his father, 20 May 1900)

While the Boers were making life difficult for British soldiers, on the other side of the world a Chinese sect, the 'Righteous Harmony Society', founded around 1770, launched the Boxer Rebellion of 1898 in reaction to Western influence in the Middle Empire. After the massacre of foreign mission members in Peking, an international expeditionary corps led by the German General Waldersee crushed the movement and forced the Chinese government, which had complied with the Boxers, into paying high indemnities to European countries. Regarding this rebellion, Keynes wrote to his father on 8 July 1900: 'I am a confirmed pro-Boxer. By the way, take away x the unknown quantity and what does Boxer become?'

THE OUTBREAK OF THE GREAT WAR

Between the end of the nineteenth century and 1914, Europe had divided itself into two blocs: the Triple Alliance, or Triplice, formed in 1883 and uniting Germany, Austria-Hungary and Italy, and the Triple Entente, an informal alliance set up between 1893 and 1907 uniting the

United Kingdom, France and Russia.[4] A complicated game of secondary alliances, colonial rivalries, conflicting territorial ambitions, particularly those of Austria in the Balkans, demographic pressures, economic difficulties, social conflicts and the rise of workers and socialist movements all helped turn Europe into a powder keg. France was in dispute with Germany, which had annexed Alsace and part of Lorraine in 1871 and imposed indemnity payments. The Balkan Wars of 1912 and 1913, in which Western powers became divided in their allegiances, some favouring Greeks, others Turks, Serbs, Bulgarians or Albanians, were the prelude to a generalized confrontation:

> In my own opinion, it is not possible to lay the entire responsibility for the state of affairs out of which the war arose on any single nation; it was engendered, in part at least, by the essential character of international politics and rivalries during the latter part of the nineteenth century, by militarism everywhere (certainly in Russia as well as in Germany and Austria-Hungary), and by the universally practised policies of economic imperialism; it has its seeds deep in the late history of Europe. (1920-4, p. 52)

On 28 June 1914, the assassination in Sarajevo of the Archduke Franz Ferdinand, heir to the Austrian throne, by a Serb, was the spark that ignited the conflict. After an ultimatum on 24 July, Austria declared war on Serbia on 28 July, the official date of the beginning of what was first a European conflict, but which became, with the United States' entry in April 1917, history's first World War. Germany declared war on Russia on 1 August and then on France on 3 August. The next day, Great Britain entered the fray by declaring war on Germany following the latter's violation of Belgian neutrality, guaranteed by the Treaty of London in 1831. In May 1915, Italy joined the Triple Entente after promises of territorial transfers which would not be respected at the end of the war.[5] The carnage following these declarations would bring into conflict 65 million soldiers, of whom 8.5 million would die and 2.1 million would be wounded. It is estimated that 10 million civilians perished directly or indirectly as a result of the war.

At the dawn of the war, Bloomsbury discovered Diaghilev's *Ballets Russes*, after having revealed post-impressionist painting to a stupefied English public. Keynes immersed himself in the proofs of his book on probabilities, and optimism was the rule. On 14 July 1914, he wrote to his father, who was leaving with Florence to holiday in France, Italy and Switzerland: 'I am now very deep in Probability and enjoying myself'. He played bridge with Moore in the country and fretted about the decoration of his apartment at King's, which he oversaw with his mother. The latter wrote to him on 21 July:

> It was very nice to hear from you – especially as you could give us such good news of our old friend 'Probability'. It is delightful to hear that you are really enjoying yourself – with this subject more than with most it seems to me that the real difficulty lies in settling in to work & that means that a lot of time is lost when you have to break off. So I venture to hope that you will not uproot yourself too soon. Even with your unusual capacity for settling down to work in strange places, I am sure you cannot get on with it in other people's houses so well as in the calm of King's.

In the end, the events were such that he was not able to follow the advice of his mother, to whom he wrote on 30 July: 'In the meantime I am trying to work but find myself dreadfully distracted by the war news, which makes it hard to think about anything else'. The next day, he advised his parents to return as soon as possible to England in the event of war breaking out and added: 'I find this state of affairs interferes dreadfully with work, – I cannot keep my mind quiet enough'. Four days later his country had declared war, an event which took him and most of his Bloomsbury friends by surprise. It would be the same for the Crash of 1929 and the outbreak of war in 1939. Clive Bell recalled that Keynes blamed him for having presumed the war would go on for a long time and accused him of pessimism for having said in 1939 that war was inevitable: 'The fact is, of course, that Maynard's judgment would have been as sound as his intellect was powerful had it really been detached; but Maynard was an incorrigible optimist' (C. Bell, 1956, p. 45–6).[6]

Keynes's parents' vacation was abruptly cut short and their return to Cambridge on 5 August 1914 complicated. While Neville immersed himself in correcting proofs of his son's book, Florence became involved in several war-related committees. Their son Geoffrey joined the Royal Army Medical Corps[7] and Maynard started his war effort on the financial front by participating, early in June 1914, in a debate opposing the Central Bank and commercial bankers over the question of gold reserve management. On 1 August, Basil Blackett of the Treasury wrote to him: 'I wanted to pick your brains for your country's benefit and thought you might enjoy the process' (JMK 16, p. 3). Keynes received this letter on Sunday 2 August, while he was correcting proofs of his book on probabilities with Bertrand Russell and Charlie Broad. This is how the latter related the events ten years later in a critical review of the finally published *A Treatise on Probability*:

> The present reviewer well remembers going over the proofs of the earlier parts of it in the long vacations of 1914 with Mr. Keynes and Mr. Russell. From these innocent pleasures Mr. Keynes has suddenly hauled away on a friendly sidecar to advise the authorities in London on the *moratorium* and the foreign exchanges. (Broad, 1922, p. 72)

Keynes was thus pressed to tear himself away from probabilities in order to immerse himself in the affairs of war. He asked Archibald Hill,[8] who had married his sister in 1913, to bring him quickly to London in the sidecar of his motorcycle. He started work immediately, convincing political authorities, and in particular Lloyd George, then Chancellor of the Exchequer, not to yield to pressure from bankers in favour of suspending specie payments.[9] In a document dated from 3 August, he underlined the 'great difference between war and peace conditions, which has been perhaps insufficiently realised in the past' (1914-3, p. 8) and added that 'the vital point is that we should not repudiate our external obligations to pay gold, until it is physically impossible for us to fulfil them' (ibid., p. 13). In a memorandum from 5 August, he pressed the government not to guarantee bonds held by accepting houses, thus aligning himself against his own interests and those of his father, since both had lent money on the discount market (1914-4).

He published a series of three articles on the financial situation and the war – 'War and the financial system, August 1914' (1914-8), 'The City of London and the Bank of England, August 1914' (1914-12) and 'The prospects of money, November 1914' (1914-13) – as well as several open letters to newspapers on the same themes. In the first, he wrote that 'one of the earliest effects of war might be the complete breakdown of the system of foreign remittance' (1914-8, p. 245). He criticized joint stock banks, sparing of credit, holding their gold and rushing on that of the Bank of England, which spread panic: 'their action suggested that considerations of their own immediate safety, and even, it should be added, of their own pecuniary profit, overshadowed those of the general interest and of the more remote future' (ibid., p. 252). However, in light of the wisdom manifested by the Bank of England and the Treasury, Keynes considered that the financial future could be envisaged with confidence. Of course, war would absorb savings and current revenue and contribute to diminishing stocks of consumer goods. But it was an error, widely held, to believe the war would destroy the country's capital.

ARRIVAL AT THE TREASURY

Since the outbreak of war, Keynes had been hoping to obtain a job at the Treasury. The fact that this was slow in coming did not prevent him from actively involving himself in the institution's affairs. He wrote to his brother-in-law on 4 August: 'I spend most of my time at the Treasury and this work is very exciting' (JMK 16, p. 15). Two days later he proudly wrote to his father: 'I've just heard that they [the bankers] consider I played an important part in preventing the suspension of specie payments' (ibid., p. 16). While continuing his lectures at Cambridge, he maintained contact with the Treasury, sending notes and reflections on the financial situation. In December 1914 he visited his brother in a Versailles military hospital and collected information on French finances.[10] On his return in January, he was offered the post of assistant to Sir George Paish, special adviser to Lloyd George, for an annual salary of £600. This enabled him to leave his teaching and administrative responsibilities at Cambridge while continuing to manage the *Economic Journal*.[11] He started his new employment on 18 January and his employers left him one free day per week to attend to his other occupations. On 6 January, he celebrated his new job by inviting 17 of his Bloomsbury friends to dine at the Café Royal, followed by a reception offered by Vanessa Bell at 46, Gordon Square.

Four days after his entry into the Treasury, Keynes wrote to his father: 'After a slack beginning I am now very busy, having become Secretary of a Secret Committee of the Cabinet, presided over by the Prime Minister' (JMK 16, p. 57). He participated, alongside the Chancellor of the Exchequer, the Financial Secretary to the Treasury and the Governor of the Bank of England, in the first inter-allies financial conference[12] in Paris from 2 to 5 February 1915, a meeting which would set up the inter-allies debt system and which would weigh heavily over the postwar period.[13] Keynes would gradually take control of this complex architecture and of the numerous bilateral negotiations it produced. Great Britain was at the heart of the system, being the country that made credit available to the Allies in order to buy goods.

Keynes was also named Treasury representative at the inter-departmental Committee on Wheat and Flour Supplies and devoted much time to these matters during his first months at the Treasury. He spent the weekend of 15 May 1915 discussing a second war loan with the Governor of the Bank of England. The first loan was contracted by the banks in November 1914. In a memorandum dated from 14 May, he explained why it was now necessary to call on the public, whose spending power had to be reduced by taxation in a way that did not reduce its power of production (1915-2). He would return to these reflections in *How to Pay for the War* at the beginning of the Second World War.

It was with prodigious speed that Keynes composed letters, reports and memorandums. At Eton he had written to his father on 9 February 1902: 'I am finding that like you when I am appointed to a committee I am invariably made to do all the work'. Upon leaving a meeting, Keynes would usually write an often long text in which, as a pretext for resuming discussions, he put forth his positions. He controlled in this way the flow of debate, having already outlined it in writing.

The year 1915 saw his responsibilities at the Treasury increase rapidly following the retirement of George Paisch. In May he was transferred to the Finance Division of the Treasury. On 1 September he became first assistant to Malcolm Ramsay, Assistant Secretary to the Treasury, in charge of banking, currency, exchanges and inter-allies finance. He declared before the Board of Admiralty on 15 March 1916: 'It is my business to deal with our financial relations to the allies day by day' (1916-3, p. 187). He would say in 1923: 'I was in the Treasury throughout the war and all the money we either lent or borrowed passed through my hands' (JMK 16, p. 3). This is how he described his lifestyle in a letter that his father copied in his diary on 18 September 1915:

> I doubt if I've ever worked harder than during the last two weeks, but I'm wonderfully well all the same . . . The work has been as interesting as it could be. I've written three major memoranda, one of which has been circulated to the Cabinet, and about a dozen minor ones on all kinds of subjects, as well as helping Ramsay with the Vote of Credit and the Budget, and keeping going with routine, and the *Economic Journal* in the evenings. (JMK 16, p. 128)

In June he accompanied Chancellor McKenna to Nice for a meeting with the Italian Minister of Finance, whose country had just entered the war on the side of the Allies. He crossed the Channel in a destroyer and took much pleasure in this (letters to his father, 1 and 7 June 1915). On his return, his work was interrupted by an emergency appendicitis operation on 12 June, which was followed by pneumonia. He recovered at Garsington under Ottoline Morrell's care. On 20 August he participated in an international conference at Bologna, which decided on requesting a loan from the Americans. In a note prepared for this meeting, he wrote that France and Russia must use their accumulated gold reserves (1915-4). In September he was engaged in negotiations with Russia, which demanded British funds in return for use of its gold to support an American loan, negotiations that ended with the signing of an agreement on 30 September. From November 1915 he was in charge of operations of an Exchange Committee set up by the Chancellor under Lord Cunliffe's direction. He wrote, with his mother, in a call for savings published by the Cambridge War Thrift Committee: 'The war in its later stage will be largely a financial struggle' (1915-9, p. 141). He continued his campaign against the suspension of the gold standard: '"Suspension of Specie Payments" has in the public ear, both at home and abroad, a disastrous sound. Our credit depends on words as well as facts. "Suspension" would involve the maximum of discredit' (1915-10, pp. 143–4). He led the fight against bankers supporting this policy. He participated in a ghost cabinet which brought together top civil servants every Friday at the home of Edwin Montagu, then Financial Secretary to the Treasury. In November and December 1915 he was involved in loan discussions with the Italians. He was appointed to a War Office committee in charge of deciding the fate of what remained of the Serbian army in Albania and wrote to his mother on 10 December: 'It's very interesting as it brings me for the first time into direct touch with military affairs' (JMK 16, p. 150). He found time to give, in November and December, a series of six lectures entitled 'The war finance of the continental powers' at London's University College.

BETWEEN BLOOMSBURY AND THE TREASURY

It was in June 1915 that the question of conscription started to be evoked. The Secretary of State for War, Horatio Herbert Kitchener,[14] requested 70 divisions in order to continue combat, while voluntary mobilization failed to meet expectations. McKenna, then Chancellor of the Exchequer, believed that it would be impossible to maintain an army of 70 divisions and to assist Britain's allies financially. Keynes prepared his arguments for a Cabinet Committee on War Policy set up in August 1915: 'the labour forces of the United Kingdom are so fully engaged in useful occupations that any considerable further diversion of them to military uses is *alternative* and not *additional* to the other means by which the United Kingdom is assisting the Allied cause' (1915-5, pp. 110–11). Expressing an idea he would develop at the start of the Second World War, he added: 'It is not possible to control production without controlling consumption in an equally drastic manner . . . Without a policy for the confiscation of private income, a considerably increased army and a continuance of subsidies are *alternative*' (ibid., pp. 114–15). In a paper dated from 9 September, which circulated as a government document (1915-8), Keynes developed this reasoning by painting a pessimistic picture of Britain's financial situation compared with Germany's, a country which had succeeded in imposing, by way of a wage freeze, an enormous tax on the working class. These arguments did not convince the Committee, which proposed maintaining an army of 70 divisions by any means possible, including conscription. It was the opinion of the majority of the cabinet, led by the Minister of Munitions Lloyd George.[15] Conscription was proclaimed on 26 January 1916.

In the First Interlude we discussed how almost all the Bloomsberries, at first surprised by the war and hesitant as to what position to take, sided with the cause of pacifism and refused conscription, proclaiming themselves conscientious objectors. In addition to the Bloomsberries, other friends of Keynes, such as Pigou, believed the longer the war went on, the less justified was the sacrifice in human life it required. Keynes shared this conviction. To the great dismay of his father, he considered resigning from his post at the Treasury,[16] but finally decided to persevere, as he wrote to his mother on 13 January: 'Things drift on, and I shall stay now, I expect, until they begin to torture one of my friends'. Under the pseudonym 'Politicus', he published in the *Daily Chronicle* of 6 January 1916, a letter criticizing the increase in military forces and conscription:

> Those who believe . . . that our duty to the allies is not to help them most effectively but to impress them with the nobility of our self-sacrifice by getting as many of our men killed or maimed as we plausibly can, or who believe that the chief test of patriotism is an eagerness to dissipate the national resources at the maximum possible rate, will find much moral solace in compulsory service (1916-1, p. 161).

He took up his pen again on the same theme and under the same pseudonym in his friend Gerald Shove's pacifist monthly *War and Peace* in April 1916. He also put pressure on MPs and ministers uncomfortable with conscription to intervene in the debate.

His Bloomsbury friends failed to understand why Keynes remained in his post, believing that his obstinacy to do so was damaging his character.[17] Lytton Strachey wrote to him on 4 November 1915, 'Are you visible of an evening? Or are you eternally in the P.M.'s bosoms?', to which Keynes replied the following day: 'No not there, but buried immeasurably deep in work'. Probably searching for ways to justify himself to his friend, he wrote to him on 16 January 1916: 'I have sent Philip[18] one or two suggestions. I hope they are not too late, but I've been too hard-pressed until to-day to write them down . . . My country! My country! We had better charter the Mayflower before fights rise much higher'. On 20 February, Lytton wrote a short message to his friend: 'Why are you still in the Treasury?'

accompanied by an *Observer* cutting in which Edwin Montagu makes a bellicose declaration to the House in support of conscription. He put this on Maynard's place at the table during a dinner at Gordon Square with himself, Vanessa Bell, Duncan Grant and David Garnett. A lively discussion broke out opposing the two friends in which Keynes

> admitted that *part* of his reason for staying was the pleasure he got from his being able to do the work so well. He also seemed to think he was doing a great service to the country by saving some millions per week . . . He at last admitted that there was a point at which he *would* think it necessary to leave – but what that point might be he couldn't say. (Lytton to James Strachey, 22 February 1916, BL, SP, Add 60711)

In his struggle against conscription, Keynes supplied £50 to the National Council Against Conscription,[19] for which several of his Bloomsbury friends worked, but he did not join the Union for Democratic Control created by left-leaning Liberals and moderate Labourites opposed to British militarism. He later frequented the 1917 Club, a Soho meeting place for anti-war intellectuals. His involvements especially took the form of testimonies in favour of his conscientious objector friends, such as James Strachey, Duncan Grant, Bunny Garnett and Gerald Shove. He believed the prestige of his position at the Treasury helped protect them from prison. This was his response to Lytton. He wrote to Dennis Robertston on 18 July 1916 that he had spent half of his time testifying in favour of his friends' virtue and sincerity.

This is how Garnett described Keynes's attitude at court:

> Maynard took an aggressive line from the first moment. Carrying a large locked bag with the Royal cipher on it, he demanded that our cases should be heard as expeditiously as possible, as he had left work of utmost national importance to attend and he had to be back at the Treasury at the earliest possible moment. (Garnett, 1955, pp. 121–22)

Grant and Garnett only won their case in appeal and worked in a Sussex farm near Charleston, where they lived with Vanessa Bell and in which Keynes also had a room. The latter often spent weekends there during the last three years of the war, examining his dossiers from the Treasury, weeding and gardening:

> He would arrive in the evening for the weekend, driven in a hired car from Lewes, tired out, but with a bulging Treasury bag, and stay in bed till lunchtime next morning, by which time the waste-paper basket would be full of the papers he had dealt with.
> . . . One of his favourite occupations at Charleston was weeding the paths . . . This weeding was a therapeutic exercise, which gave him a spiritual renewal from the frustrations of work at the Treasury. (Garnett, 1979, p. 136)

Conscientious Objection

On 23 February 1916, Keynes received a letter from Thomas Heath, Joint Permanent Secretary to the Treasury, informing him that he was exempt from military service for six months starting on 2 March due to his work's national importance. He was nevertheless given the option of appearing before a tribunal should he wish to present other reasons for exemption, including conscientious objection. On 28 February he wrote the letter quoted at the beginning of this chapter, which was addressed to the Holborn tribunal and spelled out his conscientious objection (1916-2). It seems this letter was never sent, though he made it clear he intended to appear before the local tribunal, since he received a post card requiring his presence on 28 March at 5 o'clock. He wrote on 27 March to say that more urgent business prevented him from appearing. He received a response on 29 March stating that he was under no obligation to appear in light of his six-month Treasury exemption, which indicates that his case was discussed *in absentia*. This exemption was given an unlimited extension on 18 August.

Keynes's attitude to the war and conscription has raised a lively polemic. For his first biographer Roy Harrod, Keynes was not a pacifist and certainly not a politicized antimilitarist like his friend Bertrand Russell, who lost his post at Cambridge and was condemned to six months in prison in 1918.[20] Russell and Keynes confronted each other on this question on 8 March 1915 at a Cambridge dinner party which D.H. Lawrence also attended, Russell writing to Ottoline Morrell: 'Keynes was hard, intellectual, insincere – using intellect to hide the torment and discord of his soul' (Russell, 2001, p. 34). According to Harrod, it was to calm his Bloomsbury friends that Keynes announced to them that 'although he was not a Conscientious Objector, he would conscientiously object to compulsory service' (Harrod, 1951, p. 214). However, upon being summoned to court, he excused himself by writing that he was too busy to attend.[21]

In his memoirs, Clive Bell, who shared a house with John Sheppard, Henry Norton and Keynes during the war, wrote that the latter 'was an objector of a peculiar and, as I think, most reasonable kind. He was not a pacifist; he did not object to fighting in any circumstances; he objected to being made to fight. Good liberal that he was, he objected conscription' (C. Bell, 1956, pp. 46–7). In a review of Bell's book, Harrod maintained his position: 'I submit that there was not any sense, peculiar or other, in which Keynes was a Conscientious Objector in the First World War . . . I submit that, had Keynes not been doing work of supreme national importance and had he been physically capable of being an efficient soldier, he would have answered the call when it came to him' (Harrod, 1957, p. 696). Harrod does not deny the incident reported by Bell,[22] but explains it as 'just a little gesture of appeasement to his Bloomsbury friends, which did no one any harm' (ibid., p. 697).

Elizabeth Johnson, who, at the request of the Royal Economic Society, started to work on preparing Keynes's *Collected Writings*, discovered the letter quoted at the beginning of this chapter, which in her judgement supports Bell's view over Harrod's:

> Thus Keynes' own papers seem to show, in Bell's words, he was indeed a conscientious objector to conscription 'of a peculiar and, as I think, most reasonable kind' . . . His attitude was that of many of the most honest and sincere liberals of the day and reflects a liberal view of the rights of the individual that is almost forgotten to-day. (Johnson, 1960, p. 165)

She wrote a note on Keynes's attitude during the war, reproducing the letter, and sent it to be published in *The Economic Journal*, of which Harrod was the editor. A peculiar correspondence followed, involving, in addition to the two protagonists, Keynes's brother Geoffrey, his literary executor Richard Kahn and Austin Robinson, co-editor of *The Economic Journal*. Harrod made it known that he was not opposed to the publication of Johnson's note, so as not to be accused of a conflict of interest. However, he implicitly called on Keynes's brother not to authorize the publication of documents which the latter inherited. He emphasized that Elizabeth Johnson was commissioned by the Royal Economic Society and paid to study these documents, which suggests that she was not free to do what she wanted with them. Describing himself 'as a champion of Maynard's reputation' (14 June 1958, KP, PP/7/23), Harrod believed this publication would be 'damaging to Maynard' and would have 'given much pain to your mother' (ibid., PP/7/24). In effect, while approving the fact that he helped his friends, his mother wrote to Keynes to say that she wondered about conscientious objections when other friends were dying on the battle field (quoted by Harrod, 1951, pp. 215–16). In a commentary following Johnson's article, Harrod admitted that certain documents might have escaped him amidst the piles of Keynes's papers.[23] He also admitted that Keynes could have briefly intended to present himself at court in solidarity with his friends, but that he quickly renounced this idea when he understood that in the end it was not necessary to his friends' escape from military service. He thus maintained that Keynes was not a conscientious objector: 'And I believe that most people will hold that his earlier impulse, so generous in relation to his friends, and his suppression of it, before final action was required, in the light of the facts of logic, are *both* to his credit' (Harrod, 1960, p. 167).

One thing is certain: there was no incompatibility for Keynes between conscientious objection and the decision to fight, both decisions being a matter of private judgement. He explained this after the death of Julian Bell, son of Clive and Vanessa, during the Spanish Civil War:

> Julian Bell was entitled to make his protest with his life. His action was in no way inconsistent with the fact that in other circumstances he would probably have been a conscientious objector. On the contrary, it was deeply consistent, answering in both events to the indefeasible claims of private judgment and duty (1937-9, p. 77).

In this Keynes was in every way consistent with the ethical positions exposed in Chapter 2. He adopted the same attitude at the beginning of the war in 1914, when his friend, the Hungarian poet and Apostle Ferenc Bekassy, decided to return to his native country to fight against Russia. After having tried to dissuade him, Keynes gave him money for his travels. David Garnett reproached him for having sent a friend to his death while at the same time helping an enemy country: 'Maynard disagreed violently. He said he had used every argument to persuade Bekassy not to go – but having failed to persuade him, it was not the part of a friend to impose his views by force, or by refusing help' (Garnett, 1953, p. 270). When Garnett asked him whether he would lend a man money to buy poison for his suicide, Keynes said he would respond affirmatively 'if it was a free choice, made by a sane man after due reflection, for compelling causes' (ibid., p. 271). When he learned that his friend had been killed at Bukovine on 25 June 1915, he wrote to Duncan Grant on 24 July, relating his last meeting before Bekassy's departure:

> I very depressed and he excited and not very depressed, he said, – 'It will be a very wonderful experience for those of us who live through it.' He was certain to be killed. When one thinks of him, it is his *goodness*, I think, one seems to remember. But it's no use talking about him. I think it's better to forget these things as quickly as one possibly can'. (BL, Add. MS 57931)[24]

Garnett wrote: 'Maynard's high ideal of friendship in fact cost his friend his life' (Garnett, 1953, p. 271). Regarding young war victims, Keynes wrote to Lytton Strachey on 27 November 1914:

> For myself I am absolutely and completely desolated. It is utterly unbearable to see day by day the youths going away first to boredom and discomfort and then to slaughter. Five of this College, who are undergraduates or who have just gone down, are already killed, including, to my great grief, Freddie Hardman, as you may have seen in the paper.[25]

THE FINANCIAL CRISIS AND THE GLOBALIZATION OF THE WAR

During the year 1916, the financial situation of Britain, who covered most of her allies' expenses, increasingly deteriorated while dependence on the United States increased. On 3 October an interdepartmental committee led by Eustace Percy was set up to examine the situation. Keynes represented the Treasury. In two alarming reports (1916-6 and 1916-7), he warned against the fact that Britain would soon be at the mercy of its former colony: 'If things go on as at present, I venture to say with certainty that by next June or earlier the President of the American Republic will be in a position, if he wishes, to dictate his own terms to us' (1916-7, p. 201). He rejoiced in the fact that the Germans were not aware of the situation. Keynes again pleaded in January 1917 for maintaining the gold standard, taking into account the fact that the City was still the world's banker, a position to which New York was then aspiring (1917-2). To do otherwise would prove to Germany that its enemy was in desperate financial straits.

In January 1917, after Lloyd George replaced Asquith as Prime Minister, the Finance Division of the Treasury split into two parts. Keynes was promoted head of the new 'A' Division in charge of external finances: 'I have got a much more solid advantage in these last few days, having been properly constituted head of a new Dept, with a staff behind me, to deal with all questions of External Finance' (letter to his mother, 11 February 1917). He would have 17 people under his orders at the war's end. He acquired the status of temporary principal clerk. His bosses were Robert Chalmers, Joint Permanent Secretary of the Treasury and the Conservative Bonar Law, the new Chancellor of the Exchequer.

The United States' entry into the war on 6 April 1917 was a decisive turning point.[26] Re-elected to the presidency in November 1916 on a promise of continued American neutrality, Woodrow Wilson[27] called on the belligerents to specify their conditions of peace on 18 December, and then proposed 'peace without victory' on 22 January 1917. It was the unleashing of a submarine war by Germany that reversed the situation. Keynes was then in charge of financial relations between his country and the new belligerent. Within the context of these complex negotiations, in addition to disagreements between both countries, there were misunderstandings within each country with which Keynes would have to manage. For example, a minor war occurred between the Chancellor of the Exchequer and Lord Cunliffe, Governor of the Bank of England, who did not like Keynes and sought Bonar Law's help in having him removed. It was Cunliffe who would be forced to resign in April 1918, which had the effect of bringing Keynes and Bonar Law closer together. The period between autumn 1916 and summer 1917 saw economic and financial hegemony cross the Atlantic, much to Keynes's dismay, who would vainly attempt to reverse this movement until the end of his life. In any case he would seek in his various capacities, as he would also do during the Second World War, to reduce Britain's financial dependence on the United States. He tried for example to persuade the Americans to lend directly to France and Italy without passing through Britain, which made the latter responsible for all these engagements. He constantly repeated though that Britain could not pursue this war without the financial support of the United States, whose manifest objective was to assume a position of world leadership after the war.

On 7 September 1917, Keynes made his first journey to the United States as a member of a financial mission headed by the Lord Chief Justice, Rufus Daniel Reading. The purpose of the journey was to iron out divergences between the new Financial Secretary to the Treasury, Hardann Lever, and the American Treasury Secretary, who was also President Wilson's son-in-law, William MacAdoo, and to convince the latter of the merits of generosity towards Britain. Keynes's task was to initiate Reading into Anglo-American financial relations. He remained in the United States until 6 October. Basil Blackett, who was part of the mission, wrote to the Chancellor of the Exchequer's private secretary on 1 January 1918 that, as a negotiator, Keynes was perceived as 'rude, dogmatic and disobliging . . . he made a terrible reputation for his rudeness out here' (JMK 16, p. 264). Keynes, who did not appreciate the country, wrote to Duncan Grant on 17 October: 'The only really sympathetic and original thing in America is the niggers, who are charming' (BL, Add. MS 57931).

He also discovered that the American Congress constituted a major obstacle to any negotiated entente between the representatives and experts of both countries. He never stopped complaining about – he would do so even more during the Second World War – and decrying America's will to keep Britain down. In a passage withdrawn from a personal and secret telegram – written by Keynes and sent on 8 May 1918 – from the Chancellor of the Exchequer to Lord Reading, then ambassador in Washington, one reads:

> it almost looks as if they took a satisfaction in reducing us to a position of complete financial helplessness and dependence in which the call loan is a noose round our necks and whenever obligations of ours mature in future we shall have to submit to any conditions they may choose to impose. (JMK 16, p. 287)

Hostile to Lloyd George's government and to his push for total victory, Keynes wrote to Duncan Grant on 15 December: 'I work for a Government I despise for ends I think criminal' (BL, Add. MS 57931).[28] He nevertheless continued to participate in numerous inter-Allies conferences, notably in Paris in November. He represented the Treasury in a new organization, the Inter-Ally Council for War Purchase and for Finance, created in December and which he described to Grant in an already quoted letter as 'a newly established monkey house'.

On 8 January 1918, President Wilson enumerated, in an address to Congress, the 14 points necessary to maintain a just and durable peace in Europe and in the world. He sought to assure the regulation of territorial conflicts according to the principle of nationalities, to guarantee the absolute security of the seas and create a League of Nations. The President spelled out this contract in four speeches pronounced on 11 February, 16 April, 4 July and 24 September, promising that there would be no annexations or punitive indemnities. In August, it became clear that the wind had turned against Germany, which suffered a British counter-attack on 29 September. On 5 October, the new government of Max de Bade requested an armistice on the basis of President Wilson's 14 points. The Allies came together at Versailles between 26 October and 3 November to agree on the meaning of these 14 points. On 5 November, President Wilson sent Germany a note specifying the conditions of the armistice. On 9 November, Kaiser Wilhelm II abdicated and Germany declared itself a republic.[29] The armistice was signed on 11 November at Rethondes in a train wagon by Matthias Erzberger[30] for Germany and Marshal Foch, Allied supreme commander. It called for the opening of a conference in Paris to discuss the new postwar landscape. Keynes was then immersed in financial negotiations with the French. Seven days later, American voters gave the Republicans majorities of two seats in the Senate and 39 seats in the House of Representatives.

THE CARTHAGINIAN PEACE[31]

With reports, often exaggerated or simply fanciful, of German war crimes, British public opinion, already extremely hostile towards Germany, was furious when the December 1918 election campaign was launched. Candidates stressed the harsh punishment in store for Germany. With the massive victory of the coalition led by Lloyd George, Keynes agreed with the Treasury that his participation at the Paris Peace Conference would be his last task. He wrote to his mother on 21 November 1918: 'I have now been put in principal charge of financial matters for the Peace Conference'. He was in effect in charge of preparing the British Treasury's position on reparation payments to be imposed on Germany.

In September 1918 he participated in a conference at Oxford's Balliol College on inter-Ally economic problems. In January 1917 he signed, along with Birmingham University economic historian W.J. Ashley, a memorandum on the effects of war indemnities (1917-1). This document was made available to the War Cabinet in November 1918. Lloyd George, in *The Truth About the Peace Treaties*, published in 1938, claimed that it was on the faith of Ashley and Keynes that were based

> all the extravagant estimates formulated after the War as to Germany's capacity to pay ... The prospect of keeping the German workers of all ranks in a condition of servitude for 40 years did not dim the prophetic vision or abate the extortionate zeal of these twin economists. They shared the natural feelings of the ordinary Briton that, as Germany made the War she must pay for it to the limit of her capacity. (Lloyd George, 1938, p. 448)

These strong words resembled a settling of scores.

After reading extracts from Lloyd George's coming book in the *Daily Telegraph and Morning Post*, Keynes wrote to Warren Fisher, Permanent Secretary of the Treasury, that they constituted a complete misrepresentation of reality. He published a letter in the *Sunday Times* on 30 October 1938: 'It was indeed a bold, though scarcely a bright, idea on the part of Mr Lloyd George, in all the circumstances of which he is well aware, to attempt to present my influence as having been the opposite of what he knows it to have been' (1938-15, p. 335). In reality, Ashley and Keynes's paper is a historical survey of the question of indemnities, particularly after the Franco-Prussian War of 1870–71. The authors examine various hypotheses, transfers of goods and services or transfers of cash, immediate or spread over a long period, without taking sides. They make clear however that in order for the victors to derive the greatest benefit from indemnities, they must be paid in instalments and not all at once.

On 26 November 1918, the War Cabinet set up a Reparation Committee presided over by the Australian Prime Minister William Hughes[32] to evaluate what Germany could pay without harmful side effects for the Allies. Keynes attended three of the four Committee meetings held between 27 November and 2 December as the Treasury representative sent to answer questions. In its final report, over which Keynes had no influence, the Committee decreed that Germany was able to pay all of the Allies' war costs, estimated at £24 billion, and that annual payments of £1200 million would be possible without harmful effects on the recipients. Submitting his report to the cabinet, which would be shelved in the end, Hughes admitted that it would be impossible to obtain such a sum from Germany.

Keynes worked on preparation of his own Treasury memorandum on Germany's capacity to pay. He prepared for the Chancellor on 31 October during the Versailles discussions his 'Notes on an indemnity', in which he studied the matter. He estimated the Allies could demand an immediate indemnity of £1000 million in real estate and a tribute of £1000 million to be paid off over 30 years. Anything more would have the effect of crushing Germany's future economic life and of forcing the Allies to become lenders in order to prevent famine and anarchy (1918-1, p. 341). The Treasury's final report, 'Memorandum by the Treasury on the indemnity payable by the enemy powers for reparation and other claims' (1918-2) is entirely the work of Keynes, passages of which he reused in *The Economic Consequences of the Peace*. The memorandum fixed at £3 billion, and more reasonably at £2 billion, the maximum of what Germany could pay. It was thus out of the question to envisage an indemnity covering the total cost of the war. It was not possible to bleed Germany dry in the short term and hope for a regular tribute in the long term: 'It is not practicable both to impoverish Germany by the methods already outlined and also to extract tribute on the basis of the pre-war productive capacity' (1918-2, p. 369). Moreover, to make its annual payment, Germany would be required to generate a trade surplus at the Allies' expense: 'It is hardly possible to insist on an increased productivity of German industry if the workmen are to be underfed' (ibid., p. 373). An annual tribute from Germany cannot be expected if its economy is broken: 'If Germany is to be "milked", she must not first of all be ruined' (ibid., p. 375); 'An indemnity so large as to leave the German population without hope is liable to defeat itself' (ibid., p. 382).

The Paris Conference and the Treaty of Versailles

The Conference started sitting on 18 January 1919. Twenty-seven States participated under the presidency of Georges Clemenceau, French Prime Minister.[33] It started as a formation of 52 commissions which transmitted the results of their work to the Council of Ten, also called the Supreme Council, which united, in addition to Clemenceau, American President Wilson, British Prime Minister Lloyd George and Italian Prime Minister Orlando,[34] their Foreign Affairs ministers, and two representatives from Japan. Both the latter and the Foreign Affairs ministers were ejected on 24 March from the Supreme Council, which became the Council of Four, the true locus of negotiations and decisions at a time when both entered a crucial phase. The decision to give newly created Yugoslavia the city of Fiume in Dalmatia, the majority of whose inhabitants were Italian-speaking, in spite of promises made to Italy in 1915 led to Orlando's departure on 24 April, the Supreme Council now being reduced to three.[35] On 8 February the Supreme Economic Council was set up, which was proposed by Wilson, uniting all the organizations in charge of finances, food and raw material deliveries, transportation and other economic affairs.[36] While negotiations were planned with Germany on President Wilson's insistence, the latter was excluded from discussions. German delegates were met on 19 April and informed of the peace conditions, which were amended following their commentaries.

Keynes arrived in Paris on 10 January as chief Treasury representative of the British delegation. He attended the meetings of the Council of Ten on at least four occasions. He also became the British representative on the Supreme Economic Council. His first job was to try to obtain supplementary financial aid from the United States, when American war loans were constitutional only during times of war. His counterpart was Norman Davis, Assistant Secretary of the American Treasury, whose secretary was Carter Glass. He was confident about obtaining his goals, as he wrote to John Bradbury, Joint Permanent Secretary of the Treasury on 14 January: 'The last thing therefore that they want to do is to quarrel with us prematurely over money' (JMK 16, p. 388). His hopes were grounded since Davis convinced Glass to accord Britain a supplementary loan.

On 12 January, the Supreme Council of Supply and Relief, formerly known as the Supreme Economic Council, decided to supply Germany with food on the condition that it hand over its ships as spelled out in the Treaty of Versailles. In discussions over how to pay for the supply shipments, French Finance Minister Louis-Lucien Klotz showed himself intransigent. In the context of negotiations between Foch and Erzberger for the second renewal of the armistice, Keynes travelled to Trier in Germany as chairman of the financial delegation. He discussed the question with the German delegates. It was particularly a matter of evaluating the security of German reserves in the context of agitation led by the left-wing Marxist movement, the Spartacist League, which would become the German Communist Party. Launched in January 1919, the Spartacist insurrection was suppressed by the Social Democrat Defence Minister Gustav Noske, and the founders of the League, Rosa Luxemburg and Karl Liebknecht, who were not favourable to the insurrection, were assassinated.[37] Spartacists succeeded in taking possession of a note-printing plant for two days. There would be other communist uprisings in Westphalia and in the Ruhr, after an attempted *coup d'état* from the far right, the Kapp Putsch, in March 1920.

Among the German delegates was found

> a very small man exquisitely clean, very well and neatly dressed, . . . his eyes gleaming straight at us, with extraordinary sorrow in them, yet like an honest animal at bay. This was he with whom in the ensuing months I was to have one of the most curious intimacies in the world, and some very strange passages of experience (1921-4, p. 395).

This man was Carl Melchior, a lawyer and banker. Keynes and Melchior immediately got on well and obtained from their respective delegations the permission to engage in one-on-one talks aimed at resolving the situation: 'He and I were, I think, the very first two civilians from the opposed camps to meet after the War in peaceful and honourable intercourse' (1932-3, p. 47). Keynes would relate these events in one of his most appealing writings, 'Dr Melchior: a defeated enemy', quoted here before the paragraph, read before the Bloomsbury Memoir Club in February 1921 and published on his request after his death in 1949 with 'My early beliefs'. Melchior and Keynes remained in contact until the former's death in 1933.[38] Throughout these discussions, Melchior and his colleagues tried to convince the Allies not to require payments in gold, which would have a disastrous effect on Germany's financial situation, while recognizing that 'they were therefore in our hands as regards the means of payments' (1919-2, p. 398): 'The general demeanour of the German representatives was strikingly conciliatory and even submissive . . . Dr Melchior himself showed great ability in the conduct of the proceedings' (ibid., p. 402). It would take three more meetings, at Trier, Spa and Bruxelles, to finally authorize deliveries of food to Germany on 14 March, when famine threatened the country. It was at Spa that Keynes and Melchior obtained authorization to discuss one-on-one. A meeting between them and another British delegate made possible the final settlement. Keynes would maintain these contacts, not only with Melchior, but also with the other German delegates. He would be largely responsible for the success of negotiations aimed at providing aid to Austria then threatened by famine.

Another complicated debate in which Keynes would play a central role concerned a request for financial assistance on the part of France, following the United States' refusal to help that country. Keynes also showed himself reticent to offer any major aid, intended essen-

tially to prop up the franc, which would have had damaging effects on Britain's already difficult financial situation. In a book published after the war, Klotz (1924) blamed Keynes for
the fall of the franc. The latter gave his version of events in an article published in *The Times*
on 27 February 1924. He explained that Britain had to borrow from the United States what it
lent to France: 'If we had given France everything she asked for we should have been bankrupted and perhaps have lost the war before ever the United States came in' (1924-6, p. 409).
In response to this article, on 11 March, Klotz spoke of Keynes's

> swollen vanity . . . hypertrophy of self which is akin to megalomania . . . It is Mr Keynes whom I
> accused and whom I continue to accuse. I said, and I repeat . . . that Mr Keynes committed towards
> France an *acte atroce* on 19 February 1919, when he assured the triumph of his monetary megalo-
> mania which remains the true cause of the financial catastrophe which has fallen on the whole
> world'. (quoted in JMK 16, pp. 413–14)[39]

It was in fact the Bank of France's refusal to sell gold in return for credit that unleashed the
currency crisis that would only be reabsorbed seven years later.

On 24 February 1919, Austen Chamberlain, Chancellor of the Exchequer, wrote to the
president of the Supreme Economic Council to notify it of the fact that Keynes would represent him 'on the same footing as I should be if I were present, namely, that of a full member
with full rights of speech and decision' (quoted in JMK 16, p. 415). What was more, Keynes
was one of two British Empire members on the conference's financial committee. His responsibilities were numerous. Requesting reinforcements from the Treasury in Paris, he wrote to
Bradbury on his return on 17 February: 'There is no diminution in the amount of work which
still keeps us employed from breakfast to midnight' (ibid., p. 405). He was then aged 35. He
was both exhausted and excited by his work and his involvement in high spheres of power.
He wrote to his mother on 16 March:

> I am Deputy for the Chancellor of the Exchequer on the Supreme Economic Council with full
> powers to take decisions; also one of the British Empire representatives on the Financial Comm. of
> the Peace Conference; chairman of the Inter-Allied Financial Delegates in Armistice Negotiations
> with Germany; and principal Treasury Representative in Paris.

He wrote to his father on 30 March:

> I still live a whistling life; no more journeys lately, but a steady twelve hours' work a day. For the
> last ten days I've had the novel experience of working intimately with the P.M., and have even seen
> a fair amount of Wilson and Clemenceau. The fact is that Ll. G. [Lloyd George] has, at least for the
> time being, taken a move towards a heaven peace and away from a hell peace, so that my services
> are not quite as inappropriate to this as usual. It has all been very exhausting and very exciting, but
> my digestion remains unimpaired.

Keynes worked at this time on calculating indemnities and wrote a document supporting
a proposition that would see all inter-Ally debt cancelled: 'a proposal for an entire cancellation of inter-ally indebtedness is put forward as being likely to promote the well-being of this
country and the world' (1919-3, p. 421). From as early as 1916 he had advanced the idea of
cancelling these debts. Maintaining and aggravating the debt pyramid created by the war
constituted a threat to the survival of capitalism:

Even capitalism at home, which engages many local sympathies, which plays a real part in the daily process of production, and upon the security of which the present organisation of society largely depends, is not very safe. But, however this may be, will the discontented peoples of Europe be willing for a generation to come so to order their lives that an appreciable part of their daily produce may be available to meet a foreign payment, the reason of which, whether as between Europe and America, or as between Germany and the rest of Europe, does not spring compellingly from their sense of justice or duty? (1919-3, p. 427)

Since the Americans refused the idea of debt cancellation, Keynes elaborated what he called the 'grand scheme for the rehabilitation of Europe' (letter to his mother, 17 April 1919). This project was elaborated after a conversation with Jan Smuts,[40] who described to him the catastrophic condition of the inhabitants of Hungary, which he recently visited. It allowed stricken countries, whose credit was temporarily destroyed, to re-equip themselves and restart their economy on the basis of credits guaranteed by the United States and the richest countries, under the auspice of the League of Nations. It obtained the support of the Chancellor of the Exchequer, who promoted it to the Prime Minister. In a draft of a letter from the Prime Minister to be sent to other heads of State, Keynes wrote: 'In short, the economic mechanism of Europe is jammed . . . The capital has vanished; the complicated machinery of internal and external production is more or less smashed; production has to a great extent ceased' (1919-4, p. 433). And it was not private enterprise that was in the position to avoid catastrophe and preserve the world from the dangers of Bolshevism: 'Nevertheless, in the financial sphere, the problem of restoring Europe is almost certainly too great for private enterprise alone . . . The more prostrate a country is and the nearer to Bolshevism, the more presumably it requires assistance. But the less likely is private enterprise to give it' (ibid., p. 434).

Keynes tried unsuccessfully to convince his American counterparts of the value of his plan, which was based on US credit to restart Europe's economies. The United States was only prepared to give financial aid to new States created after the war and no others. He wrote to the Chancellor on 4 May: 'The whole situation is disappointing and depressing' (JMK 16, p. 440). In a letter dated from 3 May, President Wilson indicated to Prime Minister Lloyd George that Congress would not allow the American Treasury to guarantee European bonds and that the desire to supply Germany with new capital while its present capital was being claimed by the victors was poorly understood. A new committee was set up on 9 May on Wilson's suggestion to find solutions to Europe's problems. Keynes was one of its two British members. This committee amounted to nothing: 'The Americans do not really intend to do anything; and even apart from that no concrete proposal capable of being put into force can come into existence in the unreal atmosphere of Paris' (letter to Sir John Bradbury, 22 May 1919, in JMK 16, p. 447). In the end Keynes would publish his plan as the last chapter of *The Economic Consequences of the Peace*.

At the same time, discussions were underway on reparations and Germany's capacity to pay, initiated within the context of a Commission on Reparations of Damages which had started meeting in mid-January 1919.[41] Lloyd George asked Keynes to prepare a new document to counter an extravagant proposition introduced by Hughes, Cunliffe and Summer, the three most conservative British delegates, calling for payments of £600 million per year until 1961. On 18 March, he proposed to a meeting of heads of State, in which Keynes was present, that the world's experts meet to evaluate Germany's capacity for payment.

From April to June, Keynes was often present at the Council of Four discussions, which were held in residences occupied by Wilson and Lloyd George in Paris, sometimes in the rooms of the French War and Foreign Affairs Ministries.[42] He was increasingly pessimistic of the chances of a reasonable and acceptable settlement. He explained this to the Chancellor on 4 May: 'I cannot however for one moment believe that the reparation chapter as it now stands can possibly persist as a solution of the problem showing indeed as it does a high degree of unwisdom in almost every direction' (JMK 16, pp. 452–3); 'Indeed I and most of us here are exceedingly pessimistic. The conference has led us into a bog which it will take more statesmanship to lead us out of than it has taken adroitness to lead us in' (ibid., p. 456).

On 7 May the Allies presented a treaty project to the Germans, giving them 15 days to consider their reaction. Its core is article 231,[43] which reads:

> The Allied and Associated governments affirm and Germany accepts the responsibility of Germany and her allies for causing all the loss and damage to which the Allied and Associated governments and their nationals have been subjected as a consequence of the war imposed upon them by the aggression of Germany and her allies.

Following logically, article 232 stipulates that:

> The Allied and Associated governments, however, require, and Germany undertakes, that she will make compensation for all damage done to the civilian population of the Allied and Associated Powers and to their property during the period of the belligerency of each as an Allied or Associated power against Germany.

Among these damages, the treaty's drafters included allocations paid to soldiers' families and pensions paid or to be paid following illness or death, which tripled the bill. The treaty did not fix the precise amount of Germany's total debt, providing only for a first payment on 1 May 1921. It left this to the Committee on Reparations responsible for administering this part of the treaty, which also allowed for the reordering of European borders and the founding of the League of Nations. The Committee was to manage, among other tasks, the handing over of most of Germany's merchant navy, all its overseas possessions, and goods possessed by Germans in Alsace-Lorraine. The treaty also provided for the Allies' appropriation of an important part of Germany's iron and coal resources, the basis of the country's industrialization. In the area of transportation, Germany had to give up part of its rolling stock and lost control of a good part of its river network, henceforth to be managed by foreign organizations.

Keynes was astonished and scandalized by this text which, according to him, violated the intentions of Wilson's 14 points and the conditions of armistice signed with Germany, in addition to being totally inapplicable without starving the German people. On 14 May, he announced to his mother and Duncan Grant his decision to resign from the Treasury, in two letters containing identical passages, such as: 'the Peace is outrageous and impossible and can bring nothing but misfortune . . . Certainly if I was in the Germans' place I'd rather die than sign such a peace' (JMK 16, p. 458). To his mother he wrote: 'Well, I suppose I've been an accomplice in all this wickedness and folly, but the end is now at hand' (ibid.). To Duncan Grant, he added:

> I sit in my room hour after hour receiving deputations from the new nations, who all ask not for food or new materials, but primarily for instruments of murder against their neighbours. And with such a Peace as the basis I see no hope anywhere.

Anarchy and Revolution is the best thing that can happen, and the sooner the better. Thank God
I shall soon be out of it and I suppose it wouldn't be many weeks before I've forgotten this night-
mare. I'm writing to the Treasury to be relieved of my duties by June 1 if possible and not later than
June 15 in any event.

One most bitter disappointment was the collapse of my Grand Scheme for putting everyone on
their legs. (BL, Add MS 57931)

He wrote to Sheppard on 18 May: 'This is hell. But they won't sign, I think, which is some
consolation. The full text of the Treaty is much worse even than what they have predicted'
(Sheppard Papers, King's College, Cambridge, JTS/2/112). The day before, he wrote to
William MacAulay, vice-provost of King's College, that he was preparing to resign unless
there was a major turn-around in the negotiations with Germany. He described himself as
exhausted, depressed and disgusted by the unjust and senseless propositions being made to
Germany. His letter of resignation has disappeared, though it appears to have been dated from
19 May. In a letter from 21 May, Chancellor Chamberlain insisted that Keynes, whose presence was indispensable to him, remain in his post for the time being. Keynes answered him
on 26 May saying that he could stay two or three weeks more on the express condition that
the perspective of radical changes to the agreement be in store, which he believed highly
unlikely:

I cannot express how strongly I feel as to the gravity of what is in front of us, and I must have my
hands quite free . . . The Prime Minister is leading us all into a morass of destruction. The settlement
which he is proposing for Europe disrupts it economically and must depopulate it by millions of
persons'. (JMK 16, p. 460)

The following day he wrote to John Bradbury: 'At any rate I am so sick at what goes on that
I am near breaking point; and you must be prepared for my resignation by telegram at any
moment' (ibid., p. 464). The last straw was a clause of the treaty with Austria which forced
the latter to give up a certain number of its dairy cows, this in a country with the highest infant
mortality in Europe: 'this seems to me to be [a] cruel and unwise demand' (letter to Philip
Kerr, JMK 16, p. 466). He wrote to his mother that though a nervous collapse had kept him
in bed since 30 May, 'I dragged myself out of bed on Friday to make a final protest before
the Reparation Commission against murdering Vienna and did achieve some improvement'
(ibid., p. 470). At his request, Keynes submitted to Lloyd George on 2 June a last memorandum on alternative ways of paying reparations (1919-5). Finally, on 5 June, he wrote to him:

I ought to let you know that on Saturday I am slipping away from this scene of nightmare. I can do
no more good here. I've gone on hoping even through these last dreadful weeks that you'd find some
way to make of the treaty a just and expedient document. But now it's apparently too late. The battle
is lost. I leave the twins to gloat over the devastation of Europe and to assess to taste what remains
for the British taxpayer. (JMK 16, p. 469)[44]

Repeating the same to his American counterpart Norman Davis, he added on the same day:
'You Americans are broken reeds, and I have no anticipation of any real improvement in the
state of affairs' (JMK 16, p. 471). He nevertheless proposed to him a last meeting to discuss
financial affairs. He announced his resignation to Bradbury on 6 June in similar terms. He
was now free to express himself as he liked and to assume with restraint his role as 'publicist'. On 7 June he left Paris and went directly to King's College to start his new career.

The Germans reacted on 29 May to the proposed treaty. Another proposition, containing few modifications in regards to that of 7 May, was presented on 16 June with a response delay of seven days. After a new German response, the treaty was signed at Versailles on 28 June. The diplomat Harold Nicolson, who was present at the Peace conference and shared Keynes's bitterness, wrote a colourful account of the Versailles ceremony in his diary, concluding: 'Celebrations in the hotel afterwards. We are given free champagne at the expense of the tax-payers. It is very bad champagne ... To bed, sick of life' (Nicolson, 1933, p. 371).[45]

The Economic Consequences of the Peace

After his return home, Keynes wrote to his mother on 25 June 1919:

> ... on Monday I began to write a new book, though I am not yet quite certain if I shall persevere with it. It's a general essay or pamphlet on the economic condition of Europe as it now is, including a violent attack on the Peace Treaty and my proposals to the future. I have an idea of bringing it out simultaneously in English, French, German and Italian not later than the beginning of October. But it will be a great labour and I am still rather dubious about the project. I was stirred into it by the deep and violent shame which one couldn't help feeling for the events of Monday, and my temper may not keep up high enough to carry it through.

He was encouraged in this undertaking by, among others, Margot Asquith,[46] Smuts and Robert Cecil. It was at Charleston, where he arrived on 12 June, that he wrote most of *The Economic Consequences of the Peace* in just over three months. Virginia Woolf thus described his state of mind:

> He is disillusioned, he says. No more does he believe, that is, in the stability of the things he likes ... These conclusions were forced on him by the dismal and degrading spectacle of the Peace Congress, where men played shamelessly, not for Europe, or even England, but for their own return to Parliament at the next election. (V. Woolf 1977–84, vol. 1, p. 288)

This book borrows from several genres: history, economic analysis, statistical description, political commentary and psychological portrait. Its most famous part is Chapter 3, which recounts the Paris Conference. Revisiting ideas expressed in the youthful writings presented in the preceding chapter, he defends argument according to which the mess of this conference was the result of moral and psychological failings of the Statesmen who designed it:

> let the reader excuse me when he remembers how greatly, if it is to understand its destiny, the world needs light, even if it is partial and uncertain, on the complex struggle of human will and purpose, not yet finished, which, concentrated in the persons of four individuals in a manner never paralleled, made them in the first months of 1919 the microcosm of mankind. (1919-1, p. 17)

Resembling 'a nonconformist minister, perhaps a Presbyterian' (ibid., p. 26), Wilson did not possess the intellectual qualities necessary to resist the manipulations of Lloyd George and especially of Clemenceau, whose will to avenge the defeat of 1871 and destroy Germany won out in the end: 'the collapse of the President has been one of the decisive moral events of history' (ibid., p. 23):

The President was not a hero or a prophet; he was not even a philosopher; but a generously inten-
tioned man, with many of the weaknesses of other human beings, and lacking that dominating intellectual equipment which would have been necessary to cope with the subtle and dangerous
spellbinders whom a tremendous clash of forces and personalities had brought to the top as
triumphant masters in the swift game of give and take, face to face in council – a game of which he
had no experience at all. (1919-1, pp. 24–5)

Keynes explained this failure by giving a psychological portrait of the President and by
even evoking a Freudian complex.[47] He also painted the portrait of one of the two sorcerers
confronted by Wilson, Clemenceau, 'by far the most eminent member of the Council of Four'
(ibid., p. 18). Clemenceau 'felt about France what Pericles felt of Athens – unique value in
her, nothing else mattering; but his theory of politics was Bismarck's. He had one illusion –
France; and one disillusion – mankind, including Frenchmen' (ibid., p. 20). On Asquith's
advice, which is entirely to his credit, Keynes renounced including a description of Lloyd
George as a femme fatale out to seduce Wilson while leaving Clemenceau free to realize his
plans. He finally published it in 1933 in *Essays in Biography*:

The President, the Tiger, and the Welsh witch were shut up in a room together for six months and
the Treaty was what came out. Yes, the Welsh *witch* – for the British Prime Minister contributed the
female element to this triangular intrigue. I have called Mr Wilson a non-conformist clergyman. Let
the reader figure Mr Lloyd George as a *femme fatale*. An old man of the world, a *femme fatale*, and
a non-conformist clergyman – these are the characters of our drama . . . Clemenceau was much too
cynical, much too experienced, and much too well educated to be taken in, at his age, by the fasci-
nations of the lady from Wales . . . The President's very masculine characteristics fell a complete
victim to the feminine enticements, sharpness, quickness, sympathy of the Prime Minister. (1933-4,
pp. 22–25)

For Keynes, the catastrophic nature of the Treaty of Versailles was aggravated by the fact
that the economic organization of pre-war Europe was 'intensely unusual, unstable, complicated, unreliable, temporary' (1919-1, p. 1). This organization now risked being totally
destroyed by the outrageous decisions of the victors. It had been based in particular on a
collective psychology valorizing the accumulation of capital and savings, which allowed it to
justify wealth inequality. With what Keynes would later call 'the end of laissez-faire', these
beliefs risked becoming outdated: 'The war has disclosed the possibility of consumption to
all and the vanity of abstinence to many. Thus the bluff is discovered' (ibid., p. 13). To this
psychological instability was added the demographic instability produced by strong population pressure in relation to means of existence in Central Europe and in Russia, a major factor
of war and revolution. The sources of food imports and raw materials on which Europe
depended for its survival were also unstable. It was in this context, simmering for half a
century, that war broke out leaving much of the continent bloodless and in urgent need of
transfusion.

What mattered coming out of this disaster was the awareness that 'the perils of the future
lay not in frontiers or sovereignties but in food, coal, and transport' (ibid., p. 92). Now, in
lieu of providing for the economic reconstruction of Europe, the victors' representatives in
Paris chose to settle political accounts and to avenge the victims in order to comfort political opinions at home: 'Their preoccupations, good and bad alike, related to frontiers and
nationalities, to the balance of power, to imperial aggrandisements, to the future enfeeble-
ment of a strong and dangerous enemy, to revenge, and to the shifting by the victors of their

unbearable financial burdens on to the shoulders of the defeated' (ibid., p. 35). By doing this they betrayed the contract signed with Germany on 11 November 1918: 'There are few episodes in history which posterity will have less reason to condone – a war ostensibly waged in defence of the sanctity of international engagements ending in a definite breach of one of the most sacred possible of such engagements on the part of the victorious champions of these ideals' (ibid., p. 91). The biggest part of Keynes's book consists in showing 'the spirit of completeness in which the victorious powers entered upon the economic subjection of their defeated enemy' (ibid., pp. 49–50). He provides a detailed analysis of the economic clauses of the treaty and of their catastrophic consequences for the German economy. He shows how it came about, under pressure from public opinion, that Germany was required to pay the total cost of the war, to which was scandalously added allocation payments and pensions to soldiers' families, tripling the amount of reparations already impossible to pay: 'It is, in my judgment, as certain as anything can be, for reasons which I will elaborate in a moment, that Germany cannot pay anything approaching this sum' (ibid., p. 105). The scope of damage suffered by the Allies was grossly exaggerated. As for the decision not to fix the amount of Germany's total debt, leaving this up to a Committee on Reparations whose 'powers . . . can be employed to destroy Germany's commercial and economic organisation as well as to exact payment' (ibid., p. 49), this had the effect of plunging the Allies as well as Germany into uncertainty. This is a central theme in Keynes's economic analysis, as we will see. The fundamental question though is not a matter of economic calculation nor of political order. It is in essence moral:

> The policy of reducing Germany to servitude for a generation, of degrading the lives of millions of human beings, and of depriving a whole nation of happiness should be abhorrent and detestable – abhorrent and detestable, even if it were possible, even if it enriched ourselves, even if it did not sow the decay of the whole civilised life of Europe. Some preach it in the name of justice. In the great events of man's history, in the unwinding of the complex fates of nations, justice is not so simple. And if it were, nations are not authorised, by religions or by natural morals, to visit on the children of their enemies the misdoings of parents or of rulers. (1919-1, p. 142)

The Europe of 1919 was thus in very bad shape, threatened by social explosion, as Keynes described in the penultimate chapter of his book: 'The treaty includes no provisions for the economic rehabilitation of Europe' (ibid., p. 143); 'An inefficient, unemployed, disorganised Europe faces us, torn by internal strife and international hate, fighting, starving, pillaging, and lying' (ibid., p. 157). Some European countries were already threatened by famine. Men do not always die calmly: 'And these in their distress may overturn the remnants of organisation, and submerge civilisation itself in their attempts to satisfy desperately the overwhelming needs of the individual' (ibid., p. 144). The nullification of several centuries of progress was at stake:

> If we aim deliberately at the impoverishment of Central Europe, vengeance, I dare predict, will not limp. Nothing can then delay for very long that final civil war between the forces of reaction and the despairing convulsions of revolution, before which the horrors of the late German war will fade into nothing, and which will destroy, whoever its victor, the civilisation and the progress of our generation. (1919-1, p. 170)

Keynes devoted the last chapter to proposing remedies to this seemingly desperate situation. They were taken in large part from reports prepared when he was at the Treasury, which brought him reproach by those of high office. His proposition to cancel all debt between Allies and to allocate American funds to help Europe's reconstruction also brought him reproach. He also proposed a drastic revision of the clauses of the Versailles Treaty in which Germany's obligations would be reduced considerably and in such a way as to 'make possible the renewal of hope and enterprise within her territory' (ibid., p. 168). He believed Germany and the countries of Central Europe must be allowed to re-establish normal commercial relations with Russia, Germany returning in this way to its role as a stabilizing power in this highly volatile region. A free trade union should be formed under the auspices of the League of Nations, into which the vanquished countries were to be admitted.

The Economic Consequences of the Peace was published on 12 December 1919. After a slow start the book became an extraordinary success throughout the world. Six months after its publication, sales in England and the United States exceeded 100 000 copies and it had already been translated into a dozen languages. Keynes decided, as he would do henceforth for all his books, to pay for the printing, distribution and publicity costs himself, keeping all the profits for himself and paying rights equivalent to 10 per cent of his profits to his publisher Macmillan. This brought him a lot of money. It also allowed him to send a large number of copies to whom he liked, in particular to political and union leaders, to journalists and entrepreneurs.

This was, along with the *General Theory of Employment, Interest and Money*, Keynes's most influential book. It made him an internationally famous personality. It reconciled him with Bloomsbury. This is what Lytton Strachey wrote to him on 16 December:

> Your book arrived yesterday, and I swallowed it up at a gulp. I think it is most successful. In the first place, extremely impressive; there is an air of authority about it which I think nobody could ignore. I was rather afraid at Charleston that it might appear too extreme, but I don't think this is at all the case. The slight softenings in the Clemenceau & Wilson bits seem to me a distinct improvement, adding to the effect, rather than otherwise. Then the mass of information is delightful . . . As to the argument it is certainly most crushing, most terrible . . . To my mind the ideal thing would be to abolish reparation altogether – but of course that is not practical politics.

He was also the target of several criticisms. Some political leaders reproached him for having used confidential information. It was thought that his book would harm relations between Britain and the United States. But the most virulent critics came from France, Keynes being accused of francophobia and germanophilia.[48] Surely enough, the book was very well received in Germany and Austria. Friedrich Hayek, who would become one of the most ferocious critics of Keynes's economic ideas, wrote that Keynes was at that time, for him and his friends, a hero. He was also accused of contributing to the American Senate's refusal to unconditionally ratify the treaty, but this charge is hardly warranted, since the vote took place on 19 November 1919.[49] It was while campaigning for this vote that President Wilson collapsed on 26 September, before suffering a serious heart attack on 2 October from which he never completely recovered and which made it unlikely that he ever read the portrait that Keynes painted of him. Regarding this, Keynes wrote to Norman Davis on 18 April 1920:

> I am sorry that you dislike so much what I had to say about the President. I wrote it last July before his illness. If I had been writing after his breakdown, I should have spoken more gently of a pitiful and tragic figure, for whom I feel a genuine sympathy and who in spite of everything was the one member of the Four who was *trying* to do right. (JMK 17, p. 41)

In this letter, he indicated that his ideas were now too far removed from those of the politicians to allow him to collaborate with them. He also described himself as convinced that, even if governments do not bring it to an end, the treaty would not survive what was to come.

A few months after the publication of Keynes's book, the French historian Jacques Bainville, a monarchist and companion in arms to Charles Maurras of the Action Française, published in echo the *Conséquences Politiques de la Paix*. Bainville believed it was on the political rather than economic level that the Versailles Treaty was most damaging, since it preserved the unity of a country that would inevitably reinforce itself and sooner or later turn against its hereditary enemy, France. For Bainville, 'Keynes's resounding work is a seemingly scientific pamphlet having become successful as an object of curiosity and scandal due to the paradoxes with which it is filled' (Bainville, 1920 [2002], p. 292, translated by N.B. Mann). Even though it removed, as Keynes showed, Germany's economic power, the treaty left Germany intact as a political entity, supported by a population of 60 million inhabitants. Bainville nevertheless arrived at conclusions similar to those of Keynes, when he evokes for example 'the natural desire of the vanquished to destroy a treaty that would oblige it to work for 30 or 50 years in order to relieve itself of its debt' (ibid., pp. 357–58, translated by N.B. Mann).

Etienne Mantoux was the harshest critic of the book written by Keynes, for whom he had the greatest respect as an economist. *The Carthaginian Peace or The Economic Consequences of Mr Keynes* appeared in 1946, the year of Keynes's death, and one year after the death of its author, who died on the battlefield. Etienne Mantoux was the son of historian Paul Mantoux, who had participated as an interpreter in the Council of Four. Without returning to his father's allegations concerning Keynes's absence at these meetings, he believed that his book, filled with provocative and unfounded allegations, had a pernicious influence on the events that followed, creating a guilt complex within Allies who had not kept their word. Germany was thus in a position to engage in a policy of territorial expansion facilitated by Keynes's opinion according to which borders and sovereignties had no importance. For Mantoux, 'Reparations were not outside the range of economic *possibility*' (Mantoux, 1946, p. 156), and the rapid economic growth of Germany in the 1920s belied Keynes's catastrophic predictions.[50]

In 1923, Keynes belonged to a group of 30 people under consideration as recipients of the Nobel Peace Prize. Wilhelm Kreilhau, member of the Norwegian Parliament's Nobel committee, wrote to him on 24 October 1923 requesting precise details on his participation in the Paris Conference. Troubled by Paul Mantoux's affirmations, Kreilhau wrote as well to Maurice Hankey, secretary of the Council. Hankey confirmed Keynes's statements and Mantoux amended his first declarations. Kreilhau wrote to Keynes on 28 December 1923 saying that 'had those statesmen acted on his [of Keynes, GD] advice, there is every possible reason to believe that we now should have seen happier days and been able to work under the benefits of a real peace' (quoted in JMK 17, p. 109). In the end, no one received the Nobel Prize for that year.

The End of Reparations

The Treaty of Versailles, ratified on 10 January 1920, was followed by four treaties with the other defeated powers: Saint-Germain-en-Laye with Austria on 10 September 1919, Neuilly with Bulgaria on 27 November 1919, Trianon with Hungry on 4 June 1920 and Sèvres with

Turkey on 10 August 1920. The latter, which was never applied, was replaced by the Treaty of Lausanne in 1923. The Allies' Supreme Council was maintained to discuss these treaties.

The question of reparations did not end with the Treaty of Versailles. It was the subject of twenty or so conferences and multiple meetings of experts and politicians until the beginning of the 1930s, poisoning relations as much between victors as between victors and vanquished.[51] Its development confirmed Keynes's apprehensions. On the occasion of a financial conference in Amsterdam in October 1919, Keynes returned in force with his proposition of debt cancellation and of an international loan to restart the European economy. The United States dismissed this project, accepted by several influential personalities, at the beginning of 1920. In March 1920, France decided unilaterally to occupy Frankfurt and Darmstadt. At the Spa Conference in July 1920, Lloyd George proposed fixing an indemnity equivalent to that proposed by Keynes, namely of £2 billion. On 7 March 1921, at the end of the first London Conference, Lloyd George presented an ultimatum to Germany in the name of the Allies, which was followed by the occupation of three German cities: Duisburg, Ruhrort and Düsseldorf. On 27 April 1921, to everyone's surprise, the Committee on Reparations fixed Germany's total debt at 132 billion gold marks; this after Keynes's proposed figure of 137 billion was met with shock. In May the second London Conference determined a payment calendar of 30 years. A new ultimatum, to which Germany yielded, contained the threat of occupying the Ruhr, the country's most important coal basin.

Keynes, in spite of his numerous other activities, never stopped following these events closely and intervening publicly and privately.[52] His publisher requested a revised version of *The Economic Consequences*, which in the end was published in January 1922 as a new book entitled *A Revision of the Treaty*, in which Keynes wrote: 'I have nothing very new to say on the fundamental issues' (1922-1, p. xv) while admitting that Europe had survived the shocks the treaty risked provoking thanks to its victims' stoicism and revisions imposed by facts. The change in tone between both books, he wrote in an article responding to a critic, came from the fact that, though he held the minority view in 1919, since then 'almost everyone had come round, broadly speaking, to my view' (1922-13, p. 300). The book contains a discussion of what he called external opinion and internal opinion, that of politicians that must sacrifice truth to public interest. Convinced the discussions of the second London Conference, even if they were more moderate, could not be respected, he denounced sanction against Germany as 'acts, that is, of arbitrary lawlessness based on the mere possession of superior force' (1922-1, p. 26):

> It is not usual in civilised countries to use force to compel wrongdoers to confess, even when we are convinced of their guilt; it is still more barbarous to use force, after the fashion of inquisitors, to compel adherence to an article of belief because we ourselves believe it. Yet towards Germany the Allies had appeared to adopt this base and injurious practice, and had enforced on this people at the point of the bayonet the final humiliation of reciting, through the mouths of their representatives, what they believed to be untrue. (1922-1, p. 27)

An international conference including Germany and Russia was convened in Genoa from 10 April to 19 May 1922 to discuss restarting the European economy. French obstinacy in getting the debts of tsarism recognized provoked the first German–Soviet *rapprochement* in Rapallo, both countries deciding to cancel their debts on 16 April without notifying the other conference participants. Germany underwent hyperinflation from the middle of the year. Keynes and other experts were invited in November to propose a stabilization plan. He presented to the new Conservative Prime Minister Bonar Law in December a project of settling reparations and debts in preparation for a conference to be held in Paris in January (1922-34). Germany being incapable of respecting its scheduled payments, France and Belgium put into practice their threat of occupying the Ruhr on 11 January 1923, an occupation to which the Germans passively resisted, but which also gave rise to violent blows between French and Belgian soldiers and German workers. On several occasions, Keynes vigorously denounced the illegal character of the French occupation. In November 1922, Wilhelm Cuno, whom Keynes had met as an expert at the Paris conference, succeeded Karl Joseph Wirth as Chancellor, a post he would only occupy until August 1923. There followed a peculiar story in which Carl Melchior, with whom Keynes was constantly in contact, played an important role. It was in effect Keynes who suggested both content and tone of the German Chancellor's response to Germany's invitation by the British Minister of Foreign Affairs to submit its own settlement proposal (1923-13).

In October 1923 the German government formally declared bankruptcy and the cessation of all payments. Meeting after meeting was called to examine Germany's financial situation, resulting in the Dawes Plan published in April and adopted in London on 30 August 1924. The Dawes Plan spread out German debt and allowed for a resumption of payments in 1925. Like the London Plan, Keynes believed that 'it will itself furnish the demonstration of its own impractibility' (1924-26, p. 259). For him, the Dawes Plan was a way of stalling for time and stopping the occupation of the Ruhr. It mentioned no sum for the final settlement. A new committee, presided over by the American industrialist Owen D. Young, was set up in September 1928 and started meeting in Paris in February 1929. Keynes believed this committee to have been convened too early. The Young Plan, discussed at the Hague in August 1929 and January 1930, fixed new modes of payment until 1988. The payments were interrupted by the Crash of 1929, which hit Germany hard.

On 21 June 1931, the American President Herbert Hoover proposed a year-long moratorium on reparations payments and inter-Allies debts. On 9 January 1932, Chancellor Brüning announced that Germany would be unable to resume payment after the expiration of Hoover's moratorium. In June and July 1932, the Lausanne Conference, convened in the absence of the United States, decided on new modes of reduced payments, but payments would never be resumed. It is estimated that Germany finally reimbursed about 15 per cent of the amount fixed by the Committee on Reparations in 1921. Keynes wrote to Labour Prime Minister Ramsay MacDonald on 12 July 1932:

> It is a long time since June 1919 when I resigned from the British delegation in Paris in an enraged and tormented state of mind. The waste over the intervening years has been prodigious. But it is a comfortable feeling that at last it is cleaned up. For whatever America may do, this is necessarily the end so far as Germany is concerned. (JMK 18, p. 379)

To this MacDonald responded: 'You have indeed been vindicated again and again for what you did in June 1919' (ibid., p. 380). Despite demands from France and Britain, the United States continued to require payment for its war credences, in spite of the end of reparations. Finally in 1933, after a symbolic payment made by Britain and at the time of Roosevelt's rise to power, debts were extinguished. On 30 January 1933, Adolph Hitler became Chancellor of Germany. During his rise to power, he never stopped affirming that the Versailles diktat was responsible for all of Germany's woes. The remilitarization of the Rhineland, finally evacuated by French troops in 1930, was his first major provocation gesture. The table was set for a new act of war. Keynes's activities during the Second World War will be studied in Chapter 8.

Keynes's economic vision, to which we will now turn, was already partly present in his critique of the Versailles Treaty. Whether it was a question of war or economic crisis, the solution must not come from the imposition of austerity, particularly on society's most vulnerable. His ideas on how economies function evolved from the turn of the century until the end of the Second World War, as we will see. But this basic conception did not. Nor did his preoccupation with preparing for the future, in spite of his proclamation that 'in the long run, we are all dead'. The lessons of the First World War would serve him for the Second, though for the latter he would also have at his disposal both his theory of effective demand and the prestige necessary to impose his ideas more easily. From the beginning he was preoccupied with assuring economic and financial conditions so that Britain could come out of war in prosperity, even if this meant, in the early phases, financing it through sacrifices on the level of consumption. He would not live long enough to witness the enactment of the Marshall Plan, which corresponded to what he promoted at the end of the First War. But at least he had the opportunity to see the first majority Labour government put into practice part of his propositions.

NOTES

1. '*Morally*' was added by hand to the first version of this letter.
2. 'Boer' means 'farmer' in Dutch. The term was also applied to German, Scandinavian and French settlers in Southern Africa. The First Boer War was fought between 16 December 1880 and 23 March 1881, opposing the British to the Transvaal Boers. It ended with a Peace Treaty giving the Boers self-government in the Transvaal, with British supervision.
3. The Peninsula War opposed, from 1808 to 1814, British and French troops on the Iberian Peninsula. It was important in the final defeat of Napoleon.
4. The Triple Alliance was broken by Italy's decision to remain neutral at the beginning of the war in 1914. Resulting from the Franco-Russian Alliance of 1894, the Entente Cordiale of 1904 between France and Britain and the Anglo-Russian Entente of 1907, the Triple Entente came to an end in 1918 with the Treaty of Brest-Litovsk between Soviet Russia and the Central Powers.
5. The Treaty of London, signed on 26 April 1915, provided that in exchange for Italy's entry into war the latter would receive a large part of Slovenia and the northern part of the Dalmatian Coast.
6. Several other Bloomsbury friends poked fun at Keynes's optimism. See, for example, Garnett (1979, p. 134).
7. Brother Maynard would try to dissuade him.
8. Recipient of the Nobel Prize for medicine and physiology in 1922.
9. We will return in more detail to Keynes's positions on the gold standard system in Chapter 7.
10. See 'Notes on French finance', in which Keynes describes the system of French credit as still very under-developed (1915-1, p. 46) and the hoarding as being enormous.
11. In October 1915 he asked Edgeworth to assist him in editing the journal.
12. 'A most select party', wrote Keynes to his father on 29 January, adding: 'The amount of things I've got to think about in the next few days, in order to be able to advise at a moment's notice, appalls me'.
13. He is recorded saying at this time to Lloyd George that his ideas on French finances were 'rubbish', which certainly contributed to the long period of coolness between both men, who would nevertheless go on to become close allies in the 1920s (Harrod, 1951, p. 201).
14. The same man who had defeated the Boers and shown himself of particular ferocity during the war, interning women and children and burning farms.
15. In his war memoirs, Lloyd George sharply criticized Keynes: 'Mr McKenna's nerve was shaken by these vaticinations of his chief adviser Mr J.M. Keynes. The latter was much too mercurial and impulsive a counsellor for a great emergency. He dashed at conclusions with acrobatic ease. It made things no better that he rushed into opposite conclusions with the same agility' (Lloyd George, 1933, p. 684). Keynes responded in a letter to *The Times* of 28 November 1933 (1933-28).
16. Neville Keynes wrote in his diary on 6 January: 'Maynard talks of resigning his post at the Treasury, and we are very much worried about him' (JMK 16, p. 157). This decision was perhaps linked to the fact that his boss,

McKenna, in disagreement over the cabinet's majority vote in favour of conscription, announced his resignation to Asquith on 29 December 1915 without finally going through with it.

17. In his diary entry for 28 May 1918, David Garnett relates a conversation between Bloomsberries on the deterioration of their friend's character: 'There has been a general alarm that he is going rapidly to the devil' (Skidelsky, 1983, p. 350). It evoked his pretension, the manner in which he boasted about his proximity with the great of this world and even of his poor table manners. Duncan Grant was given the mandate to bring him back to reason.

18. He was referring to MP Philip Morrell, husband of Ottoline, who was opposed to conscription.

19. It latter became the National Council for Civil Liberties.

20. This was also the opinion of Skidelsky: 'Maynard, at first, had no great anti-war feeling. He was not a pacifist, and was not interested in the political origins of the war . . . His initial attitude to the war was thus fairly cool because both its appeal and its horror lay outside the limits of his imagination' (Skidelsky, 1983, p. 295).

21. In his long obituary article, Austin Robinson (1947) makes no mention of this question.

22. Bell wrote that 'Roy Harrod has not attempted to conceal the fact' (1956, p. 46). The fact in question was not objection of conscience, but Keynes's requested court summons to plead military service exemption.

23. Skidelsky believed Harrod was familiar with the document published by Johnson, which he wittingly passed over, in the same way he hid Keynes's homosexuality (1983, p. 320).

24. See also Garnett (1979, pp. 132–4). Moggridge believed Garnet's account lacked credibility (1992, pp. 240–41). A book of Bekassy's poems was published by Hogarth Press on Keynes's suggestion.

25. Hardman was a Cambridge economics student to whom Keynes had sent a letter which was returned because its addressee was dead. He complained in this letter of the reduction in the number of students: 'I lecture to blacks and women' (letter from 25 October 1914).

26. The United States defined itself as an 'associate' rather than an 'ally' of the Allied powers, so as to not be bound by their previous agreements.

27. Thomas Woodrow Wilson (1856–1924), son of a Presbyterian minister, was professor of law and political economy and president of Princeton University before being elected democrat governor of New Jersey in 1910. He was elected the 28th president of the United States in 1912 and re-elected in 1916. He initiated a number of reforms, such as women's right to vote in 1920. He obtained the Nobel Peace Prize in 1919. For a psychological portrait of Wilson, see, in addition to Keynes (1919-1), Freud and Bullitt (1966). On Wilson's role during the war and peace negotiations, see Baker (1923).

28. He wrote to him at the start of the year, on 14 January: 'I am badly overworked, need a holiday, and am filled with perpetual contempt and detestation of the new govt. I should like to get away from it all . . . I pray for the most absolute financial crash (and yet strive to prevent it – so that all I do is a contradiction with all I feel)' (BL, MS 57931).

29. Queen Victoria's grandson, Wilhelm II (1859–1941) became King of Prussia and Emperor of Germany in 1888. After his abdication, he settled in the Netherlands, where he died. The Netherlands refused to extradite him for war crimes in January 1922.

30. Minister of Foreign Affairs in the Weimar government, he was assassinated in 1921 by ultra nationalists for having been favourable to the Treaty of Versailles.

31. At the end of the Second Punic War between Rome and Carthage, Hannibal was defeated by Scipion at Zama in 202 BC. Very severe conditions were inflicted on the defeated who, stripped of much of their territory, naval fleet and elephants, were made to pay considerable indemnities. Hannibal attempted to redress the situation by economic, political and military reforms and to continue the struggle against the Romans. Betrayed by an ally, King Prusias I of Bithynia, where he sought refuge, he was poisoned in 183 BC.

32. A Labourite, Hughes was also a former union leader.

33. Georges Clemenceau (1841–1929) was a doctor. Radical deputy in 1871, he sat on the extreme left of the Assembly from 1876 to 1893. He was called 'The Tiger'. He was owner of the daily *L'Aurore*, which published Zola's '*J'accuse*'. He was Prime Minister from 1906 to 1909 and from 1917 to 1920. He was defeated in the elections for the French Presidency in 1920. Clemenceau, whose first wife was American, had a perfect mastery of English, which was a precious advantage at the Paris Conference.

34. Vittorio Emanuele Orlando (1860–1952), a lawyer, was elected deputy in 1897. Several times minister during the war, he became Prime Minister in 1917. After the defeat of his government in June 1919, he supported Mussolini before breaking with him in 1925. He returned to political life as deputy and president of the Constituent Assembly in 1946, and member of the Senate in 1947. He was defeated by Luigi Einaudi as candidate for the presidency of the republic in 1948.

35. Orlando returned to Paris on 5 May. In the Treaty of Versailles, Italy got the Tyrol. The remaining disputed regions were negotiated directly between Italy and Yugoslavia, created at the end of the war. These events contributed to the crisis that occurred in Italy from 1919 and which would end with Benito Mussolini and his National Fascist Party taking power after the October 1922 march on Rome. In 1924, Mussolini seized Fiume, which went back to Yugoslavia under the name Reject in 1945. The latter is now part of the Republic of Croatia.

36. President Wilson named the engineer Herbert Hoover (1874–1964) as head of the American Relief Commission, charged with the repartition of American food aid to Europe during the war. A Republican, Hoover was elected President of the United States in 1928 before losing to Franklin Delano Roosevelt in 1933. Keynes wrote that 'Mr Hoover was the only man who emerged from the ordeal of Paris with an enhanced reputation' (1919-1, p. 174).

37. On 10 November 1918, the leadership of the SPD, whose president was Friedrich Ebert, concluded a secret agreement with that of the former imperial army to suppress the forces of the left and the extreme left.

38. In his memoir, Keynes wrote: 'In a sort of way, I was in love with him' (1921-4, p. 415). One of his listeners, Virginia Woolf, who very much appreciated the text, wrote in her diary: 'I think he meant it seriously, though we laughed' (V. Woolf, 1977–84, vol. 2, p. 90). See Johnson (1978b).

39. Keynes would not be outdone, describing Klotz as 'a short, plump, heavy-mustached Jew, well groomed, well kept, but with an unsteady, roving eye, and his shoulders a little bent in an instinctive deprecation' (1921-4, p. 422).

40. Philosopher, lawyer and politician, the South African Smuts had fought for the Boers. Minister of Finance (1910–19) and Prime Minister of South Africa (1919–24, 1939–48), he was delegate of the British Empire at the Paris Conference. He shared Keynes's opinion on the treatment to impose on Germany. Close adviser to Churchill during the Second World War, he composed the preamble of the Charter of the United Nations.

41. 'Indemnity' and 'reparations' were often confused in these discussions, including those by Keynes. 'Reparation' signifies compensation for war damages, while 'indemnity' signifies a sum exacted by a victor in war, which is not necessarily linked to the replacement or reparation of physical damage. While the British Prime Minister sought to erase the difference between these expressions, American President Wilson insisted on limiting discussion to claiming reparations payments from Germany.

42. Put into doubt by the historian Paul Mantoux (1955, pp. 9–10), then interpreter at these meetings, and by an American delegate, C.H. Haskin, Keynes's presence was vouched for by official American documents on at least eight occasions (see the documents in JMK 17, pp. 101–109). On this subject Keynes wrote to Alonzo E. Taylor, author of articles on the reactions to his book, on 20 October 1920: 'Since . . . Mantoux has stated that I never attended the Council of Four, I begin to wonder whether I was ever in Paris at all, and whether the whole thing wasn't, after all, a bad dream!' (JMK 17, p. 85).

43. According to Lentin (1984, p. 74), Keynes and John Foster Dulles would contribute to drafting this clause: 'The war-guilt clause, though objectionable in principle, seemed to those like Keynes and Dulles, who helped to draft it, harmless enough in practice'. About this Keynes wrote: 'This is a well and carefully drafted article' (1919-1, p. 95).

44. The 'Twins' were Lord Cunliffe, former Governor of the Bank of England and judge Summer, British representatives to the Committee on Reparations, who defended a harsh position against Germany.

45. Though not members of Bloomsbury, Nicolson and his wife Vita Sackville-West, would become close friends to members of the group, in particular Virginia Woolf.

46. In a letter from 13 June 1919, the former Prime Minister's wife asked Keynes, as a favour, to write a description of the Paris Conference painting a portrait of its main protagonists.

47. See, in the First Interlude, the section on the relations between Bloomsbury and psychoanalysis, which mentioned the influence Keynes's book had on Freud and William Bullitt who together composed a psychological study of President Wilson. Bullitt had been a member of the American delegation at the Paris Conference and, for the same reason as Keynes, resigned.

48. On French reactions to Keynes's book, see Crouzet (1972). See in particular Clemenceau (1921) and Poincaré (articles from *Temps*, 14 and 28 November 1921, and Keynes's replies 20 November and 1 December, the latter unpublished, JMK 17, pp. 287–9). It is worth noting that Keynes proposed in his book that Britain renounce indemnities to which it was entitled in favour of France.

49. There was a second vote in March 1920. In both cases, President Wilson refused to consider any change that could have won the support of some Republicans. The treaty could thus not win the two-thirds margin necessary to be adopted.

50. For other accounts and analyses of the Paris Conference and the Treaty of Versailles, in addition to Paul Mantoux's notes (1955), see Baruch (1920), Boemeke et al. (1998), Brenier (1921), Burnett (1940), De Gmeline (2001), House and Seymour (1921), Lentin (1984), Lévy (1920), Nicolson (1933), Poulon (1985b), Riddel (1934), Tardieu (1921) and Ferguson (1998), who takes up the accusation of Keynes's germanophobia. The most recent work, that of Margaret Macmillan (2001), great granddaughter of Lloyd George, is also the most fascinating and complete account of these 'six months that changed the world' and whose consequences can still be felt today. She criticizes some of Keynes's excessive judgements, particularly those regarding Lloyd George and on the behaviour of the French.

51. The first were held in San Remo (April 1920), Hythe (May–June 1920), Boulogne (June 1920), Brussels (July 1920), Spa (July 1920), Brussels (December 1920), Paris (January 1921), London (February–March and April–May 1921).

52. See the documents collected in volumes 17 and 18 of the *Collected Writings*.

6. Money: economic motor and social pathology

It is hardly possible to overestimate the importance of money.
Letter to Lytton Strachey, 5 July 1907

Money is a funny thing, – it seems impossible to believe that the present system will be allowed to continue much longer. As the fruit of a little extra knowledge and experience of a special kind, it simply (and undeservedly in any absolute sense) comes rolling in.
Letter to Florence Ada Keynes, 23 September 1919

Money is only important for what it will procure.
A Tract on Monetary Reform (1923-1, p. 1)

The love of money as a possession – as distinguished from the love of money as a means to the enjoyments and realities of life – will be recognised for what it is, a somewhat disgusting morbidity, one of those semi-criminal, semi-pathological propensities which one hands over with a shudder to the specialists in mental disease.
'Economic possibilities for our grandchildren' (1930-17, p. 329)

The evolution of Keynes's economic theory is punctuated by three books: *A Tract on Monetary Reform* (1923-1), *A Treatise on Money* (1930-1) and *The General Theory of Employment, Interest and Money* (1936-1). While the first started as newspaper articles, the second was an academic work from the start, aiming in part at deepening and correcting the ideas contained in the first. The third started as a correction of the second, of which Keynes was not satisfied. Keynes considered, after the publication of his last book, publishing *Footnotes to 'The General Theory'* (JMK 14, pp. 133–4).[1]

The words 'money' or 'monetary' figure in the three titles. Money occupies a central role in Keynes's economic vision. He devoted much reflection to money's nature, functions and role in the economy. For his Cambridge entrance exam, he wrote an essay on money. But money also played an important role in his life. He devoted much time and energy in accumulating a fortune established on 21 December 1945 at £431 238,[2] the equivalent of around £12 million today.[3] Marx wrote to Engels, after having finished the manuscript of the *Contribution to the Critique of Political Economy*, on 21 January 1859: 'I don't suppose anyone has ever written about "money" when so short of the stuff. Most *autores* on this SUBJECT have been on terms of the utmost amity with THE SUBJECT OF THEIR RESEARCHES' (Marx and Engels, 1983, p. 250; words in capitals in English in the orginal German text). Keynes was most certainly at peace with the subject of his research. At the same time, he depreciated men of money as inferior to artists and scientists, prayed for 'the euthanasia of the rentier' (1936-1, p. 376) and considered the love of money a pathology, one which nevertheless constituted capitalism's most powerful motive.

We will begin by describing Keynes's financial dealings before considering his conception of money. We will first examine a neglected aspect of this conception, the love of money's psychological dimension, which brings together Keynes and Freud. We will then present the classical view of money, particularly the quantitative theory of money, and Keynes's criticism of the latter, especially in his first works. We will lastly discuss the elaboration of what Keynes called his 'monetary theory of production' from *A Treatise on Money* to *The General Theory*, finishing with the concept of preference for liquidity. As Keynes's theory of money is inseparable from his theory of employment, which will be presented in the following chapter, we will not study all of its aspects here and return to certain elements in the following chapter.

KEYNES'S PERSONAL FINANCES

Keynes came from a well-to-do background never lacking in money.[4] John Neville's father, John Keynes, made his fortune in the flower business. At his death in 1878, his assets amounted to £40 000, which was considerable at that time. John Neville inherited £17 000, a sum which enabled him to envisage a less lucrative but more interesting career. He invested this inheritance very cautiously. This provided him with an income superior to what he could have earned as an academic. In 1881 he had built a very comfortable house at 6, Harvey Road, in Cambridge, where he lived with his wife until his death, and which constituted an important fixed point in Keynes's life. The residence was sufficiently big to accommodate, in addition to the parents and three children, three servants and three guests. Throughout the following seven decades, the Keynes family was always financially well-off. The precise accounts kept by Neville Keynes shows that, in the 1890s, investments provided for 60 per cent of his total income. His capital would grow to £24 000 at the beginning of the century. He made generous donations to members of his family, his friends and various organizations. He supplemented his son Maynard's income when he started teaching at Cambridge and helped him get back on his feet after some unfortunate speculation.

Income

From as early as his arrival at Eton, Keynes adopted his father's habit of keeping a detailed register of his financial situation. He recorded continually and in detail his income, expenses, investments, the value of his portfolio, dividends, loans, gambling winnings and various other transactions. He kept all financial documents. As a student he added many scholarly awards to his paternal allowance and to bursaries obtained for studying at Eton and Cambridge. After his studies, his annual income went from £380 in 1908–1909 to £11 801 in 1945–46, reaching a peak of £18 800 the year following the publication of *The General Theory*.[5] From 1923 on, payments from academic sources constituted a decreasingly important fraction of his income, most of which came from financial activities.[6] Earnings from newspaper articles were also substantial, as well as from the sale of his books. *The Economic Consequences of the Peace*, in particular, brought him an exceptional reward.

Keynes bought his first stocks in July 1905, using what he called a 'special fund' accumulated by his father from his scholarships and birthday gifts and given to him at his majority. He became more seriously involved in this activity in 1910 thanks to an increase in his income. His net assets went from £220 at the end of 1905 to £16 315 in 1919. From this date on, he invested on a vast scale both his own funds and those of his friends and partners, having decided it was no longer a question of being a wage labour slave and overworked by lectures and students' supervision: 'He must not become so cluttered up with routine work as to be unable to give his main energies to the salvation of Europe' (Harrod, 1951, p. 286). His teaching was reduced to eight lectures per year from 1920. He needed considerable money to escape wage-earner drudgery, accomplish the missions for which he felt a calling and lead an agreeable existence:

> He was determined not to relapse into salaried drudgery. He must be financially independent. He felt that he had that in him which would justify such independence. He had many things to tell the nation. And he wanted a sufficiency. He must be able to take stalls at the Russian Ballet whenever he wished – and entertain the dancers, if that struck his fancy. He must be able to buy his friends pictures – and pay them handsomely. (Harrod, 1951, p. 297)

Relating a conversation with Keynes, Friedrich Hayek was surprised that the same man could both call for the 'euthanasia of the rentier' and agree with him on

> the importance which the man of independent means had had in the English political tradition. Far from contradicting me, this made Keynes launch out into a long eulogy of the role played by the propertied class in which he gave many illustrations of their indispensability for the preservation of a decent civilization. (Hayek, 1952, p. 230)

Keynes became involved in the currency market during the summer of 1919 at a time when all currencies were floating. Some accused him of using insider information obtained while he was at the Treasury. Harrod once again came to his defence on this matter: 'We may add that to those who knew him well at all the charge appears quite fantastic. He was punctiliously honourable in all financial matters' (Harrod, 1951, p. 298). With O.T. Falk,[7] his friend and colleague from the Treasury and companion from the Tuesday Club, Keynes set up the Syndicate, which went into operation on January 1920. He used funds from his Bloomsbury friends and members of his family. When the evolution of exchange rates went totally against his predictions,[8] Keynes found himself in serious financial difficulty during the summer. He succeeded in re-establishing his position before the end of 1922, through more propitious speculations, but also thanks to unexpected earnings from the sale of *The Economic Consequences of the Peace* and financial help from his father. From then on the sale of his books provided him considerable yields, even more so since he inverted the habitual relationship between publisher and author. It was he who assumed the book's production costs and who paid rights to the publisher.

In 1922, with a commission from *The Manchester Guardian* to publish a series of twelve supplements on postwar Europe's economic and financial situation, Keynes discovered a new way to make money: journalism. This activity would soon constitute his second source of income, before teaching and after investment. He negotiated bitterly the price of his articles and set up a complex architecture for their translation and their distribution around the world.

In 1923, after having taken control of *The Nation and Athenaeum*, he composed in it a weekly series entitled 'Finance and investment' in which he gave investment advice. The following year saw the publication of the London and Cambridge Economic Service's *Monthly Bulletin*, which he set up with William Beveridge, Arthur L. Bowley and Hubert Henderson. Its goal was to provide businessmen with economic information to help them in their decisions.

As an investor, Keynes made considerable gains but also suffered serious setbacks. His results were generally better in the 1930s than in the 1940s. Other than stocks and currencies, he speculated in raw materials: cotton, lead, tin, copper, rubber, wheat, sugar, oil and jute. In conjunction with this activity, he published between 1923 and 1930 seven long memoranda entitled 'Stocks of staple commodities' for the *Monthly Bulletin* (JMK 12, pp. 267–647). His transactions in this domain put him in serious difficulty in 1928, such that he no longer had much to lose in the stock market crash of 1929. In 1936, he found himself in possession of a quantity of wheat nearly equivalent to a month of English consumption, which arrived by ship from Argentina and for which he was required to take delivery. He measured King's College Chapel, which is in reality a gothic cathedral, and determined that it could stock half the wheat. He bought time by insisting on a meticulous verification of the wheat's quality on board of the vessels and succeeded in selling the shipment before having to take delivery himself.[9]

In 1937 and 1938, while speculating on Wall Street, he lost two thirds of the value of his assets, which had grown spectacularly from 1930 to 1936, passing from £7815 to £506 522. The heart attack he suffered in May 1937 considerably reduced his engagements on all fronts, but did not interrupt for long his speculative activities. On 29 March 1938, he wrote to Richard Kahn, to whom he described his changing phases of worry and enthusiasm: 'None too good for health with continuous anxious work on the telephone' (JMK 12, p. 29). A letter from the same period illustrates his conception of speculation and explains his stoicism in regards to reversals of fortune:

> I feel no shame at being found still owning a share when the bottom of the market comes . . . I should say that it is from time to time the duty of a serious investor to accept the depreciation of his holdings with equanimity and without reproaching himself. Any other policy is anti-social, destructive of confidence, and incompatible with the working of the economic system. An investor is aiming, or should be aiming primarily at long-period results, and should be solely judged by these . . . The idea that we should all be selling out to the other fellow and should all be finding ourselves with nothing but cash at the bottom of the market is not merely fantastic, but destructive of the whole system. (Letter to F.N. Curzon, 18 March 1938, JMK 12, pp. 38–9).

In *The General Theory*, Keynes explained that capitalism's instability comes partly from the fact that investors, instead of making enlightened and socially advantageous investments destined 'to defeat the dark forces of time and ignorance which envelop our future' (Keynes 1936-1, p. 155), seek on the contrary to get rich as quickly as possible at others' expense. He proposed an original solution to the evils resulting from this situation: 'to make the purchase of an investment permanent and indissoluble, like marriage, except by reason of death or other grave cause, might be a useful remedy for our contemporary evils' (ibid., p. 160).

Keynes's portfolio was always dominated by shares of a few enterprises, sometimes less than four. He wrote to F.C. Scott[10] on 15 August 1934: 'One's knowledge and experience are definitely limited and there are seldom more than two or three enterprises at any given time in which I personally feel myself entitled to put *full* confidence' (JMK 12, p. 57). Again to Scott, he wrote on 23 August: 'It is indeed awfully bad for all of us to be constantly revaluing our investments according to market movements' (ibid., pp. 58–9). On 7 June 1938, he wrote to him: 'The whole art is to vary emphasis and the centre of gravity of one's portfolio according to circumstances' (ibid., p. 68).

In addition to his personal investment activities, which he most often attended to in bed in the morning and for which he generally transacted with stockbrokers Buckmaster and Moore, Keynes occupied positions in several financial enterprises. A member of the board of the National Mutual Life Assurance Society from September 1919, he became chairman in May 1921 until October 1938. His health forced him to leave this post: 'Now that I am able tentatively to return to work, I have to decide what it is most prudent to give up. One naturally chooses that part of one's activities in which one finds least satisfaction. And that, in present circumstances, is I feel the National Mutual' (letter to Falk, 11 October 1938, JMK 12, p. 47). His speeches at the company's annual meeting, in large part reproduced in the press, constituted an important event in the life of the City.[11] The second, pronounced on 21 January 1923, contains a passage which illustrates his conception of the relation between an individual investor and an investment society:

> The average investor must obviously be at a hopeless disadvantage in looking after his savings as compared with a well-managed mutual society. It ought to be considered as imprudent for such a man to make his own investments as to be his own doctor or lawyer. I should like to see by far the greater part of the moderate savings of the middle class invested through the best mutual offices. (1923-5, p. 125)

In December 1923, Keynes became member of the board of the Provincial Insurance Company, a society in which he would be actively involved until his death. With O.T. Falk, he contributed to the creation of three investment companies: the A.D. Investment Trust, formed in July 1921 mainly by colleagues from the Treasury A Division and which he left in 1927; the Independent Investment Company, founded in January 1924; and the P.R. Finance Company, set up in January 1923 and counting among its stockholders several members of Bloomsbury and his family. Keynes chaired this last company from 1932 to 1936. His activities made him an eminent and respected member of the City, London's financial centre. His financial career was crowned by his nomination, on 18 September 1941, as director of the Bank of England. This is not the least of paradoxes for one who never stopped criticizing this institution. He wrote to his mother on 6 September: 'Rather appalling, I feel, such respectability! Coming after a fellowship at Eton I feel it is only a matter of time before I become a Bishop or Dean of York'.

In addition to managing his own funds and those of stockholders of companies he managed, Keynes was involved in the finances of his Alma Maters. He was appointed Inspector of Accounts for King's College from his arrival in 1909, Second Bursar, a post created for him, in 1919 and Bursar in 1924, a function he assumed until his death. He was very active in these tasks and considerably enriched his college, whose investments he diversified (see JMK 12, p. 91). Appointed fellow of Eton College in 1940, he actively involved himself in his first college's finances. He wrote to Jasper Ridley, a banker he frequented in this function and whose prudence he criticized, in March 1944: 'My central principle of investment is to go contrary to general opinion, on the ground that, if everyone is agreed about its merits, the investment is inevitably too dear and therefore unattractive' (JMK 12, p. 111). He also managed the finances of the Royal Economic Society.

Expenses

Keynes thus did not lack money. The latter seemed essential to him to enable his activities as a spreader of ideas and to convince his contemporaries, particularly political and economic leaders, of the necessity of indispensable reforms for the survival of civilization. His resources gave him the means of taking control of press organs through which he was able to spread his ideas. During the Second World War, his financial independence allowed him to put himself at his country's service without receiving a salary. He was not submitted to the civil servants' duty of reserve and thus maintained his freedom of speech.[12]

Money also allowed him to maintain the standard of living in which his parents had brought him up. Keynes, while keeping a close eye on his spending,[13] never deprived himself of anything and lived in a certain luxury. He enjoyed good food, fine wines and elegant clothes. He regularly organized grand receptions. Parties were continual at Bloomsbury, 'the grandest I suppose being given by Maynard and Lydia Keynes at 46 Gordon Square' (Garnett, 1962, p. 63). Like all middle-class people of his time, Keynes had servants. It was unlikely that he often involved himself in kitchen or household chores, with the exception of gardening. He regularly frequented restaurants and shows, particularly the ballet, of which he was especially fond. He travelled often and sometimes assumed a large part of his travelling companions' expenses. His travels were most often occasions for important purchases. A more than two-month long tour of Italy with Vanessa Bell and Duncan Grant in the spring of 1920 gave rise to an veritable orgy of spending, Keynes writing to his father on 16 April that he had bought nearly a ton of merchandise.

Keynes never owned the places in which he lived, as was common at the time. Very long-term leases were standard, which was the case for 46 Gordon Square, his London residence, and the Tilton farmhouse leased from 1925. Before occupying these places, he covered, in addition to the rent of his own apartments, a large part of the renting costs of his Bloomsbury friends. Most often these arrangements were complex, with several renters having distinct statuses, which sometimes led to frictions. He contributed to the cost of renting Charleston, in which he kept a room from 1916 to 1926. He helped Lytton Strachey pay the rent of houses the latter shared with Dora Carrington. He carried out numerous and costly renovations and enlargements at 46 Gordon Square and especially at Tilton. He also developed Tilton as a farming business and succeeded in making a profit from it through, notably, pork rearing and bacon production. He also organized hunts.

Financial aid to his friends accounted for another part of Keynes's expenses. Several Bloomsberries, and others such as Bekassy, Sickert and Wittgenstein, were beneficiaries of this largesse. Some enjoyed an allowance during a more or less extended period of time. This was particularly true of David Garnett and especially of Duncan Grant, to whom Keynes's will assured an annual income, as well as to his secretary Mrs Stephens.[14] According to this will, Lydia's annual income after taxes was never to fall below £1500. After the latter's death, his remaining capital, including the books and paintings, was bequeathed to King's College.

Lastly, as an art patron, Keynes made important contributions to various enterprises and institutions: the London Artists Association, the Camargo Society, the Cambridge Arts Theatre. The latter in particular cost him dearly. We will return in detail to this aspect of Keynes's life, as well as to his important activity as a painting and rare book collector, in the last chapter. Of course, the purchase of a Cézanne or Newton's manuscripts cannot be considered an expense, but rather an investment. However, Keynes did not buy these objects to speculate, but to enjoy. He let go of very few paintings during his life.

THE LOVE OF MONEY: FROM ARISTOTLE TO FREUD[15]

Keynes believed money to be essential for living well, for helping friends, for encouraging the arts and for freeing him to act as a publicist. But it must not be in itself an object of covetousness. The condemnation of the love of money is part of a long tradition, having its origins in the Bible: 'He that loveth silver shall not be satisfied with silver; nor he that loveth abundance with increase: this is also vanity' (Ecclesiastes, 5.10). Solon, who had exonerated the debts of the Athenians, wrote in one of the poems composed to support his reforms:

> The man whose riches satisfy his greed
> Is not more rich for all those heaps and hoards
> Than some poor man who has enough to feed
> And clothe his corpse with such as God affords

Aristotle, for whom Keynes had the greatest admiration,[16] denounced chrematistics, the pursuit of wealth for its own sake.[17] The philosopher believed money was a dangerous invention carrying within it the seed of the worst excess. From a means of facilitating exchanges, it has been transformed into the finality of human activity. Exchange, which was a means of transmuting use values, has become a means of obtaining surplus money. Money, which originated as a convention and is thus a legal rather than natural institution, has become the standard with which to measure a wealth which can be accumulated without limits. It has been confused with wealth. It has been extirpated from the real world, from nature. As in the myth of Midas, it can even lead to death.[18] The words of the philosopher become vehement when he condemns money-making: 'in this art of money-making there is no limit of the end, which is wealth of the spurious kind, and the acquisition of money' (Aristotle, 1905, p. 43). Worse than commerce is interest-paying loans which allow one to obtain from a sum of money a superior sum by the simple fact of handing it over some time. This is a gain against nature:

> The most hated sort, and with the greatest reason, is usury, which makes a gain out of money itself, and not from the natural use of it. For money was intended to be used in exchange, but not to increase at interest. And this term usury, which means the birth of money from money, is applied to the breeding of money because the offspring resembles the parent. Wherefore of all modes of getting wealth this is the most unnatural. (Aristotle, 1905, p. 46)

There is no limit to the fierceness of he who desires money for money's sake and measures everything according to this standard. Aristotle feared money would destroy society by rotting it from within. Christianity continues this theme. Jesus, in a famous outburst against temple merchants, warned against the rich who find their consolation on earth. One cannot both serve God and money, a fleeting possession: 'Lay not up for yourselves treasures upon earth, where moth and rust doth corrupt, and where thieves break through and steal. But lay up for yourselves treasury in heaven, where neither moth nor rust doth corrupt, and where thieves do not break through nor steal' (Matthew 6:19–20). For St Augustine, human beings are motivated by three great impulses: money, political power and concupiscence. Thomas Aquinas developed, to justify his condemnation of interest, a theory anticipating the vision Keynes would use against 'classical economists'.[19] He wrote of the arguments of the Medieval Church that the latter's doctrine 'deserves rehabilitation and honour' (1936-1, p. 351). With his condemnation of the love of money, the immoralist rediscovered the way of morality:

I see us free, therefore, to return to some of the most sure and certain principles of religion and traditional virtue – that avarice is a vice, that the exaction of usury is a misdemeanour, and the love of money is detestable, that those who walk most truly in the paths of virtue and sane wisdom who take least thought for the morrow. (1930-17, pp. 330–31)

There appeared in Keynes's first writings, particularly in the papers read before the Apostles, reflections on the fragility of possessing monetary wealth and the expression of contempt for the love of money. These ideas are to be found in his first lecture notes: 'The ethical value of wealth is not easily justified unless we regard the present state of affairs as purely transitional' (KP, UA/6/15, p. 45). Despite being very critical of Bolshevism, whose contempt of freedom he found repugnant, Keynes recognized in this new and strange combination of religion and business a virtue: that of having unseated the love of money from the central position it occupies under capitalism. Soviet Communists could be represented 'as though the early Christians led by Attila . . . using the equipment of the Holy Inquisition and the Jesuit missions to enforce the literal economics of the New Testament' (1925-2, p. 257). In Russia, pecuniary motivations ceased being the main levers of social action. This was not the case with capitalism, on the contrary:

At any rate to me it seems clearer every day that the moral problem of our age is concerned with the love of money, with the habitual appeal to the money motive in nine-tenths of the activities of life, with the universal striving after individual economic security as the prime object of endeavour, with the social approbation of money as the measure of constructive success, and with the social appeal to the hoarding instinct as the foundation of the necessary provision for the family and for the future. (1925-2, pp. 268–9)

At the same time, the quest for money is perhaps essential to channel certain dangerous tendencies of human beings, aggressive and sadistic drives which lead some to transform others into objects:

Moreover, dangerous human proclivities can be canalised into comparatively harmless channels by the existence of opportunities for money-making and private wealth, which, if they cannot be satisfied in this way, may find their outlet in cruelty, the reckless pursuit of personal power and authority, and other forms of self-aggrandisement. It is better that a man should tyrannise over his bank balance than over his fellow-citizens; and whilst the former is sometimes denounced as being but a means for the latter, sometimes at least it is an alternative. (1936-1, p. 374)

These reflections refer to depth psychology. As we have seen, Keynes and his Bloomsbury friends were well acquainted with Freud's work. For his part, Freud was acquainted with economic thought and had, in his youth, translated the works of John Stuart Mill. In his condemnation of the pursuit of money, Mill takes on Aristotelian accents and announces those of Keynes:

But the best state for human nature is that in which, while no one is poor, no one desires to be richer, nor has any reason to fear being thrust back, by the efforts of others to push themselves forward.

That the energies of mankind should be kept in employment by the struggle for riches, as they were formerly by the struggle of war, until the better minds succeed in educating the others into better things, is undoubtedly more desirable than that they should rust and stagnate. While minds are coarse they require coarse stimuli, and let them have them. (Mill, 1848, vol. 2, p. 262)

In a passage from the *Treatise on Money* (1930-1, vol. 2, pp. 258–9), Keynes referred to the works of Freud, Ferenczi and Jones on money. He was certainly familiar with the links Freud and his friends established between anal eroticism and the propensity to hoard, and the identification of money with excrement. For Freud, parsimony is thus one of 'the first and most constant results of the sublimation of anal erotism' (Freud, 1908, p. 75) and 'the connections between the complexes of interest in money and of defaecation, which seem so dissimilar, appear to be the most extensive of all' (ibid., p. 76). Ferenczi went further describing the drives at the basis of capitalism: 'the character of capitalism, however, not purely practical and utilitarian, but libidinous and irrational, is betrayed in this stage also: the child decidedly enjoys the collecting in itself' (Ferenczi, 1914, p. 85). For Jones, 'Metal coins, however, and particularly gold, are unconscious symbols for excrement, the material from which most of our sense of possession, in infantile time, was derived (Jones, 1916, p. 129).[20]

Without going as far as Freud or Ferenczi, whose arguments he knew, Keynes associated in *The General Theory* money with filth:

> If the Treasury were to fill old bottles with banknotes, bury them at suitable depths in disused coalmines which are then filled up to the surface with town rubbish, and leave it to private enterprise on well-tried principles of *laissez-faire* to dig the notes up again . . ., there need be no more unemployment. (Keynes, 1936-1, p 129)

Moreover, he often returned to the irrational and pathological character of hoarding, of the drive to accumulate money. The 1930 quotation at the beginning of this chapter is very clear in this regard. In an ideal society, the care of these pathologies would be confided to mental illness specialists. These specialists were Freud and his disciples, some of whom were intimate friends of Maynard. The actions of capitalists were linked to the sublimation of an over-active libido:

> Why do practical men find it more amusing to make money than to join in open conspiracy? . . . That is why, unless they have the luck to be scientists or artists, they fall back on the grand substitute motive, the perfect *ersatz*, the anodyne for those who, in fact, want nothing at all – money . . . Clissold and his brother Dickon, the advertising expert, flutter about the world seeking for something to which they can attach their abundant *libido*. But they have not found it. They would so like to be apostles. But they cannot. They remain business men. (1927-2, pp. 319–320)

Businessmen occupy, in Keynes's world vision, an inferior position. Endowed with considerable energy, they lack the moral and intellectual capacities to rise above their vulgar impulses and seek money rather than love, beauty and truth.

There is also in this a problem of relation to time. It is in taking account of time, like incertitude and money, that the Keynesian vision distinguishes itself from the classical vision. The three dimensions are related. The accumulation of money flows from both fear of the future, of incertitude, and from the negation of death's inevitability. Possessing money is the best response to the hazards of the future:

> *For the importance of money essentially flows from its being a link between the present and the future* . . . Money in its significant attributes is, above all, a subtle device for linking the present to the future; and we cannot even begin to discuss the effect of changing expectations on current activities except in monetary terms. (1936-1, pp. 293–4)

It translates our fear of the future and uncertainty, of precariousness, in short, our anxiety:

Because, partly on reasonable and partly on instinctive grounds, our desire to hold money as a store of wealth is a barometer of the degree of our distrust of our own calculations and conventions concerning the future. Even though this feeling about money is itself conventional or instinctive, it operates, so to speak, at a deeper level of our motivation. It takes charge at the moments when the higher, more precarious conventions have weakened. (1937-4, p. 116)

Money gives those who fear death an illusionary immortality. Keynes associated frugality and savings with Victorian morality. These 'unreasonable but insistent inhibitions against acts of expenditure as such' (1936-1, p. 108) assured the enrichment of the independently wealthy, whose disappearance he predicted at the end of *The General Theory*. This would be a work of public salvation, which would allow for the enjoyment of the present moment instead of indefinitely postponing pleasure:

The 'purposive' man is always trying to secure a spurious and delusive immortality for his acts by pushing his interest in them forward into time. He does not love his cat, but his cat's kittens; nor, in truth, the kittens, but only the kittens' kittens, and so on forward for ever to the end of catdom. For him jam is not jam unless it is a case of jam tomorrow and never jam today. Thus by pushing his jam always forward into the future, he strives to secure for his act of boiling it an immortality. (1930-17, p. 330)

MONEY IN CLASSICAL ECONOMICS

Keynes presented his economic work as a confrontation with what he called classical theory. Recalling the fact that the term 'classical economists' had been used by Marx to characterize Ricardo, Mill and their predecessors, he applied it to his successors 'who adopted and perfected the theory of the Ricardian economics, including (for example) J.S. Mill, Marshall, Edgeworth and Prof. Pigou' (1936-1, p. 3). He thus included in this vast group, in addition to those traditionally considered classical, neoclassical economists. The theoretical positions of both vary greatly on a number of questions. They come together, however, in their adherence to the quantity theory of money.[21]

It was in reality more a conception or a vision that had been handed down over the centuries through increasingly sophisticated and varied theoretical formulations. The basic idea is simple: when in an economy the quantity of money[22] varies, the price level varies in the same direction and in the same proportion. The chain of causality thus goes from money to prices and not from prices to money. According to this conception, money is said to be exogenous. Its quantity is the result of causes external to the system in question. Another tradition believed that money is endogenous; it is created within the system and its quantity adapts itself to the price level. According to the quantity theory, money is neutral, which means that variation of its quantity has no real effect on the economy, on relative prices, on production, on employment. It only affects nominal values. Inflation is a purely monetary phenomenon, caused exclusively by increases in the quantity of money in circulation.

This conception came into being with the origins of economic reflection. It was already formulated in Aristophanes' comedy *The Wasps* in the fourth century BC, as well as in very early Chinese writings. The astronomer Copernicus evoked it in a treatise on the minting of money written in 1517. In 1568, the jurist and philosopher Jean Bodin, in his *Réponse au paradoxe de M. de Malestroit*, affirmed that by far the most important cause of major price increases in France at that time was the afflux of precious metals coming from the Americas through Portugal and Spain. According to him, it was not simply a phenomenon limited by time and space. The effect of variations of the quantity of money on price level was a law which applied to all times and places. This conviction is found in all followers of the quantity theory, from Bodin up to Milton Friedman, who affirmed that the relationship between the variations in the stock of money and the price level is an empirical relation whose 'uniformity is, I suspect, of the same order as many of the uniformities that form the basis of the physical sciences' (Friedman, 1956, p. 21). After Petty, Locke and Cantillon, David Hume gave this theory a famous formulation in 1752:

> Money is not, properly speaking, one of the subjects of commerce; but only the instrument which men have agreed upon to facilitate the exchange of one commodity for another. It is none of the wheels of trade: it is the oil which renders the motion of the wheels more smooth and easy. If we consider any one kingdom by itself, it is evident, that the greater or less plenty of money is of no consequence; since the prices of commodities are always proportioned to the plenty of money. (Hume, 1752a, p. 281)

Money thus serves only to facilitate exchanges. In the same writing, Hume clarifies his remarks, admitting that in the short term, depending on the place where it is injected in an economy, money can have a stimulating effect on business and commerce. It can thus have a real effect, it can act on quantities. But once readjustments are made, once the equilibrium has been realized, the only effect of a variation of the quantity of money is a variation, in the same direction and proportion, of the price level. It is the long-term neutrality of money.

Ricardo, whom Keynes attacked more harshly than Hume, whose philosophy he admired, was a resolute defender of the quantity theory, in practice as much as theory.[23] He believed the excessive issuing of notes by the Bank of England, after the suspension of the convertibility of the pound sterling in gold in 1797, was responsible for the raging inflation during the Napoleonic Wars. In 1810 a committee set up by the government produced the Bullion Report which adopted in large part Ricardo's arguments. The 'antibullionists' considered banknotes on the contrary to be signs of credit, issued by banks against merchants' bills of exchange. The debate between advocates and adversaries of the Bullion Report transformed in the following decades into a debate between advocates of the currency principle and those of the banking principle, which anticipated the controversy between monetarists and Keynesians. For the former, the causal link moves from money to prices, and for the latter, from prices to money, whose quantity adapts itself to the needs of the economy.

The quantity theory of money, until then formulated in the literary prose used by most classical economists, was subject from the end of the nineteenth century to mathematical translations. One of the most famous was developed by Irving Fisher in *The Purchasing Power of Money* (1911), of which Keynes published a review in *The Economic Journal* (1911-6). Fisher's equation is formulated as follows:

$$MV = PT$$

where M is the stock of money, V its velocity of circulation, P the price level and T the total volume of transactions.

Fisher's analysis is known as the transaction approach. At the same time, Marshall and Pigou developed an income approach, also called the Cambridge equation, to which Keynes was initiated by Marshall while he was a student.[24] This approach emphasizes the separation between selling and buying rather than on the simultaneity of transactions. Money is a temporary store of value between buying and selling. The individual who receives an income cannot spend all of it immediately and chooses to keep part of it in liquid form. Money can be assimilated to an asset, as one alternative among others. This approach thus takes into account the modalities of payment and institutional arrangements. It can be expressed as follows:

$$M = kPNy$$

where M is the quantity of money, k the proportion of their income which individuals want to keep in liquid form, P the price level, N the population and y the per capita income.

Keynes and the Quantity Theory of Money

Most commentators believe Keynes moved from enthusiastically supporting the quantity theory of money to challenging it, however partially. Keynes wrote in *The General Theory* that the quantity theory is not valid in situations of involuntary unemployment, though it becomes so in times of full employment. Regarding this theory, one reads in *A Tract on Monetary Reform*: 'This theory is fundamental. Its correspondence with fact is not open to question' (1923-1, p. 61). It is not surprising that Milton Friedman, who in the middle of the last century revived the quantity theory, believed this book to be Keynes's best: 'Keynes was a quantity theorist long before he was a Keynesian, and he continued to be one after he became a Keynesian. Many parts of the *General Theory* are a continuation of his earlier interests and beliefs' (Friedman, 1972, p. 159).[25]

However, when one reads Keynes more attentively, the matter becomes more complex. He explained that a variation in the quantity of money can modify not only the price level, but also the velocity of money as well as the proportion of debt banks keep in liquid form.[26] Generally, the habits of both the public and banking policies are modified in step with often unforeseeable events. It is only by supposing that all these factors are constant that one may conclude that quantity of money and price level vary in ways suggested by quantity theory. This is true in the long run, but '*In the long run* we are all dead. Economists set themselves too easy, too useless a task if in tempestuous seasons they can only tell us that when the storm is long past the ocean is flat again' (1923-1, p. 65). In brief, the quantity theory of money is not very useful in studying short-term movements in the economy.

In reality Keynes was sceptical very early on regarding this theory, in spite of his professed faith, which might have arisen from filial piety towards Marshall. In his first academic article 'Recent economic events in India', he emphasized that one must not place too much trust in the apparent statistical convergence between increases in price level and increases in quantity of money (1909-1, p. 8). His scepticism was closely linked to methodological positions elaborated in his *Treatise on Probability* and other works. In his lecture notes, one often reads that the quantity theory is true, all things being equal:

> But other things seldom are equal; and these other things are very often, perhaps generally, more important than the changes in the volume of the currency. That is to say, the level of prices depends upon a number of independent factors, and will vary if any of these factors change. The quantity of money is only one of them. (KP, UA/6/22, p. 4)[27]

Moreover, Keynes reproached Fisher in his notes for not explaining by which transmission mechanisms the flux of new money acts on prices.[28]

A complex problem of measurement was particularly at issue. Keynes tackled this in a long document on price indexes, evoked in Chapter 2, composed after the completion of his dissertation on probabilities in the spring of 1909. In this he posed the problem of measuring quantities in economics: 'The quantities in economics in connection with which difficulties of measurement arise, either from the nature of the subject or from the lack of statistics, are very numerous' (1909-4, p. 55). This is particularly evident in the case of prices: 'The contradiction arises out of the very fundamental characteristic of the price relation, not always recognised, that it is not, in the fullest and strictest sense, numerically measurable' (ibid., p. 57); and even more so in that of the price level: 'general exchange value, defined as an *ensemble* of particular exchange values, is generally incapable of measurement' (ibid., p. 95).[29]

Beyond the problem of measurement, it was the question of inductive inference that was at stake: '*The inductive verification* of such a theory is evidently difficult. We cannot isolate the various contributory causes, or prepare experiments. It is, therefore, always difficult to refute a controversialist who points to one of the possible causes as the *sole* cause of what has occurred' (KP, UA/6/22, p. 25).[30] As Keynes affirmed on several occasions in his pre-war lecture notes, it is very difficult, if not impossible, to verify the quantity theory of money empirically. This of course went against the then emerging and now largely dominant ideas according to which one can resolve controversies in economics by means of empirical testing: 'The inductive verifications of the adherents of the [quantity] theory have been, I think, nearly as fallacious as those of its opponents' (lecture notes, 1912–1914, JMK 12, p. 765). This is why, Keynes declared to his students, the great controversies having opposed for centuries Bodin against Malestroit, Montesquieu against Hume, bullionists against antibullionists, advocates of the banking principle against those of the currency principle and, we might add, Keynes's disciples against those of Friedman, have never been settled by facts.

One already finds in these notes the famous statement on the long run: 'It is true, of course, that we must nearly always add the qualification "in the long run"; but when the long run is a *very* long run, so long that the ultimate event cannot be *foreseen*, the doctrine loses most of its importance' (JMK 12, 752). Manifestly, in spite of several commentators' thoughts on the matter, Keynes was never an enthusiastic adherent to the quantity theory of money and, from this period, began reflecting on the causes of alternating cycles of expansion and depression with other instruments of analysis, as attests for example the paper presented on 3 December 1913 before the London Political Economy Club, 'How far are bankers responsible for the alternations of crisis and depression?' (1913-5).

MONEY AND INSTABILITY: *A TREATISE ON MONEY*

In the first sentence of *A Treatise on Money*,[31] Keynes defined a money of account as 'that in which debts and prices and general purchasing power are *expressed*' (1930-1, vol. 1, p. 3). It is, he added, 'the primary concept of a theory of money' (ibid.). These lists of prices or debts can be noted verbally, engraved on rocks, jotted down on paper or, as he would have added today, typed on a computer. Money is thus firstly a unit of account. It then becomes a medium of exchange and a store of wealth, that is, 'Money itself, namely that by delivery of which debt contracts and price contracts are *discharged*, and in the shape of which a store of general purchasing power is *held*' (ibid.). These properties flow from those of the unit of account. Prices and debts must firstly be expressed in terms of the latter: 'Money proper in the full sense can only exist in relation to a money of account' (ibid.). This means there does not exist, in the beginning, a real economy with real prices to which money is added to facilitate exchange. Economic quantities are at once monetary, and this has been true since earliest antiquity.

Money, as we have seen, has a psychological dimension. It also has a social and political dimension. It is the State that holds the power to determine the money of account: 'by the mention of contracts and offers, we have introduced law or custom, by which they are enforceable; that is to say, we have introduced the State or the community' (ibid., p. 4). Money is thus a social institution and 'like certain other essential elements in civilisation, is a far more ancient institution than we were taught to believe some few years ago' (ibid., pp. 11–2). In addition to its psychological dimension, this vision of money separates Keynes from those for whom money is a good like any other, at the same time difficult to integrate into analysis. Of course, Keynes was neither the first nor the last to have emphasized the link between money, the State and power. Historicists, such as Weber, institutionalists, such as Veblen, and unclassable theorists such as Simmel have insisted on this dimension. Money, like the rest of the economy, is not a natural creation, it is a product of society and the State.

Inspired this time by Marshall and the Cambridge tradition, Keynes also described money as an asset, one that can be the object, alternatively to others, of a demand. Individuals receiving an income must first make a choice, determining what they consume and what they save; they must then decide under what form to keep their savings. By doing this, Keynes sketched the liquidity preference theory which will be discussed below and which constitutes an essential element of the structure of *The General Theory*.

In the *Treatise*, Keynes distinguishes two types of deposits: cash and savings deposits. The first are again subdivided into two categories: income deposits, held to cover the interval between the reception of income and its expenses, and business deposits, also linked to the interval between receipts and outgoings. A savings deposit is on the contrary not related to a necessary expense and can be retained until an opportunity presents itself to use it. In *The General Theory*, these categories are transformed into four motives to demand money: the income motive, the business motive, the precautionary motive and the speculative motive (1936-1, pp. 195–6). After the publication of this last book, Keynes added the finance motive, that is, businesses needing liquidity to finance operations.[32]

Cash deposits correspond to what Keynes calls in the *Treatise* industrial circulation, and savings deposits to the financial circulation. This distinction is linked to institutional changes within capitalism, which have led to an autonomization of the finance sector, a determinant factor in the instability of modern economies.[33] There is no automatic motor that leads to equilibrium. Keynes deduced from this the necessity for central banks to act in a way that assures price stability and employment. In *The General Theory*, emphasis is placed on budgetary policy and public investment, which does not eliminate the necessity of a monetary policy of stabilization. At the same time, this transformation is linked to the fact that Keynes's attention moved away from the question of economic fluctuations to that of the persistence of high rates of unemployment.

Keynes opposed in *A Treatise on Money* the quantity theory of money with his 'fundamental equations for the value of money'. Like Marx, he distinguished between the sector of the economy producing investment goods and the sector of consumption goods, a distinction that he abandoned in *The General Theory*. The two fundamental equations give us the price level of consumption goods and the price level for output as a whole. In both cases, the price level is the sum of two terms: the cost of production per unit produced, which Keynes called the 'level of efficiency earnings' and the difference between the cost of new investment and the volume of current savings. Thus we have, for the price level of output as a whole:

$$P = \frac{E}{O} + \frac{I-S}{O}$$

where P is the price level, E the total money income (or expenditure), O the total output, I the value of the increment of new investment goods and S the amount of savings.

Keynes stressed that these equations were identities, like the quantity theory equations. But they also reveal another meaning. They tell us first that investment and saving are of different dimensions, are activities undertaken by different individuals with nothing guaranteeing their equality. This is one of the *Treatise*'s most important messages, which caused the most surprise when Keynes presented it to the Macmillan Committee, as we will see in the following chapter. In what specifically concerns money, these equations tell us that the price level and its fluctuation, inflation and deflation, are not determined by fluctuations of the quantity of money, but by the average cost of production, essentially the level of wages, and especially by the difference between investment and savings, and thus by the actions of entrepreneurs. This difference is expressed by either windfall profits or windfall losses, which unleashes a process of investment variation followed by price change in the same direction. Keynes was inspired here by Wicksell, from whom he borrowed his distinction between natural interest rates, assuring the equality between savings and investment, and market rates fixed by banks. These fundamental equations are thus in the end a means of integrating monetary and real processes. This dichotomy is absurd, since money is real, and economic reality is monetary. Keynes explored this in depth in the 1930s, at the same time as he elaborated the theory of effective demand. He also integrated into his analysis expectations and uncertainty, a fundamental dimension of his worldview which, curiously, was rarely present in the *Treatise*.[34]

A MONETARY THEORY OF PRODUCTION

In the 1930s, Keynes increasingly insisted on the gap separating his conception of the role of money from that of the classics. Each autumn he gave a series of lectures called 'The pure theory of money', the title of the first volume of the *Treatise*.[35] On 10 October 1932, during the first course of the autumn term, he declared to his students: 'Gentlemen, the change in the title of these lectures – (from "The pure theory of money" to "The monetary theory of production") – is significant' (L. Tarshis, 'The Keynesian revolution in the 1930s', unpublished manuscript quoted by Skidelsky, 1992, p. 460).[36] Such was the title that he then decided to give to what would become *The General Theory of Employment, Interest and Money*. He also gave this title to a short but important paper published the following year in the Festschrift in honour of Arthur Spiethoff (1933-3).

Keynes explained to his students that his objective was henceforth to explain the level of production in a monetary economy. This expression does not refer to the customary distinction between a barter and a money economy. In the latter, money is only a means to carry out exchanges. Marx, he recognized, escaped this error by distinguishing between the circulation of commodities and the circulation of capital: 'The distinction between a co-operative economy and an entrepreneur economy bears some relation to a pregnant observation made by Karl Marx' (1933-32, p. 81). On this subject Keynes told his students on 23 October 1933 that in Marx there is 'a kernel of truth' (1989-2, p. 93); 'Therefore Marx's view is right' (ibid., p. 95).[37]

A monetary economy is on the contrary one in which money plays an active role, producing real effects on processes. The economies in which we live are monetary economies. A theory constructed for barter or monetary exchange economies, which Keynes regroups under the general term of real-exchange economy, is thus not adapted to understand modern economies. Neither general treatises nor even treatises on money take into account real-exchange economies.

> An economy, which uses money but uses it merely as a neutral link between transactions in real things and real assets and does not allow it to enter into motives or decisions, might be called – for want of a better name – a *real-exchange economy*. The theory which I desiderate would deal, in contradistinction to this, with an economy in which money plays a part of its own and affects motives and decisions and is, in short, one of the operative factors in the situation, so that the course of events cannot be predicted, either in the long period or in the short, without a knowledge of the behaviour of money between the first state and the last. And it is this which we ought to mean when we speak of a *monetary economy*. (1933-3, pp. 408–9)

Laurie Tarshis recounts that he and his colleagues had the impression of living a singular moment, on 10 October and during the following weeks: 'I attended the first lecture, naturally awed but bothered. As the weeks passed, only a stone would not have responded to the growing excitement [the lectures] generated' (quoted in Skidelsky, 1992, p. 460). It was at this moment that, according to Tarshis, the Keynesian Revolution began, during the trough of the depression which began in 1929. It was the absence of a monetary theory of production that prevented efficient solutions from being understood and proposed. It was still not understood that decisions in an economy are taken in terms of money prices and particularly money wages. Wage-bargains between entrepreneurs and workers do not determine a bundle of goods, but a sum of money. Workers do not go on strike if their real wages diminish because of a rise in consumption goods prices. No government, except those in totalitarian countries, can impose a general reduction of 20 per cent of money wages overnight.

In real-exchange economies, crises, booms and depressions are inconceivable: 'I am saying that booms and depressions are phenomena peculiar to an economy in which – in some significant sense which I am not attempting to define precisely in this place – money is not neutral' (1933-3, p. 411). Keynes announced at the end of the paper from which the above is taken that he was then working on elaborating a monetary theory of production 'in some confidence that I am not wasting my time' (ibid.). The result of this effort would be *The General Theory of Employment, Interest and Money*. Money plays in this a central role, constituting the link between anticipations in an uncertain world and levels of production and employment:

This book, on the other hand, has evolved into what is primarily a study of the forces which determine changes in the scale of output and employment as a whole; and, whilst it is found that money enters into the economic scheme in an essential and peculiar manner, technical monetary detail falls into the background. A monetary economy, we shall find, is essentially one in which changing views about the future are capable of influencing the quantity of employment and not merely its direction. (1936-1, p. xxii)[38]

LIQUIDITY PREFERENCE AND INTEREST

In the theoretical construction that Keynes made public in 1936, the concept of liquidity preference plays a central role, next to the propensity to consume and the marginal efficiency of capital. It is a question of the 'three fundamental psychological factors' (1936-1, pp. 246–7). Keynes claimed first to have discovered the propensity to consume before developing his conception of interest and finally the marginal efficiency of capital. In fact, as we just saw, liquidity preference was already sketched in *A Treatise on Money*. We will return in more detail to the articulation of these three concepts in *The General Theory* in the following chapter and limit ourselves here to a few remarks.[39]

Liquidity refers to the facility with which a commodity can be exchanged against all others, to the rapidity with which it can be transformed into a means of payment without loss or cost. Money, which is not easily produced and which is universally desired, thus represents liquidity par excellence, that which allows one to obtain all other goods, to pay out wages and incomes, to liquidate debts, to be sure of recuperating the initial amount: 'It is characteristic . . . of money that its yield is *nil*, and its carrying-cost negligible, but its liquidity-premium substantial' (1936-1, p. 226).

Preference for liquidity is a psychological propensity, linked to individuals' insecurity, to their fear of the future, which makes them hold in liquid form a more or less considerable part of their assets: 'The possession of actual money lulls our disquietude; and the premium which we require to make us part with money is the measure of the degree of our disquietude' (1937-4, p. 116). This premium is the rate of interest. According to the classical conception, the rate of interest is the reward for abstinence, and it is fixed by the intersection of the supply and demand of capital. According to Keynes, the rate of interest is the reward for the renunciation of liquidity. It results from the intensity of the demand for liquidity and from the supply of money determined by the monetary authorities.

The rate of interest is a highly psychological phenomenon. It is subject to mixed anticipations in which a process of mimetism, which Keynes described in the example of a beauty contest in Chapter 12 of the *General Theory*, plays a role. One chooses, among a hundred photos, the six prettiest faces. The winner is the one whose choice is closest to the average of all the other choices. What matters is thus guessing what others will think, the most skilful at this game thus guessing at the third or fourth degree. In the same way, the rate of interest results in the final analysis from what people think it will be. There is in any case no objective or natural value of these rates, which result from the intertemporal preferences of agents and from the productivity of capital.[40] This is what the Board President of the National Mutual Life Insurance proclaimed to his colleagues on 20 February 1935: 'The current long-term rate of interest is a highly psychological phenomenon which must necessarily depend on what expectations we hold concerning the future rate of interest' (1935-1, p. 212).

Keynes thus believed he was reviving conceptions of former economists, particularly

Montesquieu. As we have seen, Thomas Aquinas, to support his condemnation of usury, defined interest as money's rent. This liquidity premium associated with not holding money has had important consequences:

> That the world after several millennia of steady individual saving, is so poor as it is in accumulated capital-assets, is to be explained, in my opinion, neither by the improvident propensities of mankind, nor even by the destruction of war, but by the high liquidity-premiums formerly attaching to the ownership of land and now attaching to money. (1936-1, p. 242)

The short-term consequences are just as serious. In particular, unemployment, to which we will now turn, is closely linked to monetary phenomena: 'Unemployment develops, that is to say, because people want the moon; – men cannot be employed when the object of desire (i.e. money) is something which cannot be produced and the demand for which cannot be readily choked off' (1936-1, p. 235).

In the Preface to the French edition of *The General Theory*, Keynes emphasized that his interest theory is a central and original element of his approach: 'it is the function of the rate of interest to preserve equilibrium, not between the demand and the supply of new capital goods, but between the demand and the supply of money, that is to say between the demand for *liquidity* and the means of satisfying this demand' (ibid., p. xxxiv). This discovery is linked to 'my final escape from the confusions of the Quantity Theory, which once entangled me' (ibid.).

This is the only question to which Keynes returned on several occasions after the publication of *The General Theory* (1937-1, 1937-7, 1937-11, 1938-7). The majority of cases were replies to critiques, particularly from Hicks, Ohlin and Roberston, which sought to show that the gap was not in fact so wide between Keynes's theory of interest and orthodox ideas on the question, according to which 'the rate of interest is fixed at the level where the supply of credit, in the shape of saving, is equal to the demand for credit, in the shape of investment' (1937-7, p. 206). He insisted on stressing his difference:

> The above is altogether remote from my contention that the rate of interest (as we call it for short) is, strictly speaking, a *monetary* phenomenon in the special sense that it is the *own rate* of interest on money itself, i.e. that it equalises the advantages of holding actual cash and a deferred claim on cash. (1937-7, p. 206)

It was during these discussions that Keynes introduced a new motive of demand for money, related to the fact 'that an investment *decision* may sometimes involve a temporary demand for money before it is carried out, quite distinct from the demand for active balances which will arise as the result of the investment activity whilst it is going on' (ibid., p 207). This demand for finance moves investment even further away from saving. Liquidities, supplied by the banking system, allow for the financing *ex ante* of an investment project before the appearance of any savings: 'It is, to an important extent, the "financial" facilities which regulate the *pace* of new investment' (ibid., p. 210). And it is not the rate of interest but, as we will explain in the following chapter, the variation of income that brings about *ex post* the equality of savings and investment.

With these new developments, Keynes returned to an endogenous conception of monetary creation, already present in *A Treatise on Money*, in which the banking system played a key role. In *The General Theory*, Keynes completed his analysis of the rate of interest by supposing that the money supply is fixed by monetary authorities. It can therefore be considered as exogenous. Following Hicks, Keynes's neoclassical interpreters would consider it in this way, while post-Keynesians would in contrast emphasize money's endogenity.[41] But we have moved from Keynes to Keynesianism, a theme to which we will return in the Conclusion. It is sufficient to note, once again, that Keynes's positions were variable and that he in no way feared assuming contradiction. We have also, in this chapter as we will do in the next, followed closely the way Keynes defined what he called 'classical economics'. We mentioned, in Chapter 3, the fact that Whitehead, in his report on Keynes's dissertation on probability, accused its author of caricaturing those he criticized by presenting their arguments 'at their stupidest'. To make his point, Keynes has a tendency to create scarecrows. The 'classical theory' is of course something more complex and diversified than the picture given by Keynes. Some so-called 'classical' economists anticipated certain elements of Keynes's theory. This must be kept in mind in reading the next chapter.[42]

NOTES

1. Keynes's first book, *Indian Currency and Finance* (1913-1) already contains views on money and the international monetary system that he will later develop. See Dimand (1991) and Ferrandier (1985).
2. Including a collection of paintings and old books estimated at £20 000. See KP, SE/11/7/94.
3. Approximately $22 millions US at today's (June 2006) rate of exchange.
4. Milton Friedman believed this explained Keynes's errors, his positions in favour of monetary laxism. He never understood how much the acquisition of money actually cost. See his remarks in Blaug (1990).
5. These figures, and those which follow, only give a general and approximate idea of Keynes's financial situation. For a more exact vision, one would have to take into account the evolution of the price index. Thus, for consumer goods' prices, on a basis of 100 in 1913, the index was established at 202.8 in 1945, reaching a high of 250 in 1920 and a low of 144.4 in 1935.
6. On Keynes's career as an investor, see JMK 12, pp. 1–113. See also Moggridge (1992, pp. 348–52, 407–11).
7. In most of these undertakings, Keynes collaborated with Falk. Business relations between the two friends deteriorated in the 1930s.
8. He speculated against the pound sterling and the mark, whose values remained steady relative to the dollar. He had previously, in autumn 1919, lost £13 235 by speculating against the mark (JMK 17, p. 131).
9. See JMK 12, pp. 10–12 and Moggridge (1992, p. 586).
10. Francis Clayton Scott (1881–1979), a graduate from Oxford, was president of the Provincial Insurance Company.
11. They are reproduced in JMK 12, pp. 114–239.
12. See Chapter 8.
13. Harrod, who knew him well, wrote: 'He was throughout his life careful about small money matters' (1951, p. 304). His friends, with whom he was very generous, sometimes accused him of stinginess when he received them. Lytton Strachey, for example, wrote to Carrington on 25 September 1925, after having been received at Tilton: 'Would you believe it? Not a drop of alcohol appeared. The Charlestonians declare that Il gran Pozzo is now immensely rich – probably £10,000 a year. I can believe it and water, water everywhere! Such is the result of wealth' (Strachey Papers, BL, Add 60721). Pozzo di Borgo, Russia's ambassador to Paris from 1814 to 1834, was a nickname given to Keynes by Strachey in 1908.
14. Madam Stephens, 'Missie', was Keynes's secretary for the 12 years preceding his death, following him to the Treasury and often accompanying him to the United States. She organized his papers before Roy Harrod undertook the writing of Keynes's 'authorized biography'. It was also she who typed the manuscript and corrected the book's proofs.
15. A part of what follows has been developed in Dostaler (1997) and Dostaler and Maris (2000). On the relations between Freud and Keynes, see Bonadei (1994), Castex (2003, vol. 3), Mini (1994), Parsons (1997) and Winslow (1986, 1992).
16. He wrote to Strachey on 23 January 1906: 'Have you ever read the Ethics of that superb Aristotle? the greatest of works and with few of the follies with which all his commentators seem to credit him. There never was such good sense talked – before or since.'
17. *Chrémata* means money wealth in Greek.

18. According to legend, Midas, the eighth century BC King of Phrygia, a country rich in gold and iron mines, obtained from Bacchus the power to transform everything he touched into gold. Fearing death from thirst and hunger, he implored the god to deliver him from this privilege, which he obtained by bathing in the Pactole River. The Pactole, carrying flakes of gold, would make Cresus, King of Lydia, very rich.
19. We will see below what Keynes understood by this. While for the classics, interest was the reward for abstinence, it was for Keynes the reward for the renunciation of liquidity, the rent of money.
20. We will return in Chapter 8 to Jones's remarkable prophesy concerning the return to the gold standard.
21. On the quantitative theory of money, and more generally on the history of monetary theories, see Blaug et al. (1995), Bridel (1987), de Boyer (2003), S. Diatkine (1995) and Laidler (1991).
22. Leaving aside the question of what is exactly understood by money, whose forms are evidently much more diversified than they were in the time of Jean Bodin or David Hume.
23. On the relations between the monetary theories of Keynes and Ricardo, see Deleplace (1998).
24. Marshall gave its first formulation in a manuscript from 1871, which was for a long time unpublished, but of which Keynes was certainly familiar, 'Essay on money' (in Marshall, 1975, vol. 1, pp. 164–76).
25. For an analysis emphasizing convergences between Friedman and Keynes, see Frazer (1994). See also Dostaler (1998).
26. This analysis of the relation between changes in the quantity and velocity of money could be found elsewhere, in particular in Fisher (1911).
27. It is difficult to establish the date of these notes, written and constantly edited and reused between 1909 and 1923.
28. But one must admit that for Fisher, as for Wicksell, quantity theory does not suppose a mechanical and instantaneous relation between variation of quantity of money and price level. They were, like Keynes, preoccupied by the transitory period between these two events.
29. Keynes published, when he was giving these lectures, a review of the *Theorie des Geldes und der Umlaufsmittel* (1912) by Ludwig von Mises (1914-6), without remarking or underlining the resemblance between his ideas and those of Mises on measurement. On measurement of value in Keynes and in classical economics, see Seccareccia (1982).
30. See also JMK 12, p. 701.
31. On *A Treatise on Money*, see Bauvert (2003), Dimand (1986), Friboulet (1985), Hanin (2003), Hicks (1967), Pineault (2003) and Rymes (1998).
32. See Davidson (1965) and Graziani (1987).
33. See on this subject Vicarelli (1984), Minsky (1975, 1977) and Tutin (2003).
34. For Bateman (1996), the integration of uncertainty in Keynes's analysis has nothing to do with his work on probabilities, but follows rather from his experiences as an investor and government adviser.
35. Thomas Ryme transcribed and reconstructed these notes as 'notes of a representative student' in Keynes (1989-2). See also Rymes (1986).
36. Laurie Tarshis was a Canadian student who attended Keynes's lectures from 1932 to 1935. His notes, as well as those of other students, have been retrieved in Keynes (1989-2). See Tarshis (1978) and Hamouda and Price (1998). He was the author of what was probably the first Keynesian textbook, *Elements of Economics* (1947), eclipsed by Paul Samuelson's *Economics*, published the following year.
37. We will return to this in the following chapter.
38. 'On the other hand', at the beginning of the quotation, means in contrast to *A Treatise on Money*, which Keynes had just criticized.
39. Theories of interest rates and of preference for liquidity have raised a number of controversies and interpretations. See among others Brossard (1998), de Boyer (1982, 1998), Deleplace (1988), Le Héron (1986), Léonard and Norel (1991), Milgate (1977), Moore (1988), Orléan (1988) Tortajada (1985) and Winslow (1995).
40. Keynes, as we have mentioned, abandoned Wicksell's idea of a natural rate of interest, linked to the productivity of capital, after the *Treatise on Money*.
41. On this question see Elie (1998), Lavoie (1986), Moore (1984), Wray (1990) and the papers collected in Deleplace and Nell (1996).
42. On this, see Eshag (1963), Bridel (1987) and Laidler (1999).

7. Labour: the battle against unemployment

But the absurdity of labour being from time to time totally unemployed, in spite of everyone wanting more goods, can only be due to a muddle, which should be remediable if we could think and act clearly.
'Currency policy and unemployment' (1923-21, p. 113)

The paradox is to be found in 250,000 building operatives out of work in Great Britain, when more houses are our greatest material need. It is the man who tells us that there is no means, consistent with sound finance and political wisdom, of getting the one to work at the other, whose judgement we should instinctively doubt.
The Means to Prosperity (1933-2, p. 336)

The outstanding faults of the economic society in which we live are its failure to provide for full employment and its arbitrary and inequitable distribution of wealth and incomes.
The General Theory of Employment, Interest and Money (1936-1, p. 372)

The word 'labour' has always been associated with the idea of effort, fatigue, even punishment. History, we are told, started in Eden before God condemned Adam and Eve to earn a living through toil after tasting the fruit of the tree of knowledge of good and evil. St Paul preached to the Thessalonians: 'this we commanded you, that if any would not work, neither should he eat' (2.3.10). The Greek citizen managed to escape this malediction, as slaves were employed to provide for their master's material needs. Aristotle justified slavery by arguing for the slave's natural inferiority. For his part, Jesus, a carpenter's son who surrounded himself with 12 workers, valorized manual labour. In the eighteenth century, Thomas Aquinas established Church doctrine, still in effect today, which condemned slavery and described labour as the natural activity of free men who, by working, remove themselves from sin and keep evil thoughts at bay. This did not prevent some very Christian nations from tolerating slavery for several centuries.[1]

Following William Petty (*A Treatise on Taxes and Contributions*, 1662), most classical economists made labour the foundation of commodities' exchange value. For Adam Smith, 'Labour, therefore, is the real measure of the exchangeable value of all commodities' . . . and this labour is associated with the 'toil of our own body' (Smith, 1776, vol. 1, p. 24). Moreover, wages, labour's remuneration, vary 'with the ease or hardship, the cleanliness or dirtiness, the honourableness or dishonourableness of the employment' (ibid., p. 80). Ricardo affirmed that 'the value of a commodity, or the quantity of any other commodity for which it will exchange, depends on the relative quantity of labour which is necessary for its production' (Ricardo, 1821, p. 11). For Marx, 'all labour is, speaking physiologically, an expenditure of human labour-power, and in its character of identical abstract human labour, it creates and forms the value of commodities' (Marx, 1867, p. 54).

Not all classical economists make labour the foundation of value. Say, for example, anticipated the marginalist revolution and announced the neoclassical approach by making utility the cause of value. However, in the marginalist view, labour remained present as a factor of production with which the idea of disutility is associated: 'The most important parts of the theory will turn upon the exact equality, without regard to sign, of the pleasure derived from the possession of an object, and the pain encountered in its acquisition' (Jevons, 1871, p. 97). Keynes gave labour a central place in his economic vision:

> I sympathise, therefore, with the pre-classical doctrine that everything is *produced* by *labour* ... It is preferable to regard labour, including, of course, the personal services of the entrepreneur and his assistants, as the sole factor of production, operating in a given environment of technique, natural resources, capital equipment and effective demand. This partly explains why we have been able to take the unit of labour as the sole physical unit which we require in our economic system, apart from units of money and of time. (1936-1, p. 213–4)

Keynes thus used in *The General Theory* quantities of money value and employment as units of measurement. Wages bridge the gap between both. To a labour unit, measured in hours, days, weeks or years, corresponds a money-wage. These money-wages Keynes called wage-units, and it is in this unit that the quantity of employment in an economy is measured.

UNEMPLOYMENT BEFORE KEYNES

There is thus a long tradition behind the association of labour with effort and pain. And yet it is an even greater misfortune to be deprived of work, unless one disposes of an income allowing one to escape this modern form of slavery. For most of the population, employment is practically the only means of obtaining income and thus consumption. Unemployment is seen as an evil, an economic, social and political problem. In a paper prepared for the Royal Commission on Gold and Silver, which sat in 1887 and 1888, Alfred Marshall linked the increase in 'irregularity of employment' to the development of 'modern forms of industry' (Marshall, 1926, p. 92). It seems that John Hobson was the first to use the word 'unemployment', in *The Problem of the Unemployed*, published in 1896.

Later involuntary unemployment would be distinguished from voluntary unemployment. A voluntary unemployed worker for example refuses to take an available job because of the wages it pays. Unemployment can also be linked to the time required to search when one is between jobs: this is frictional unemployment, whose importance is the result of, for example, the availability of information in an economy. While frictional unemployment is short-term, structural unemployment results from a disequilibrium between workers' qualifications and the nature of jobs, an imbalance caused by transformations in the economy. It is also linked to the job market's institutional characteristics. In the latter case, a new term was developed by Milton Friedman in 1968, that of the 'natural rate of unemployment', whose level is determined by real forces such as the structural characteristics of the labour market, the nature of trade unionism, unemployment insurance, the difficulties in gathering information.[2] Seasonal unemployment is also identified in activities such as agriculture, fishing and construction.

As always, reality manifests itself before words can be found to express it. Unemployment appeared at the same time as paid labour, thus before the birth of capitalism. There were unemployed people in Rome and in Medieval cities. But it was with the accumulation of capital in the sixteenth century that the phenomenon became widespread. From the beginning, it aroused in those who observed it a contradictory reaction. Unemployment was a source of misery and idleness. In this regard it represented the danger, of which all mercantilist thinkers were aware, of social disorder and unrest in the popular classes. Peasant revolts remained fresh in the collective memory. In 1615, Antoine de Montchrestien, in his *Traité d'économie politique*, wrote that, in a prosperous kingdom, men must be both active and interactive. Underlining the dangers of idleness, he justified protectionism by the fact that it stimulated a nation's employment. A nation's true wealth is not linked to the quantity of gold it possesses, contrary to the opinion most often associated with mercantilism, but to labour and production.

But, at the same time as mercantilists proposed means of stimulating employment, which brought them praise from Keynes at the end of *The General Theory*,[3] they were conscious of the fact that full employment exerts an upward pressure on wages unfavourable to the prosperity of merchants and manufacturers. This is why they were partisans of demographic growth. Beyond the fact that growing populations assured the availability of the cannon fodder indispensable for pursuing the aggressive foreign policies of the period, it constituted a means of exerting a downward pressure on wages. This is a central idea not only in Marx and Keynes, but also in one construction of modern economic theory, the Phillips Curve.

The Classical Era

With the arrival of the Industrial Revolution at the end of the eighteenth century, unemployment became an increasingly massive and generalized phenomenon. The recurrence of cyclical fluctuations started to be discerned, throughout which the number of the unemployed varied along with other economic indicators. The introduction of increasingly sophisticated machines led to massive layoffs of poorly qualified workers unable to find jobs. These circumstances provoked revolts in which workers seized and destroyed machines. The Luddites were one such movement.[4] Born in Nottingham in 1811, it spread all over England until 1816. David Ricardo, the first edition of whose *Principles of Political Economy and Taxation* appeared in 1817, first thought that workers were mistaken in believing that mechanized production was the main cause of unemployment. He modified this point of view and added to the third edition of 1821 a new chapter on machines, in which he declared: 'but I am convinced, that the substitution of machinery to human labour, is often very injurious to the interests of the class of labourers' (Ricardo, 1821, p. 388). While his friends and disciples were dismayed by this abrupt turn, Marx would praise the scientific honesty of this 'bourgeois' economist.

Say's Law

Following Smith, classical economists were at pains to explain the phenomenon of unemployment, which remained unnamed. In his *Treatise on Political Economy* of 1803, Jean-Baptiste Say published the first formulation of the famous law bearing his name, also called the 'law of markets', according to which, on the scale of the whole economy, supply creates its own demand.[5] There are several formulations of this, by Say and also by James Mill, Ricardo and others. One states that 'it is production which opens a demand for products' (Say, 1803, p. 133). Replying to Malthus, his main critic, Say wrote: 'I think I have proved in my first letter that productions can only be purchased with productions: I do not therefore yet see any reason to abandon the doctrine, that it is production which opens a market to production' (Say, 1821, p. 24). This proposition is based on the quantity theory of money, by virtue of which money only serves as a means of exchange: 'money is but the agent of the transfer of values' (Say, 1803, p. 133). Even if it is hoarded, 'the ultimate object is always to employ it in a purchase of some kind' (ibid.). Production has no other goal but to exchange money obtained from the sale of our goods against other products. Production constitutes a demand for other products. A rise in production increases incomes which in turn leads to a rise in spending of an equal amount. All savings are transformed into investment destined to raise future consumption. It is useless to stimulate demand artificially: 'the encouragement of mere consumption is no benefit to commerce (ibid., p. 139).

In accordance with this conception, a phenomenon of overproduction, of general glut, is impossible. Only sectorial disequilibrium between supply and demand is possible. Ricardo, who accepted Say's Law, believed crises were provoked by 'sudden changes in the channels of trade'.[6] Thus the end of the Napoleonic Wars in 1815 led to serious economic disturbances expressed by, for example, important rises in unemployment caused by soldier demobilization. Neither the concept of full employment nor that of unemployment is present in Say and his contemporaries, but their approach can be interpreted in modern terms in the statement according to which an economy in equilibrium tends, in the absence of external shocks and dysfunctional markets, toward full employment.

This macroeconomic argument was reinforced by a new microeconomic conception with which Say opposed Smith and his friend Ricardo. For Say, value does not result from work but rather utility. It is determined by the interaction of supply and demand on the market. This determination not only applies to goods produced by entrepreneurs, but also to factors of production leased to the latter by economic agents. Included in these factors is labour. The price of this service is a wage, which is thus determined by supply and demand. Say does not make a rigorous demonstration of this, but, if wages are really determined in this way and no obstacle prevents the negotiation between entrepreneur, work seeker and the person offering his work, the equilibrium between supply and demand signifies the absence of involuntary unemployment and thus full employment.

It is thus not surprising that, in Chapter 2 of *The General Theory*, 'The postulates of the classical economics', Keynes links Say's Law, the quantity theory of money and the determination of wages on the labour market. Though classical theory admits 'frictional' and 'voluntary' unemployment, 'classical postulates do not admit of the possibility of the third category, which I shall define below as "involuntary" unemployment' (1936-1, p. 6).

Malthus against Say

However, unanimity was far from the rule among Say and Ricardo's contemporaries. Several economists and social thinkers, observing both masses of unsold goods and jobless men ready to work for any wage in order to avoid starvation, could not accept the arguments proposed to them. Two famous names were among them, one on the right of the political spectrum, the other on the left. The Reverend Thomas Robert Malthus and Simonde de Sismondi opposed the law of markets and classical analyses with arguments anticipating those of Marx and Keynes.

Malthus shared, in contrast to Ricardo, Say's vision of value and distribution. He believed, like the latter, that remuneration of productive services is fixed in the same way as values of goods, which 'are determined by the demand, compared with the supply of them' (Malthus, 1820, p. 62). But he was radically opposed to the law of markets formulated by Say and adopted by Ricardo. To assure a market for production, he believed that one needs an 'effectual demand', which he defined as 'the sacrifice which the demanders must make in order to effectuate the continued supply of the commodity in the quantity required under the actual circumstances' (ibid., p. 80). It is not only a matter of there being purchasing power, but also a desire to buy, 'a demand by those who are able and willing to pay an adequate price for them' (ibid., p. 328).

From then on, high levels of savings, which since Smith was understood as the motor of capital accumulation and economic growth, became in contrast an impediment to production. The growth of production required an increase in demand, while for Say it increased it automatically. Overproduction crises, manifested in the paradox of man's poverty amidst an abundance of goods, are thus possible. To combat them, Malthus advocated public works, foreign trade and stimulation of unproductive spending, particularly by aristocrats, landlords and members of the clergy.

It is therefore hardly surprising that Keynes saw in Malthus a precursor.[7] Reworked several times, his portrait of Malthus figured among his most famous economist biographies. He presented him as 'the first of the Cambridge economists'. The initial version of his portrait was presented at the Oxford Political Philosophy and Science Club on 2 May 1914, then revised for the London Political Economy Club in 1922. The last version was prepared for his *Essays in Biography*, published in 1933. The sections pertaining to Malthus's vision of saving, investment and effective demand were added to the book's proofs early in 1933.[8]

By this time, as we will see further on, Keynes had developed the main elements of his theory of effective demand. At the same time, Sraffa, who was editing Ricardo's works, made available to Keynes the correspondence between Malthus, whose letters he discovered in 1930, and Ricardo, 'the most important literary correspondence in the whole development of Political Economy' (1933-5, p. 96). As Keynes would repeat in *The General Theory*, Ricardo's victory over Malthus in their controversy constituted a catastrophe which led economic theory down the wrong path for a century. As he explained in an allocution celebrating the centenary of his death, Malthus understood perfectly well the harmful effects of excessive savings on production:

> In the second half of his life he was preoccupied with the post-war unemployment which then first disclosed itself on a formidable scale, and he found the explanation in what he called the insufficiency of effective demand; to cure which he called for a spirit of free expenditure, public works and a policy of expansionism ... A hundred years were to pass before there would be anyone to read with even a shadow of sympathy and understanding his powerful and unanswerable attacks on the great Ricardo. (1935-3, p. 107)

In *The General Theory*, Keynes would add that Malthus was unable to counter Ricardo's affirmation according to which it is impossible for effective demand to be insufficient because he was unable to provide a convincing alternative explanation beyond appealing to facts. This is why 'Ricardo conquered England as completely as the Holy Inquisition conquered Spain' (1936-1, p. 32). It was left to Keynes to provide an alternative explanation to Ricardo and the classical economists.

Sismondi, precursor of Marx and Keynes

Ignored by Keynes, the Swiss economist and historian Simonde de Sismondi proposed, a year before Malthus in his *Nouveaux Principes d'économie Politique* (1819), a heterodox analysis of capitalism which underlined the cyclical fluctuations engendering underemployment and poverty. A disciple of Smith, in his first book *De la Richesse Commerciale* (1803), Sismondi became a radical critic of classical liberalism and a resolute opponent of Say's Law, for which he substituted a macroeconomic analysis in terms of disequilibrium and the first algebraically formulated growth model. For Sismondi, capitalism was a transitory and contradictory historical system in which the interests of the rich collide with the interests of the proletariat. Sismondi was one of the first to use this term to characterize the social class having only wage income on which to survive. There is an inevitable tendency towards the pauperization of the proletariat. Against Say and Ricardo and with Malthus, Sismondi affirmed that general overproduction of goods in an economy is possible:

> On the other side, Mr. Malthus, in England, has held, as I have tried to do on the Continent, that consumption is not at all a necessary consequence of production; that the needs and the desires of man are indeed without limit, but that such needs and desires are not satisfied by consumption unless they are tied to the ability to exchange. We have asserted that it is not at all sufficient to create such means of exchange in order to let them pass into the hands of those who have these desires or wants; that it happens quite often that the means of exchange increase in a society while the demand for labour, or the wage, decreases; that then the wants and needs of one part of the population could not be satisfied, and consumption also declined. Finally, we have claimed that the one unmistakable sign of a society's prosperity was not the growing production of wealth, but a growing demand for labour, or an increase in offered wages that rewards it. (Sismondi, 1824, pp. 617–18)

Of note in the preceding quotation is the expression 'demand for labour': crises thus generate unemployment. For Sismondi, it is because they abstract themselves from time that Ricardo, Say and their disciples fail to perceive the phenomena of which businesspeople are perfectly aware. It is the conjunction of temporal disequilibrium between production and consumption and the unequal distribution of wealth within society that causes recurrent crises. The proletariat does not receive enough income to ensure adequate effective demand.

Marx and the industrial reserve army

Sismondi was a precursor of Keynes and also of Marx. In contrast to Keynes, Marx presented Sismondi's arguments on several occasions, but most often it was to criticize them. It is peculiar to observe Marx treating Ricardo with more consideration than he does the historian from Geneva. That said, Marx formed with Malthus and Sismondi a trio comprising the main opponents to Say's Law. Allergic to Marx's work,[9] Keynes nevertheless recognized in him the merit of having updated Say's error: 'The great puzzle of effective demand with which Malthus had wrestled vanished from economic literature . . . It could only live on furtively, below the surface, in the underworlds of Karl Marx, Silvio Gesell or Major Douglas' (1936-1, p. 32). But this recognition resembled a kiss of Judas, since Keynes put Marx on the same footing as two rather obscure economists.[10]

It was with Marx that unemployment fully entered economic analysis and was presented as one of capitalism's main phenomena, illustrating the contradictions of an economic and socially transitory system inevitably destined to disappear. Far from being accidental, unemployment, like the economic crises with which it is linked, is a necessity, a fundamental aspect of capitalism. In *Wage-Labour and Capital*, Marx affirmed that 'the industrial war of the capitalists among themselves . . . has the peculiarity that its battles are won less by recruiting than by discharging the army of labour' (Marx, 1848, p. 266). The presence of the term 'army' almost 20 years before the publication of Volume 1 of *Capital* is noteworthy. The description of unemployment as an 'industrial reserve army' is one of Marx's most famous metaphors.[11] It encapsulates the idea, already present in mercantilism and found in Keynes and his disciples,[12] of the link between pressures on wages and unemployment. For Marx, the industrial reserve army is essential for maintaining profit rates and thus to the very existence of capitalism:

> But if a surplus labouring population is a necessary product of accumulation or of the development of wealth on a capitalist basis, this surplus-population becomes, conversely, the lever of capitalistic accumulation, nay, a condition of existence of the capitalist mode of prooduction. It forms a disposable industrial reserve army, that belongs to capital quite as absolutely as if the latter had bred it at its own cost. Independently of the limits of the actual increase of population, it creates, for the changing needs of the self-expansion of capital, a mass of human material always ready for exploitation. (Marx, 1867, p. 693)

The continuous transformation of a part of the working class into partial or complete unemployed is an essential component of capital accumulation: 'The same causes which develop the expansive power of capital, develops also the labour-power at its disposal. The relative mass of the industrial reserve army increases therefore with the potential energy of wealth ... *This is the absolute general law of capitalist accumulation*' (ibid., p. 707). The reserve army increases and decreases according to how the conjuncture develops, thus playing the role of wage regulator. Crises, provoked by the lowering of profit rates leading to a plethora of capital and over-accumulation, express themselves through depreciation, mothballing and even the partial destruction of capital. The rise in unemployment they provoke allows at the same time for the restoration of profit which leads to an ulterior broadening of production. The industrial reserve army is thus maintained in balance with the progress of accumulation: 'Relative surplus-population is therefore the pivot upon which the law of demand and supply of labour works' (ibid., p. 701). Marx believed that with the growth of capitalism, the reserve army would grow proportionately with the population: 'Accumulation of wealth at one pole is, therefore, at the same time accumulation of misery, agony of toil, slavery, ignorance, brutality, mental degradation, at the opposite pole, i.e., on the side of the class that produces its own product in the form of capital' (ibid., p. 709). The overthrow of capitalism and its replacement by socialism are the only paths out of this impasse.

Keynes's main effort in economic theory consisted in trying to demonstrate that the problem of unemployment could be resolved within capitalism by supplying a different explanation, one challenging the neoclassical approach.[13] In this undertaking, he sometimes used Marx, despite his negative opinion of his work. He recognized that Marx understood well the difference between a real and monetary economy with his distinction between the formula of commodity circulation C-M-C, and that of capital circulation M-C-M', where M represents money and C commodities. Keynes even borrowed Marx's formula in one of the drafts of *The General Theory* when he explained that the difference between M' and M, the surplus value, is negative in periods of depression and crisis:[14] 'Marx, however, was approaching the intermediate truth when he added that the continuous excess of M' would be inevitably interrupted by a series of crises, gradually increasing in intensity, or entrepreneur bankruptcy and underemployment, during which, presumably, M must be in excess' (1933-32, p. 82). He believed his own theory reconciled Marx and underconsumptionists such as Major Douglas.[15]

Joan Robinson, author of *An Essay in Marxian Economics* (1942), believed Keynes would have arrived at the theory of effective demand sooner if he had started from Marx and not from orthodox theory. For her, Kalecki was lucky to never have been exposed to classical theory and to have known only Marx and Rosa Luxemburg. This is why he arrived more quickly at a similar and in some regards superior theory to that of Keynes, which was first published in Polish in 1933:

> Kalecki had one great advantage over Keynes – he had never learned orthodox economics . . . The only economics he had studied was Marx. Keynes could never make head or tail of Marx . . . But starting from Marx would have saved him a lot of trouble. Kahn, at the 'circus' where we discussed the *Treatise* in 1931, explained the problem of saving and investment by imagining a cordon round the capital-good industries and then studying the trade between them and the consumption-good industries; he was struggling to rediscover Marx's schema. Kalecki began at that point. (Robinson 1964[1965], pp. 95–6)

The Neoclassical Era

We saw in the previous chapter how Keynes borrowed the expression 'classical economists' from Marx, modifying his definition to include what was called around 1900 neoclassical theory, born of the 1870s Marginalist revolution led by Jevons, Menger and Walras.[16] The split between classics and neoclassics is mainly situated on the level of value and distribution theory, although several great names from the classical world believed, like the marginalists, that value was linked to utility and determined by the mechanism of supply and demand. On the macroeconomic level, or what was then called monetary theory, Keynes considered that there was continuity. Classical theory is based on the following two pillars: the quantity theory of money and Say's Law, which brings it to deny the existence of involuntary unemployment.

Neoclassical theory adds to this a presentation of the functioning of the market founded on the hypotheses of decreasing marginal utility and marginal productivity and on an understanding of the economic agent as a hedonistic and rational *homo œconomicus* who balances pleasure and pain through calculation. This presentation may take the form of an abstract, formalized and mathematized model, in which one seeks to integrate relations between all markets in an economy. Such is the case for Walras's general equilibrium model of the 1870s, whose outline can already be found in Quesnay and Say and which became the dominant approach in the twentieth century. Or it takes the form of Marshall's partial equilibrium model.

Among these markets, we are interested here in the labour market. Here workers, whose supply of labour increases with rising wages, confront entrepreneurs, who will substitute capital for labour with these wage increases. We thus have a labour supply curve with a positive slope and a demand curve with a negative slope. These two curves normally cross at one point, determining the equilibrium level of real wage and employment. For Marshall, if these curves have the slopes we just described, expressing the rationality of entrepreneurs and workers, then any movement away from equilibrium unleashes forces that bring it back. In short, it is a stable equilibrium. This means that, in the case of labour, if there are no obstacles to the free play of markets, supply equals demand at the level of full employment. Wage is then equal to the marginal product of labour, the rise of total production caused by the addition of a unit of labour. The wage rate thus measures the contribution of workers to production, while the interest rate measures that of capital, and rent that of land. American economist John Bates Clark went the furthest in affirming the legitimacy of a system in which each factor of production receives exactly the value of what it created.[17] Knut Wicksell, who developed this theory independently,[18] believed this mode of distribution in no way guaranteed equity and justice. For Walras, an optimal situation is attained through a process of trial and error, within the context of 'free competition in production . . . since free competition consists, on the one hand, in allowing entrepreneurs freedom to expand output in case of a profit and to restrict output in case of a loss; and, on the other hand, in allowing land-owners, workers and capitalists, as well as entrepreneurs, freedom to buy or sell services and products by bidding against one another' (Walras, 1874–77, p. 255).

The existence of trade unions collectively negotiating wages superior to the equilibrium wage or government decisions fixing minimum wages is a hindrance to this free competition and one cause of unemployment. According to this perspective, the solution to unemployment is to lower wages. This solution is proposed by Pigou in *Unemployment*, published in 1913. Marshall's successor to the chair of political economy at Cambridge, Pigou was a colleague and friend of Keynes. In 1933 at the trough of the depression, he offered the same solution in a much more important work, *The Theory of Unemployment*, which provided a sophisticated version of the marginal productivity of labour theory. Keynes was then working on his own explanation of unemployment and the publication of Pigou's book arrived at the right time, helping him illustrate the flaws of classical theory. Pigou would be Keynes's scapegoat in *The General Theory*. The latter describes *The Theory of Unemployment* as 'mainly a study of what determines changes in the volume of employment, assuming that there is no involuntary unemployment' (1936-1, p. 190). Pigou reacted sharply to Keynes's attacks, but in a way that did not call into question their friendship.[19] He then moved towards Keynes's positions in *Employment and Equilibrium* (1941) and especially in *A Retrospective View*, which was made up of conferences published in 1950, a few years after his retirement. He now admitted the possibility of important levels of unemployment in circumstances of short-term equilibrium, which classical theory could not explain. This attests to the intellectual honesty of the man. Lionel Robbins, a resolute opponent of Keynes in the 1930s, would make the same revisions towards the end of his life.

Keynes against the Classics

The General Theory opens by attacking the so-called classical theory of employment as it was constructed from Say and Ricardo to Marshall and Pigou. For Keynes, its cardinal sin is that it considers as given what needed explanation, namely the level of employment and production. In contrast to Ricardo, the principal object of political economy is not the distribution of a nation's wealth, but the explanation of what determines its level. In this general context, classical theory's view of employment rests on two postulates. The first affirms that '*The wage is equal to the marginal product of labour*'; the second that '*The utility of the wage when a given volume of labour is employed is equal to the marginal disutility of that amount of employment*' (Keynes 1936-1, p. 5, italics in the book). The first postulate allows for the construction of a demand curve for labour by firms; the second, of a supply curve of labour by workers. The intersection of these two curves gives 'the amount of employment . . . fixed at the point where the utility of the marginal product balances the disutility of the marginal employment' (ibid., p. 6). This model allows for the existence of frictional unemployment and voluntary unemployment, but not, according to Keynes, involuntary unemployment.[20]

This construction is untenable, for the labour supply curve as postulated by classical theory does not exist. Keynes admitted the existence of classical theory's first postulate, but not its second. Workers do not negotiate real wages, like in the classical model, but money wages. These wages are the result of bargaining between workers, unionized in most cases, and enterprises. Wage earners are not in a position to 'bring their real wages into conformity with the marginal disutility of the amount of employment offered by the employers at that wage' (ibid., p. 11). What is more, classical economists postulate that workers are in a position to determine the rate of real wages corresponding to full employment. In reality, one finds the opposite: if a decrease in real wages is provoked, not by a decrease in nominal wages but by price rises, then the supply of labour does not diminish, in contrast to classical theory's second postulate. Real wages are thus determined by factors other than the supply and demand of labour. The conclusions of this analysis invalidate the political prescriptions of classical economists to curb unemployment:

> Thus it is fortunate that the workers, though unconsciously, are instinctively more reasonable econ- omists than the classical school, inasmuch as they resist reduction of money-wages . . . Every trade union will put up some resistance to a cut in money-wages, however small. But since no trade union would dream of striking on every occasion of a rise in the cost of living, they do not raise the obsta- cle to any increase in aggregate employment which is attributed to them by the classical school. (1936-1, pp. 14–15)

Classical theory's errors have their source in an erroneous conception of knowledge:

> The classical theorists resemble Euclidean geometers in a non-Euclidean world who, discovering that in experience straight lines apparently parallel often meet, rebuke the lines for not keeping straight . . . Yet, in truth, there is no remedy except to throw over the axiom of parallels and to work out a non-Euclidean geometry. (ibid., p. 16)

The non-Euclidean geometry called for here is the theory of effective demand to which we will return below. It is squarely opposed to most of the elements of classical theory which dominated minds for more than a century: the neutrality of money, Say's Law, the determi- nation of interest rates by saving and investment. From this emerges

> The celebrated *optimism* of traditional economic theory, which has led to economists being looked upon as Candides, who, having left this world for the cultivation of their gardens, teach that all is for the best in the best of all possible worlds provided we will let well alone . . . It may well be that the classical theory represents the way in which we should like our economy to behave. (ibid., pp. 33–4)[21]

KEYNES AND UNEMPLOYMENT

A detour is required before proceeding to Keynes's non-Euclidean theory. This theory started to assume its definitive form in 1932, three years after the outbreak of a crisis that would push the unemployment rate to more than 20 per cent in most big industrialized countries. Even before this, the number of unemployed in 1920s England never fell below a million. The phenomenon of unemployment appeared to Keynes at this time as one of the main problems faced by capitalism. He rejected the means proposed by most economists, whom he did not yet refer to as 'classical', to fight it. He himself suggested different measures and led the struggle in the political sphere to impose them. But he lacked a complete and satisfying theory to rationally support these measures. He lacked an effective weapon with which to fight orthodox theory. This illustrates well the fact that the link between economic theory and political propositions associated with it is not as simple as it appears. Rather than seeing Keynesian policies aimed at fighting unemployment as applications of the theory of effective demand, one must consider this theory as an attempt to ground these policies. We will thus reconstitute the genesis of Keynes's theory of employment by situating it in its context.

The 1920s: Policies before Theory

Great Britain left World War One in a state of economic weakness and social agitation. After a brief spell of euphoria, the economy fell into a deep depression between 1920 and 1922, with an unemployment rate exceeding 20 per cent in the spring of 1921. Despite the end of this depression in 1923, the unemployment rate would never fall below 10 per cent during the 1920s, except for a brief period in 1924. Employers' efforts to lower wages met with fierce resistance on the part of the Trades Union Congress (TUC), which then brought together 6.5 million members. Strike movements multiplied between 1919 and 1922. The most important was declared on 15 April 1921 by miners, railwaymen and transporters' unions. This movement was reinforced by the influence of the Russian Revolution, which unleashed in Britain's ruling classes, as it did elsewhere in the West, fear of the 'Reds'.

Keynes considered these questions in the third and fourth of a series of five articles under the general title 'Europe's economic outlook', published by the *Sunday Times* in August and September 1921. These articles caused a sensation, as much in the United States as in Europe. On depressions, he wrote that their causes are complex and multiple, and that expectations and uncertainty play a major role in their unfolding:

> It is a feature of the economic organisation of the contemporary world that between the consumer and the manufacturer there stands a string of merchants and middlemen. These merchants and middlemen, regarded as a body, buy and contract to buy before they sell or contract to sell. Further they contract to buy *goods* against *money*. Their business requires them, therefore, to *forecast* two things, the demand of consumers and the value of money (that is to say the course of prices). When they forecast erroneously on a large scale, effort is wasted, fortunes lost, organisation disorganised – in a word, trade is depressed. (1921-11, p. 261)

These remarks are not surprising coming from an author who would soon publish *A Treatise on Probability*. It will be remembered that in this work Keynes defended the idea that uncertainty toward the future must not be an obstacle to decisions and rational action. Such is his position regarding depression and unemployment. Public and particularly banking authorities have a duty to apply policies of rational management in order to counter the effects of uncertainty. As concerns interest rates and wages, Keynes defended a rather orthodox position. Real wages in 1920 reached levels markedly higher that those prevailing before the war, particularly following a 13 per cent reduction in the length of the working week over a period of two years. Now, as much as one must avoid giving a permanent character to wage levels fixed in the middle of a depression, one must also avoid perpetuating those accorded during boom periods. In one of his *Sunday Times* articles, he wrote that by resisting wage decreases, workers' leaders 'have been expanding their influence and their idealism and their resources on an impossible enterprise' (1921-12, p. 269). In *A Tract on Monetary Reform*, composed of articles published in 1922 in the *Manchester Guardian Commercial*, he wrote of the

1921–1922 depression: 'The period of depression has exacted its penalty from the working classes more in the form of unemployment than by a lowering of real wages' (1923-1, p. 28).

On 5 December 1922 in a lecture to the Institute of Bankers, he developed his idea that money-wages are more rigid than prices and that it is useless to attempt to re-establish economic equilibria by seeking to modify them rapidly and substantially: 'The business of forcing down certain levels of wages, and so forth, in equilibrium is almost hopeless, or it will take a long time' (1922-31, p. 66). This did not prevent him from thinking that unemployment's persistence is linked to excessively high real wage levels, though he now believed that they cannot be reduced by attempting to reduce money wages. Reduction in real wages can only be attained by price increases. One must adjust the exchange rate and price level in relation to real wages rather than the other way around.

This manner of seeing things was linked to a conception of incomes opposed to orthodox economic understanding. In the latter, incomes are determined by the productivity of factors and the possibility of substituting one factor for another. From the first point of view, 'the situation is determined first and foremost by historical influences as gradually modified by contemporary social and political forces' (1930-3, p. 6). In every society, these incomes thus evolve slowly, except during periods of revolutionary upheaval. Only Bolshevik or Fascist governments can abruptly impose wages reductions of the order of 20 per cent. In democratic countries, a government which chooses this option is condemned to lose elections or risk provoking revolution. The system is threatened when the population judges that some incomes do not respond to any norm of justice:

> No man of spirit will consent to remain poor if he believes his betters to have gained their goods by lucky gambling. To convert the business man into the profiteer is to strike a blow at capitalism, because it destroys the psychological equilibrium which permits the perpetuance of unequal rewards. The economic doctrine of normal profits, vaguely apprehended by everyone, is a necessary condition for the justification of capitalism. (1923-1, p. 24)

During the summer of 1923, the unemployment rate reached 11.4 per cent of the workforce, affecting 1.3 million workers. On 7 July, the Bank of England's discount rate was raised from 3 to 4 per cent. Keynes denounced this measure: 'the Bank of England thinks it more important to raise the dollar exchange a few points than to encourage flagging trade' (1923-17, p. 101). On 8 August he presented to the Liberal Summer School a talk on the theme 'Currency policy and unemployment', which was published in *Nation and Athaeneum* on 11 August and contained in condensed form several intuitions that would be developed in *The General Theory*. Unemployment was no longer linked to the imperfection of markets or to excessively high wages. It is the sign of dysfunction within 'the *existing* economic organisation of society' (1923-21, p. 113), something socialists understood well.

Contemporary capitalism's main flaw was that it had not found a solution to this problem. Keynes again places uncertainty and lack of confidence in the future as one of the main causes of unemployment, this lack of confidence having multiple sources, political as much as economic. Among the latter, important fluctuations in the value of money play an important role. Controlling such fluctuations by submitting money value to rational management must be one of the main tasks of public authorities.

Unemployment is the result of the dysfunction of the capitalist system and can be eradicated. In addition to the rational control of money there must also be the control of population because 'the problem of unemployment is already, in part, a problem of population' (1923-6,

p. 79). It was thus not only Malthus's idea of effective demand that interested Keynes, but also his theory of population. He was convinced of the fact that, even if unemployment was reduced by rational economic policies, the state of technical development and the availability of agricultural products would not support nineteenth century demographic growth levels. From then on, it was not sufficient to abandon laissez-faire in the economic domain. Responding to William Beveridge, who was opposed to birth control, Keynes wrote in the columns of *Nation and Athenaeum* that

> It is easy to understand the distaste provoked by particular methods, and the fear inspired by any proposal to modify the *laissez-faire* of nature, and to bring the workings of a fundamental instinct under social control. But it is strange to be untroubled or to deny the existence of the problem for our generation. (1923-24, p. 124)[22]

The appearance of public works

From 25 to 27 March 1924, the League of Nations organized a conference in London on unemployment in which Keynes was a speaker. He affirmed here the importance of monetary factors linked to psychological factors. Expectation of falling prices causes unemployment. On 12 April 1924, when Labour briefly came to power for the first time, Lloyd George called on Liberals to reflect on Britain's economic future, and particularly on means of stimulating production. Keynes responded in an article published on 24 May in *Nation and Athenaeum*, 'Does unemployment need a drastic remedy?',[23] in which he declared himself in agreement with the Liberal Lloyd George, the Conservative Stanley Baldwin and the Labourite Sidney Webb on the fact that 'there is no place or time here for *laissez-faire*' (1924-14, p. 220). The cure for unemployment is found in monetary reform but also in 'the diversion of national savings from relatively barren foreign investment into state-encouraged constructive enterprises at home' (ibid., p. 223). The idea of public works appears for the first time. Keynes proposed house construction and renovating the transportation and electricity systems. He emphasized that such stimulation 'shall initiate a cumulative prosperity' (ibid.). It is first appearance of the idea of a multiplier, a word Keynes would introduce in 1933. For Harrod, this article shows that, from 1924, Keynes had clearly outlined 'the public policy which has since been specifically associated with his name' (Harrod, 1951, p. 350). Responding to criticisms raised by his article, Keynes repeated that a major reduction in wages was not a practical solution to unemployment and affirmed what from then on he would call his heresy: 'I bring in the State; I abandon *laissez-faire*' (1924-17, p. 228). On 6 November 1924, he gave a talk at the Sidney Ball Association's annual conference in Oxford entitled 'The end of laissez-faire'. Presented again at Berlin University in June 1926, the talk was published that same year by Leonard and Virginia Woolf's publishing house, the Hogarth Press. The political content of this pamphlet, which affirms that there is not, and never has been a coincidence between private interest and social interest, was treated in Chapter 4. Keynes repeated that many economic evils, including unemployment, 'are the fruits of risk, uncertainty, and ignorance ... Yet the cure lies outside the operations of individuals' (1926-1, p. 291). It is by controlling money and credit, saving and investment and the spreading of information that unemployment can be reduced and other economic problems can be corrected.

During this period, Keynes's struggle against unemployment was closely linked to his struggle against the return to the gold standard, which we will discuss in the next chapter. Bankers who heralded this measure failed to understand that problems in the credit system were to blame for the paradox of unemployment amidst shortage: 'Individualistic capitalism in England has come to the point when it can no longer depend on the momentum of mere expansion; and it must apply itself to the scientific task of improving the structure of its economic machine' (1925-6, p. 200). In *The Economic Consequences of Mr Churchill*, Keynes explained how there was hidden behind the return to the gold standard a deliberate policy of increasing unemployment as a means of lowering money-wages (1925-1).[24] On 15 October 1925, six months before the bitter conflict in the coal mines and the start of the general strike, he declared in the *Manchester Guardian Commercial*: 'But I sympathise with the working classes in resisting a general reduction of real wages. I am sure that no material reduction is possible in the near future without engaging on a social struggle of which no one could foretell the outcome' (1925-24, p. 444). Five years of maintaining the British government's current policies 'might bring us to the edge of revolution, if revolution is ever possible in this country' (ibid., p. 445).

The Liberal Party against the Treasury View

Keynes's battles were not fought alone but within the Liberal Party, particularly in the Summer School. In July 1928, he published an article in the *Evening Standard* entitled 'How to organise a wave of prosperity?', a plea in favour of public spending to combat unemployment. He attacked what would be called the 'Treasury View' [25] but what was then called 'sound finance', the translation to economic policy terms of classical orthodoxy: 'And the more successful the efforts of the Treasury, in the pursuit of so-called 'Economy', to damp down the forms of capital expansion which they control – telephones, roads, housing, etc. again the greater the certainty of increasing unemployment ' (1928-11, p. 762). Of a first way to deflate costs, a general assault on money wages, he writes that it 'is not only politically impossible, but also maladroit, because the wage rates which will be most likely to yield before the assault will be those in which wages are already relatively low because of bargaining weakness' (ibid., p. 763). An outline of the multiplier idea is found in this article: 'Moreover, the increased purchasing power of a working population in full employment would react quickly and cumulatively on the prosperity of numberless industries and occupations' (ibid., p. 764).

In the Second Interlude we discussed the role played by Keynes in the production of the Liberal Party's Yellow Book (*Britain's Industrial Future*) and Orange Book (*We Can Conquer Unemployment*) and Lloyd George's solemn pledge on 1 March 1929 to undertake, if elected, a public works programme that, in addition to its intrinsic utility, would seek to 'reduce the terrible figures of the workless in the course of a single year to normal proportions' (quoted in 1929-1, p. 88; see also 1929-8, p. 804). The objective was to reduce unemployment from 11 per cent to 4.7 per cent, which translated into the creation of 750 000 jobs.

Although he turned down being a candidate for Cambridge University, Keynes was actively involved in the election campaign. Commenting on the Liberal Party's Orange Book in the *Evening Standard* on 19 March 1929, he again argued for the multiplier effect of public investment, which he contrasted to the intellectual poverty of the Treasury's arguments (1929-8).[26] Once a public investment was launched, prosperity from it would be cumulative. On 19 April 1929 he attacked the ideas developed by the Chancellor of the Exchequer before the House of Commons against public spending. According to Treasury experts, not only would such spending be powerless to reduce unemployment, but it would aggravate it by diverting funds that would otherwise be available for private investment. This would be called 'crowding out' in the 1970s. Winston Churchill formulated this view in his budget speech of 15 April 1929: 'It is the orthodox Treasury dogma, steadfastly held that whatever might be the political or social advantages, very little additional employment and no permanent additional employment can, in fact, and as a general rule, be created by state borrowing and state expenditure' (Churchill's speech quoted in 1929-10, p. 809). This dogma has a long history. Hawtrey, the only professional economist at the Treasury, and Apostle and friend of Keynes, gave it a classic formulation in an article published in 1925. He tried to demonstrate that public spending financed by borrowing could only increase employment in exceptional circumstances unlikely to present themselves. Called to give his advice in 1928 on the propositions of Keynes and his friends, he underlined their inflationary character.[27] It was on this basis that the Treasury elaborated a vision opposed to Keynes and the Liberal Party's electoral argumentation, a vision presented in the *White Paper* of May 1929.

For Keynes the Treasury View essentially consisted in an unfounded affirmation defying common sense: 'Certainly this dogma is not derived from common sense. On the contrary, it is a highly sophisticated theory. No ordinary man, left to himself, is able to believe that, if there had been no housing schemes in recent years, there would, nevertheless, have been just as much employment' (1929-10, p. 809). By supposing there is always a level of real wage sufficiently low to generate full employment, 'the theory starts off by assuming the non-existence of the very phenomenon which is under investigation' (ibid., p. 811). Contrary to this dogma, savings do not necessarily transform themselves into investment and, when investment falls behind savings, unemployment results. It was between summer 1928 and winter 1929 that Keynes developed his thesis of the disequilibrium between savings and investment, a thesis that would be central to both *A Treatise on Money* and *The General Theory*. But this idea, present in Wicksell and other earlier authors, was already formulated in a talk given to London's Political Economy Club on 3 December 1913 and mentioned in the previous chapter: 'One of the characteristics of a boom period . . . as distinguished from a period of depression is, I suggest, that in the former period investment exceeds saving while in the latter period investment falls short of saving' (1913-5, p. 6).

Keynes defended the Liberal programme in a pamphlet composed with Hubert Henderson, *Can Lloyd George do it?* (1929-1). They criticized academic argumentation cut off from reality. Unemployment occurs because savings are too high in relation to the investment projects of entrepreneurs. There is no guarantee that savings transform themselves into productive investments. Credit expansion is essential but insufficient to assure a recovery that must be supported by public spending. In addition to direct employment, spending generates indirect employment, the forces of prosperity having, like those of depression, a cumulative effect. It was not possible, they add, to measure these secondary effects precisely, but they would be considerable. The admission of this impossibility would feed arguments against public works.

In Search of a New Theory

The elections of May 1929 gave Labour a relative majority. It was thus a Labour government led by Ramsay Macdonald that faced the worst economic crisis of modern times. Instead of the reduction promised by Lloyd George, the unemployment rate, which was below 10 per cent during the elections, went from 14.6 per cent in 1930 to 21.5 per cent in 1931. It would not fall below 20 per cent before 1933. The Macmillan Committee was created on 5 November to investigate finance and industry. This decision was taken, explained the

Chancellor of the Exchequer Philip Snowden, 'largely because of the impression made on public opinion by Mr Keynes's proposals on these points as enumerated in the Liberal Yellow Book before the last election' (memorandum from 8 April 1930, cited by Clarke, 1988, p. 103). Named to the Committee, Keynes wrote to Lydia on 25 November 1929: 'As you said, I am becoming fashionable again'. The Prime Minister received him at lunch, but Keynes did not succeed in convincing the government to abandon the orthodox management chosen to deal with the crisis.

Keynes was also named member of the Economic Advisory Council, created on 24 January 1930 to advise the government on the economic situation.[28] On its first meeting on 17 February, the Council formed, on Keynes's suggestion, a Committee on the Economic Outlook to diagnose the situation engendered by the depression. As president, Keynes proposed setting up a group of economists made of Pigou, Robbins, Henderson,[29] Stamp and himself that would report back in November 1930 with findings on the situation and its possible remedies. This Committee of Economists painfully produced a report on 24 October. It was a compromise between Keynes's positions and those of his colleagues. Keynes abandoned public works with the intention of obtaining a consensus in favour of protectionist measures. Despite this concession, Robbins, resolutely opposed to these measures, signed a minority report.

The Macmillan Committee met from 21 November 1929 to 31 May 1931. Keynes was one of the most active commissioners. But he really shone as a witness. He was questioned during five long sessions between 20 February and 7 March 1930. The stupefied commissioners were given detailed presentations of arguments of the forthcoming *Treatise on Money*. While in the latter these arguments were presented with a high degree of abstraction, they were presented much more concretely as replies to his colleagues' questions. Keynes started by revisiting the argument according to which wage decreases, then widely recommended, are not a good method of reducing unemployment. Wages remained practically unchanged since 1924 and this was hardly surprising: 'My reading of history is that for centuries there has existed an intense social resistance to any matters of reduction in the level of money incomes' (1930-4, p. 64). The core of the argument, which Keynes had only recently brought to light, concerned the relationship between savings and investment. Decisions to save and invest are taken by different agents for different motives, and no mechanism exists to assure their equality. It is not high real wages and unemployment insurance that cause depressions and unemployment, but the fact that investment lags behind savings. Illustrating his thesis with the 'banana parable' (ibid., pp. 76–7), which describes a campaign for frugality in a community producing and consuming only bananas, Keynes showed that savings do not increase a society's wealth, much to the contrary. Only investment can do this. We have here the outline of the idea according to which adjusting savings to investment can be done at a level inferior to that of full employment. Keynes presented his theory as 'a revolution in the mind' (ibid., p. 87). He proposed seven measures to end depression. The last of these, stimulating investment with or without direct government intervention, was his preference. Lacking this, he declared himself in favour of protectionist measures as the lesser evil. Keynes also explained to his colleagues that stimulation measures would have a cumulative effect. But he had yet to discover how to measure this cumulative effect, as he wrote with Henderson in *Can Lloyd George do it?*

It was Richard Kahn, a young colleague and former student of Keynes, who found during the summer of 1930 the means of measuring the direct and indirect effects on employment of an increase in public spending financed by loans. He highlighted the link between these cumulative effects and the proportion of new incomes to be spent. A four-page technical paper circulated first in the summer of 1930 before being published in the July 1931 edition of *The Economic Journal* under the title 'The relation of home investment to employment'. In 1935, Keynes would call the relation described by Kahn the 'multiplier'. This concept played a major role in the transition from *A Treatise on Money* to *The General Theory*. This idea had already been explored, first by Wicksell, once again, but also by F. Lavington, another of Keynes's students, as well as by N. Johansen, L.F. Griffin, and even Hawtrey, the theoretician behind the Treasury's views. It was in a paper prepared for the Treasury on the Liberal measures to fight unemployment that Hawtrey developed the multiplier idea, which he presented before the Macmillan Committee.[30]

In the previous chapter we presented the *Treatise on Money*, which appeared on 24 October 1930 after seven years of often interrupted labour. The circumstances of its writing made Keynes unsatisfied, warning his readers: 'I feel like someone who has been forcing his way through a confused jungle' (1930-1, vol. 1, p. xvii). He undoubtedly had the impression of not having at his disposal all the theoretical elements necessary to explain the new context of massive unemployment. Devoted to the explanation of price fluctuations and monetary dynamics, this book does not explicitly deal with the level of employment. But by connecting price movements to the gap between savings and investment, by explaining depression by excess saving and investor psychology, he opened the doors to *The General Theory*. In a long chapter entitled 'Historical illustrations', Keynes depicted humanity's evolution, emphasizing the opposition between thrift and enterprise, the motor of growth: 'If enterprise is afoot, wealth accumulates whatever may be happening to thrift; and if enterprise is asleep, wealth decays whatever thrift may be doing' (1930-1, vol. 2, p. 132).

After reading the *Treatise*, Richard Kahn, Austin and Joan Robinson, Piero Sraffa and James Meade, Keynes's closest friends and disciples, made him aware of the incongruity of a theoretical construction which postulated full employment and in which adjustments to monetary perturbations are made by means of price movements. Hawtrey and Robertson raised several problems. Hayek, his main adversary, called into question his theory of capital, profit and interest.[31] As he did after the publication of *A Tract on Monetary Reform*, Keynes immediately started correcting his work in light of these criticisms, those raised by the Macmillan Committee and others. This would result in another book,[32] the fruit of Keynes's effort of reflection, but also of an ensemble of colleagues, particularly the friends named at the beginning of this paragraph who formed the 'Circus', a group that met in the first months of 1931 to discuss the *Treatise*. Richard Kahn, nicknamed Angel Gabriel, served as messenger between the Circus and Keynes, who did not participate in these discussions.[33] Throughout the book's preparation, he remained at Keynes's side, especially during the holiday periods at Tilton, revising, correcting and discussing the successive versions, to such a point that Schumpeter believed Kahn should be considered co-author of the book (Schumpeter, 1954, p. 1172).[34] Joan Robinson, who did not fear speaking her mind to Keynes, wrote that 'the general theory'[35] should be considered a collective work (Robinson, 1948). Her article 'The theory of money and the analysis of output', published in October 1933 in the first issue of the *Review of Economic Studies*[36] is one of the first clear presentations of *The General Theory*'s essential arguments, along with the document *Public Works in their International Aspect* prepared by James Meade for the New Fabian Research Bureau.[37]

A member of the editorial board of the Macmillan Committee's report, Keynes put the final touches on the report on 29 May and, despite compromises between several discordant views, declared himself satisfied with it: 'On the whole, I am rather happy about it, though it is a bit long-winded and has the faults of all composite documents' (letter to Kahn, 29 May 1931, JMK 20, p. 310). On the following day, he sailed for the United States for the second time in his life. He was invited to the University of Chicago to participate in the annual meeting of the Harris Foundation, whose theme was 'Unemployment as a world problem'. In his writing 'An economic analysis of unemployment' (1931-2), Keynes revisited arguments from the *Treatise*, as he did before the Macmillan Committee. But he went beyond them by evoking the possibility of production stabilization at a level inferior to that of full employment. He was surprised to observe several American economists, particularly Jacob Viner and his colleagues at the University of Chicago – which would become several decades later the seat of the anti-Keynesian reaction – favourable to public works as a remedy to unemployment.[38]

On 17 October 1932, Keynes and four other economists, including Pigou, published in *The Times* a letter underlining the importance of public and private spending in account of the fact that, in the current conditions, 'private economy does not transfer from consumption to investment part of an unchanged national income' (1932-15, p. 138).[39] Once again, this illustrates that there is no necessary congruence between political and theoretical positions since, at the same time, Pigou was finishing *The Theory of Unemployment*, which would appear in autumn of 1933 and which Keynes would cut to pieces in the *General Theory*. Moreover, this letter made known to a much wider public the debate between Hayek and Keynes, and more generally between the London School of Economics and Cambridge. Hayek, Robbins and two of their colleagues would express their opposition to public spending in the columns of *The Times* on 19 October (Hayek et al., 1932).[40] This letter provoked a retort from Keynes and his friends, published on 21 October, accusing Hayek and his allies of supporting an illusion buried since Adam Smith but often resuscitated: 'It seems to be thought that there exists a stock of stored-up wealth the amount of which is fixed independently of our action' (1932-16, p. 140).

On 18 September 1932, Keynes wrote to his mother: 'I have written nearly a third of my new book on monetary theory'. He gave his autumn lectures the title 'The monetary theory of production'. He elaborated during the following winter the theory of effective demand, in which economic equilibrium is realized, not by price fluctuations as in *A Treatise on Money*, but by fluctuations in production.[41] In the following quotation, Keynes tells Harrod on 30 August 1936 how his ideas came into place:

> It only came after I had enunciated to myself the psychological law that, when income increases, the gap between income and consumption will increase, – a conclusion of vast importance to my own thinking but not apparently, expressed just like that, to anyone else's. Then, appreciably later, came the notion of interest as being the measure of liquidity preference, which became quite clear in my mind the moment I thought of it. And last of all, after an immense lot of muddling and many drafts, the proper definition of the marginal efficiency of capital linked up one thing with another. (JMK 14, p. 85)

This letter contradicts the widely held opinion according to which the concepts of liquidity preference and marginal efficiency of capital had been in place since the beginning of 1933. In March Keynes published a series of four articles reprinted as a pamphlet entitled *The Means to Prosperity*, which sought to vulgarize his theory at its present state of development (1933-2). It is here that he used the term 'multiplier' for the first time. Like many of his writings, these articles were published in several languages and countries and had, given their non-academic character, a considerable impact. Reading Keynes's arguments had the effect of shaking up high-level civil servants at the Treasury such as Richard Hopkins and Otto Niemeyer.

In autumn 1934, he started sending chapters of his book to the printers, using the proofs for his lecture series, which was now called 'The general theory of employment'. As he wrote to his friend George Bernard Shaw on 1 January 1935 in the context of a debate over Marxism, he had a premonition that his book would set off a revolution:

> To understand *my* state of mind, however, you have to know that I believe myself to be writing a book on economic theory which will largely revolutionise – not, I suppose, at once but in the course of the next ten years – the way the world thinks about economic problems. When my new theory has been duly assimilated and mixed with politics and feelings and passions, I can't predict what the final upshot will be in its effect on action and affairs. But there will be a great change, and, in particular, the Ricardian foundations of Marxism will be knocked away. I can't expect you, or anyone else, to believe this at the present stage. But for myself I don't merely hope what I say, in my own mind I'm quite sure. (Letter to George Bernard Shaw, 1 January 1935. (JMK 13, pp. 492–3)[42]

Virginia Woolf related having lunch with Maynard and Lydia during which Keynes's work was discussed. She described in the 6 January 1935 entry of her diary her friend's 'gigantic boast' as follows:

> M. own letter said that he thinks he has revolutionised economics; in the new book he is writing. 'Wait ten years, & let it absorb the politics & the psychology & so on that will accrue to it; & then you'll see – the old Ricardo system will be exposed; & the whole thing set on a new footing.' This he wrote in so many words: a gigantic boast; true I daresay. (V. Woolf, 1977–1984, vol. 4, p. 272)

The New Deal

On 4 March 1933, Franklin Delano Roosevelt succeeded Herbert Hoover as President of the United States, at the same time as Hitler was coming to power in Germany. The New Deal to which his name is associated consisted of a series of ad hoc measures inspired in particular by the institutionalist economists who advised him. The similarity with Keynesian propositions, as well as with the policies initiated in Sweden in 1931 and inspired by the economists Lindahl, Myrdal and Ohlin of the Stockholm School, is striking. It is not far-fetched to think that Keynes might have indirectly inspired New Deal future advisers during his 1931 passage in the United States. The New Deal cannot, however, be interpreted as an application of Keynesianism, since *The General Theory* had yet to be published. In reality, one of the first countries to explicitly refer to Keynes was Canada, which applied a Keynesian budget in April 1939. Robert Bryce, Assistant Deputy Minister of Finance and main architect of this budget, attended Keynes's lectures from 1932 to 1935.

Keynes was enthusiastic about these events. Industrial production doubled between Roosevelt's taking office in March and the month of July. However, this growth languished in the autumn and the government hesitated on how it should proceed. This was when Felix Frankfurter, a Harvard law professor and one of Roosevelt's advisers, suggested that Keynes intervene. He did this in a famous open letter published in the *New York Times* on 31 December 1933 in which he hoped the President might offer a third way between orthodoxy and revolution.[43]

Keynes sailed with Lydia for the United States on 9 May 1934, officially to receive an honorary doctorate from Columbia University, but in reality to observe and, if possible, influence the American government. On 28 May he met with Roosevelt for an hour. Though each man declared himself charmed by the other, it is difficult to know exactly what took place between them. On 1 February 1938, while the American and British economies were suffering a lapse, Keynes sent a long letter to Roosevelt in which he tried to convince him of the necessity of public investments, especially in housing, transportation and public services, and of proceeding by nationalizations if necessary. Following Roosevelt's polite response, Keynes repeated his challenge to the President on 25 March: 'you are treading a very dangerous middle path. You must either give more encouragement to business or take over more of their functions yourself' (JMK 21, p. 440).

On 6 June 1934 he presented his theories of effective demand and the multiplier to the American Political Economy Club (1934-4).[44] His paper served him as a guide in his discussions with American decision-makers. In February 1935, Keynes presented his new theory at Oxford, where it was criticized by his ally Henderson. In June his student Robert Bryce presented it in enemy territory at Hayek's seminar at the London School of Economics (Bryce, 1935). The proofs of *The General Theory* were read and commented on by Harrod, Hawtrey, Kahn and Joan Robinson. Both summer and autumn were devoted to final revisions of the book at Tilton.

The General Theory of Employment, Interest and Money

The General Theory left the hands of its author on 19 January 1936 and was published on 4 February in an inexpensive edition whose price Keynes fixed himself. The previous day, the Cambridge Arts Theatre, to which Keynes donated a considerable amount of money, time and energy, opened its doors.[45] This book is probably the most famous and influential work in the field of economics in the twentieth century. It has inspired an enormous amount of literature. In 1936 alone, there were 125 reviews in English.[46] Until the 1970s, literature on Keynes focused almost entirely on this one book. Until today, scholars continue to comment on, interpret, criticize and wonder what Keynes really meant by it.[47]

This is not surprising for two reasons. The first is that the book deals with problems societies were confronting in Keynes's time and continue to confront today. Unemployment and massive income inequality for example remain major problems. The second reason has to do with the unique character of a work deliberately constructed to surprise and unsettle. Apart from the fact that Keynes addressed himself to his fellow economists, *The General Theory* is a work that defies categorization. It was not written for the general public, in the manner of, for example, *The Economic Consequences of the Peace*. But neither is it a scholarly treatise like *A Treatise on Money* or *A Treatise on Probability*, works in which Keynes demonstrated his worth as a theoretician. Nor is it a textbook, and Keynes hoped it would never become one. He did not want 'the comparatively simple fundamental ideas which underlie my theory . . . [to] be crystallised at the present stage of the debate' (1937-4, p. 111). These ideas have been, however, 'crystallised' many times, particularly into mathematical language, an exercise that continues to this day, and that does not always constitute an accurate reflection of his ideas.[48]

For most economists, and especially contemporary economists, Keynes's writing is bizarre, indigestible if not incomprehensible. *The General Theory* has been described by some as messy, poorly organized and repetitive, its language obscure, opaque, difficult to understand and especially to formalize. Others have written that it is filled with vague hypotheses and ambiguous and overly literary argumentations. Shortly after it was published, Keynes was reproached for having renounced mathematical presentation. He was accused of having a casual attitude regarding definitions and terms whose meaning sometimes varied according to the context. Hayek had already made such a criticism regarding *A Treatise on Money*. Keynes's response to this clarified his vision of language. For him there is no univocal correspondence between an expression and that to which it refers, and in economics, as in other moral sciences, one may use technical language in a less rigorous manner than one would, for example, in mathematics or physics: 'A definition can often be *vague* within fairly wide limits and capable of several interpretations differing slightly from one another, and still be perfectly serviceable' (1925-10, p. 36). Economics is constantly in the process of redefining its terms. Keynes also found an aesthetic advantage to varying words and expressions referring to the same reality. A reader must not be bored or put to sleep. To convince a reader, to lead him into understanding, not only must one get rid of the definitional restraints of logical deductive science, but one should also not fear using the tools of rhetoric, especially metaphor. From this point of view, *The General Theory*, like Keynes's other books, is a literary work. To describe economics, its author distances himself from the formalized language of physics and mathematics in order to employ everyday and literary language simultaneously.

As for its structure, *The General Theory* does not follow a continuous and regular progression. The core of the theory is presented in the third chapter. A long and in principle methodological parenthesis (Book II: Definitions and ideas) broaches fundamental questions, including expectation. Books III and IV deal respectively with consumption and investment and are thus at the heart of the theory. Here too a systematic presentation is eschewed in favour of many comings and goings, before Chapter 18 provides a general summary of the theory. Book IV introduces changes in money-wages and prices, while the final Book presents a kind of pot-pourri with commentaries on trade cycles, notes on the history of economic thought and reflections on social philosophy.

The book's main arguments having already been set forth in the story of their genesis, a discussion of its key elements will suffice here. The best summary of *The General Theory* comes from Keynes himself, in response to criticisms formulated by Jacob Viner, D.H. Robertson, Wassily W. Leontieff and F.W. Taussig in the November 1936 edition of the *Quarterly Journal of Economics*. Published in February 1937, Keynes's article is more a commentary on his book than a response to his critics. This is how he presents its main theme:

> This that I offer is, therefore, a theory of why output and employment are so liable to fluctuation. It does not offer a ready-made remedy as to how to avoid these fluctuations and to maintain output at a steady optimum level. But it is, properly speaking, a theory of employment because it explains *why*, in any given circumstances, employment is what it is. Naturally I am interested not only in the diagnosis, but also in the cure; and many pages of my book are devoted to the latter. But I consider that my suggestions for a cure, which, avowedly, are not worked out completely, are on a different plane from the diagnosis. They are not meant to be definitive; they are subject to all sorts of special assumptions and are necessarily related to the particular conditions of the time. (1937-4, pp. 121–2)

It is thus a theory of what determines an economy's level of employment. Considering the hypotheses made on the organization of production and our short-term horizon, the determination of the level of employment is at the same time a determination of the level of production and aggregate income. But it is clear that employment is the primary objective. Keynes opens the last chapter of his book with the passage quoted at the head of the present chapter, which makes of unemployment the first fault of the contemporary economy. The analysis is devoted to the first vice and not to the second, the arbitrary and inequitable distribution of wealth. But they are closely linked. In effect, once the classical vision – according to which economic growth results from savings and hence from the abstinence of the well-off – is rejected, the economic justification for income inequality disappears. While he admitted that it is both illusionary and utopic to seek perfect equality in income and fortune, this did not prevent Keynes from recognizing that the inequalities of his age were totally unacceptable.

Keynes's distinction between diagnosis and cure must be underlined. His book is almost entirely devoted to diagnosis. He affirmed having no recipes valid for all times and places to rectify the evils engendered by capitalism. It is thus an error to consider *The General Theory* as a set of economic policy propositions, to which it is often reduced. In this regard, there is an interesting resemblance between Keynes and Marx. The latter said that it was not up to him to write 'recipes for the cook-shops of the future' (Marx, 1867, p. 21). His task consisted rather of analysing the present, and predicting coming movements. In practice, both adapted their policy choices to circumstances throughout their life and demonstrated a pragmatism very far removed from the dogmatism that characterized the action and thought of their disciples. For example, Keynes warned, shortly after *The General Theory*'s publication, against the dangers of inflation while Britain's rate of unemployment was still very high.[49]

Diagnosis

Doctors are interested in the short-term evolution of their patients' health, it being understood that in the long run, death is inescapable. One's future health, before this inevitable deadline, is unpredictable. But it is also considerably influenced by actions and decisions made in the past. If one smokes, drinks and eats excessively for several decades, it is likely certain organs will be irremediably damaged, even though there is no certitude nor general law on this matter. Churchill lived to be 92 while absorbing enormous quantities of alcohol and chain-smoking cigars, while Keynes, whose health was fragile and who had little tolerance to such excess, died at 62.

In the field of economics, the past provides us with a certain quantity of capital in the form of buildings, machines and tools whose conditions of use are not easily modified. There is also an available workforce with certain qualifications not easily transferable. We have at our disposal usable techniques and information, industrial, commercial and financial forms of organization, rules of competition. The economy fits into a social structure that influences, in particular, wealth distribution. It is composed of individuals, united in classes, who have relatively rigid habits and tastes. Of course, none of this is constant or written in stone. But, given the time horizon on which his analysis rests, Keynes considered these elements as given.

In this context, the interaction of 'the three fundamental psychological factors' (1936-1, pp. 246–7) determines the level of employment and national revenue. They are 'the psychological propensity to consume, the psychological attitude to liquidity and the psychological expectation of future yield from capital-assets' (ibid., p. 247). We have already been acquainted with liquidity preference (Chapter 6), and we have quoted above the letter in which Keynes explained when and how these concepts appeared to him. They are factors closely linked to uncertainty toward the future and agents' non-rational expectations. Levels of money-wages determined by bargaining between employers and employees and the quantity of money determined by the central bank are among the 'ultimate independent variables' (ibid., p. 246) necessary to complete the model.

The propensity to consume is the proportion of an individual's income he consumes. It is characterized by the fact that, when income increases, spending on consumption rises, but of lesser proportion: 'This psychological law was of the utmost importance in the development of my own thought, and it is, I think, absolutely fundamental to the theory of effective demand as set forth in my book' (1937-4, p. 120). This is valid as much for individuals as societies. From a given increase in his income, a wealthy person will consume a less important part than a poor person. And societies generating wealth save an increasingly important fraction of their revenues. This private virtue becomes a public vice, an obstacle to attaining full employment. Determined by a series of social and institutional factors, the propensity to consume is relatively stable in the short run.

The second component of demand is investment which is, in contrast, very volatile. This is why it acts as a motor in the dynamics of capitalism and why Keynes makes it the subject of Book IV's eight chapters, the biggest part of his book: 'it is usual in a complex system to regard as the *causa causans* that factor which is most prone to sudden and wide fluctuation' (ibid., p. 121). It is here that the two other psychological factors come into play. The individual who invests does so in the hope of obtaining a series of returns on a certain temporal horizon. He can be sure of nothing. He does not make his decisions by comparing the certain or even probable receipts and actual costs. Investment, like any decision

> to do something positive, the full consequences of which will be drawn out over many days to come, can only be taken as a result of animal spirits – of a spontaneous urge to action rather than inaction, and not as the outcome of a weighted average of quantitative benefits multiplied by quantitative probabilities . . . In estimating the prospects of investment, we must have regard, therefore, to the nerves and hysteria and even the digestions and reactions to the weather of those upon whose spontaneous activity it largely depends. (1936-1, pp. 161–2)

We have here an echo of Keynes's reflections on probabilities [50]

Uncertainty thus does not prohibit decision, as the young Keynes wrote, responding to Moore, in 'Ethics in relation to conduct'. And in the economic domain, long-term expectation can be, despite everything, relatively stable. To measure this, Keynes brings in the marginal efficiency of capital. This concept serves to compare the series of expected returns from an investment with the supply price, or replacement cost, of the capital asset: 'More precisely, I define the marginal efficiency of capital as being equal to that rate of discount which would make the present value of the series of annuities given by the returns expected from the capital-asset during its life just equal to its supply price' (1936-1, p. 135). The marginal efficiency of capital must not be confused, as is often the case, with the marginal productivity of capital of neoclassical theory. The latter rests on the hypothesis that, given the quantities of other factors of production, the addition of a unit of capital increases production at a decreasing level. It is measured in real terms, which raises 'difficulties as to the definition of the physical unit of capital, which I believe to be both insoluble and unnecessary' (ibid., p. 138). The marginal efficiency of capital is in contrast calculated by comparing monetary streams one of which is anticipated: 'The outstanding fact is the extreme precariousness of the basis of knowledge on which our estimates of prospective yield have to be made' (ibid., p. 149). If investor confidence and dynamism weaken for whatever reason, the marginal efficiency of capital will diminish without anything changing in capital's physical productivity.

Keynes believed that while investment in any type of capital increases, the marginal efficiency of capital diminishes, and this for two reasons: 'partly because the prospective yield will fall as the supply of that type of capital is increased, and partly because, as a rule, pressure on the facilities for producing that type of capital will cause its supply price to increase' (ibid., p. 136).[51] One could draw a curve linking, for each capital good, marginal efficiency of capital and the level of investment and, by aggregating all these curves, obtain the schedule of marginal efficiency of capital, also called the schedule of demand for capital.[52]

One of the most important characteristics of contemporary capitalism, on which Keynes had insisted earlier in *A Treatise on Money* and which Veblen and the institutionalist economists had brought to light at the turn of the century, is the separation between control and ownership of capital: 'With the separation between ownership and management which prevails to-day and with the development of organised investment markets, a new factor of great importance has entered in, which sometimes facilitates investment but sometimes adds greatly to the instability of the system' (ibid., pp. 150–51). Most often, investors borrow money in order to acquire capital goods. The lender is not a philanthropist and requires interest in return. The borrower is incited to increase the quantity of his investment to the point in which the marginal efficiency of capital is reduced to the level of the rate of interest: 'the rate of investment will be pushed to the point on the investment demand-schedule where the marginal efficiency of capital in general is equal to the market rate of interest' (ibid., pp. 136–7).

To complete the explanation, all that remains is to see on what the interest rate depends. As we saw in the previous chapter, rather than equalize savings and investment, the rate of interest is a monetary variable which equalizes supply and demand for money. While supply is fixed by monetary authorities, the demand for money is closely linked to the third fundamental psychological variable, liquidity preference. The diagnosis of the diseases of contemporary capitalism can be established as follows:

> The difficulties in the way of maintaining effective demand at a level high enough to provide full employment, which ensue from the association of a conventional and fairly stable long-term rate of interest with a fickle and highly unstable marginal efficiency of capital, should be, by now, obvious to the reader. (ibid., p. 204)

The situation is aggravated by the fact that in the long run, liquidity preference and thus interest rates tend to increase. Furthermore, as economies progress and become wealthy, the propensity to save tends to grow. This has an impact, not only on consumer demand, but also on the effect of investment on income increases. The link between income and investment is the investment multiplier, which 'tells us that, when there is an increment of aggregate investment, income will increase by an amount which is k times the increment of investment' (ibid., p. 115). Now the multiplier is determined by the marginal propensity to consume. It is even higher to the extent that individuals consume a smaller proportion of their growing income.

Savings, considered as an accounting unit defined as the difference between national income and consumer spending, is by definition equal to investment. This is not the case, however, with intentions to save and intentions to invest. Variations of national income adjust the level of savings to that of investment. This is how the private virtue of savings can be transformed into public vice: 'The more virtuous we are, the more determinedly thrifty, the more obstinately orthodox in our national and personal finance, the more our incomes will have to fall when interest rises relatively to the marginal efficiency of capital' (ibid., p. 111).

Remedies

Keynes concludes from his analysis that, although it is not violently unstable, the modern economic system 'seems capable of remaining in a chronic condition of sub-normal activity for a considerable period without any marked tendency either towards recovery or towards complete collapse. Moreover, the evidence indicates that full, or even approximately full, employment is of rare and short-lived occurrence' (ibid., pp. 249–50). If consumer demand is represented by C and investment demand by I, the aggregate income Y, linked to the volume of employment, can thus be represented as follows:

$$Y = C + I$$

There is no mechanism that can automatically push this demand to the level of full employment. It falls on the actions of public authorities to stimulate effective demand: 'Our final task might be to select those variables which can be deliberately controlled or managed by central authority in the kind of system in which we actually live' (ibid, p. 247). Here, all options are open, from the most moderate to the most radical. It is thus possible, through fiscal policies and transfers, to redistribute the incomes from rich to poor and by doing this stimulate consumer demand. The establishment of the Welfare State is thus justified, not only for ethical and political reasons, but also for economic reasons. Assisting the unemployed prevents them from revolting but also helps restart the economy.

Stimulating investment is also indispensable and we have at our disposal a panoply of monetary, fiscal and other measures that can be managed faster and easier. Interest rates can be influenced by money supply. But the State itself can also act directly as buyer, in the context, for example, of public works. The term G can thus be added to the equation of national revenue:

$$Y = C + I + G$$

Foreign trade can also be called to help, the difference between the value of exports and imports, X, constituting another element of demand:

$$Y = C + I + G + X$$

These instruments of economic 'fine tuning' were set up on a grand scale after the Second World War. The war itself was a stimulant to the Keynesian revolution. In *How to Pay for the War* (1940–1), Keynes underlined the importance of setting up modern national accounts. He himself played an active role in the creation of these instruments in Britain, closely supervising the works of Stone and Meade. But in this we leave Keynes and enter the history of Keynesianism, marked by the creation of instruments such as the IS–LM model and the Phillips curve.

This Keynesianism, sometimes qualified as hydraulic,[53] is opposed to a more radical Keynesianism, whose roots are also found in Keynes, particularly in Chapter 24 of *The*

General Theory in which the euthanasia of the rentier and the socialization of investment are evoked. We have seen the hindering role, not only under capitalism but throughout human history, played by interest, which rewards no sacrifice. Interest's long-term disappearance could constitute part of the solution to the problem of employment. This would imply the disappearance of a parasitic social class, 'the euthanasia of the rentier, and, consequently, the euthanasia of the cumulative oppressive power of the capitalist to exploit the scarcity-value of capital' (1936-1, p. 376). For Keynes, this process would not be sudden and would be 'merely a gradual but prolonged continuance of what we have seen recently in Great Britain, and will need no revolution' (ibid., p. 376). Here again the continuity between some of Keynes's arguments and the classical thinkers must be noted, particularly with Smith who, when describing rentiers, underlined that in all societies there are individuals who harvest in places where nothing was planted, and Ricardo, for whom interests of landowners were opposed to those of industrialists and workers.

The socialization of investment aims to solve the problem raised by societies in which 'the capital development of a country becomes a by-product of the activities of a casino' (ibid., p. 159) – that is, the stock exchange – led by the lure of short-term financial gain. The struggle against the instability of the marginal efficiency of capital and thus of investment, must involve the structural intervention of the State: 'I expect to see the State, which is in a position to calculate the marginal efficiency of capital-goods on long views and on the basis of the general social advantage, taking an ever greater responsibility for directly organising investment' (ibid., p. 164). This does not mean the suppression of private enterprise, with which the public authorities must cooperate, but rather 'a somewhat comprehensive socialisation of investment, [which] will prove the only means of securing an approximation to full employment' (ibid., p. 378). We are here far removed from the Keynesian management which would be set up after the war. That said, moderate Keynesianism was imposed in several important countries. Before the outbreak of war, in the United States, Canada and elsewhere, the principle of using budgetary deficits as a motor for restarting the economy was adopted following the economic downturn of 1937–38.

NOTES

1. This situation has far from been eradicated, even from so-called more developed countries.
2. See Friedman (1968b). Natural unemployment cannot be reduced by monetary policies.
3. See Chapter 23 of *The General Theory*, 'Notes on mercantilism, the usury laws, stamped money and theories of under-consumption'.
4. The name comes from John Ludd, who destroyed machines used in textile production around 1780.
5. The law of markets has, since its formulation by Say, generated an immense secondary literature. See in particular Lange (1942), Patinkin (1948), Sowell (1974), Kates (1998) and Denis (1999).
6. This is the title of Chapter 19 of his *Principles*.
7. On relations between Malthus and Keynes, see Lambert (1962), Rutherford (1987), Hollander (1996) and Martin (2003).
8. Keynes had a habit of making multiple and repeated corrections on his books' proofs. He could allow himself this bad habit from the view point of the printers since he paid for his works' production costs.
9. 'How can I accept a doctrine which sets up as its bible, above and beyond criticism, an obsolete economic textbook which I know to be not only scientifically erroneous but without interest or application for the modern world?' (1925-2, p. 258). He appreciated Engels more: 'But I've made another shot at old K.M. last week, reading the Marx–Engels correspondence just published, without making much progress. I prefer Engels of the two' (letter to George Bernard Shaw, 1 January 1935, in JMK 28, p. 42).
10. Clifford H. Douglas (1879–1952) was the inspiration behind the populist Social Credit movement, which had

some success in Australia, Canada and New Zealand. Of Silvio Gesell (1862–1930), author of *The Natural Economic Order* (1916) and promoter of 'stamped' money, Keynes wrote that he was a builder of an 'anti-Marxian socialism' (1936-1, p. 355).

11. This expression was, however, anterior to Marx. It was born in England in the 1840s and used in Chartist literature.
12. 'I see at a glance that Keynes is showing that unemployment is going to be a very tough nut to crack, because it is not just an accident – it has a function. In short, Keynes put into my head the very idea of the reserve army of labour that my supervisor had been so careful to keep out of it' (Robinson, 1953, p. 265).
13. See below.
14. A similar idea exists in Malthus.
15. On relations between Marx and Keynes, which we have touched on throughout this book, see in particular De Villé and De Vroey (1985), Duménil (1977), Herscovici (2002), Howard and King (1992), Lagueux (1985), Latouche (1985), Mattick (1969) and Sardoni (1986).
16. On Keynes's treatment of the classical school, see D. Diatkine (1985, 1995), Gislain (1987), Verdon (1996) and the papers collected in Ahiakpor (1998).
17. See in particular *The Distribution of Wealth* (1899).
18. See *Value, Capital and Rent* (1893) and *Lectures on Political Economy* (1901 and 1905).
19. On the debate between Keynes and Pigou, see Aslanbeigui (1992), Béraud (2003), Brady (1994) and Rima (1986).
20. It was on 16 October, during his first lecture of the 1933 autumn term, that Keynes presented for the first time both postulates (1989-2, pp. 85–6). We will limit ourselves here to Keynes's presentation, which of course aroused a great deal of criticism. For example, he was accused by some of constructing an artificial classical theory with false postulates. For others, involuntary unemployment exists in classical economics outside equilibrium; only their explanation and remedies differ from those of Keynes. For a detailed account of the evolution of the concept of involuntary unemployment from Keynes to the new Keynesians, see De Vroey (2004). Analysing the diverse and contradictory definitions of this concept and the impasse in which the debates over it led, De Vroey concludes that the concept of involuntary unemployment is not 'the sine qua non of Keynesian theory' (p. 250) and can be dispensed of without putting in question the Keynesian critique of laissez-faire. For other points of view, see Brenner (1979), Darity and Horn (1983), McCombie (1987–1988), Smithin (1985) and Trevithick (1992). On the postulates of classical theory, see Ghislain (1987).
21. Candide was the optimistic hero of a famous philosophical tale by Voltaire, who was one of Bloomsbury's praised authors.
22. With the exception of Toye's book (2000), which reproduces unpublished lecture notes from 1914, little has been written on Keynes's ideas on population, a theme he often approached (see for example 1922-25, 1923-3, 1937-6, without counting numerous passages in publications mainly devoted to other subjects). Fascinated by Malthus's economic theory, he was also fascinated by his theory of population, and belonged with Wicksell to the Malthusian League. He resigned, however, in 1943 as vice president of this association because he disagreed with its decision to propose measures restraining the fertility of the poor. Hitler's experiments had cooled his youthful enthusiasm for eugenics, which he shared with Fisher, Wicksell and Myrdal. He also distanced himself from Malthus's demographic arguments and considered population growth more positively.
23. There is an error in the title of this article such as it was reproduced in Volume 19 of the *Collected Writings*, where 'employment' is written in lieu of 'unemployment'.
24. Also see JMK 19, p. 772. See the following chapter for more details.
25. On the struggle between the Keynesian vision and the Treasury View, and the economic policies debates of the 1920s and 1930s, see, for example, Booth (1989), Clarke (1988, 1998), Middleton (1985), Peden (1988) and Tomlinson (1981).
26. Also see JMK 19, pp. 822–3 and 829.
27. See Clarke (1988), pp. 52–3.
28. This committee would later be transformed into the Committee on Economic Information.
29. Henderson already started distancing himself from Keynes's ideas and would become one of his most virulent critics.
30. See Cain (1982).
31. On the *Treatise*'s reception, see Dimand (1989). On the relations between Keynes and Roberston, see Anyadike-Danes (1985), Presley (1989), Mizen and Presley (1995) and Poulon (1987); on Hawtrey's criticism of the *Treatise*, E.G. Davis (1980); on the debate between Keynes and Hayek, Cochran and Glahe (1999), Dostaler (1991, 1999), Hayek (1995), Lawson (1996), McCormick (1992), Nentjes (1988), Parguez (1982, 1989b) and Tutin (1988). Several documents, letters and articles on these controversies are found in Volume 13 of Keynes's *Collected Writings*.
32. The transition from *A Treatise on Money* to *The General Theory* has raised a considerable secondary literature, encouraged by the fact that most of the drafts, manuscripts, successive plans and lecture notes of at least seven of Keynes's students have been conserved. Part of this is found in JMK 13 and 29 and Keynes (1989–2). In the secondary literature, see in particular Cain (1979), Cartelier (1995), Castex (2003, vol. 3), Clarke (1988),

Dimand (1988), Hirai (2004), Kahn (1984), Kregel (1987), Laidler (1999), Lambert (1969), Le Héron (1985), Lerner (1974), Marcuzzo (2001), Meltzer (1988), Milgate (1983), Moggridge (1973), Patinkin (1976a), Patinkin and Leith (1977) and Vallageas (1986). On the transition from the *Tract on Monetary Reform* to the *Treatise*, see Hirai (2007).

33. On the Cambridge Circus, see JMK 13, pp. 337–43; Kahn and Robinson (1985).

34. This remark might be on account of Schumpeter's jealousy, who had already renounced publishing a book on money because of Keynes's publication and whose *Business Cycles* went largely unnoticed after *The General Theory*'s publication. For a comparison of these two thinkers, see Arena (1985), Larceneux (1985) and Minsky (1986). On the collaboration between Kahn and Keynes, see Harcourt (1994) and Marcuzzo (2002).

35. She wrote 'general theory' intentionally to distinguish this corpus from Keynes's *General Theory*, of which it is only an element. On this subject see Asimakopulos (1991). I take this occasion to praise Tom Asimakopulos, an exceptional teacher, who died prematurely in 1990. It was he who initiated me into the works of Keynes, Joan Robinson and Piero Sraffa and who made possible several meetings with the latter two.

36. Nicknamed the 'Children Journal', this review was founded by young economists from Cambridge and the London School of Economics with the objective of filling in the gap between the two institutions.

37. For a fascinating account of the complex relations between economists at Cambridge and some other places, through the analysis of their correspondence, for the most part unpublished, see Marcuzzo and Rosselli (2005).

38. On relations between Keynes and Chicago, see Leeson (2003) and Patinkin (1979).

39. Another letter, signed by 41 economists, including Keynes, was published in *The Times* of 5 July 1932 on Harrod and Meade's initiative.

40. Before obtaining his LSE chair, Hayek, who was then teaching in Vienna, gave a series of lectures later published as *Prices and Production*. He also ventured into enemy terrain, at Cambridge, where in January 1931 he exposed his arguments, which were met with much consternation. There was at first dead silence, following which Richard Kahn risked the following question: 'Is it your view that if I went out tomorrow and bought a new overcoat, that would increase unemployment?'. To which Hayek responded affirmatively, pointing to his famous triangles covering the blackboard: 'but it would take a very long mathematical argument to explain why' (Kahn, 1984, p. 182).

41. The exact moment of Keynes's elaboration of this theory has been the object of several discussions. For Clarke and Skidelsky it was the summer of 1932, for Patinkin and Dimand sometime in 1933, for Milgate in 1934. Outlines are found in his lectures from 25 April and 2 May 1932.

42. On 15 January 1935, Keynes wrote to Susan Lawrence, former Labour MP, regarding his ideas: 'Before this way of thinking can be translated into practice, it has to be mixed with politics and passions just like any other way of thinking, and the nature of the outcome is something which I cannot foresee in detail' (JMK 21, p. 348). It is noteworthy that Keynes used the same terms here as he does in his letter to Shaw and his conversation with Virginia Woolf.

43. This letter was quoted at the beginning of Chapter 4.

44. To this club belonged several major figures, such as Schumpeter, Hansen, Mitchell, J.M. Clar, and Berle. It is not known if they all attended Keynes's talk.

45. See Chapter 9.

46. See the 40 articles reproduced in Backhouse (1999).

47. In addition to the numerous works devoted to Keynes in the bibliography, the following is a list of relatively recent publications on *The General Theory* illustrating the multiplicity of possible interpretations: Asimakopulos (1987), Benetti (1998), Boyer (1990), Brown-Collier and Bausor (1988), Clower (1989), Cartelier (1988), Dos Santos Ferreira (1988, 2000), Favereau (1988b), Frydman (1988), Lavoie (1985b), Parguez (1989a), Patinkin (1990), Shackle (1989) and Pressman (1987). For works dealing specifically with questions of labour and unemployment, see Addison and Burton (1982), Collins (1988), Davidson (1980), De Vroey (1997a, 1997b, 2004), S. and D. Diatkine (1975), Erhel and Zajdela (2003), Harcourt (1985b), Mongiovi (1991), Seccareccia (1987) and Zouache (2003). Rivot (2003) examines Keynes's policies on employment in his political writings. On effective demand, see Amadeo (1989), Asimakopulos (1982), Garegnani (1983), J. Halevi (1984), Kregel (1988) and Martin (1998). On the question of units of measurement and magnitudes in *The General Theory*, see Carabelli (1992), S. Diatkine (1989) and Rosier (2003).

48. We will come back to these questions in the Conclusion.

49. See on this subject Hutchison (1981) and Chorney (1987).

50. Also see the passage from *The General Theory* quoted at the start of Chapter 3.

51. Keynes returned here to an idea put forth by Adam Smith and developed, under various forms and explanations, by Ricardo, J.S. Mill and Marx. For them, accumulation of capital and growth engender the fall of capital's profitability. While Ricardo was dismayed by the inevitable arrival of stationary states, Mill and Marx celebrated it, but for different reasons: the former because men could finally devote themselves to finer things in life, the second because falling profit rates would provoke capitalism's downfall. Keynes's position is close to that of Mill.

52. Keynes does not trace these curves in *The General Theory*, which contains but one graph, suggested by Harrod, illustrating the classical theory of interest rates (1936-1, p. 180). On this, see O'Donnell (1999b).
53. On this subject, see Beaud and Dostaler (1995), Chapter 5 and the Conclusion of this book (Chapter 10). Also see, for an evaluation of Keynesian policies after 50 years, the writings collected in Hamouda and Smithin (1988).

8. Gold: an international monetary system in the service of humanity

> In truth, the gold standard is already a barbarous relic.
> *A Tract on Monetary Reform* (1923-1, p. 138)

> Dr Freud relates that there are peculiar reasons deep in our subconsciousness why gold in particular should satisfy strong instincts and serve as a symbol.
> *A Treatise on Money* (1930-1, vol. 2, p. 258)

It is often said that Keynes only became interested in international economics later in life, owing to his role during the Second World War. Attention is drawn to the fact that his *magnum opus*, *The General Theory of Employment, Interest and Money*, deals mainly with a closed economy. This would explain some of Keynesianism's limitations, increasing economic globalization being seen as one of the main sources of failure of Keynesian policies.

This vision is misguided. Throughout his life, Keynes was passionate about international economic questions, especially those of a monetary and financial nature, as theoretician but also as civil servant, negotiator and speculator. During his time at the India Office between October 1906 and July 1908 he studied both India's monetary problems and the functioning of the international monetary system. His first book, *Indian Currency and Finance*, was nourished by this concrete experience, as were all his writings, even the most abstract. Published in 1913, it contains an early formulation of his positions on international monetary system reform, which he developed fully in the 1940s. The idea, so fundamental to the Keynesian vision, of rational management of money and the economy is already present in this early work.[1]

Throughout Keynes's work one finds certain fundamental objectives, the priority accorded to internal equilibrium and the free choice of economic policy by governments in relation to the stability of exchange being first among them. International financial stability must be organized in a way that allows each country to pursue its national objectives of full employment and price stability. That said, in his concrete propositions for reform, Keynes demonstrated a pragmatism that brought him constantly to modify, sometimes radically, his positions.

In the following pages, we will tell the story of two of the battles to which Keynes committed himself most intensely. We will first examine his crusade against returning to the gold standard in the 1920s. We will then study his actions during the Second World War, and more particularly his involvement in establishing a new international monetary system, the essential basis of both national and international economic recovery.[2]

THE FIRST BATTLE: THE RETURN TO GOLD

The Reign of the Golden Calf

Precious metals have been used as standards of value since the most ancient of civilizations. Gold and silver transported from America by Spain in the sixteenth century contributed to the accumulation of capital culminating in the triumph of liberal capitalism in the nineteenth century.

The gold standard is a system in which a national unit of account corresponds to a fixed weight of gold, banknotes being redeemed on demand in gold at that rate.[3] In particular, the reimbursing of a balance of payments deficit is carried out by a transfer of gold from debtor country to creditor country. In 1752, David Hume published his classic account of the automatic adjustment mechanism of the balance of trade through movements of gold between countries and variations in price levels. This process was explained by the quantity theory of money, by virtue of which a variation of the quantity of gold provokes, after a period of adjustment, a proportional variation in price level. Trying to prevent gold from leaving the country is as useless as trying to prevent rivers from flowing into the sea (Hume, 1752b, p. 309). An automatic and natural mechanism distributes precious metals between different countries. The gold standard is seen as a system assuring monetary discipline at the international level. This system was officially established in Great Britain in 1716. The pound sterling was fixed the following year by Master of the Mint Isaac Newton at 123.24 grains of 22/24 carat gold, that is, at £3/17/10½d per ounce of gold. This would remain its official value until 1931.

In 1797, during the French Revolutionary Wars, the Bank of England decided to suspend the gold convertibility of its banknotes. This unleashed a polemic, one of whose most notable moments was when in 1809 David Ricardo sent to *The Morning Chronicle* three anonymous letters in which he explained the increase in gold prices as due to excessive issuing of non-convertible banknotes. This diagnosis was contained in the report of the Bullion Committee, a government commission set up in 1810. A law of 22 June 1816 made gold the standard of value and the legal means of payment. The return to the Bank of England banknotes convertibility at pre-war parity was decreed in 1819 and applied in 1821. In 1844, the Bank Charter Act proposed by Robert Peel reformed the Bank of England in the direction suggested by the partisans of the Currency Principle. While the Currency Department issued banknotes covered by a metallic reserve, the Banking Department issued credit and controlled the discount rate. The law obliged the Bank to cover fully all additional banknotes issued with metal.

Besides Britain, only Portugal had adopted the gold standard before 1870. Most other countries followed a bimetallic gold–silver system or a silver standard.[4] After war with France, Germany adopted the gold standard on 12 July 1873, followed by France, Belgium, Switzerland, Italy and the Scandinavian countries. The 1880s saw the system impose its domination around the world. The discovery of gold in the Transvaal in 1888 swept away the last traces of bimetallism. The last important countries to rally to the gold standard were Austria-Hungary (1892), Russia (1896) and Japan (1897–98). In the United States, the system was adopted in practice in 1873 but not formally endorsed until the Gold Standard Act of 1900, after William MacKinley's re-election. An advocate of the gold standard, he was at the same time a defender of protectionism.[5]

All countries adopted the gold standard gradually, without concertation or preliminary planning, under the pressure of events. A series of exceptional circumstances explained the price of gold's stability in the nineteenth century, allowing for simultaneous price and exchange rate stability. These were, for example, gold discoveries in California in 1848[6] and Australia in 1851, and the subsequent exploitation of deposits in South Africa: 'The considerable success with which gold maintained its stability of value in the changing world of the nineteenth century was certainly remarkable' (1923-1, p. 132). According to Keynes, for whom gold had no value in itself, these circumstances led to the illusion that this metal was intrinsically valuable and thus escaped the risks and hazards of a 'managed currency'. He believed the United States paid dearly, particularly during the crisis of 1907, for trying to minimize State monetary management. The creation of the Federal Reserve System in 1913 testifies to the American authorities' awareness of the necessity of rational monetary management.

Well before its suspension during the First World War, the gold standard raised considerable discussion, criticism and alternative propositions. International conferences on finance are hardly recent phenomena. Conferences were called in 1867, 1878, 1881 and 1892. The gold standard had few unconditional supporters during its reign from 1870 to 1914. The most respected economists of the period, such as Jevons, Menger, Marshall, Wicksell and Fisher, had serious reserves and proposed several reworkings of the system. One year before his death, Marshall wrote to his former student, thanking him for having sent him his *Tract on Monetary Reform*: 'As years go on it seems to me to become even clearer that there ought to be an international currency; and that the – in itself foolish – superstition that gold is the "natural" representation of value has done excellent service' (letter from Marshall to Keynes, 19 December 1923, JMK 19, pp. 162–3).

In his first book *Indian Currency and Finance*, Keynes explained that a gold exchange standard marked progress in respect to the pure gold standard by allowing for the conservation of precious metals. In such a system, central banks do not reimburse banknotes in gold on demand, as was the case with the gold standard, but in currencies whose value in gold is fixed. It is this international reserve currency that must be exchanged for gold on demand. Such was the model set up after the Second World War, with the US dollar being the currency equivalent to gold. India had a system of this type when Keynes wrote his book. He believed that this system was not ideal and that one day it would be necessary to abandon gold completely and replace it with a rationally managed international money.

> The time may not be far distant when Europe, having perfected her mechanism of exchange on the basis of a gold standard, will find it possible to regulate her standard of value on a more rational and stable basis. It is not likely that we shall leave permanently the most intimate adjustments of our economic organism at the mercy of a lucky prospector, a new chemical process, or a change of ideas in Asia. (1913-1, p. 71)

World War One forced all the belligerents, with the exception of the United States, to a *de facto* abandonment of the gold standard. It was a period of price instability, including in the United States, due to the price of gold's instability in terms of purchasing power. Keynes's attitude on this was complex. On the one hand, he declared himself against suspending pound convertibility, recalling the disastrous experiment of 1797, the blow to England's international prestige and the revelation of weakness thus given to its enemy. In fact, the pound was strong at the start of the war. It fell with respect to the American dollar, but grew in respect to other European currencies such as the franc, rouble and lira. In a number of speeches, articles and reports, Keynes even proposed restoring, after the war, the gold standard. However, he never stopped denouncing the fetishization of gold nor insisting on the necessity of rationally managing international currencies:

> If it proves one of the after effects of the present struggle, that gold is at last deposed from its despotic control over us and reduced to the position of a constitutional monarch, a new chapter of history will be opened. Man will have made another step forward in the attainment of self-government, in the power to control his fortunes according to his own wishes. (1914-13, p. 320)

Keynes also criticized the generalized tendency of hoarding gold, which must circulate and be used in order to support exchange rates and the purchase of foreign goods. Bankers behaved like maharajahs: 'It would be consistent with these ideas to melt the reserve into a great golden image of the chief cashier and place it on a monument so high that it could never be got down again. If any doubt comes to be felt about the financial stability of the country, a glance upwards at the image will, it is thought, restore confidence' (ibid., pp. 313–14). In most countries, management of gold reserves was far from rational. Products and not gold make the wealth and power of nations. Adam Smith showed that a country could lead and win a war without having significant gold and silver reserves at its disposal.

The Cunliffe Committee on Currency and Foreign Exchanges,[7] a commission set up after the war to study questions of currency and exchange, proposed in 1918 returning to the gold standard at pre-war parities. This was again proposed at the Genoa Conference in April 1922, which brought together 39 countries, but not the United States. Keynes participated as a journalist for the *Manchester Guardian*.[8] Shortly before the Conference he published in this newspaper an article entitled 'The stabilization of the European exchanges: a plan for Genoa', which was his first reform plan for the international monetary system. The strength of this publication got him invited to the British delegation's meetings. Members of the conference harboured reservations regarding a return to the gold standard for countries whose currencies had been strongly devalued.

The Crusade against the Return to Gold

It was the City's financial domination that led most countries, including those who had no interest in doing so, to adopt the gold standard. There was a close link between the gold standard's reign and Britain's world economic and financial domination: 'Before the war . . . We, in fact were the predominant partner in the gold standard alliance' (1925-6, pp. 198–9). This came from the fact that the rhythm of Britain's economic growth in the nineteenth century was extremely rapid, while in the twentieth century the United States would take the lead.

After the fall of the Conservative–Liberal coalition cabinet led by Lloyd George in October 1922, Keynes proclaimed, in a speech before a Liberal society of Manchester, the necessity of fighting against all forms of protectionism. He proposed in this election campaign speech a light devaluation of the pound sterling (1922-30, p. 4). He then declared himself in favour of returning to the gold standard, but on the condition that pre-war parity would not be re-established.

During this time, Keynes travelled to Germany, where he advised a government in dire financial straits. Borrowing from this experience in a series of lectures before the Institute of

Bankers, he set forth the proper way of reforming Britain's finances, emphasizing that a return to gold would not automatically re-establish price stability. German inflation (the mark was then a tenth of its pre-war value) was linked to the spectacular diminution of the proportion of wealth people kept in liquid form. This illustrated the fact that 'the value of the currency is a matter of confidence' (1922-31, p. 14). When confidence is lost in a currency, it is quickly transformed into goods. This is the basis of Keynes's position on the gold standard. Gold, like all forms of money, has no intrinsic value. The value of money, its purchasing power, depends on confidence and is linked to politics.

In one lecture, Keynes drew attention to differing attitudes on gold between continental banks and the Bank of England, a difference which explained the latter's supremacy. On the continent it was believed

> that gold is not kept in reserve to be used on any occasion whatever . . . The opposite view has been traditionally held for more than a hundred years past now in England. One of the great foundations, I believe, of our financial security has been this simple point of the correct theory about the gold reserve. (ibid., p. 34)

The dissolution of France's Left Coalition in July 1926 was followed by Poincaré's devaluation on 25 June 1928 and abandonment of the Germinal Franc. In a series of articles and letters devoted to France's financial situation, Keynes insisted on the psychological difference between the French and the English: 'O unchanging France! O wide and vasty channel! To a Frenchman the gold reserves are always for ornament, not for use – the family jewels. To an Englishman they are always for use, and not for ornament – the family cash' (1926-4, p. 459).

The Genoa Conference proposed that the return to gold required strongly depreciated currencies to be devalued rather than re-established at pre-war parity. This applied particularly to France, Italy and Belgium. Accepting the agreement but with no intentions of applying it, these countries believed currency devaluation in relation to gold constituted an injustice for holders of credits incurred before the war: 'But to regard the weight of gold as the measure of justice rather than the purchasing power of the currencies is, I think, a very technical form of justice' (1922-31, p. 45).

Britain in contrast could return to its pre-war parity, as it did coming out of the Napoleonic Wars: 'It would naturally be a matter of great pride to this country if, after the worst war of the twentieth century, we were again able to return to our previous undisturbed parity' (ibid., p. 61). However, the price of this return to pride was high, in terms of depression, unemployment and social conflicts. Having lost 7 per cent of its value, pound re-evaluation would have translated into higher British prices on foreign markets and thus into declining demand for British products. In order to re-establish the competitiveness of British goods, it was necessary to lower costs in pounds sterling, and the only costs that could be lowered were wages. This lowering would not be limited to the export sector; the movement started in the latter would be generalized, giving rise to strikes and social tensions. It was thus, in addition to economic rationality, a matter of social justice. Wage-earners would be made to pay for consequences of adjustments provoked by stupid measures. Gold, as Keynes wrote in *A Treatise on Money*, 'has become part of the apparatus of conservatism' (1930-1, vol. 2, p. 259).

Keynes continued his crusade from 1923 in the columns of *The Nation and Athenaeum*, of which he took control in May with a group of Liberal militants. He wrote on 14 July 1923, following the Bank of England's raising of its discount rate in an attempt to support the value of the pound, that the objectives of exchange stability, price stability and full employment are henceforth contradictory (1923-17). The gold standard would sacrifice full employment and price stability to the stability of exchange rates. It would link Britain's economic fate to that country now occupying first place in the world economy: the United States. Returning to the gold standard would be equivalent to contracting a marriage severely limiting the bachelor's individual freedoms. The fiancée being American, products consumed by her will occupy an increasingly important place in the basket of marital provisions: 'Miss G. happens to be an American, so that in the future the prices of grapefruit and popcorn are likely to be more important to him than those of eggs and bacon' (1925-6, p. 193).

On 11 December 1923, Keynes published *A Tract on Monetary Reform*, one of whose sections is devoted to restoring the gold standard. It is here that he wrote the famous phrase 'In truth, the gold standard is already a barbarous relic' (1923-1, p. 138) and formulated the grounds of his opposition:

> Therefore, since I regard the stability of prices, credit, and employment as of paramount importance, and since I feel no confidence that an old-fashioned gold standard will even give us the modicum of stability that it used to give, I reject the policy of restoring the gold standard on pre-war lines. (ibid., p. 140)[9]

In a speech before the National Liberal Club on 13 December, Keynes affirmed that the belief in the fact that returning to the gold standard would assure harmonious monetary arrangements arose from superstition (1923-30). Gold functioned relatively well in the nineteenth century in securing monetary long-term stability and extremely poorly in short-term fluctuations linked to credit cycles. In the twentieth century, it failed in both cases. Keynes proposed replacing gold by a standard having a fixed value in relation to a basket of commodities.

The Economic Consequences of Mr Churchill

It is one of history's ironies that it was Labour Prime Minister Ramsay MacDonald who announced to the House of Commons on 18 February 1924 his intention of following the recommendations of the Cunliffe Report and thus restoring the gold standard to its pre-war parity. Keynes was surprised to find himself, on this question as on other policies, on the left of Labour Chancellor of the Exchequer Philip Snowden. The same situation would recur after 1929. On 11 July 1924, he was called to testify before the Committee on the Currency and Bank of England Note Issues, where he declared that 'One of the great objections to the gold standard is that I think that as time goes on, with methods of economising, gold will tend to be redundant, and one of the things I want to be protected against is inflation due to the depreciation of gold' (JMK 19, p. 254). On 25 July he wrote to Charles Addis, one of the Bank of Englands's directors: 'To close the mind to the idea of revolutionary improvements in our control of money and credit is to sow the seeds of the downfall of individualistic capitalism. Do not be the Louis XVI of the monetary revolution' (JMK 19, p. 272). Keynes would be as poorly understood by the British authorities as Turgot was by Louis XVI.

Following the Conservative victory on 29 October 1924, which came after a censure vote against the Labour government, the value of the pound sterling rose from $4.49 on 31 October to \$4.72 at the end of the year. As the prospect of returning to the gold standard became increasingly likely, Keynes's campaign became increasingly urgent. He published an article in *Nation and Athenaeum* on 21 March 1925, declaring that the gold standard would never be an automatic and autoregulating system and again warning that it would place Britain under American tutelage (1925-8).

The decision had already been made during a secret meeting between Prime Minister Baldwin, Chancellor of the Exchequer Churchill and Bank of England Governor Norman on 20 March 1925. It followed the recommendation of a committee of experts formed at the end of 1924 and composed of Austen Chamberlain, Bradbury, Niemeyer and Pigou, whose report was presented to Churchill in February. It was announced by the latter in his budget speech on 29 April. Keynes wrote in *Nation and Athenaeum* on 2 May: 'Mr Churchill has done what was expected, and the experience of a hundred years ago has repeated itself' (1925-11, p. 357). He predicted that returning to pre-war parity would require 'a struggle with every trade union in the country to reduce money wages' (ibid., p. 360).

Churchill was far from certain of the well-foundedness of his decision. He was sensitive to Keynes's arguments and asked his advisers to seek his advice on all his important decisions. After reading his 21 February (1925-6) article in *Nation and Athenaeum*, he wrote the following day to Otto Niemeyer, controller of the Treasury's Finance Division and thus his main adviser:[10]

> The Treasury have never, it seems to me, faced the profound significance of what Mr Keynes calls 'the paradox of unemployment amidst dearth'. The Governor shows himself perfectly happy in the spectacle of Britain possessing the finest credit in the world simultaneously with a million and a quarter unemployed . . . I would rather see Finance less proud and Industry more content. (Public Record Office, T172/1499, quoted in Moggridge, 1992, pp. 428–9)

During dinner on 17 March, Churchill listened until midnight to Keynes's arguments against returning to the gold standard at pre-war parity. But in the end he gave in to contrary pressures. These events have provoked considerable debate:

> The legend has grown up and has obtained such currency that Winston himself has almost come to believe it, that the decision to go back to gold was the greatest mistake of his life, and that he was bounced into it in his green and early days by an unholy conspiracy between the officials of the Treasury and the Bank of England. (Grigg, 1948, p. 180)

Skidelsky (1969 and 1992, p. 198) and Gilbert (1976, pp. 93 and 99) defend the idea of Churchill's opposition to returning to the gold standard, an opposition that was defeated by his advisers, while Moggridge (1972, pp. 66–7 and 1992, p. 432) claims on the contrary that Churchill was always convinced of the well-foundedness of this decision and the fact of his presenting contrary arguments to his advisers was part of his decision-making method.[11]

History proved Keynes right. As he wrote in his Preface to *Réflexions sur le franc*:

> On three principal occasions in these ten years I have ventured to oppose the current flow of contemporary opinion and to forecast denouements contrary to those generally anticipated . . . The second occasion was before the return of Great Britain to the gold standard when I predicted consequences to the internal economy of the country and to the effect on the export trades which have been . . . on the whole fulfilled. (1928-1, p. 8; English version in JMK 19, p. 740)

The decision to return to the gold standard at pre-war parity was, as he declared before the Committee on Industry and Trade on 9 July 1925, '*ipso facto* a decision to reduce everybody's wages 2s in the £' (JMK 19, p. 390). British authorities, believing in the outdated assumptions of competitive wages and mobility of labour presented in economic textbooks, imagined that wages reduction would take place automatically.

Keynes submitted to *The Times* a series of three articles on the consequences of returning to the gold standard. After having been refused by the venerable London newspaper, they were published by *The Evening Standard* on 22, 23 and 24 July. Shortly afterward, Keynes published an expanded version as a pamphlet entitled: *The Economic Consequences of Mr Churchill*. A virulent attack against the economic policies of Churchill and the Conservatives, this writing is Keynes at his best.[12] The re-evaluation of around 10 per cent of the pound sterling led to an equivalent rise in the price of English exports on international markets and thus a weakening of the competitive position of businesses operating in these sectors. The latter had no other means of re-establishing their position but by lowering production costs and in particular wages. It was thus export sector workers who were the first to undergo the pound sterling's shift from $4.40 to $4.86. Churchill's advisers underestimated the difficulties associated with a general reduction of money values. What were fundamentally at stake were two visions of the economy and society:

> The truth is that we stand midway between two theories of economic society. The one theory maintains that wages should be fixed by reference to what is 'fair' and 'reasonable' as between classes. The other theory – the theory of the economic juggernaut – is that wages should be settled by economic pressure, otherwise called 'hard facts', and that our vast machine should crash along, with regard only to its equilibrium as a whole, and without attention to the chance consequences of the journey to individual groups. (1925-1, pp. 223–4)

The 'economic consequences of Mr Churchill' were thus deliberate policies designed to raise unemployment and put pressure on wages. The coal industry was the hardest hit by these events. On 1 May 1926, following the workers' refusal to accept a decrease in wages and an increase in working hours, the employers declared a lock-out. A general strike called on 3 May by the Trades Union Congress in solidarity with the miners was aborted after nine days. Keynes sympathized with the strikers: 'But my feelings, as distinct from my judgment, are with the workers. I cannot be stirred so as to feel the T.U.C as deliberate enemies of the community, who must be crushed before they are spoken with' (1926-15, p. 532). He predicted that these events would provoke an upturn in the parliamentary strength of the Labour Party, which he advised to be more attentive to monetary questions. In November, the miners went back to work in conditions fixed by employers and approved by the government.

On 26 June he published 'The first-fruits of the gold standard'. While the productive activity of the United States attained unprecedented highs, Great Britain floundered in a depression with more than one million unemployed. There was only 'one solid advantage which, in my opinion, the gold standard has gained, namely, the improvement of London's position as a centre for holding international balances' (1926-19, p. 555). He wrote on 23 October: 'The restoration of the gold standard has probably increased our profits on international banking business' (1926-25, p. 571). In short, if coal miners had the choice of giving in or dying of hunger, others learned to profit from the new situation.

Eighteen months after the return to gold, Keynes reviewed, in February 1927, the situation in *Nation and Athenaeum*. He affirmed that disequilibria generated by this decision had not been corrected, although it was impossible to measure them precisely (1927-4, p. 663). In an article published in *The Economic Journal* of June 1927, he indicated how this decision had also increased Britain's public debt (1927-8). Up until the 1929 elections, in which he was actively involved, Keynes never missed an opportunity to remind people of the links between Britain's catastrophic situation and the return to gold. In the *Nation* on 19 January 1929, he admitted to being mistaken in not predicting the danger of a gold shortage; he had forgot 'that gold is a fetish' (1929-2, p. 776). The central bank's insistence on holding significant inactive reserves provoked restrictive policies which would remain until 'the working classes of every country have been driven down against their impassionated resistance to a lower money wage' (ibid.). This is how Keynes, in a letter to *The Evening Standard* of 30 April 1929, linked these events to his propositions for employment.

> I can only say that I began advocating schemes of National Development as a cure for unemployment four years or more ago – indeed, as soon as I realised that, the effect of the return to gold having been to put our money rates of wages too high relatively to our foreign competitors we should not, for a considerable time, hope to employ as much labour as formerly in the export industries. (1929-13, pp. 812–13)

In *A Treatise on Money*, Keynes devoted a chapter to the gold standard. He referred to Freud explaining the irrational fascination gold has always exerted over men.[13] He quoted a passage from Ernest Jones, creator of the English psychoanalytic movement. This passage is remarkable considering the fact that it was written in the middle of the war, nearly ten years before the return to the gold standard:

> The ideas of possession and wealth, therefore, obstinately adhere to the idea of 'money' and gold for definite psychological reasons, and people simply will not give up the 'economist's fallacy' of confounding money with wealth. This superstitious attitude will cost England in particular many sacrifices after the War, when efforts will probably be made at all costs to reintroduce a gold. (Jones, 1916, p. 129)

This prophecy can be considered, for Keynes, as 'a success for the psycho-analytic method' (1930-1, vol 2, p. 259).

Keynes believed this irrational fascination was fading, gold having 'become a much more abstract thing – just a standard of value' (ibid., p. 260). He outlined a new monetary system by proposing the establishment of a supernational central bank which would issue an international standard equivalent to gold. To assure price stability, that of gold would be linked to a price index of 62 basic products. Always present, gold would thus be reduced to the rank of constitutional monarch:

> Thus gold, originally stationed in heaven with his consort silver, as Sun and Moon, having first doffed his sacred attributes and come to earth as an autocrat, may next descend to the sober status of a constitutional king with a cabinet of banks; and it may never be necessary to proclaim a republic. But this is not yet – the evolution may be quite otherwise. The friends of gold will have to be extremely wise and moderate if they are to avoid a revolution. (1930-1, vol. 2, p. 261)

The Fall of the Golden Calf

The crisis started in October 1929 led to major disruptions in the international financial and monetary system. As long as the gold standard was in force, Keynes sought the most effective means for Britain to profit from it. This brought him, until then a fervent advocate of free trade,[14] to propose protectionist measures aimed at preserving the parity of the pound sterling. Keynes thought that the crisis could actually help Britain regain world financial leadership.

> For these reasons I, who opposed our return to the gold standard and can claim, unfortunately, that my Cassandra utterances have been partly fulfilled, believe that our exchange position should be relentlessly defended today, in order, above all, that we may resume the vacant financial leadership of the world. (1931-9, p. 236)

Keynes was nurturing illusions, as he would do again in the coming war. Six months after the publication of this article, which aroused lively reactions, Great Britain suspended the gold standard. A few days later, in *The Sunday Express* of 27 September, Keynes applauded this decision as having beneficial consequences on employment: 'We feel that we have at last a free hand to do what is sensible' (1931-25, p. 245). The decision was taken because the Bank of England had no other choice, having to pay back £200 million in gold in a few weeks, playing 'the game up to the limits of quixotry, even at the risk of driving British trade almost to a standstill' (ibid., p. 246). Keynes predicted that the pound would fall to a much lower level than the experts anticipated. It lost 30 per cent from September to December 1931. This allowed the economy to revive 'in a way which is strictly fair to every section of the community, without any serious effects on the cost of living' (ibid., p. 246).

Keynes anticipated, and the unfolding of events proved him right, that most countries would follow Britain's example, 'the curse of Midas' (ibid., p. 248) falling on the rare States having remained loyal to the Golden Calf, France and the United States being first among them. In April 1933, the United States abandoned the gold standard. In 1936, the system had everywhere come to its end. Yet this did not settle problems, the rise across the world of protectionism being a major factor in the depression's prolongation. It was now necessary to get down to the task of constructing a new international monetary order.

SECOND BATTLE: TOWARDS A NEW INTERNATIONAL MONETARY SYSTEM

On 16 May 1937, Keynes suffered a serious heart attack caused by a bacterial endocarditis, an illness for which rest was then the only remedy. The first symptoms of his illness had appeared unidentified early in the 1930s. He spent three months in the Ruthin sanatorium. He never completely recovered. Virginia Woolf wrote to Lydia on 5 June 1937: 'we are much relieved to hear that Maynard is better. I hope he won't get stronger *mentally* as his normal strength is quite enough for me' (V. Woolf, 1975–80, vol. 6, pp. 133–4). In March 1939, Janos Plesch became his physician.[15] By this time, Keynes had partially recovered, but it was a physically diminished man who would play a major role in British life and world affairs during the Second World War.

The *Anschluss* of March 1938 was followed in September by the Munich Pact, which affected Keynes's health and morale. He did not understand how Prime Minister Chamberlain could have sought an agreement with Hitler. In spite of this, and like at the beginning of World War One, Keynes remained optimistic. Like many others, he was convinced that Hitler was bluffing and had no intention of attacking the West. Arriving at Tilton on 29 August 1939, he did not believe war was imminent. On 1 September, German troops invaded Poland. Two days later, Great Britain declared war on Germany.

Beginning on 20 September, Keynes brought together work colleagues from the First World War, whom he called the 'old dogs', to discuss how best to influence the war effort. He was already preoccupied by postwar economic reconstruction, anticipating that the latter would most certainly lead Europe, and particularly Britain, into an enormous balance of payment deficit *vis-à-vis* the United States. But his more pressing problem was how to finance the war effort. On 20 October, he presented to the Marshall Society his ideas on war financing. This presentation was followed by the publication of two articles in the *Times* on 14 and 15 November, collected and expanded in *How to Pay for the War*, a pamphlet published on 27 February 1940. This plan was praised by economists of all persuasions, including Hayek in a 24 November article in *The Spectator*. It proposed limiting consumption to free resources for the war through a mechanism of forced saving or deferred pay which would be returned with interest in successive payments after the war. The plan was poorly received by the Labour Party and the unions, which led Keynes to revise it, as he considered their support as essential.[16] To help repayment, Keynes also proposed a capital levy to be deducted during the postwar reconstruction boom, which alienated him from business circles. Shortly after the publication of *How to Pay for the War*, James Meade and Richard Stone, with Keynes's collaboration, established a system of national accounts.[17]

On 10 May 1940, Hitler attacked Belgium, Holland and France. The same day, Winston Churchill succeeded Chamberlain as Prime Minister and formed a coalition government with Labour and the Liberals. Keynes met him often at the Other Club, founded by Churchill in 1911. He was then appointed member of a Chancellor of the Exchequer's Consultative Committee, created on 1 July. But, in contrast to his World War One experience, he did not have the status of civil servant or employee. He received no salary, though he had at his disposal a room, secretary services and a bed at the Treasury from 12 August. This is how he described his new situation, as well as his health, in a letter to his friend John Sheppard, then Principal of King's College, on 14 August:

> As from two days ago my position at the Treasury changed fundamentally. The people there, including many old friends, have been quite extraordinarily good and considerate in the arrangements made. I have no routine duties and no office hours so that I need work no harder than I am inclined. But I have a sort of roving commission plus membership of various high up committees which allow me to butt in in almost any direction where I think I have something useful to say. I am now allowed to know all the innermost secrets, which was not the case until this week, without knowledge of which one cannot really advise to much purpose; and I have been given a room at the Treasury with the share of a Class I civil servant private secretary, who can devil for me. How it will all develop one can only say with experience, but my position, which in its early days was in many ways so undefined as to be distinctly embarrassing, is no longer so. On top of this, Plesch gave me a drastically improved report yesterday on my heart which agrees with my own subjective sensations. (J.T. Sheppard Papers, King's College, Cambridge, JTS/2/112)[18]

He was simply 'Keynes', free to attack what he wished, whom he wished and when he judged it necessary. He was not hindered by the civil servant's duty of reserve and used this privilege widely. He met discreetly with journalists, parliamentarians, bankers and other decision-makers to transmit information in a way that prepared the ground for reorienting positions. With the Americans and other opposites in negotiations, he maintained relations outside official circuits, as was the case with Carl Melchior and other Germans during the Paris negotiations at the end of the First World War. In January 1941, his status was clarified and his power reinforced by being appointed economic adviser to the Chancellor of the Exchequer. He would become a Treasury spokesman and sometimes delegation head during six visits to the United States.

Franklin D. Roosevelt was re-elected President of the United States for the third time on 5 November 1940. American legislation prevented the country from directly helping belligerents. This was by-passed by the Lend Lease announced on 17 December, which gave the President power to sell, transfer, exchange, lease or lend war materials to nations whose defence was considered vital to the defence of the United States and who were to repay 'in kind or property, or any other direct or indirect benefit which the President deems satisfactory'. Discussions on the Lend Lease would be closely linked to negotiations over the international monetary system and led by the same people. Keynes spoke of this with Harry Hopkins, adviser to President Roosevelt, in London in January 1941. On this occasion, he discussed a response to the German promise of a 'New Order' composed at Foreign Secretary Lord Halifax's request. In this document, he sketched a new monetary system which would, according to him, avoid 'some of the abuses of the old *laissez-faire* international currency arrangements, whereby a country could be bankrupted, not because it lacked exportable goods, but merely because it lacked gold' (1940-11, p. 12). The Lend Lease Act was signed on 11 March 1941. Keynes continued to discuss it with the United States, where he stayed from April to August; in May he met President Roosevelt on this subject.

White's Plan against Keynes's Plan

On his return from the United States in August 1941, Keynes started writing, at Tilton, the first version of his project for international monetary system reform in the form of two papers, finished on 8 September and entitled respectively 'Post-war currency policy' and 'Proposals for an international currency union'. In a preliminary paper, Keynes attacked the doctrine of laissez-faire, which was at the source of the principal economic difficulties of the time: 'To suppose that there exists some smoothly functioning automatic mechanism of adjustment which preserves equilibrium if only we trust to methods of *laissez-faire* is a doctrinaire delusion which disregards the lessons of historical experience without having behind it the support of sound theory' (1941-1, pp. 21–2).

The gold standard was the coronation of this doctrine. For Keynes, it had, in light of gold's rareness, a fundamentally deflationist bias. It contributed to enrich the already rich and impoverish the poor. The basic idea of Keynes's new system proposed in the second paper was to extend national banking principles to the international level. The final objective was to set up an expansionist mechanism by providing the world with the necessary liquidity to favour growth. This would be done by the creation of an international clearing house functioning by means of overdrafts. It was thus the outline of a world central bank that Keynes had proposed in *A Treatise on Money*. The plan recommended multilateral exchange between economic partners on the international level and proposed mechanisms to stabilize member States' balance of payments. The first paper put forth the principles which he had advocated for 30 years and to which he remained committed. The second proposed terms and conditions that would be considerably transformed over the course of the negotiations, to such a point that the principles are no longer apparent.

In habitual fashion, Keynes had these papers circulated widely. They were revised many times into several versions. He easily accepted suggestions to modify them, as his first biographer and collaborator emphasized: 'He was entirely lacking in the kind of obstinacy which so often results from pride of authorship' (Harrod, 1951, p. 533). A second version of his international monetary system reform project was finished on 18 November (1941-3), following criticisms from, among others, Richard Kahn, James Meade and R.G. Hawtrey. This version added substance to his first schemata. It insisted on multilateral compensation between members and a control of capital movements as a permanent characteristic of the postwar system. Dennis Robertson, who collaborated with Keynes in the 1920s but who distanced himself during preparation of *The General Theory* because he did not accept its author's radical condemnation of the classical system, was enthusiastic about the plan. This marked the beginning of a new phase of close collaboration between the two economists. Lord Robbins, who with Hayek led the battle against Keynes and his disciples from his headquarters at the London School of Economics at the start of the 1930s, was also enthusiastic about Keynes's paper, which was more widely circulated than the previous one.

As always, Keynes worked quickly, and a third version of the project was completed on 15 December (1941-4). It was here that the bancor appeared, an international currency nonconvertible into gold or national currencies. Its value could vary. But it was defined in terms of gold quantity. For psychological reasons originating in tradition, a connection with gold was to be maintained in order to assure the new currency's prestige. Keynes underlined that it would be necessary to increase the responsibility of creditor countries in the new international monetary system. He added that, in this domain as in others, the main question concerned a balance between what was to be decided by rules and what was to be decided by discretionary decisions, in step with circumstances. He himself favoured the second method of decision.

Following numerous commentaries, particularly from Harrod but also from several members of governmental organizations, Keynes reformulated his paper on 24 and 25 January 1942 into a fourth version, which was printed as part of a Treasury report on international economic and monetary problems. It was discussed and criticized by the reconstruction committee set up by the war cabinet. It finally made its way before Churchill's government on 10 April 1942, where it was approved pending a few minor amendments, thus becoming Britain's official position. Keynes wrote to Richard Kahn on 11 May:

> My currency schemes, which you saw in an early version, have gone through a vast number of drafts without, in truth, substantial change. It has been somewhat of a business getting them through all stages, but successfully achieved at last . . . Now it is a question of capturing American sympathy . . . As you may suppose, it has been rather a *tour de force* getting the thing so far as it has got. It is still a tender plant, which can be easily blasted by a harsh word from any quarter. (JMK 25, pp. 143–4)

In fact, the Americans had also been working on such a plan. On 8 July, Richard Hopkins,[19] Second Secretary to the Treasury, received from Sir Frederick Phillips, representing the

Treasury in the United States, the draft of an international monetary reform plan prepared by the US Treasury. This plan was kept secret and only Keynes was authorized to read it. It was authored by Harry Dexter White.[20] Like several other American experts involved in the Bretton Woods negotiations, White admired Keynes's ideas. The two men met briefly in 1941 during the latter's visit to the United States. A short time later, White described Keynes to Roosevelt as 'an extremely able and tough negotiator with, of course, a thorough understanding of the problems that confronted us' (Harry White Papers, quoted by Skidelsky, 2000, p. 324). He sometimes required a replacement, having been left totally exhausted after his one-on-ones with Keynes.[21]

White's plan proposed the creation of a Stabilization Fund on the basis of deposits, and a Bank for Reconstruction. He put more emphasis on stabilizing exchange rates and abolishing restrictive practices than on long-term perspectives. The sums fixed at the start and the possibilities for expansion were much more limited than in Keynes's plan. White proposed the creation of a unit of account called the unitas, a simple receipt for gold deposited in the Fund. The role of the unitas was much less important than that of the bancor. Keynes began to read the document on 24 July at Tilton. He wrote to Frederick Phillips on 3 August: 'Seldom have I been simultaneously so much bored and so much interested' (JMK 25, p. 159). This plan was, in his opinion, filled with good intentions, but the actions it proposed were doomed to failure. However, compromises were already forming in his mind. Shortly after reading it, he wrote down notes on White's plan, which he sent to Hopkins and Phillips, and composed a fifth version of his own plan, which he sent to White on 28 August. During a visit by Morgenthau and White to London in the autumn, Keynes and the latter met several times and had a long discussion on the two plans on 23 October.

White's plan was officially sent to England in February 1943, after having been reworked seven times since the summer of 1942. Keynes then composed a comparative analysis of the two plans, whose fundamental difference he described as follows: 'The American ideas take shape in a Stabilisation Fund with a "limited liability" subscription, whereas the Bancor proposals aim at an International Clearing with a wide use of credit' (1943-1, p. 225). On 7 April, the two plans were officially published. Keynes's plan, in its fifth version,[22] was entitled 'Proposals for an international clearing union'. This document, which Keynes did not sign, is generally referred to as 'Keynes's plan'.[23] A four-point outline is formulated at the beginning of the document:

1. The mechanism of currency and exchange;
2. The framework of a commercial policy regulating the conditions for the exchange of goods, tariffs, preferences, subsidies, import regulations, and the like;
3. The orderly conduct of production, distribution and price of primary products so as to protect both producers and consumers from the loss and risk for which the extravagant fluctuations of market conditions have been responsible in recent times;
4. Investment aid, both medium- and long-term, for the countries whose economic development needs assistance from outside. (1943-3, pp. 233–4)

This was the true beginning of the Bretton Woods negotiations. On 18 May 1943, Keynes, now Baron of Tilton, gave his first speech at the House of Lords. Its subject was the reform of the international monetary system. Keynes insisted on the similarities between the English and American plans: 'Neither plan conceals a selfish motive. The Treasuries of our two great nations have come before the world in these two Papers with a common purpose and with high hopes of a common plan' (1943-5, p. 280). He described the Americans' plan as appearing like an old bottle containing new wine.

The White Plan continued to be modified. The Americans discussed it with several other countries. At the end of June 1943, Keynes composed a synthesis of the two plans (1943-7). He conceded to the Americans the principle of subscriptions, the limitation of creditor responsibility, the fact that no country would be forced to change its currency's gold value against its will, the formula for quotas and voting rights, and the general form of stabilization funds. He knew that the final compromise would have to be made according to American terms.

In September and October, exploratory and informal Anglo-American talks took place in the United States on Britain's suggestion. The British delegation was led by Richard Law, Foreign Office Under-Secretary, and included, among others, Keynes, Robbins, Meade and Robertson, the latter already being in Washington. White was of course part of the American delegation. He had just published in August his proposition of a Bank for Reconstruction and Development, which Keynes described on the boat, according to British delegation participants, as Bedlam. True to his habit, Keynes was very active and met many people in Washington, including Treasury Secretary Morgenthau, with whom he lunched on his arrival. Throughout his stay, he met White often, wanting to settle with him, in particular, the question of transforming the unitas into a true international monetary standard.

Between 15 September and 9 October 1943, the delegations met nine times. In a speech given during the first plenary meeting on 21 September, Keynes insisted on the fact that postwar economic problems must be treated as a whole, with the ultimate objective that of finding a radical solution to the problems of employment and improved living standards. James Meade, who was part of the delegation, thus described this speech in which Keynes revisited themes from his 'Economic possibilities for our grandchildren' (1930-17): 'Keynes's speech was absolutely in the first rank of speechifying. I have never heard him better, – more brilliant, more persuasive, more witty or more truly moving in his appeal' (Howson and Moggridge, 1990, p. 110). However, with his fatigue intensifying from one meeting to the next, Keynes grew increasingly intransigent and ill-tempered, nearly to the point of breaking off negotiations. The meetings were dominated by verbal jousts between Keynes and White. These meetings were thus described by a British participant:

> What absolute Bedlam these discussions are! Keynes and White sit next [to] each other, each flanked by a long row of his own supporters. Without any agenda or any prepared idea of what is going to be discussed they go for each other in a strident duet of discord, which after a crescendo of abuse on either side leads up to a chaotic adjournment of the meeting in time for us to return to the Willard for a delegation meeting. (quoted in JMK 25, p. 364)

Meade wrote in the detailed diary he was then keeping: 'But it augurs ill for the future unless these negotiations can somehow or another be got out of the hands of two such prima donnas as White and Keynes' (Howson and Moggridge, 1990, p. 133). It was obviously the Americans who held the final word in these discussions. Although they conceded on written formulations, they never made any basic concessions and, being the dominant power, had little motivation to do so. Keynes seemed at times unaware of this fact and believed the mere force of his argumentation could reverse the situation.

The meetings ended with the writing of a 'Joint statement by experts of united and associated nations on the establishment of an international stabilisation plan' in 14 articles. Of the

13 points of disagreement identified before the start of the meetings, six were resolved, in most cases in accordance with the American version. The others were negotiated between October 1943 and April 1944, while the Joint Statement was revised into several successive versions. Keynes wrote to his mother on 18 April 1943: 'And we are very content indeed with what we have accomplished – greatly in excess of our best expectations . . . We all really are trying to make good economic bricks for the world after the war – however hopelessly difficult the political problems may be'.

Bretton Woods

On 22 April 1944, a 'Joint statement by experts on the establishment of an international monetary fund' was published in the United States and England, after seven revisions of the Joint Statement signed on 9 October in the United States and after difficult discussions, some of which took place in England between advocates and adversaries of Keynes's positions.[24] This statement immediately provoked lively opposition in several sectors of British public opinion. The Left saw it as a threat to the objectives of full employment while the Right detected a danger for the British Empire. The banking world saw it as a threat to the City's financial predominance. Keynes, who warned authorities against hastily publishing the document without sufficient preparation of public opinion, met the press and consulted with parliamentarians from all parties. He wrote to John Anderson on 16 April 1944: 'But in certain respects the fact that I am not a Civil Servant and live in a limbo (though it be, in all respects, nearer hell than heaven) makes my interposition in such a way rather easier' (JMK 25, p. 436). He was preoccupied by his countrymen's isolationist tendencies and anti-American sentiments. He was forced to slow down his activities in March following heart problems that prevented him from being present during negotiations between Britain and her Dominion partners. In early May, he explained the project in a series of meetings with the European Allies.

Keynes gave a speech on 23 May in the House of Lords defending the compromise he had reached with the Americans, which he presented as a child 'being, in some important respects, a considerable improvement on either of its parents' (1944-3, p. 10). He insisted on the fact that this position did not constitute a return to the gold standard and that it left each country free to determine its own internal policies. On being accused of betraying his ideals, he emphasized the complementariness of the agreement with ideas he had defended vigorously since the 1920s.

> Was it not I, when many of to-day's iconoclasts were still worshippers of the Calf, who wrote that 'Gold is a barbarous relic'? Am I so faithless, so forgetful, so senile that, at the very moment of the triumph of these ideas when, with gathering momentum, Governments, parliaments, banks, the Press, the public, and even economists, have at last accepted the new doctrines, I go off to help forge new chains to hold us fast in the old dungeon? I trust, my Lords, that you will not believe it. (1944-3, JMK 26, pp. 16–17)

On 26 May, Morgenthau announced that President Roosevelt had invited 44 countries to a conference from 1 July at Bretton Woods in New Hampshire. It was to be preceded by a smaller conference in Atlantic City, a site chosen for the comfort of Keynes, whose precarious state of health was well known. The choice of date was arduous for the American authorities, considering preparations for both the Allied Landing and the Republican and

Democratic conventions in view of presidential elections. The final date was chosen in order to give the event maximum impact in light of Roosevelt's presidential campaign, which hoped to give the President a fourth mandate. The Democratic Convention was to begin on 19 July, directly following the Bretton Woods Conference. Keynes wrote to Richard Hopkins on 23 June, mentioning the Republican opposition to the plan reported in the *New York Times*: 'The staging of the vast monkey-house at Bretton Woods is, of course, in order that the President can say that 44 nations have agreed on the Fund and the Bank and he challenges the Republicans or anyone else to reject such an approach. I should say that this tactic is very likely to be successful' (JMK 26, p. 63).

Directed by Keynes, the British delegation included D.H. Robertson, L.C. Robbins, N. Ronald, R.H. Brand, R. Opie and W. Eady. From 16 to 23 June, the British as well as delegates from seven other countries and an observer from the American embassy crossed the Atlantic. Several discussions took place on board, where two 'boat drafts' were composed and dedicated to the International Monetary Fund and the International Bank for Reconstruction and Development, which were presented to the Americans at Atlantic City.

The British suggested the functioning of the Fund be largely automatic and routine, and that it not be overseen by a powerful and permanent directorship. Preliminary works began on 23 June in Atlantic City, where Keynes and White met on their arrival. The week from 23 to 30 June was in large part devoted to ironing out the latest difficulties between the British and Americans. Keynes wrote to Richard Hopkins on 25 Juneh:

> At the same time he [White] agrees that we and the Americans should reach as high a degree of agreement behind the scenes as to which of the alternatives we are ready to drop and which we agree in pressing. Thus to the largest extent possible White and I will have an agreed text, but on the surface a good many matters may be presented in alternative versions. (JMK 26, p. 61)

It was thus a matter of making a maximum of preliminary decisions, while trying not to give the delegates the impression that Bretton Woods was a *fait accompli*. Keynes again wrote to Hopkins on 30 June that there were several behind-the-scenes meetings between White and himself. He complained of the fact that the Americans would not stop consulting their lawyers. Lord Robbins, a member of the British delegation and old adversary of Keynesian policies, noted in his diary, which is a precious source of information on these events:

> Keynes was in his most lucid and persuasive mood; and the effect was irresistible. At such moments, I often find myself thinking that Keynes must be one of the most remarkable men that have ever lived – the quick logic, the birdlike swoop of intuition, the vivid fancy, the wide vision, above all the incomparable sense of the fitness of words, all combine to make something several degrees beyond the limit of ordinary human achievement. (Howson and Moggridge, 1990, p. 158)

On 1 July 1944, the delegations arrived in the small resort of Bretton Woods, where Mount Washington Hotel lacked staff and was unprepared to receive them. It was said that the manager went into hiding with a case of whisky when the delegates arrived! Instead of participating in the evening's inaugural meetings, Keynes, always a man of tradition, held a long-prepared dinner party celebrating the fifth centenary of the *Amicabilis Concordia* between King's College of Cambridge and Oxford's New College.[25]

The Bretton Woods Conference got down to business on 3 July. The delegates were divided into three commissions. The first, devoted to the International Monetary Fund (IMF), was chaired by White; the second, devoted to the International Bank for Reconstruction and Development (IBRD), was chaired by Keynes; the third, devoted to other forms of financial cooperation, was chaired by Mexican Eduardo Suarez. In his preliminary speech, Keynes affirmed: 'In general, it will be the duty of the Bank, by wise and prudent lending, to promote a policy of expansion of the world's economy in the sense in which this term is the exact opposite of inflation' (1944-5, p. 73).

Plenary commissions were not often called, the essential work being done by small committees. Keynes sent his colleagues to the latter, in which he participated little, staying in his quarters at the disposition of the British delegates, giving them information, advice or orders. As in Atlantic City, there was much behind-the-scenes settling. The working days were long and often continued late into the wee hours. Keynes wrote to Richard Hopkins on 22 July: 'My only real complaint has been the grossly excessive number of cocktail parties' (JMK 26, p. 110). He wrote to his mother on 25 July: 'I do not think I have ever worked so continuously hard in my life'. Worried about his health and feeling moments of weaknesses, he avoided late-night discussions and remained under Lydia's constant supervision. On 19 July, after dining with Morgenthau, he suffered a light heart attack. Inadvertently revealed to the press, the news made waves in Europe. Throughout the conference, Keynes's personal relations with White and Morgenthau were excellent, but discussions were also difficult, particularly when it came to the future institutions' location. Keynes was accused of running his commission at a frantic pace, without taking time to give delegates the necessary explanations, to such a point that Morgenthau was obliged to intervene.

The Conference was scheduled to finish on 19 July but was extended until the 22nd. Work came to an end on 20 July, with agreements that turned out to be not dissimilar to April's Joint Statement. The final act, however, was *ad referendum*, that is, requiring approval by respective governments before becoming law. Work was thus far from over. Keynes gave an acceptance speech for the final act on the evening of 22 July, praising White and Morgenthau, even having a few good words for the lawyers and jurists, whose presence he found annoying: 'Too often lawyers busy themselves to make commonsense illegal. Too often lawyers are men who turn poetry into prose and prose into jargon. Not so our lawyers here in Bretton Woods. On the contrary they have turned our jargon into prose and our prose into poetry' (1944-6, p. 102). This is how Lord Robbins's diary described the event:

> At the end Keynes capped the proceedings by one of his most felicitous speeches, and the delegates paid tribute by rising and applauding again and again. In a way, this is one of the greatest triumphs of his life. Scrupulously obedient to his instructions, battling against fatigue and weakness, he has thoroughly dominated the Conference. (Howson and Moggridge, 1990, p. 193)

R.H. Brand wrote to Hopkins: 'I hope you will think the Conference was a success. I must tell you that Keynes was without doubt quite the dominant figure. He certainly is an astonishing man' (JMK 26, p. 113). His exit received a standing ovation and a chorus of the traditional 'For he's a jolly good fellow.'

The American Victory

Problems of interpreting the agreement were raised immediately following the end of the Conference. On 31 July, Dennis Robertson brought to Keynes's attention the existence of an internal contradiction in Bretton Woods's final act. This apparently anodyne question caused a stir in the following months and threatened to undermine the whole process. It was a question of knowing at what point the Fund could prevent a member from imposing restrictions on payments, transfers and convertibility in cases where its gold and foreign currency reserves were rapidly diminishing. Keynes considered that the decision was up to the member country and not to the Fund. During the Conference, the British made a concession on this subject to the United States, a concession Keynes believed took place without his knowledge. Robertson maintained that he had seen the written compromise and approved it. He wrote to Keynes in January 1945: 'But in any case I made a great error of judgment in not deciding when I received your assent, that I must see you myself to make sure you had understood its implications' (JMK 26, p. 160). Keynes wrote to Robbins on 19 January: 'I remember Eady coming to me about some drafting point near the end, but no memory or consciousness that it was this one' (ibid., p. 174). Relations between Keynes and Robertson, cordial during wartime, once again became strained. The debate gave rise to new exchanges between Keynes and White. Keynes prepared an official letter destined for Morgenthau, which was finally sent on 1 February 1945. The response, which brought an end to the matter in the terms hoped for by Keynes, did not arrive until 8 June.

The Bretton Woods Agreement was adopted by the US House of Representatives, with amendments satisfying bankers and Republicans which Keynes described to his colleagues as having limited scope. Roosevelt's death in April 1945, followed by the replacement of American political personnel, and in particular of Morgenthau by Fred Vinson, complicated the situation. Keynes replaced the Chancellor as head of a delegation which, from September, spent two months in the United States and whose main goal was to discuss repayment conditions for the Lend Lease. He described the mission to his mother as 'the toughest assignment I have ever had' (21 October 1945): 'But my difficulties in bringing London along to a reasonable compromise are not less than those in moving Washington. And our business, taken as a whole, is of enormous complexity' (letter to his mother, 4 November 1945). In fact, Keynes and his delegation obtained neither a grant nor even an interest-free loan from the United States. An agreement was essential, without which the whole edifice of Bretton Woods risked collapse. The Anglo-American financial agreement was signed on 6 December and constituted a veritable capitulation for Great Britain. Instead of the $5 billion grant it requested, Britain received a loan of $3.75 billion at 2 per cent interest.

In December 1945, the Bretton Woods Agreement was put before the British parliament, where opposition to it was intense. Keynes gave a speech before his peers on 18 December. While recognizing the unsatisfactory character of its terms, he called them to vote in favour of them: 'Yet I must ask Your Lordships to believe that the financial outcome, though it is imperfectly satisfactory to us, does represent a compromise and is very considerably removed from what the Americans began by thinking reasonable' (1945-3, p. 612). The agreement was finally adopted by a vote of 343 to 100 with 169 abstentions. With the acceptance by the other participants, the inaugural meeting of the governors of the International Monetary Fund and the International Bank for Reconstruction and Development was called for the month of March 1946 in Savannah, Georgia. There were, however, a few problems still to be settled, particularly the site of the institutions' headquarters and the status of the directors and their salaries. The British were opposed to these organizations being situated in Washington, where they would be too close to American political power, and suggested New York instead.

At the end of the meeting in Washington, new Secretary Vinson announced without any consideration towards Keynes that his country proposed Washington as headquarters.

Keynes was appointed on 19 February 1946 British governor of the two organizations created at Bretton Woods, the IMF and the IBRD.[26] In his inaugural speech at Savannah, he described the new organizations as children surrounded by fairies. The first fairy brings Joseph's multicoloured jacket, to illustrate that the children belong to the whole world. The second brings a box of vitamins for delicate children. The third fairy represents the spirit of wisdom and discretion. It was hoped 'that there is no malicious fairy, no Carabosse', whose curse would be ' "You two brats shall grow up politicians; your every thought and act shall have an *arrière-pensée*" ... If this should happen, then the best that could befall – and that is how it might turn out – would be for the children to fall into an eternal slumber, never to be waken or be heard of again in the courts and markets of Mankind' (1946-2, p. 216). It appeared Vinson felt himself attacked and did not appreciate being compared to Carabosse!

In the following discussions, the British capitulated to the Americans' choice of location for the new institutions, which were established in Washington. Regarding the directorship, the Americans accepted that the latter would not be comprised of a full-time bureaucracy. However, on the question of salaries, which the Americans wanted high, Keynes announced that his delegation would vote against such a decision, one of the rare times this happened. Keynes's growing bitterness towards the Americans became apparent toward the end, as if he suddenly became aware of their ulterior motives. He wrote on 13 March 1943 to Richard Kahn:

> The Americans have no idea how to make these institutions into operating international concerns, and in almost every direction their ideas are bad. Yet they plainly intend to force their own conceptions through regardless of the rest of us ... The Americans at the top seem to have absolutely no conception of international co-operation; since they are the biggest partners they think they have the right to call the tune on practically every point. If they knew the music that would not matter so much; but unfortunately they don't. (JMK 26, p. 217)

Returning by train to Washington, Keynes suffered a major heart attack. On the boat bound for Europe, it was said that he started working on a paper violently condemning American policy and advising the British government not to ratify the agreement. It was also said that George Bolton, adviser at the Bank of England and Ernest Rowe-Dutton, Under-Secretary to the Treasury, convinced him to destroy this paper (Bolton, 1972, quoted in Moggridge, 1972, p. 834, who questioned the authenticity of this episode). He wrote in his report to the Chancellor on the Savannah meeting: 'Nevertheless, the outcome, though discouraging to our previous hopes and a doubtful augury for the efficient working of the new institutions, must be viewed in its right perspective' (1946-3, p. 227). Shortly after his return, Keynes spent the Easter holiday at his home in Tilton with Lydia and his parents. He died on Easter day, before noon, at the age of 62. It is likely the great efforts he expended during the war contributed to abbreviating his existence.

Lessons of a Defeat

The agreement that gave birth to the International Monetary Fund and the International Bank for Reconstruction and Development, now the World Bank, was paradoxical. As we have seen, Keynes was one of its main architects from beginning to end. And yet, in its final form, the agreement was very different from the intentions expressed by Keynes in his first outlines for building a new international monetary order, designed to favour full employment and growth and to prepare a world without war. Not only was the agreement closer to American ideas than to those of the European ally, but the subsequent evolution of the organizations and their practice separate them even further from Keynes's aims.

This illustrates the predominance of political, economic and military power bargaining, the three dimensions being intimately linked. Keynes was highly aware of this. Since the First World War, and even before, world leadership passed from Britain to the United States. The economic depression in Britain started before 1929; it was the stagnation of the 1920s that inspired several of Keynes's arguments rather than the crises of the 1930s. It was Roosevelt's New Deal and not *The General Theory* that helped bring the world out of the crisis in the 1930s. The Second World War, fought in Europe, was nevertheless won in large part by the United States. It was normal that the Americans impose their new international economic order. It was they who prevented the Germans from imposing theirs. It was thus hardly surprising that Bretton Woods sanctioned this fact.

The events which have been mentioned here also illustrate another reality: the growing power of non-elected experts, particularly in the domain of international financial relations. In reality, Bretton Woods was a finely orchestrated play with New Hampshire's White Mountains as backdrop and the base of Mount Washington as stage, on which a sumptuous hotel received 45 delegations and carried its name. There were at times vigorous discussions and amendments to proposed texts. But essential matters had already been determined. The delegates did not have to decide between Keynes's plan and White's plan. Keynes, White and their collaborators had already ironed out their divergences so that a single Anglo-American plan could be presented to the Bretton Woods delegates. Both Americans and British had already negotiated this plan with allies, friends and protectorates. As we have seen, the Bretton Woods Conference was even preceded by a preliminary meeting in Atlantic City between Americans, British and a few other delegations, conceived to prepare the agenda and settle lingering disputes before the final ceremony. Even though, particularly on White's insistence, the delegates were made to feel as if they were brought together to make decisions, a large part of the play had already been performed on the theatre stage of Atlantic City.

This technocratic power transcended national boundaries. A veritable *Internationale* of experts, especially economists, was involved in the story leading to Bretton Woods.[27] The paradox is that most of them were, or at least declared themselves, Keynesians. This also explains the nature of the final understanding, whose wording, if only to reflect the intentions of its signatories, reflected a part of Keynes's intentions.

But it is not surprising that Keynesians gave birth to this agreement when one considers the journey of their inspirer. Keynes was consistently loyal to a few fundamental objectives – a world without unemployment, without glaring inequalities between classes and nations – and this implied rational management of the economy by the State. An international financial agreement was essential to arrive at these ends. His unremitting effort to bring them about forced Keynes into making increasingly important and successive compromises which were unavoidable in order to obtain the indispensable agreement from the Americans. His concessions gradually emptied the agreements of the substance Keynes thought were preserved in them, especially when the duplicity of interested agents became involved. Keynes was painfully aware of this at the end of his life. This understanding gave rise to the development of policies profoundly different from those he envisaged. But that is another story.

NOTES

1. On Keynes and India, see Chandavarkar (1989) and Dimand (1991).
2. The present chapter borrows from Dostaler (1985) and (1994-5). On these questions, see Chandavarkar (1987), Elie (1989-90), Ferrandier (1985), Gardner (1975), Perroux (1945), Schmitt (1985), Williamson (1985), the writings collected in Thirlwall (1976) and the studies of Moggridge (1969, 1972 and 1986).
3. On the gold standard, see Merten (1944), Bordo and Schwartz (1984) and De Cecco (1984).
4. 'Monometallism' is used to describe a system in which one precious metal assumes the role of standard, while 'bimetallism' describes a system in which two metals, generally gold and silver, between which a stable exchange rate must be fixed, fulfil this function.
5. MacKinley led an imperialist policy, installing an American military government in Cuba after war with Spain. He was assassinated in 1901 by an anarchist. Vice-President Theodore Roosevelt, a cousin of future President Franklin Delano Roosevelt, succeeded him.
6. The California gold rush, in which gold provoked hallucinations and led to madness, inspired one of cinema's masterpieces, *The Gold Rush* of Charlie Chaplin, an artist for whom Keynes had the highest admiration. While *Modern Times* illustrated the fate of workers in modern capitalism, *The Great Dictator* highlighted the murderous folly of Nazism. Gold, employment and war, these were Keynes's three main battlefields.
7. Walter Cunliffe was governor of the Bank of England from 1913 to 1918.
8. See his articles in JMK 17, pp. 354–425.
9. Friedrich Hayek, who started a doctoral thesis in economics in 1923, claims to have arrived independently at the same conclusions as Keynes. He then renounced publishing his discovery after having learned of Keynes's book, who, with the publication of *The Economic Consequences of the Peace*, became one of his heroes (Hayek, 1994, p. 89). This would later change.
10. Niemeyer outclassed Keynes by a small margin in civil servant exams in 1906, which allowed him to choose a position in the Treasury, Keynes having to settle with the India Office. One wonders what would have happened if Keynes had made his career at the Treasury. After conflicting with the Treasury's Permanent Secretary Warren Fisher, Niemeyer resigned to join the Bank of England in 1927. Richard Hopkins then succeeded him as Controller of Finance. With Frederic Leith-Ross, Deputy Controller of Finance, these men were Churchill's main advisers. Keynes's personal relations with Niemeyer and Leith-Ross were never easy, while he saved Hopkins in his attacks against the Treasury. In spite of this, these men would all meet once a month at the Tuesday Club.
11. See also Kersaudy (2000), pp. 239–42.
12. This was the inspiration behind Nicholas Kaldor's title *The Economic Consequences of Mrs Thatcher* (1983).
13. See the second quotation in epigraph to this chapter.
14. Keynes nevertheless affirmed often that his adherence to free trade was not dogmatic and could be revised according to circumstances.
15. Keynes appreciated this Hungarian doctor, who counted Einstein among his patients, because he was capable of advancing with great assurance a diagnosis and then pronouncing the contrary with as much assurance the following week. Moreover, he expressed his ideas in ordinary rather than esoteric and specialized language. In his copious correspondence with his doctor, Keynes produced detailed and sometimes surprising autodiagnoses.
16. See Toye (1999).
17. On this subject see Delfaud and Planche (1985).
18. Somewhat more than a month earlier, on 9 July, he wrote to him regarding his 'new job at the Treasury': 'I should say that the necessary duties are very slight indeed, and in the main any work I do I shall have to make and invent for myself' (JTS/2/112). As we will see, the course of events would invalidate these remarks on the lightness of his tasks.
19. A friend of Keynes, Hopkins often played the role of intermediary between him and the Treasury.
20. White was born in 1892. After obtaining a doctorate from Harvard and teaching at Lawrence College in Appleton, Wisconsin, he entered the Treasury in 1934, where he made a rapid ascension, becoming in 1938 one of Secretary Henry Morgenthau's main advisers. He was named in 1941 Assistant Secretary to the Treasury, with responsibility for all matters pertaining to international relations. Appointed US Executive Director of the International Monetary Fund, White died of a heart attack in 1948 three days after having been interrogated by a House of Representative committee on anti-American activities over spy allegations. According to Skidelsky (2000, pp. 256–63), he was a Soviet agent; also see Rees (1973). One thing is certain: White preferred Soviet-American hegemony to Keynes's Anglo-American domination.
21. On Keynes as a negotiator, see F.G. Lee (1975).
22. The successive modifications made by Keynes can be found in JMK 25, 449–68.
23. Roosevelt was at first opposed to Morgenthau's suggestion of publishing the American plan after the British informed them of their intention to publish their paper as a white paper. He changed his mind after a London newspaper published a summary of the White plan on 5 April.

24. United around Hubert Henderson, one of Keynes's former allies and collaborators at the end of the 1920s, the adversaries were found particularly at the Bank of England.

25. Participants in this ceremony included Dennis Robertson, Nigel Ronald, Lionel Robbins, Robert Brand, Wyn Plumptree, Dean Acheson, Oscar Fox and China's Minister of Finance, Dr Kung (JTS/2/112).

26. 'I am going, as you will soon read in the paper, as British Governor of the International Monetary Fund and the International Bank for Reconstruction. But, whilst those are the big words, it is in fact a holiday jaunt' (letter to Sheppard, 20 February 1946, JTS 2/112).

27. For more on this subject, see Ikenberry (1992).

9. Art: theoretician, consumer and patron of the arts

Of all kinds of descriptive or theoretical criticism there is none, to my mind, which is less satisfactory than that which deals with art ... Nothing can be more fatal than the supposed antagonism between the precise and verbal notions of philosophy and the organic, indivisible perceptions of beauty and feeling, between these things that we know piecemeal and those which we may only grasp as wholes, between those who see and those who understand.
'A theory of beauty' (1905-2, pp. 2–3)

This, then, is the first step towards peace, the scientist must admit the artist to be his master.
'Science and art' (1909-2, p. 3)

I can almost boast that I am Commissar for Fine Arts in my country.
Letter to M.S. Stepanov, 18 July, 1944[1] (quoted in Moggridge 1992, p. 705)

At last the public exchequer has recognised the support and encouragement of the civilising arts of life as part of their duty. But we do not intend to socialise this side of social endeavour. Whatever views may be held by the lately warring parties, whom you have been hearing every evening at this hour, about socialising industry, everyone, I fancy, recognises that the work of the artist in all its aspects is, of its nature, individual and free, undisciplined, unregimented, uncontrolled. The artist walks where the breath of the spirit blows him. He cannot be told his direction; he does not know it himself. But he leads the rest of us into fresh pastures and teaches us to love and to enjoy what we often begin by rejecting, enlarging our sensibility and purifying our instincts.
'The Arts Council: its policy and hopes' (1945-2, p. 368)

We started this journey with ethics. We finish it with aesthetics. From the good, we move to the beautiful. There is of course more than one bridge between the two worlds. The greatest philosophers have generally tackled both questions. For Moore and the Bloomsbury group, as we have seen, the good is linked to good states of mind resulting from the contemplation of beauty, in nature and in art. In *Art*, Bloomsbury's aesthetic manifesto, Clive Bell writes: 'Art is above moral, or, rather, all art is moral because, as I hope to show presently, works of art are immediately means to good' (C. Bell, 1914, p. 32). In his account of the first post-impressionist exhibition, of which he was secretary, Desmond MacCarthy declared that

> Now anything new in art is apt to provoke the same kind of indignation as immoral conduct, and vice is detected in perfectly innocent pictures. Perhaps any mental shock is apt to remind people of moral shocks they have received, and the sensations being similar, they attribute this to the same cause. (MacCarthy, 1995, p. 77)

For Keynes, many of whose closest friends were artists, art occupied the summit in the hierarchy of human activities, above science and well above economic activities. The latter were at the service of the first two. This he explained in a previously mentioned paper, presented before the Apostles Society on 20 February 1909, at the beginning of his career as a Cambridge economist. Although the text is untitled, it has been given the title of 'Science and art'. It is hitherto difficult to excel in the domains of art and science, Keynes proclaimed. It is unlikely we will see a new Leonardo da Vinci born in the twentieth century. Moreover, artists and scientists understand each other less and less and at times even look down on each other. It is necessary to overcome these misunderstandings and recognize that the gap between artistic activity and scientific activity is not as wide as one thinks. The scientist, like the artist, is a creator. And both use intuition to develop their works. The greatest scientists, Newton, Einstein and others have insisted on the importance of a theory's elegance, however arid it may be. And to convince their contemporaries of their theory's validity, they must use the art of rhetoric.

That said, the scientist must recognize art's superiority over science. The creative process of an artwork has, on the scale of human activities, a greater intrinsic value than that of the discovery of new knowledge. Furthermore, art and science remain closer to each other than to economic activities, in particular the pursuit of wealth:

> I, the moderator, believe that the scientist should take an intermediate position in the world. It is certain that he spends his time much better than the businessman spends his . . . But is it not almost as certain that the good artist stands to the scientist very much as the scientist stands to the stock-broker? Putting moneymaker and capacity aside, is there any brother who would not rather be a scientist than a businessman, and an artist than a scientist? (1909-2, p. 3)

In a review of a book by Wells, published in January 1927 (1927-2) and quoted in Chapter 6, Keynes gives a Freudian interpretation of this hierarchization of human activities. Art and science constitute the supreme form of sublimation. Businessmen, not having the chance to be artists or scientists, are forced to channel their abundant libido into the neurotic pursuit of money, into the accumulation of that which serves nothing.

We know, however, that Keynes devoted much energy to amassing money. But such money was destined above all to facilitate access to beauty. And Keynes considered himself first and foremost a scientist. He would have preferred to have been an artist, he told his brothers at the end of his talk. Choosing between Newton, Leibniz and Darwin or Milton, Wordsworth and Velasquez, he would have liked to have been one of the last three. He did not consider himself sufficiently gifted to be an artist. But mastery of words and writing can be considered an art. Keynes lamented that his *Treatise on Money* was an artistic failure. Recalling his gift at explaining simply complicated problems, his friend Clive Bell wrote: 'In moments such as these I felt sure that Maynard was the cleverest man I had ever met; also, at such moments, I sometimes felt, unreasonably no doubt, that he was an artist' (C. Bell, 1956, p. 61).[2]

This chapter will not deal with Keynes's portrait as an artist, but rather with his attitude and positions regarding art. It will begin by analysing certain relatively unknown papers he wrote on aesthetics. It will then turn to his activities as a consumer of art, in particular as a collector of paintings. It will finish by examining the key role he played, as administrator, organizer and patron, in the artistic and cultural life of Great Britain.[3]

AESTHETIC VISION

Prolegomena

From the start of his Apostles Society membership, in 1903, to his 'taking wings' in 1910,[4] Keynes presented over twenty texts, most of a philosophical nature. Aesthetic considerations are developed in about half of them. The very first text he presented, probably in June 1903, is entitled 'Shall we write filth packets?' and bears the alternative title: 'The obscene in literature'. Here Keynes revisits themes developed in Strachey's first interventions before the Apostles. Continuing where the latter left off, he defends the idea that anything may be the object of artistic treatment, in particular the least conventional of sexual activities: 'But we ought to write filth packets not only about the normal passions, but about the abnormal also . . . there is no proper literature on the higher sodomy, a passion which might provide material for the most splendid situations' (1903-3, pp. 11–12). Nothing is more fitting than Shakespeare's most obscene passages.

'Beauty', presented on 30 April 1904, is the first paper to deal entirely with aesthetics. Keynes engages, as he does with ethics and probability, in a critical development of Moore's arguments, the philosopher being present in the audience. He criticizes Moore's conception of beauty as excessively broad and vague. In *Principia Ethica*, Moore defines the beautiful as 'that of which the admiring contemplation is good in itself' (Moore, 1903a, p. 249). For Keynes, there are things we may contemplate with admiration that are not beautiful: 'but I am not so clear that there is one specific thing *beauty* attaching to everything of which the admiring contemplation is good' (1904-1, pp. 3–4). Keynes considers that, excluding natural beauty and perhaps a small number of exceptional art works, there is no beauty in and of itself. We attribute beauty to paintings. This short text constituted a sketch which was undoubtedly subjected to sharp criticism from Moore, here the accused. Keynes clarified and developed his positions in later writings.

We have already mentioned 'Miscellanea ethica', written between July and September 1905, which contains, along with 'Ethics in relation to conduct', the grounds of Keynes's conception of probabilities. But this manuscript also proposes important reflections on aesthetics. It contains a concept which will go on to play a central role in Keynes's aesthetic vision, that of 'fitness': '"Fit" can be completely specified by reference to "good", but both notions seem to be unique and elementary. Corresponding to every good feeling there is a fit object and we may say that those objects are fit towards which it is possible to have a feeling which is good' (1905-1, pp. 5–6). Defined in this way, fitness is a mental object that corresponds to an external object. Good states of mind or aesthetic emotions are on the contrary linked to our perception. The beauty of an object comes from its intrinsic characteristics, but also from our organs of perception and from our spatial position relative to it:

> Our aesthetic feelings are evoked by the content of our perceptions; we must assume, therefore, *either* that similar objects always and in all persons evoke similar sensations, *or* that out of the various sensations evoked one can be said to be like the object in a sense in which the others are not. Neither of these assumptions, however, seems justifiable; to take Hume's illustration, if we were to look at our mistress's complexion through a microscope we might change our views upon the beauty. Our eyes are a particular kind of lens; suppose, as is certainly conceivable, a different variety had been provided by the beneficent foresight of Providence, an entirely different group of objects might appear to us beautiful. (1905-1, p. 12)

The question of the physical and moral qualities involved in the passion of love was at the heart of Keynes and his friends' preoccupations. What applies to love relationship also applies to the contemplation of art works:

> The beauty of some pictures depends a good deal upon the particular method in which we fix them; those in particular which rely for their effect upon distant or elaborate perspective sometimes require that kind of adjustment of the eyes which we must often make in using stereoscopic or opera glasses, if we are to see the object with distinctness. (ibid., p. 17)

Furthermore, beauty is an organic unity, in the sense that the beauty of a whole is not the sum of the beauty of its parts, this being the case regardless of whether it is a human being, a painting or any other object likely to provoke an aesthetic emotion.

'A Theory of Beauty'

Between August and October 1905, Keynes wrote 'A theory of beauty', his most elaborate manuscript on aesthetics. This text was not written for the Apostles, but for the G.L. Dickinson Society, where it was read on 8 November 1905. This would likely explain why Keynes allowed himself to reproduce long passages from 'Miscellanea ethica', in particular those concerning 'fitness'. The paper was presented before the Apostles on 5 May 1912, with several cuts in regard to the initial manuscript, about which he wrote to Lytton Strachey, 12 November 1905: 'I forgot to tell you that I read my paper on Beauty at Dickinson's last Wednesday. It was too esoteric and I didn't feel it was much of a success'. The text is rather more abstract than esoteric, which is inevitable given the theme it tackles. It deals with reconciling 'the process of knowledge and of sensation', an undertaking in which the artist and the philosopher must make common cause 'for in the nature of things the study of art has a very close and intimate relation with the study of philosophy' (1905-2, p. 4). The first epigraph of this chapter, quoted from this paper, denounces the antagonism between art and philosophy. To understand beauty, but also society, the economy and the world, one must bring together analysis and intuition:

> We require for success at the same time a separation and collaboration of the analytic and intuitive powers. He will be a very singular individual who possesses both in any high degree; but if only the philosopher and the artist lose their mutual feeling of suspicion, and the genius of the one check and direct the genius of the other, then the parts and kinds of beauty will be known at last and knowledge and creation may advance together. (1905-2, p. 3)

The artist is unable to translate completely into words the nature of his perceptions. His language must necessarily lack exactitude.[5] But his vision must never be blurred. The artist and the philosopher must both learn to perceive. The philosopher, for his part, may lack an artist's taste and creative capacity, 'But he must have enough of the artist in him to know the nature and objects of aesthetic judgment; he must himself be capable of strong and individual impressions on these matters, and he must continually check his analysis by the experience of more subtle and sensitive minds' (ibid., p. 5).

Before exposing his own conception of beauty, Keynes criticizes a number of erroneous views. According to Dürer, for example, beauty flows from mathematical proportions between the parts of a whole. For Burke, a list may be drawn of characteristics enabling one to qualify an object as beautiful. For others, beauty is identified with some other entity external to it, such as the good, the useful or pleasure. Great thinkers such as Socrates and Plato are not spared. Much of the confusion comes from the belief in the fact that beauty is one and indivisible, that there exists but one type of beauty. Having found a criterion to justify our taste in one case, we seek to apply it to all others. Accordingly, we would like Degas for the same reasons we like Botticelli, which, for Keynes, is absurd.[6]

Beauty's value is solely the result of the emotions it arouses within conscious beings: 'In the realm of beauty, man is the center of the Universe' (ibid., p. 9). Contrary to Moore, the fact that there are splendours hidden to our eyes in the mountains of the Moon does not increase the beauty of the Universe. It is not beauty in itself that is good, but rather the emotions beauty arouses. The value of these emotions resides in the relation between emotion and the contents of our mind and not in the relation between this content and some cause which is supposed to be the source of the emotion: 'There is a further point of a somewhat similar nature, but much more controversial. I maintain that the value of our feelings depends solely on their relation to what we see, and not at all on the relation between what we see and what is there' (ibid., p. 9).

If human beings were to become, like certain animal species, sensitive to ultraviolet or to infrared or able to perceive new types of vibrations, it is probable that the nature of aesthetic emotion would be considerably transformed as a result. Things repellent now might then appear as exquisitely beautiful. Keynes continues to insist on the main idea put forward in his previous paper, namely that beauty is not an intrinsic characteristic of external objects, that the produced impression varies according to the angle of observation:[7]

> We cannot select one perception and call it and it only the right perception; the beauty of a perceived object is a function not only of the intrinsic characteristics of the object itself, but also of our organs of perception, and of our relative spatial position. Strictly the term beauty ought always to be applied to the *mental* objects which call up aesthetic feelings, and not to the external objects to which these mental objects correspond. For it is impossible to assert dogmatically that to each external object there is only one mental object in true and natural correspondence. (1905-2, p. 11)

That said, there is enough uniformity in the human organs of perception and sensation to attribute beauty to external objects, even if it remains uncertain that all men see the same thing when they examine the same object. The question of our relationship to the external world is a matter for metaphysics, a domain outside Keynes's field of interest at this moment.

Sensitivity to beauty, the capacity to perceive it, are themselves variable qualities among human beings, qualities relating to intelligence, culture and education. Of course, artists possess above-average capacities in this domain. But even ordinary men may attain, through education and training, higher 'faculties of contemplation'. At the bottom of all Keynes's later actions as founder and leader of artistic organizations was the explicit objective of 'educating the population's taste' so that it may have access to the contemplation of beauty. There is undoubtedly in this a touch of Victorian elitism.

Beauty concerns our perceptions of the physical and natural world but it also applies to mental objects, and this despite the fact that aesthetics is mainly concerned with nature or artistic creations. We are not only interested in the physical appearance of our friends, but also in their mind. Of course, analysis becomes more complex in this case, even if fundamentally 'the theory of physical and mental beauty is one and embraces the same fundamental notions and ideas' (ibid. p. 27). The concept of fitness, introduced in 'Miscellanea ethica', sheds some light on the matter. Related to goodness though not to be confused with it, fitness also relates to beauty: 'The idea of "fit" is, as it were, a generalised idea of "beauty"' (ibid., p. 24). The idea of 'moral beauty' is better rendered by that of fitness:

> Any object, whose contemplation *ought* to give rise to a state of mind that is good, is fit. A state of mind may, in its turn, become an object of contemplation, and we may, therefore, speak of its fitness as well as of its goodness . . . In fact, I distinguish moral excellence and moral beauty; admitting that all moral excellence has some beauty, I deny, though with the utmost hesitation, that the more excellent is necessarily the more beautiful. (1905-2, pp. 24–5)

It follows from these definitions and considerations that 'it is the most beautiful we ought to love, and the most beautiful which ought to fill us with the best and noblest emotions' (ibid. p. 25), it being understood that the beauty in question here is that of the mind as much as the body: 'Surely Plato is right in supposing that the peculiar beauty of the opening mind of youth is not only a most natural but a most fit object of affection. I think as men grow older they become less loveable but more excellent' (ibid.).

Keynes ends his paper by classifying of beauty into four types, whose definition, he stresses, is relatively arbitrary. 'Pure beauty' has a timeless immobility, even if it is that of a storm. It is found in certain Greek statues, Keats, daffodils or glaciers. What he calls the 'beauty of interest' is, on the contrary, related to the instability and action of the intellect. It takes on importance, at the expense of the first form of beauty, with the development of humanity: 'Pure beauty we can still worship, but it is interest we need for daily food' (ibid., p. 32). 'Beauty of consecutive arrangement' flows from perfectly logical arrangements, as with Pythagorean theorems and great works of philosophy. 'Tragic beauty' cannot be perceived by the agents of catastrophe, but rather by those who contemplate it from the outside, from the standpoint of the good. Keynes finishes by calling for diversity in matters of art and of beautiful, for cultural diversity:

> Most of us will have our favourite kinds and types; in some particular direction we shall be lovers and judges. Yet we must refrain from narrowing down too far the fit objects of our senses, and, while it is the delight and the duty of all lovers of beauty to dispute and dispute continually concerning tastes, we must not impose on the almost infinite variety of fit and beautiful objects for human emotion tests and criteria which we may think we have established in that corner of the field which is dearest to ourselves; nor must we fail to see beauty in strange places because it has little in common with the kind of beauty we would strive to create, were we artists and not philosophers. (1905-2, p. 34)

Further Remarks

In his subsequent writings, Keynes developed his ideas by branching off into other directions. Lover of theatre, he asked his Apostle brothers, on 5 February 1906, whether writing melodramas was a legitimate activity. His answer was positive, since melodrama justifies itself through its relation to tragic beauty. According to him, the common accusation that melodramas lack realism is unfounded. Realism is not essential. In words foreshadowing those of Virginia Woolf for fiction or Fry and Bell for painting, Keynes wrote that a play does not describe reality, but rather mental events, emotions, feelings: 'Mental events compose the essence of the play' (1906-2). It was a matter, as Strachey will do in his biographies, of exploring a character, of telling the story of its evolution. By signs and symbols, we show the workings of the mind, and not what our eyes and ears perceive. The artist must bring to perception the smallest vibrations of emotions and feelings. His mission is to undress the soul, not unlike that of psychoanalysis. To do this, one does not turn away from staging violence unheard of in reality, from using conventions and trick effects, from painting characters worse than any found in nature. This theatrical art, Keynes adds, must be available to the masses and not only to the elite.

Two years later, Keynes imagined a dialogue between two princes, Henry and Rupert, the first having an intellectual's rational and reasonable temperament, the other the soul of an artist. It is likely Henry represented the mathematician Henry Norton and the second, the poet Rupert Brooke, the two most recent apostles, and both present at the Society's meeting on 28 November 1908. Prince Rupert's main argument, which is manifestly that of Keynes, is that there is no emotion, aesthetic or not, without bodily sensation: 'Emotions, at any rate, are really bodily sensations at bottom' (1908-3, p. 1). Those who no longer feel bodily sensation when reading poetry or contemplating paintings do not derive aesthetic emotions from these activities even if they do derive some pleasure from them: 'And the same thing is true of pictures. We often look at them with enjoyment; but we are having no feelings towards them if they leave our bodies unmoved' (ibid., p. 2). We can form a judgement, which would have a certain value, regarding a poem or painting without feeling a real emotion which necessarily manifests itself by a physical sensation. Prince Henry concludes the dialogue by writing: 'we must hope for the resurrection of the body' (ibid., p. 5).

In 'Can we consume our surplus? Or the influence of furniture on love', Keynes looked into an area of artistic creation that would take on much importance for the Bloomsbury group, particularly for Vanessa Bell, Duncan Grant and Roger Fry, through the activities of the Omega Workshops, namely that of furniture and interior design. He states here that the physical environment in which we live, its aesthetic character, has an effect on our activities, type of work, but also on the nature of our romantic activities: 'Who could commit sodomy in a boudoir or sapphism in Neville's Court? . . . One would not easily, for instance, become in love with Cleopatra in the King's Combination Room' (1909-6, pp. 3–5). It is difficult to work intellectually with ease, to give oneself to flow of ideas, in crowded rooms whose ceilings are very high. Chairs have 'an important emotional effect beyond their mere comfort' (ibid., p. 3), which according to Keynes is an important modern discovery: 'It is important, therefore, that we should live in rooms and on chairs built to our measure by the most skilled upholsters' (ibid., p. 5). The author of these lines would put these prescriptions into practice by having his London and Cambridge lodgings decorated by his friends Duncan Grant and Vanessa Bell.

Of course, the writings we have just evoked do not constitute a general theory of aesthetics, on the same level as the theories of probability, money or employment that Keynes would go on to develop. They are circumstantial documents, manuscripts composed with the intention of being read before a closed circle of friends. One must recognize the provocation and humour they contain. One must also recognize their limits, inaccuracies and contradictions, though on this last point, Keynes always considered contradiction not as an evil, but as a positive sign of thought's evolution in relation to circumstances and criticisms of which it is an object.

That said, one cannot help but notice reflections foreshadowing those of Bloomsbury's art criticism. They also follow ideas that were developed in the 1890s by Roger Fry, well before his integration in Bloomsbury,[8] that will later influence Clive Bell's conception of 'significant form', linked to his rejection of a vision of art as imitation of nature. We find this same rejection in Virginia Woolf's conception of the novel or in Lytton Strachey's conception of the biography. Keynes himself would put these principles to work in the numerous portraits he would compose until the end of his life, mixing artistic effects with psychological insights. His theoretical work in economics was itself marked by aesthetic preoccupations. Far from being a rational and calculating *homo oeconomicus*, the human being who evolves on the economic stage has the same characteristics as the tormented characters in Virginia Woolf's novels or the neurotic individuals who inhabit the stories of Lytton Strachey. When Keynes, in *The Economic Consequences of the Peace* for example, describes characters, one often has the impression of looking at a painting.

CONSUMER OF ART

Opinions on Keynes' aesthetic sense are divided. For Clive Bell, who had already described Keynes as an artist in his own way:

> He had very little natural feeling for the arts; though he learnt to write admirably lucid prose, and, under the spell of Duncan Grant, cultivated a taste for pictures and made an interesting collection. Said Lytton Strachey once: 'What's wrong with Pozzo – a pet name for Maynard which Maynard particularly disliked – is that he has no aesthetic sense'. (C. Bell, 1956, pp. 134–5)

Strachey's statement is apocryphal and, if authentic, can no doubt be seen as an expression of aggressiveness toward the friend who had robbed him of Duncan Grant's affection. As for that of Bell, it must be nuanced by the fact that Keynes and Clive Bell were never the closest of allies in Bloomsbury, in particular on the subject of politics. As for Duncan Grant, Vanessa Bell or Roger Fry, even if they never considered Keynes a specialist of visual art, they did consider him, at least from a certain time, an enlightened amateur.[9]

In his commentary, Clive Bell suggests that, were it not for his relationship with Duncan Grant, Keynes would never have become interested in painting. This is not true, even if it is undeniable that Grant and Vanessa Bell played an important role in the constitution of his painting collection. His interest in ballet has, in the same way, been linked to his marriage to the Russian ballerina Lydia Lopokova. This is also false; married in 1925, Keynes had been attending Russian Ballets since their arrival in London in 1911.

Keynes appears not to have taken a particular interest in painting during his university years, although one does find in his archives a few words on Greek architecture and sculpture and on Danish or Italian painting. In August 1905, he visited the Louvre five times, as well as the modern collections at the Palais du Luxembourg, with his mother. He described his impressions to Strachey on 8 September, concluding that: 'The impressionist room was more interesting than the entire Louvre. I like Monet best'. Of course, his liaison with Duncan Grant, from 1908, contributed in an important way to making him sensitive to creative activity in painting. During the weeks he spent with Duncan on the Isle of Hoy in Northern Scotland, he finished writing his dissertation on probabilities. But he discovered at the same time that painting was as serious a business as his own. He spent many hours posing for Grant, who painted a portrait which Keynes would give to his parents as a gift.

He would go on to buy some paintings before the war, mostly by artists with whom he was personally acquainted. He attended exhibitions attentively, as the annotated catalogues conserved in his papers would attest. He was present at the two post-impressionist exhibitions, writing to Duncan Grant on 15 November 1910: 'What is your final view about the Frenchmen? – they don't find much favour here – even Dickinson was rather outraged'. Though sceptical, he judged it necessary to break with the conservatism of the New English Art Club, which happened to reject one of Grant's paintings.[10]

The Degas Sale

It was thanks to an unexpected episode during the war that Keynes's painting collection really took off. During a visit to Roger Fry's London studio in March 1918, Grant got hold of the catalogue of a sale of paintings having belonged to Degas, deceased the previous year. The sale would be held in Paris, at the Georges Petit gallery. Excited, Grant convinced that very evening his friend Maynard, who was to participate in an inter-Allied conference in Paris, to persuade the Treasury into giving money to the National Gallery so that it could participate in the auction. With Vanessa, they examined the catalogue, in Charleston, Maynard manifesting much enthusiasm, in particular for the Cézannes. Arriving in London on 21 March, he wired Charleston: 'Money secured for pictures'. He had convinced the Treasury that this operation would have a beneficial effect on the balance of payments between England and France by permitting the latter to obtain the pound sterling it so desperately needed to settle its debts. On 22 March, Vanessa wrote:

> We are fearfully excited by your telegram and are longing to know more. This is a line to say do consult Roger before you go, as he'll know what to get hold of in Paris. Duncan says be as professional as possible in the buying and get at the right people. Otherwise some German or Scandinavian will trick you . . . We have great hopes of you and consider your existence at the Treasury is at last justified. I think a feast of our pig will be one of your rewards. (CHA1/59/5/1)

Bunny Garnett added at the end: 'They are very proud of you and eager to know how you did it. You have been given complete absolution & future crimes also forgiven' (ibid.). On 23 March, Keynes confided to Vanessa Bell regarding the manner in which he succeeded in obtaining 555 000 francs (then £20 000) in a day and a half – before anyone had had the time to reflect on what had happened. The Chancellor of the Exchequer, Bonar Law, considered the matter a sort of joke and accorded the funds readily since it was the first time his employee declared himself in favour of spending.

Keynes was accompanied on this trip by the director of the National Gallery, Charles J. Holmes,[11] who, to avoid being recognized, given the competition from French museums, dressed up in a false moustache and other accessories. Duncan and Vanessa, unsure of Maynard's capacities for appreciation, had hoped that Roger Fry would be there to advise Holmes, but this was not possible. The sale took place on 26 and 27 March while Paris was being shelled by Big Berthas. The National Gallery bought some twenty works, including four Ingres, two Delacroix, two Manets, two Gauguins, one Corot, one Rousseau, one Forain, one Ricard and sketches by David, Ingres and Delacroix.[12] Holmes, who did not spend all the money at his disposal, could have easily bought a Cézanne or an el Greco, but chose not to.

Keynes bought for himself an Ingres drawing, *Femme Nue*, for 1900 francs, a small Delacroix painting, *Cheval dans un Pâturage*, a sketch of Delacroix for the decoration of the Bourbon Palace – which he gave to Duncan Grant for his role in the undertaking – and most importantly a Cézanne still life, *Les Pommes*, for 9000 francs. He had hoped that Holmes would buy it with the allotted money and give it to him as a gift: 'I shall try very hard on the journey out to persuade him to buy a Cézanne as a personal reward to me for having got him his money' (letter to Vanessa Bell, 23 March 1918, CHA1/341/3/1). In the England of the time there were no Cézannes in public collections, the few that were to be found were in the hands of private collectors.

Back from France, on the evening of 28 March, Austen Chamberlain, member of Lloyd George's war cabinet, brought Keynes to Charleston by car and dropped him off at the start of the kilometre-long lane leading to the house. Keynes left his luggage, including the Cézanne, in a bush where the road met the lane. Duncan, Vanessa, Clive and Bunny had just finished eating:

> Maynard came back suddenly and unexpectedly late at night having been dropped at the bottom of the lane by Austen Chamberlain in a Government motor [sic!] and said he had left a Cézanne by the roadside! Duncan rushed off to get it and you can imagine how exciting it was ... The Cézanne is really amazing and it's most exciting to have it in the house. (Vanessa Bell to Roger Fry, in Shone and Grant, 1975, pp. 283–4)

The Cézanne picture would become a kind of reference and object of pilgrimage for the painters of Bloomsbury. Virginia Woolf described Roger Fry's visit to 46 Gordon Square to admire the work: 'Roger very nearly lost his senses. I've never seen such a sight of intoxication. He was like a bee on a sunflower' (letter to Nicholas Bagenal, 15 April 1918, V. Woolf, 1975–80, vol. 2, p. 230). She describes *Les Pommes* and their effects on her sister and Duncan in her diary:

> There are 6 apples [sic!] in the Cézanne picture. What can 6 apples *not* be? I began to wonder. Theres their relationship to each other, and their colour, and their solidity. To Roger and Nessa, moreover, it was a far more intricate question than this. It was a question of pure paint or mixed; if pure which colour: emerald or veridian [sic!]; and then the laying on of the paint; and the time he'd spent, and how he'd altered it, and why, and when he'd painted it – We carried it into the next room, and Lord! how it showed up the pictures there, as if you put a real stone among sham ones; the canvas of the others seemed scraped with a thin layer of rather cheap paint. The apples positively got redder and rounder and greener. I suspect some very mysterious quality of potation [sic!] in that picture. (V. Woolf, 1977–1984, vol. 1, pp. 140–41, entry for 18 April, 1918)[13]

Building a Collection

Cézanne's *Les Pommes* constitutes the beginning and the heart of a collection that Keynes would continue building until the end of his life. Often, if not most of the time, he would be advised when buying by Vanessa Bell, Duncan Grant or Roger Fry. There remain in the Keynes archives several telegrams and post cards from Duncan Grant urging him to take advantage of some sale. Sometimes his friends would buy for him without having had the time to consult him, telling him they would keep the paintings if he was not interested. It was in a certain way a question of collective buying for Bloomsbury, most of whose members lacked the funds necessary to acquire such works individually. Shone collected Duncan Grant's testimony on this aspect of Keynes's activities, and on certain annoying traits of character:

This was the real beginning of Maynard's collection and pictures were swiftly added over the next few years. Those bought at the 'Vente Degas' were the unexpected benefits of shrewd wartime speculation. The later ones belonged to the period of growing personal wealth. To have Maynard and his money there on the spot, to be able to persuade him to buy, was a splendid compensation for relative poverty. But of course Maynard fully appreciated the situation and was only too willing to concede. His love and respect for Vanessa and Duncan as creative artists, amounting it seems to a kind of humility, was all-embracing . . . Maynard had, perhaps, little innate feeling and understanding of painting, but his discrimination and knowledge grew over the years and was aided by Lydia's more quickly responsive feelings and definite if somewhat idiosyncratic views. But with this growing knowledge, a characteristic quality of Maynard's came into play: he attempted to speak and pronounce upon painting on occasion with an authority that was ill-founded. (Shone and Grant, 1975, p. 284)[14]

At the second Degas sale, Keynes acquired four of the master's sketches, including *Deux Danseuses au Maillot*. That same year he acquired two Amadeo Modigliani sketches and a painting by André Lhote, from whom he had already bought a work in 1913. On the occasion of the Matisse exhibition in London,[15] Vanessa and Duncan convinced their friend to buy a small painting: *Déshabillé*: 'The Matisses are lovely, but for the most part, rather light sketches. We have induced Maynard to buy one of the best, a small seated figure with bare arms, very sober in colour' (Letter from Vanessa Bell to Roger Fry, 30 November 1919, CHA1/59/4/11). One of his best buys, from a German refugee on 30 December 1919 with unexpected returns from *The Economic Consequences of the Peace*, was probably a sketch for *La Grande Jatte* by Seurat, a watercolour by Signac and a sketch Picasso prepared for Diaghilev's Russian Ballets, which he described in a letter to Kenneth Clark on 19 August 1943 as 'a very good, pencil drawing by Picasso . . . not one of his flowing outlines' (Scrase and Croft, 1983, p. 58). Several years later, Duncan Grant, Keynes and the dealer P.M. Turner would see the final version of *La Grande Jatte* in a private house in Paris, but Grant was not able to convince the other two to buy it. On this subject, Keynes wrote to Rich, author of *Seurat et l'évolution de La Grande Jatte*, on 13 March 1935:

I have seen at one time or another many studies for 'La Grande Jatte' and, indeed, all but bought the picture itself some years ago when it was still in the hands of the family. So that I am most interested to know that you are collecting together all the material for what is certainly one of the greatest pictures in the world. (ibid., p. 42)

In 1920, Keynes's collection was enriched by, among others, a Renoir and a Derain still life. Most of these acquisitions were obtained at low prices, and it is certain that Keynes saw them also as investments. He preferred buying from auctions than directly from artists, which was more economical. There is, he wrote, in the case of paintings, 'a slight mystery about the prices' and 'the element of "investment" may not be entirely absent after all' (1921-14, pp. 296–7).

After having made, in 1919 and 1920, some of his most important purchases, in particular from the famous or on the verge of becoming famous French painters, Keynes turned towards modern English art, encouraging equally young and well established artists. He bought several paintings from his friends Duncan Grant, Vanessa Bell and Roger Fry. He also commissioned the first two to decorate his lodgings, both at Gordon Square and at King's College, Cambridge. Duncan Grant had started by painting four mural frescos in Keynes's Cambridge rooms in 1910 and 1911. After the war, Keynes hired Duncan and Vanessa to redo this job, Duncan not being pleased with his first paintings. The two artists would go on to produce, at Charleston, eight extended paintings representing four men and four women, both life sized, symbolizing various Cambridge tripos subjects. It is not easy to guess which arts and sciences are represented by these characters about whom one cannot help noticing that the women are clothed and the men naked. The murals, which are still in Keynes's rooms today, were completed in 1922.

Keynes also regularly encouraged the painter William Roberts, author of a famous painting of himself with Lydia (*Lord and Lady Keynes*, 1932). He considered Roberts and Grant as the two most important English painters of their generation (1930-8, p. 304). Another of his protégés was Walter Sickert. In 1922, the latter returned from a stay in Dieppe, impoverished and lonely, having lost his second wife, Christine. Vanessa Bell advised Keynes to buy *The Bar Parlour*. After praising Vanessa's paintings, Sickert was invited to a Bloomsbury reception given by Maynard and Lydia.[16] He painted a portrait of Lydia which he offered to Keynes in 1924 and dedicated 'To J.M.K from a hereditary mathematician'. One of Sickert's ancestors was a mathematician. The same year, Keynes bought from him two more works and, in 1934, contributed to a fund set up to help him escape his financial woes. He bought, in 1928 and 1943, two canvases by Spencer Gore, a Sickert associate. During the war, he acquired three drawings by Henry Moore, whose sculptures he especially admired. In 1940, he bought a work by Ivon Hitchens at a time when the latter had fallen on extremely hard times.

Over the years, Keynes continued to enrich his collection of master works: three Cézannes, two Delacroix, two Picassos, two Braques, one Courbet, one Renoir, one Derain. These paintings become part of his environment. He often repeated how happy he was to return from a trip to find Cézanne in his bedroom and Sickert over his piano. His nephew Milo recounted that a Degas was to be found in the laundry room of Tilton. He did not easily lend his pictures to exhibitions, although, during the Second World War, he would lend generously to CEMA. He tried to repeat his Degas sale success by attempting, unsuccessfully this time, to convince the National Gallery to buy three works by Chardin from an important collection owned by Baron Henri de Rothschild. Recalling First World War purchases, he wrote in 1943 to Ernest Rowe-Dutton, a colleague at the Treasury: 'They (the Ingres and Delacroix) must be worth many times what we paid for them and, if this opportunity had been let slipped, we should never have been able to make their loss good' (Scrase and Croft, 1983, pp. 10–11).

Books and Performing Arts

Along with his paintings, Keynes left behind a very important collection of rare books and manuscripts.[17] He shared this passion with his brother Geoffrey. He began his collection as a student at Eton and pursued it, with increasing passion, until the end of his life. He maintained a lively correspondence with other collectors and dealers. He acquired, in particular, an impressive ensemble of first editions and translations of important works in the domains of the history of ideas, of English literature from the Elizabethan and Stuart periods and of theatre. His library included 150 manuscripts by Newton, a personage who fascinated him and on whom he would write one of his last texts. He stated, in his last years, that he no longer had time for painting, investing his money and energy in acquiring books.

We have not really left the world of art. Books are for Keynes works of art to be handled with respect and love. He would have been horrified at the thought of cheap paperbacks. In a radio programme broadcast in 1936 entitled 'On reading books', he explained that a reader 'should approach them [books] with all his senses; he should know their touch and their smell . . . He should live with more books than he reads, with a penumbra of unread pages, of which he knows the general character and content, fluttering round him' (1936-5, p. 334).

Collector, Keynes is also a passionate lover of peforming arts. The first art into which he was initiated, by his parents, was theatre and he would remain attached to it until the end of his life. In 1896 the New Theatre was founded in Cambridge, where the best companies in England would perform. His mother wrote of him: 'he thus acquired that love of drama which developed throughout his life and led to his building the Arts Theatre as a gift to the Borough of Cambridge' (George 'Dadie' Rylands' account in Scrase and Croft, 1983, p. 7).[18] Keynes later turned to ballet, especially on the arrival of Diaghilev's company in London in 1911. He would rapidly become a passionate consumer of this art, bringing together dance, music and painting. He occasionally published reviews of plays or ballet productions, often anonymously or under a pseudonym, in particular in *The Nation and Athenaeum*. He even once tried his hand at film criticism (1924-27). He wrote promotion material, which was called 'puff', for shows and productions with which he was associated. Not limiting himself to performing arts, he also spoke, in articles or letters to newspapers, of painting exhibitions, and sometimes composed catalogue introductions.

Keynes also attended concerts and the opera, on which several of his Bloomsbury friends were specialists. Confined to bed due to illness in 1937, he spent his time listening to the BBC, the result of which was a long letter to that organization's public relations director in which he comments in detail on the broadcaster's music programming: 'I am no musician, but I listen in to an enormous amount and, therefore, venture to give my views' (letter to Stephen Tallents, 12 July 1937, JMK 28, p. 352). He suggested that there be at least three weekly opera programmes while deploring the transmission problems related to big orchestras, chamber music being best suited to radio. Being careful not to reject popular music, which he could appreciate and of which he accepted hearing more, he regretted that 'there was an unnecessary amount of absolute tenth-rate music' (ibid.). Like classical music, popular music can and must be of high standards.

PATRON OF THE ARTS

Keynes's writings on aesthetics are largely unknown. Better known are his activities as collector and art lover. But it is as patron of the arts that he made his most renowned contributions. Art is also an economic activity from which its creators must make a living. Art has been an essential part of the *polis* from its very inception. The latter has responsibilities *vis-à-vis* this domain of human action.

The State, Art and Society

In 1936, the BBC decided to organize the publication of a series of articles in the summer edition of the magazine *The Listener* on the theme 'Art and the State'. Its focus was the study of the place and treatment of art under various regimes – fascist, nazi, communist and liberal – by calling on their representatives. Keynes was approached to write an introductory article. While J.R. Ackerlay had mentioned, in his letter to Keynes, painting, sculpture and architecture, the latter responded 'May I assume that you do not mean to exclude opera, ballet and drama?' (Letter dated 28 May 1936, JMK 28, p. 336). Keynes's article appeared in August 1936 under the title 'Art and the State', a few months after the publication of *The General Theory* and the opening of the Arts Theatre of Cambridge, which will be discussed later.

According to Keynes, statesmen have always been known, both for their own glory and for their people's satisfaction, to spend a considerable part of the national income on magnificent buildings, works of art and ceremonies. Of course religion played an important role in these undertakings. Many of the wonders of the world were built in this way. Unfortunately, since the eighteenth century, a transformation in the vision of the relation between State and society has occurred. This reached its zenith in the nineteenth century, continues to this day and has been catastrophic for civilization:

> This view was the utilitarian and economic – one might almost say financial – ideal, as the sole, respectable purpose of the community as a whole; the most dreadful heresy, perhaps, which has ever gained the ear of a civilized people. Bread and nothing but bread, and not even bread, and bread accumulating at compound interest until it has turned into a stone. Poets and artists have lifted occasional weak voices against the heresy. (1936-6, p. 342)

In the realm of art as elsewhere, the 'vision of the Treasury' has triumphed. Only spending serving exclusively economic ends is acceptable. Even spending on health and education are considered only if their profitability is taken into account: 'We still apply some frantic perversion of business arithmetic in order to settle the problem whether it pays better to pour milk down the drains or to feed it to school children' (ibid.). Only one form of unprofitable spending has survived from the heroic ages of humanity: war. Three years earlier, in 'National self-sufficiency', he spoke even more virulently against these effects of capitalism:

> The same rule of self-destructive financial calculation governs every walk of life. We destroy the beauty of the countryside because the unappropriated splendours of nature have no economic value. We are capable of shutting off the sun and the stars because they do not pay a dividend. London is one of the richest cities in the history of civilization, but it cannot 'afford' the highest standards of achievement of which its own living citizens are capable, because they do not 'pay'.
>
> If I had the power today I should surely set out to endow our capital cities with all the appurtenances of art and civilisation on the highest standards of which the citizens of each were individually capable, convinced that what I could create, I could afford – and believing that the money thus spent would not only be better than any dole, but would make unnecessary any dole. (1933-22, p. 242)

Thus, for Keynes, civilization will thrive only once it has succeeded in liberating itself from the tyranny of financial profitability. As important as monuments and buildings, festivities and ceremonial occasions constitute essential moments in every normal life, which cannot be reduced to often meaningless work. Such events are not generally financially profitable and if they become so, it is most often a sign of decadence: 'The exploitation and incidental destruction of the divine gift of the public entertainer by prostituting it to the purposes of financial gain is one of the worser crimes of present-day capitalism' (1936-6, p. 344). The artist today finds himself in such a precarious situation that his 'attitude . . . to his work renders him exceptionally unsuited for financial contacts' (ibid.).

In his article, Keynes proposes a scale of intervention relating to art's more or less public character. Architecture is the most public of the arts, 'best suited to give form and body to civic pride and the sense of social unity' (ibid., p. 345). Music comes next, followed by the various performing arts, visual arts, the exception being sculpture, which is a complement to architecture, and finally poetry and literature 'by their nature more private and personal' (ibid.). Major spending on the arts is what makes the authoritarian regimes of Germany, Italy and Russia strong. England, France and the United States, perverted by the Treasury vision, lag behind.

Beyond maintaining full employment, the State has the responsibility of upholding civilization. This does not mean that artistic activity must be regulated by the State, administered by bureaucrats and politicians, as is the case in totalitarian States. On the contrary. As underlined in the third epigraph to this chapter, the artist is by definition free and generally has little idea where he is headed. As for art, it cannot be subjected to economic logic. Its logic is internal. It is that of the combination of forms, colours, sounds, words, as proclaimed by Bloomsbury. Keynes did not consider himself an artist. But from early on in life, he did consider himself possessed of a mission, one of greater importance than that of an economic theorist, namely that of patron of art and of artists. It is this last challenge that remains to be chronicled.[19]

The Support of Painters

The first way to help painters survive is to buy their works. Yet often this is done too late. Van Gogh, one of those whose works caused a scandal during the first post-impressionist exhibition, never sold but one canvas during his lifetime. In his activity as a collector, as we have seen, Keynes sometimes used an artist's financial needs as a criterion for buying, provided of course that he liked his work. He supported in this way his friends Duncan Grant, Vanessa Bell and Roger Fry and other painters such as William Roberts, Walter Sickert or Ivon Hitchens. Support for Grant exceeded buying paintings, since Keynes provided him with a pension until the end of his life. He was motivated in this case by personal reasons in addition to artistic objectives.

Private buyer, Keynes also became, in 1911, a public buyer within the Contemporary Art Society, of which he would remain a member until his death. This organization was founded in 1909 with the goal of acquiring modern works to lend or donate to public galleries. Keynes's lively correspondence with the Society increased in frequency from 1939. It seems he was a very active member until the end of his life.[20]

Before the war, English painters divided themselves between a series of small associations, some conservative, others progressive. On 15 November 1913, a number of painters decided to form the London Group. Roger Fry, Duncan Grant and Vanessa Bell would become members at the end of the war. Keynes wrote the introduction of the group's 1921 exhibition, a group which 'includes the greater part of what is most honourable and most promising amongst the younger English painters of today' (1921-14, p. 296). In his introduction he wrote that 'civilised ages have always recognized that a patron of the arts performs for the society he lives in a distinguished and magnanimous function. Without patrons art cannot easily flourish' (ibid., p. 297).

It goes without saying that Keynes considered himself such a patron and would become one on a grand scale. The existence of the London Group was far from providing its members with the financial security necessary to continue their work. To deal with this problem, Keynes conceived of a cooperative organization whose goal would be to counter the precariousness and irregularity of artists' incomes, 'to reduce the anxieties of promising painters and perhaps help to get a better market in the long run for their works' (1930-8, p. 298). The organization would manage its artists' financial affairs, take care of selling their works and guarantee them a minimal regular income. In February 1925, Keynes obtained the approval of his friend Samuel Courtauld,[21] then of James Hindley-Smith and L.H. Myers, two other wealthy collectors. The four musketeers would found, in July 1925, the London Artists' Association, which would make its first sales in October of the same year. Though the four founders were financially responsible for the undertaking, it was the artists and they alone who made decisions about who would become a member. One is not surprised to learn that it was Keynes who was in charge of the organization's business management.[22]

It was out of the question that, in Keynes's mind, the organization could operate indefinitely at a loss:

> The Association is not a charity organisation: it cannot afford entirely to neglect the commercial aspect of pictures. It does not set out to support absolute beginners in art, however promising, and is not anxious to elect a painter unless his work shows some reasonable sign of selling sooner or later. (1930-8, p. 305)

It would have to choose artists whose works would eventually find buyers. Between 1925 and 1930, when Keynes published a history of the organization, the latter had sold more than 700 works of art, for a total sum of £22 000: 'The question of price policy is a very difficult one, which is still not solved to anyone's satisfaction. Two principles are obvious. We want to get for an artist's pictures as high a price as the public will pay. On the other hand, almost any price is better than nothing' (ibid., p. 305). As in the case of books, it is unwise to lower prices too much, unless the larger public acquires the habit of buying paintings, but for the moment 'the number of individuals in England who spend any appreciable sum on pictures in a year is extremely small' (ibid., p. 306).

The first members of the Association were Bernard Adenay, Keith Baynes, Vanessa Bell, Frank Dobson, Duncan Grant, Roger Fry and Frederick Porter. George Barne, William Coldstream, Raymond Coxon, Douglas Davidson, Morland Lewis, Rory O'Mullen, Paul Nash, R.V. Pitchforth, F.J. Porter, William Roberts, Sydney Sheppard, Edward Wolf joined later, either as full or associated members. No school or style dominated: 'I hope that anyone who visits our exhibitions will agree that we have managed to combine together, not unsympathetically, a considerable variety of temperaments and methods of painting' (ibid., p. 303). The Association did not intend to replace art dealers and tried hard to maintain the best possible relations with them. One of its activities consisted in sending its members' canvases to exhibitions held in London but also in the regions.

The project had two goals, intimately linked: to cultivate, on the one hand, a public 'very ignorant and hesitating for the most part' (ibid., p. 307), to convince it to spend its money on artworks rather than on the hideous and useless objects it most often chooses, and, on the other hand, to assure a minimum income to artists whose relationship to money is generally complicated:

> Like all creative work where the occupation and the achievement are ends in themselves, painting can never be properly pursued for the express purpose of making money . . . At the same time most artists having produced something are, naturally, anxious to get for it as much as possible. Thus the mixture of motives is apt to make them at the same time the nicest and the most difficult people in the world to deal with in a business way. (1930-8, pp. 306–7)

During an exhibition of floral painting in 1931, Keynes, taking into account the economic situation, convinced those who submitted paintings for sale to lower their prices by half in relation to what they would normally ask. But the organization would not survive the crisis. After Roger Fry and Frank Dobson, Duncan Grant, Vanessa Bell and Keith Baynes quit in July 1931 to join Agnew's gallery, which angered Keynes and created some tension within Bloomsbury. In October 1933, the founders liquidated the enterprise, while continuing to provide financial support to Wolfe and Roberts, the latter until 1937.[23] A final exhibition was held in 1934.

On several occasions, Keynes appeared within the columns of *Nation and Athenaeum* to give his opinion on the events taking place in the world of visual art. He criticized the 'obstinacy, ignorance and bad taste of the official custodians' (1923-23, p. 310) of the National Gallery who did not buy works by Cézanne. Despite being expensive, it was the time to buy works by Cézanne, Daumier, Manet, Picasso, Derain and Matisse. Under the signature of Siela, he intervened in a debate between Sargent and Leonard Woolf on the definition of impressionism (1927-9).

In the 1930s, it was the performing arts that most motivated Keynes, though it is important to mention an original project in painting he set up on Duncan Grant's suggestion, namely, the creation at Cambridge University of a painting library enabling students, on a minimal membership fee, to borrow sketches and watercolours to decorate their rooms. This system is still in existence. Keynes continued to be actively engaged in the interests of his friends. He intervened, unsuccessfully, when Cunard decided to cancel Duncan Grant's contract to decorate the Queen Mary. In 1941, Duncan Grant and Vanessa Bell were commissioned to paint the interior of the small Berwick church, St. Michael's and All Angels. This led to complicated negotiations with the ecclesiastical authorities, whom Keynes accused of underpaying its artists. Things worked out in the end and Keynes even accepted, on 9 May 1942, an offer from the bishop of Chichester to join the Sussex Churches Art Council. There is in this important work, to which Quentin Bell and others also contributed, a clear influence of Byzantine art which they discovered, at the same time as Keynes, at the beginning of the century.

The consecration of Keynes's role in the visual art world came when, on 29 October 1941, Bevin wrote asking him if he would accept the Prime Minister's proposition of becoming Trustee of the National Gallery, the most prestigious museum in Great Britain and one of the first in the world. Keynes was flattered and happy about a nomination he considered 'a very pleasant and honourable mild job', as attests a letter to Courtauld on 6 November.[24] The latter responded writing that 'all our most respectable institutions are being revolutionized' (quoted in Skidelsky, 2000, p. 168). He began his duties officially on 17 December 1941.

Performing Arts

Keynes was a passionate lover of theatre and ballet before his meeting with the ballerina Lydia Lopokova, who became his wife in 1925. But it was this meeting that propelled him to become a patron of the performing arts. He began by managing Lydia's career and financial affairs, she being completely incompetent in such matters.[25] She hadn't even a bank account, entrusting her money to her hotel porter.

Lydia intended to end her career as a dancer after her marriage, but it did not turn out as such. She continued to participate in the London seasons of Diaghilev's Russian Ballets in

1925 and 1926, as well as in Paris in 1926. Considering she put on too much weight, she refused to participate in the 1927 season, but accepted dancing in a gala presentation for King Alfonso of Spain on 15 July.[26] She didn't intend to break her ties with the theatre and ballet world, and it was at this point that Keynes came to the fore. He became a member of the organizing committee and provided financial support to the Cambridge Amateur Dramatic Club's production of Stravinsky's *A Soldier's Tale* and Shakespeare's little-known dramatic poem *A Lover's Complaint*. Lydia danced in Stravinsky's work and, for the first time, acted in a play by Shakespeare. In addition to financing the production, Keynes prepared the advertising. In 1930, he rented the London Arts Theatre for a 'Masque of poetry and ballet', 'Beauty, truth and rarity', including Shakespeare's dramatic poem and other pieces. Lydia participated as actor and dancer. Both shows were presented first in Cambridge, then in London.

The Camargo Society
With Diaghilev's death, in Venice, in August 1929, followed by that of Anna Pavlova in 1931, the future of ballet became uncertain. A meeting of ballet lovers was called, to which Keynes and his wife were invited. One of the organizers recalled:

> I talked with one guest in particular, who was more quiet and practical than the rest. We had in common an intense interest for Trefilova. He seemed unusually well informed, and I could not quite place him. Whenever I tried to nail him to a definite branch of art, he always escaped. Afterwards I found it was J.M. Keynes, who practises, of course, the most fantastic of them all. (Haskell, 1934, p. 136)

During a second meeting, at the end of 1929, the Camargo Society was founded, with Lydia Keynes as choreographical adviser. The name recalls Marie-Anne de Cupis (1710–90), known as La Camargo, born in Brussels, prima ballerina of the Paris Opera, occasional courtesan, who triumphed in works by Rameau and Campra. A fundraising dinner, for which Bernard Shaw prepared the invitation letter, was held on 16 February 1930. Sunday lunches brought together at the Keynes's home Ninette de Valois, Fred Ashton and Constant Lambert, stars of Camargo. Much fine wine was consumed while planning the society's activities.

The economic situation did not help an organization which immediately found itself in financial distress. The goal was in effect to provide a regular income to all those involved in ballet: dancers, composers, choreographers, decorators, seamstresses and technicians. To save itself from crisis, the Society named Keynes as treasurer, a post he would keep until 1935 and run with efficiency and rigour. Eleven ballets were produced during the first year. In his 1931 report, calling for subscription renewal, he wrote:

> In view of the fact that the Society started with no tangible assets and has produced eleven new ballets, this is, in the opinions of the Committee, an extraordinarily satisfactory result. But it has only been achieved by means of the most resolute economy . . . it would be more satisfactory if selection by the Camargo Society carried with it a reasonable remuneration (1931-12, p. 319).

Keynes devoted considerable time and energy to this project and his involvements were not limited to the treasury,[27] but also to the organization of productions.[28] During the world economic conference in London, he organized on 29 July 1933 a gala performance for delegates of 46 countries at Covent Garden, an occasion marking Lydia Lopokova's last appearance on the stage as a dancer.[29] The two works presented were the first two acts of *Coppelia* and the second act of the ballet *Swan Lake*. This resulted in criticism from the *New Statesman and Nation*,[30] which accused Keynes of betraying the goals of Camargo by presenting classic works instead of modern ballets. Keynes was surprised at the critics' ignorance as to the conditions in which ballet was produced in London. One must be profitable at least some of the time, and, as in the case of opera, 'it is the limited class of established favourites, chosen from the very few ballets which have gained a permanent place in the repertories of the opera houses of the world, which attract a great audience' (1933-21, p. 321). Experimental ballets, which must be supported, generally do not cover two thirds of their production costs. They must be financed therefore by staging those classics for which the public is willing to pay.

In 1933, Ninette de Valois, who danced with Diaghilev's company from 1923 to 1925, going on to contribute to Camargo's foundation where she achieved her first successes as a choreographer, founded Sadler's Wells Ballet, which would become, in 1956, the Royal Ballet. Camargo had thus fulfilled the goals for which it was conceived, as Keynes indicated in his 1934 report:

> When the Society was founded four years ago, shortly after the death of Diaghilev and Pavlova, there was no other organisation in London for the production of ballet. The object of the Society was [. . .] to keep alive traditions too easily lost. Since that time the Vic-Wells Ballet has been established as a permanent organisation giving very similar opportunities for dancers and choreographs as those which the Camargo Ballet Society was aiming at. (1934-1, p. 322)

From then on Keynes became an enthusiastic supporter of Vic-Wells, and even contributed to the programming of the second Buxton theatre festival in August and September of 1938, in which he recalls the words of his wife: 'There is no company in the world, Madame Lopokova says, which can make so fair a comparison in the conditions of its work and in its accomplishments with the old Imperial Ballet of St Petersburg' (1938-9, p. 325).

The Cambridge Arts Theatre

Keynes did not slow down his involvement in the arts while he was finishing his *General Theory*. On the contrary, the completion of his major work in economic theory coincided exactly with that of one of his main contributions to the arts, that is, the creation of the Cambridge Arts Theatre, which opened its doors the night before the book's publication.

Cambridge had until the beginning of the 1930s two theatres, one of which was transformed into a cinema while the other closed its doors for financial reasons. Keynes had already been approached in 1925 with the aim of creating a new theatre but, too busy with the London Artists' Association, he declined the invitation.[31] Early in November 1933, the rooms of the Amateur Dramatic Club, in whose activities Keynes was involved, were destroyed in a fire. It was at that moment he started entertaining the idea of contributing money, but also time and energy, to the creation in Cambridge of a place dedicated to all the performing arts:

> When in 1934 I initiated proposals for the incorporation of a company to build and manage the Arts Theatre of Cambridge, my purpose was the promotion of the arts of drama, cinema, opera, ballet and music at Cambridge in a suitable home and under management which could maintain standards of educational purposes worthy of the town and the University. (letter to the mayor of Cambridge, 23 April 1938, JMK 28, p. 354)

He wrote of his intentions to Lydia, in a letter from 20 November 1933:

I gave rather a good lecture this morning. Since then I've been amusing myself thinking out a plan to build a small, very smart, modern theatre for the College. Will you agree to appear in the first performance if it comes off? . . . The project fascinates me and I already begin to draw plans of my own for it.[32]

Keynes was, in all areas of his activities, overflowing with plans. And he rapidly kept his interested parties informed. A few days after this letter, he presented his project to the Amateur Dramatic Club's committee. On 17 February, he obtained the authorization of the authorities of King's College to develop it. In May 1934, he proposed to Norman Higgins, who was the director of the cinema, to close down and transfer his equipment to the planned theatre of which he would become general manager.[33]

Keynes decided then to form a private company to carry out this project, which included building on grounds belonging to the college. The architectural firm of George Kennedy & Nightingale was hired to give an estimation.[34] An organizational meeting took place at Tilton on 15 and 16 September 1934, attended by, other than Keynes and his wife, Higgins, Miss J.M. Harvey, former secretary of Camargo and George Rylands, Cambridgian, theatre man and long-time friend of Keynes. The company, whose creation was approved by King's College, was registered on 14 December 1934, with Keynes, Harvey and Rylands as directors and Higgins as secretary. Keynes bought most of the ordinary shares, and, as the sale of preference shares set aside for rich Cambridgians turned out to be less than expected, ended up buying 12 500 ordinary shares and supplying an interest-free loan of £17 450. He wrote to Lydia on 26 May 1935: 'The greatest comfort of all, I think, from having some money is that one does not need to badger other people for it'. All in all, the project's cost would be double the original estimation.

During the construction, which began in March 1935, Keynes, as he did during the theatre's later life, actively occupied himself with all aspects of the undertaking. Judging that theatre lovers should be able to eat on the premises, he watched over the construction of a restaurant whose menu and wine list he scrutinized closely. Wanting to encourage people to drink good wines rather than spirits, he raised the margin on the latter prices and lowered the margin on wine prices as their quality increased. He was involved in negotiations with theatre and ballet companies passing through Cambridge. He organized programmes, proposed productions and read submitted manuscripts. He was even seen in the kiosk selling tickets, where he revealed himself to be rather inefficient: 'A long queue would entice him into the box office where his belief that the task was perfectly simple proved mistaken, and his efforts to help something of an embarrassment' (Higgins, 1975, p. 274).

The Arts Theatre's opening, on 3 February 1936, was devoted to a ballet by Vic-Wells, the following evening being given to cinema. The introductory document, written by Keynes, states:

The object of the Arts Theatre of Cambridge is the entertainment of the University and Town. Its name describes, and the form of a Pentagon given to its auditorium by the architects symbolizes, its purpose of providing a home in Cambridge for the five arts of drama, opera, ballet, music and cinema. (Higgins, 1975, p. 274)

Keynes, who was an admirer of Ibsen, financed the production of four of the latter's plays during the first year, introducing them anonymously with the words: 'these four plays in particular can be regarded as a commentary on the profoundest social phenomenon of the period, the emergence of the modern woman' (1936-3, p. 327). Lydia performed in two of the four. Keynes financed all the other productions in which Lydia acted, among them *The Misanthropist* by Molière, in 1937, and *On the Frontier* by friends Auden and Isherwood, in 1938.

Here as elsewhere, Keynes had the reputation, like his friend Leonard Woolf at Hogarth Press, of being extremely demanding of his collaborators, which resulted in sharp words from Dadie Rylands, in a letter from 20 December 1939:

> You must realise more than you do that you are known to be a hard taskmaster; Richard knows it, Sheppard knows it, and I know it. You are very nearly as hard as the old Woolf! Your fault is that you always drive a willing horse . . . Now Maynard I am not pleased with you . . . I cannot serve as a director if Victorian factory conditions are to be allowed. (quoted by Moggridge, 1992, p. 589)

In 1938, with the project on its feet and profitable, Keynes decided that, being a private company, it should become public and he proposed the creation of a charitable trust to which he donated all his ordinary shares and invested, over the course of the following seven years, the sum of £5000, enabling him to acquire the preference shares that remained undisclosed.[35] He obtained a mortgage of £12 000 from Barclay's Bank to recover what remained of his interest-free loan. On his suggestion, the administrative council was composed of two representatives of the city, one of which was the mayor, two university professors, the director of King's College, George Ryland and himself, representing the theatre management.[36] Keynes thus donated the theatre to the City and to Cambridge University, in homage to his parent's devotion to the two institutions: 'and I like to think of the establishment of this trust, with its potentiality of equal service to both bodies, as being in some sense a memorial to their, as I well know, devoted services to Cambridge over half a century' (letter to the mayor of Cambridge, 23 April 1938; JMK 28, p. 355). Keynes never stopped following the theatre's affairs, keeping, for example, control over its memberships until 1940.

During the war, Cambridge was spared German bombing and the Arts Theatre put on a number of shows and welcomed many stars and respected companies. Londoners came to enjoy the calm. Keynes, who would bring Vanessa Bell's children to the theatre and ballet, was convinced of the importance of childhood arts education. The Arts Theatre thus organized several outdoor shows during the day with places reserved in advance for classes. In 1946, the year of Keynes's death, the theatre liquidated its mortgage. After a few years of renovation, the Arts Theatre is still present at Cambridge. A monumental canvas of Maynard and Lydia is suspended in the entrance hall.

The Creation of the Arts Council

One might think that his enormous responsibilities during the Second World War, in particular difficult and exhausting negotiations with the Americans and trips to the United States would have been enough to occupy the already too busy days of a sick and weakened man. This was not the case. Keynes considered the founding of the Arts Council of Great Britain rather than the Bretton Woods accords as his most important and satisfying contribution.

During the war years, Keynes continued to be actively involved in the Arts Theatre and, agenda permitting, attended its productions with pleasure. This brought him in contact, in May 1940, with the Council for the Encouragement of Music and the Arts, (CEMA), with a request to support a tour of Donald Wolfit's company, which had presented a series of plays at Cambridge. CEMA was founded on 19 January 1940, on the initiative of the president of the Education Council, Lord De La Warr, who had recently obtained £25 000 from the Pilgrim Trust. The objective was to encourage, by helping financially, artists, musicians and actors whose situation had been made precarious by the war. It was also an opportunity to offer artistic events to a physically dispersed population cut off from its customary activities during the winter curfew. It was the successor to an analogous project during the depression.

When he began contact with CEMA, Keynes criticized it by accusing it of only financing amateur tours instead of offering guarantees to existing professional organizations. Faced with CEMA's refusal to support Wolfit's tour, Keynes successfully proposed contributing himself to guaranteeing it. He then decided to address himself, as he also did in such circumstances, to the real power in charge by coming into contact, not with the president, but with CEMA's secretary, Mary Glasgow, flattered and intimidated by this intervention from such a great man.[37] He received her in his home and, stretched out because of his heart condition, bombarded her with questions about the institution, seeking to know why CEMA supported only second class amateur productions rather than high level artistic endeavours: 'It was standards that mattered, and the preservation of serious professional enterprise, not obscure concerts in village halls. He was never one to mince words and, hearing him for the first time, I found him formidable' (Glasgow, 1975, p. 262).

Early in 1942, the British Treasury replaced the Pilgrim Trust as the financing body of CEMA. On 17 December 1941, the president of the Board of Education, R.A. Butler, asked Keynes if he would become president. They expected him to refuse, considering his other commitments. He accepted in a letter on 14 January and started work on 1 April. Mary Glasgow believed he was waiting and expected this offer. She also underlined Keynes's horror regarding the bureaucracy in CEMA's management, and then in the Arts Council which, according to him, was to be 'independent in organisation, free from red tape . . . The arts owe no vow of obedience' (ibid., p. 263).

Under Keynes's presidency, the goal consisting of giving concerts in factories, bringing the theatre to mining cities, organizing productions in public gardens, continued, but the accent shifted to the promotion of high-level artistic creation.

> But we also seek, and increasingly, to aid all those who pursue the highest standards of original composition and executive performance in all branches of the arts to carry their work throughout the country, and to accustom the great new audiences which are springing up to expect and approve the best. The leading symphony orchestras and string orchestras, most of the painters, and a large majority (I think I can now say), of the opera, ballet, and drama companies in the country pursuing a serious artistic purpose are working in occasional and continuous association with us. Our policy is to be satisfied with their work and purpose in general terms, and to leave the artistic control with the companies and individuals concerned; and they, with the plays, pictures, and concerts they offer, may be as many and as various as there are individuals of genius and good will. (1943-4, pp. 360–61)

Among the major problems of British artistic life was that of a lack of suitable buildings. Money needed to be found to renovate and build, public works becoming servants of art as well as stimulators of employment: 'If with state aid the material frame can be constructed, the public and the artists will do the rest between them. The muses will emerge from their dusty haunts, and supply and demand shall be their servants' (ibid., p. 361). Among his many interventions, Keynes prevented the destruction of one of the oldest theatres in England, that of Bristol, founded in 1766, which reopened its doors on 11 May 1943. It was for this occasion that he wrote the article quoted here.

A reorganization of the Council, in September 1942, established three panels, for music, art and theatre, Keynes presiding over each. It was especially theatre that mobilized him: 'Keynes liked to have a say in what the companies associated with us chose to perform' (Glasgow, 1975, p. 264). But he also favoured ballet and, on the subject of a possible visit by a Russian ballet, which never did come about, he was moved to discuss the tour's arrangements with the Russian delegation at Bretton Woods, where he then found himself.[38] He also became involved in painting, organizing in 1942 a tour of three exhibitions, one of the most recent of the Tate's acquisitions, the other of Wilson Steer and the last by Walter Sickert. It was impossible to organize an exhibition of French painting, but CEMA presented in the spring of 1945 an exhibition of illustrations from French books, including works by Toulouse-Lautrec, Bonnard, Matisse, Rouault and Picasso; what, Keynes wrote in the exhibition's catalogue, constituted a 'tribute to France' (1945-1, p. 366). On the musical front, the Council took charge of guarantee schemes for symphony orchestras, string orchestras and chamber orchestras. It took under its patronage Sadlers Well's opera and ballet companies.

Keynes also refused many grant applications, among others that of the Glyndebourne Opera Festival, considering it a luxury for the rich. Throughout he was often engaged in interminable quarrels. He conducted himself like he did in his financial negotiations with the United States: 'He could be very rude on occasion, and he did antagonise a number of people. Faced with an issue on which he felt deeply – and there were many such – he never hesitated to declare war' (Glasgow, 1975, p. 267).

When he was in London, CEMA's activities took much of Keynes's time, much more than he anticipated when he began, which brought him briefly to consider resigning in 1944. Meetings were often held in his home, at 46 Gordon Square. He corresponded practically on a daily basis with the secretary, discussing and approving the day's business, reports, projects and administrative questions. This correspondence did not stop when he was abroad: 'He asked that all minutes of meetings be sent to him without delay, wherever he was, and instructed me to write him full reports of everything that happened. These he dissected at once and returned them with comments of devastating frankness' (ibid., p. 270). Keynes' letters were often very long and 'full of quirks and prejudices, and a kind of Edwardian puckishness' (ibid., p. 270).[39]

With the war at its end, Keynes and his colleagues at CEMA focused on creating a permanent structure to be its successor that would place art at the forefront in Great Britain. Keynes wrote, on his return from Bretton Woods in August 1944, a document entitled 'Proposals for the re-organization of CEMA as a permanent peace-time body'. He proposed at a Council meeting on 28 September the creation of a Royal Council of the Arts of eleven members. The new structure, which was to be called the Arts Council, was approved in January 1945. Keynes then pressured the coalition government which decided in May to transform CEMA into a permanent organization called the Arts Council of Great Britain. This was one of his last decisions. The announcement was made by the Chancellor of the Exchequer, John Anderson, on 12 June 1945. Keynes gave a press conference, presenting the new organization two weeks later in a speech to the BBC:[40]

The purpose of the Arts Council of Great Britain is to create an environment to breed a spirit, to cultivate an opinion, to offer a stimulus to such purpose that the artist and the public can each sustain and live on the other in that union which has occasionally existed in the past at the great ages of a communal civilised life. (1945-2, p. 372)

Hating bureaucracy, Keynes also despised incomprehensible acronyms, like CEMA, 'as bad and forbidding a name as Bancor itself!' (1943-4, p. 359). This is why he proposed the name of Arts Council to replace it: 'I hope you will call us the Arts Council for short, and not try to turn our initials into a false, invented word. We have carefully selected initials which we hope are unpronounceable' (1945-2, p. 368). The war, he told his listeners, made us discover an important thing: 'the unsatisfied demand and the enormous public for serious and fine entertainment' (ibid., p. 369). He added that the BBC played an important role in awakening the public's taste for art and that the new organization must work in collaboration with the broadcaster. One of the primordial tasks of the Council would be to decentralize artistic life across England, which would require the construction of new buildings which were to be both aesthetic and functional: 'We look forward to the time when the theatre and the concert-hall and the gallery will be a living element in everyone's upbringing, and regular attendance at the theatre and at concerts a part of organized education' (ibid., p. 371). London, half destroyed, was to become a great artistic metropolis: 'We hope that Covent Garden will be re-opened early next year as the home of opera and ballet' (ibid.).

CEMA was closely involved in Covent Garden's renaissance. When he was in Bretton Woods, Keynes had been named Chairman of the Trustees of the Royal Opera House, Covent Garden. Reconstructed for the last time in 1858, the Royal Opera House became the property of Covent Garden Properties which leased it, at the beginning of the war, to Mecca Cafes, to serve as a dance hall. It was decided that Sadler's Wells ballet would move to Covent Garden, but Sadler's Wells Opera decided not to participate, leaving Covent Garden to form its own opera company. Like for the Arts Theatre, Keynes was associated with all aspects of the building's reopening, including the hall's decoration. On 20 February 1946, Covent Garden was inaugurated with a production of Tchaikovsky's *Sleeping Beauty* in the presence of three generations of the royal family, production in which Margot Fonteyn would triumph in the role of Princess Aurora. This gala was destined 'to be a landmark in the restoration of English cultural life' and 'to symbolise the return of England's capital to its rightful place in a world of peace' (letter to C.R. Attlee, 24 January 1946, in Moggridge, 1992, p. 705). Keynes, who underwent a mild heart attack during the arrival of the royal family, occupied with Lydia neighbouring seats. It would be his last public appearance in his home country. On 5 April, he decided to bequeath £5000 to the Royal Opera Trust. The Arts Council would not see its charter incorporated until 10 July 1946, after the death of its designated president, to whom the king was about to award the Order of Merit.

NOTES

1. Minister of Foreign Affairs for the USSR in the 1940s, Stepanov led the Soviet delegation at Bretton Wooods.
2. On the relation between art and science, see also the last section of Chapter 3.
3. With the exception of the biographies, not much has been written on Keynes and art, and particularly aesthetics, O'Donnell (1995) being the first analytical article on this last subject. See Glasgow (1975), Higgins (1975), Shone with Grant (1975), Heilbrun (1984), Goodwin (1998, 2001) and Moggridge (2005). In his fascinating introduction to Fry's writings on commerce in art (1998, pp. 1–65), Goodwin brings to light some links between Fry's view and Keynes's ideas on speculation. On the relation between art and science, their views are also quite similar. Thus Fry wrote, in a paper entitled 'Art and science', first published in 1919: 'It will be seen

how close the analogies are between the methods and aims of art and science' (Fry, 1920, p. 57). Fry's friend, Charles Mauron, chemist, literary critic, translator of Virginia Woolf and inventor of 'psychocriticism', wrote 'One of the most remarkable traits of his personality was certainly a rare combination of scientific spirit and esthetic sensibility' (lecture given at Oxford, 1949, *Psyché*, Paris, no. 63, January 1952, in Caws and Wright, 2000, p. 268).

4. An Apostle takes wings when he ceases to regularly attend the Society's meetings. He becomes then an 'angel'. See First Interlude.

5. Such was, as previously mentioned, Keynes's response to those who accused him of lacking precision in his economic writings.

6. This paper was written in 1905, when Degas was still largely unknown in England. We will see later the major role Degas will play as Keynes becomes active as a collector.

7. Keynes develops this idea by giving the example of post-impressionist painting, whose importance in England would not be felt for another five years.

8. See Goodwin (2006), who stresses the influence of Tolstoy on Fry.

9. On Keynes as a collector of paintings, see Shone and Grant (1975) and Scrase and Croft (1983). The latter constitutes the catalogue of an exhibition, held in 1983 at Cambridge, of paintings and manuscripts bequested by Keynes.

10. See Stansky, 1996, p. 248.

11. Holmes gives his version of the events in his memoirs (1936, pp. 334–42).

12. These purchases would not be made public until after the war.

13. There are in reality seven apples in Cézanne's picture.

14. Among the other of Keynes's annoying behaviours, there is the following, recounted by Vanessa in a letter to Roger Fry on 25 September 1925. There was in Keynes's room at 46 Gordon Square a canvas by Grant which Keynes maintained belonged to him while Vanessa, as Duncan, considered it hers. When he took full possession of the place after being married, Keynes screwed the canvas onto the wall. Nevertheless, Vanessa was able to undo it and take it back to her place. We do not know how the story ended (CHA1/59/4/16).

15. Present in London, Matisse was very surprised to see his works sell so well.

16. See the description of this evening in L. Woolf (1967), pp. 115–17.

17. For more on this see Munby (1975) and Scrase and Croft (1983).

18. On the Arts Theatre, see the following section. Keynes's mother has been mayor of Cambridge.

19. In the vision of relation of art to the state, there are again close connections between Keynes's and Fry's ideas. See for example 'Art and socialism', first published in 1912, in Fry (1920), pp. 39–54.

20. On this subject, see the documents contained in the folder PP/72 of Keynes Papers.

21. Rich industrialist, patron and art lover, Samuel Courtauld (1876–1947) was a friend of Lydia Lopokova. He possessed an important collection of paintings, most of which went to the Courtauld Gallery, part of which he donated to the Tate. Enlightened businessman, he was an admirer of Keynes. On 8 February 1925, Lydia wrote to Maynard, regarding his project: 'Sam called me to say that he likes the idea very much of the Artists cooperative society but he wants to speak with you to understand completely the scheme, and being Sam he doubts the practicability of the idea, but he means well and desires to contribute' (1989-1, p. 285).

22. See, in Keynes's archives, the documents contained in PP/73.

23. In a letter from October 1933 to Frank Hindley Smith, Keynes stresses that such help could only be extended to painters likely to become successful. He refused continuing subsidy to Frederick Porter, whose sales amounted to nothing: 'Assistance to him would be little better than a dole, which I do not feel to be the case with the other two' (quoted by Scrase and Croft, 1983, p. 35).

24. See archive file PP/77.

25. In his will, Keynes left his estate to Lydia to be managed by Richard Kahn.

26. It seems that the couple sought to have a child. It is probable that Lydia underwent an abortion in 1927. See Keynes' letter to Lydia on 6 May 1927 and Skidelsky, 1992, p. 295.

27. 'It is a miracle how Alfred Tysser, and later J.M. Keynes, steered us clear of debt' (Haskell, 1934, p. 137).

28. Let us recall that this period was that of Keynes's involvement in the Macmillan Committee and of the first drafts of *The General Theory*.

29. That same year, on 18 September, she made her professional debut as a stage actress in Shakespeare's *Twelfth Night*. Keynes rehearsed with her all summer long. But it was a disaster, mostly because of her accent (Skidelsky, 1992, p. 502).

30. Of which Keynes was chairman of the board.

31. As early as 1913, Keynes envisaged the creation of a repertory theatre at Cambridge.

32. His 30 November 1933 lecture was devoted to presenting a part of the theory of employment that would be made public over two years later.

33. See Higgins (1975), who recounted the birth and first years of the Arts Theatre's existence.

34. This was the same firm to which Keynes entrusted the renovation of the Tilton house at the end of 1935.

35. His heart attack in 1937 and subsequent time off recovering undoubtedly played a role in Keynes's decison to wind down his involvement in the Art's Theatre's management. It is in his place of convalescence at Ruthin Castle that he first shared his ideas with the mayor and vice-chancellor of Cambridge. Keynes was emphatic that this transformation of the legal status of the Arts Theatre would permit considerable fiscal savings.
36. Higgins (1975, p. 276) remarked that no one present on the administration council refused this offer, which counts as a homage to Keynes and to his parents.
37. Regarding this and the founding of the Arts Council, for which she was the first general secretary, see Glasgow (1975). See also White (1974), who was assistant secretary of CEMA.
38. Keynes tried unsuccessfully to obtain a military service exemption for ballet dancers, stressing that Germany and Russia had done so during the preceding war (Sidelsky, 2000, p. 51).
39. His abundant correspondence with CEMA is contained in folder PP/84 of Keynes's archives.
40. This speech is preserved in the BBC archives.

10. Conclusion: from Keynes to Keynesianism

The terms 'Keynesian' and 'Keynesianism' started to be used during Keynes's lifetime. The expression 'Keynesian revolution' appeared as the title of a book by Lawrence Klein in 1947, though Keynes himself qualified as revolutionary the consequences of his new theory. As their use became more frequent, the meaning of these words became increasingly ambiguous. Keynes himself told Austin Robinson, after dining with economists in Washington, in 1944: 'I was the only non-Keynesian there' (J. Robinson, 1979, p. 27). According to other accounts, he distanced himself from some of his disciples shortly before his death.

The links between Keynes's ideas, the Keynesian revolution and Keynesianism are thus complex. It exceeds the scope of this conclusion to fully cover this field, which I have approached elsewhere[1] and which has been studied in innumerable other works. The literature on the Keynesian revolution and Keynesianism is, in effect, more abundant than the literature on Keynes. It will suffice here to raise certain of its issues, while finishing with an evaluation of the contemporary relevance of Keynes's message.

THE KEYNESIAN REVOLUTION

Keynes was not the only inspiration behind the revolution that bears his name. As this book has tried to show, his understanding of society and the proposed political actions resulting from it preceded the construction of the economic theory that legitimized them. This understanding and these propositions were situated in a particular historical context. When Keynes was born, the competitive and liberal capitalism that had triumphed in nineteenth-century England found itself in deep crisis. During his life he witnessed two world wars, the Russian Revolution, the Great Depression, the rise of Fascism and Nazism, and the United States' assumption of world leadership. On this agitated world scene, liberal democracies were able to survive only by engaging in profound transformations.

Though one must be wary of counterfactual history, it would be interesting to speculate on what would have happened had Keynes not been prevented at the last minute from boarding the ship destined for Russia and struck by a mine on 5 June 1916. The expressions 'Keynesian revolution' and 'Keynesianism' would, of course, never have seen the light of day. But several transformations associated with the Keynesian Revolution would most likely have occurred, such as the rise of interventionism and the birth of the Welfare State. Keynes's interventions certainly accelerated things in Great Britain and gave them their particular form, but Sweden, like the United States and other countries, did not wait for Keynes to carry out such changes.

If it is easily admitted that the Keynesian revolution was not the result of Keynes alone, it is generally believed that his main and original contribution resides in the economic theory he proposed in 1936. But here again, things are not so simple. Economists associated with the institutionalist movement in the United States, beginning at the turn of the century with its founder Thorstein Veblen, developed analyses similar to Keynes, who was probably inspired by them. It was these economists who instructed President Hoover's and President Roosevelt's advisers. Following Knut Wicksell, another of Keynes's inspirations, Stockholm School members Myrdal, Lindahl and Ohlin proposed in the 1920s arguments very similar to the theory of effective demand and the multiplier. They were the architects of the Swedish Welfare State set up in the early 1930s. In 1932, Michal Kalecki, then an obscure Polish economist influenced by Marx and Rosa Luxemburg, proposed a model containing, in a succinct and formalized manner, the essential elements of *The General Theory*. Keynes's friends were surprised at how quickly Kalecki understood and assimilated Keynes's new arguments when he arrived in Cambridge in 1936! In short, these ideas were in the air. Several economists questioned what Keynes called 'classical theory' and sought out new directions to account for economic crises and unemployment. This was also the case in England and in Cambridge, even among those that Keynes labelled as 'classical'.[2]

Numerous economists thus worked to elaborate economic visions highlighting the insufficiency of effective demand as causing the increased unemployment that only interventionist policies could halt. Keynes's intelligence, his talents as a communicator and his powerful position contributed to the fact that it was his conception that became dominant and his name that became associated with these developments. In contrast to the publications of Kalecki or Myrdal, *The General Theory* was published at the right time and in the right place and language. Finally, his economic theory was part of a global understanding of society, an understanding that is the source of his greatest originality. As we have seen, Keynes's *Weltanschauung* rests on ethical and epistemological foundations that brought him to question the scientificity of an economic discipline considered as autonomous. The pragmatism of his political conceptions resulted from this.

KEYNESIANISMS

The Keynesianism that developed and triumphed following the Second World War was a hybrid creation of numerous guises. It is more accurate to speak of Keynesianisms in the plural. Within these currents, the master's legacy was often fiercely disputed and his global vision often blurred and sometimes even disintegrated.

In 1937, John Hicks published a famous article in which he reduced *The General Theory* to a few equations illustrated by a graph now known as the IS–LM model (for investment, saving, liquidity and money).[3] This model constitutes with the Philips Curve, born in 1958 and illustrating the trade-off between inflation and unemployment, the most important tools of what is called, following Paul Samuelson, the 'neoclassical synthesis'. The latter framework seeks to synthesize Walrasian neoclassical microeconomics with a Keynesian macroeconomics relieved of certain important elements, such as time and uncertainty. While remarking positively on Hicks's paper, Keynes also published an article (1937-4) critical of ideas that would become the dominant trend in Keynesianism.

Another trend, formed around Keynes's inner circle at Cambridge, insisted on his work's revolutionary character, its rupture with classical theory and its account of expectations and uncertainty. For Joan Robinson, who defined herself as a 'left-wing Keynesian', Keynes was not truly conscious of all the implications of his work and became conservative in his later years. This trend came to be known as 'post-Keynesian'.[4] Some post-Keynesians even claimed Kalecki, more than Keynes, as their true source of inspiration. Relations between the two groups were never harmonious and sometimes even acrimonious, with Joan Robinson qualifying the neoclassical synthesis as bastard Keynesianism, being in turn mocked by her adversaries as being the high priestess of Keynes's shroud.

Furthermore, none of these lines of thought is homogeneous and, in each, factions argue over the meaning of Keynes's message. More recently, a new Keynesian economics seeks to give Keynesian theory more rigorous microeconomic foundations based on the hypothesis of the agent's rationality, which, as we have seen, was not shared by Keynes. For the new Keynesians, as well as for the holders of the neoclassical synthesis, the rigidity of prices and wages constitutes the main cause of unemployment.[5]

NEOLIBERALISM AND THE CRISIS OF KEYNESIANISM

In 1965, Milton Friedman, one of Keynesianism's main opponents, declared to a reporter from *Time* magazine that 'We are all Keynesians now'.[6] Three years later, he wrote that his complete declaration to the journalist was: 'In one sense, we are all Keynesians now; in another, no one is a Keynesian any longer', by which he meant: 'We all use the Keynesian language and apparatus; none of us any longer accepts the initial Keynesian conclusions' (Friedman, 1968a, p. 15). Friedman made this declaration when growth, which had been the norm since the end of the Second World War, was stalled. Productivity rates weakened and inflation and unemployment increased simultaneously, in contradiction to the Phillips Curve. The crisis of the Welfare State was evoked, aggravated by crisis in the international monetary system set up at Bretton Woods and by steep increases in petrol prices.

New policies were applied and new theories developed to rationalize them. They were part of an understanding that broke with Keynesianism and revived, in a different political context, the classical liberalism against which Keynes fought. This new understanding was called 'neoliberal', an ambiguous term since it could be confused with its opposite, namely the New Liberalism espoused by Keynes. With monetarism, supply-side economics and anarcho-capitalism, another new theoretical trend was 'new classical economics'. As early as in the 1930s, Friedrich Hayek started a crusade against Keynes and his disciples which he continued tirelessly until his last breath in 1992. In 1947, he founded, with a group of intellectuals, journalists, jurists, political scientists and economists, the Mount Pelerin Society, dedicated to the defence of a liberalism threatened not only by communism and social-democracy, but also by Keynesian interventionism. This society was a breeding ground for neoliberal thinkers, several of whom became from the 1970s advisers to Western governments. The awarding to Hayek in 1974 and Friedman in 1976 of the Bank of Sweden Prize in Economics in Memory of Alfred Nobel, erroneously called the 'Nobel Prize in Economics', symbolized the ideological turnaround then taking place in the world of economic ideas and policies. In 1995, Robert Lucas, a leading thinker in the new classical economics, received the same award.

Neoliberal discourse, in its journalistic as well as political or academic versions, blamed Keynes, Keynesianism and Keynesian policies for the difficulties the capitalist economies started experiencing at the end of the 1960s. For Hayek, it was inevitable that Keynesian medicine, which was in his view nothing more than an exhilarating drug, would sooner or later engender inflation and unemployment. The latter would be curbed only after a long cure of austerity had re-established equilibrium. It would then be a matter of letting things follow their own course. The market, he felt, is a marvellous creation in which politics must intervene as little as possible, if only to assure the necessary judicial framework.

KEYNES'S ROLE

Before posing the question of whether Keynesian policies were in effect responsible for the economic difficulties felt throughout the world after the '*trente glorieuses*', one must investigate the role played by Keynes's ideas in the sustained growth of the postwar Western economies. Like the genesis of the Keynesian revolution, these ideas have been accorded far too much power over the course of events. Moreover, the Keynesian policies applied during the postwar period constituted a panoply of diverse measures whose links with Keynes's ideas were often tenuous.

Keynes greatly influenced the manner in which economists and politicians elaborated and justified new economic policies and redefined relations between economy and State. He had an influence on the affirmation of full employment as a primary objective, which several countries adopted simultaneously at war's end and the United Nations endorsed in 1948. This objective necessarily implied the adoption of demand stimulation policies theorized by Keynes. It also implied definitions and measures of aggregates in the context of national accounting, whose setting up Keynes supported. At the beginning of the 1950s, several economists elaborated increasingly sophisticated models to measure the effects of alternative fiscal and monetary policies.

But it was not theoretical elaborations that gave rise to postwar growth. Keynes overestimated the role of ideas and the power of reason and underestimated the role of political expediency. We have seen where this error led him in his negotiations with the Americans during the Second World War. He believed until the end that reason would prevail, when in reality it was the power of the victor that was imposed. It was the war that created full employment and not the publication of *The General Theory*. The Marshall Plan which followed and allowed for Europe's economic revival can appear as the late application of what Keynes had vainly hoped for in 1919. But this plan resulted more from the American desire to counter the Soviet bloc expansion than from reading *The Economic Consequences of the Peace*. The events that followed can be explained by the intersection of a series of factors in which political power struggles, as much within countries as between countries and blocs of countries, played a major role. Of course, Keynes's theory was extremely useful in understanding this dynamic.

But one cannot impute to Keynes the sustained growth of the *trente glorieuses*, nor can one make him responsible for its failures. One of the most surprising accusations against Keynes's policy proposals is that the latter contributed, by means of deficits, to generating inflation. Regarding inflation, Keynes clearly warned against a policy of full employment that risked provoking inflationist overheating. The unemployment rate below which governments needed to demonstrate prudence was not zero but rather 5 per cent and perhaps even more. Regarding deficits, Keynes never advocated maintaining major deficits over a prolonged period of time, but rather alternating between deficits and surpluses according to economic circumstances. During the golden era of Keynesian interventionism, in the 1950s and 1960s, most governments, particularly the American government, enjoyed budgetary surpluses. It was under governments favourable to neoliberalism that deficits sometimes reached record highs.

WHAT REMAINS OF KEYNES?

As we have seen, Keynes never intended to propose recipes allowing governments to fine-tune the economy and systematically react to all of the economy's failures. He was from the beginning interested in diagnosing society's ills. Remedies for treating illnesses were for him on a different level. They were not to be prescribed in a dogmatic and definitive fashion and vary according to circumstances, periods and places. In this sense, 'Keynesian policies' as such do not exist. Keynes borrowed from Burke the idea that expediency is, in politics, the greatest of virtues. The economy, like society, must not be constrained by rules defined once and for all by an omniscient power.

What remains of Keynes is a global understanding of society, of its articulation with economics, politics, ethics, knowledge and art, an understanding which this book has attempted to reconstruct and from which there is still much to learn. The diagnosis he posed during the first half of the twentieth century is still relevant today. It applies now more than ever, since several of the illnesses he identified have worsened.

For Keynes, the market is not a natural mechanism capable of settling all problems. Laissez-faire resulting from this belief is a dangerous illusion. This conviction is diametrically opposed to the dominant ideology of today, with its faith in an auto-regulating and anthropomorphic market. Not only has it forcefully resurfaced in Western countries since the 1960s, but it has been imposed in former Soviet bloc countries and in China. In the latter, it has united with the political totalitarianism Keynes so abhorred. Elsewhere, in the United States for example, it has accompanied a resurgence in the religious and moral fundamentalism against which Keynes and his Bloomsbury friends fought.

His description and condemnation of laissez-faire, particularly in his famous pamphlet (1926-1), remain relevant. The same holds true of his evocation of the destructive effects of laissez-faire on social inequalities, urban development and the countryside. Keynes denounced art's submission to the criteria of economic profitability. This submission has never more been the case. It was to avoid it that he set up the Arts Council of Great Britain. Keynes's vision is fundamentally anti-utilitarian, anti-materialist and anti-economicist. Man has been briefly sent to Earth to enjoy beauty, knowledge, friendship and love. Keynes dismissed both liberal and Marxist economists for having overvalued the economic factor in social life. He dreamed of a world to come in which the economy would play a secondary role. This too remains far from sight.

He believed that capitalism's main defect was its being founded on the love of money, whose neurotic dimension seemed obvious to him, an idea he shared with Freud. His descriptions of the economy's submission to financial powers, of the dangers of speculation, are prophetic. From this point of view, the situation has again deteriorated since his time. Keynes affirmed that capitalism will lose its legitimacy if people believe their 'betters to have gained their goods by lucky gambling' (1923-1, p. 24).

We have discussed at length Keynes's philosophy of knowledge, particularly in Chapter 3. This is another major contribution having lost none of its interest. In the same way that he rejected the idea of auto-regulating markets, he condemned the use, in the study of human affairs, of techniques conceived to describe the physical world. In human affairs, no one knows what the future holds. We all must make decisions in the dark, in economics as in politics, in one's public as in one's private life. We do not do this by rationally comparing benefits and costs, especially since one's actions are most often the fruit of irrational drives. The limits of applying to social sciences mathematical techniques conceived for a world believed to be determinist results from this. Keynes's anti-logicist position goes hand in hand with his and the Apostles' affirmation of the right to contradiction, to change one's mind, to the clash of ideas. Here as well, things have developed in a direction completely opposite to the one hoped for by Keynes. The 'Keynesian economics' taught in universities today would have Keynes turning in his grave had his ashes not been scattered.[7]

Keynes did not believe that political freedom and economic efficiency, for which he hoped, would suffice to bring about a better world. It was also necessary to guarantee social justice. The problem of articulating between these various ends is far from being satisfactorily resolved. In his tireless search for a solution to this challenge, Keynes figures among the great humanists and social thinkers whose works merit closer understanding and meditation.

For Keynes, the problems of poverty, inequality, unemployment and economic crises are neither exogenous accidents nor punishments for excess, but rather the result of a poorly organized society and human error. It is thus up to individuals united in the *polis* to attenuate or end them by carrying out major reforms. Are such reforms possible within the context of the capitalist economies known to us today? Keynes believed or at least hoped they were. The setting up of the Welfare State seemed to prove him right, but the tide has turned and his diagnosis of capitalism's state of health, put forward now more than half a century ago, is more relevant than ever. No one can claim to know what the future holds. It is up to us, however, to construct it. This is perhaps the main message of John Maynard Keynes.

NOTES

1. See Beaud and Dostaler (1995). One of the pioneering studies opposing Keynesian economics and the economics of Keynes is Leijonhufvud (1968). See also Clower (1965) and, for a critique of this view of the Keynesian revolution, Chick (1978, 1983). For a survey of the critics of Keynes and the Keynesian revolution, see Fletcher (1987).
2. On this, see the fascinating account, by David Laidler, of the 'fabrication' of the Keynesian revolution (Laidler, 1999). For Laidler, 'the re-arrangement of ideas to which it [the "Keynesian revolution"] refers was neither revolutionary in the usual sense of the word nor by any means uniquely Keynesian in origin' (p. 3). See also Patinkin (1982).
3. On Keynes and the IS–LM model, see Young (1987), Hamouda (1986) and the papers collected in De Vroey and Hoover (2004).
4. See Eichner and Kregel (1975), Carvalho (1992) and Lavoie (2004).
5. See Arena and Torre (1992) and Mankiw and Romer (1991),
6. This declaration was published on 31 December.
7. Although Keynes requested in his will that his ashes be buried in the chapel of King's College, his brother had them scattered on the hill overlooking Tilton.

Appendix 1. Keynes and his time: chronology

	Life of Keynes	Historical events
1883	Birth on 5 June in Cambridge, Great Britain, at 6 Harvey Road, of John Maynard Keynes, son of John Neville Keynes (1852–1949) and Florence Ada (1861–1958), née Brown. He will have one sister, Margaret (1885–1970), and one brother, Geoffrey (1887–1982).	14 March: Death of Karl Marx in London. 30 October: two bombs placed by an Irish republican organization explode in the London Underground. Foundation of the Fellowship of a New Life. The term 'eugenics' is coined by Francis Galton.
1884	*Studies and Exercises in Formal Logic*, of John Neville Keynes.	Foundation of the Fabian Society, offshoot of the Fellowship of a New Life, by G.B. Shaw, H.G. Wells, Sydney and Beatrice Webb and of the Socialist League, by William Morris; the Democratic Federation, founded in 1881 by Henry Hyndman becomes the Social Democratic Federation. The Reform Act extends voting rights to about 60% of adult males.
1885		June: the Gladstone Liberal government is defeated on the budget by an alliance of Conservatives and Irish Nationalists: the Conservative leader Robert Cecil, Lord Salisbury, succeeds Gladstone as Prime Minister. November, elections: Conservatives, 249; Liberals, 335; Irish Nationalists, 86. After Nonconformists (1828) and Catholics (1829), Jews obtain the civil rights denied by the Test Act of 1673 to the dissidents from the Church of England. The Labouchere Amendment criminalizes male homosexual

	Life of Keynes	Historical events
		contacts, which are made punishable by two years' imprisonment, with or without forced labour. Royal Commission on the depression.
1886		The alliance of Liberals and Irish Nationalists puts an end to the Conservative government and Gladstone returns to power in February. He introduces in April a Home Rule Bill establishing an Irish Parliament. Conservatives opposed to this project are joined by a Liberal Unionist faction led by Joseph Chamberlain and Lord Hartington, which leads to the rejection of the bill and the fall of the government. July, elections: Conservatives, 316; Liberal Unionists, 78; Liberals, 191; Irish Nationalists, 85. Lord Salisbury becomes Prime Minister.
1887	Starts a stamp collection.	Golden Jubilee of Victoria, born in 1819, Queen of Great Britain since 1837.
1888		Keir Hardie founds the Scottish Labour Party. Jack the Ripper stabs five prostitutes in London's East End.
1889	January: starts school at the Perse School Kindergarten.	Creation in Paris of the Second International, declaring 1 May as International Labour Day.
1890		Foundation of the British Economic Association, which will become the Royal Economic Society.
1891	*The Scope and Method of Political Economy*, of John Neville Keynes.	Birth of *The Economic Journal*, journal of the Royal Economic Society.

	Life of Keynes	Historical events
1892	January: inscription to St. Faith's preparatory school.	July, elections: Conservatives, 268; Liberal Unionists, 47; Liberals, 272; Irish Nationalists, 81; others, 4. Elected, Hardie is the first representative of an independent labour movement. Gladstone forms a government with the support of Irish Nationalists. Franco-Russian Alliance.
1893		13–14 January: foundation of the Independent Labour Party by Keir Hardie. The House of Lords rejects a second Home Rule Bill accepted by the House of Commons.
1894		Gladstone retires and Lord Rosebery succeeds him as Prime Minister. Beginning in France of the 'Affaire Dreyfus' which will split the country in two; Dreyfus is a Jewish officer condemned for espionage in favour of Germany, on false evidence; he is rehabilitated in 1906.
1895		July, elections: Conservatives, 340; Liberal Unionists, 71; Liberals, 177; Irish Nationalists, 82. Lord Salisbury is again Prime Minister; Chamberlain, Secretary of State for Colonies. November: Oscar Wilde is condemned to two years of imprisonment and forced labour for homosexual relations; he dies in France, penniless, in 1900. Foundation by Sidney Webb of the London School of Economics.
1897	September: arrival at Eton College, one of England's most prestigious public schools, having passed the	June: Diamond Jubilee of Queen Victoria. Foundation by Millicent Fawcett of

	Life of Keynes	Historical events
	entrance exam in July 1896. He will stay there until 1902, keeping a diary during the last three years. He wins many academic awards. His closest friends are Dilwyn Knox, who will make a career at the Foreign Office, Bernard Swithinbank, future civil servant in Burma, and Daniel Macmillan, his future publisher.	the National Union of Women's Suffrage Society, the 'suffragists'.
1898		Foundation of the Employers' Parliamentary Council, to defend employers' interests in Parliament.
1899	Starts research on the pedigree of the Keynes family, going back to the time of William the Conquerer.	October: the South African republics of Orange and Transvaal declare war (The Second Boer War) on England.
1900	Refuses to join the Eton College Volunteer Corps during the Boer War.	27 February: representatives of the Trades Union Congress, the Social Democratic Federation and the Independent Labour Party form the Labour Representation Committee, to defend labour's interests against the Employers' Parliamentary Council. Ramsay Macdonald is secretary. October, Khaki elections (after the colour of military uniform) Conservatives, 334; Liberal Unionists, 68; Liberals, 184; Irish Nationalists, 82; Labour Representation Committee, 2.
1901	Starts buying ancient and rare books, an activity he will pursue until the end of his life. Buys a 12-volume edition of Burke's works. December: elected to the College Pop, social club and debating society of the college established in 1811. Awarded an Eton scholarship in mathematics and classics for King's College, Cambridge.	22 January: death of Queen Victoria. Her son succeeds her and reigns under the name of Edward VII until 1910.

	Life of Keynes	Historical events
1902	Reading in period attire of Burke's speech on the East India Bill. President of Eton Literary Society, where he reads a paper on Bernard de Cluny. October: arrival at King's College, with which he will remain associated, first as student, then as fellow, teacher and administrator until the end of his life. He prepares the mathematics tripos. He takes part in many Cambridge societies, as well as in the activities of the University Liberal Club and Cambridge Union. He meets Lytton Strachey and Leonard Woolf, who will become very close friends.	31 May: the Treaty of Vereeniging ends the Boer War. 11 July: Lord Salisbury resigns as Prime Minister and is succeeded by his nephew Arthur Balfour. 2 August: coronation of Edward VII. 30 June–11 August: colonial conference, during which Chamberlain launches his protectionist campaign.
1903	John Sheppard introduces him to the philosoper G.E. Moore. 28 February: recruited by Leonard Woolf and Lytton Strachey, Keynes becomes the 243rd member of the Cambridge Conversazione Society, known as 'The Apostles', founded at Cambridge in 1820. He will be involved in the Society's affairs until 1937, and will read around twenty papers. Attends Moore's lectures on ethics and McTaggart on metaphysics. Moore's *Principia Ethica* is published in October.	September: resignation of Chamberlain, following the divisions that his campaign for protection created in the Conservative Party. Electoral agreement ('Lib-Lab') between the Liberal whip H. Gladstone and the secretary of the Labour Representative Committee, Ramsay Macdonald. Foundation by Emmeline Pankhurst and her daughters Christabel and Sylvia of the Women's Social and Political Union, the 'suffragettes'. Creation at Cambridge University of new tripos in 'Economics and associated branches of Political Science', at the instigation of Alfred Marshall.
1904	March: trip to Germany with his mother, to rejoin his sister. 'Ethics in relation to conduct', read to the Apostles, is the beginning of a reflection that will end with the publication of *A Treatise on Probability*, published 17 years later.	8 April: Entente Cordiale between France and Great Britain, of which Edward VII is the initiator. 31 May: opposed to protectionism, the conservative MP Winston Churchill crosses the House's floor and joins the Liberals.

	Life of Keynes	Historical events
	Wins the University Members Prize for English Essay for *The Political Doctrines of Edmund Burke*. October: elected president of the Liberal Club. Becomes member of the British Association for the Advancement of Science.	Establishment in Ireland of the Ulster Unionist Council, by people wishing the continuation of the 1800 Act of Union, merging Ireland and Great Britain.
1905	Spring: president of the Cambridge Union. May–June: twelfth wrangler in the Mathematics Tripos. June: beginning of graduate studies. He reads great economists and enrols in October for the lectures of Alfred Marshall, who tries to convince him to become an economist by passing the new economics tripos. August–September: holidays with his parents in the Swiss Alps; on the return journey, he spends one week with his mother in Paris, where he discovers impressionist painting. First share buying at the stock exchange. Succeeds Lytton Strachey as secretary of the Apostles, and becomes very active in the recruiting of new members. Affair with Arthur Hobhouse, Apostle and future liberal MP.	16 March: beginning of the 'Thursday Evenings' at 46 Gordon Square, home of Leslie Stephen's children (Vanessa, Virginia, Thoby and Adrian), which marks the birth of the Bloomsbury Group. 28 November: foundation by J. Griffith and T. O'Kelley, of Sinn Fein, partisan to Ireland's independence. 4 December: resignation of Prime Minister Balfour, unable to maintain the cohesion of his party. Next day, Henry Campbell-Bannerman, Liberal leader since 1899, becomes Prime Minister and launches elections.
1906	Participation in the campaign for the January elections. March–April: holiday in Italy; he rejoins his brother in Germany on his return journey. Keynes chooses, instead of economics, and in spite of Marshall's exhortations, to prepare himself for the Civil Service examinations, held in August. He is second, behind Otto Niemeyer. The latter having chosen to enter the Treasury, Keynes chooses the India	12 January, elections: Conservatives, 132; Liberal Unionists, 25; Liberals, 400; Irish Nationalists, 83; Labour Representation Committee, 30. Campbell-Bannerman nominated Prime Minister. The Labour Representation Committee becomes the Labour Party. Trade Dispute Act: unions cannot be sued for damages caused during a strike. Workmen's Compensation Act,

	Life of Keynes	Historical events
	Office, in London, where he starts work on 16 October. His light schedule allows him to start writing a dissertation on the foundations of probability for King's College, in view of obtaining a fellowship. August–September: holiday in Scotland, with Lytton and James Strachey, and Harry Norton. Corrects the proofs of the fourth edition of *Studies and Exercises in Formal Logic* by his father.	forcing employer to pay compensation for injuries and diseases caused by work.
1907	March: transfered to Revenue, Statistics and Commerce Department. Becomes member of the Royal Economic Society and frequents the Economic Club of University College, in London. Starts buying pictures. Participates in the campaign for women's voting rights. June: holiday in the Pyrenees with his father and brother. Autumn: meets Clive and Vanessa Bell and Virginia Stephen, future Woolf, during a 5-week stay in Cambridge. Beginning of his integration in the Bloomsbury group. December 12: submits his dissertation on probability.	Triple Entente among France, Great Britain and Russia, established against the Triple Alliance of 1882 among Germany, Austria-Hungary and Italy. The Social Democratic Federation becomes the Social Democratic Party (SDP), which will merge in 1988 with the Liberal Party to form the Liberal Democrats. Nobel Prize in literature to Rudyard Kipling, poet of British imperialism.
1908	February: often at Vanessa Bell's bedside during the month following her first delivery. March: publication of his first paper, a book review, in the *Journal of the Royal Statistical Society*. He learns on 21 March that his candidacy to a King's fellowship is not retained and decides to revise his dissertation for a new submission. April: Marshall, who is about to retire,	5 April: sickness forces Campbell-Bannerman to retire and he is replaced as Prime Minister by Herbert Asquith, Chancellor of the Exchequer since 1905; Lloyd George is the new Chancellor. Old Age Pensions Act, providing financial support to people over 70. Children Act, regulating children's work. Miners' Eight Hours Act.

	Life of Keynes	Historical events
	to be succeeded by Pigou, proposes that he teach economics in Cambridge. May: debut of his affair with Duncan Grant, with whom he holidays in August and September in the Scottish Island of Hoy, where he finishes the second version of his dissertation on probability and starts an article on India. Duncan Grant paints his portrait. 5 June: resignation from the India Office, where he stops working on 20 July. 24 October: installation in his rooms at King's College. December: submission of a new version of his dissertation on probability.	A.C. Pigou succeeds Marshall at the Cambridge Political Economy Chair. Lt-Gen. Robert Baden-Powell starts the Scout movement.
1909	19 January: starts lecturing on money, credit and prices. 30 January: draws up a list of books and articles to be written in the following years. Most of these projects will be realized. 6 February: first open letter, to *The Economist*, about protectionism. March: publication of his first academic paper, 'Recent Economic Events in India', *Economic Journal*. 16 March: election to a fellowship of King's College. During the summer, installation in the rooms that he will occupy until his death. 7–21 April: stays with Duncan Grant at Versailles, where he writes a paper on price index, which will be awarded the Adam Smith prize. June: last trip with his family, in the Pyrenees. July–September: rents 'Little House', a country house in Burford, near Oxford, where he entertains many friends.	Lloyd George's 'People's Budget' proposes important tax rises on high income to finance a new social security system. The budget is rejected by the House of Lords on 30 November and Asquith calls for general elections. House and Town Planning Act. Trade Boards Act, granting a minimum wage for more vulnerable workers. Reports of the Royal Commission on the Poor Laws and Relief of Distress.

	Life of Keynes	Historical events
	22 October: founding of the Political Economy Club, which meets on Monday nights in Keynes's rooms at King's. It groups his most brilliant students, and it is at this gathering that Keynes will give one of his last talks on 2 February 1946. November: Duncan Grant rents a lodging at 21 Fitzroy Square, where Keynes keeps a room until the end of 1911. Secretary of the Cambridge University Free Trade Association. Appointed Inspector of Accounts of King's College.	
1910	Appointed Secretary of the Board for Economics and Politics of Cambridge University, a post he will hold until 1915. 17 March: departure for a 7-week trip to Greece and Turkey with Duncan Grant. Summer: renting of 'Little House' at Burford. October: John Neville Keynes is elected registrar of Cambridge University. November: Keynes 'takes wings' and becomes an angel in the Apostles Society. Controversy with Karl Pearson about the effects of parental alcoholism on children. Secretary of the Cambridge University Free Trade Association. Participation in the two election campaigns, at the beginning and end of the year, for the Liberals; speeches against protectionism. Member of the Eighty Club, a progressive liberal organization.	14 January, elections: Conservatives, 273; Liberals, 275; Irish Nationalists, 82; Labour, 40. 10 February: 'Dreadnought hoax'; Bloomsbury members organize a false visit to a British warship dressed up as a group of princes from Abyssinia. Scandal in the House of Commons. March: foundation of the International Psychoanalytical Association. Declaration by the Second International of 8 March as the International Women's Day. 6 May: death of Edward VII, replaced by George V. Exhibition 'Manet and the Post-impressionists', first important public manifestation of Bloomsbury, organized by Roger Fry, from November to 11 January. 2 December, elections provoked by a constitutional crisis: Conservatives, 271; Liberals, 272; Irish Nationalists, 84; Labour, 42. Asquith stays in power thanks to the support of Irish Nationalists and Labour.

	Life of Keynes	Historical events
		Great Unrest: beginning of a period of two years marked by numerous strikes.
1911	February: founding member of the University Reforms Committee. March–April: trip to Italy and Tunisia with Grant. June: discovers Diaghilev's Ballets Russes, in their first London season. Entertained for the first time by Ottoline Morrell, where he meets Prime Minister Asquith. Summer: camping at Clifford's Bridge, in Devon. Autumn: shares a lodging, rented in his name, with Virginia and Adrian Stephen, Duncan Grant, Leonard Woolf and his brother Geoffrey, at 38 Brunswick Square, until 1914. September–October: 15-day mission in Ireland, with a delegation of 50 liberal MPs. 17 October: appointed editor of *The Economic Journal*, a post he will hold until 1945. Series of six lectures at the London School of Economics on Indian finances. Grant finishes four mural paintings, started in 1910, in Keynes's rooms at King's College. Appointed member of the Council of the Society for Psychical Research. Elected member of the College finance Committee. Nominated Girdlers' College Lecturer in Economics.	6 February: Ramsay Macdonald becomes Labour leader. 22 June: coronation of George V. 1 July: the dispatching of a German gunboat near Agadir, in Morocco, creates strong tension with France and Great Britain. 18 August: the Parliament Act limits the powers of the House of Lords to block House of Commons legislation. November: Balfour is replaced as Conservative leader by Andrew Bonar Law. 6 December: the National Insurance Act creates the first contributory system of insurance against illness and unemployment, paid for by the State, employers and employees; one of the first steps towards the Welfare State. Founding of the British Socialist Party, merging the Social-Democratic Party and other socialist organizations; led by Henry M. Hyndman, the party will dissolve in 1920, some members joining the Labour Party and others the Communist Party. Hyndman himself founded the National Socialist Party in 1916.
1912	January: elected to the Council of the Royal Economic Society, where he will stay until the end of his life.	15 April: sinking of the RMS Titanic. 28 September: adoption of Home Rule, offering self-government to

	Life of Keynes	Historical events
	March–April: trip to the Côte d'Azur with Gerald Shove. July–August: rents Crown Inn, Everleigh, where he entertains many friends. September–October: stay in Austria-Hungary. October: arrival in Cambridge of Ludwig Wittgenstein, elected Apostle, who will become a close friend of Keynes. December: elected member of the London Political Economy Club. Appointed fellowship elector, which will bring him to read many theses. Meets Irving Fisher; they will remain in contact until the end of Keynes's life.	Ireland. Sanctioned by the King on 30 January 1913, the law will be effective only after the war. 8 October 1912: the declaration of war by Montenegro on the Ottomans launches the first Balkan War. October–December: second Post-Impressionist exhibition, organized by Roger Fry. The Liberal Unionists merge officially with the Conservative Party. Creation of the Ulster Volunteer Force, Irish paramilitary organization opposed to Home Rule. Foundation of *The Daily Herald*, Labour newspaper.
1913	February: Margaret Keynes marries Archibald Hill, physiologist, 1922 Nobel Prize. March–April: trip to Italy, Tunisia and Egypt. June: *Indian Currency and Finance*. August: camping at Brandon, near Thetford, in Suffolk, where the 'Bloomsberries' (Keynes, Grant, Vanessa and Clive Bell, Fry and others) meet the 'Neo-Pagans', the friends of the poet Rupert Brooke. September: Geoffrey Keynes saves the life of Virginia Woolf, following a suicide attempt. Member of the Royal Commission on Indian Money and Finances. Elected secretary of the Royal Economic Society, a post he will hold until 1945.	30 May: the treaty of London ends the first Balkan War, but the second immediately begins, then ends in June with the treaty of Bucharest. 8 July: foundation by Roger Fry of Omega Workshops, devoted to domestic art. 15 November: foundation of the London Group, reuniting painters opposed to the conservatism of the Royal Academy. December: creation of the Federal Reserve System in the United States. Trade Union Act, allowing unions to devote part of their members' subscription to political ends. Arrest of Sylvia Pankhurst, one of the leaders of the suffragettes, at Bromley Public Hall; a group of women sets fire to Southport Pier.
1914	January: holiday with Duncan Grant in the South of France, where he contracts diphtheria. 2 March: publication of the report of	28 June: assassination at Sarajevo, by a Serbian nationalist, of Archduke Franz Ferdinand, heir to the Austro-Hungarian throne, and his wife.

	Life of Keynes	Historical events
	the Royal Commission on Indian Money and Finances. April: rents Asheham House in Sussex, from Virginia and Leonard Woolf, where Vanessa Bell joins him. Summer: camping at Coverack, in Devon. August: first intervention, unofficial, at the request of Basil Blackett, of the Treasury, in war finances. September: the marriage of Adrian Stephen and Karin Costelloe puts an end to the occupation of Brunswick Square. Keynes moves to 10, Great Ormond Street. December: goes to France to meet his brother, who works as a medical officer in a Versailles hospital.	28 July: after an ultimatum on 24 June, Austria-Hungary declares war on Serbia. Germany declares war on Russia on 1 August and on France on 3 August. 31 July: assassination of the French Socialist leader Jean Jaurès. 4 August: following the violation of Belgian neutrality, Great Britain declares war on Germany. 5 August: the unionist Arthur Henderson becomes Labour leader for the second time. 8 August: the Parliament adopts the Defence of the Realm Act, which enforces the government's power and restricts civil rights, until August 1921. 13 August: declaration by Great Britain of war on Austria-Hungary. November: first war loan. 5 November: after France and Russia, Great Britain declares war on Turkey. 16 December: Great Britain proclaims its protectorate on Egypt. Opposition to the entry of war by part of the Labourites, among whom Ramsay Macdonald, and some Liberals, regrouped in the Union for Democratic Control.
1915	January 17: starts working at the Treasury, as assistant of George Paish, adviser to the chancellor of the Exchequer, Lloyd George. He celebrates the event by inviting 17 of his Bloomsbury friends to the Café Royal. He is appointed secretary of a Cabinet Committee on Food Prices, chaired by the Prime Minister, and Treasury representative on an inter-departmental Committee on Wheat and Flour Supplies.	23 April: mobilized, the poet Rupert Brooke dies at 27 from septic mosquito bite while sailing towards Gallipolli with the British Mediterranean Expeditionary Force. 26 April: secret treaty between Great Britain, France and Italy, which ends the Triple Alliance on 3 May. 19 May: Asquith invites the other parties to join a coalition power, Labour thus entering government for the first time. Reginald McKenna is

Life of Keynes	Historical events
2–5 February: participates in the first Allied financial conference in Paris. March: moves to 3 Gower Street. Meets Knut Wicksell. May: becomes member of the First (Finance) Division of the Treasury. June: trip to Nice with the new Chancellor McKenna to meet the Italian minister of Finances. 12 June: urgent surgery for appendicitis, followed by pneumonia. Convalescence at Garsington, where Ottoline Morrell takes care of him. 20 August: inter-Allied financial conference at Boulogne. 1 September: becomes second in command to Malcolm G. Ramsay, the Assistant Secretary in charge of matters of banking, currency exchange and allied finance. November: member of an Exchange Committee formed by the Chancellor. November–December: six public conferences on 'The war finance of the continental powers' at London University. Autumn: starts to frequent the Asquiths at their country house, The Wharf, in Sutton and sometimes at 10 Downing Street.	Chancellor of the Exchequer, Lloyd George minister of Munitions, Edward Grey Foreign Secretary. 21 September: first McKenna budget, with important tax hikes. 16 October: Great Britain declares war on Bulgaria. 12 December: the catastrophic attempt to seize the Dardanelles leads to the temporary disgrace of Churchill, first Lord of the Admiralty. 28 December: the majority of the cabinet accepts conscription.
1916 28 February: writes a letter claiming the status of conscientious objector. Due to his activities at the Treasury, Keynes had obtained a 6-month exemption of military service, which will be prolonged indefinitely on 18 August. He testifies on several occasions in favour of his Bloomsbury friends who refuse military service on grounds of conscientious objection. April: he is offered a candidacy at the national elections for the Cambridge University seat.	27 January: royal sanction of the Military Service Act which orders the conscription of all able-bodied and unmarried males of 18 to 41; effective on 5 February. 23 April: 'Easter Rising', insurrection of Irish nationalists in Dublin, causing 450 deaths, followed by 15 executions. 6 July: Lloyd George succeeds Lord Kitchener, killed by a mine on 5 June, as Secretary of State for War. 6 December: following the

	Life of Keynes	Historical events
	5 June: he is supposed to accompany the Secretary of State for War to Russia but, at the last minute, he cannot join the delegation. The ship he was to board explodes on a mine. Vanessa Bell acquires the lease of Charleston farmhouse, in Sussex, with the financial aid of Keynes, who will use a room there until 1926. August: moves to 46 Gordon Square, which will become his London residence until the end of his life. He takes the lease in his name in 1918, sharing the home with John Sheppard and Harry Norton; Clive Bell will keep a room until 1925.	resignation, on 18 December, of Asquith, criticized for his conduct of the war and facing divisions in his party, Lloyd George becomes Prime Minister. Bonar Law is Chancellor of the Exchequer. Lloyd George forms a five-member War Cabinet, which is the real centre of power.
1917	January: appointed chief of the new 'A' Division of the Treasury, in charge of external finances, responsible before the Chancellor. September–October: first trip, of six weeks, to the United States, where he accompanies Chief Justice Reading to discuss financial questions. 19 June: participation in the creation of the 'Tuesday Club', which brings together, the third Tuesday of the month, at the Café Royal, politicians, civil servants, journalists and academics to discuss economic and political questions. Keynes will open the discussion on 24 July, 1919, and on many other occasions until 1942. Contributes to the renting of Mill House, where Lytton Strachey and Dora Carrington set up home. December: representative of the Treasury to the Inter-Ally Council for War Purchases and for Finance. Geoffrey Keynes marries Margaret Darwin, granddaughter of Charles Darwin.	22 January: US President Wilson calls for a 'peace without victory'. The February Revolution, which ends the Tsarist Empire, is followed in November by the Bolshevik insurrection which brings Lenin and the Communist Party to power, transforming Russia into the Union of Soviet Socialist Republics (USSR). 6 April: United States declares war on Germany. June–July: crisis in monetary relations between Great Britain and the United States. 24 October: William Adamson becomes Labour leader, until 1921. 27 October: IRA (Irish Republican Army) Convention. October: foundation of the Co-operative Party, which passes an electoral agreement with Labour in 1927. 2 November: declaration of the Foreign Secretary Arthur Balfour in favour of a Jewish settlement in the Palestine territory.

	Life of Keynes	Historical events
	John Neville Keynes ceases to keep his diary.	President Wilson arrives in Brest on 13 December. George V changes the name of the British dynasty from Hanover-Saxe-Coburg to Windsor. Foundation of the publishing house The Hogarth Press, by Leonard and Virginia Woolf.
1918	14 January: Sidney Webb tries to convince Keynes to stand as Labour candidate for Cambridge University. 27–28 March: accompanies the National Gallery's director to Paris for auction of Degas' personal collection of paintings, after having obtained a sum of £3000 from the Treasury. He buys for himself a Cézanne and a few other pictures. September: the lease of 46 Gordon Square is renewed in Keynes's name. September or October: first meeting with his future wife, Lydia Lopokova, star ballerina of Diaghilev's Ballets Russes, in London. November–December: represents the Treasury in the meetings of the Committee of Indemnity. Writes a 'Memorandum by the Treasury on the indemnity payable by the enemy powers for reparation and other claims'. Christmas Day: birth of Angelica Bell, daughter of Vanessa Bell and Duncan Grant, at Charleston. Keynes is the stepfather, and attends to Vanessa's two sons.	8 January: US President Wilson presents to the Congress a peace project in 14 points. February: the Representation of the People Act extends voting rights to all men over 21 and enfranchises women over 30; the number of voters rises from 7.7 million to 21.4 million. 15 August: the Cunliffe Committee proposes a return to the gold standard system at the sterling pre-war parity. 9 November: following worker uprising in Germany, Kaiser Wilhelm II is forced to abdicate. The Social-Democratic Party rules the new republic with the Independent Social-Democratic Party. 11 November: capitulation of Germany and signature of the Armistice; abdication of Charles I, emperor of Austria-Hungary. 14 November: the government announces the dissolution of Parliament on 25 November. 1 December: occupation of Germany by the Allies. 14 December, elections: Conservatives, 332; National Liberals (partisans of Lloyd George), 127, Labourites favourable to the coalition government, 10; Asquithian Liberals, 36; Labour, 57; Sinn Fein, 73. Labour becomes the 'Royal opposition to his Majesty'.

	Life of Keynes	Historical events
		'Labour and the New Social Order', new Labour programme: clause IV proposes 'the common ownership of means of production'. Started in 1918 and continuing in 1919 the influenza epidemic ('Spanish Flu') kills more people than the war.
1919	January–June: participation in the Peace Conference of Paris, where he arrives on 10 January, as principal Treasury representative, and official representative of the British Empire on the Supreme Economic Council. 14 January: Keynes goes with a delegation directed by Marshal Foch to Treves, to discuss financial arrangements and food delivery with German delegates. Among the latter, Carl Melchior will become a close friend of Keynes. They get authorization from their delegations to hold private negotiations. Ill on his return to Paris, he spends two weeks of convalescence on the Riviera. The negotiations on food delivery are concluded in Brussels on 13 and 14 March. March: Keynes proposes a cancellation of inter-Allied war debts. April–June: attends eight meetings of the Council of Four, of which seven are held at President Wilson's or Lloyd George's residences. 7 June: disagreeing with the nature and extent of reparations imposed on Germany by the Allies, he resigns from the British delegation and leaves Paris. June: present at the triumph of Lydia Lopokova in *La Boutique Fantasque*. She disappears on 10 July to reappear on March 1921. 22 July: opens for the first time the discussion at the 'Tuesday Club' on	10 January: formation of a new government directed by Lloyd George; Austen Chamberlain is Chancellor of the Exchequer and Bonar Law, Lord Privy Seal. Sinn Fein MPs refuse to sit in Westminster, meet in an Irish parliament, the Dail, and proclaim the independence of Ireland. Beginning of two years of war between the Irish Republican Army (IRA) and the British troops. 18 January: beginning of the Paris Peace Conference which leads to the signature of the Treaty of Versailles on 28 June. On 19 November, the American Senate refuses to ratify the Treaty. January: Spartakist uprising in Berlin and assassination of Rosa Luxemburg and Karl Liebknecht on the 15. 2 March: birth of the Third International, the Communist International (Comintern); the socialist parties refusing to join the Comintern will form in 1920 the International Worker's Union of Socialist Parties. 23 March: birth of the Fascist movement in Italy. 28 April: adoption of the pact giving birth to the League of Nations, based in Geneva. 31 July: adoption of the Weimar Republic constitution in Germany. 19 September: treaty of Saint-

	Life of Keynes	Historical events
	'Certain aspects of the Treaty of Peace with Germany'. 25 July: witness to the Indian Exchange and Currency Committee. August: starts speculating on foreign exchange markets. 13–15 October and 2–3 November: participation in a financial conference in Amsterdam. He draws up a project for international loans for the League of Nations. Meets Melchior. November: named second Bursar of King's College. Reduces his teaching load to one series of lectures a year, given during the Autumn term. 12 December: *The Economic Consequences of the Peace*, written in three months in Charleston. The book, translated into many languages, has great worldwide success. 13 December: open letter to *The Times*, with eleven members of Cambridge University, exhorting the government to 'do everything within their power to accelerate the economic recovery of Europe'.	Germain-en-Laye with Austria, dissolving the Austro-Hungarian Empire.
1920	January: creates with his friend, the financier Oswald Falk, the 'Syndicate', to speculate on currencies, using his own funds and those of his Bloomsbury friends. He is near bankruptcy in April and May. He will have repaid his debts and reconstituted his assets at the end of 1922, speculating on currencies but also on commodities. 4 March: first meeting, at Keynes's London home, of the Bloomsbury Memoir Club, comprising 13 members. April–May: 6-week trip to Rome, with Duncan Grant and Vanessa Bell; orgy of buying; stayed at the Villa	February: Asquith returns to Parliament after a by-election in Paisley. 24 February: the German Workers' Party, founded the year before, becomes the National Socialist German Workers' Party (Nazi Party). April: at 7 per cent, the Bank Rate reaches its highest level in peacetime since 1907. July: Spa conference on reparations. July: Founding of the British Communist Party, led by Albert Inkpin until 1929. September: conference of 35

	Life of Keynes	Historical events
	'I Tatti', at the Berenson, near Florence. July: asked by Asquith to become member of a finance sub-committe of the National Liberal Federation's Industrial Committee. Testifies on the rupee's value at the Committee on Indian Exchange and Currency.	countries, in Brussels, called to discuss trade and international finances. Unemployment Insurance Act, covering most workers. Launching in India of a civil disobedience campaign led by Mahatma Gandhi and the Indian National Congress. Establishment of Home Rule in Ireland.
1921	Starts a career as journalist by contributing regularly to *The Manchester Guardian*. February: reads a paper on Melchior to the Bloomsbury Memoir Club. March: trip in the Algerian desert with Sebastian Sprott, Apostle and future psychologist. Member of the sub-committee of the British League of Nations for the limitation of armaments. Lydia Lopokova reappears in London in Diaghilev's ballet company. 5 May: suggests to Germany that they accept the last decisions of the Reparation Commission, while saying that they will be unable to pay. 21 June: presidential address to the Apostles' annual dinner. July: creation of A.D. Investment Trust, with O.T. Falk. Summer in Charleston with Vanessa Bell and Duncan Grant. August: invited by the Indian government to be vice-president of a Royal Commission on tariffs. He finally gives up the idea of going to India, in January 1922. August: series of six articles in *The Sunday Times*, under the general title 'Europe's economic outlook', which	24–30 January: Paris conference, on German reparation payments. 14 February: John Robert Clynes is Labour leader until 1922. 21 February–14 March: London conference, on German reparation payments. 29 April–5 May: London conference on reparations, sending an ultimatum to Germany. 14 April: labour unions for mining, railway and transportation workers call for a strike. 28 June: Adolf Hitler chairman of the Nazi Party in Germany. November: the Liberal Party adopts as its official policy the cancellation of war debts and the reduction of German reparations to a reasonable amount. 6 December: Anglo-Irish Treaty, ratified on 7 January 1922, establishing an Irish Free State (EIRE), coming into force on 6 December 1922. Northern Ireland (ULSTER) has the option of withdrawing from the Free State, which it will do. Opponents of the Treaty mounted a military campaign which produced the Irish Civil War (1922–23).

	Life of Keynes	Historical events
	have a lot of impact in the United States as well as in Europe. August: *A Treatise on Probability*. Memorandum on the University reform to the Royal Commission on Oxford and Cambridge. Intervention in women's struggle to get full recognition at Cambridge University. Nominated vice-president of the Indian Fiscal Commission on tariff policy, but resigns before assuming the office.	Economic depression in Great Britain continuing until 1922. Establishment of the National Unemployed Workers' Movement; the number of unemployed workers increased from 1 million in 1921 to 2 million the following year. Beginning of the great German inflation
1922	January: *A Revision of the Treaty*. April–May: present at the Genoa conference as correspondent of *The Manchester Guardian*, for which he writes thirteen papers. He meets the Soviet minister of Foreign Affairs, Georgi Chicherin. April to January 1923: edits 12 supplements to *The Manchester Guardian*, under the general title 'Reconstruction in Europe', published in five languages, including 12 articles by himself, among which is a first plan of reorganization of the international monetary system. He obtains contributions of many renowned personalities. 4 August: speech to the Liberal Summer School, in which he will be an active participant during the 1920s. 26 August: speech to the World Economic Congress at Hamburg. Meets Melchior and Cuno, future Chancellor. The mark had started its decline. October: electoral speeches for the Liberal Party. 2 November: arrives in Berlin with a group of economists, at the invitation of the German government, to discuss the stabilization of the mark, the value	10 April–19 May: the Genoa conference assembles 34 nations, including Germany and USSR, to discuss reconstruction of European finance and trade. 16 April: Treaty of Rapallo, between Germany and USSR, each renouncing territorial and financial claims against the other and normalizing their diplomatic relations. 24 June: assassination by two right-wing officers of Walther Rathenau, German Foreign Affairs Minister, favourable to a negotiated agreement on reparations. 1 August: in answer to an American demand for reimbursement of war debts, the 'Balfour note' declares that Great Britain will be able to reimburse only if it is reimbursed by its Allies and Germany. First Liberal Summer School in Oxford. 31 August: meeting in Paris, the Reparation Commission rejects a British proposal to give Germany a moratorium until the end of the year. October: after a march on Rome of his 'black shirts', Mussolini seizes power and installs a fascist regime in Italy.

	Life of Keynes	Historical events
	of which was declining at an accelerating pace. November–December: four conferences on monetary problems at the Institute of Bankers. 18 December: meets the new Chancellor of the Exchequer Stanley Baldwin and, the following day, the Prime Minister Bonar Law, to whom he proposes a plan for the settlement of reparations and debts on 23 December. Duncan Grant and Vanessa Bell finish five mural paintings, started in 1919, to decorate Keynes's apartment at King's College. Takes charge of the financial affairs of Lydia Lopokova, who moves in to 50 Gordon Square, where he organizes many receptions for Diaghilev's company.	19 October: a meeting of the Conservative MPs at Carlton Club leads to the fall of Lloyd George's coalition government. Bonar Law succeeds him as Prime Minister. He dissolves Parliament on 25 October. 15 November: elections: Conservatives, 345; National Liberals, 54; Asquithian Liberals, 62; Labour, 142; others, 16. Bonar Law remains Prime Minister; Stanley Baldwin is Chancellor of the Exchequer. November 21: Ramsay Macdonald becomes Labour leader for the second time, until 1931. Foundation of the British Broadcasting Company (BBC), which becomes the British Broadcasting Corporation in 1926.
1923	January: creation of the P.R. Finance Company, with O.T. Falk. March: becomes chairman of the board of the liberal weekly review *The Nation and the Athenaeum*, born from a merger of *The Nation* and *The Athenaeum*. Hubert Henderson is editor and Leonard Woolf literary editor. The first issue is published on 5 May, with papers by Virginia Woolf and Lytton Srachey. Keynes will himself publish 155 papers in the review, some of them anonymous or under the pseudonym 'Siela'. He holds, in particular, a weekly column under the title 'Finance and Investment'. Many Bloomsbury members collaborate. January: creation, with William Beveridge, A.L. Bowley and Hubert Henderson, of the London and	January 2: Allied leaders meet the Germans in Paris to discuss reparations. 8 January: the Reparation Commission, with the exception of the British representative, declares Germany in default of payment. 11 January: French and Belgian troops occupy the Ruhr. 22 May: Stanley Baldwin succeeds Bonar Law as Prime Minister, who is forced to resign because of throat cancer. In the Cabinet formed on 26 May, Robert Cecil becomes Lord Privy Seal. Neville Chamberlain will be nominated Chancellor of the Exchequer in August. 7 June: conciliatory note from Germany in response to an ultimatum sent by Foreign Secretary Lord Curzon.

Life of Keynes	Historical events
Cambridge Economic Service, which publishes, until 1938, the *Monthly Bulletin*, offering statistics on the economic situation. Keynes publishes there a series of seven long memoranda on commodity markets.	November: reunification of the Liberal Party under the leadership of Asquith.
May: after the transmission of a note by Great Britain to Germany about reparations, by Lord Curzon, Foreign Secretary, Keynes suggests the wording of an answer to the German Chancellor Cuno.	23 October: Baldwin calls for elections, after announcing the introduction of protectionist measures to combat unemployment.
30 May: meets Prime Minister Baldwin, whom he informs of his contacts with Chancellor Cuno.	8–9 November: Munich Putsh, following which Adolf Hitler is put on trial, imprisoned and writes *Mein Kampf*.
1–4 June: goes to Berlin at the request of Chancellor Cuno, to discuss the German answer to the British proposition.	6 December: elections, following which, with 258 seats, the Conservatives lose the absolute majority; Labour obtain 191 seats and the Liberals 159.
14 July: denounces the rise of the discount rate from 3 to 4 per cent, while the unemployment rate attains 11.4 per cent.	
Summer: rents a house with Lydia Lopokova at Studland, in Dorset. His Bloomsbury friends disapprove of an eventual marriage between them.	
8 August: speech at the Liberal Summer School, 'Currency policy and unemployment'.	
Refuses a propositon of the Cambridge Liberal Association to be candidate in the elections, but participates actively in the campaign; speeches on 4 and 5 December.	
11 December: *A Tract on Monetary Reform*, reproducing his most important articles of the series 'Reconstruction in Europe'.	
Series of conferences, during the winter, to the National Liberal Club, on 'Currency policy and social reform'.	
Keynes's name is among the nominees	

	Life of Keynes	Historical events
	for the Nobel Peace Prize. In the end, the Prize is not awarded for that year. Autumn: controversy with William Beveridge, director of the London School of Economics, on the relationship between unemployment and demography.	
1924	January: creation, with O.T. Falk, of the Independent Investment Company. February: starts working on a book called *The Standard of Value*, which will become *A Treatise on Money*. 23 February: first of a series of comments on the annual speeches of the clearing banks' chairmen. 25–27 March: participation in a conference held in London by the League of Nations on Unemployment in its national and international aspects. 11 July: speech to the Committee on the Currency and Bank of England Note Issues (Chamberlain Committee), established on 10 June by the Treasury. Writing of a long biographical article following the death, on 12 July, of Alfred Marshall. 2 August: speech to the Liberal Summer School. 1 October: speech to the Committee on National Debt and Taxation. 25 October: election speech to support a Liberal candidate. 6 November: conference at Oxford on 'The end of laissez-faire'. Campaign against the return to the gold standard at the pre-war parity. Nominated First Bursar of King's College, a position he will hold until the end of his life. He redresses the College's financial situation.	22 January: following Baldwin's defeat, after the speech from the throne, Labour leader Ramsay Macdonald forms a government supported by Liberals. Philip Snowden is Chancellor of the Exchequer. On 18 February, he announces the government's intention to follow up Cunliffe Report's proposition (1918) by returning to the gold standard at the pre-war parity. February: official recognition of Soviet power. April: reports of the Dawes and McKenna committees established in December 1923 to study the German situation. 16 July–16 August: the London Conference of Allied powers adopts the Dawes plan, proposing a recycling of German debt, and obtains French retirement from the Ruhr. August: Housing Act, with plans to build council houses at modest rent. 8 October: the Labour government is defeated after a censorship vote. 29 October: elections won by the Conservatives (419); Liberals collapse (40) while Labour keep 151 seats. Communists have one deputy. Baldwin regains the Prime Ministership and Winston Churchill, back with the Conservatives, becomes Chancellor of the Exchequer.

	Life of Keynes	Historical events
1925	February: foundation, with Samuel Courtauld and James Hindley-Smith, of the London Artists Association, to ensure the financial security of painters, amongst whom are Duncan Grant and Vanessa Bell. 17 March: meets Churchill and other high officials to discuss the return to the gold standard. 6 May: evidence before the Committee on National Debt and Taxation. 9 July: evidence before the Committee on Industry and Trade (Balfour Committee), created during the summer of 1924. July: *The Economic Consequences of Mr Churchill.* 1 August: 'Am I a liberal?', conference to the Liberal Summer School. 4 August: marriage with Lydia Lopokova. They rent a house near Lewes, where they host, among others, Ramsey and Wittgenstein. 3 September: departure for USSR, where the newly weds visit Lydia's family in Leningrad and Keynes represents Cambridge University at the celebrations of the Academy of Sciences bicentenary; he gives two conferences in Moscow. October: takes a long-term lease on a farmhouse, Tilton, in Sussex, near Charleston. It is there that he will henceforth write his major works. He will also be more and more involved in farming activities. November: tries to explain Wittgenstein's theories to the Apostles. December: *A Short View of Russia.*	28 April: Churchill announces the return to the gold standard at the pre-war sterling parity. October: the Locarno Conference leads to a number of treatises to guarantee the borders of European countries. Retirement benefits extended to widows and orphans. Asquith becomes Earl of Oxford, one of the oldest titles in English peerage.
1926	January: to Vanessa and Duncan's discontent, Keynes decides to occupy 46 Gordon Square with Lydia only.	11 March: the Samuel Commission proposes a reorganization of the mining industry, with wage reduction

	Life of Keynes	Historical events
	9 February: speech on the relation between Liberalism and Labour to the Manchester Reform Club. 22 March: evidence before the Royal Commission on Indian Currency and Finance. An open letter by Keynes to *Nation and Athenaeum* of 12 June provokes a definitive rupture with Asquith, now Lord Oxford. 22 June: meeting with Einstein, following the presentation in Berlin of 'The end of laissez-faire'. Summer: nominated to the executive committee of the Liberal Industrial Inquiry, created by the Liberal Summer School with the financial support of Lloyd George; this committee will work for 18 months. November–December: actively involved in the restructuring of the Lancashire cotton industry, which will end up with the creation, in January 1929, of the Lancashire Cotton corporation. July: *The End of Laissez-faire*. 9 August: speech to the summer school of the Independent Labour Party. Frequents the Webbs, Bernard Shaw and H.G. Wells.	to restore profitability. Mine owners then announce wage reductions of 10 to 25 per cent and an extension of the working day from seven to eight hours, with a threat of lock-out in case of miners' refusal to accept the new terms. 3–16 May: a general strike called by the TUC to support the miners mobilizes 9 million workers, but ends without a satisfactory result. The miners continue their resistance until their capitulation at the end of the year, many of them remaining unemployed and victimized. The general strike provokes a new crisis in the Liberal Party, with another split between Asquith and Lloyd George. The Liberal Summer School establishes a Liberal Industrial Inquiry. 15 October: resignation of Asquith as Liberal leader. Lloyd George takes charge. 19 October–23 November: the London Imperial Conference proclaims the autonomy of Dominions, after the creation in 1924 of a Dominion Office to replace the Colonial Office.
1927	Elected to the Other Club, founded by Churchill and F.E. Smith in 1909, to dine and discuss political and economic questions beyond party frontiers.	26 May: rupture of diplomatic relations between Great Britain and the USSR. *Labour and the Nation*, Labour policy document reproducing many elements of the radical Independent Labour Party manifesto, *Socialism in Our Time*. It asserts that Labour's programme is not to patch a bad system, but to transform capitalism into socialism.

	Life of Keynes	Historical events
		The Trade Disputes Act outlaws general and sympathetic strikes, bans civil servants from joining unions, and restricts political grants by unions, which reduces Labour's finance.
1928	22 January: asked to be Liberal candidate for the University. 17 March: 'Economic possibilities for our grandchildren', delivered to the Essay Society of Winchester College. April: trip to Russia with Lydia, with a stop on the return journey to Berlin and Hamburg, where he meets Melchior. June: *Réflexions sur le Franc et sur Quelques Autres Sujets*. 11 October: asked again to be Liberal candidate.	2 February: *Britain's Industrial Future*, Liberal 'Yellow Book', being the report of the Liberal Industrial Inquiry, of which Keynes was one of the main writers. 15 February: death of Asquith. March: The 'Flapper's Bill' gives the right to vote to women of 21 and over. There are now 14 million women and 12 million men with voting right in Great Britain.
1929	Last attendance to the Liberal Summer School. Campaign for a massive public investments programme, against the 'Treasury View'. Elected fellow of the British Academy. Refuses again to be Liberal candidate for Cambridge University, but is actively involved in the election campaign. 10 May: *Can Lloyd George Do it?*, with Hubert Henderson. 19–29 July: four conferences at the School of International Studies in Geneva, followed by a stay in Burgundy with Lydia. November: appointed member of the Macmillan Committee. December: three meetings with the Prime Minister, to discuss the economic situation and the ways to ameliorate advice and information to overnment. This results in the	1 March: publication of 'We can conquer unemployment', 'Orange Book' forming the basis of the Liberal electoral campaign. February–June: the Young Committee fixes the definitive reparation amounts to be paid by Germany until 1988. 15 April: in his budget speech, Churchill formulates the 'Treasury View', according to which the financing of public works by loans reduces the available funds for private investments. 1 March: Lloyd George's pledge, suggested by Keynes, of a substantial reduction of unemployment by means of public works, in case of a Liberal victory. 30 May, elections: first Labour majority (288), Conservatives gaining 260 seats and Liberals 59. Ramsay Macdonald becomes Prime Minister

	Life of Keynes	Historical events
	formation of the Economic Advisory Council. At the year's end, the value of his assets collapsed.	on 5 June. Philip Snowden regains the Exchequer. Margaret Bondfield, Minister of Labour, is the first woman to enter the Cabinet in British History. 24 October: 'Black Thursday' marks the beginning of the Great Crash and an unprecedented world economic crisis. 5 November: establishment of the Committee on Finance and Industry (Macmillan Committee), which meets for the first time on 21 November. It will hear 49 witnesses until July 1930, and then meet from October to prepare its report. Local Government Act: abolition of Poor Law workhouse. Establishment of a more generous unemployment insurance system.
1930	Member of the editorial board of a new review, *The Political Quarterly*. 24 January: appointed to the Economic Advisory Council (EAC), whose creation is announced the same day. He proposes at the first meeting, on 17 February, the creation of a Committee on the Economic Outlook, which he will chair and which will produce two reports, after three meetings (21 March, 3 April and 1 May). 20 February–7 March: testifies for five days before the Macmillan Committee, presenting throughout ten hours the ideas of his *Treatise on Money*. 10 July: Keynes suggests to the Prime Minister the formation of a Committee of Economists, inside the EAC, with the mandate to examine the economic situation and propose solutions. He will chair this five-member committee which meets for the first time on 24	18 January: death of the Cambridge mathematician Frank Ramsey, aged 26. January: The Hague Conference adopts the Young Plan and establishes a Bank for International Settlements. 29 May: Oswald Mosley resigns from the Cabinet, after an unsuccessful attempt to propose a programme based on Keynes's ideas. He writes a manifesto signed with other Labour MPs on 30 December. Poor Law Act, transferring the administration of hospitals from the Poor Law to local authorities.

	Life of Keynes	Historical events
	July and hands over its report on 24 October, with a dissenting report from Lionel Robbins. 31 October: *A Treatise on Money*, vol. 1, *The Pure Theory of Money*, vol. 2, *The Applied Theory of Money*. November: first meetings of the 'Circus', a group of Keynes's young disciples (Kahn, Sraffa, Meade, Austin and Joan Robinson), to discuss *A Treatise on Money*. Lydia Keynes is admitted to the Bloomsbury Memoir Club. Treasurer of the Camargo Society, a ballet company created after the death of Diaghilev. Member of the drafting committee, which produces the Macmillan report during the winter 1930–31.	
1931	February: first issue of *The New Statesman and Nation*, stemming from the merging, at Keynes' initiative, of *The Nation and Athenaeum* and *The New Statesman*. He is chairman of the board and Kingsley Martin is editor. 1 March: declares himself publicly (as he did privately in the Committee of Economists) in favour of protectionist policies, which triggers sharp reactions from economists. 28 April: severe criticism of the Snowden conservative budget. 21 May: re-elected vice-president of the National League of Young Liberals; disagreeing with the party's support to a reactionary fiscal measure, he refuses this nomination. 30 May: the day following the signature of the Macmillan report, departure for a second trip, of five weeks, to the United States, where he is invited to the Harris Foundation	February: Mosley quits Labour and founds the New Party. 4 May: the collapse of Credit-Anstalt, Austria's principal bank, triggers a European financial crisis. 20 June: US President Hoover proposes a one-year moratorium on reparations and war debt payments. 13 July: the financial crisis reaches Great Britain, whose currency is submitted to intense pressures. The same day, the Macmillan Committee's report is published. July: the Committee on National Expenditure (May Committee), established in February to examine the state of public finances, proposes important cuts in public expenditures, in particular a reduction of 20 per cent of unemployment benefits. August: unemployment reaches a peak of 2.8 million. 24 August: following a lack of

	Life of Keynes	Historical events
	lectures and seminars at the University of Chicago, on the theme 'Unemployment as a World Problem'. Meets President Hoover in Washington. 14 July: member of a new Committee on Economic Information of the Economic Advisory Council. 19 September: nominated to the Prime Minister's Advisory Committee on Financial Questions. 4 October: meets the Prime Minister and Lloyd George. November: *Essays on Persuasion*, collection of extracts of publications from the preceding 12 years. Controversies with Hayek, Robertson and Hawtrey. First symptoms of the disease from which he will die.	consensus in his Cabinet concerning measures to end the economic crisis, Macdonald resigns and is asked by the King, the same day, to form a national government. This government approves on 27 August the policies proposed in the May Report. Macdonald, Snowden and all those participating in the National government are excluded from the Labour Party, of which Arthur Henderson, becomes the leader for the third time, until October 1932. 29 August: following the restrictions in public spending, the government obtains from Paris and New York loans that permit the support, temporarily, of the pound sterling. 21 September: suspension of the convertibility of the pound, which loses 30% of its value. October, elections: Conservatives, 473; Liberals, 33; National Liberals, 35; Labour, 52; dissident Labourites, favourable to the National government, 13; others, 5. Macdonald remains Prime Minister of a government largely dominated by Conservatives. 11 December: the Statute of Westminster creates the British Commonwealth of Nations, regrouping the former British colonies. It will be named Commonwealth in 1946. Creation of the New Fabian Research Bureau.
1932	6 January: departure for Hamburg, where on the 8th, he presents to the International Economic Society, a conference entitled 'The economic prospect of 1932'. He meets the	January: Mosley meets Mussolini in Italy and decides to disband his New Party, replaced by the British Union of Fascists. June–July: the Lausanne Conference

	Life of Keynes	Historical events
	Chancellor Heinrich Brüning on the 11th. Last encounter with Melchior who dies in 1933. 21 January: Lytton Strachey dies of an undiagnosed cancer. 5 July: publication in *The Times* of a letter signed by 13 economists, amongst whom Keynes, calling for an increase in public expenses, of investment projects, of credits, and tax reductions. August: appointed to a Committee on International Economic Policy, to prepare for the world economic conference of 1933. 10 October: first of a series of lectures henceforth entitled 'The monetary theory of production'. 17 October: letter of six economists, amongst whom Keynes, to *The Times*, calling for an increase in public spending. Four economists of the London School of Economics, including Robbins and Hayek, criticize this proposition in *The Times* of 19 October. The six reply on the 21st. Starts investing in Wall Street. Florence Ada, Keynes's mother, is elected mayor of Cambridge.	puts an end to the Young Plan and reduces reparations payments and war debts. August: the Ottawa Agreement on Commonwealth Preference in Trade gives birth to a sterling area with imperial preference. Canada refuses to adhere. October: hunger march. 8 November: Franklin Delano Roosevelt is elected President of the United States.
1933	17 April: arrival in Dublin, where he gives the Finlay-O'Brien conference at University College, 'National self-sufficiency'. March: *Essays in Biography.* *The Means to Prosperity.* 29 June: last performance of Lydia Lopokova as dancer, in a gala organized by Keynes for the World Economic Conference. 4 July: meets the Prime Minister to discuss Roosevelt's refusal of an exchange rates stabilization proposal.	30 January: Adolf Hitler becomes Chancellor of Germany. Reparation payments are indefinitely suspended. 4 March: inauguration of Roosevelt's presidency. Beginning of the 'New Deal' programme. April: creation of the Gestapo in Germany. 7 June: four power pact signed by representatives of Britain, France, United States and Japan in Rome, for the protection of peace. 12 June–27 July: the World Economic

	Life of Keynes	Historical events
	18 September: Lydia makes her theatrical debut at the Old Vic in a Shakespeare production that Keynes helped her rehearse. He conceives the project of a Cambridge theatre. 30 December: death of Carl Melchior. 31 December: open letter to the American president Roosevelt, published in _The New York Times_. First version of a table of contents for _The General Theory_, then entitled 'Monetary theory of production'. End of the activities of the London Artists' Association and the Camargo Society.	Conference of London, called to combat the depression by economic agreements and monetary stabilization, is a failure, provoked in particular by Roosevelt's refusal to stabilize exchange rates. June: Great Britain suspends its war debts payments to the United States, which will lead to the 1934 Johnson Act, forbidding loans to nations in default on their war debts. June: the Nazi Party is proclaimed the unique party in Germany. First concentration camps in Germany.
1934	9 May: departure for a 3-week trip to the United States, where he receives an honorary doctorate from Columbia University on 5 June. He meets President Roosevelt on 28 May. He expounds his theory of effective demand to the American Political Economy Club.	30 January: the Gold Reserve Act gives the Federal Reserve title to all the gold collected. The next day, president Roosevelt fixes the dollar value at $35 an ounce of gold, value that will remain until 15 August 1971. February: hunger march. 25 July: assassination of Austrian Chancellor Engelbert Dollfuss by a group of Nazis who failed to take power. 2 August: after the death of German President Paul von Hindenburg, Hitler transfers the role and powers of the presidency to the Chancellor, now called the Führer, also supreme military commander. _For Socialism and Peace_: Labour Party's programme of action. The Unemployment Act establishes an Unemployment Assistance Board and separates unemployment benefits from measures supporting the long-term unemployed.
1935	June: Robert Bryce, a Canadian student, explains Keynes's new theory	6 May: jubilee of George V. June: the Conservative Stanley

	Life of Keynes	Historical events
	in the Hayek Seminar at the London School of Economics. 11–13 July: participates in a meeting of economists organized by the Antwerp Chamber of Commerce to discuss the international monetary situation. Refuses financial support to the Liberal Party and makes instead a donation to Labour, for which he votes for the first and only time. Controversy with George Bernard Shaw about Marx and socialism.	Baldwin replaces Ramsay Macdonald as Prime Minister and dissolves Parliament on 25 October. July: the Government of India Act establishes, among other things, a central bank, as proposed by Keynes in 1913. September: invasion of Ethiopia by Mussolini. 8 October: Clement Attlee succeeds George Lansbury as Labour leader, a position he will hold for 20 years. 14 November, elections: Conservatives, 387; Liberals, 17; Labour, 154; dissident Labourites, 44; others, 9.
1936	3 February: opening of the Cambridge Arts Theatre, created and financed by Keynes. 4 February: *The General Theory of Employment, Interest and Money*. 21 April: reads a long paper on Jevons, for the centenary of his birth, before the Royal Statistical Society. 13–14 July: purchase of manuscripts, many of them devoted to alchemy, and the death mask of Newton. End of September: departure for Leningrad, to visit Lydia's parents, with a stop in Stockholm where he presents a conference to the Economic Club. Purchase of an apartment for Lydia near the Cambridge Arts Theatre.	20 January: death of George V. His son, who reigns as Edward VIII, is forced to abdicate on 11 December to marry Wallis Simpson, a twice-divorced American. His younger brother is crowned as George VI. March: Hitler occupies and remilitarizes the Rhineland, violating the Locarno agreements. May 1936: victory of the Popular Front in the French elections. Leon Blum, leader of the Socialist Party, becomes Prime Minister and introduces the 40-hour week and other important social reforms, as well as the nationalization of the Bank of France and the armaments industry. July: beginning of the Spanish Civil War, opposing insurgent army officers led by Francisco Franco to the Popular Front government elected five months earlier. November: proclamation of the Rome–Berlin axis; anti-Comintern pact between Germany and Japan,

	Life of Keynes	Historical events
		joined by Italy one year later. Tripartite Agreement between Great Britain, France and United States.
1937	February: reply to critiques by Leontief, Robertson, Taussig and Viner in 'The general theory of employment', *Quarterly Journal of Economics*. 16 February: speech before the Eugenics Society. 16 May: heart attack, caused by an infectious endocarditis. Rests at Harvey Road, then in Ruthin Castle, Wales, from 18 June to 23 September. He then stays at Tilton until February 1938. Lydia controls his schedule and visits. 18 July: Julian Bell, son of Clive and Vanessa Bell, is killed in Spain, where he was volunteer in the Republican camp. Controversies with Ohlin, Robertson and Pigou. Acquires the lease of 47 Gordon Square. From Spring to 1938, the value of his assets is reduced by two thirds.	Relapse of the economy May: Neville Chamberlain, Chancellor of the Exchequer since 1931, replaces Baldwin who resigned as Prime Minister. 12 May: coronation of George VI. 29 December: a new constitution proclaims Ireland an independent nation. Eamond de Valera is Prime Minister. The Labour Party publishes *Labour's immediate programme*.
1938	1 February and 25 March: private letters to Roosevelt suggesting economic policies. 11 February: his doctors authorize a gradual return to his normal activities. No teaching during this year. 23 February: first public appearance since his heart attack, for his annual speech as chairman of the National Mutual Life Assurance Society. He then resigns from this post. 10 March: first stay in Cambridge since his disease.	Anglo-American trade agreement 13 March: Hitler enters Vienna and proclaims the Anschluss, the inclusion of Austria in the German Reich. 29 September: Munich agreement between the governments of France, Great Britain, Germany and Italy, following which Czechoslovakia must surrender part of the Sudetenland to Germany. Foundation of the Fourth International by Leon Trosky's followers.

	Life of Keynes	Historical events
	11 September: reads 'My early beliefs' to the Bloomsbury Memoir Club, in Tilton garden. Autumn: resumes his participation in the meetings of the Committee on Economic Information after an 18-month interruption. Debate with Jan Tinbergen on econometrics. Honorary doctorates from Oxford and Glasgow Universities. Sets up the Cambridge Research Scheme of the National Institute of Economic and Social Research into Prime Costs, Proceeds and Output, which will be integrated in the Department of Applied Economics.	
1939	February: severe attack of influenza. Janosh Plesch, physician of Einstein and other renowned personalities, becomes and will remain Keynes's doctor until the end. End of September: begins to gather home colleagues of the First War, the 'old dogs', among whom are Walter Layton, William Beveridge and Athur Salter, to discuss the situation created by the war. 12 October: starts again to go to the Other Club, where he meets Churchill. 27 October: presents a project to finance the war, including compulsory savings, which will become deferred pay, at a dinner reuniting ministers and deputies. Its publication in *The Times* of 14 and 15 November sparks a general outcry, from the Left as well as from the Right, and support from the majority of economists, including Hayek and Robbins. 23 November: after much hesitation, he refuses to be candidate at a by-	15 March: Hitler attacks Czechoslovakia. 26 April: The British Prime Minister announces conscription. 28 April: first Keynesian budget in Canada. Summer: the IRA conducts a bombing campaign in London. 23 August: Treaty of Nonaggression between Germany and the USSR. 1 September: German troops enter Poland. 3 September: France and Great Britain declare war on Germany.

	Life of Keynes	Historical events
	election for the seat of Cambridge University, for which he would have had the support of the three parties. 6 December: first presence at the Tuesday Club since his illness; talk on price policy. To support his project on war finance, he starts working on national accounts estimation.	
1940	24 January: meets Labour MPs and the General Council of the Trades Union Congress to try to convince them of the validity of his project to finance the war. 27 February: *How to Pay for the War: A Radical Plan for the Chancellor of the Exchequer*. This publication is followed by an important correspondence and many discussions. 28 June: appointed to the Treasury's Consultative Council. He has no salary, but has at his disposal an office, the services of a secretary, and a bed at the Treasury. He follows closely the work of Meade and Stone on national accounting. He serves as a link between the Treasury and economists recruited in other ministries and government agencies. Nominated to the Exchange Control Conference, comprising members of the Treasury and the Bank of England. Appointed Master's representative on the Governing Body at Eton College. June: intercession to obtain the liberation of Sraffa and other intellectuals of enemy nationalities. 18 September: explosion of a bomb at Gordon Square, while he is receiving for dinner. October–February 1941: intense discussions on budgetary policy,	10 May: Winston Churchill succeeds Chamberlain as Prime Minister and establishes a coalition government. Kingsley Wood is Chancellor of the Exchequer. 23 May: arrest and imprisonment of Mosley. 30 May: dissolution of the British Union of Fascists. June: James Meade, joined by Richard Stone in August, starts working on the preparation of national accounts, in the Central Economic Information Service of the Offices of the War Cabinet. Their document, 'National income, saving and consumption', is published on 6 January 1941. 22 June: Marshall Pétain, French Prime Minister, signs an armistice with Germany. 18 June: From London, General de Gaulle launches an appeal to the French resistance towards German occupation. 10 July: beginning of the Battle of Britain. 18 August: German air force begins bombarding London. 21 August: assassination of Trotsky in Mexico; his murderer, Soviet agent Ramon Mercader, received in 1961 the medal of Hero of the Soviet Union.

	Life of Keynes	Historical events
	Keynes writing numerous memoranda for the Chancellor. November: represents the Treasury on a committee created to study the question of export surplus.	28 October: invasion of Greece by Italy. With an advance of £5 million to Greece, Great Britain starts financing the Allies. 5 November: re-election of Roosevelt, who declared on 2 November that the United States would not go to war. 8 December: Roosevelt announces the Lend-Lease agreement, under which the President can accord military aid to any nation whose defence seems vital to the defence of the United States, against repayment, the form of which would be discussed later. Full employment is attained.
1941	Nominated adviser to the Chancellor of the Exchequer. Member of the budget committee, where he will stay throughout the war. 28 March: suicide of his friend Virginia Woolf. 8 May–29 July: first of six missions to the United States, as representative of the Chancellor of the Exchequer, to negotiate the conditions of the Lend-Lease. He discusses, among other questions, commercial policies, international policies for raw materials and projects to finance postwar aid. He meets Treasury Secretary Morgenthau on 13 May and Roosevelt on 28 May and 7 July. On 28 July, Americans transmit to Keynes 'considerations' for the Lend-Lease, among which article VII proposes, after the war, the abolition of trade discrimination, particularly British imperial preference. During this visit, Keynes meets many economists. He also meets Einstein again. 8 September: finishes writing a first	11 March: the Lend-Lease Act is adopted by Congress. 7 April: first 'Keynesian' budget in Great Britain, using the framework of national accounts. June: establishment of an inter-departmental committee under the chairmanship of William Beveridge to study social security systems. 22 June: Germany attacks the USSR. 14 August: signature in Newfoundland, by Churchill and Roosevelt, of the Atlantic Charter establishing a vision for a postwar world. It is signed between 22 December and January 1942 by 26 countries. October: establishment of an inter-departmental Committee on postwar Economic Problems. 8 December: the day following the attack against its navy at Pearl Harbour, United States declares war on Japan, and then on Germany and Italy. Great Britain and the United States set up a common headquarters,

	Life of Keynes	Historical events
	plan of reform of the international monetary system, proposing an International Currency Union, which will become the Clearing Union. Many other versions will follow. 18 September: nominated director of the Bank of England.	but often disagree on military strategy. The Archbishop of York, William Temple, calls for the establishment of a Welfare State.
1942	1 April: chairman of the Council for the Encouragement of Music and the Arts (CEMA). June: nominated Baron Keynes of Tilton. He sits at the House of Lords with the Liberals. 8 July: a first American plan of reform of the international monetary system, written by Harry White, is transmitted to Keynes. Many exchanges with White and others will follow, as well as successive versions of the Keynes plan (Clearing Union) and the White plan (Stabilization fund). July: attracts Churchill's attention on the growing indebtedness of England towards India. He will often intervene on this question in the following months. 30 November: reads to the Royal Society a paper on Newton, which will be published after his death. Doctorate in law from Manchester University. Active involvement in the preparation of the Beveridge report on the reform and financing of social security.	January: visit by Churchill to Washington. 23 February: Great Britain signs the Lend-Lease agreement. August: trips of Churchill to the Middle East and Moscow. November: the results of the elections for Congress and the Senate are less favourable to Roosevelt's administration. November: British and American troops invade Africa. 1 December: publication of the Beveridge Report on British Social Security system.
1943	January: resigns as vice-president of the Malthusian League, disagreeing with the position of the Council in favour of birth control for the poor. 26 February: presents his plan for reform of the international monetary system at a meeting of representatives of the Allied powers.	1 January: signature by the United States, Great Britain, USSR and 23 other countries of the United Nations charter. 14–24 January: the Casablanca Conference, with Churchill, Roosevelt and de Gaulle, decides the terms for the pursuit of the war.

	Life of Keynes	Historical events
	27 February: death of his Eton friend Dilwyn Knox. 6 March: nominated 'High Steward of the Borough of Cambridge'. 7 March: death of Mary Paley, wife of Alfred Marshall, about whom Keynes writes a long paper. 7 April: Keynes's plan becomes the offical position of Great Britain as 'Clearing Union White Paper'. 18 May: speech to the House of Lords on his plan for the reform of the international monetary system. September–October: 6-week trip to the United States, to discuss informally monetary and trade policies, in particular Article VII of the Lend-Lease agreement and the reform of the international monetary system. November: nominated trustee of the National Gallery.	31 January: the Sixth German Army capitulates at Stalingrad. May: the Trident conference, in Washington, between Roosevelt and Churchill, accepts the principle of a seaborne invasion of France. 17–24 August: first Quebec Conference, with Churchill, Roosevelt and Canadian Prime Minister, Mackenzie King. 28 November–2 December: Tehran conference, involving Roosevelt, Churchill and Stalin.
1944	January: refuses the Cambridge chair of political economy offered to him after Pigou's retirement. March–April: heart problems. 22 April: publication of the British-American 'Joint Statement by Experts on the Establishment of an 'International Monetary Fund', for which Keynes writes explanatory notes. 23 May: speech to the House of Lords on the on-going negotiations for the reform of the international monetary system. 16 June: leader of the British delegation to Bretton Woods, Keynes leaves London. Discussions with other delegations on the boat. 23 June: arrival at New York. 24–29 June: preparatory discussions in Atlantic City. 1 July: at his arrival in Bretton Woods,	26 May: the White Paper on employment policy recognizes that the government has the responsibility to insure a high and stable level of employment. 6 June: Landing in Normandy, D-Day 1–22 July: the Bretton Woods Conference, regrouping 44 countries, creates the International Monetary Fund and the International Bank for Reconstruction and Development. 11–16 September: second Quebec conference, involving Churchill, Roosevelt and Mackenzie King. October: Moscow conference involving Roosevelt, Churchill and Stalin. 7 November: Roosevelt elected for a fourth term as president of the United States. 16 December: last counter-attack of Hitler in the Ardennes.

	Life of Keynes	Historical events
	Keynes offers a dinner to commemorate the 500th anniversary of the Concordat between King's College, Cambridge and New College, Oxford. 22 July: the Bretton Woods agreements are signed; Keynes gives a speech at the closing plenary session. 28 July: arrival of the Keyneses in Canada, where financial relations with Great Britain are discussed. They pass by New York and Washington before returning to England on 24 August. October–November: new trip to the United States to discuss Lend-Lease and American financial aid. He sees the American President on 26 and 27 November. 28 November: departure to Ottawa, to discuss financial aid from Canada. Returns to England on 12 December.	
1945	January–June: member of a National Debt Inquiry. February: resigns from the editorship of *The Economic Journal*. March: appointed member of a committee on reparations. April: honorary doctorate of the Edinburgh Law University. 19–29 May: negotiations with a Canadian delegation in London and Cambridge. June: the government announces that the CEMA will be transformed into the Arts Council of Great Britain, at Keynes's suggestion. August: discussions with an American delegation about postwar trade policies and Great Britain's financial situation. 27 August–17 December: trip to the United States, including a visit to Canada (2–6 September), for very difficult negotiations on Lend-Lease	4–11 February: Yalta (or Crimea) Conference, involving Roosevelt, Churchill and Stalin. 12 April: Roosevelt dies of a cerebral haemorrhage. Vice-President Harry Truman takes charge. 25 April–26 June: the San Francisco Conference attended by 46 nations, establishes the United Nations. 30 April: suicide of Hitler. 8 May: capitulation of Germany. 23 May: Labour retires from the coalition government and returns to opposition. 28 July: Japan rejects an ultimatum from the United States. 6 and 9 August: atomic bombs are dropped by US bombers on Hiroshima and Nagasaki: 110 000 immediate deaths and a total of 320 000 before the end of the century, while 300 000 persons are suffering

	Life of Keynes	Historical events
	repayments and American financial aid. Keynes leads the mission in the name of the Chancellor of the Exchequer. He hopes to obtain a donation or a loan without interest. The Anglo-American Financial Agreement, signed on 6 December, provides a loan with interest, for a sum much lower than what was asked. 18 December: speech to the House of Lords, in favour of this agreement and those of Bretton Woods. For a period of eight months, Keynes is the main economic adviser of the Labour Chancellor Hugh Dalton, his former student. Elected president of the Econometric Society.	from sequels of the bombings. 5 July, elections: Labour, 393; Conservatives, 213; Liberals, 12; others, 22. Clement Attlee becomes Prime Minister of the first Labour majority government; Hugh Dalton is Chancellor of the Exchequer and Ernest Bevin Foreign Secretary. 16 July–2 August: the Postdam conference, reuniting the heads of government of the UK, the USA and the USSR, imposes disarmament and reparations payments to Germany, organizes the occupation of the country, abolishes the Nazi Party and decides to try war criminals. 14 August: capitulation of Japan. 17 August: Truman terminates the Lend-Lease Agreement. 15 August: the King opens the first New Parliament since the war began, with a Labour government. 18 December: the House of Lords ratifies the Bretton Woods Agreement and the Anglo-American Financial Agreement.
1946	Honorary doctorates from the Sorbonne and Cambridge University. 19 February: nominated British Governor of the International Monetary Fund and the International Bank. 20 February: opening gala, organized by Keynes, of Covent Garden, for which he chooses *The Sleeping Beauty*. 1 March: arrival in New York, en route towards Savannah, in Georgia, for the inaugural meeting of Governors of Fund and Bank, starting on 9 March. On the return trip to Washington, Keynes suffers a severe stroke. Easter holiday in Tilton, with Lydia	The National Insurance Act extends social security to the entire population, thus creating the Welfare State in Great Britain. The National Health Service Act creates a publicly-funded healthcare system. 5 March: Churchill proclaims in Missouri the existence of an Iron Curtain in Europe.

Life of Keynes	Historical events
and his parents. He dies on 21 April, Easter morning, in his bed. Lydia will survive him until 1981. 24 April: Keynes's body is cremated at Brighton, and his ashes are scattered in the hills around Tilton; he had asked that they be deposited in a vault in King's College Chapel. 2 May: state funeral at Westminster Abbey. 4 May: ceremony at the Chapel of King's College, where the following extract of John Bunyan's *Pilgrim's Progress* is read: 'Then, said he, I am going to my Father's; and though with great difficulty I am got hither, yet now I do not repent me of all the trouble I have been at to arrive where I am. My sword I give to him that shall succeed me in my pilgrimage, and my courage and skill to him that can get it. My marks and scars I carry with me, to be a witness for me, that I have fought his battles who now will be my rewarder'.	

Appendix 2.   Maynard as seen by his friends and contemporaries

CLIVE BELL (1956, pp. 60–61)

In the highest degree he possessed that ingenuity which turns commonplaces into paradoxes and paradoxes into truisms, which discovers or – invents – similarities and differences, and associates disparate ideas – that gift of amusing and surprising with which very clever people, and only very clever, can by conversation give a peculiar relish to life. He has a witty intellect and a verbal knack. In argument he was bewilderingly quick, and unconventional. His comment on any subject under discussion, even on a subject about which he knew very little, was apt to be so lively and original that one hardly stopped to enquire whether it was just. But in graver mood, if asked to explain some technical business, which to the amateur seemed incomprehensible almost, he would with good-humoured ease make the matter appear so simple that one knew not whether to be more amazed at his intelligence or one's own stupidity. In moments such as these I felt sure that Maynard was the cleverest man I had ever met; also, at such moments, I sometimes felt, unreasonably no doubt, that he was an artist.

QUENTIN BELL (1980, pp. 69–70)

I do not remember the time when I did not know Maynard and from the first I found him extraordinarily attractive and wonderfully kind. My first clear recollection of him can be dated to the summer of 1915; we both belonged to a party which was being ferried across Chichester Harbour to Bosham and I threw his hat into the sea. It is for me a memory of unalloyed pleasure. It had been a warm day, Maynard had taken his hat off and it lay within easy reach; it was upside down and its shape – perhaps even its name – suggested that it would ride upon the waters like a boat. It did, and I can still see it clearly in my mind's eye, gently, rather jauntily, riding up and down upon the little waves.

   The ferry had to change course. The hat, ruined I dare say, was retrieved with a boat hook; I was reproached but in no way troubled – a little surprised that the grown-ups did not share my ecstatic delight.

   Neither then nor later did I see Maynard lose his temper. I am told that he could be tart, brutal even, but neither as maddening children nor as tiresome young people did my brother and I ever provoke him to wrath, or if we did I was unaware of it.

DAVID 'BUNNY' GARNETT (1979, p. 147)

He was one of the most brilliant talkers I have known. He would pounce on any remark which interested him, extend it, develop it. At the Treasury his room was opposite that of Lord

Catto. This led to his being given the name of Doggo. And in his unswerving fidelity to his old friends and his affection for them there was something canine. And so was his gift for pouncing and seizing the essential and the gundog's nose which led him to recognise it instantly.

In this portrait sketch I have dwelt on his mistakes which were obvious, whereas his great achievements demand expert appreciation.

But they have led to his brilliance as a biographer being overlooked. He had the advantage over Lytton Strachey of having known the men he was writing about personally. He wrote of all with affection but with a delightful wit, and could sum up a man in a sentence. If I were to sum up Maynard it would be 'Affection, understanding, flashing intelligence'.

ANGELICA GARNETT (1984, p. 48)

At bedtime I was sometimes allowed, as a privilege, to have my bath in Maynard's bathroom, more splendid than ours. It was a luxury chiefly because of its larger size, but there were glass jars full of sponges and bath salts, and I well remember Maynard, in his elegant city suit, standing over me and showering me with these as I sat in the water.

L.F. GIBLIN (1946, p. 1)

Keynes had of all men I have known, a personality and mind the most fully armed for all adventures. Whatever matter came up on however unfamiliar a subject his contribution stood out for significance and insight within the limits he imposed on what he said. He had a capacity for activity of a high order in many unrelated fields and he kept those activities going at the same time, even when dogged by bad health as he was in the last ten years.

MARY GLASGOW (1975, p. 267)

Supremely intelligent himself, he was impatient of anything less than clear thinking and well-defined aims. He knew what he wanted, and why, and he liked to have his own way. He could be very rude on occasion, and he did antagonise a number of people. Faced with an issue on which he felt deeply – and there were many such – he never hesitated to declare war.

ROY F. HARROD (1946, p. 182)

Whatever the final verdict on *The General Theory*, Keynes' greatness as an economist will not be questioned. His mental capacities had a far wider range than those usually found in professional economists. He was a logician, a great prose writer, a deep psychologist, a bibliophile, an esteemed connoisseur of painting; he had practical gifts of persuasion, political finesse, businesslike efficiency; he had personal gifts which made him have profound influence on those who came into direct contact with him. Economics, still young, only in part a fully specialist subject as yet, has gained from its contact with such a comprehensive intellect. I remember his once describing Ricardo as 'the most distinguished mind that had found Economics worthy of it.' We may surely judge Keynes' mind to be more distinguished than Ricardo's.

FRIEDRICH A. HAYEK (1952, p. 196)

Whatever one may think of Keynes as an economist, nobody who knew him will deny that he was one of the outstanding Englishmen of his generation. Indeed, the magnitude of his influence as an economist is probably at least as much due to the impressiveness of the man, the universality of his interests, and the power and persuasive charm of his personality as to the originality or theoretical soundness of his contribution to economics. He owed his success largely to a rare combination of brilliance and quickness of mind with a mastery of the English language in which few contemporaries could rival him and – what is not mentioned in the *Life* [Roy Harrod, *The Life of John Maynard Keynes*] but to me seemed always one of his strongest assets – a voice of bewitching persuasiveness.

NORMAN HIGGINS (1975, pp. 273–4)

From the start of the project [the Cambridge Arts Theatre] throughout the remainder of his life, Keynes, despite his many other commitments and the stress of his voluntary Treasury work during the war years, always found time to discuss details of management, and his interest in every aspect was insatiable – the make-up of audiences, their drinking habits, and in the Restaurant the proportion of wine drinkers and what they drank.

HARRY JOHNSON (1974, pp. 132–4)

Keynes was a brilliant phenomenon; he was a sparkling man and a great experience for me . . . One of the secrets of his charm was that he would go out of his way to make something flattering out of what a student had said. If the student had made an absolute ass of himself, Keynes would still find something in it which he would transform into a good point. It might well be the very opposite of what the student had said; but the student was so relieved to find that he was not being cut to pieces that he was really impressed by the brilliance of what he was told he *had* said. On the other hand, when a faculty member got up – faculty members had the right to get up at any time, having interspersed themselves among the students, and at that time Joan Robinson stood up and attempted to argue with him – he simply cut their heads off. No matter how ingenious what they said was, he would make nonsense of it. And that, again, flattered the students, because they had been told that they were really incisive and then somebody they knew was really clever was reduced to rubble before their eyes. That was a doubly flattering thing. I think this has something to do with the various well-known reactions to Keynes as a personality. When he was out of the public eye, he could be extremely kind and charming, and could make somebody feel glad to be alive. On the other hand, when the chips were really down, he could be quite ruthless in the way he dealt with people.

RICHARD KAHN (1975, p. 32)

Keynes often used to remark to me that he enjoyed the advantage of waking up every morning like a new-born babe, entirely uncommitted to what he had thought or advocated previously. This is why he has so often been charged with inconsistency. The fact is that he did not resist a change of attitude, whether it was due to a change in the situation, or to the development of his own thinking, partly under the influence of other economists.

FLORENCE ADA KEYNES (1950, p. 64)

Our children had their own nursery routine but were with us a great deal and loved to be allowed to take their small part in entertaining visitors. Maynard specially enjoyed coming down to lunch and listening to grown-up conversation. Sometimes it was necessary to remind him that he would not be expected to join in the talk himself. He accepted the situation but remarked sadly that it would be 'a great drawback'. Once when his father pointed out to him that he had not behaved quite so well in company as a few days previously, he excused himself by pleading that on the earlier occasion he had been preparing himself for it for days and could not always make such an effort. He never failed to be ready with an excuse or an argument in support of his own view.

GEOFFREY KEYNES (1975, p. 26)

All my young days were lived under the shadow of a much more intellectual and forceful character in the person of my elder brother – not that he was ever unkind or even domineering; the division was the natural result of a situation where the elder was leading not so much by virtue of a few years between them, but rather by inborn advantages of mind and body. We were not close friends and my view of him was rather that of an eminent acquaintance to whom I looked up as a superior and rather distant being.

DOUGLAS LEPAN (1979, p. 91)

His nature was protean, and his range of expression. He could be magisterial, analytic, scornful, withering, contemptuous, insinuating, persuasive. But as he lifted his head to speak of 'the sweet breath of justice', I was reminded of the sweetness and youthfulness I had noticed in this expression that first evening in Hall when I was sitting beside him. There was something cherubic, almost seraphic, about his smile. And there was something else that is difficult to speak about, the word has been so debased. His charm.

JAMES MEADE (1944–46, p. 251)

He was the greatest genius I ever met. His personal magnetism for young men, including myself, was unequalled. His charm, artistry and personality are such as I have never met in anyone else. He combined the scientist, artist and human moralist and man of affairs in a unique manner.

A.F.W. PLUMPTRE (1947, pp. 367–8)

He is, in many ways, the best teacher I ever had: he always took pains to discuss our written work in detail and to make us talk about it. He would choose subjects that were not too far beyond us; often they would involve examination of some limited but important points in the theory of value. He talked easily and, almost more important, he was easy to talk to. Not so Keynes! His overwhelming brilliance made interruption undesirable and argument almost out of question.

LIONEL ROBBINS (1971, p. 193)

How can one describe for a future age the sources of this astonishing ascendancy? It goes without saying that Keynes was one of the foremost economists of his age: whether you agreed with him or not, you could not deny the power and vividness of his analysis or his strong sense of quantitative proportions. But there were other economists, not many it is true, with accomplishments no less considerable. There was, however, only one Keynes. What distinguished him rather and made him stand out above all his generation were more general qualities of mind and character: the swiftness of his thought and perceptions; the cadences of his voice and his prose style; his idealism and moral fervour; above all, the life-enhancing quality of his presence – as someone, I think it was Sir Roy Harrod, once said, when he came into a room we all cheered up. If I search about my mind for parallels, I can think of none more apt than the description in the *Symposium* by Alcibiades of the personal influence of Socrates – the magician who held you entranced, even against your judgment and your will. It would be false, however, to depict him as a paragon of all the virtues. His advice was by no means always right; his judgment could be faulty and his action rash. He was sometimes arrogant. He was often impatient and quick-tempered. When roused he could be more devastatingly rude than any man I have known. But he was also kind and ready to forgive. If convicted of offence, there was no one who could better make the *amende honorable*. If convicted of error, there was no one more willing to liquidate the invested intellectual capital of the past. I have known genius of purer quality – there was considerably less of earthy alloy for instance in G.H. Hardy. But, all in all, I would certainly regard Maynard Keynes as the most remarkable man I have ever met.

AUSTIN ROBINSON (1947, p. 1)

For more than any man in our times Keynes was, not indeed in a chameleon sense all things to all men, but in a truer sense many things to many men. His tastes were catholic, and he had the gift of achieving a knowledge of many subjects to a level that made him the respected confidant of those that professed it. With philosophers, mathematicians, historians, bibliophiles, with the critics and exponents of modern painting and of the ballet, just as truly as with economists, financiers, civil servants and politicians, he could speak on a ground of equality of knowledge and of understanding. And because of this, what one man saw in Maynard Keynes was likely to be something different from what another might see.

JOAN ROBINSON (1975, p. 128)

His own mood often swung from left to right. Capitalism was in some ways repugnant to him but Stalinism was much worse. In his last years, certainly, the right predominated. When I teased him about accepting a peerage he replied that after sixty one had to become respectable. But his basic view of life was aesthetic rather than political. He hated unemployment because it was stupid and poverty because it was ugly. He was disgusted by the commercialism of modern life. (It is true that he enjoyed making money for his College and for himself but only as it did not take up too much time.) He indulged in an agreeable vision of a world where economics has ceased to be important and our grandchildren can begin to lead a civilised life. But in that vision there is room for a rich man to enjoy his wealth in a civilised manner.

BERTRAND RUSSELL (1967, p. 72)

Keynes's intellect was the sharpest and clearest that I have ever known. When I argued with him, I felt that I took my life in my hands, and I seldom emerged without feeling something of a fool. I was sometimes inclined to feel that so much cleverness must be incompatible with depth, but I do not think this feeling was justified.

JOSEPH A. SCHUMPETER (1946, pp. 503–4)

In general, there is something inhuman about human machines that fully use every ounce of their fuel. Such men are mostly cold in their personal relations, inaccessible, preoccupied. Their work is their life, no other interests exist for them, or only interests of the most superficial kind. But Keynes was the exact opposite of all this – the pleasantest fellow you can think of; pleasant, kind, and cheerful in the sense in which precisely those people are pleasant, kind, and cheerful who have nothing on their minds and whose one principle it is never to allow any pursuit of theirs to degenerate into work. He was affectionate. He was always ready to enter with friendly zest into the views, interests, and troubles of others. He was generous, and not only with money. He was sociable, enjoyed conversation, and shone in it. And contrary to a widely spread opinion, he could be *polite*, polite with an old-word *punctilio* that costs time. For instance, he would refuse to sit down to his lunch, in spite of telegraphic and telephonic expostulation, until his guest, delayed by fog in the Channel, put in appearance at 4 p.m.

LYTTON STRACHEY, LETTER TO LEONARD WOOLF, 15 FEBRUARY 1905 (STRACHEY, 2005, p. 51)

There can be no doubt that we are friends. His conversation is extraordinarily alert and very amusing. He sees at least as many things as I do – possibly more. He's interested in people to a remarkable degree. N.B. He doesn't seem to be in anything aesthetic, though his taste is good. His presence in character is really complete. He analyses with amazing persistence and brilliance. I never met so active a brain. (I believe it's more *active* than either Moore's or Russell's). His feelings are charming, and, as is natural, in perfect taste.

LYTTON STRACHEY, TO THE APOSTLES, 25 FEBRUARY 1905 (IN HOLROYD, 1994, p. 109)

For it is one of his queer characteristics that one often wants, one cannot tell why, to make a malicious attack on him, and that, when the time comes, one refrains, one cannot tell why. His sense of values, and indeed all his feelings, offer the spectacle of a complete paradox. He is a hedonist and a follower of Moore; he is lascivious without lust; he is an Apostle without tears.

LEONARD WOOLF (1960, p. 144)

Maynard's mind was incredibly quick and supple, imaginative and restless; he was always thinking new and original thoughts, particularly in the field of events and human behaviour and in the reaction between events and men's actions. He had the very rare gift of being as brilliant and effective in practice as he was in theory, so that he could outwit a banker, business man, or Prime Minister as quickly and gracefully as he could demolish a philosopher or crush an economist. It was these gifts which enabled him to revolutionize economic theory and national economic and financial policy and practice, and to make a considerable fortune by speculation and a considerable figure in the City and in the world which is concerned with the patronage or production of the arts, and particularly the theatre and the ballet. But most people who knew him intimately and his mind in shirtsleeves rather than public uniform would agree that there were in him some streaks of intellectual wilfulness and arrogance which often led him into surprisingly wrong and perverse judgments. To his friends he was a lovable character and these faults or idiosyncracies were observed and discounted with affectionate amusement.

VIRGINIA WOOLF, EXTRACTS OF HER DIARY (1977–1984)

He is like quicksilver on a sloping board – a little inhuman, but very kindly, as inhuman people are. (20 January 1915)

Went to Charleston for the night; & had a vivid sight of Maynard by lamplight – like a gorged seal, double chin, ledge of red lip, little eyes, sensual, brutal, unimaginative . . . (26 September 1920)

Maynard, besides being our greatest living economist, has a dancer for mistress, & is now preparing to stage a Mozart ballet, with 13 nimble dancers; interviews the Coliseum Manager; is an expert at contracts; knows the points of dancers, & can tell you all about the amours at the Imperial academy at Petersburg. (6 September 1922)

He has a queer swollen eel like look, not very pleasant. But his eyes are remarkable, & as I truly said when he gave me some pages of his new book [*A Tract on Monetary Reform*] to read, the process of mind there displayed is as far ahead of me as Shakespeare. (11 September 1923)

He is finer looking now; not with us pompous or great: simple, with his mind working always, on Russian, Bolshevists, glands, genealogies; always the proof of a remarkable mind when it overflows thus vigorously into byepaths. (21 April 1928)

M. adroit & supple & full of that queer imaginative ardour about history, humanity; able to explain flints & the age of man from some book he has read. (12 August 1934)

Maynard read a very packed profound & impressive paper ['My early beliefs'] so far as I could follow, about Cambridge youth; their philosophy; its consequences; Moore; what it lacked; what it gave. The beauty & unworldiness of it. I was impressed by M. & felt a little flittery & stupid. (12 September 1938)

Which of our friends will interest posterity most? Maynard? ... He is now supreme, mounted on his sick throne, a successful man – farmer, bursar, a man of business, he called himself, applying for petrol. A heavy man with a thick moustache. A moralist. As interested in Patsy the black dog with the bald patch as in Europe. (6 January 1940)

Bibliography

1. WORKS BY JOHN MAYNARD KEYNES

The following bibliography includes all Keynes's books, book chapters, pamphlets and articles, including obituaries, reviews and published radio programmes, excluding columns such as 'Finance and investment', 'Events of the week', 'Life and politics', and a certain number of anonymous contributions. In most cases, only the first edition has been included. Regarding other types of documents, such as open letters to newspapers, official documents composed by Keynes, memoranda, notes and commentaries, speeches, interviews and lectures, only passages quoted or mentioned in this book have been reproduced in this bibliography. The reader will find an exhaustive list of these documents in Volume 30 of the *Collected Writings of John Maynard Keynes*. For each bibliographical entry reproduced here, the reader is directed to where such entries can be found.

Concerning the Keynes archives, again only documents quoted or mentioned in this book have been given. Each entry is followed by the mention KP, followed by the archive number. A title in square brackets has been added to an untitled paper. Documents extending over several years, such as correspondences, have been regrouped and placed before the chronological list of Keynes's writings. Several texts are found in other archives, listed below. Regarding the chronological list, for each year, books, book chapters and pamphlets have been mentioned first; the other documents have been classified by chronological order, as far as possible.

Abbreviations

BL: British Library.
CHA: Charleston Papers, King's College Library, Cambridge.
JMK: *The Collected Writings of John Maynard Keynes*, London: Macmillan, 1971–1989, 30 volumes.
JRP: Joan Robinson Papers, King's College, Cambridge.
JTS: J.T. Sheppard Papers, King's College, Cambridge.
KP: Keynes Papers, King's College Library, Cambridge.
SP: Strachey Papers, British Library.

Archival Documents not Included in the Chronological List

L/42: Correspondence and related papers on a miscellany of academic and business issues, 1942 January–September, December.
PP/20A: 2 lists of initials and names, 1901–15, unidentified statistics, 1906–15.
PP34: Diary, 4–26 November 1894 and 16 Feb–18 April 1896, with, at back, lists of i) holiday destinations [18]84–99 ii) London theatre productions, 1894–1900 and iii) books read, some with dates of reading, 1898–1900.

PP/35: Diary, 5 June–21 December 1899.

PP/43: John Neville Keynes's holiday diaries, 1895–1902.

PP/45: Correspondence:

    PP/45/168: John Neville Keynes and Florence Ada (parents).

    PP/45/190: Lydia Lopokova (wife).

    PP/45/316: Lytton Strachey.

    PP/45/321: Bernard Swithinbank.

PP/72: Correspondence relating to the Contemporary Art Society.

PP/73: Correspondence concerning the London Artists' Association.

PP/77: Correspondence concerning Keynes's work as a trustee of National Gallery.

PP/84: Correspondence as Chairman of the Council for the Encouragement of Music and the Arts (C.E.M.A.), 1941–46.

PP/88: Condolence letters received by Florence Ada Keynes on John Maynard Keynes's death, orders of services at Westminster Abbey, 2 May 1946 and King's College Chapel, 4 May 1946, and two letters 1948.

SE/11: Ledgers, completed by Keynes, of his personal speculations in stocks and currency, 1912–45.

TP/1/1: Discursive correspondence concerning the *Treatise on Probability*, 1909–22.

TP/4: Reports to the electors to fellowships on Keynes's 1907 dissertation, 1908, by A.N. Whitehead, W.E. Johnson and A.C. Pigou, with same by Whitehead and Johnson for 1909 submission, 1909.

UA/6: Autograph manuscripts notes and typescripts of lectures given by Keynes in the Faculty of Economics and Politics, 1909–1923. Some lectures given between 1912 and 1914 are reproduced in JMK 12, pp. 690–783.

Chronological List of Keynes's Writings

1899-1 [date uncertain]. Untitled essay concerning the achievements of Great Britain under Queen Victoria; KP, PP/31/7.

1900-1. 'The character of the Stuarts: how far was it responsible for their misfortunes?', 24 November; KP, PP/31/3.

1900-2 [date uncertain]. 'The difference between East and West: will they ever disappear?', November; KP, PP/31/4.

1900-3 [date uncertain]. 'The English national character'; KP, PP/31/9.

1901-1. 'Cromwell', 14 June; KP, PP/31/5.

1901-2. [date uncertain]. 'What are the prospects of European peace at the present time?'; KP, PP/31/15.

1902-1. 2 essays on Bernard of Cluny, one read to the Eton Literary Society, 3 May; KP, PP/33.

1903-1. 2 drafts, 1 incomplete, of an essay on Peter Abelard. Written Christmas Vacation 1902–03. Read to King's College Appenine Society, Lent Term; KP VA/16.

1903-2. Essay on Time, read at King's College Parrhesiasts Society, 8 May; KP, UA/17.

1903-3. 'Shall we write filth packets?', read to the Apostles Society between February and December; KP, UA/19/1.

1903-4. Philosophy lecture notes. Lent Term. 1. Modern Ethics, given by G.E. Moore; KP, UA/1/1.

1903-5. Philosophy lecture notes. Lent Term. 2. Metaphysics, given by J.E. McTaggart; KP, UA/1/2.

1903-6. '*The Cambridge Modern History*. Vol. 7. *The United States*, Cambridge University Press, 1903', *Cambridge Review*, 5 November; JMK 11, 502–7.

1904-1. ['Beauty'], read to the Apostles Society, 30 April; KP, UA/19/3.

1904-2. 'The political doctrines of Edmund Burke', written Summer–Autumn. Winner of the University Members Prize; KP, UA/20/3.

1904-3. ['Ethics in relation to conduct'], read to the Apostles Society, 23 January; KP, UA/19/2.

1905-1. 'Miscellanea ethica', Written 31 July–19 September; KP, UA/21.

1905-2. 'A theory of beauty', read to the G.L. Dickinson Society on 5 October and to the Apostles Society on 5 May 1912; KP, UA/23/2.

1905-3. 'Modern civilisation', read to the Apostles Society, 28 October; KP, UA/22.

1906-1. 'Jevons, H. Stanley. *Essays on Economics*, London: Macmillan, 1906', *Cambridge Review*, 8 February; JMK 11, 507–9.

1906-2. 'Shall we write melodrama?', read to the Apostles Society, 3 February; KP, UA/25.

1906-3. 'Egoism', read to the Apostles Society, 24 February 1906; KP, UA/26.

1907-1. 'Principles of probability', submitted as Fellowship Dissertation to King's College, December; KP, TP/A/1–2.

1908-1. '*A Study in Social and Industrial Problems*, compiled by Edward G. Howarth and Mona Wilson, London: J.M. Dent, 1907', *Journal of the Royal Statistical Society*, **71**, 31 March, 215–7; JMK 11, 174–7. [Keynes records in a notebook this title as his first published article; he received £1/6/3d]

1908-2. 'Board of Trade index numbers of real wages: Note by JMK', *Economic Journal*, **18**, September, 472–3; JMK 11, 178–9.

1908-3. 'Prince Henry or Prince Rupert?', read to the Apostles Society, 28 November; KP, UA/30.

1908-4. 'Principles of probability', submitted as Fellowship Dissertation to King's College, 2 vols., December; KP, MM/6.

1908-5. 'Board of Trade index numbers of real wages: reply to G. Udny Yule's comment', *Economic Journal*, **18**, December, 655–7; JMK 11, 180–82.

1909-1. 'Recent economic events in India', *Economic Journal*, **19**, March, 51–67; JMK 11, 1–22.

1909-2. ['Science and art'], read to the Apostles Society, 20 February; KP, UA/32.

1909-3. '*Die geographische Verteilung der Getreidepreise in Indien von 1861 bis 1905*, von Th. H. Engelbrecht, Berlin, Paul Parey, 1908', *Journal of the Royal Statistical Society*, **72**, 31 March, 139–40; JMK 11, 22–3.

1909-4. 'The method of index numbers with special reference to the measurement of general exchange value', written in April, winner of the Adam Smith prize; JMK 11, 49–156.

1909-5. 'India during 1907–8', *Economist*, **69**, 3 July, 11–12; JMK 15, 34–8.

1909-6. 'Can we consume our surplus? or The influence of furniture on love', read to the Apostles Society; KP, UA/34.

1910-1. 'Great Britain's foreign investments', *New Quarterly*, February, 37–53; JMK 15, 44–59.

1910-2. '*Éléments de la théorie des probabilités*, by Émile Borel, Paris, Librairie scientifique A. Hermann et fils, 1909', *Journal of the Royal Statistical Society*, **73**, February, 171–2; JMK 11, 182–3.

1910-3. Letter sent to *The Times*, 6 June, not published; JMK 11, 186–8.

1910-4. '*A First Study of the Influence of Parental Alcoholism on the Physique and Ability of the Offspring*, by Ethel M. Elderton with the assistance of Karl Pearson, London, Dulau, 1910', *Journal of the Royal Statistical Society*, **73**, July, 769–73; JMK 11, 189–96.

1910-5. 'Webb, M. de P. *The Rupee Problem, a Plea for a Definite Currency Policy for India*, Karachi, 1910', *Economic Journal*, **20**, September, 438–40; JMK 11, 23–6.

1910-6. 'Wicksteed, Philip H. *The Common Sense of Political Economy*, London, Macmillan, 1910', *Hibbert Journal*, **9**, October, 215–8; JMK 11, 509–14.

1910-7. Letter to the Editor, *Journal of the Royal Statistical Society*, **74**, December; JMK 11, 196–205.

1910-8. ['On the principle of organic unity'], read to the Apostles Society; reread 22 January 1921; KP, UA/35.

1911-1. Letter to the Editor, *The Times*, 16 January, not published; JMK 11, 206–7.

1911-2. 'The principal averages and the laws of error which lead to them', *Journal of the Royal Statistical Society*, **74**, February, 322–31; JMK 11, 159–73.

1911-3. Letter to the Editor, *Journal of the Royal Statistical Society*, **74**, February; JMK 11, 207–16.

1911-4. '*Wahrscheinlichkeitsrechnung und ihre Anwendung auf Fehlerausgleichung, Statistik, und Lebensversicherung*, by Emanuel Czuber, Second edition, 2 vols, Leipzig, B.G. Teubner, 1908, 1910', *Journal of the Royal Statistical Society*, **74**, May, 643–7; JMK 11, 562–7.

1911-5. '*Publications Issued by and in Preparation for the National Monetary Commission of the United States*, Washington, 1910–11', *Journal of the Royal Statistical Society*, **74**, July, 841–6; JMK 11, 367–74.

1911-6. 'Fisher, Irving. *The Purchasing Power of Money: Its Determination and Relation to Credit, Interest and Crisis*, New York, Macmillan, 1911', *Economic Journal*, **21**, September, 393–8; JMK 11, 375–81.

1911-7. 'Morrison, Sir Theodore. *The Economic Transition in India*, London, John Murray, 1911', *Economic Journal*, **21**, September, 426–31; JMK 11, 27–33.

1912-1. 'Jevons, W. Stanley. *Theory of Political Economy*, fourth edition, edited by H. Stanley Jevons, London, Macmillan, 1911', *Economic Journal*, **22**, March, 78–80; JMK 11, 515–6.

1912-2. '*Report upon the Operations of the Paper Currency Department of the Government of India during the Year 1910–11*, Calcutta, 1911', *Economic Journal*, **22**, March, 145–7; JMK 11, 33–6.

1912-3. '*Report of the National Monetary Commission of the United States*, Senate document no. 243, 62–2, Washington, Government Printing Office, 1912', *Economic Journal*, **22**, March, 150–51; JMK 11, 381–2.

1912-4. '*Report by the Committee on Irish Finance*, Cd. 6153, H.M.S.O. 1912; *Government of Ireland Bill: Outline of Financial Provisions*, Cd. 6154, H.M.S.O. 1912; *Return Showing the Debt Incurred for Purely Irish Purposes*, H. of C. 110, H.M.S.O. 1912', *Economic Journal*, **22**, September, 498–502; JMK 11, 516–21.

1912-5. 'Chen, Huan-Chang. *The Economic Principles of Confucius and his School*, 2 vols, Columbia University Studies, New York, Longmans, 1911', *Economic Journal*, **22**, December, 584–88; JMK 11, 521–7.

1912-6. 'McIlraith, James W. *The Course of Prices in New Zealand; Report of Commission on the Cost of Living in New Zealand, together with Minutes of Proceedings and Evidence*, Wellington Government Printing Office, 1911', *Economic Journal*, **22**, December, 595–8; JMK11, 221–25.

1912-7. '[Board of Trade] *Tables Showing for Each of the Years 1900–1911 the Estimated Value of the Imports and Exports of the United Kingdom at the Prices Prevailing in 1900*, Cd. 6314, HMSO 1912', *Economic Journal*, **22**, December, 630–31; JMK 11, 219–21.

1912-8. '*Report of the Commissioners of Inland Revenue for the Year Ended 31st March 1912*, Cd. 6344, H.M.S.O., 1912', *Economic Journal*, **22**, December, 632–3; JMK 11, 527–8.

1912-9. '*Report of the Mint, 1911*, Cd. 6362, HMSO 1912', *Economic Journal*, **22**, December, 633–4; JMK 11, 382.

1912-10. '*Calcul des probabilités*, par H. Poincaré, Deuxième édition, Paris, Gauthier-Villars, 1912; *Calcul des probabilités*, par Louis Bachelier, Vol. I, Paris, Gauthier-Villars, 1912; *Le calcul de probabilités et ses applications*, par E. Carvallo, Paris, Gauthiers-Villars, 1912; *Wahrscheinlichkeitsrechnung*, by A. A Markoff, Leipzig, Teubner, 1912', *Journal of the Royal Statistical Society*, **76**, December, 113–6; JMK 11, 567–73.

1912-11. '*Ueber das Geschechtsverhälnis bie Zwillingsgeburten*, by Kazimierz J. Horowicz, Göttingen, E.A. Huth, 1912', *Journal of the Royal Statistical Society*, **76**, December, 116–7; JMK 11, 573–4.

1913-1. *Indian Currency and Finance*, London: Macmillan; JMK 1.

1913-2. '*Departmental Committee on Matters Affecting Currency of the British West African Colonies and Protectorates. Report*, Cd. 6426, 1912; *Minutes of Evidence*, Cd. 6427, HMSO 1912', *Economic Journal*, **23**, March, 146–7; JMK 11, 383–4.

1913-3. 'Barbour, Sir David. *The Standard of Value*, London, Macmillan, 1912', *Economic Journal*, **23**, September, 390–93; JMK 11, 384–8.

1913-4. 'Hobson, J. A. *Gold, Prices, and Wages*, London, Methuen, 1913', *Economic Journal*, **23**, September, 393–8; JMK 11, 388–94.

1913-5. 'How far are bankers responsible for the alternations of crisis and depression?', paper presented to the Political Economy Club of London, 3 December; JMK 13, 2–14.

1914-1. '*Forty-Third Annual Report of the Deputy Master of the Mint, 1912*, Cd. 6991, HMSO 1913', *Economic Journal*, **24**, March, 152–7; JMK 11, 394–400.

1914-2. 'Fischel, Marcel-Maurice. *Le Thaler de Marie-Thérèse: étude de sociologie et d'histoire économique*, Paris, Giard et Brière, 1912', *Economic Journal*, **24**, June, 257–60; JMK 11, 529–33.

1914-3. Memorandum against the suspension of gold, 3 August; JMK 16, 7–15.

1914-4. The proper means for enabling discount operations to be resumed, Treasury memorandum, 5 August; JMK 16, 16–19.

1914-5. 'Currency expedients abroad', *Morning Post*, 11 August; JMK 16, 20–23.

1914-6. 'Mises, Ludwig von. *Theorie des Geldes und der Umlaufsmittel*, Munich, Duncker and Humblot, 1912; Bendixen, Friedrich. *Geld und Kapital*, Leipzig, Duncker und Humblot, 1912', *Economic Journal*, **24**, September, 417–19; JMK 11, 400–403.

1914-7. 'Innes, A. Mitchell. *What is Money?*, New York, Banking Law Journal, 1913', *Economic Journal*, **24**, September, 419–21; JMK 11, 404–6.

1914-8. 'War and the financial system, August 1914', *Economic Journal*, **24**, September, 460–86; JMK 11, 238–71.

1914-9. 'Wilhelm Lexis (1837–1914)', *Economic Journal*, **24**, September, 502–3; JMK 10, 317–18.

1914-10. 'Current topics – currency expedients abroad', *Economic Journal*, **24**, September, 503–9; JMK 11, 272–8.

1914-11. 'The cost of war to Germany: some expedients explained', *Morning Post*, 16 October; JMK 16, 37–9.

1914-12. 'The City of London and the Bank of England, August 1914', *Quarterly Journal of Economics*, **29**, November, 48–71; JMK 11, 278–98.

1914-13. 'The prospects of money, November 1914', *Economic Journal*, **24**, December, 610–34; JMK 11, 299–328.

1914-14. 'The trade of India in 1913–14', *Economic Journal*, **24**, December, 639–42; JMK 11, 36–40.

1915-1. Notes on French finance, memorandum, 6 January; JMK 16, 42–57.

1915-2. The Bank of England in relation to government borrowing and the necessity of a public loan, memorandum, 14 May; JMK 16, 96–105.

1915-3. 'The island of stone money', *Economic Journal*, **25**, June, 281–3; JMK 11, 406–9.

1915-4. A summary of the gold position, note, 19 August; JMK 16, 109.

1915-5. [The alternatives], memorandum, 23 August; JMK 16, 110–15.

1915-6. 'The works of Bagehot', *Economic Journal*, **25**, September, 369–75; JMK 11, 533–41.

1915-7. 'The economics of war in Germany', *Economic Journal*, **25**, September, 443–52; JMK 11, 332–44.

1915-8. The financial prospect of this financial year, memorandum, 9 September; JMK 16, 117–25.

1915-9. With Florence Ada Keynes, 'An urgent appeal', The Cambridge War Thrift Committee, November; JMK 16, 141–3.

1915-10. A note on 'suspension of specie payments' and other methods of restricting gold export, 6 November; JMK 16, 143–9.

1915-11. 'The Bank of England and the "Suspension of the Bank Act" at the outbreak of war', *Economic Journal*, **25**, December, 565–8; JMK 11, 329–30.

1916-1. Letter to the Editor, *Daily Chronicle*, 6 January; JMK 16, 157–61. [signed 'Politicus']

1916-2. Statement to the Holborn Local Tribunal claiming exemption from military service on the grounds of conscientious objection, 28 February; KP, PP/7.

1916-3. Notes for a talk to the Board of Admiralty, 15 March; JMK 16, 184–8.

1916-4. 'Face the facts', *War and Peace*, April; JMK 16, 179–84. [signed 'Politicus']

1916-5. 'Frederick Hillersdon Keeling (1886–1916)', *Economic Journal*, **26**, September, 403–4; JMK 10, 319–20.

1916-6. The financial dependance of the United Kingdom on the United States of America, memorandum, 10 October; JMK 16, 197–8.

1916-7. 'Our financial position in America' and 'Report to the Chancellor of the Exchequer of the British members of the joint Anglo-French Financial Committee', 24 October; JMK 16, 198–209. [the first paper, signed by Reginald McKenna, is an introduction to the report].

1917-1. with W.J. Ashley. Memorandum on the effect of an indemnity, 2 January; JMK 16, 313–34.

1917-2. Memorandum on the probable consequences of abandoning the gold standard, 17 January; JMK 16, 215–22.

1917-3. 'New taxation in the United States', *Economic Journal*, **27**, December, 345–50; JMK 11, 345–50.

1917-4. 'Note on the issue of Federal Reserve notes in the United States', *Economic Journal*, **27**, December, 565–7; JMK 11, 409–10.

1918-1. Notes on an indemnity, memorandum, 31 October; JMK 16, 338–43.

1918-2. Memorandum by the Treasury on the indemnity payable by the enemy powers for reparation and other claims, December; JMK 16, 344–83.

1919-1. *The Economic Consequences of the Peace*, London: Macmillan; JMK 2.

1919-2. Report on financial conversations at Trèves, 15–16 January 1919, 20 January; JMK 16, 394–404.

1919-3. The treatment of inter-ally debt arising out of the war, memorandum, March; JMK 16, 420–28.

1919-4. Scheme for the rehabilitation of European credit and for financing relief and reconstruction, memorandum, and draft for an explanatory letter to be addressed by the Prime Minister to the President, M. Clemenceau, and Signor Orlando, April; JMK 16, 429–36.

1919-5. [Memorandum on alternative reparation proposals], June; JMK 16, 467–9.

1920-1. 'The present state of the foreign exchanges', *Manchester and District Bankers' Institute Magazine*, 16 January; JMK 17, 171–9.

1920-2. 'Hawtrey, R.G. *Currency and Credit*, London, Longmans Green, 1919', *Economic Journal*, **30**, September, 362–5; JMK 11, 411–14.

1920-3. 'Shirras, G. Findlay. *Indian Finance and Banking*, London, Macmillan, 1920', *Economic Journal*, **30**, September, 396–7; JMK 11, 40–42.

1920-4. 'The Peace of Versailles', *Everybody's Magazine*, September, 36–41; JMK 17, 51–77.

1920-5. 'Economic readjustment of Europe', *Farm and Home*, **41**, October; JMK 30, 4–7.

1920-6. 'America at the Paris Conference: A delegate's story', *Manchester Guardian*, **66**, 2 December; JMK 17, 91–8.

1921-1. *A Treatise on Probability*, London: Macmillan; JMK 8.

1921-2. Presidential address to the Apostle Society, 21 January; KP, UA/36.

1921-3. 'The economic consequences of the Paris "Settlement"', *Manchester Guardian*, 31 January and 1 February; JMK 17, 208–13.

1921-4. 'Dr Melchior, A Defeated Enemy', memoir read to the Bloomsbury Memoir Club, 3 February, first published in 1949; JMK 10, 389–429.

1921-5. 'The latest phase of reparations', *Manchester Guardian*, 5 March 1921; JMK 17, 221–5.

1921-6. 'Will the German mark be superseded? Reasons why permanent recovery is unlikely', *Manchester Guardian Commercial*, 24 March; JMK 18, 1–7.

1921-7. 'The proposed occupation of the Ruhr', *Manchester Guardian*, 26 and 27 April; JMK 17, 225–30.

1921-8. 'The new reparation proposals', *Manchester Guardian*, 6 May; JMK 17, 235–40.

1921-9. 'Europe's economic outlook. I. New reparations settlement: Can Germany pay?', *Sunday Times*, 21 August; JMK 17, 242–8.

1921-10. 'Europe's economic outlook. II. New reparations settlement: Effect on world trade', *Sunday Times*, 28 August; JMK 17, 249–56.

1921-11. 'Europe's economic outlook. III. The depression in trade', *Sunday Times*, 4 September; JMK 17, 259–65.

1921-12. 'Europe's economic outlook. IV. The earnings of labour', *Sunday Times*, 11 September; JMK 17, 265–71.

1921-13. 'Europe's economic outlook. V. Settlement of war debts', *Sunday Times*, 18 September; JMK 17, 272–8.

1921-14. 'London Group', Catalogue for the London Group Exhibition, Mansard Gallery, October; JMK 28, 296–7.

1921-15. 'Record depreciation of the mark. How speculators are more than paying the indemnity?', *Manchester Guardian*, 9 November; JMK 18, 8–10.

1921-16. 'Reparation payments. The suggested moratorium. Time to drop "make-believe"', *Sunday Times*, 4 December; JMK 17, 289–92.

1921-17. 'The civil service and financial control', lecture to the Society of Civil Servants; JMK 16, 296–307.

1922-1. *A Revision of the Treaty*, London: Macmillan; JMK 3.

1922-2. 'The stabilisation of the European exchanges: A plan for Genoa', *Manchester Guardian*, 6 April; JMK 17, 355–60.

1922-3. 'On the way to Genoa: What can the conference discuss and with what hope?', *Manchester Guardian*, 10 April; JMK 17, 370–76.

1922-4. 'The conference gets to work', *Manchester Guardian*, 12 April; JMK 17, 376–8.

1922-5. 'Currency reform at Genoa', *Manchester Guardian*, 15 April; 'The finance experts at Genoa', JMK 17, 380–83.

1922-6. 'Getting back to a gold standard', *Manchester Guardian*, 17 April; JMK 17, 384–6.

1922-7. '"Rubbish about milliards." The facts of the Russian reparation struggle', *Manchester Guardian*, 18 April; JMK 17, 386–90.

1922-8. 'A plan for a Russian settlement', *Manchester Guardian*, 19 April; JMK 17, 390–94.

1922-9. 'Editorial foreword', *Manchester Guardian Commercial*, Series of Supplements 'Reconstruction in Europe', no. 1, 20 April, 2; JMK 17, 351–2.

1922-10. 'The theory of the exchanges and "purchasing power parity"', *Manchester Guardian Commercial*, Series of Supplements 'Reconstruction in Europe', no. 1, 20 April, 6–8; JMK 4, 70–80, 164–9.

1922-11. 'The forward market in foreign exchanges', *Manchester Guardian Commercial*, Series of Supplements 'Reconstruction in Europe', no. 1, 20 April, 11–8; JMK 4, 94–115.

1922-12. 'A chapter of miscalculations at the conference', *Manchester Guardian*, 21 April; JMK 17, 394–7.

1922-13. Letter to the Editor, *New York Times Book Review and Magazine*, 23 April; JMK 17, 298–301.

1922-14. 'The reparation problem at Genoa', *Manchester Guardian*, 24 April; JMK 17, 398–402.

1922-15. 'The financial system of the Bolsheviks', *Manchester Guardian*, 26 April; JMK 17, 403–8.

1922-16. 'Financial results of Genoa', *Manchester Guardian*, 27 April; JMK 17, 408–10.

1922-17. 'The Russian rouble and the basis of future trade', *Manchester Guardian*, 1 May; JMK 17, 411–15.

1922-18. 'The proposals for Russia', *Manchester Guardian*, 4 May; JMK 17, 416–20.

1922-19. 'Reconstruction in Europe: An introduction', *Manchester Guardian Commercial*, Series of Supplements 'Reconstruction in Europe', no. 2, 18 May, 66–7; JMK 17, 426–33.

1922-20. 'The Genoa conference', *Manchester Guardian Commercial*, Series of Supplements 'Reconstruction in Europe', no. 3, 15 June, 132–3; JMK 17, 420–25.

1922-21. 'Russia', *Manchester Guardian Commercial*, Series of Supplements 'Reconstruction in Europe', no. 4, 6 July, 200–201; JMK 17, 434–40.

1922-22. 'Inflation as a method of taxation', *Manchester Guardian Commercial*, Series of Supplements 'Reconstruction in Europe', no. 5, 27 July, 268–9; JMK 4, 37–53, 161–3.

1922-23. 'The consequences to society of changes in the value of money', *Manchester Guardian Commercial*, Series of Supplements 'Reconstruction in Europe', no. 5, 27 July, 321–8; JMK 4, 1–28.

1922-24. 'A moratorium for war debts', *Westminster Gazette*, 5 August, 1, 3; JMK 18, 12–17.

1922-25. 'An economist's view of population', *Manchester Guardian Commercial*, Series of Supplements 'Reconstruction in Europe', no. 6, 17 August, 340–41; JMK 17, 440–46.

1922-26. 'Germany's difficulties. How the mark will go. Violent fluctuations expected', *Manchester Guardian*, 26 August; JMK 18, 27–8.

1922-27. 'German people terrified by uncertainty', *Manchester Guardian*, 28 August; JMK 18, 28–30.

1922-28. 'Is a settlement of the reparation question possible now?', *Manchester Guardian Commercial*, Series of Supplements 'Reconstruction in Europe', no. 8, 28 September, 462–4; JMK 18, 32–43.

1922-29. 'Speculation in the mark and Germany's balances abroad', *Manchester Guardian Commercial*, Series of Supplements 'Reconstruction in Europe', no. 8, 28 September, 480–82; JMK 18, 47–58.

1922-30. Notes for a speech at the 95 Club, Manchester, 25 October 1922; JMK 19, 1–6.

1922-31. Lectures to the Institute of Bankers, 15, 22 and 29 November, 5 December; JMK 19, 6–76.

1922-32. 'The stabilisation of the European exchanges – II', *Manchester Guardian Commercial*, Series of Supplements 'Reconstruction in Europe', no. 11, 7 December, 658–61; JMK 18, 70–84.

1922-33. 'The need for a constructive British policy', *Manchester Guardian*, 9 December; JMK 18, 88–93.

1922-34. Keynes's plan for settlement, 23 December; JMK 18, 97–9.

1922-35. 'Introduction to the series', Cambridge Economic Handbooks, Cambridge, Cambridge University Press; JMK 12, 856–7.

1923-1. *A Tract on Monetary Reform*, London: Macmillan; JMK 4. [Reprints, sometimes in revised form, of 1922–10, 1922–11, 1922–22 and 1922–23]

1923-2. 'The reparation crisis. Suppose the conference breaks down?', *Westminster Gazette*, 1 January; JMK 18, 105–8.

1923-3. 'The underlying principle', *Manchester Guardian Commercial*, Series of Supplements 'Reconstruction in Europe', no. 12, 4 January, 717–18; JMK 17, 448–54.

1923-4. 'Europe in decay', *The Times*, 8 January; JMK 18, 113–15.

1923-5. 'Mr Keynes on the economic outlook', speech to the Annual Meeting of the National Mutual, 29 January 1923, *The Times*, 1 February; JMK 12, 121–7.

1923-6. Letter to the Editor, *Times*, 14 February; JMK 19, 79.

1923-7. 'Jevons, H. Stanley. *The Future of the Exchange and the Indian Currency*, Oxford University Press, Indian Branch, 1922', *Economic Journal*, **33**, March, 60–65; JMK 11, 42–8.

1923-8. 'Some aspects of commodity markets', *Manchester Guardian Commercial*, Series of Supplements 'Reconstruction in Europe', no. 13, 29 March, 784–6; JMK 12, 255–65.

1923-9. 'Statement of policy of *The Nation and Athenaeum*', *Manchester Guardian*, 4 May; JMK 18, 122–3.

1923-10. 'Editorial foreword', *Nation and Athenaeum*, **33**, 5 May, 146; JMK 18, 123–6.

1923-11. 'British policy in Europe', *Nation and Athenaeum*, **33**, 5 May, 148–50; JMK 18, 129–33.

1923-12. 'The German offer and the French reply', *Nation and Athenaeum*, **33**, 12 May, 188–9; JMK 18, 136–9.

1923-13. Suggested German reply to Lord Curzon, 16 May; JMK 18, 143–5.

1923-14. 'Mr Bonar Law: a personal appreciation', *Nation and Athenaeum*, **33**, 26 May, 262; JMK 10, 33–6.

1923-15. 'The international loan', *Nation and Athenaeum*, **33**, 26 May, 264–6; JMK 18, 150–56.

1923-16. 'The diplomacy of reparations', *Nation and Athenaeum*, **33**, 16 June, 358–9; JMK 18, 166–70.

1923-17. 'Bank rate at four per cent', *Nation and Athenaeum*, weekly column 'Finance and Investment' **33**, 14 July, 502; JMK 19, 100–103.

1923-18. 'Mr Baldwin's prelude', *Nation and Athenaeum*, **33**, 21 July, 511–12; JMK 18, 182–6.

1923-19. 'Is a settlement of reparations possible?', *Nation and Athenaeum*, **33**, 28 July, 538–9.

1923-20. 'The American debt', *Nation and Athenaeum*, **33**, 4 August, 566–7; JMK 18, 193–7.

1923-21. 'Currency policy and unemployment', *Nation and Athenaeum*, **33**, 11 August, 611–12; JMK 19, 113–18.

1923-22. 'The legality of the Ruhr occupation', *Nation and Athenaeum*, **33**, 18 August, 631–2; JMK 18, 206–9.

1923-23. Anonymous note on the purchase policy of the National Galleries, *Nation and Athenaeum*, **33**, 18 August, 633; JMK 28, 310–11.

1923-24. 'Population and unemployment', *Nation and Athenaeum*, **34**, 6 October, 9–11; JMK 19, 120–24.

1923-25. 'Lord Grey's letter to *The Times*', *Nation and Athenaeum*, **34**, 13 October, 43; JMK 18, 217–19.

1923-26. 'How much has Germany paid?', *Nation and Athenaeum*, **34**, 27 October, 146–8; JMK 18, 224–30.

1923-27. 'The Liberal Party', *Nation and Athenaeum*, **34**, 17 November, 266; JMK 19, 143–6.

1923-28. 'A reply to Sir William Beveridge', *Economic Journal*, **33**, December, 476–86; JMK 19, 125–37.

1923-29. 'Free trade', *Nation and Athenaeum*, **34**, 24 November, 302–3, 1 December, 335–6; JMK 19, 147–56.

1923-30. 'Currency policy and social reform', notes for a speech at the National Liberal Club, 13 December; JMK 19, 158–62.

1924-1. 'Mr J.M. Keynes's speech', in *Unemployment in its national and international aspects, Studies and Reports*, series C (Unemployment), Geneva: International Labour Office; JMK 19, 182–93.

1924-2. 'Gold in 1923', *Nation and Athenaeum*, **34**, 2 February, 634–4; JMK 19, 164–8.

1924-3. 'The French press and Russia', *Nation and Athenaeum*, **34**, 9 February, 659; JMK 19, 168–72. [signed 'From a French correspondent']

1924-4. 'The prospects of gold', *Nation and Athenaeum*, **34**, 16 February, 692–3; JMK 19, 173–6.

1924-5. 'The speeches of the bank chairmen', *Nation and Athenaeum*, **34**, 23 February, 724–5; JMK 9, 188–92.

1924-6. 'France and the Treasury: M. Klotz's charges refuted. Mr Keynes's reply', *The Times*, 27 February; JMK 16, 407–13.

1924-7. 'A comment on Professor Cannan's article', *Economic Journal*, **34**, March, 65–8; JMK 11, 415–19.

1924-8. 'The franc', *Nation and Athenaeum*, **34**, 15 March, 823–4; JMK 19, 177–81.

1924-9. 'Newspaper finance', *Nation and Athenaeum*, **35**, 5 April, 6–7; JMK 19, 194–7.

1924-10. 'The experts' report: I. The Dawes report', *Nation and Athenaeum*, **35**, 12 April, 40–41; JMK 18, 235–41.

1924-11. 'The experts' reports: II. The McKenna report', *Nation and Athenaeum*, **35**, 19 April, 76–7; JMK 18, 241–6.

1924-12. 'The meaning of "bonus"', *Nation and Athenaeum*, **35**, 17 May, 218; JMK 12, 244–6.

1924-13. 'Investment policy for insurance companies', *Nation and Athenaeum*, **35**, 17 May, 226; vol. 12, 240–44.

1924-14. 'Does unemployment need a drastic remedy?', *Nation and Athenaeum*, **35**, 24 May, 235–6; JMK 19, 219–23.

1924-15. 'Discussion on monetary reform: Mr Keynes', *Economic Journal*, **34**, June, 169–76; JMK 19, 206–14. [discussion at the Royal Economic Society Annual Meeting, 14 April]

1924-16. 'Note on the above' [on D.H. Robertson, 'Note on the real ratio of international interchange'], *Economic Journal*, **34**, June, 291–2; JMK 11, 445–6.

1924-17. 'A drastic remedy for unemployment: reply to critics', *Nation and Athenaeum*, **35**, 7 June, 311–12; JMK 19, 225–31.

1924-18. 'The policy of the Bank of England', *Nation and Athenaeum*, **35**, 19 July, 500–501; JMK 19, 261–7.

1924-19. 'The policy of the Bank of England: reply', *Nation and Athenaeum*, **35**, 26 July, 500; JMK 19, 272–3.

1924-20. 'The London Conference and territorial sanctions', *Nation and Athenaeum*, **35**, 26 July, 527; JMK 18, 246–8.

1924-21. 'Wheat', *Nation and Athenaeum*, **35**, 26 July, 527–8; JMK 19, 273–5.

1924-22. 'Debt payments from ourselves to America and from Germany to the Allies', *Daily Herald*, 5 August; JMK 18, 261–2.

1924-23. 'Foreign investment and national advantage', *Nation and Athenaeum*, **35**, 9 August, 584–7; JMK 19, 275–84.

1924-24. 'Home versus foreign investment. Further suggestions for revision of trustee list', *Manchester Guardian Commercial*, 21 August; JMK 19, 285–8.

1924-25. 'Alfred Marshall (1842–1924)', *Economic Journal*, **34**, September, 311–72; JMK 10, 161–231.

1924-26. 'The Dawes scheme and the German loan', *Nation and Athenaeum*, **36**, 4 October, 7–9; JMK 18, 254–61.

1924-27. Notice on the movie 'Tess of the D'Urbervilles', *Nation and Athenaeum*, **36**, 11 October, 53; JMK 28, 316–17 [unsigned].

1924-28. 'Defaults by foreign governments', *Nation and Athenaeum*, **36**, 18 October, 130–31; JMK 19, 323.

1924-29. 'The balance of political power at the elections', *Nation and Athenaeum*, **36**, 8 November, 207–8; JMK 19, 325–7.

1924-30. 'Edwin Montagu', *Nation and Athenaeum*, **36**, 29 November, 322–3; JMK 10, 41–2.

1925-1. *The Economic Consequences of Mr Churchill*, London: Hogarth Press; JMK 9, 207–30. [expanded version of three articles published in the *Evening Standard*, 22, 23 and 24 July, under the heading 'Unemployment and Monetary Policy'].

1925-2. *A Short View of Russia*, London: Hogarth Press; JMK 9, 253–71.

1925-3. 'The inter-allied debts', *Nation and Athenaeum*, **36**, 10 January, 516–17; JMK 18, 264–8.

1925-4. 'Some tests for loans to foreign and colonial governments', *Nation and Athenaeum*, **36**, 17 January, 564–5; JMK 19, 328–33.

1925-5. 'The Balfour note and inter-allied debts', *Nation and Athenaeum*, **36**, 24 January, 575–6; JMK 9, 44–7.

1925-6. 'The return towards gold', *Nation and Athenaeum*, **36**, 21 February, 707–9; JMK 9, 192–200.

1925-7. 'The bank rate', *Nation and Athenaeum*, **36**, 7 March, 790–92; JMK 19, 333–7.

1925-8. 'The problem of the gold standard', *Nation and Athenaeum*, **36**, 21 March, 866–70; JMK 19, 337–44.

1925-9. 'Is sterling over-valued?', *Nation and Athenaeum*, **37**, 4 and 18 April, 28–30, 86; JMK 19, 349–54.

1925-10. Notes on fundamental terminology, for a lecture given on 25 April; JMK 29, 35–9.

1925-11. 'The gold standard', *Nation and Athenaeum*, **37**, 2 May, 129–30; JMK 19, 357–61.

1925-12. 'An American study of shares versus bonds as permanent investments', *Nation and Athenaeum*, **37**, 2 May, 157–8; JMK 12, 247–52.

1925-13. 'The gold standard: a correction', *Nation and Athenaeum*, **37**, 9 May, 169–70; JMK 19, 362–5.

1925-14. 'The committee on the currency', *Economic Journal*, **35**, June 299–304; JMK 19, 371–8.

1925-15. 'The gold standard act, 1925', *Economic Journal*, **35**, June, 312–13; JMK 19, 378–9.

1925-16. 'The arithmetic of the sterling exchange', *Nation and Athenaeum*, **37**, 13 June, 338; JMK 19, 379–82.

1925-17. 'Am I a Liberal?', *Nation and Athenaeum*, **37**, 8 and 15 August, 563–4, 587–8; JMK 9, 295–306.

1925-18. 'Our monetary policy: rejoinder to Lord Bradbury's recent article', *Financial News*, 18 August; JMK 19, 425–7.

1925-19. Letter to the Editor [on 'Freudian psycho-analysis'], *Nation and the Athenæum*, **35**, 29 August, 643–4; JMK 28, 392–3. [signed 'Siela']

1925-20. 'Discussion on the national debt: Mr J.M. Keynes', *Economic Journal*, **35**, September, 359–60; JMK 19, 367–8.

1925-21. 'The economic position in England', first of two lectures given in Moscow, 14 September; JMK 19, 434–7.

1925-22. 'The economic transition in England', second of two lectures given in Moscow, 15 September; JMK 19, 438–42.

1925-23. 'Soviet Russia – I, II, III', *Nation and Athenaeum*, **38**, 10 October, 39–40; 17 October, 107–8; 24 October, 139–40; JMK 9, 253–71.

1925-24. 'Relation of finance to British industry', *Manchester Guardian Commercial*, 15 October, 393; JMK 19, 442–7.

1926-1. *The End of Laissez-Faire*, London: Hogarth Press; JMK 9, 272–94.

1926-2. Editor, *Official Papers by Alfred Marshall*, London: Macmillan.

1926-3. 'The French Franc: an open letter to the French Minister of Finance (whoever he is or may be)', *Nation and Athenaeum*, **38**, 9 January, 515–17; JMK 9, 76–82.

1926-4. 'The French Franc: a reply to comments on "An open letter"', *Nation and Athenaeum*, **38**, 16 January, 544–5; JMK 19, 455–60.

1926-5. 'Wallis Budge, Sir E.A. *The Rise and Fall of Assyriology*, London Hopkinson 1925', *Nation and Athenaeum*, **38**, 16 January, 564; JMK 28, 287.

1926-6. 'Some facts and last reflections about the franc', *Nation and Athenaeum*, **38**, 30 January, 603–4; JMK 19, 460–65.

1926-7. 'Germany's coming problem: the prospects of the second Dawes year', *Nation and Athenaeum*, **38**, 6 February, 635–6; JMK 18, 271–6.

1926-8. 'Liberalism and labour', *Nation and Athenaeum*, **38**, 20 February, 707–8; JMK 9, 307–11.

1926-9. 'Broadcast the budget!', *Radio Times*, 26 February; JMK 19, 473–6.

1926-10. 'Francis Ysidro Edgeworth, 1845–1926', *Economic Journal*, **36**, March, 140–53; JMK 10, 251–66.

1926-11. 'Bagehot's *Lombard Street*', *Banker*, March, 210–16; JMK 19, 465–72.

1926-12. 'Trotsky on England', *Nation and Athenaeum*, **38**, 27 March, 884; JMK 10, 63–7.

1926-13. 'Coal: a suggestion', *Nation and Athenaeum*, **39**, 24 April, 91–2; JMK 19, 525–9.

1926-14. 'Back to the coal problem', *Nation and Athenaeum*, **39**, 15 May, 159; JMK 19, 534–7.

1926-15. 'The need of peace by negociation', *New Republic*, 19 May, 395; 'Reflections on the strike', JMK 19, 531–4.

1926-16. '*The Stock Exchange Official Intelligence for 1926*, London, Spottiswoode, 1926', *Nation and Athenaeum*, 39, 29 May, 214; JMK 12, 252–3.

1926-17. 'The control of raw materials by governments', *Nation and Athenaeum*, **39**, 12 June, 267–9; JMK 19, 546–52.

1926-18. Letter to the Editor, *Nation and Athenaeum*, **39**, 12 June, 316; JMK 19, 538–41.

1926-19. 'The first-fruits of the gold standard', *Nation and Athenaeum*, **39**, 26 June, 344–5; JMK 19, 552–6.

1926-20. Letter to the Editor, *Nation and Athenaeum*, **39**, 28 June, 381; JMK 19, 542.

1926-21. 'Mr Baldwin's qualms', *Nation and Athenaeum*, **39,** 10 July, 406–7; JMK 19, 559–63.

1926-22. 'The franc once more', *Nation and Athenaeum*, **39**, 17 July, 435–6; JMK 19, 563–7.

1926-23. 'A.A. Tschuprow (1873–1926)', *Economic Journal*, **36**, September, 517–8; JMK 10, 517–18.

1926-24. 'The progress of the Dawes scheme', *Nation and Athenaeum*, **39**, 11 September, 664–5; JMK 18, 277–82.

1926-25. 'The Autumn prospects for sterling: should the embargo on foreign loans be reimposed?', *Nation and Athenaeum*, **40**, 23 October, 104–5; JMK 19, 568–74.

1926-26. 'The position of the Lancashire cotton trade', *Nation and Athenaeum*, **40**, 13 November, 209–10; JMK 19, 578–85.

1926-27. 'The prospects of the Lancashire cotton trade', *Nation and Athenaeum*, **40**, 27 November, 291–2; JMK 19, 587–92.

1926-28. 'The Cotton Yarn Association', *Nation and Athenaeum*, **40**, 24 December, 443–5; JMK 19, 593–601.

1927-1. 'Liberalism and industry', in H.L. Nathan and H. Heathcote Williams (eds), *Liberal Points of View*, London: Ernest Benn, 205–19; JMK 19, 638–48.

1927-2. 'Clissold', *Nation and Athenaeum*, **40**, 22 January, 561–2; JMK 9, 315–20.

1927-3. 'McKenna on monetary policy', *Nation and Athenaeum*, **40**, 12 February, 651–3; JMK 9, 200–206.

1927-4. Letter to the Editor, *Nation and Athenaeum*, **40**, 19 February, 720–21; JMK 19, 661–4.

1927-5. 'Mr Churchill on the war', *Nation and Athenaeum*, **40**, 5 March, 754–6; JMK 10, 46–52.

1927-6. 'Are books too dear?', *Nation and Athenaeum*, **40**, 12 March, 786–8; JMK 19, 664–70.

1927-7. 'A note on economy', *Nation and Athenaeum*, **41**, 30 April, 103 and 21 May, 207–8; JMK 19, 671–5.

1927-8. 'The Colwyn Report on National Debt and Taxation', *Economic Journal*, **37**, June, 198–212; JMK 19, 675–94.

1927-9. Letter to the Editor, *Nation and Athenaeum*, **41**, 25 June, 410; JMK 28, 311–12. [signed 'Siela']

1927-10. 'The progress of reparations', *Nation and Athenaeum*, **41**, 16 July, 505–6; JMK 18, 282–7.

1927-11. 'The progress of the Cotton Yarn Association', *Nation and Athenaeum*, **41**, 27 August, 683–4; JMK 19, 610–14.

1927-12. 'Model form for statements of international balances', *Economic Journal*, **37**, September, 472–6; JMK 11, 446–51.

1927-13. 'Helfferich, Karl. *Money*. 2 vols. Translated from the German by L. Infield; edited with an introduction by T.E. Gregory, London, Benn, 1927', *Nation and Athenaeum*, **42**, 15 October, 94; JMK 11, 419–20.

1927-14. 'The retreat of the Cotton Yarn Association', *Nation and Athenaeum*, **42**, 19 November, 267–8; JMK 19, 622–7.

1927-15. 'Why Labour's surtax is bad finance?', *Evening Standard*, 22 November; JMK 19, 701–3.

1927-16. 'The British balance of trade, 1925–27', *Economic Journal*, **37**, December, 551–65; JMK 19, 704–22.

1928-1. *Réflexions sur le franc et sur quelques autres sujets*, Paris: Simon Kra. [French translations of 1926–3, 1926–4, 1926–6, 1927–5, 1927–8, 1927–10, 1927–16, 1928–1, 1928–2, 1928–3, 1928–7]

1928-2. 'The financial reconstruction of Germany', *Nation and Athenaeum*, **42**, 7 January, 531–2; JMK 18, 290–95.

1928-3. 'A personal note on Lord Oxford', *Nation and Athenaeum*, **42**, 25 February, 772–3; JMK 10, 37–40.

1928-4. 'Note on the British balance of trade', *Economic Journal*, **38**, March, 146–7; JMK 19, 722–3.

1928-5. 'Mr Churchill on rates and the liberal industrial inquiry', *Nation and Athenaeum*, **43**, 28 April, 99–100; JMK 19, 735–8.

1928-6. 'He's a relation of mine', *Nation and Athenaeum*, **43**, 28 April, 112; JMK 10, 60–62.

1928-7. 'The war debts', *Nation and Athenaeum*, **43**, 5 May, 131–1; JMK 9, 47–53.

1928-8. 'Assyria', *Nation and Athenaeum*, **43**, 12 May, 182–4; JMK 28, 289–9.

1928-9. 'Treasury and bank notes, conditions of amalgamation: an economist's criticism', *The Times*, 12 May; JMK 19, 742–9. [reprinted with a supplementary letter to *The Times* of 12 May as 'The amalgamation of the British note issues', *Economic Journal*, **38**, June, 321–8]

1928-10. 'The stabilisation of the franc', *Nation and Athenaeum*, **43**, 30 June, 416–7; JMK 9, 82–5.

1928-11. 'How to organise a wave of prosperity', *Evening Standard*, 31 July; JMK 19, 761–6.

1928-12. 'The French stabilisation law', *Economic Journal*, **38**, September, 490–94; JMK 19, 755–60.

1928-13. 'Crete and Greece in the Bronze Age', *Nation and Athenaeum*, **44**, 6 October, 20; JMK 28, 292–4.

1928-14. 'La production et la consommation de l'étain', *Recueil mensuel de l'Institut International du Commerce* (Brussels), **16**, 20 October, 1–4; JMK 12, 506–12.

1928-15. 'Benjamin Srong (1877–1928)', *Nation and Athenaeum*, **44**, 20 October, 96; JMK 10, 323.

1928-16. 'Mr McKenna's warning', *Britannie*, 2 November; JMK 19, 770–73.

1928-17. 'Mills, Frederick C. *The Behaviour of Prices*, New York, National Bureau of Economic Research, Publication no. 11, 1927', *Economic Journal*, **38**, December, 606–8; JMK 11, 225–8.

1929-1. With Hubert Henderson, *Can Lloyd George Do It? The Pledge Examined*, London: *Nation and Athenaeum*; JMK 9, 86–125.

1929-2. 'Is there enough gold? The League of Nations enquiry', *Nation and Athenaeum*, **44**, 19 January, 545–6; JMK 19, 775–80.

1929-3. 'The Lancashire Cotton Corporation', *Nation and Athenaeum*, **44**, 2 February, 607–8; JMK 19, 632–6.

1929-4. 'The bank rate: five-and-a-half per cent', *Nation and Athenaeum*, **44**, 16 February, 679–80; JMK 19, 796–9.

1929-5. 'The German transfer problem', *Economic Journal*, **39**, March, 1–7; JMK 11, 451–9.

1929-6. 'Warren, G.F. and Pearson, R.A. *Inter-Relationships of Supply and Prices*. Cornell University Agricultural Experiment Station, Ithaca, New York, 1928', *Economic Journal*, **39**, March, 92–5; JMK 11, 228–32.

1929-7. 'Mr Churchill on the peace', *Nation and Athenaeum*, **44**, 9 March, 782–3; JMK 10, 52–7.

1929-8. 'Mr. J.M. Keynes examines Mr. Lloyd George's pledge', *Evening Standard*, 19 March; JMK 19, 804–8.

1929-9. 'Professor Fisher discusses reparations problems with John M. Keynes', *New York Evening World*, 25 March; JMK 18, 313–18.

1929-10. 'A cure for unemployment', *Evening Standard*, 19 April; JMK 19, 808–12.

1929-11. 'Mr Snowden and the Balfour note', *Nation and Athenaeum*, **45**, 20 April, 67–8; JMK 18, 318–22.

1929-12. 'Allied debts and reparations', *Daily Express*, 22 April; JMK 18, 322–9.

1929-13. Letter to the Editor, *Evening Standard*, 30 April; JMK 19, 812–14.

1929-14. 'Great Britain and reparations', *Nation and Athenaeum*, **45**, 11 May, 190–91; JMK 18, 336–40.

1929-15. 'The Treasury contribution to the White paper', *Nation and Athenaeum*, **45**, 18 May, 227–8; JMK 19, 819–24.

1929-16. 'The reparation problem: a discussion: II. A rejoinder', *Economic Journal*, **39**, June, 179–82; JMK 11, 468–72.

1929-17. 'The report of the Young Committee', *Nation and Athenaeum*, **45**, 15 June, 359–61; JMK 18, 329–36.

1929-18. 'Proposed international bank and new U.S. policy are big ideas of Young debt plan', *Evening World*, 24 June; JMK 18, 342–6.

1929-19. 'Mr Keynes' views on the transfer problem: III. A reply by Mr Keynes', *Economic Journal*, **39**, September, 404–8; JMK 11, 475–80.

1929-20. 'The bank rate', *The Listener*, 2 October, 435; JMK 19, 834–8.

1929-21. 'A British view of the Wall Street slump', *New York Evening Post*, 25 October; JMK 20, 1–2.

1930-1. *A Treatise on Money*, London: Macmillan: vol. 1, *The Pure Theory of Money*; vol. 2: *The Applied Theory of Money*; JMK 5 and 6.

1930-2. 'The economic chaos of Europe', in J.A. Hammerton (ed.), *Harmsworth's Universal History of the World*, London: Educational Book, vol. 8, pp. 4905–16; JMK 11, 350–66.

1930-3. 'The question of high wages', *Political Quarterly*, 1, January–March, 110–24; JMK 20, 3–16.

1930-4. Evidence to the Committee on Finance and Industry (Macmillan Committee), 20, 21 and 28 February, 6 and 7 March; JMK 20, 38–157.

1930-5. 'Unemployment', *Listener*, 26 February, 361–2, 383; JMK 20, 315–25.

1930-6. 'Ramsey as an economist', *Economic Journal*, **40**, March, 153–4; JMK 10, 335–6.

1930-7. 'C.P. Sanger (1872–1930)', *Economic Journal*, **40**, March, 154–5; JMK 10, 324–5.

1930-8. 'The London Artists' Association: its origin and aims', *Studio*, **99**, March, 235–49; JMK 28, 297–307.

1930-9. 'The draft convention for financial assistance by the League of Nations', *Nation and Athenaeum*, **46**, 8 March, 756–7; JMK 20, 332–6.

1930-10. 'The draft convention for financial assistance by the League of Nations-II', *Nation and Athenaeum*, **46**, 15 March, 792–4; JMK 20, 337–41.

1930-11. 'The Stock Exchange Official Intelligence for 1930, London, Spottiswoode, 1930', *Nation and Athenaeum*, **47**, 19 April, 92; JMK 12, 253.

1930-12. 'A dupe as hero', *Nation and Athenaeum*, **47**, 3 May, 144–5; JMK 18, 348–50.

1930-13. 'The industrial crises', *Nation and Athenaeum*, **47**, 10 May, 163–4; JMK 20, 345–9.

1930-14. 'Arthur Balfour (1848–1930)', *Economic Journal*, **40**, June, 36–8; JMK 10, 43–5.

1930-15. 'A.F.R. Wollaston (1875–1930)', *Nation and Athenaeum*, **47**, 15 June, 345; JMK 10, 347–8.

1930-16. 'The future of the rate of interest', *The Index*, September; JMK 20, 390–99.

1930-17. 'Economic possibilities for our grandchildren', *Nation and Athenaeum*, **48**, 11 and 18 October, 36–7, 96–8; JMK 9, 321–32.

1930-18. 'Glasgow, George. *The English Investment Trust Companies*, London, Eyre & Spottiswoode, 1930', *Nation and Athenaeum*, **48**, 25 October, 142; JMK 12, 254.

1930-19. 'Sir Oswald Mosley's manifesto', *Nation and Athenaeum*, **48**, 13 December, 367; JMK 20, 473–6.

1930-20. 'The great slump of 1930', *Nation and Athenaeum*, **48**, 20 and 27 December, 402, 427–8; JMK 9, 126–34.

1930-21. 'Economist analyses year', *Christian Science Monitor*, 31 December; JMK 12, 647.

1931-1. *Essays in Persuasion*, London: Macmillan; with additions, JMK 9. [Extracts of 1919–1, 1922–1, 1923–1, 1925–1, 1925–2, 1926–1, 1929–1, 1930–1 and other articles]

1931-2. 'An economic analysis of unemployment', in Quincy Wright (ed.), *Unemployment as a World Problem*, Chicago: University of Chicago Press, 3–42; JMK 13, 343–67.

1931-3. 'Credit control', in E.R.A. Seligman (ed.), *The Encyclopaedia of Social Sciences*, London: Macmillan, vol. 4, 550–53; JMK 11, 420–27.

1931-4. 'Foreword', in Rupert Trouton (ed.), *Unemployment: Its Causes and their Remedies*, London: Hogarth; JMK 20, 487–8.

1931-5. 'Opening remarks as chairman; contribution to discussion', in Royal Institute of International Affairs (ed.), *The International Gold Problem: Collected Papers*, London: Oxford University Press, 18, 167, 186–90.

1931-6. 'The problem of unemployment, II', *Listener*, 14 January, 46–7; 'Saving and spending', JMK 9, 135–41.

1931-7. 'W.E. Johnson (1859–1931)', *The Times*, 15 January; JMK 10, 349–50.

1931-8. 'Clare College', *Nation and Athenaeum*, **48**, 17 January, 512–13; JMK 28, 416–21.

1931-9. 'Proposals for a revenue tariff', *New Statesman and Nation*, **1**, 7 March, 53; JMK 9, 231–8.

1931-10. 'Put the budget on a sound basis: a plea for lifelong free traders', *Daily Mail*, 13 March; JMK 20, 489–92.

1931-11. 'Economic notes on free trade: I. The export industries', *New Statesman and Nation*, **1**, 28 March, 175; JMK 20, 498–500.

1931-12. 'The Camargo Society', April; JMK 28, 318–20.

1931-13. 'Economic notes on free trade: II. A revenue tariff and the cost of living', *New Statesman and Nation*, **1**, 4 April, 211; JMK 20, 500–502.

1931-14. 'Economic notes on free trade: III. The reaction of imports on exports', *New Statesman and Nation*, **1**, 11 April, 242–3; JMK 20, 502–5.

1931-15. 'Plays and pictures: the Camargo Society', *New Statesman and Nation*, **1**, 11 April, 253; JMK 28, 9–10.

1931-16. 'The budget that wastes times', *Evening Standard*, 28 April; 'Mr Snowden's budget', JMK 20, 520–23.

1931-17. 'This income tax puzzle. Mr. J.M. Keynes "makes it plain"', *Evening Standard*, 30 April; JMK 20, 523–5.

1931-18. 'Some consequences of the economy report', *New Statesman and Nation*, **2**, 15 August, 189; JMK 9, 141–5.

1931-19. 'Notes on the situation', *New Statesman and Nation*, **2**, 29 August, 246; JMK 20, 596–8.

1931-20. 'A rejoinder' [reply to D.H. Robertson, 'Mr. Keynes' theory of money'], *Economic Journal*, **41**, September, 412–23; JMK 13, 219–36.

1931-21. Notes for a speech to Members of Parliament, 16 September; JMK 20, 607–11.

1931-22. 'We must restrict our imports', *Evening Standard*, 10 September; 'On the eve of gold suspension', JMK 9, 238–42.

1931-23. 'A gold conference', *New Statesman and Nation*, **2**, 12 September, 300; JMK 20, 598–603.

1931-24. 'The budget', *New Statesman and Nation*, **2**, 19 September, 299; 'The economy bill', JMK 9, 145–9.

1931-25. 'The future of the world', *Sunday Express*, 27 September; JMK 9, 245–9.

1931-26. 'Logic', *New Statesman and Nation*, **2**, 3 October, 407; 'Ramsey as a philosopher', JMK 10, 336–9.

1931-27. 'The pure theory of money: a reply to Dr Hayek', *Economica*, **11**, November, 387–97; JMK 13, 243–56.

1932-1. 'The world's economic crisis and the way to escape', in Walter Salter et al., *The World's Economic Crisis and the Way to Escape*, London: George Allen and Unwin, 71–88; JMK 21, 50–62.

1932-2. 'The consequences to the banks of the collapse of money values', *Vanity Fair*, January, 21–3; JMK 9, 150–58. [first, and shorter, version in 1931–1]

1932-3. 'The economic prospects 1932', lecture given at Hamburg, 8 January; JMK 21, 39–48.

1932-4. 'An end of reparations?', *New Statesman and Nation*, **3**, 16 January, 57–8; JMK 18, 366–9.

1932-5. 'Member bank reserves in the United States', *Economic Journal*, **42**, March, 27–31; JMK 11, 427–33.

1932-6. 'Saving and usury', *Economic Journal*, **42**, March, 135–7; JMK 29, 13–16.

1932-7. 'State planning', broadcast, 14 March; JMK 21, 84–92.

1932-8. 'Reflections on the sterling exchange', *Lloyds Bank Monthly Review*, April, 143–60; JMK 21, 63–82.

1932-9. 'This is a budget of excessive prudence. No disclosure of government policy on four vital issues', *Evening Standard*, 20 April; JMK 21, 102–7.

1932-10. 'The dilemma of modern socialism', *Political Quarterly*, **3**, April–June, 155–61; JMK 21, 33–48.

1932-11. 'A policy for Lausanne', *The Times*, 15 June; JMK 18, 373–6.

1932-12. 'World famous economist J.M. Keynes reviews Australia's position', *The Melbourne Herald*, 27 June; JMK 21, 94–100.

1932-13. 'Production costs: further comments on expert's report', *The Melbourne Herald*, 5 July; JMK 21, 100–2.

1932-14. 'A note on the long-term rate of interest in relation to the conversion scheme', *Economic Journal*, **42**, September, 415–23; JMK 21, 114–25.

1932-15. With D.H. MacGregor, A.C. Pigou, Walter Layton, Arthur Salter and J.C. Stamp, Letter to the Editor, *The Times*, 17 October; JMK 21, 138–9.

1932-16. With D.H. MacGregor, A.C. Pigou, Walter Layton, Arthur Salter and J.C. Stamp, Letter to the Editor, *The Times*, 21 October; JMK 21, 139–40.

1932-17. 'Pros and cons of tariffs', *Listener*, 30 November, 769–10, 783; JMK 21, 204–10.

1932-18. 'Keynes's fundamental equations: a note', *American Economic Review*, **22**, December, 691–2; JMK 5, 330–31.

1932-19. 'Enjoying Russia', *New Statesman and Nation*, **4**, 10 December, 770; JMK 28, 14–16.

1932-20. 'This must be the end of war debts', *Daily Mail*, 12 December; 'A British view of Mr Hoover's note', JMK 18, 382–6.

1932-21. 'The World Economic Conference 1933', *New Statesman and Nation*, **4**, 24 December, 825–6; JMK 21, 210–16.

1933-1. *Essays in Biography*, London: Macmillan; with additions, JMK 10.

1933-2. *The Means to Prosperity*, London: Macmillan; JMK 9, 335–66.

1933-3. 'A monetary theory of production', in G. Clausing (ed.), *Der Stand und die nächste Zukunft der Konjunkturforschung: Festschrift für Arthur Spiethoff*, Munich: Duncker & Humblot, 123–5; JMK 13, 408–11.

1933-4. 'Mr Lloyd George: a fragment', in 1933–1, 31–41; JMK 10, 20–26.

1933-5. 'Robert Malthus, the first of the Cambridge economists', in 1933-1, 95–149; JMK 10, 71–103. [paper read and revised on various occasions since 1914]

1933-6. 'A short anthology' [about Frank Ramsey] in 1933-1, 301–10; JMK 10, 339–40.

1933-7. 'Hagstroem, K.-G. *Les préludes antiques de la théorie des probabilités*. Fritzes, Stockholm, 1932', *Journal of the Institute of Actuaries*, **1**, January, 56–7; JMK 11, 541–2.

1933-8. 'Some hopeful portents for 1933', *Daily Mail*, 2 January; JMK 21, 141–5.

1933-9. 'Spending and saving: a discussion between Sir Josiah Stamp and J.M. Keynes', *Listener*, 11 January, 41–2; JMK 21, 145–54.

1933-10. 'A programme for unemployment', *New Statesman and Nation*, **5**, 4 February, 102; JMK 12, 154–61.

1933-11. 'Does the Kaffir boom herald world recovery', *Daily Mail*, 7 February; 'The Kaffir boom: will history repeat itself?', JMK 21, 225–9.

1933-12. 'Should Britain compromise on the gold standard?', *Daily Mail*, 17 February; JMK 21, 229–33.

1933-13. 'The multiplier', *New Statesman and Nation*, **5**, 1 April, 405–7; JMK 21, 171–8.

1933-14. 'The means to prosperity. Mr. Keynes's reply to criticism', *The Times*, 5 April; JMK 21, 178–85.

1933-15. 'A budget that marks times', *Daily Mail*, 26 April; JMK 21, 194–7.

1933-16. 'Pay or default? – Neither', *Daily Mail*, 8 June; 'An economist's view of the debt payment problem', JMK 18, 387–90.

1933-17. 'The World Economic Conference', *Listener*, 14 June, 925–7, 962; JMK 21, 251–9. [conversation with Walter Lippman]

1933-18. 'The chaos of the foreign exchanges', *Daily Mail*, 20 June; JMK 21, 259–63.

1933-19. 'Can we co-operate with America?', *Daily Mail*, 27 June; JMK 21, 264–8.

1933-20. 'President Roosevelt is magnificently right', *Daily Mail*, 4 July; JMK 21, 273–7.

1933-21. Letter to the Editor, *New Statesman and Nation*, **6**, 8 July, 43; JMK 28, 320–22.

1933-22. 'National self-sufficiency', *New Statesman and Nation*, **6**, 8 July, 36–7, 15 July, 65–7; JMK 21, 233–46.

1933-23. 'Shall we follow the dollar or the franc?', *Daily Mail*, 14 July; JMK 21, 277–80.

1933-24. 'Farewell to the World Conference', *Daily Mail*, 27 July; JMK 21, 281–4.

1933-25. 'Hoare, Alfred. *Unemployment and Inflation*. London, P.S. King, 1933', *Economic Journal*, **43**, September, 474–5; JMK 11, 433.

1933-26. 'Two years off gold: how far are we from prosperity now?', *Daily Mail*, 19 September; JMK 21, 284–8.

1933-27. 'Einstein', *New Statesman and Nation*, **6**, 21 October, 481; JMK 28, 21–2.

1933-28. Letter to the Editor, *The Times*, 28 November; JMK 30, 18–19.

1933-29. 'Mr Robertson on "saving and hoarding". I', *Economic Journal*, **43**, December, 699–701; JMK 13, 327–30.

1933-30. 'Mr Keynes's control scheme' [reply to E.C. Simons], *American Economic Review*, **23**, December; JMK 11, 434–5.

1933-31. 'Open letter to President Roosevelt', *New York Times*, 31 December, 2; JMK 21, 289–97.

1933-32. Chapter 2: The distinction between a co-operative economy and an entrepreneur economy, draft of *The General Theory;* JMK 29, 76–87.

1934-1. 'The Camargo Ballet Society'; JMK 28, 322–4.

1934-2. 'Roosevelt's economic experiments', *Listener*, 17 January, 93; JMK 21, 305–9.

1934-3. 'President Roosevelt's gold policy', *New Statesman and Nation*, **7**, 20 January, 76; JMK 21, 309–17.

1934-4. 'The theory of effective demand', paper read to the American Political Economy Club, 6 June; JMK 13, 457–68.

1934-5. 'Agenda for the President', *The Times*, 11 June; JMK 21, 322–9.

1934-6. Letter to the Editor, *New Statesman and Nation*, **8**, 15 July; JMK 28, 25–7.

1934-7. Letter to the Editor, *New Statesman and Nation*, **8**, 11 August; JMK 28, 28–9.

1934-8. 'The Bank for International Settlements. Fourth annual report (1933–34), Basle, 1934', *Economic Journal*, 44, September, 514–18; JMK 11, 480–85.

1934-9. 'Shaw on Wells on Stalin: a comment by JMK', *New Statesman and Nation*, **8**, 10 November, 653; 'Mr Keynes replies to Shaw', JMK 28, 30–35.

1934-10. 'Poverty in plenty: is the economic system self-adjusting?', *Listener*, 21 November, 850–51; JMK 13, 485–92.

1934-11. 'Can America spend its way into recovery?', *Redbook Magazine*, **64**, December, 24, 76; JMK 21, 334–8.

1935-1. 'Future interest rates: Mr J.M. Keynes on the outlook', speech to the Annual Meeting of the National Mutual, *The Times*, 21 February; JMK 12, 208–16.

1935-2. '*Report of Monetary Committee, 1934, New Zealand. Minutes of evidence, Monetary Committee, 1934*, New Zealand. Government printer, Wellington, N.Z., 1934', *Economic Journal*, **45**, March, 192–6; JMK 11, 435–9.

1935-3. 'The commemoration of Thomas Robert Malthus. The allocutions: III. Mr Keynes', *Economic Journal*, **45**, June, 230–34; JMK 10, 104–8.

1935-4. 'Henry Cunynghame (1849–1935)', *Economic Journal*, **45**, June, 398–406; JMK 10, 297–305.

1935-5. 'The Bank for International Settlements. *Fifth Annual Report (1934–35)*, Basle, 1935', *Economic Journal*, **45**, September, 594–7; JMK 11, 485–9.

1935-6. 'Andrew Andréadès', *Economic Journal*, **45**, September, 597–9; JMK 30, 20–22.

1935-7. 'Economic sanctions', *New Statesman and Nation*, **10**, 28 September, 401; JMK 21, 370–72.

1935-8. 'The future of the foreign exchanges', *Lloyds Bank Monthly Review*, **68**, October, 527–35; JMK 21, 360–69.

1936-1. *The General Theory of Employment, Interest and Money*, London: Macmillan; JMK 7.

1936-2. 'Foreword', in G.H. Recknell (ed.), *King Street, Cheapside*, London: National Mutual Life Assurance Society; JMK 12, 239–40.

1936-3. 'Ibsen's middle period', in *Programme for the Ibsen season*, Arts Theatre, Cambridge, February; JMK 28, 326–8.

1936-4. 'William Stanley Jevons, 1835–82: A centenary allocution on his life and work as economist and statistician', *Journal of the Royal Statistical Society*, **99**, June, 516–55; JMK 10, 109–60.

1936-5. 'On reading books', edited version of a talk for the B.B.C., 1 June, *The Listener*, 10 June; JMK 28, 329–35.

1936-6. 'Art and the State', *Listener*, 26 August; JMK 28, 341–9.

1936-7. 'The supply of gold', *Economic Journal*, **46**, September, 412–18; JMK 11, 490–98.

1936-8. 'Fluctuations in net investments in the United States', *Economic Journal*, **46**, September, 540–47; JMK 7, 386–93.

1936-9. 'Herbert Somerton Foxwell (1849–1936)', *Economic Journal*, **46**, December, 589–614; JMK 10, 267–96.

1937-1. 'The theory of the rate of interest', in A.D. Gayer (ed.), *The Lessons of Monetary Experience: Essays in Honour of Irving Fisher*, London: George Allen & Unwin, 145–52; JMK 14, 101–8.

1937-2. 'How to avoid a slump', *The Times*, 12, 13 and 14 January; JMK 21, 384–95.

1937-3. 'William Herrick Macaulay (1853–1936)', *Cambridge Review*, 15 January; JMK 10, 351–6.

1937-4. 'The general theory of employment', *Quarterly Journal of Economics*, **51**, February, 209–23; JMK 14, 109–23.

1937-5. 'Borrowing for defence. Is it inflation?', *The Times*, 11 March; JMK 21, 404–9.

1937-6. 'Some economic consequences of a declining population', *Eugenic Review*, **29**, April, 13–17; JMK 14, 124–33.

1937-7. 'Alternative theories of the rate of interest', *Economic Journal*, **47**, June, 241–52; JMK 14, 201–15.

1937-8. 'British foreign policy', *New Statesman and Nation*, **14**, 10 July, 61–2; JMK 28, 61–5.

1937-9. 'Further thoughts on British foreign policy', letter prepared for the *New Statesman and Nation*, but not sent, 26 July; JMK 28, 73–8.

1937-10. 'Walter Case (1885–1937)', *The Times*, 9 October; JMK 10, 326–7.

1937-11. 'The "ex ante" theory of the rate of interest', *Economic Journal*, **47**, December, 663–9; JMK 14, 215–23.

1937-12. 'Professor Pigou on money wages in relation to unemployment', *Economic Journal*, **47**, December, 743–5; JMK 14, 262–5.

1938-1. 'Foreword', in Quentin Bell (ed.), *Julian Bell: Essays, Poems and Letters*, London: Hogarth Press; JMK 10, 358–60.

1938-2. With Piero Sraffa, 'Introduction', *An Abstract of a Treatise on Human Nature 1740: a Pamphlet Hitherto Unknown by David Hume*, Cambridge: Cambridge University Press, v–xxxii; JMK 28, 373–90.

1938-3. 'Scott, W.R. *Adam Smith as Student and Professor*. Jackson, Glasgow, 1937', *Economic History*, supplement to *The Economic Journal*, **48**, February, 33–46; JMK 11, 542–58.

1938-4. 'Meade, J.E. *Consumers' credits and unemployment*. Oxford University Press, 1938', *Economic Journal*, **48**, March, 67–71; JMK 11, 439–44.

1938-5. 'A positive peace programme', *New Statesman and Nation*, **15**, 25 March, 509–10; JMK 28, 99–104.

1938-6. 'Funkhouser, H. Gray. *Historical Development of the Graphical Representation of Statistical Data*. Osiris studies on the history and philosophy of science, vol. III, part I, The Saint Catherine Press, Bruges, 1937', *Economic Journal*, **48**, June, 281–2; JMK 11, 232–4.

1938-7. 'Mr Keynes and "finance"' [Reply to D.H. Robertson], *Economic Journal*, **48**, June, 318–22; JMK 14, 229–33.

1938-8. 'Mr Keynes's consumption function: a reply' [comment on an article by G.R. Holden], *Quarterly Journal of Economics*, **52**, August, 708–9; JMK 14, 268–9.

1938-9. 'A tribute to the ballet at Sadler's Wells', Programme of the Second Buxton Theatre Festival, August–September; JMK 28, 324–5.

1938-10. 'The policy of government storage of foodstuffs and raw materials', *Economic Journal*, **48**, September, 449–60; JMK 21, 456–70.

1938-11. 'George Broomhall (1857–1938)', *Economic Journal*, **48**, September, 576–8; JMK 10, 328–9.

1938-12. 'My early beliefs', paper read on 11 September to the Bloomsbury Memoir Club, first published in 1949; JMK 10, 433–50.

1938-13. 'Efficiency in industry: a measure of growth', *The Times*, 13 September; JMK 21, 477–82.

1938-14. 'Mr Chamberlain's foreign policy', *New Statesman and Nation*, **16**, 8 October, 518–19: JMK 28, 125–7.

1938-15. Letter to the Editor, *Sunday Times*, 30 October; JMK 16, 335–6.

1938-16. 'Mr Keynes's consumption function: further comment', *Quarterly Journal of Economics*, **53**, November, 160; JMK 14, 270.

1938-17. 'Alfred Hoare (1850–1938)', *Economic Journal*, **48**, December, 753–7; JMK 10, 310–14.

1939-1. 'Democracy and efficiency', *New Statesman and Nation*, **17**, 28 January, 121–3; JMK 21, 491–500. [conversation with Kingsley Martin]

1939-2. 'Relative movements of real wages and output', *Economic Journal*, **49**, March, 34–51; JMK 7, 394–412.

1939-3. 'Crisis finance. An outline of policy. I. Employment and the budget', *The Times*, 17 April; JMK 21, 509–13.

1939-4. 'Crisis finance. An outline of policy. II. The supply of savings', *The Times*, 18 April; JMK 21, 513–18.

1939-5. 'Will rearmament cure unemployment?', *Listener*, 1 June, 1142–3; JMK 21, 528–32.

1939-6. 'Borrowing by the State. I. High interest and low', *The Times*, 24 July; JMK 21, 551–7.

1939-7. 'Borrowing by the State. II. A programme of method', *The Times*, 25 July; JMK 21, 557–64.

1939-8. 'Mr Keynes on the distribution of incomes and "propensity to consume": a reply', *Review of Economics and Statistics*, **21**, August, 129; JMK 14, 270–71.

1939-9. 'Professor Tinbergen's Method', *Economic Journal*, **49**, September, 558–68; JMK 14, 306–20.

1939-10. 'The process of capital formation', *Economic Journal*, **49**, September, 569–74; JMK 14, 278–85.

1939-11. 'Haberler, G. von. *Prosperity and Depression*. 2nd edition, Geneva, League of Nations, Allen & Unwin, 1939', *Economic Journal*, **49**, September, 622–3; JMK 29, 274–5.

1939-12. 'Paying for the war', *The Times*, 14 and 15 November; JMK 22, 41–51.

1939-13. 'Mr Keynes and his critics: a reply and some questions', *The Times*, 28 November; JMK 22, 74–81.

1939-14. 'The income and fiscal potential of Great Britain', *Economic Journal*, **49**, December, 626–35; JMK 22, 52–66.

1939-15. 'How should we raise the money?', *Manchester Daily Herald*, 7 December; JMK 22, 87–90.

1940-1. *How to Pay for the War*, London: Macmillan; JMK 9, 367–439.

1940-2. 'The concept of national income: a supplementary note', *Economic Journal*, **50**, March, 60–65; JMK 22, 66–73.

1940-3. 'Comment [on Tinbergens' reply to J.M.K.'s review of "Professor Tinbergen's method"]', *Economic Journal*, **50**, March, 154–6; JMK 14, 318–20.

1940-4. 'Should savings be compulsory?', *Listener*, 11 March, 508–9; JMK 22, 111–17.

1940-5. 'Fay, C.R. *English Economic History mainly since 1700*, Cambridge, Heffer, 1940', *Economic Journal*, **50**, June–September, 254–61; JMK 11, 558–61.

1940-6. 'The measurement of real income', *Economic Journal*, **50**, June–September, 341; JMK 11, 235–7.

1940-7. 'The United States and the Keynes Plan', *New Republic*, 29 July, 156–9; JMK 22, 144–55.

1940-8. 'Paying for twelve months' war', *Listener*, 26 September, 436, 455; JMK 22, 240–45.

1940-9. 'The Society's jubilee, 1890–1940', *Economic Journal*, **50**, December, 401–9; JMK 12, 846–55.

1940-10. 'Henry Higgs (1864–1940)', *Economic Journal*, **50**, December, 555–8; JMK 10, 306–9.

1940-11. Proposals to counter the German 'New Order', 1 December; JMK 25, 7–16.

1941-1. Post-War currency policy, 8 September; JMK 25, 21–33.

1941-2. Proposals for an International Currency Union, 8 September; JMK 25, 33–4.

1941-3. Proposals for an International Currency Union, 18 November; JMK 25, 42–61.

1941-4. Proposals for an International Currency Union, 15 December; JMK 25, 68–94.

1942-1. 'Foreword', in Samuel Courtauld, *Government and Industry: their Future Relations*, London: Macmillan; JMK 30, 23.

1942-2. 'How much does finance matter?', *Listener*, 2 April; JMK 27, 264–70.

1942-3. Proposals for an International Clearing Union, Preface, August; JMK 25, 168–95.

1942-4. Remarks at a luncheon at King's College to celebrate his father's 90th birthday and his parents' diamond wedding anniversary, 30 August; KP, PP/20.

1943-1. A comparative analysis of the British project for a Clearing Union (C.U.) and the American project for a Stabilisation Fund (S.F.), 1 March; JMK 25, 215–26.

1943-2. 'Dilwyn Knox (1884–1943)', *The Times*, 10 March; JMK 10, 357.

1943-3. Proposals for an International Clearing Union, White Paper, Preface, April; JMK 25, 233–5.

1943-4. 'The arts in war-time', *The Times*, 11 May; JMK 28, 359–62.

1943-5. Maiden speech before the House of Lords, 18 May; JMK 25, 269–80.

1943-6. 'The objective of international price stability', *Economic Journal*, **53**, June–September, 185–7; JMK 22, 30–33.

1943-7. The synthesis of C.U. and S.F., 29 June; JMK 25, 308–14.

1943-8. 'Frederick Phillips (1884–1943)', *The Times*, 18 August; JMK 10, 330–31.

1943-9. 'Reginald McKenna (1863–1943)', *The Times*, 15 September; JMK 10, 58–9.

1943-10. 'Leonard Darwin (1850–1943)', *Economic Journal*, **53**, December, 438–9; JMK 30, 24–5.

1944-1. Post-war employment, Note by Lord Keynes on the Report of the Steering Committee, 14 February; JMK 27, 364–72.

1944-2. Explanatory notes by United Kingdom experts on the Proposal for an International Monetary Fund, 22 April; JMK 25, 437–42.

1944-3. Speech to the House of Lords, 23 May; JMK 26, 9–21.

1944-4. 'Mary Pailey Marshall (1850–1944)', *Economic Journal*, **54**, June–September, 268–84; JMK 10, 232–50.

1944-5. Opening remarks of Lord Keynes at the first meeting of the second commission on the Bank for Reconstruction and Development, 3 July; JMK 26, 72–7.

1944-6. Speech in moving to accept the final act at the closing plenary session, Bretton Woods, 22 July; JMK 26, 101–3.

1944-7. 'The Bretton Woods Conference. I. The International Bank', *Listener*, 27 July, 100; JMK 26, 103–5.

1944-8. 'Note by Lord Keynes' [on F.D. Graham, 'Keynes vs Hayek on a commodity reserve currency'], *Economic Journal*, **54**, December, 429–30; JMK 26, 39–40.

1945-1. 'Foreword', in *An Exhibition of French Book Illustration, 1895–1945*, C.E.M.A.; JMK 28, 365–6.

1945-2. 'The Arts Council: its policy and hopes', *Listener*, 11 May; JMK 28, 367–72.

1945-3. Speech to the House of Lords, 18 December; JMK 24, 605–24.

1946-1. 'Bernard Shaw and Isaac Newton', in S. Winsten (ed.), *G.B.S. 90: Aspects of Bernard Shaw's Life and Work*, London: Hutchinson, pp. 106–9; JMK 10, 375–81.

1946-2. Lord Keynes's speech at inaugural meeting of Governors of Fund and Bank, Savannah, 9 March; JMK 26, 215–17.

1946-3. The Savannah conference on the Bretton Woods Final Act, 27 March; JMK 26, 220–38.

1946-4. 'The balance of payments of the United States', *Economic Journal*, **56**, June, 172–87; JMK 27, 427–46.

1947. 'Newton, the man', in *Newton Tercentenary Celebrations, July 15–19, 1946*, Cambridge, Royal Society of London, 27–34, paper read to the Royal Society, London, 30 November 1942; JMK 10, 363–74.

1949. *Two Memoirs: Dr Melchior: a defeated enemy, and My Early Beliefs*, London: Rupert Hart-Davis.

1989-1. With Lydia Lopokova, *Lydia and Maynard: the Letters of John Maynard Keynes and Lydia Lopokova*, New York: Charles Scribner's Sons.

1989-2. *Keynes's Lectures 1932–35: Notes of a Representative Student*, transcribed, edited and constructed by Thomas K. Rymes, Ann Arbor: University of Michigan Press.

2. OTHER REFERENCES

Abraham-Frois, Gilbert (1991), *Keynes et la Macroéconomie contemporaine*, Paris: économica.

Abrahamsen, David (1992), *Murder and Madness: The Secret Life of Jack the Ripper*, New York: Donald I. Fine.

Addison, John T. and John Burton (1982), 'Keynes's analysis of wages and unemployment revisited', *Manchester School*, **50** (1), 1–23.

Ahiakpor, James C.W. (ed.) (1998), *Keynes and the Classics Reconsidered*, Boston: Kluwer Academic.

Amadeo, Edward J. (1989), *Keynes's Principle of Effective Demand*, Aldershot, UK and Brookfield, US: Edward Elgar.

Annan, Noel (1986), *Leslie Stephen: The Godless Victorian*, Chicago: University of Chicago Press.

Annan, Noel (2002), 'Keynes and Bloomsbury', in William Roger Louis (ed.), *Still More Adventures with Britannia: Personalities, Politics and Culture in Britain*, London: I.B. Taurus, pp. 113–26.

Anyadike-Danes, M.K. (1985), 'Dennis Robertson and Keynes's General Theory', in G.C. Harcourt (ed.), *Keynes and his Contemporaries*, London: Macmillan, pp. 105–23.

Arena, Richard (1985), 'Rationalité microéconomique et circulation macroéconomique: Keynes et Schumpeter', *Cahiers d'économie Politique*, no. 10–11, 149–68.

Arena, Richard and Dominique Torre (eds) (1992), *Keynes et les Nouveaux Keynésiens*, Paris: Presses Universitaires de France.

Aristotle (1905), *Aristotle's Politics*, Oxford: Clarendon Press.

Asimakopulos, Athanasios (1982), 'Keynes' theory of effective demand revisited', *Australian Economic Papers*, **21** (38), 18–36.

Asimakopulos, Athanasios (1987), 'La signification théorique de la *Théorie Générale* de Keynes', in Gérard Boismenu and Gilles Dostaler (eds), *La 'Théorie Générale' et le Keynésianisme*, Montreal: ACFAS, pp. 39–54.

Asimakopulos, Athanasios (1991), *Keynes's General Theory and Accumulation*, Cambridge: Cambridge University Press.

Aslanbeigui, Nahid (1992), 'Pigou's inconsistencies or Keynes's misconceptions?', *History of Political Economy*, **24** (2), 413–33.

Asquith, H.H. (1982), *Letters to Venetia Stanley*, edited by Michael Brock and Eleanor Brock, Oxford: Oxford University Press.

Atkinson, Glen and Theodore Oleson Jr. (1998), 'Commons and Keynes: their assault on laissez faire', *Journal of Economic Issues*, **32** (4), 1019–30.

Backhouse, Roger E. (ed.) (1999), *Keynes: Contemporary Responses to the General Theory*, South Bend, Indiana: St. Augustine's Press.

Backhouse, Roger E. (2006), 'Sidgwick, Marshall and the Cambridge school of economics', *History of Political Economy*, **38** (1), 15–44.

Backhouse, Roger E. and Bradley Bateman (eds) (2006), *The Cambridge Companion to Keynes*, Cambridge: Cambridge University Press.

Bainville, Jacques (1920), *Les Conséquences Politiques de la Paix*, Paris: Nouvelle Librairie Nationale; with J.M. Keynes, *Les Conséquences Économiques de la Paix*, Paris: Gallimard, 2002, pp. 285–459.

Baker, Ray Stannard (1923), *Woodrow Wilson and World Settlement, Written from his Unpublished and Personal Material*, Garden City, New York: Doubleday, Page & Company, 3 vols.

Barrère, Alain (ed.) (1988), *The Foundations of Keynesian Analysis*, London: Macmillan.

Barrère, Alain (ed.) (1989), *Money, Credit and Prices in Keynesian Perspective*, London: Macmillan.

Barrère, Alain (ed.) (1990), *Keynesian Economic Policies*, London: Macmillan.

Barrère, Alain (1990a), *Macroéconomie Keynésienne: Le Projet Économique de John Maynard Keynes*, Paris: Dunod.

Baruch, Bernard M. (1920), *The Making of the Reparation and Economic Sections of the Treaty*, New York and London: Harper & Brothers.

Bateman, Bradley W. (1987), 'Keynes's changing conception of probability', *Economics and Philosophy*, **3** (2), 97–120.

Bateman, Bradley W. (1988), 'G.E. Moore and J.M. Keynes: a missing chapter in the history of the expected utility model', *American Economic Review*, **78** (5), 1098–106.

Bateman, Bradley W. (1990), 'Keynes, induction, and econometrics', *History of Political Economy*, **22** (2), 359–79.

Bateman, Bradley W. (1996), *Keynes's Uncertain Revolution*, Ann Arbor: University of Michigan Press.

Bateman, Bradley W. and John B. Davis (eds) (1991), *Keynes and Philosophy: Essays on the Origin of Keynes's Thought*, Aldershot, UK and Brookfield, US: Edward Elgar.

Bauvert, Joanna (2003), 'L'ambivalence du concept de liquidité dans le *Treatise on Money*', *Actualité Économique*, **79** (1–2), 87–100.

Beaud, Michel and Gilles Dostaler (1995), *Economic Thought since Keynes: A History and Dictionary of Major Economists*, Aldershot, UK and Brookfield, US: Edward Elgar; paperback edn, London: Routledge, 1997.

Bell, Clive (1914), *Art*, London: Chatto & Windus; London: Arrow Books, 1961.

Bell, Clive (1956), *Old Friends: Personal Recollections*, London: Chatto & Windus.

Bell, Quentin (1972), *Virginia Woolf: A Biography*, London: Hogarth Press, 2 vols.

Bell, Quentin (1980), 'Recollections and reflections on Maynard Keynes', in Derek Crabtree and A.P. Thirlwall (eds), *Keynes and the Bloomsbury Group*, London: Macmillan, pp. 69–86.

Bell, Quentin (1995), *Elders and Betters*, London: John Murray.

Bell, Quentin (1997), *Bloomsbury*, London Phoenix (first edn, 1968).

Bell, Quentin, A. Garnett, H. Garnett and R. Shone (1987), *Charleston Past and Present*, London: Chatto & Windus.

Bell, Vanessa (1998), *Selected Letters of Vanessa Bell*, edited by Regina Marler, Wakefield, Rhode Island and London: Moyer Bell.

Benetti, Carlo (1998), 'La structure logique de la *Théorie Générale* de Keynes', *Cahiers d'économie Politique*, nos 30–31, 7–48.

Benetti, Carlo, Gilles Dostaler and Christian Tutin (eds) (1998), *Keynes: Économie et Philosophie*, *Cahiers d'économie Politique*, nos 30–31.

Béraud, Alain (2003), 'Keynes et Pigou sur le salaire monétaire et l'emploi: une synthèse du débat', *Actualité Économique*, **79** (1–2), 147–62.

Berthoud, Arnaud (1989), 'Liberté et libéralisme économique chez Walras, Hayek et Keynes', *Cahiers d'économie Politique*, nos 16–17, 43–67.

Berthoud, Arnaud (1998), 'Économie et action politique dans la *Théorie Générale* de Keynes', *Cahiers d'économie Politique*, nos 30–31, 265–79.

Black, Max (1967), 'Probability', in Paul Edwards (ed.), *The Encyclopedia of Philosophy*, New York: Macmillan & The Free Press and London: Collier Macmillan, vol. 6, pp. 464–79.

Blaug, Mark (1990), *John Maynard Keynes: Life, Ideas, Legacy*, Houndsmills, Basingstoke: Macmillan.

Blaug, Mark (ed.) (1991), *John Maynard Keynes (1883–1946)*, Aldershot, UK and Brookfield, US: Edward Elgar, 2 vols.

Blaug, Mark, W. Eltis, D. O'Brien and R. Skidelsky (1995), *The Quantity Theory of Money: From Locke to Keynes and Friedman*, Aldershot, UK and Brookfield, US: Edward Elgar.

Blot, Jean (1992), *Bloomsbury: Histoire d'une Sensibilité Artistique et Politique Anglaise*, Paris: Balland.

Bodkin, Ronald G., Lawrence R. Klein and Kanta Marwah (1988), 'Keynes and the origins of macroeconometric modelling', in Omar F. Hamouda and John N. Smithin (eds), *Keynes and Public Policy after Fifty Years*, vol. 2, *Theories and Method*, New York: New York University Press, pp. 3–11.

Boemeke, Manfred F., Gerald D. Feldman and Elisabeth Glaser (eds) (1998), *The Treaty of Versailles: a Reassessment after 75 Years*, Cambridge: Cambridge University Press.

Bogdanor, Vernon (ed.) (1983), *Liberal Party Politics*, Oxford: Clarendon Press.

Boismenu, Gérard and Gilles Dostaler (eds) (1987), *La 'Théorie Générale' et le Keynésianisme*, Montreal: ACFAS.

Bolton, George (1972), 'Were critics as wrong as Keynes was?', *The Banker*, **122**, 1385–7.

Bonadei, Rossana (1994), 'John Maynard Keynes: contexts and methods', in Alessandra Marzola and Francesco Silva (eds), *John Maynard Keynes: Language and Method*, Aldershot, UK and Brookfield, US: Edward Elgar, pp. 13–75.

Booth, Alan (1989), *British Economic Policy, 1931–49: Was there a Keynesian Revolution?*, New York: Simon and Schuster.

Bordo, Michael D. and Anna J. Schwartz (eds) (1984), *A Retrospective of the Classical Gold Standard 1821–1914*, Chicago: University of Chicago Press.

Bousseyrol, Marc (2000), *Introduction à l'Oeuvre de Keynes*, Paris: Ellipse.

Boyer, Robert (1990), 'The forms of organisation implicit in the *General Theory*: an interpretation of the success and crisis of Keynesian economic policies', in A. Barrère (ed.), *Keynesian Economic Policies*, London: Macmillan, pp. 117–39.

Bradshaw, Tony (ed.) (2001), *A Bloomsbury Canvas: Reflections on the Bloomsbury Group*, Aldershot, UK: Lund Humphries.

Brady, Michael E. (1994), 'Keynes, Pigou and the supply side of the *General Theory*', *History of Economics Review*, no. 21, 34–46.

Braithwaite, Richard B. (1975), 'Keynes as a philosopher', in Milo Keynes (ed.), *Essays on John Maynard Keynes*, Cambridge: Cambridge University Press, pp. 237–46.

Brenier, Henri (1921), *Le Traité de Versailles et le Problème des Réparations: le Point de Vue Français, une Réfutation par les Faits du Livre de M. Keynes*, Marseille: Chambre de Commerce.

Brenner, Reuven (1979), 'Unemployment, justice and Keynes's *General Theory*', *Journal of Political Economy*, **87** (4), 837–50.

Bridel, Pascal (1987), *Cambridge Monetary Thought: Development of Saving–Investment Analysis from Marshall to Keynes*, London: Macmillan.

Broad, Charlie D. (1922), '*A Treatise on Probability*. By J.M. Keynes', *Mind*, **31** (121), 72–85.

Brossard, Olivier (1998), 'Comportement vis-à-vis de la liquidité et instabilité conjoncturelle: Une réflexion sur la préférence pour la liquidité', *Cahiers d'économie Politique*, nos 30–31, 123–46.

Brown, Neville (1988), *Dissenting Forbears: The Maternal Ancestors of J.M. Keynes*, Chichester, Sussex: Phillimore.

Brown-Collier, E. and R. Bausor (1988), 'The epistemological foundations of the *General Theory*', *Scottish Journal of Political Economy*, **35** (3), 227–41.

Bryce, Robert (1935), 'An introduction to a monetary theory', in Don Patinkin and James Clark Leith (eds) (1977), *Keynes, Cambridge and The General Theory*, London: Macmillan, pp. 129–45.

Burke, Edmund (1968) [1790], *Reflections on the Revolution in France*, Harmondsworth: Penguin Books.

Burnett, Philip Mason (1940), *Reparation at the Paris Peace Conference from the Standpoint of the American Delegation*, New York: Columbia University Press.

Bywater, William G. (1975), *Clive Bell's Eye*, Detroit: Wayne State University.

Cain, Neville (1979), 'Cambridge and its revolution: a perspective on the multiplier and effective demand', *Economic Record*, **55**, 108–17.

Cain, Neville (1982), 'Hawtrey and the multiplier theory', *Australian Economic History Review*, **22**, 68–78.

Caine, Barbara (1998), 'The Stracheys and psychoanalysis', *History Workshop Journal*, **45** (Spring), 145–69.

Carabelli, Anna (1988), *On Keynes's Method*, London: Macmillan.

Carabelli, Anna (1992), 'Organic independence and Keynes's choice of units in the *General Theory*', in Bill Gerrard and John Hillard (eds), *The Philosophy and Economics of John Maynard Keynes*, Aldershot, UK and Brookfield, US: Edward Elgar, pp. 3–31.

Carabelli, Anna (1998), 'Keynes on probability, uncertainty and tragic choices', *Cahiers d'économie Politique*, nos 30–31, 187–226.

Caramagno, Thomas C. (1992), *The Flight of the Mind: Virginia Woolf's Art and Manic-Depressive Illness*, Berkeley: University of California Press.

Cartelier, Jean (1988), 'Keynes' *General Theory*: foundation for a heterodox economy?', in Alain Barrère (ed.), *The Foundations of Keynesian Analysis*, London: Macmillan, pp. 128–49.

Cartelier, Jean (1995), *L'Économie de Keynes*, Brussels: De Boeck.

Carter, Miranda (2001), *Anthony Blunt: His Lives*, New York: Farrar, Straus and Giroux.

Carvalho, Fernando J. Cardim de (1988), 'Keynes on probability, uncertainty, and decision-making', *Journal of Post Keynesian Economics*, **11** (1), 66–81.

Carvalho, Fernando J. Cardim de (1992), *Mr Keynes and the Post Keynesians: Principles of Macroeconomics for a Monetary Production Economy*, Aldershot, UK and Brookfield, US: Edward Elgar.

Castex, Pierre (2003), *Théorie Générale de la Monnaie et du Capital*, Paris: L'Harmattan, 4 vols.

Caws, Mary Ann and Sarah Bird Wright (2000), *Bloomsbury and France: Art and Friends*, New York: Oxford University Press.

Cecil, Hugh and Mirabel (eds) (1990), *Clever Hearts: Desmond and Molly MacCarthy, A Biography*, London: V. Gollancz.

Chandavarkar, Anand G. (1987), 'Keynes and the international monetary system revisited (a contextual and conjectural essay)', *World Development*, **15**, 1395–1405.

Chandavarkar, Anand G. (1989), *Keynes and India: A Study in Economics and Biography*, London: Macmillan.

Chandavarkar, Anand G. (2000), 'Was Keynes Anti-Semitic?', *Economic and Political Weekly*, May, 16–22.

Chauviré, Christiane (1989), *Ludwig Wittgenstein*, Paris: Seuil.

Chesney, Kellow (1970), *The Victorian Underworld*, London: Temple Smith

Chick, Victoria (1978), 'The nature of the Keynesian revolution: a reassessment', *Australian Economic Papers*, **17** (30), 1–20.

Chick, Victoria (1983), *Macroeconomics after Keynes: a Reconsideration of the General Theory*, Oxford: Philip Allan and Cambridge: MIT Press.

Chorney, Harold (1987), 'Keynes et le problème de l'inflation: les racines du retour à une "saine gestion"', in Gérard Boismenu and Gilles Dostaler (eds), *La 'Théorie Générale' et le Keynésianisme*, Montréal: ACFAS, pp. 149–62.

Clarke, Peter (1978), *Liberals and Social Democrats*, Cambridge: Cambridge University Press.

Clarke, Peter (1988), *The Keynesian Revolution in the Making, 1924–1936*, Oxford: Clarendon Press.

Clarke, Peter (1996), *Hope and Glory: Britain 1900–1990*, London: Penguin Books.

Clarke, Peter (1998), *The Keynesian Revolution and its Economic Consequences*, Cheltenham, UK and Lyme, USA: Edward Elgar.

Clemenceau, Georges (1921), 'Introduction', in André Tardieu, *La Paix*, Paris: Payot.

Clower, Robert W. (1965), 'The Keynesian counterrevolution: a theoretical appraisal', in F.H. Hahn and F.P. Brechling (eds), *Theory of Interest Rates*, London: Macmillan and New York: St. Martin's Press, pp. 103–25.

Clower, Robert W. (1989), 'Keynes' *General Theory*: the Marshallian connection', in Donald A. Walker (ed.), *Perspectives on the History of Economic Thought*, vol. 2, *Twentieth-Century Economic Thought*, Aldershot, UK and Brookfield, US: Edward Elgar, pp. 133–47.

Coates, John (1996), *The Claims of Common Sense: Moore, Wittgenstein, Keynes and the Social Sciences*, New York: Cambridge University Press.

Cochran, John P. and Fred R. Glahe (1999), *The Hayek–Keynes Debate: Lessons for Current Business Cycle Research*, Lewiston: Edwin Mellen.

Collins, Judith (1983), *The Omega Workshops*, London: Secker & Warburg.

Collins, Michael (1988), 'Did Keynes have the answer to unemployment in the 1930s?', in John Hillard (ed.), *J.M. Keynes in Retrospect: the Legacy of the Keynesian Revolution*, Aldershot, UK and Brookfield, US: Edward Elgar, pp. 64–87.

Combemale, Pascal (1999), *Introduction à Keynes*, Paris: La Découverte.

Cook, Matt (2003), '"A New City of Friends": London and Homosexuality in the 1890s', *History Workshop Journal*, **56** (1), 33–58.

Cornwell, Patricia (2002), *Portrait of a Killer: Jack the Ripper Case Closed*, New York: Putnam's.

Cot, Annie L. (1992), 'Jeremy Bentham, un "Newton" de la morale', in Alain Béraud and Gilbert Faccarello (eds), *Nouvelle Histoire de la Pensée Économique. Tome 1: Des Scolastiques aux Classiques*, Paris: La Découverte, pp. 289–301.

Cottrell, Allin (1993), 'Keynes's theory of probability and its relevance to his economics: three theses', *Economics and Philosophy*, **9** (1), 25–51.

Cottrell, Allin and Michael S. Lawlor (eds) (1995), *New Perspectives on Keynes*, Annual Supplement to Volume 27, *History of Political Economy*, Durham and London: Duke University Press.

Crabtree, Derek and A. P. Thirlwall (eds) (1980), *Keynes and the Bloomsbury Group: The Fourth Keynes Seminar held at the University of Kent at Canterbury 1978*, London: Macmillan.

Crabtree, Derek and A. P. Thirlwall (eds) (1993), *Keynes and the Role of the State: The Tenth Keynes Seminar Held at the University of Kent at Canterbury, 1991*, London: Palgrave Macmillan.

Craig, David M. (2003), 'The Crowned Republik? Monarchy and Anti-Monarchy in Britain, 1760–1901', *Historical Journal*, **46** (1), 167–85.

Crouzet, François (1972), 'Les réactions françaises devant "Les Conséquences économiques de la paix" de Keynes', *Revue d'Histoire Moderne et Contemporaine*, **19** (January–March), 6–26.

Cutler, Tony, Karel Williams and John Williams (1987), *Keynes, Beveridge and Beyond*, London and New York: Routledge & Kegan Paul.

Darity, William Jr. and Bobbie L. Horn (1983), 'Involuntary unemployment reconsidered', *Southern Economic Journal*, **49** (3), 717–33.

Davidson, Paul (1965), 'Keynes's finance motive', *Oxford Economic Papers*, **17** (1), 47–65.

Davidson, Paul (1980), 'The dual-faceted nature of the Keynesian revolution: money and money wages in unemployment and production flow prices', *Journal of Post Keynesian Economics*, **2** (3), 291–307.

Davidson, Paul (2007), *John Maynard Keynes*, London: Palgrave.

Davis, Eric G. (1980), 'The correspondence between R.G. Hawtrey and J.M. Keynes on the *Treatise*: the genesis of output adjustment models', *Canadian Journal of Economics*, **13** (4), 716–24.

Davis, John B. (1991), 'Keynes's critiques of Moore: philosophical foundations of Keynes's economics', *Cambridge Journal of Economics*, **15** (1), 61–77.

Davis, John B. (1994a), *Keynes's Philosophical Development*, Cambridge: Cambridge University Press.

Davis, John B. (ed.) (1994b), *The State of Interpretation of Keynes*, Dordrecht: Kluwer Academic.

Deacon, Richard (1985), *The Cambridge Apostles: A History of Cambridge University's Elite Intellectual Secret Sociey*, London: Robert Royce.

Deane, Phyllis (2001), *The Life and Times of J. Neville Keynes: A Beacon in the Tempest*, Cheltenham, UK and Northampton, MA, USA: Edward Elgar.

De Boyer, Jérome (1982), 'Demande effective et théorie monétaire du taux d'intérêt chez Keynes: une interprétation', *Cahiers d'économie Politique*, no. 8, 85–104.

De Boyer, Jérome (1998), 'Keynes et le risque de taux d'intéret de la banque', *Cahiers d'économie Politique*, nos 30–31, 51–64.

De Boyer, Jérome (2003), *La Pensée Monétaire: Histoire et Analyse*, Paris: Les Solos.

De Brunhoff, Suzanne (1990), 'The keynesian critique of laissez-faire', in Alain Barrère (ed.), *Keynesian Economic Policies*, London: Macmillan, pp. 140–52.

De Cecco, Marcello (1984), *The International Gold Standard: Money and Empire*, London: Frances Pinter.

De Gmeline, Patrick (2001), *Versailles 1919: Chronique d'une Fausse Paix*, Paris: Presses de la Cité.

Deleplace, Ghislain (1988), 'Ajustement de marché et "taux d'intérêt spécifiques" chez Keynes et Sraffa', *Cahiers d'économie Politique*, nos 14–15, 75–98.

Deleplace, Ghislain (1998), 'Keynes et Ricardo sur la macroéconomie et la monnaie', *Cahiers d'économie politique*, nos 30–31,49–84.

Deleplace, Ghislain and Patrick Maurisson (eds) (1985), *L'Hétérodoxie dans la pensée économique: K. Marx, J.M. Keynes, J.A. Schumpeter*, *Cahiers d'économie politique*, nos 10–11.

Deleplace, Ghislain and Edward J. Nell (eds) (1996), *Money in Motion: the Post Keynesian and Circulation Approaches*, London: Macmillan.

Delfaud, Pierre and Alain Planche (1985), 'Les lois de l'économie de guerre: des agrégats de Keynes au financement de l'effort de guerre', in Frédéric Poulon (ed.), *Les Écrits de Keynes*, Paris: Dunod, pp. 66–88.

De Morgan, Augustus (1847), *Formal Logic*, London: Open Court, 1926.

Denis, Henri (1999), *La 'loi de Say' sera-t-elle enfin rejetée? Une Nouvelle Approche de la Surproduction*, Paris: Économica.

De Salvo, Louise (1989), *Virginia Woolf: The Impact of Childhood Sexual Abuse on her Life and Work*, New York: Ballantine Books.

De Villé, Philippe and Michel De Vroey (1985), 'Salaire et marché du travail chez Marx et Keynes: orthodoxie ou hétérodoxie', *Cahiers d'économie Politique*, nos 10–11, 67–90.

De Vroey, Michel (1997a), 'Le concept de chômage involontaire, de Keynes aux nouveaux keynésiens', *Revue économique*, **48** (6), 1381–408.

De Vroey, Michel (1997b), 'Involuntary unemployment: the missing piece in Keynes's *General Theory*', *European Journal of the History of Economic Thought*, **4** (2), 258–83.

De Vroey, Michel (2004), *Involuntary Unemployment: The Elusive Quest for a Theory*, London: Routledge.

De Vroey, Michel and Kevin D. Hoover (eds) (2004), *The IS–LM Model: Its Rise, Fall, and Strange Persistence*, Annual Supplement to Volume 36, *History of Political Economy*, Durham and London: Duke University Press.

Diatkine, Daniel (1985), 'Smith, Ricardo, Keynes: vie et mort du "prodigue" et du "projector"', *Cahiers d'économie Politique*, nos 10–11, 409–21.

Diatkine, Daniel (1995), '"Au risque d'un solécisme . . .": Keynes, Smith et l'école classique', in *Nouvelles Perspectives de la Macroéconomie: Mélanges en l'Honneur du Doyen Alain Barrère*, Paris: Publications de la Sorbonne, pp. 43–58.

Diatkine, Sylvie (1989), 'La mesure en unités de salaire réel ou monétaire: une comparaison entre Smith et Keynes', *Économies et sociétés*, **23** (10), 157–78.

Diatkine, Sylvie (1995), *Théories et Politiques Monétaires*, Paris: Armand Colin.

Diatkine, Sylvie and Daniel Diatkine (1975), 'La Théorie de l'emploi et les Théories des Systèmes de Prix', in Alain Barrère (ed.), *Controverses sur le Système Keynésien*, Paris: Économica, pp. 288–332.

Dickinson, G. Lowes (1931), *J. McT. E. McTaggart*, Cambridge: Cambridge University Press.

Dimand, Robert W. (1986), 'The macroeconomics of the *Treatise on Money*', *Eastern Economic Journal*, **12** (4), 431–41.

Dimand, Robert W. (1988), *The Origins of the Keynesian Revolution: The Development of Keynes' Theory of Employment and Output*, Aldershot, UK and Brookfield, US: Edward Elgar.

Dimand, Robert W. (1989), 'The reception of Keynes' *Treatise on Money*: a review of the reviews', in Donald A. Walker (ed.), *Perspectives on the History of Economic Thought*, vol. 2, *Twentieth-Century Economic Thought*, Aldershot, UK and Brookfield, US: Edward Elgar, pp. 87–96.

Dimand, Robert W. (1991), '"A prodigy of constructive work": J.M. Keynes on *Indian Currency and Finance*', in William J. Barber (ed.), *Perspectives on the History of Economic Thought*, vol. 6, *Themes in Keynesian Criticism and Supplementary Modern Topics*, Aldershot, UK and Brookfield, US: Edward Elgar, pp. 29–35.

Dos Santos Ferreira, Rodolphe (1988), 'Reflections on the microeconomic foundations of the Keynesian aggregate supply function', in Alain Barrère (ed.), *The Foundations of Keynesian Analysis*, London: Macmillan, pp. 251–62.

Dos Santos Ferreira, Rodolphe (2000), 'Keynes et le développement de la théorie de l'emploi dans une économie monétaire', in Alain Béraud and Gilbert Faccarello (eds), *Nouvelle Histoire de la Pensée Économique. Tome 3: Des Institutionnalistes à la Période Contemporaine*, Paris: La Découverte, pp. 236–93.

Dostaler, Gilles (1985), 'Le retour à l'étalon-or en Grande-Bretagne: une fâcheuse illusion', in Frédéric Poulon (ed.), *Les Écrits de Keynes*, Paris: Dunod, pp. 176–94.

Dostaler, Gilles (1987), 'La vision politique de Keynes', in Gérard Boismenu and Gilles Dostaler (eds), *La 'Théorie Générale' et le Keynésianisme*, Montréal: ACFAS, pp. 75–90.

Dostaler, Gilles (1991), 'The debate between Hayek and Keynes', in William J. Barber (ed.), *Perspectives on the History of Economic Thought*, vol. 6, *Themes in Keynesian Criticism and Supplementary Modern Topics*, Aldershot, UK and Brookfield, US: Edward Elgar, pp. 77–101.

Dostaler, Gilles (1994–95), 'Keynes et Bretton Woods', *Interventions Économiques*, no. 26, 53–78.

Dostaler, Gilles (1996), 'The formation of Keynes's vision', *History of Economics Review*, no. 25, 14–31.

Dostaler, Gilles (1997), 'Keynes and Friedman on money', in Avi J. Cohen, Harald Hagemann and John Smithin (eds), *Money, Financial Institutions and Macroeconomics*, Boston: Kluwer Academic, pp. 85–100.

Dostaler, Gilles (1998), 'Friedman and Keynes: divergences and convergences', *European Journal of the History of Economic Thought*, **5** (2), 317–47.

Dostaler, Gilles (1999), 'Hayek, Keynes et l'économie orthodoxe', *Revue d'Économie Politique*, **109** (6), 761–73.

Dostaler, Gilles (2000), 'Néolibéralisme, keynésianisme et traditions libérales', *La Pensée*, no. 323, 71–87.

Dostaler, Gilles (2002a), 'Discours et stratégies de persuasion chez Keynes', *Sciences de la Société*, no. 55, 122–36.

Dostaler, Gilles (2002b), 'Un homme multidimensionel: Keynes raconté par Skidelsky', *Critique Internationale*, no. 17, 63–74.

Dostaler, Gilles and Hélène Jobin (2000), 'Keynes, les probabilités et les statistiques: une relation complexe', in Jean-Pierre Beaud and Jean-Guy Prévost (eds), *L'ère du chiffre:*

systèmes statistiques et traditions nationales, Québec: Presses de l'Université du Québec, pp. 411–29.

Dostaler, Gilles and Bernard Maris (2000), 'Dr Freud and Mr Keynes on money and capitalism', in John Smithin (ed.), *What is Money?*, London and New York: Routledge, pp. 235–56.

Dostaler, Gilles and Robert Nadeau (eds) (2003), *Que reste-t-il de Keynes?*, *Actualité Économique*, **79** (1–2).

Dow, Sheila C. (2003), 'Probability, uncertainty and convention: economists' knowledge and the knowledge of economic actors', in J. Runde and S. Mizuhara, *The Philosophy of Keynes' Economics*, London, Routledge, pp. 207–15.

Dow, Sheila C. and John Hillard (eds) (1995), *Keynes, Knowledge and Uncertainty*, Aldershot, UK and Brookfield, US: Edward Elgar.

Duménil, Gérard (1977), *Marx et Keynes Face à la Crise*, Paris: Économica.

Dunn, Jane (1996), *Virginia Woolf and Vanessa Bell: A Very Close Conspiracy*, London: Pimlico.

Durbin, Elizabeth (1985), *New Jerusalems: The Labour Party and the Economics of Democratic Socialism*, London: Routledge & Kegan Paul.

Durbin, Elizabeth (1988), 'Keynes, the British Labour Party and the economics of democratic socialism', in Omar Hamouda and John N. Smithin (eds), *Keynes and Public Policy after Fifty Years*, vol. 1, *Economics and Policy*, New York: New York University Press, pp. 29–42.

Eatwell, John and Murray Milgate (eds) (1983), *Keynes's Economics and the Theory of Value and Distribution*, New York: Oxford University Press.

Edel, Leon (1980), *Bloomsbury: A House of Lions*, New York: Avon Books.

Eichner, Alfred S. and Jan A. Kregel (1975), 'An essay on post-Keynesian theory: a new paradigm in economics', *Journal of Economic Literature*, **13** (4), 1293–314.

Elie, Bernard (1989–90), 'Le retour du contrôle des flux d'investissements internationaux: l'ombre de John Maynard Keynes', *Interventions Économiques pour une Alternative Sociale*, nos 22–23, 81–98.

Elie, Bernard (1998), *Le Régime Monétaire Canadien: Institutions, Théories et Politiques*, Montréal: Presses de l'Université de Montréal.

Eltis, Walter and Peter Sinclair (eds) (1988), *Keynes and Economic Policy: the Relevance of 'The General Theory' after Fifty Years*, London: Macmillan.

Erhel, Christine and Hélène Zajdela (2003), 'Que reste-t-il de la théorie du chômage de Keynes?', *Actualité Économique*, **79** (1–2), 163–77.

Eshag, Eprime (1963), *From Marshall to Keynes: An Essay on the Monetary Theory of the Cambridge School*, Oxford: Basil Blackwell.

Favereau, Olivier (1985), 'L'incertain dans la "révolution keynésienne": l'hypothèse Wittgenstein', *Économies et Sociétés, Oeconomia*, **19** (3), 29–72.

Favereau, Olivier (1988a), 'Probability and uncertainty: "after all, Keynes was right"', *Économies et Sociétés*, **22** (10), 133–67.

Favereau, Olivier (1988b), 'La *Théorie Générale*: de l'économie conventionnelle à l'économie des conventions', *Cahiers d'économie Politique*, nos 14–15, 197–220.

Fawcett, Peter (1977), 'Bloomsbury et la France', in Jean Guiguet (ed.), *Virginia Woolf et le Groupe de Bloomsbury*, Paris: Union Générale d'Éditions, pp. 57–72.

Felix, David (1995), *Biography of an Idea: John Maynard Keynes and The General Theory of Employment, Interest and Money*, New Brunswick: Transaction.

Felix, David (1999), *Keynes: A Critical Life*, Westport, Connecticut: Greenwood Press.

Ferenczi, Sandor (1914), 'The Ontogenesis of the Interest in Money', *Internationale Zeitschrift für Ärtzliche Psychoanalyse*, **2**, 506–13; in Ernest Borneman (ed.), *The Psychoanalysis of Money*, New York: Urizen Books, 1976, pp. 81–90.

Ferguson, Niall (1998), *The Pity of War*, New York: Basic Books.

Ferrandier, Robert (1985), 'L'étalon-or aux Indes: une absurde fascination', in Frédéric Poulon (ed.), *Les Écrits de Keynes*, Paris: Dunod, pp. 158–75.

Fisher, Irving (1911), *The Purchasing Power of Money*, New York: Macmillan

Fitzgibbons, Athol (1988), *Keynes's Vision: A New Political Economy*, Oxford: Clarendon Press.

Fitzgibbons, Athol (1995), *Adam Smith's System of Liberty, Wealth, and Virtue: The Moral and Political Foundations of The Wealth of Nations*, Oxford: Clarendon Press.

Fletcher, Gordon A. (1987), *The Keynesian Revolution and its Critics*, London, Macmillan and New York: St Martin.

Frazer, William (1994), *The Legacy of Keynes and Friedman: Economic Analysis, Money, and Ideology*, New York: Praeger.

Freeden, Michael (1978), *The New Liberalism: An Ideology of Social Reform*, Oxford: Clarendon Press.

Freeden, Michael (1986), *Liberalism Divided: A Study in British Political Thought, 1914–1939*, Oxford: Clarendon Press.

Freud, Sigmund (1908), 'Character and anal eroticism', *Psychiatrisch-neurologische Wochenschrift*, **9**, 465–7; in Ernest Borneman (ed.), *The Psychoanalysis of Money*, New York: Urizen Books, 1976, pp. 73–80.

Freud, Sigmund (1961), *The Letters of Sigmund Freud*, edited by Ernst L. Freud, London: Hogarth Press.

Freud, Sigmund and William C. Bullitt (1966), *Thomas Woodrow Wilson, Twenty-eighth President of the United States: A Psychological Study*, London: Weidenfeld & Nicolson.

Friboulet, Jean-Jacques (1985), 'Le Traité de la monnaie et l'inflation d'équilibre', in Frédéric Poulon (ed.), *Les Écrits de Keynes*, Paris: Dunod, pp. 111–30.

Friedman, Milton (1953), 'The methodology of positive economics', in *Essays in Positive Economics*, Chicago: University of Chicago Press, pp. 3–43.

Friedman, Milton (ed.) (1956), *Studies in the Quantity Theory of Money*, Chicago: University of Chicago Press.

Friedman, Milton (1968a), *Dollars and Deficits: Inflation, Monetary Policy and the Balance of Payments*, Englewood Cliffs, New Jersey: Prentice-Hall.

Friedman, Milton (1968b), 'The role of monetary policy', *American Economic Review*, **58** (1), 1–17.

Friedman, Milton (1972), 'Comments on the critics', *Journal of Political Economy*, **80** (5), 906–50; in R.J. Gordon (ed,) (1974), *Milton Friedman's Monetary Framework: A Debate with his Critics*, Chicago: University of Chicago Press, pp. 132–77.

Fry, Roger (1909), 'An essay in aesthetics', *New Quarterly*, **2** (April), 171–90; in R. Fry *Vision and Design*, London: Oxford Univesity Press, 1920, pp. 12–27.

Fry, Roger (1920), *Vision and Design*, London: Oxford University Press, 1981.

Fry, Roger (1924), *The Artist and Psycho-analysis*, London: Hogarth Press; in Craufurd Goodwin (ed.) (1998), *Art and the Market: Roger Fry on Commerce in Art. Selected Writings*, Ann Arbor: University of Michigan Press, 1998, pp. 125–38.

Frydman, Roger (1988), 'La *Théorie Générale* de Keynes: économie et politique', *Cahiers d'économie Politique*, nos 14–15, 99–110.

Furbank, P.N. (1979), *E.M. Forster: a Life*, Oxford: Oxford University Press.

Gadd, David (1974), *The Loving Friends: A Portrait of Bloomsbury*, New York: Harcourt Brace Jovanovich.

Gardner, Richard N. (1975), 'Bretton Woods', in Milo Keynes (ed.), *Essays on John Maynard Keynes*, Cambridge: Cambridge University Press, pp. 202–15.

Garegnani, Pierangelo (1983), 'Notes on consumption, investment and effective demand', in John Eatwell and Murray Milgate (eds), *Keynes's Economics and the Theory of Value and Distribution*, New York: Oxford University Press, pp. 21–69.

Garnett, Angelica (1984), *Deceived with Kindness: a Bloomsbury Childhood*, London: Pimlico.

Garnett, Angelica (1998), *The Eternal Moment: Essays by Angelica Garnett*, Oron, Maine: Puckerbrush Press.

Garnett, David (1953), *The Golden Echo*, London: Chatto & Windus.

Garnett, David (1955), *The Flowers of the Forest*, London: Chatto & Windus.

Garnett, David (1962), *The Familiar Faces*, London: Chatto & Windus.

Garnett, David (1979), *Great Friends: Portraits of Seventeen Writers*, London: Macmillan.

Gaspard, Marion (2003), 'Ramsey's theory of national saving: a mathematician in Cambridge', *Journal of the History of Economic Thought*, **25** (4), 413–35.

Gay, Peter (1993), *The Cultivation of Hatred (The Bourgeois Experience: Victoria to Freud, volume III)*, New York: W.W. Norton.

Gerbier, Bernard (1995), 'A. Marshall, 1843–1924', in Michel Vigezzi (ed.), *Dix Grands Auteurs en Économie*, Grenoble: Presses Universitaires de Grenoble, pp. 41–56.

Gerrard, Bill and John Hillard (eds) (1992), *The Philosophy and Economics of John Maynard Keynes*, Aldershot, UK and Brookfield, US: Edward Elgar.

Gerzina, Gretchen Holbrok (1989), *Carrington: A Life*, London: W. W. Norton.

Giblin, L.F. (1946), 'John Maynard Keynes (some personal notes)', *Economic Record*, **22** (June), 1–3.

Gilbert, Martin (1976), *Winston Chuchill*, London: Heinemann.

Gillies, Donald A. (2000), *Philosophical Theories of Probability*, London: Routledge.

Gislain, Jean-Jacques (1987), 'A propos des deux postulats de la théorie "classique" du marché du travail dans la *Théorie Générale*: hérésie et orthodoxie', in Gérard Boismenu and Gilles Dostaler (eds), *La 'Théorie Générale' et le Keynésianisme*, Montréal: ACFAS, pp. 55–74.

Glasgow, Mary (1975), 'The concept of the Arts Council', in Milo Keynes (ed.), *Essays on John Maynard Keynes*, Cambridge: Cambridge University Press, pp. 260–71.

Goodwin, Craufurd (ed.) (1998), *Art and the Market: Roger Fry on Commerce in Art. Selected Writings,* Ann Arbor: University of Michigan Press.

Goodwin, Craufurd (2001), 'Maynard Keynes and the Creative Arts', in Tony Bradshaw (ed.), *A Bloomsbury Canvas: Reflections on the Bloomsbury Group*, Aldershot, UK: Lund Humphries, pp. 51–3.

Goodwin, Craufurd (2006), 'The art of an ethical life: Keynes and Bloomsbury', in Roger E. Backhouse and Bradley Bateman (eds), *The Cambridge Companion to Keynes*, Cambridge: Cambridge University Press, pp. 217–36.

Graziani, Augusto (1987), 'Keynes' finance motive', *Économies et Sociétés*, **21** (4), 23–42.

Green, Christopher (ed.) (1999), *Art Made Modern: Roger Fry's Vision of Art*, London: Merrell Holberton in association with the Courtauld Gallery.

Greer, William B. (2000), *Ethics and Uncertainty: The Economics of John M. Keynes and Frank H. Knight*, Cheltenham, UK and Northampton, MA, USA: Edward Elgar.

Grigg, Percy James (1948), *Prejudice and Judgment*, London: Jonathan Cape.

Groenewegen, Peter (1995a), *A Soaring Eagle: Alfred Marshall, 1842–1924*, Aldershot, UK and Brookfield, US: Edward Elgar.

Groenewegen, Peter (1995b), 'Keynes and Marshall: methodology, society, politics', *History of Political Economy*, **27**, supplement, 129–55.

Haavelmo, Trygve (1943), 'Statistical testing of business-cycle theories', *Review of Economic Statistics*, **25** (1), 13–18.

Halevi, Joseph (1984), 'Structure économique et demande effective', *Économie appliquée*, **37** (1), 201–13.

Halévy, Elie (1901–1904), *La Formation du Radicalisme Philosophique*, Paris: F. Alcan; translated by M. Morris, *The Growth of Philosophic Radicalism*, London: Faber, 1928.

Hamouda, Omar (1986), 'Beyond the IS/LM device: Was Keynes a Hicksian', *Eastern Economic Journal*, **12** (4), 370–84.

Hamouda, Omar and Betsey Price (eds) (1998), *Keynesianism and the Keynesian Revolution in America: A Memorial Volume in Honour of Lorie Tarshis*, Cheltenham, UK and Lyme, US, Edward Elgar.

Hamouda, Omar and Robin Rowley (1996), *Probability and Economics*, London: Routledge.

Hamouda, Omar and John N. Smithin (eds) (1988), *Keynes and Public Policy after Fifty Years*, New York: New York University Press and Aldershot, UK: Edward Elgar, 2 vols.

Hanin, Frédéric (2003), 'La place du *Treatise on Money* dans l'oeuvre de Keynes: une théorie de l'instabilité', *Actualité Économique*, **79** (1–2), 70–86.

Harcourt, G.C. (ed.) (1985a), *Keynes and his Contemporaries: the Sixth and Centennial Keynes Seminar held at the University of Kent at Canterbury, 1983*, London: Macmillan and New York: St. Martin's Press.

Harcourt, G.C. (ed.) (1985b), 'Keynes's unemployment equilibrium: some insights from Joan Robinson, Piero Sraffa and Richard Kahn', in G. C. Harcourt (1985a), pp. 3–41.

Harcourt, G.C. (1994), 'Kahn and Keynes and the making of *The General Theory*', *Cambridge Journal of Economics*, **18** (1), 11–24.

Harcourt, G.C. and P.A. Riach, Peter (eds) (1997), *A 'Second Edition' of The General Theory*, London: Routledge, 2 vols.

Harrison, Michael (1972), *Clarence: The Life of H.R.H. the Duke of Clarence and Avondale (1864–1892)*, London: W.H. Allen.

Harrison, Ross (1983), *Bentham*, London: Routledge & Kegan Paul.

Harrod, Roy F. (1946), 'John Maynard Keynes', *Review of Economic Statistics*, **28** (4), 178–82.

Harrod, Roy F. (1951), *The Life of John Maynard Keynes*, London: Macmillan.

Harrod, Roy F. (1957), 'Clive Bell on Keynes', *Economic Journal*, **67** (268), 692–99.

Harrod, Roy F. (1960), '[Keynes's attitude to compulsory military service] A comment', *Economic Journal*, **70** (277), 166–7.

Haskell, Arnold L. (1934), *Balletomania: Then and Now*, New York: Alfred A. Knopf, 1977.

Hawtrey, Ralph G. (1925), 'Public expenditure and the demand for labour', *Economica*, no. 13, 38–48.

Hayek, Friedrich (1952), 'Review of R.F. Harrod, *The Life of John Maynard Keynes*', *Journal of Modern History*, **24** (2), 195–8.

Hayek, Friedrich (1970), 'The error of constructivism', inaugural lecture at the Paris-Lodron University of Salzburg, in *New Studies in Philosophy, Politics, Economics and the History of Ideas*, London: Routledge, 1978, pp. 3–22.

Hayek, Friedrich (1994), *Hayek on Hayek: An Autobiographical Dialogue*, London: Routledge.

Hayek, Friedrich (1995), *The Collected Works of F.A. Hayek*, vol. 9, *Contra Keynes and Cambridge: Essays, Correspondence*, London: Routledge.

Hayek, Friedrich, T.E. Gregory, Arnold Plant and Lionel Robbins (1932), 'Spending and savings: public works and rate', *The Times*, 19 October.

Heilbrun, James (1984), 'Keynes and the economics of the arts', *Journal of Cultural Economics*, **8** (2), 37–49.

Helburn, Suzanne (1991), 'Burke and Keynes', in Bradley W. Bateman and John B. Davis (eds), *Keynes and Philosophy: Essays on the Origin of Keynes's Thought*, Aldershot, UK and Brookfield, US: Edward Elgar, pp. 30–54.

Hendry, David F. (1980), 'Econometrics: alchemy or science?', *Economica*, **47** (188), 387–406.

Henry, Gérard Marie (1997), *Keynes*, Paris: Armand Colin.

Herland, Michel (1991), *Keynes et la Macroéconomie*, Paris: Économica, [first edn, *Keynes*, Paris: Union Générale d'Édition, 1981].

Herland, Michel (1998), 'Concilier liberté économique et justice sociale: les solutions de Keynes', *Cahiers d'économie Politique*, nos 30–31, 281–310.

Herscovici, Alain (2002), *Dinamica Macroeconomica: una Interpretaçao a partir de Marx e de Keynes*, Sao Paulo: EDUC.

Hession, Charles H. (1984), *John Maynard Keynes: A Personal Biography of the Man who Revolutionized Capitalism and the Way we Live*, New York: Macmillan.

Hicks, John R. (1937), 'Mr. Keynes and the "classics": a suggested interpretation', *Econometrica*, **5** (2), 147–59.

Hicks, John R. (1967), 'A note on the *Treatise*', in *Critical Essays in Monetary Theory*, Oxford: Oxford University Press, pp. 189–202.

Higgins, Norman (1975), 'The Cambridge Arts Theatre', in Milo Keynes (ed.), *Essays on John Maynard Keynes*, Cambridge: Cambridge University Press, pp. 272–9.

Hill, Christopher (1972), *The World Turned Upside Down*, London: Maurice Temple Smith.

Hill, Roger (ed.) (1989), *Keynes, Money and Monetarism*, London: Macmillan.

Hillard, John (ed.) (1988), *J. M. Keynes in Retrospect: the Legacy of the Keynesian Revolution*, Aldershot, UK and Brookfield, US: Edward Elgar.

Hirai, Toshiaki (2004), 'The turning point in Keynes's theoretical development: from *A Treatise on Money* to the *General Theory*', *History of Economic Ideas*, **12** (2), 29–50.

Hirai, Toshiaki (2007), 'How did Keynes transform his theory from the *Tract* into the *Treatise*', *European Journal for the History of Economic Thought*, **14** (2).

Hollander, Samuel (1996), 'Malthus and Keynes: some recent secondary literature', *History of Economics Review*, no. 25, 127–8.

Holmes, Charles J. (1936), *Self & Partners (Mostly Self): Being the Reminiscences of C.J. Holmes*, London: Constable.

Holroyd, Michael (1971), *Lytton Strachey and the Bloomsbury Group: His Work, their Influence*, Harmondsworth, Middlesex: Penguin.

Holroyd, Michael (1994), *Lytton Strachey: The New Biography*, New York: Farrar, Straus and Giroux.

Hoover, Kenneth R. (2003), *Economics as Ideology: Keynes, Laski, Hayek, and the Creation of Contemporary Politics*, Lanham, Maryland: Rowman & Littlefield.

House, Edward Mandell and Charles Seymour (eds) (1921), *What Really Happened at Paris: the Story of the Peace Conference, 1918–1919*, New York: Charles Scribner's Sons.

Howard, Michael and John King (1992), 'Keynes, Marx and political economy', in Bill Gerrard and John Hillard (eds), *The Philosophy and Economics of John Maynard Keynes*, Aldershot, UK and Brookfield, US: Edward Elgar, pp. 231–45.

Howson, Susan (1975), *Domestic Monetary Management in Great Britain, 1919–38*, Cambridge: Cambride University Press.

Howson, Susan and Donald E. Moggridge (eds) (1990), *The Wartime Diaries of Lionel Robbins and James Meade 1943–45*, London: Macmillan.

Howson, Susan and Donald Winch (1977), *The Economic Advisory Council 1930–1939: A Study in Economic Advice during Depression and Recovery*, Cambridge: Cambridge University Press.

Hume, David (1752a), 'Of money', in *Essays: Moral, Political, and Literary*, Indianapolis: Liberty Fund, 1985, pp. 281–94.

Hume, David (1752b), 'Of the balance of trade', in *Essays: Moral, Political, and Literary*, Indianapolis: Liberty Fund, 1985, pp. 308–26.

Hutchison, Terence W. (1981), 'Keynes versus the "Keynesians" . . .? An essay in the thinking of J.M. Keynes and the accuracy of its interpretation by his followers', in *The Politics and Philosophy of Economics: Marxists, Keynesians, and Austrians*, Oxford: Basil Blackwell, pp. 108–51.

Ikenberry, G. John (1992), 'A world economy restored: expert consensus and the Anglo-American postwar settlement', *International Organization*, **46** (1), 289–321.

Jaffé, William (1976), 'Menger, Jevons and Menger de-homogenized', *Economic Inquiry*, **14** (4), 511–24.

Jevons, W. Stanley (1871), *The Theory of Political Economy*, Harmondsworth, Middlesex: Penguin Books, 1970.

Johnson, Elizabeth (1960), 'Keynes' attitude to compulsory military service', *Economic Journal*, **70** (277), 160–65.

Johnson, Elizabeth (1978a), 'Keynes as a literary craftsman', in Elizabeth S. Johnson and Harry G. Johnson (eds), *The Shadow of Keynes: Understanding Keynes, Cambridge and Keynesian Economics*, Oxford: Basil Blackwell, pp. 30–37.

Johnson, Elizabeth (1978b), 'Dr. Melchior', in Elizabeth S. Johnson and Harry G. Johnson (eds), *The Shadow of Keynes: Understanding Keynes, Cambridge and Keynesian Economics*, Oxford: Basil Blackwell, pp. 45–61.

Johnson, Harry G. (1974), 'Cambridge in the 1950s', *Encounter*, **42** (1), 28–39; in Elizabeth S. Johnson and Harry G. Johnson, *The Shadow of Keynes: Understanding Keynes, Cambridge and Keynesian Economics*, Oxford: Basil Blackwell, 1978, pp. 127–50.

Johnstone, John Keith (1954), *The Bloomsbury Group: A Study of E.M. Forster, Lytton Strachey, Virginia Woolf and their Circle*, New York: Noonday Press.

Jones, Ernest (1916), 'The theory of symbolism', *British Journal of Psychology*, 9; in *Papers on Psycho-Analysis*, Boston: Beacon Press, 1961, pp. 87–144.

Kahn, Richard F. (1975), *On Re-Reading Keynes: Fourth Keynes Lecture in Economics, 6 November 1974*, London: Oxford University Press.

Kahn, Richard F. (1984), *The Making of Keynes' General Theory*, Cambridge: Cambridge University Press.

Kahn, Richard F. and Austin Robinson (1985) 'The Cambridge "Circus"', in G. C. Harcourt (ed.), *Keynes and his Contemporaries*, London: Macmillan, pp. 42–57.

Kates, Steven (1998), *Say's Law and the Keynesian Revolution: How Macroeconomic Theory Lost its Way*, Cheltenham, UK and Lyme, USA: Edward Elgar.

Kersaudy, François (2000), *Winston Churchill: Le Pouvoir de l'imagination*, Paris: Tallandier.

Keynes, Florence Ada (1950), *Gathering up the Threads: A Study in Family Biography*, Cambridge: W. Heffer & Sons.

Keynes, Geoffrey (1975), 'The early years', in Milo Keynes (ed.), *Essays on John Maynard Keynes*, Cambridge: Cambridge University Press, pp. 26–35.

Keynes, John Neville (1884), *Studies and Exercises in Formal Logic*, London: Macmillan, fourth edn, 1906.

Keynes, John Neville (1891), *The Scope and Method of Political Economy*, fourth edn, 1917; New York: Augustus M. Kelley, 1965.

Keynes, Milo (ed.) (1975), *Essays on John Maynard Keynes*, Cambridge: Cambridge University Press.

Kitson Clark, George (1966), *The Making of Victorian England*, New York: Atheneum.

Klein, Lawrence R. (1947), *The Keynesian Revolution*, New York: Macmillan.

Klotz, Gérard (2003), 'Que reste-t-il de Keynes? Au moins la comptabilité nationale', *Actualité Économique*, **79** (1–2), 221–38.

Klotz, Louis-Julien (1924), *De la Guerre à la Paix*, Paris: Payot.

Koopmans, Tjalling C. (1941), 'The logic of econometric business-cycle research', *Journal of Political Economy*, **49** (2), 157–81.

Kregel, Jan A. (1987), 'The changing place of money in Keynes's theory from the *Treatise* to the *General Theory*', in Giancarlo Gandolofo and Ferruccio Marzano (eds), *Keynesian Economics, Growth and Development, Fiscal and Policy Issues*, Milan: Giuffre, pp. 97–114.

Kregel, Jan A. (1988), 'The multiplier and liquidity preference: two sides of the theory of effective demand', in Alain Barrère (ed.), *The Foundations of Keynesian Analysis*, New York: St. Martin's Press, pp. 231–50.

Lagueux, Maurice (1985), 'Hétérodoxie et scientificité chez Marx, Keynes et Schumpeter', *Cahiers d'économie Politique*, nos 10–11, 422–36.

Lagueux, Maurice (1998), 'Was Keynes a liberal or an individualist? Or Mandeville read by Keynes', *Cahiers d'économie Politique*, nos 30–31, 255–63.

Laidler, David (1991), *The Golden Age of the Quantity Theory*, Princeton, New Jersey: Princeton University Press.

Laidler, David (1999), *Fabricating the Keynesian Revolution: Studies of the Inter-War Literature on Money, the Cycle and Unemployment*, Cambridge: Cambridge University Press.

Lalande, André (2002), *Vocabulaire technique et critique de la philosophie*, Paris: Presses Universitaires de France.

Lambert, Paul (1962), 'Malthus et Keynes, nouvel examen de la parenté profonde des deux œuvres', *Revue d'économie Politique*, **72** (6), 783–829.

Lambert, Paul (1969), 'The evolution of Keynes's thought from the *Treatise on Money* to the *General Theory*', *Annals of Public and Cooperative Economy*, **40**, 243–63.

Lange, Oskar (1942), 'Say's law: a restatement and critique', in O. Lange et al. (eds), *Studies in Mathematical Economics and Econometrics in Memory of Henry Schultz*, Chicago: University of Chicago Press, pp. 49–68.

Larceneux, André (1985), 'La genèse du concept de macroéconomie: Schumpeter, Marx, Keynes', *Cahiers d'économie Politique*, nos 10–11, 195–212.

Latouche, Serge (1985), 'Les ruses de la raison et les surprises de l'histoire: Marx, Keynes et Schumpeter, théoriciens de l'impérialisme', *Cahiers d'économie Politique*, nos 10–11, 369–87.

Lavialle, Christophe (2001), 'L'Épistémologie de Keynes et "l'hypothèse Wittgenstein": la cohérence de la *Théorie Générale de l'emploi, de l'intérêt et de la Monnaie*', *Cahiers d'économie Politique*, no. 38, 25–64.

Lavoie, Marc (1985a), 'La distinction entre l'incertitude keynésienne et le risque néoclassique', *Économie Appliquée*, **38** (2), 493–518.

Lavoie, Marc (1985b), 'La *Théorie Générale* et l'inflation de sous-emploi', in Frédéric Poulon (ed.), *Les Écrits de Keynes*, Paris: Dunod, pp. 131–52.

Lavoie, Marc (1986), 'L'Endogénéité de la monnaie chez Keynes', *Recherches Économiques de Louvain*, **52** (1), 67–84.

Lavoie, Marc (2004), *L'économie Postkeynésienne*, Paris: La Découverte.

Lawson, Tony (1985), 'Uncertainty and economic analysis', *Economic Journal*, **95** (380), 909–27.

Lawson, Tony (1996), 'Hayek and Keynes: a commonality', *History of Economics Review*, no. 25, 96–114.

Lawson, Tony (2003), 'Keynes's realist orientation', in Jochen Runde and Sohei Mizuhara (eds), *The Philosophy of Keynes's Economics: Probability, Uncertainty and Convention*, London: Routledge, pp. 159–69.

Lawson, Tony and Hashem Pesaran (eds) (1985), *Keynes' Economics: Methodological Issues*, London: Croom Helm.

Lee, Frank G. (1975), 'The international negotiator', in Milo Keynes (ed.), *Essays on John Maynard Keynes*, Cambridge: Cambridge University Press, pp. 217–23.

Lee, Hermione (1996), *Virginia Woolf*, London: Chatto & Windus.

Leeson, Robert (ed.) (2003), *Keynes, Chicago and Friedman*, London: Pickering & Chatto, 2 vols.

Le Héron, Edwin (1985), 'Circulation industrielle, circulation financière et taux d'intérêt', *Economie Appliquée*, **38** (1), 211–34.

Le Héron, Edwin (1986), 'Généralisation de la préférence pour la liquidité et financement de l'investissement', *Economies et Sociétés*, series Monnaie et production, nos 6–7, 67–93.

Leijonhufvud, Axel (1968), *On Keynesian Economics and the Economics of Keynes: A Study in Monetary Theory*, New York: Oxford University Press.

Lentin, Antony (1984), *Lloyd George, Woodrow Wilson and the Guilt of Germany: An Essay in the Pre-History of Appeasement*, Leicester: Leicester University Press.

Léonard, Jacques and Philippe Norel (1991), 'Système monétaire et préférence pour la liquidité: Keynes et la "macroéconomie des comportements"', *Economie Appliquée*, **44** (2), 153–62.

Lerner, Abba P. (1974), 'From the *Treatise on Money* to the *General Theory*', *Journal of Economic Literature*, **12** (1), 38–42.

Levy, Paul (1979), *Moore: G.E. Moore and the Cambridge Apostles*, New York: Holt, Rinehart and Winston.

Lévy, Raphaël-George (1920), *La Juste Paix ou la Vérité sur le Traité de Versailles*, Paris: Plon-Nourrit et Cie.

Littleboy, Bruce (1990), *On Interpreting Keynes: A Study in Reconciliation*, London and New York: Routledge.

Lloyd George, David (1933), *War Memoirs of David Lloyd George*, vol. 2, London: Little, Brown, and Company.

Lloyd George, David (1938), *The Truth about the Peace Treaties*, vol. 1, London: Victor Gollancz.

Lovell, Mary S. (2001), *The Sisters: The Saga of the Mitford Family*, New York: W.W. Norton.

Lubenow, William C. (1998), *The Cambridge Apostles, 1820–1914: Liberalism, Imagination, and Friendship in British Intellectual and Professional Life*, Cambridge: Cambridge University Press.

Lubenow, William C. (2003), 'Authority, honour and the Strachey family 1817–1974', *Historical Research*, **76** (194), 512–34.

McCann Jr., Charles R. (1994), *Probability Foundations of Economic Theory*, London: Routledge.

McCann Jr., Charles R. (ed.) (1998), *John Maynard Keynes: Critical Responses*, London: Routledge, 4 vols.

McCombie, John S.L. (1987–1988), 'Keynes and the nature of involuntary unemployment', *Journal of Post Keynesian Economics*, **10** (2), 202–15.

McCormick, Brian J. (1992), *Hayek and the Keynesian Avalanche*, New York: St. Martin's Press.

MacCarthy, Desmond (1995)' 'The post-impressionist exhibition of 1910', in S.P. Rosenbaum (ed.), *The Bloomsbury Group: A Collection of Memoirs and Commentary*, revised edn, Toronto: University of Toronto Press, 1995, 74–8; extract from *Memories*, London: MacGibbon and Kee, 1953, 178–83.

Machlup, Fritz (1957), '*The Scope and Method of Political Economy*. By John Neville Keynes', *Southern Economic Journal*, **23** (3), 330–32.

Macmillan, Margaret (2001), *Paris 1919: Six Months that Changed the World*, New York: Random House.

Maloney, John (ed.) (1985), *Marshall: Orthodoxy and the Professionalisation of Economics*, Cambridge: Cambridge University Press.

Malthus, Thomas Robert (1820), *Principles of Political Economy Considered with a View to their Practical Application*, second edn, London: William Pickering; New York: A.M. Kelley, 1951.

Mankiw, N. Gregory and David Romer (eds) (1991), *New Keynesian Economics*, Cambridge, Mass.: MIT Press.

Mantoux, Étienne (1946), *The Carthaginian Peace or The Economic Consequences of Mr Keynes*, London: Oxford University Press.

Mantoux, Paul (1955), *Les Délibérations du Conseil des Quatre (24 mars–28 juin 1919), Notes de l'officier Interprète*, Paris: Centre National de la Recherche Scientifique, 2 vols; *The Deliberations of the Council of Four (March 24–June 28, 1919): Notes of the Official Interpreter*, Princeton: Princeton University Press, 1992.

Marcuzzo, Maria Cristina (2001), 'From the fundamental equations to effective demand: "natural evolution" or "change of view"', in P. Arestis, M. Desai and S. Dow (eds), *Methodology, Microeconomics and Keynes: Essays in Honour of Victoria Chick*, London: Taylor and Francis, vol. 2, pp. 26–38.

Marcuzzo, Maria Cristina (2002), 'The collaboration between J.M. Keynes and R.F. Kahn from the *Treatise* to the *General Theory*', *History of Political Economy*, **34** (2), 421–47.

Marcuzzo, Maria Cristina (2006), 'Keynes and Cambridge', in Roger E. Backhouse and Bradley Bateman (eds), *The Cambridge Companion to Keynes*, Cambridge: Cambridge University Press, pp. 118–35.

Marcuzzo, Maria Cristina and Annalisa Rosselli (eds) (2005), *Economists in Cambridge: A Study through their Correspondence, 1907–1946*, London: Routledge.

Marion, Mathieu (2005), 'Sraffa and Wittgenstein: physicalism and constructivism', *Review of Political Economy*, **17** (3), 37–62.

Maris, Bernard (1999), *Keynes ou l'économiste Citoyen*, Paris: Presses de la Fondation Nationale des Sciences Politiques.

Marler, Regina (1997), *Bloomsbury Pie: The Making of the Bloomsbury Room*, London: Virago Press.

Marsh, Jan (1995), *Bloomsbury Women: Distinct Figures in Life and Art*, London: Pavilion Books.

Marshall, Alfred (1926), *Official Papers of Alfred Marshall*, London: Macmillan.

Marshall, Alfred (1975), *The Early Economic Writings of Alfred Marshall 1867–1890*, J.K. Whitaker (ed.), London: Macmillan, 2 vols.

Marshall, Mary Paley (1944), *What I Remember*, Cambridge: Cambridge University Press.

Martin, Catherine (1998), 'Réalisation de la demande effective et comportement des entrepreneurs: une étude du chapitre 3 de la *Théorie Générale* de Keynes', *Cahiers d'économie Politique*, nos 30–31, 85–104.

Martin, Catherine (2003), 'Une ambiguïté de la relation entre Keynes et Malthus: rejet de la loi de Say, monnaie et rapport salarial', *Actualité Économique*, **79** (1–2), 117–32.

Marx, Karl (1848), *Wage-Labour and Capital*, in David McLellan (ed.) (1977), *Karl Marx: Selected Readings*, Oxford: Oxford University Press, pp. 248–68.

Marx, Karl (1867), *Capital: A Critique of Political Economy*, vol. 1, *The Process of Capitalist Production*, Chicago: Charles H. Kerr & Company, 1909.

Marx, Karl and Friedrich Engels (1845–1846), *The German Ideology* [first published in 1932], in David McLellan (ed.) (1977), *Karl Marx: Selected Readings*, Oxford: Oxford University Press, pp. 159–91.

Marx, Karl and Friedrich Engels (1983), *Collected Works*, vol. 40, New York: International Publishers.

Marzola, Alessandra and Francesco Silva (eds) (1994), *John Maynard Keynes: Language and Method*, Aldershot, UK and Brookfield, US: Edward Elgar.

Mattick, Paul (1969), *Marx and Keynes: The Limits of the Mixed Economy*, Boston: Porter Sargent.

Maurisson, Patrick (ed.) (1988), *La 'Théorie Générale' de John Maynard Keynes: un cinquantenaire*, *Cahiers d'économie Politique*, nos 14–15.

Meade, James (1944–46), *The Cabinet Office Diary, 1944–46, The Collected Papers of James Meade*, edited by Susan Howson, London: Unwin Hyman, vol. 4, 1990.

Meeks, J. Gay Tulip (1991), 'Keynes on the rationality of decision procedures under uncertainty: the investment decision', in J. Gay Tulip Meeks (ed.), *Thoughtful Economic Man: Essays on Rationality, Moral Rules and Benevolence*, Cambridge: Cambridge University Press, pp. 126–60.

Meisel, Perry and Walter Kendrick (1985), *Bloomsbury/Freud: The Letters of James and Alix Strachey, 1924–25*, New York: Basic Books.

Meltzer, Allan H. (1988), *Keynes's Monetary Thought: A Different Interpretation*, Cambridge: Cambridge University Press.

Merten, Jacques E. (1944), *La Naissance et le Développement de l'étalon-or: 1696–1922*, Paris: Presses Universitaires de France.

Meyerowitz, Selma S. (ed.) (1982), *Leonard Woolf*, Boston: Twayne.

Middleton, Roger (1985), *Towards the Managed Economy: Keynes, the Treasury and the Fiscal Debate of the 1930s*, London: Methuen.

Milgate, Murray (1977), 'Keynes on the "classical" theory of interest', *Cambridge Journal of Economics*, **1** (3), 307–15.

Milgate, Murray (1983), 'The "new" Keynes papers', in John Eatwell and Murray Milgate (eds), *Keynes's Economics and the Theory of Value and Distribution*, London: Duckworth, pp. 187–99.

Mill, John Stuart (1848), *Principles of Political Economy, with some of their Applications to Social Philosophy*, New York: Colonial Press, 2 vols, 1899.

Mini, Piero V. (1991), *Keynes, Bloomsbury and The General Theory*, London: Macmillan.

Mini, Piero V. (1994), *John Maynard Keynes: A Study in the Psychology of Original Work*, London: Macmillan.

Minsky, Hyman P. (1975), *John Maynard Keynes*, New York: Columbia University Press.

Minsky, Hyman P. (1977), 'The financial instability hypothesis: an interpretation of Keynes and an alternative to "standard" theory', *Nebraska Journal of Economics and Business*, **16** (1), 5–16.

Minsky, Hyman P. (1986), 'Money and crisis in Schumpeter and Keynes', in H.J. Wagener and J.W. Drukker (eds), *The Economic Law of Motion of Modern Society: a Marx–Keynes–Schumpeter Centennial*, Cambridge: Cambridge University Press, pp. 112–22.

Mizen, Paul and John R. Presley (1995), 'Robertson and persistent negative reactions to Keynes's *General Theory*: some new evidence', *History of Political Economy*, **27** (4), 639–51.

Moggridge, Donald E. (1969), *The Return of Gold: The Formulation of Economic Policy and its Critics*, Cambridge: Cambridge University Press.

Moggridge, Donald E. (1972), *British Monetary Policy, 1924–1931: the Norman Conquest of $4.86*, Cambridge: Cambridge University Press.

Moggridge, Donald E. (1973), 'From the *Treatise* to the *General Theory*: an exercise in chronology', *History of Political Economy*, **5** (1), 72–88.

Moggridge, Donald E. (1986), 'Keynes and the international monetary system, 1909–46', in Jon S. Cohen and Geoffrey C. Harcourt (eds), *International Monetary Problems and Supply-Side Economics: Essays in Honour of Lorie Tarshis*, New York: St. Martin's Press, pp. 56–83.

Moggridge, Donald E. (1990), 'Keynes as editor', in John D. Hey and David Winch (eds), *A Century of Economics: 100 Years of the Royal Economic Society*, Oxford: Basil Blackwell, pp. 143–57.

Moggridge, Donald E. (1992), *Maynard Keynes: An Economist's Biography*, London: Routledge.

Moggridge, Donald E. (2005), 'Keynes, the arts and the state', *History of Political Economy*, **37** (3), 535–55.

Moggridge, Donald E. and Susan Howson (1974), 'Keynes on monetary policy, 1910–1946', *Oxford Economic Papers*, **26** (2), 226–47.

Mongiovi, Gary (1991), 'Keynes, Sraffa and the labour markets', *Review of Political Economy*, **3** (1), 25–42.

Monk, Ray (1990), *Ludwig Wittgenstein: the Duty of Genius*, New York: Free Press.

Moore, Basil J. (1984), 'Keynes and the endogeneity of the money stock', *Studi Economici*, **39** (22), 23–69.

Moore, Basil J. (1988), 'Keynes's treatment of interest', in Omar F. Hamouda and John N. Smithin (eds), *Keynes and Public Policy After Fifty Years*, vol. 2, *Theories and Method*, New York: New York University Press, pp. 121–9.

Moore, George E. (1903a), *Principia Ethica*, revised edn, Cambridge: Cambridge University Press, 1993.

Moore, George E. (1903b), 'The refutation of idealism', in *Selected Writings*, London: Routledge, 1993, pp. 23–44.

Moore, George E. (1942), 'An autobiography', in Paul Arthur Schilpp (ed.), *The Philosophy of G.E. Moore*, La Salle, Illinois: Open Court, pp. 3–39.

Moore, Gregory (2003), 'John Neville Keynes's solution to the English *Methodenstreit*', *Journal of the History of Economic Thought*, **25** (1), 5–38.

Muchlinski, Elke (1996), *Keynes als Philosoph*, Berlin: Duncker & Humblot.

Muchlinski, Elke (2003), 'Epistémologie et probabilité chez Keynes', *Actualité Économique*, **79** (1–2), 57–70.

Munby, A.N.L. (1975), 'The book collector', in Milo Keynes (ed.) *Essays on John Maynard Keynes*, Cambridge: Cambridge University Press, pp. 290–98.

Nadeau, Robert (1999), *Vocabulaire Technique et Analytique de l'Épistémologie*, Paris: Presses Universitaires de France.

Naylor, Gillian (ed.) (1990), *Bloomsbury: The Artists, Authors and Designers by Themselves*, London: Pyramid.

Nentjes, A. (1988), 'Hayek and Keynes: a comparative analysis of their monetary views', *Journal of Economic Studies*, **15** (3–4), 136–51.

Netter, Maurice (1996), 'Radical uncertainty and its economic scope according to Knight and according to Keynes', in Christian Schmidt (ed.), *Uncertainty in Economic Thought*, Cheltenham, UK and Brookfield, USA: Edward Elgar, pp. 112–25.

Newman, Peter (1987), 'Ramsey, Frank Plumpton', in John Eatwell, Murray Milgate and Peter Newman (eds), *The New Palgrave Dictionary of Economics*, London: Macmillan, vol. 4, pp. 41–6.

Nicolson, Harold (1933), *Peacemaking 1919*, London: Constable.

Nijinski, Vaslav (1995), *Cahiers: Le Sentiment*, Arles: Actes Sud.

O'Donnell, Rod M. (1989), *Keynes: Philosophy, Economics and Politics: The Philosophical Foundations of Keynes's Thought and their Influence on his Economics and Politics*, London: Macmillan.

O'Donnell, Rod M. (1990a), 'Continuity in Keynes's conception of probability', in Donald E. Moggridge (ed.), *Keynes, Macroeconomics and Method: Selected Papers from the*

History of Economics Society Conference 1988, Aldershot, UK and Brookfield, US: Edward Elgar, pp. 53–72.

O'Donnell, Rod M. (1990b), 'Keynes on mathematics: philosophical foundations and economic applications', *Cambridge Journal of Economics*, **14** (1), 29–47.

O'Donnell, Rod M. (ed.) (1991), *Keynes as a Philosopher-Economist, The Ninth Keynes Seminar Held at the University of Kent, Canterbury, 1989*, London: Macmillan.

O'Donnell, Rod M. (1995), 'Keynes on aesthetics', in Allin F. Cottrell and Michael S. Lawlor (eds), *New Perspectives on Keynes*, Durham: Duke University Press, pp. 93–121.

O'Donnell, Rod M. (1998), 'Mixed goods and social reform', *Cahiers d'économie Politique*, nos 30–31, 167–85.

O'Donnell, Rod M. (1999a), 'Keynes's socialism: conception, strategy and espousal', in Claudio Sardoni and Peter Kriesler (eds), *Keynes, Post-Keynesianism and Political Economy*, London and New York: Routledge, pp. 149–75.

O'Donnell, Rod M. (1999b), 'The genesis of the only diagram in the *General Theory*', *Journal of the History of Economic Thought*, **21** (1), 27–37.

O'Donnell, Rod M. (2004), 'Keynes as a writer: three case studies', in Tony Aspromourgos and John Lodewijks (eds), *History and Political Economy: Essays in Honour of P.D. Groenewegen*, London: Routledge, pp. 197–216.

Orio, Lucien and Jean-José Quiles (1993), *L'Économie Keynésienne: un Projet Radical*, Paris: Nathan.

Orléan, André (1988), 'L'auto-référence dans la théorie keynésienne de la spéculation', *Cahiers d'économie Politique*, nos 14–15, 229–42.

Palmer, Alan and Veronica Palmer (1987), *Who's Who in Bloomsbury*, New York: St. Martin's Press.

Parguez, Alain (1982), 'Hayek et Keynes face à la crise', *Économies et Sociétés*, **16** (24), 705–38.

Parguez, Alain (1989a), 'Money and financial capital within a Keynesian framework', in Alain Barrère (ed.), *Money, Credit and Prices in Keynesian Perspective*, London: Macmillan, pp. 3–15.

Parguez, Alain (1989b), 'Hayek et Keynes face à l'austérité', in Gilles Dostaler and Diane Éthier (eds), *Friedrich Hayek: Philosophie, Économie et Politique*, Paris: Économica, pp. 143–60.

Parsons, Wayne (1997), *Keynes and the Quest for a Moral Science: A Study of Economics and Alchemy*, Cheltenham, UK and Lyme, USA: Edward Elgar.

Partridge, Frances (1981), *Love in Bloomsbury: Memories*, Boston: Little, Brown and Company.

Pasinetti, Luigi L. and Bertram Schefold, (eds) (1999). *The Impact of Keynes on Economics in the 20th Century*, Cheltenham, UK and Northampton, MA, USA: Edward Elgar.

Patinkin, Don (1948), 'Relative prices, Say's law, and the demand for money', *Econometrica*, **16** (2), 135–54.

Patinkin, Don (1976a), *Keynes' Monetary Thought: A Study of its Development*, Durham: Duke University Press.

Patinkin, Don (1976b), 'Keynes and econometrics: on the interaction between the macroeconomics revolution of the interwar period', *Econometrica*, **44** (6), 1091–123.

Patinkin, Don (1979), 'Keynes and Chicago', *Journal of Law and Economics*, **22** (2), 213–32.

Patinkin, Don (1982), *Anticipations of the General Theory? And Other Essays on Keynes*, Chicago: University of Chicago Press and Oxford: Basil Blackwell.

Patinkin, Don (1990), 'On different interpretations of the *General Theory*', *Journal of Monetary Economics*, **26** (2), 205–43.

Patinkin, Don and James Clark Leith (eds) (1977), *Keynes, Cambridge and The General Theory*, London: Macmillan.

Peden, George C. (1988), *Keynes, the Treasury, and British Economic Policy*, London: Macmillan.

Perroux, François (1945), 'Les accords de Bretton Woods', *La Vie Intellectuelle*, **13** (3), 40–89.

Pigou, Arthur C. (1921), '*A Treatise on Probability* By J.M. Keynes', *Economic Journal*, **31** (124), 507–12.

Pineault, Eric (2003), 'Pour une théorie de l'institution monétaire: actualité du *Treatise on Money*', *Actualité Economique*, **79** (2), 101–16.

Plumptre A.F.W. (1947), 'Keynes in Cambridge', *Canadian Journal of Economics and Political Science*, **13** (3), 366–71.

Polanyi, Karl (1944), *The Great Transformation*, New York: Rinehart.

Ponsot, Jean-François (2002), 'Keynes and the "National Emission Caisse" of North Russia: 1918–1920', *History of Political Economy*, **34** (1), 177–207.

Porter, Theodore M. (1986), *The Rise of Statistical Thinking, 1820–1900*, Princeton: Princeton University Press.

Porter, Theodore M. (1995), *Trust in Number: The Pursuit of Objectivity in Science and Publicity*, Princeton: Princeton University Press.

Potier, Jean-Pierre (2002), 'Keynes et la question du socialisme', in Maurice Chrétien (ed.), *Le Socialisme Britannique: Penseurs du XXè Siècle*, Paris: Économica, pp. 69–95.

Poulon, Frédéric (ed.) (1985a), *Les Ecrits de Keynes*, Paris: Dunod.

Poulon, Frédéric (1985b), 'La paix carthaginoise: les conséquences économiques de Versailles' in F. Poulon (1985a), pp. 24–46.

Poulon, Frédéric (1987), 'Keynes et Robertson: naissance d'un désaccord sur la fonction de l'épargne dans la théorie monétaire', *Économies et Sociétés*, 21, Série 'Monnaie et production', no. 4, 9–22.

Poulon, Frédéric (2000), *La Pensée Economique de Keynes*, Paris: Dunod.

Presley, John R. (1989), 'J.M. Keynes and D.H. Robertson: three phases of collaboration', *Research in the History of Economic Thought and Methodology*, **6**, 31–46.

Pressman, Steven (1987), 'The policy relevance of the *General Theory*', *Journal of Economic Studies*, **14** (4), 13–23.

Ramsey, Frank (1922), 'Mr. Keynes on probability', *Cambridge Magazine*, **1** (1), 3–5.

Ramsey, Frank (1926), 'Truth and probability', in *The Foundations of Mathematics and Other Logical Essays*, London: Kegan Paul, Trench, Trubner & Co, 1931, pp. 156–98.

Reder, Melvin W. (2000), 'The anti-semitism of some eminent economists', *History of Political Economy*, **32** (4), 833–56.

Reed, Christopher (ed.) (1996), *A Roger Fry Reader*, Chicago: University of Chicago Press.

Reed, Christpher (2004), *Bloomsbury Rooms: Modernism, Subculture and the Domesticity*, New Haven: Yale University Press.

Rees, David (1973), *Harry Dexter White: A Study in Paradox*, London: Macmillan.

Regan, Tom (1986), *Bloomsbury's Prophet: G.E. Moore and the Development of his Moral Philosophy*, Philadelphia: Temple University Press.

Ricardo, David (1821), *On the Principles of Political Economy and Taxation*, third edn, Cambridge: Cambridge University Press, 1951.

Richardson, Elizabeth P. (1989), *A Bloomsbury Iconography*, Winchester, Hampshire: St. Paul's Bibliographies.

Riddell, George A. (1934), *Lord Riddell's Intimate Diary of the Peace Conference and After, 1918–1923*, New York: Reynal & Hitchcock.

Rima, Ingrid H. (1986), 'The Pigou-Keynes controversy about involuntary unemployment: a half-century reinterprettion', *Eastern Economic Journal*, **12** (4), 467–77.

Rima, Ingrid H. (1988), 'Keynes's vision and econometric analysis', in Omar F. Hamouda and John N. Smithin (eds), *Keynes and Public Policy after Fifty Years*, vol. 2: *Theories and Method*, New York: New York University Press, pp. 12–22.

Rivot, Sylvie (2003), 'La politique de l'emploi dans les écrits politiques de Keynes (1930–1939)', *Actualité Economique*, **79** (1–2), 133–46.

Robbins, Lionel C. (1932), *An Essay on the Nature and Significance of Economic Science*, London: Macmillan; 2nd edn, 1935.

Robins, Anna Gruetzner (1997), *Modern Art in Britain 1910–1914*, London: Barbican Art Gallery.

Robinson, Austin (1947), 'John Maynard Keynes, 1883–1946', *Economic Journal*, **57** (225), 1–68.

Robinson, Austin (1964), 'Could there have been a "General Theory" without Keynes', in Robert Lekachman (ed.) *Keynes' General Theory: Reports of Three Decades*, London: Macmillan, pp. 87–95.

Robinson, Joan (1948), 'La théorie générale de l'emploi', *Économie Appliquée*, **1** (2–3), 185–96.

Robinson, Joan (1953), *On Re-reading Marx*, Cambridge: Students' Bookshop; in *Collected Economic Papers*, Oxford: Basil Blackwell, vol. 4, 1973, pp. 247–68.

Robinson, Joan (1964), 'Kalecki and Keynes', in *Problems of Economic Dynamics and Planning: Essays in Honour of Michal Kalecki*, Warsaw: Polish Scientific Publishers, pp. 335–41; in *Collected Economic Papers*, Oxford, Basil Blackwell, vol. 3, 1965, pp. 92–99.

Robinson, Joan (1975), 'What has become of the Keynesian revolution?', in Milo Keynes (ed.), *Essays on John Maynard Keynes*, Cambridge: Cambridge University Press, pp. 123–31.

Robinson, Joan (1979), 'Has Keynes failed?', *Annals of Public and Co-operative Economy*, **50** (1), 27–9.

Rosenbaum, S.P. (1987), *Victorian Bloomsbury: The Early History of the Bloomsbury Group, volume 1*, London: Macmillan.

Rosenbaum, S.P. (1993), *A Bloomsbury Group Reader*, Oxford: Blackwell.

Rosenbaum, S.P. (1994), *Edwardian Bloomsbury: The Early History of the Bloomsbury Group, volume 2*, London: Macmillan.

Rosenbaum, S.P. (ed.) (1995), *The Bloomsbury Group: A Collection of Memoirs and Commentary*, revised edn, Toronto: University of Toronto Press (first edn, 1975).

Rosenbaum, S.P. (1998), *Aspects of Bloomsbury: Studies in Modern English Literary and Intellectual History*, London: Macmillan.

Rosenbaum, S.P. (2003), *Georgian Bloomsbury: The Early History of the Bloomsbury Group, 1910–1914, volume 3*, New York: Palgrave Macmillan.

Rosier, Michel (2002), 'The logic of Keynes' criticism of the *classical* model', *European Journal of History of Economic Theory*, **9** (4), 608–43.

Rosier, Michel (2003), 'Les grandeurs fondamentales de la *Théorie Générale*', *Actualité Économique*, **79** (1–2), 197–219.

Roth, Danièle (2001), *Bloomsbury, côté cuisine*, Paris: Balland.

Rotheim, Roy J. (1988), 'Keynes and the language of probability and uncertainty', *Journal of Post Keynesian Economics*, **11** (1), 82–99.

Rowley, Robin (1988), 'The Keynes–Tinbergen exchange in retrospect', in Omar F. Hamouda and John N. Smithin (eds), *Keynes and Public Policy After Fifty Years*, vol. 2, *Theories and Method*, New York: New York University Press, pp. 23–31.

Runde, Jochen (1994), 'Keynesian uncertainty and liquidity preference', *Cambridge Journal of Economics*, **18** (2), 129–44.

Runde, Jochen and Sohei Mizuhara (eds) (2003), *The Philosophy of Keynes's Economics: Probability, Uncertainty and Convention*, London: Routledge.

Russell, Bertrand (1912), *The Problems of Philosophy*, London: Thornton Butterworth and New York: Oxford University Press, 1959.

Russell, Bertrand (1922), '*A Treatise on Probability*. By John Maynard Keynes', *Mathematical Gazette*, **11**, 119–25.

Russell, Bertrand (1967), *The Autobiography of Bertrand Russell: 1872–1914*, London: George Allen and Unwin.

Russell, Bertrand (2001), *The Selected Letters of Bertrand Russell: The Public Years, 1914–1970*, London and New York: Routledge.

Rutherford, R.P. (1987), 'Malthus and Keynes', *Oxford Economic Papers*, **39** (1), 175–89.

Rymes, Thomas K. (1986), 'Keynes's lectures, 1932–1935: notes of a representative student: a prelude: notes for the Easter Term, 1932', *Eastern Economic Journal*, **12** (4), 397–412.

Rymes, Thomas K. (ed.) (1989), *Keynes's Lectures 1932–35: Notes of a Representative Student*, Ann Arbor: University of Michigan Press.

Rymes, Thomas K. (1998), 'Keynes and anchorless banking', *Journal of the History of Economic Thought*, **20** (1), 71–82.

Sardoni, Claudio (1986), 'Marx and Keynes on effective demand and unemployment', *History of Political Economy*, **18** (3), 419–41.

Say, Jean-Baptiste (1803), *A Treatise on Political Economy or The Production, Distribution and Consumption of Wealth*, New York: Augustus M. Kelley, 1964.

Say, Jean-Baptiste (1821), *Letters to Mr Malthus*, New York: Augustus M. Kelley, 1967.

Schmidt, Christian (ed.) (1996a), *Uncertainty in Economic Thought*, Cheltenham, UK and Brookfield, US: Edward Elgar.

Schmidt, Christian (1996b), 'Risk and uncertainty: a Knightian distinction revisited', in Schmidt (1996a), pp. 64–85.

Schmidt, Christian (2003), 'Que reste-t-il du *Treatise on Probability* de Keynes?', *Actualité Economique*, **79** (1–2), 37–55.

Schmitt, Bernard (1985), 'Un nouvel ordre monétaire international: le plan Keynes' in Frédéric Poulon (ed.), *Les Ecrits de Keynes*, Paris: Dunod, pp. 195–209.

Schultz, Bart (2004), *Henry Sidgwick: Eye of the Universe, An Intellectual Biography*, Cambridge: Cambridge University Press.

Schumpeter, Joseph A. (1946), 'John Maynard Keynes', *American Economic Review*, **36** (4), 495–518.

Schumpeter, Joseph A. (1954), *History of Economic Analysis*, London: George Allen & Unwin.

Scrase, David and Peter Croft (1983), *Maynard Keynes: Collector of Pictures, Books and Manuscripts*, Cambridge: Provost and Scholars of King's College.

Seccareccia, Mario (1982), 'Keynes, Sraffa et l'économie classique: le problème de la mesure de la valeur', *Actualité Economique*, **58** (1–2), 115–52.

Seccareccia, Mario (1987), 'Les courants de la pensée économique de la *Théorie Générale*: quelques éléments nouveaux d'interprétation', in Gérard Boismenu and Gilles Dostaler (eds), *La 'Théorie Générale' et le keynésianisme*, Montréal: ACFAS, pp. 15–38.

Seymour, Miranda (1992), *Ottoline Morrell: Life on a Grand Scale*, London: Hodder and Stoughton.

Shackle, George L.S. (1989), 'What did the *General Theory* do?', in John Pheby (ed.), *New Directions in Post-Keynesian Economics*, Aldershot, UK and Brookfield, US: pp. 48–58.

Sharma, Soumitra (ed.) (1998), *John Maynard Keynes: Keynesianism into the Twenty-First Century*, Cheltenham, UK and Lyme, USA: Edward Elgar.

Shionoya, Yuichi (1991), 'Sidgwick, Moore and Keynes: a philosophical analysis of Keynes's "My early beliefs"', in Bradley W. Bateman and John B. Davis (eds), *Keynes and Philosophy*, Aldershot, UK and Brookfield, US: Edward Elgar, pp. 6–29.

Shone, Richard (1993), *Bloomsbury's Portraits: Vanessa Bell, Duncan Grant and their Circle*, London: Phaidon Press [first edn, 1976].

Shone, Richard (1999), *The Art of Bloomsbury: Roger Fry, Vanessa Bell and Duncan Grant*, London: Tate Gallery Publishing.

Shone, Richard with Duncan Grant (1975), 'The picture collector', in Milo Keynes (ed.) *Essays on John Maynard Keynes*, Cambridge: Cambridge University Press, pp. 280–89.

Sidgwick, Henry (1874), *The Methods of Ethics*, London: Macmillan; seventh edn, 1907.

Sidgwick, Henry (1906), *A Memoir by A.S. and E.M.S.*, London: Macmillan.

Sigot, Nathalie (2001), *Bentham et l'économie: une Histoire d'utilité*, Paris: Economica.

Sismondi, Jean-Charles L. Simonde de (1819), *Nouveaux principes d'économie politique*; *New Principles of Political Economy, of Wealth in its Relation to Population*, New Brunswick: Transaction, 1991.

Sismondi, Jean-Charles L. Simonde de (1824), 'Sur la balance des consommations avec les productions', *Revue Encyclopédique*, 22; 'On the balance of consumption with production', in *New Principles of Political Economy, Of Wealth in its Relation to Population*, New Brunswick: Transaction, 1991, pp. 617–43.

Skidelsky, Robert (1967), *Politicians and the Slump: The Labour Government of 1929–1931*, London: Macmillan.

Skidelsky, Robert (1969), 'Gold standard and Churchill: The Truth', *The Times Business News*, 17 March.

Skidelsky, Robert (1975), *Sir Oswald Mosley*, London: Macmillan.

Skidelsky, Robert (1982), 'Keynes and Bloomsbury', in Michael Holroyd (ed.), *Essays by Divers Hands*, London: Boydell Press, pp. 15–17.

Skidelsky, Robert (1983), *John Maynard Keynes*, vol. 1, *Hopes Betrayed: 1883–1920*, London: Macmillan; American edn, New York: Viking, 1986.

Skidelsky, Robert (1992), *John Maynard Keynes*, vol. 2, *The Economist as Saviour: 1920–1937*, London: Macmillan.

Skidelsky, Robert (1997), 'Keynes and the United States', in W. Roger Louis (ed.), *Adventures with Britannia: Personnalities, Politics and Culture in Britain*, London: I.B. Tauris.

Skidelsky, Robert (2000), *John Maynard Keynes*, vol. 3, *Fighting for Britain, 1937–1946*, London: Macmillan.

Skidelsky, Robert (2003), *John Maynard Keynes, 1883–1946: Economist, Philosopher, Statesman*, London: Macmillan.

Smith, Adam (1776), *An Inquiry into the Nature and Causes of the Wealth of Nations*, 2 vols, Homewood, Illinois: Richard D. Irwin, 1963.

Smithin, John N. (1985), 'The definition of involuntary unemployment in Keynes' *General Theory*: a note', *History of Political Economy*, **17** (2), 219–22.

Sowell, Thomas (1974), *Say's Law: An Historical Analysis*, Princeton: Princeton University Press.

Spalding, Frances (1980), *Roger Fry: Art and Life*, Berkeley: University of California Press.

Spalding, Frances (1983), *Vanessa Bell*, London: Weidenfeld and Nicolson.

Spalding, Frances (1997), *Duncan Grant*, London: Chatto & Windus.

Stansky, Peter (1996), *On or About December 1910: Early Bloomsbury and its Intimate World*, Cambridge, Massachusetts: Harvard University Press.

Stone, Richard (1978), 'Keynes, political arithmetic and econometrics', *Proceedings of the British Academy*, **64**, 55–92.

Strachey, Lytton (1918), *Eminent Victorians*, London: Chatto and Windus.

Strachey, Lytton (1921), *Queen Victoria*, London: Chatto and Windus.

Strachey, Lytton (1972), *The Really Interesting Question and Other Papers*, edited by Paul Levy, London: Weidenfeld and Nicolson.

Strachey, Lytton (2005), *The Letters of Lytton Strachey*, edited by Paul Levy, London, Penguin Books.

Sturgis, Matthew (2005), *Walter Sickert: A Life*, London: HarperCollins.

Suzuki, Tomo (2003), 'The epistemology of macroeconomic reality: the Keynesian revolution from an accounting point of view', *Accounting, Organizations and Society*, **28**, 471–517.

Tardieu, André (1921), *La Paix*, Paris: Payot.

Tarshis, Lorie (1978), 'Keynes as seen by his students in the 1930s', in Don Patinkin and J. Clark Leith (eds), *Keynes, Cambridge and the General Theory*, London: Macmillan, pp. 48–63.

Thirlwall, Anthony P. (ed.) (1976), *Keynes and International Monetary Relations: The Second Keynes Seminar Held at the University of Kent at Canterbury, 1974*, London: Macmillan.

Thirlwall, Anthony P. (ed.) (1978), *Keynes and Laissez-faire: The Third Keynes Seminar Held at the University of Kent at Canterbury, 1976*, London: Macmillan.

Thirlwall, Anthony P. (ed.) (1982), *Keynes as a Policy Adviser: The Fifth Keynes Seminar Held at the University of Kent at Canterbury, 1980*, London: Macmillan.

Thirlwall, Anthony P. (ed.) (1987), *Keynes and Economic Development, The Seventh Keynes Seminar Held at the University of Kent, Canterbury, 1985*, London: Macmillan.

Thomson, David (1950), *England in the Nineteeenth Century, 1815–1914*, London: Penguin Books.

Tilman, Rick and Ruth Porter-Tilman (1995), 'John Neville Keynes: The social philosophy of a late Victorian economist', *Journal of the History of Economic Thought*, **17** (2), 266–84.

Tinbergen, Jan (1935), 'Annual survey: Suggestions on quantitative business cycle theory', *Econometrica*, **3** (3), 241–308.

Tinbergen, Jan (1939), *Statistical Testing of Business-Cycle Theories*, Geneva: League of Nations, 2 vols.

Tinbergen, Jan (1940), 'On a method of statistical business cycle research: a reply', *Economic Journal*, **50** (197), 141–54.

Tolstoy, Leo (1962), *What is Art? and Essays on Art*, New York: Oxford University Press [*What is Art* first published in 1898].

Tomlinson, Jim (1981), *Problems of British Economic Policy, 1870–1945*, London: Methuen.

Tortajada, Ramon (1985), 'La monnaie et son taux d'intérêt chez J.M. Keynes', *Cahiers d'économie Politique*, nos 10–11, 131–48.

Toye, John (2000), *Keynes's View on Population*, Oxford: Oxford University Press.

Toye, Richard (1999), 'Keynes, the labour movement and "How to Pay for the War"', *Twentieth Century British History*, **10** (3), 255–81.

Trevithik, J.A. (1992), *Involuntary Unemployment: Macroeconomics from a Keynesian Perspective*, Hemel Hempstead: Harvester Wheatsheaf.

Tutin, Christian (1988), 'Intérêt et ajustement: le débat Hayek/Keynes (1931–1932)', *Économie Appliquée*, **41** (2), 247–87.

Tutin, Christian (2003), 'Keynes, une économie politique du capitalisme financier?', *Actualité Economique*, **79** (1–2), 21–36.

Vallageas, Bernard (1986), 'Le problème de la nature du profit et de son agrégation dans le *Traité sur la monnaie* et la *Théorie Générale*', *Économies et Sociétés*, **20**, Série 'Monnaie et production', no. 3, 171–88.

Ventelou, Bruno (1997), *Lire Keynes et le Comprendre*, Paris: Vuibert.

Verdon, Michel (1996), *Keynes and the 'Classics': A Study in Language, Epistemology and Mistaken Identities*, London and New York: Routledge.

Vicarelli, Fausto (1984), *Keynes: The Instability of Capitalism*, London: Macmillan [*Keynes, l'instabilità del capitalismo*, Milano: Etas Libri, 1977]

Vicarelli, Fausto (ed.) (1985), *Keynes's Relevance Today*, London: Macmillan and Philadelphia: University of Pennsylvania Press.

Viner, Jacob (1927), 'Adam Smith and laissez-faire', *Journal of Political Economy*, **35** (2), 200–232.

Walley, Peter (1991), *Statistical Reasoning with Imprecise Probabilities*, London: Chapman and Hall.

Walras, Léon (1874–1877), *Elements of Pure Economics, or The Theory of Social Wealth*, New York: Augustus M. Kelley, 1969.

Watney, Simon (1980), *English Post-Impressionism*, London: Studio Vista.

White, Eric W. (1974), 'Keynes: architect to the arts council', in Donald E. Moggridge (ed.), *Keynes: Aspects of the Man and his Work*, London: Macmillan, pp. 22–32.

Wicke, Jennifer (1994), '"Mrs. Dalloway" goes to the market: Woolf, Keynes, and modern markets', *Novel: A Forum on Fiction*, **28** (1), 5–23.

Wilkinson, Lancelot Patrick (1980), *A Century of King's, 1873–1972*, Cambridge: King's College.

Williamson, John (1985), 'Keynes and the postwar international economic order', in Harold L. Wattel (ed.), *The Policy Consequences of John Maynard Keynes*, Armonk, New York: M.E. Sharpe, pp. 145–56.

Wilson, Trevor (1966), *The Downfall of the Liberal Party, 1914–1935*, Ithaca, New York: Cornell University Press.

Winch, Donald (1969), *Economics and Policy: A Historical Study*, London: Hodder and Stoughton.

Winslow, E.G. (1986), 'Keynes and Freud: psychoanalysis and Keynes's account of the "animal spirits" of capitalism', *Social Research*, **53** (4), 549–78.

Winslow, E.G. (1990), 'Bloomsbury, Freud, and the vulgar passions', *Social Research,* **57** (4), 785–819.

Winslow, E.G. (1992), 'Psychonalysis and Keynes's account of the psychology of the trade cycle', in Bill Gerrard and John Hillard (eds), *The Philosophy and Economics of J.M. Keynes*, Aldershot, UK and Brookfield, US: Edward Elgar, pp. 212–30.

Winslow, E.G. (1995), 'Uncertainty and liquidity-preference', in Sheila Dow and John Hillard (eds), *Keynes, Knowledge and Uncertainty*, Aldershot, UK and Brookfield, US: Edward Elgar, pp. 221–43.

Wittgenstein, Ludwig (1922), *Tractatus Logico-Philosophicus*, London: Routledge.

Wittgenstein, Ludwig (1974), *Letters to Russell, Keynes and Moore*, edited by G.H. von Wright, Ithaca, New York: Cornell University Press.

Wood, John Cunningham (ed.) (1983), *John Maynard Keynes: Critical Assessments*, London: Croom Helm, 4 vols.

Wood, John Cunningham (ed.) (1994), *John Maynard Keynes: Critical Assessments. Second series*, London: Routledge, 4 vols.

Woolf, Leonard (1960), *Sowing: An Autobiography of the Years 1880 to 1904*, London: Hogarth Press.

Woolf, Leonard (1967), *Downhill all the Way: An Autobiography of the Years 1919 to 1939*, London: Hogarth Press.

Woolf, Leonard (1990), *Letters of Leonard Woolf*, London: Bloomsbury.

Woolf, Virginia (1915), *The Voyage Out*, London: Penguin Books, 1992.

Woolf, Virginia (1919), *Night and Day*, London: Vintage, 1992.

Woolf, Virginia (1922), 'Old Bloomsbury', in S. P. Rosenbaum (ed.), *The Bloomsbury Group: A Collection of Memoirs and Commentary*, revised edn, Toronto: University of Toronto Press, 1995, pp. 40–59.

Woolf, Virginia (1925), 'Modern fiction', in *The Essays of Virginia Woolf*, vol. 4, *1925–1928*, London: Hogarth Press, 1986, pp. 157–70.

Woolf, Virginia (1934), '"JMK": a biographical fantasy', Virginia Woolf's Manuscript Articles and Essays, Berg Collection, New York Public Library, **7**, 73–7; in S.P. Rosenbaum (ed.), *The Bloomsbury Group: A Collection of Memoirs and Commentary*, revised edn, Toronto: University of Toronto Press, 1995, pp. 274–5.

Woolf, Virginia (1940), *Roger Fry: A Biography*, London: Hogarth Press.

Woolf, Virginia (1975–1980), *The Letters of Virginia Woolf*, London: Hogarth Press, 6 vols.

Woolf, Virginia (1977–1984), *The Diary of Virginia Woolf*, London: Hogarth Press, 5 vols.

Woolf, Virginia (2003), *Congenial Spirits: The Selected Letters of Virginia Woolf*, London: Pimlico.

Worswick, G. David N. and James S. Trevithick (eds), *Keynes and the Modern World*, Cambridge: Cambridge University Press.

Wray, L. Randell (1990), *Money and Credit in Capitalist Economy: The Endogenous Money Approach*, Aldershot, UK and Brookfield, US: Edward Elgar.

Young, George M. (1977), *Portrait of an Age: Victorian England*, Toronto and London: Oxford University Press.

Young, Warren (1987), *Interpreting Mr Keynes: the IS/LM Enigma*, Boulder, Colorado: Westview Press and Oxford: Basil Blackwell.

Zerbato, Michel (ed.) (1987), *Keynésianisme et sortie de crise: Keynes contre le libéralisme*, Paris: Dunod.

Zouache, Abdallah (2003), 'Coordination et chomage involontaire: de Keynes aux nouveaux keynésiens', *Actualité Economique*, **79** (1–2), 179–95.

Index